The Chinese and Their Future

The Chinese and Their Future

Beijing, Taipei, and Hong Kong

Zhiling Lin
and
Thomas W. Robinson,
Editors

The AEI Press

Publisher for the American Enterprise Institute
WASHINGTON, D.C.

1994

Library of Congress Cataloging-in-Publication Data

The Chinese and their future : Beijing, Taipei, and Hong Kong / edited
by Zhiling Lin and Thomas W. Robinson.
    p. cm.
    Proceedings of an international conference held in January, 1991.
    ISBN 0-8447-3805-0. — ISBN 0-8447-3804-2 (pbk.)
    1. China. 2. Taiwan. 3. Hong Kong. 4. Chinese reunification
questions, 1949– I. Lin, Zhiling. II. Robinson, Thomas W.
DS779.26.C47376   1993
951.05'9—dc20   93-21227
                                       CIP

1 3 5 7 9 10 8 6 4 2

THE AEI PRESS
Publisher for the American Enterprise Institute
1150 17th Street, N.W., Washington, D.C. 20036

Printed in the United States of America

Contents

LIST OF TABLES

LIST OF FIGURES

Contributors

ZHILING LIN is a research associate in the Asian Studies Program at the American Enterprise Institute. She also lectures regularly at the Area Studies Program at the Foreign Service Institute of the U.S. Department of State, the Business Council for International Understanding, and the Industrial College of the Armed Forces at the National Defense University. Ms. Lin lectures, writes, and translates works on Chinese culture, society, and foreign relations.

THOMAS W. ROBINSON is president of American Asian Research Enterprises and, until 1993, was director of the China Studies Program at the American Enterprise Institute. He is also adjunct professor of national security at Georgetown University and chairperson of the Foreign Service Institute's China studies course. Mr. Robinson has published widely on Chinese and Russian politics and foreign policies, Soviet Asian policy, Russian-Chinese relations, Asian security, international relations, and international relations forecasting.

JUDITH BANISTER is division chief of the Center for International Research at the U.S. Bureau of the Census. Ms. Banister was chief of the China Branch at the Census Bureau from 1982 to 1992. She is the author of numerous articles, papers, and monographs on demographic trends in China, North and South Korea, Vietnam, and the Asia-Pacific region in general. Her most recent books are *China's Changing Population* (1987) and, with Nicholas Eberstadt, *The Population of North Korea* (1992).

HEI-YUAN CHIU is a research fellow at the Institute of Ethnology and director of the Office of Survey Research of the Academia Sinica as well as professor in the Department of Sociology at National Taiwan University. He is also the principal investigator of the research project Social Change Survey in Taiwan. Mr. Chiu is the author of numerous books and articles on religion and social change in Taiwan.

FENG SHENGBAO is a visiting scholar at the Institute of East Asian

Studies, University of California, Berkeley. Mr. Feng has written widely on Chinese political development, and his works have been published in both China and the United States.

CHI-MING HOU was a visiting senior research fellow and later vice president and director of international programs at the Chung-hua Institution for Economic Research in Taipei before his death in 1991. Mr. Hou was also the Charles A. Dana Professor of Economics at Colgate University (1968–1991), where his research focused on trade and development in the Chinese economy.

GUOCANG HUAN is a vice president of JP Morgan, Inc. Mr. Huan is also a senior fellow at the Atlantic Council and a research fellow and assistant professor at Columbia University. Before holding these posts, he was vice president for the Center for Modern China (1991–1992) and a visiting fellow at the Center of International Studies at Princeton University. Mr. Huan has written widely for both English and Chinese publications.

SIU-KAI LAU is professor of sociology, chairman of the Board of Sociology, head of the graduate school's Division of Sociology, and associate director of the Hong Kong Institute of Asia-Pacific Studies at the Chinese University of Hong Kong. Professor Lau's most recent articles have focused on politics and leadership in Hong Kong.

JEAN C. OI is associate professor of government at Harvard University and resident research associate at the Fairbank Center for East Asian Research. She has also been a national fellow at the Hoover Institution. Ms. Oi is author of *State and Peasant in Contemporary China: The Political Economy of Village Government* (1989) and a forthcoming book on fiscal politics and the development of local economies in post-Mao China.

ELLEN SALEM is a visiting scholar at the University of Hong Kong Business School. Ms. Salem has worked as an Asian-based business consultant at Asia Equity and First Pacific Securities and as a journalist covering China with the *Far Eastern Economic Review* (Hong Kong). She is now specializing in the integration of Asian political and economic risk assessment and corporate strategic planning.

SUSAN L. SHIRK is director of the University of California systemwide Institute on Global Conflict and Cooperation. She is also a professor at both the Graduate School of International Relations and Pacific

Studies and the Department of Political Science at the University of California, San Diego. Ms. Shirk is on the board of directors of the National Committee on U.S.-China Relations and is a member of the Council on Foreign Relations.

YUN-WING SUNG is a senior lecturer in economics and codirector of the Hong Kong and Asia-Pacific Economics Research Programme at the Chinese University of Hong Kong. He has been a visiting scholar at the University of Chicago and the Harvard-Yenching Institute. He is also a corresponding editor of *Asia-Pacific Economic Literature* and has published extensively in several international journals.

RICHARD P. SUTTMEIER is professor of political science at the University of Oregon and director of the university's Asian Studies Program. Mr. Suttmeier has concentrated his research on issues relating to the development of science and technology in China and, more recently, in East and Southeast Asia. He is widely published in these fields. His current research focuses on the management of technical and environmental risks in China.

BYRON S. J. WENG is professor of government and public administration as well as fellow and secretary of the Chinese Law Program at the Chinese University of Hong Kong. Mr. Weng specializes in Chinese politics with an emphasis on mainland China–Taiwan–Hong Kong relations and has written numerous books and articles in both English and Chinese.

YUNG WEI is a member of the Legislative Yuan (Parliament), Republic of China, and professor of political science (on leave) at the National Chiao-tung University in Taiwan. Mr. Wei is also founder and chairman of the Vanguard Foundation and served as chairman of the Research, Development, and Evaluation Commission of the Executive Yuan (Cabinet of the ROC) from 1976 to 1988.

ZHANG SHUQIANG is assistant professor in the Department of Educational Psychology of the University of Hawaii at Manoa, where he has taught research methodology and statistics and served as conference interpreter and translator. Mr. Zhang is also president of Friends of Democracy for China.

Preface

Even before the cataclysmic events of 1989–1991 spelled the end of the cold war and, in most places, of Communist rule, it was evident that the three Chinese entities in close geographic proximity—China, Hong Kong, and Taiwan—were moving, albeit seemingly separately, in the same general direction. Initial inspection revealed them to be at different stages of economic development and of modernization, organized according to competing economic assumptions and institutions, utilizing opposing modes of political rule, appealing to highly contrasting ideological ideas, of vastly different physical size, and occupying quite different places in the international arena. And yet it could not be denied that, despite the gulf separating them in these and other areas, they were beginning not only to narrow those differences but also to restore common cultural bonds, to penetrate each other's economies, to communicate, to explore their political differences more directly, and at least not to engage in fratricide internationally.

It is not clear where the term *Greater China* came from or when it first came to be used. Perhaps it represented a kind of neutral term, *Da Zhonghua*, found useful by Chinese on the mainland and Taiwan, to refer to the larger geographic area when their respective representatives attended international meetings at the same time. It seems to have emerged sometime in the late 1980s more or less simultaneously in all three places, especially in Hong Kong, where it was used by scholars and journalists seeking to understand what the role of the colony would be once reversion took place in 1997. It became a rather wistfully idealistic term for what once was and what might someday be again, despite all that appeared to divide Chinese in the three places. And when the Tiananmen repression came and all thought of joint negotiations for peaceful reunification between China and Taiwan had to be halted, if temporarily, Greater China took on the meaning of holding onto a concept for its own sake, while events seemed to be driving Chinese away from each other once again.

Whatever the case, by 1991 there was much interest in what the Chinese future might bring, for the three Chinese locales, throughout

Asia, and among other interested peoples and institutions. There was equal interest in the events and trends in China after Tiananmen—that is, whether, how, and when the mainland would recover from the shock and the effects of the June 1989 event. Moreover, Taiwan had clearly and decisively embarked on the path of political democratization and social pluralization, approaching the mainland and opening to the international community. Finally, Hong Kong was well into its final decade under British rule, and the transition to Beijing rule was beginning to take shape. But despite these developments, little attention had as yet been devoted to the composite future of the Chinese in the three places. A gap thus opened between interest and knowledge, especially as concerned the implications for foreign policy making toward China, Hong Kong, and Taiwan.

With these thoughts in mind, the coeditors undertook to organize an international conference on the topic. Meeting in early January 1991, the conference brought together scholars, analysts, journalists, and interested persons from all three parts of Greater China, from several places throughout the United States, and a large audience chiefly from the Washington, D.C., area. The basic idea was to sketch recent developments in politics, society, and economics in all three Greater China components, extend the analysis into the near-term future, introduce Asian and global international developments, consider how these might influence relations between and among Beijing, Hong Kong, and Taipei, and then try to sum things up by putting together domestic and international variables. This volume is the product of that conference and of the labors of the authors of its various chapters.

The success of the conference was due not only to those whose names are associated with the book in the formal sense. Full note should be taken as well of the efforts of Kathleen Walsh, administrative assistant in the China Studies Program at the American Enterprise Institute. More than perhaps anyone else, she configured the meeting in the formal sense, saw to the myriad details involved in such operations, helped govern a group of student interns, drafted budgets and acted as paymaster, became a computer whiz, and worked with special care and effectiveness with authors and editors concerning submissions and revisions. While "no one is indispensable," she came close to being just that.

Thanks also go to many on the AEI staff, particularly Isabel Davidov and Hilary Laytham, for their professional conference management. In addition, some twelve interns shared in the conference work, did research assistance, and wrote summaries. They are David Anderson, Colleen Aylward, Philip Baylis, Nicholas Harding, Jennifer Hu, Paul Kullman, Janine Li, Joshua Lin, Susan McCarthy, Derek Mitchell, Todd Stephens, and Cecilia Sun.

Appreciation also goes to two speakers, Arthur Hummel, former American ambassador to the People's Republic of China, and Ding Mou-shih, representative in the United States of the Coordination Council for North American Affairs of the Republic of China, who delivered excellent lunch addresses. Each of the papers presented at the conference was subject to critical appraisal by an esteemed board of commentators. These included Christopher Clarke, Ralph Clough, David Dean, Kerry Dumbaugh, Nicholas Eberstadt, Wendy Frieman, Harry Harding, Ellis Joffe, Albert Keidel, Edwin Lim, Chong-Pin Lin, Donald Munro, Robert Sutter, and Anne Thurston.

This topic proved difficult, partly because it was relatively new but also because it was the proverbial moving target. Events have moved very rapidly since the conference, necessitating continuous updates and revisions. The editors have tried, nonetheless, to achieve a first approximation to the subject not only by putting together a representative and high-quality group but also by attempting their own integration in the concluding chapter. But there are undoubtedly many errors, of fact and interpretation, remaining. The editors can only accept responsibility for them and ask some small indulgence of the reader. Undoubtedly, better summaries and more commanding ideas concerning the Chinese and their future will soon emerge. Meanwhile, however, the editors hope that study of this important and fascinating topic will have been assisted, in a small and initial manner, by the present volume.

Finally, the editors would like to dedicate this volume to the memory of Chi-ming Hou, who, until his death in 1991, was vice president and director of international programs at the Chung-hua Institution for Economic Research in Taiwan and also professor of economics at Colgate University in the United States. His contributions to the conference and the book were of high quality, and his personal attributes of quiet scholarship and constant search for the truth will long be remembered by many on both sides of the Pacific.

PART ONE
Introduction

1

Introduction

Zhiling Lin and Thomas W. Robinson

Just as the outside world felt encouraged by the flow, and then the flood, of information about China's reform and opening up in the mid-to-late 1980s, there came the shocking news in June 1989 of bloodshed in Tiananmen Square. Following the incident, China entered a period of political regression and economic stagnation that lasted to the middle of 1991. But at the same time, the Communist political order collapsed in the former Soviet Union and in East Europe, the cold war came to an end, and the United States emerged as the sole superpower after its victory in the Gulf War. Amid the celebration of these triumphs, however, the world was greatly concerned about China, about its political, economic, strategic, and international situation, and most of all about its future.

The situation was also changing rapidly in the two other East Asian Chinese entities, Hong Kong and Taiwan. In 1987, Hong Kong, the last of Britain's colonial empire, entered its final decade under London's rule, first established in 1842. A world city, Hong Kong was Asia's financial and service cocapital (along with Tokyo), was still the best port on the long China coast, was the headquarters for the increasingly high levels of finance and trade with China, and (despite the opening up of China in the late 1970s) was the only place where Chinese and foreigners could meet each other in psychological and physical comfort. As for Taiwan, the island had become an attractive and dynamic place in many regards: it was the world's most successful export platform, it had modernized itself economically in little more than a single generation, it had managed to preserve the best of Chinese traditional culture while simultaneously undergoing full modernization, and it had even begun the transition from the long authoritarian rule under the Kuomintang toward full-fledged democracy.

By themselves, these developments are reason enough to devote scholarly and policy attention to Beijing, Hong Kong, and Taipei. In addition, though, a larger process appears to be at work, with

3

arresting implications for the three, for other parts of Asia, and for states and peoples outside the region: the construction—tentative at first and certainly without deliberate intent—of "Greater China." Such an entity, united by a common language, would comprise a "natural economic region" but would not be a single economy; it would share a common history and perhaps a common future but would not be united under any single administration. Provided with a common set of cultural assumptions, the Chinese in the three places could determine the relevance of that cultural background and tradition as they face the powerful impact of Westernization and advanced technology. Undeniably, "something" was happening, it was new, and it could alter the future course of all three.

This volume, the first such effort known to us in this field, addresses many issues posed by the trends and forces within and among the three Chinese entities as they could be seen in the early 1990s. The very newness of the topic prevents what is written herein from being definitive. But many ideas are introduced, trends assessed, and forecasts made. In the scheme of things, some forecasts may prove in error, some trends weighted perhaps incorrectly, and the ideas evaluated as only initial efforts. Nonetheless, that is the only way to begin, and that is why we have undertaken this work. In outline, here is what this book presents.

Shirk on the Politics of Post-Tiananmen China

Susan Shirk inquires into the politics of post-Tiananmen mainland China. She believes Deng Xiaoping made a serious, perhaps fatal, mistake when he decided to "use local officials as an effective political counterweight to the center without changing the old political rules of the game," although he never publicly articulated that strategy. The fiscal giveaways provided in 1990 and 1991 to the provinces did overpower the centralizing instincts of the conservative Chinese Communist party chiefs. But such sharing of funds among center, province, and enterprise merely generated political rents for politicians at all levels without improving economic efficiency. Indeed, local officials who enjoyed the rewards of partial reform became obstacles to carrying reform through to complete marketization.

Using their new financial authority to build political machines for themselves, the local politicians then fought off any attempt by the enterprises to change the rules of the game. They also struggled against returning to central control. Deng's creation of a class of proreform local officials backfired, however, because they blocked efforts to improve economic performance either by moving back completely to central control or by moving forward toward full marketization. "Playing to the provinces" through administrative decentralization thus both interfered with economic decentralization to the enterprise level and stimulated economic overheating. The consequent inflation, shortages, and deficits provided ammunition for conservatives in their drive to make a comeback, enabling them even before Tiananmen to eliminate the reformist contenders for the post-Deng leadership, even as Deng substituted a new group at the top dedicated to sustaining the reform drive. The resulting balance in the party Central Committee thus created a political deadlock, with reforms moving neither forward nor backward until Deng himself took further political initiatives later in 1991 and, more decisively, in 1992.

Feng on the People's Liberation Army

Feng Shengbao considers the role of the People's Liberation Army (PLA) in the Tiananmen period. The PLA is not politically neutral as the military is in the West or as politically independent as it is in some developing countries but totally subordinate to the Chinese Communist party. Military reform aims to build a powerful, modern, and regularized (but still "revolutionary") military force, but it excludes the idea of military professionalism, in which the military officer remains politically neutral. Although the modernization of military strategy and tactics has greatly affected the Chinese military's thinking and will eventually weaken the party's supremacy, "prodemocracy" officers have not yet understood what a politically neutral army is.

According to Feng Shengbao, the success of the reforms in military strategy and tactics allowed the party and Deng Xiaoping to maintain authority at the time of the June 4, 1989, Tiananmen incident. Although the PLA was presumably following orders handed down by the party, which at the time lacked consensus on what action to take, it risked and did lose its reputation by carrying them out.

After crushing the democracy movement, the party reorganized military personnel, especially the top leadership, and increased the amount of political study to maintain control. Yang Shangkun was made state chairman, and his brother Yang Baibing was made chief of the General Political Department. Political indoctrination now more than ever stressed the absolute leadership of the party over the army. Many officers, including a few liberals, believed the PLA would need a strongman after Deng. They believed the PLA should remain an instrument of the party, but doubted that the PLA would execute any "crazy" ideas on behalf of the octogenarians, such as invade Taiwan. They also pointed out that the reforms in other socialist countries may influence China and that if the June 4 "verdict" were to be reversed, a further emancipation of thought within the PLA would occur. As if to fulfill Feng's prediction that the Yangs would attempt to aggrandize their positions and that that would be resisted by the top party leadership, three years after Tiananmen both Yangs, as well as others associated with them, were removed from their positions of power.

Zhang on the Chinese Political Culture

Zhang Shuqiang focuses on three readily discernible ideological components of contemporary Chinese political culture: (1) orthodox Marxist doctrine as the dominant state-sanctioned "correct" philosophy; (2) the Confucian tradition as the ideological foundation of China's cultural identity; and (3) contemporary cultural nationalism as a rallying call for the rejuvenation of China. Although all debate must remain within the established ideological framework, Zhang points out that the "new" version of Marxism in China vitiates the most substantive aspects of orthodox Marxist doctrine. The redesign of socialism starts with the introduction of private ownership and market economics. In essence, the socialist economy has to be revitalized by an injection of capitalism. This means private ownership, the antithesis of socialism or communism, has to be approved as a means of production, and diverse forms of distribution—out-and-out exploitation in the quintessential Marxist sense—have to be approved.

In the past, the party leadership derived its legitimacy from the Chinese version of Marxism, but Marxism has turned out to be either a fallacy or an equivocation. The burden is now on the party to prove it still has a basis for legitimacy: an anxious totalitarian regime is trying to consolidate its hold on state power in the name of national stability and development. The party, averring that patriotism is essentially compatible with socialism, insists that to be Chinese is to embrace the party's socialism. Zhang terms this claim a "blatantly fascist interpretation of national character." The Chinese people are inspired instead by the real possibility of rejuvenating the nation both economically and culturally by assimilating nourishment from the West. The contention is therefore between democracy and autocracy. But the party has been trying to change the issue into a conflict between China and foreign countries to reclaim its legitimacy and orthodoxy as the bona fide representative of the whole nation.

The Confucian worldview, which sees an equilibrium among all the elements in the cosmos, is referred to as the will of Heaven. Politics is considered only an extension of moral philosophy or ethics. Society is understood to be a hierarchy of social roles with each individual fitting into a specific role to ensure harmony. It would be a serious character flaw not to stand in awe of the "mandate of Heaven," of one's superiors, or of the words of the sages. The leader rules the people in trust from Heaven for the welfare of the people, and when a ruler misrules he automatically forfeits his right to rule. The Tiananmen massacre graphically demonstrates the party's loss of the "mandate of Heaven."

New authoritarianism is a reform ideology based on the Confucian political-moral paradigm and could be interpreted as enlightened autocracy—a strong leader adopting undemocratic measures to enforce economic development. Western liberal democracy is another alternative, but the party leadership, in the name of "Chineseness," refuses to choose this approach, to its own peril in the end.

Banister on Demographics, Economics, and Politics

Judith Banister presents an overview of China's population dynamics and discusses the relations among the country's demographic, economic, and political trends. The 1990 census together with those taken on three previous occasions supplies very useful figures and trends. As of mid-1990, the total population was 1.133 billion people and was increasing at about 1.4 percent or 15 million people per year. Life expectancy was high at an average of sixty-eight years, birth and death rates remained low, childbearing was bunched in the middle twenties of the mother's age, marriage age remained in the early twenties for most all Chinese, and the fertility level was low and declining somewhat, mostly as a result of party-imposed birth control methods (including the one-child family and forced abortion, but also a comprehensive and widespread family planning delivery system) and the effects of urbanization and continued rural modernization. The age composition was rapidly changing as successive baby booms and their "echoes" reached employment and marriageable ages and then grew old, and migration and urbanization significantly affected the geographic distribution of people throughout the country (these mostly the results of the economic reforms).

The important point for the rest of the 1990s is that these figures and trends are not expected to change much, assuming no political or economic catastrophes. That is to say, population growth and change will not be the central determinants of the nature and change of the Chinese polity and its economy; rather, the reverse is true. Serious political breakdown, political errors, or economic reverses could greatly affect fertility levels in both rural and urban areas. With an expected population of 1.3 billion by the year 2000—that is, an additional 200 million people—any Chinese regime will have little room for error. But in the absence of serious problems, population increase could be as much a boon for China as a problem.

Lin on Cultural Currents

According to Zhiling Lin, contemporary Chinese society can be represented by the combination of three cultural currents: traditional, modernist, and "party." Traditional culture, although significantly weakened by Chinese Communist party policies, has experienced a renaissance in the post-Mao reform era that began in 1978. Modernist (Western) culture began influencing China about 250 years ago and continues to have a major impact. Party culture, appearing early in this century, uses Marxism-Leninism-Maoism to try to overcome elements of traditional culture, but at the same time it attempts to counter "undesirable" Western influence by disguising itself in traditional Chinese cultural garb.

But the Chinese people have begun to realize that it is party culture, not traditional culture, that has weakened China and that traditional and modernist currents, far from opposing each other as the party would have it, can be combined to vitalize the country, as seen in the cases of Hong Kong, Singapore, Taiwan, and South Korea. The party's ideology suppresses individualism through the network of the work unit to make people blindly obedient. The party's economic leveling of society has created a passive attitude toward work. Moreover, the party has encouraged people to fight each other, and to stay "proletarian." Confucianism, however, encourages people to work hard and to be outstanding to bring honor to the family, and modernization occurs amid class harmony and requires differentiation to achieve social progress. To preserve the best of the Chinese traditional outlook amid modernity, party culture must be replaced, and the cultural transformation eventually will lead to the end of Communist party rule in China.

Post-1978 reformist policy has led to the most productive period of the century. It has also modernized the people's ways of thinking, although the party continues to twist certain aspects of the Confucian tradition, such as obedience of lower social groups to higher, to serve its purposes. The spring 1989 movement came about because people saw the real obstacle to modernization not in traditional culture but in party culture. Students, teachers, intellectuals, and private enterprise owners realized this, but most workers and peasants had not yet reached this perceptual breakthrough and remained accustomed to the "big pot meal" mentality. Zhiling Lin concludes by emphasizing the importance of keeping the Chinese door open to outside influence, which, she states, will not corrode Chinese tradition but will help to enhance tradition-backed modernization.

Oi on Changes in Chinese Agriculture

Jean Oi inspects the role of agriculture in the pre- and post-Tiananmen reform eras. Deng Xiaoping succeeded in replacing the "iron rice bowl" system with that of a "get rich first" orientation, with its principal expression in the family responsibility system in agriculture. Production leaped upward during the 1980s and remained high throughout the early 1990s as a consequence. But China's agricultural sector faces an uncertain future, partly because of anxiety following the post-Tiananmen crackdown but primarily because of the inability of the agricultural sector to increase production since the mid-1980s. The household responsibility system and material incentives were necessary conditions for increased production in the early 1980s and were behind the rate of income increase, adjusted for inflation, of 14 percent from 1980 to 1985. But the key issue after that time was not so much the structure of agricultural production as the sufficiency of existing incentives for peasants to increase grain production.

In 1985, the state indirectly reduced the incentive for peasants to grow and sell more to the state by abolishing the unified procurement system and changing the price structure. Rapidly rising production costs accounted for the large decrease in the profitability of growing grain. Moreover, market prices were generally higher than state-set prices. Thus, the low profitability of grain compared with other income sources and sales opportunities explains why peasants increasingly moved away from grain production and why therefore agricultural production as a whole stagnated (to be sure, at a level much higher than prereform levels).

To solve the grain production and other similar rural problems required the leadership to make difficult political choices that threatened to undermine the very essence of the socialist system. Especially after Tiananmen, for fear of political turmoil the leadership did not dare to institute price reforms that would eliminate subsidies and raise basic commodity prices. Another politically sensitive question was property rights. Lack of ownership of the means of production was a basic reason why peasants failed to invest in their land. In the wake of the Tiananmen crackdown, peasants feared recollectivization of the land.

A third factor was lack of sustained capital investment in the agricultural sector. Investment instead went into rural enterprises. Collective investment of capital in agriculture as a percentage of total collective investment in fixed assets declined from 39.6 percent in 1982 to 9.4 percent in 1988. China's peasants and local officials responded to Deng's initial calls to develop a modern rural economy, relying on rural industrialization to generate wealth and absorb the surplus labor freed as a consequence of decollectivization. In the early 1990s, it remained an issue whether China's leadership could give up its policy of keeping the countryside in a subordinate role merely to produce grain for the urban areas.

Salem on the Chinese Economy Immediately after Tiananmen

Ellen Salem analyzes the Chinese economic situation after Tiananmen. She notes in particular the unexpectedly strong resurgence of economic regionalism, especially in the southern provinces. As the Beijing government attempts to recentralize power, local rights have replaced political reform as the rallying cry in the provinces. The central government has made extensive efforts to rescue the state industrial sector, which, funded by ever-increasing state subsidies and loans, produced a very high percentage of unsalable goods, thereby setting the stage for another round of inflation. These support funds were collected through higher taxes on the provinces.

Just after Tiananmen, China's leadership chose to revive outdated policies to deal with the new era's challenges. But because of the imminent change in leadership, a paralysis in decision making pervaded. During this time, China's economy lay in "cold storage." China's austerity program accomplished only two of its six objectives: it partly reduced inflation and reinstated rigid central planning. Funds for building the infrastructure, however, were sidetracked to subsidize the state industrial sector and to stave off restlessness in urban areas. The cancellation of soft loans and the falloff of foreign investment following the Tiananmen massacre further cut spending on infrastructure. At the same time, price reform and the movement toward a market economy were buried, at least until later in 1991.

Most threatening in terms of maintaining social stability was the rapid rise in unemployment. Massive unemployment goes hand in hand with low inflation, but efforts to give jobs to the unemployed would result in high inflation or a huge increase in state subsidies and hidden inflation. Salem points out that restive provincial governments resisted any political decision to maintain or accelerate the immediate post-Tiananmen backsliding toward central planning. She believes China will have a brighter future if the new leadership can separate party and state, abolish central planning, and institute meaningful price reform. Above all, the leadership must realize that economic reform cannot proceed without political reform. In a helpful postscript, written in early 1993, Salem notes where her early 1991 analysis was correct and where it erred. She fully approves of the halting of the drift back toward central planning and of the rapid movement toward marketization. She warns, however, that the Chinese economy, just because of the halfway and halting nature of latter-day reformism, still faces many challenges and crises.

Suttmeier on the Role of Science and Technology

Richard P. Suttmeier explores the role of science and technology in the emergence of Greater China. The quest for science and technology in China has always been tempered with the desire to maintain an essential Chineseness. All groups claim a nationalistic responsibility to foster science and technology as a means to achieve national wealth and power, but because these forces also give rise to cosmopolitanism, they tend to oppose the narrowness of nationalism. Thus, nationalism has both spurred and obstructed the development of science and technology.

Newly industrialized economies (NIEs) have established technical links with companies from more highly industrialized countries, accelerated research and development (R&D) investment, increased the number of students going abroad, enticed well-trained technical personnel back from the United States and elsewhere, and established technical outposts in their own countries to capture new technologies. Both Taiwan and mainland China have emphasized defense R&D and neglected enterprise R&D, although for different reasons (the prevalence of small firms in Taiwan, the failures of socialist incentives on the mainland). The mainland especially needs production and managerial technologies from abroad, particularly from NIEs, which may have more appropriate technologies than those of the more industrialized Western countries. There is much potential for mutual benefit from cooperation in science and technology between the three Chinese entities. Such cooperation is also likely to enhance the position of the Chinese in the new Asian technosystem.

Wei on Democratization in Taiwan

Yung Wei contends that the Republic of China on Taiwan (ROC) is in the process of achieving democratization while maintaining national unification, social stability, and economic development. The ROC's successful modernization does not conform to development theories stressing dependency on bureaucratic authoritarianism. This exceptional development model depends on two major factors: strong cohesion among the ruling elite, and the government's emphasis on growth and equity in its development efforts. The government first improved the rural sector through land reform and then supported the industrial sector with the aid of the expanded rural sector. Finally, after achieving an increased living standard and educational level for the population, the government began programs aimed at democratization.

Since as early as 1951, many Taiwanese have participated in county and provincial politics, and today almost all city mayors and county magistrates are Taiwanese, as are the overwhelming majority of provincial assembly members. Moreover, the president, the vice premier, more than 40 percent of the members of the Executive Yuan, and more than 48 percent of the members of the Standing Committee of the Nationalist party (KMT) are Taiwanese.

Many obstacles blocked the way to a more open political structure, including martial law, restrictions on forming new parties, incomplete national elections, the Taiwanese independence movement, the threat from mainland China, and the ROC's decline in international status. But with the passing of Chiang Kai-shek in 1974, his son, Chiang Ching-kuo, began the democratization process, including lifting martial law and allowing new parties to form. This process was continued by Taiwan-born President Lee Teng-hui, and by 1990 more than fifty parties had been registered with the Ministry of Interior Affairs.

The National Affairs Conference of 1990 arrived at some far-reaching conclusions, including the retirement of all senior members of national representative bodies by the end of 1991, the abolishment of the selection of members for national representative bodies from overseas Chinese and from occupational groups, the popular election of the governor of Taiwan and mayors of Taipei and Kao-hsiung, the termination of the Period of Mobilization and the Suppression of Rebellion, and the treatment of both sides of the Taiwan Strait as political entities and the enactment of laws concerned with their relations.

The main opposition party, the Democratic Progressive party

(DPP), wanted more drastic change, including a total overhaul of the parliamentary membership, direct election of the president, and a new constitution. If all these recommendations were accepted and implemented, it would be tantamount to the establishment of a new Republic of Taiwan. Partly to offset the separatist flavor of certain aspects of the National Affairs Conference and partly to gain a dominating role in deciding reunification policy, the KMT established the National Unification Council. It established a three-stage plan for reunification: mutually beneficial interchanges, official channels of communication, and mechanisms for deliberation.

Yung Wei sees no serious cleavages in the KMT but believes the opposition parties will remain divided. The major issues facing the ROC in the future are constitutional reform, ruling party reform, debate over a cabinet versus a presidential system of government, maintenance of law and order, social welfare, environmental protection, labor problems, and expansion of external relations. Taiwanese independence will be used by certain political elements to gain power, but it is unlikely to become a mainstream political movement. With the mushrooming of various think tanks, foundations, and funds in Taiwan, the links among knowledge, money, and power have increasingly become a political reality. A three-way impact will also occur among democratization, national unification, and foreign relations. Regarding the last point, however, Yung Wei does not foresee any serious threats from mainland China against Taiwan. Finally, he hopes that Taiwan's development experience can be shared with mainland China, thereby eventually leading to peaceful reunification of these two parts of the country.

Hou on the Taiwanese Economy

Chi-ming Hou argues that the Taiwanese economy will remain strong and be integrated further into the world economy in the 1990s. He predicts that Taiwan's economic ills will be overcome in a relatively short time. The island's phenomenal economic performance over the 1949–1989 period is due to the government's early promotion of exports, agriculture, savings, and education. The most significant factor, export expansion, created a great number of jobs, reduced income inequality, and contributed to the high savings ratio. The huge trade surplus that emerged in the late 1980s, however, has led to a large accumulation of foreign exchange reserves, which in turn could lead to a harmful outflow of capital. Moreover, in recent years, Taiwan has experienced a slowdown of growth along with somewhat higher inflation. The most important reason for this stagflation is the loss of vigor of private investment.

A relatively new factor has been social unrest due to labor-management confrontation and strong environmental protests. These have made many enterprises hesitant to invest. Moreover, the uncertainty created by domestic political struggles during the democratic transition and a rising crime rate can hardly inspire businesses to expand. Consequently, the investment climate during the very early 1990s deteriorated badly enough to create a temporary loss of confidence in the vitality of the economy. Given that the growth rate of gross national product (GNP) is still above 5 percent, inflation remains below 5 percent, and the unemployment rate is around 2 percent, however, Chi-ming Hou does not consider Taiwan to be in a poor economic state. On the contrary, he foresees a prosperous economy for the rest of the 1990s, based on the same basic ingredients of economic success as in the past. He qualifies this prediction by noting that political and social stability must be maintained, that labor-management relationships must remain relatively harmonious, that establishment of a social welfare system must be discouraged, that privatization of public enterprises should be speeded up, and that economic internationalization should continue.

Chiu on the Taiwanese Society in Transition

Hei-yuan Chiu presents a picture of Taiwanese society in transition from its original traditional form to thorough modernity. He believes that in the near future, Taiwan will become an open, pluralistic, and democratic society, assuming that continuing reforms do not suffer an unforeseen serious setback. Although liberalization and democratization have made people more open-minded and tolerant toward different political opinions, many Chinese on Taiwan still maintain a conservative attitude. Chiu's findings, based on survey research, show that most Taiwanese will not contest government limitations on freedoms if such actions create stability. Freedom of speech and freedom of association cannot be taken for granted in Taiwan because most people do not support them in times of chaos and instability. Although the main purpose of political reform is to give more people power, many actually feel powerless because the progress of reform does not always meet their expectations.

The government has also become more ineffective as a result of newly released social and political forces. Thus, in 1985, 91 percent of the respondents agreed with the statement of "bearing hardship leads to success." But in 1990, only 78 percent of respondents confirmed this statement. The 13 percent discrepancy shows a critical change in the Taiwanese work ethic.

Despite the impact of secular humanism, the product of Taiwan's modernization, folk religions remain the most popular faith in Taiwan, the strong utilitarian orientation of which motivates people to accumulate wealth. The island's high economic growth rate thus enriches the temples, and the elaborate festivals held there reinforce the people's commitment to folk religions. Taiwan also has substantial and increasing populations of Buddhists and Christians. The growing movement toward religion in general is correlated with the feeling of powerlessness and lack of standards that are the natural, if undesired, product of a modern society.

Lau on the Politics of Hong Kong

Siu-kai Lau writes about the Hong Kong political scene in the early 1990s. For nearly 150 years, Britain was able to maintain a stable and effective government in Hong Kong through a "fortuitous constellation of conditions." These include: the fear of China and the impracticality of independence, the high autonomy of the colonial government, the collaboration of the Chinese colonial elites, a general consensus on the political system and public policies, the integrity and good performance of the civil service, the depoliticization of society, the low level of social conflict, and high economic growth.

Since the 1970s, socioeconomic changes in Hong Kong have gradually impinged on the relations between the government and the people. These changes are attributable to the colonial government's short remaining life (in 1997, Hong Kong reverts to China), interference in the colony's autonomy by the Chinese government, insufficiency of democratic reforms, frustration of civil servants over their future, class conflict, popular identification with as well as fear of China, and a somewhat lower economic growth rate.

Siu-kai Lau calls for the consolidation of an allied political authority in Hong Kong and the formulation and implementation of a policy program that addresses the major problems confronting the territory before and after 1997. A probable outcome is an expanded political authority comprising the Hong Kong government, the Chinese government, and the moderate-conservative leaders. In this process, the power of the colonial government will decrease while that of the Chinese government, as well as that of local leaders, will increase.

15

Sung on the Economy and Society of Hong Kong

Yun-wing Sung analyzes the economy and the society of Hong Kong, in particular by examining Hong Kong's brain drain, capital outflow, economic internationalization, the "window" role for China, developments during the immediate post-Tiananmen period, and port and airport development plans. He is cautiously optimistic about Hong Kong's future. Although the Tiananmen crisis temporarily accelerated Hong Kong's capital outflow and brain drain, Sun points out that the economy remains vibrant. While real estate markets collapsed in Canada, Japan, and the United States in 1990, they rose beyond pre-Tiananmen peaks in Hong Kong. Despite an economic recession in North America, Hong Kong still maintained a moderate growth of about 2 percent in 1990 and recovered even further thereafter. In addition, because of rising unemployment in North America and a strong demand for labor in Hong Kong, the return of overseas Hong Kong emigrants increased.

Even without the reversion to Chinese rule in 1997, Hong Kong firms would tend to diversify and become multinational as they grow in size. The impending incorporation into China has only hastened this trend. Moreover, international investors have moved into Hong Kong to fill the partial vacuum left by the outward movement, for the while, of indigenous Hong Kong capital. Hong Kong's economic circumstance during the early 1990s was therefore not one of permanent outflow of skills and capital but one of economic internationalization. Capitalist and freewheeling Hong Kong is in fact the key to the opening up of the socialist and rigidly regimented Chinese economy. It acts as financier, trading partner, and middleman in both commodity and services trade. Hong Kong also facilitates the open-door policy in many intangible ways, serving as a contact point for foreign and Chinese companies, a conduit for market information and technology transfer, and a market and production training ground.

The Tiananmen incident and economic retrenchment led to a temporary decline in the volume of China-related business, but China also became more dependent on Hong Kong. For instance, after the incident, official soft loans to China dried up, but Hong Kong's loans to China remained relatively constant. Moreover, Hong Kong's investments in China tended to be strictly from the private sector, whereas part of the investment of other countries was supported by governmental loans. Hong Kong became the world's busiest container port in 1987, and the Kai Tak airport was forecast to be saturated by 1997. Thus, the Hong Kong government announced its decision to spend HK$127 billion (U.S.$16.3 billion) on a new airport and other facilities. The substantial capital spending would raise the real gross domestic product (GDP) by about 1 percent every year and generate 10,000 new jobs every year during construction.

The paradox of the future of Hong Kong is that the political side of the picture looks gloomy but the economic side looks bright. The future of Hong Kong depends first and foremost on what happens in Beijing rather than in Hong Kong. By investing massively in international links, human capital, and infrastructure, however, Hong Kong has significantly increased the chance that it will survive and prosper to and beyond 1997.

Weng on Reunification of the Chinese Entities

Byron Weng introduces his discussion of how a divided China might evolve by considering the issue of "competing successors" in divided nations. He defines a competing successor as a political entity with its own distinctive territory, people, and government, which claims to be sovereign but remains a component unit of a divided nation. Divided nations such as Germany, China, Korea, Vietnam, and Cambodia were or are composed of two or more competing successors. Competing successors of divided nations display more mutually penetrated relations, that is, their relations tend to be more sensitive and more tense. In a skewed manner, they give one another special favors in safe areas but impose tighter controls and regulations in threatened areas.

On the basis of the Henderson-Lebow paradigm of how divided nations might evolve toward reunification, and on the familiar patterns of international confrontation, competition, and collaboration, Weng sets forth a framework for analyzing and projecting the development of mainland China–Taiwan relations. (For a divided China, Hong Kong is not considered a competing successor but rather as a "lost" territory.) He divides the theoretical process into six stages: hostility, stalemate, competition, cooperation, negotiation, and settlement, with the last stage having two possibilities, partition or unification.

He then describes the actual development of PRC-ROC relations: tense cold war, 1949–1958; relaxed, stalemated cold war, 1959–1971; closed competition in a state of nominal cold war, 1971–1978; unilateral overtures for negotiation and open competition, 1979–1987; and open competition and partial cooperation, 1987–present. The interplay between external and internal influences constitutes the bulk of his chapter, leading to a discussion of possible outcomes of a negotiated settlement. If partition is the outcome, it can follow either the German model of establishing two Chinas or the Democratic Progressive party's preference of one China, one Taiwan. If unification is the outcome, three options are possible: a confederative arrangement, a federation, or a unitary state. The last option contains three formulas: one country, two systems; one China, two regions; and a condominium, national or regional. The key, Weng states, lies with mainland China. Although his evidence supports his positive and peaceful projections, he ends with a note of warning: who can say that there will be no further intervening historical "accidents" such as the Tiananmen tragedy?

Robinson on Security Relations

Thomas W. Robinson inspects the broad sweep of the Asian security situation for the 1990s. First, he indicates what post–cold war global trends and forces will affect Asia. These are multipolarity; the triple revolution of democratization, marketization, and interdependence; the universal primacy of domestic problems; the rise of technology; and the emergence of global issues. Their reflections in Asia are relative equality among the major powers; deepening and broadening of the drives toward democracy and market economies and the breakdown of national boundaries; continued peace among the major Asian powers; the effects of technology on economic growth; and the need to grapple with environmental and other problems through new international institutions. The possibility of constructing a new, higher-order Asian security system on their basis is reasonably good.

A range of security issues will have to be faced first, however. Short-term issues include the North Korean nuclear weapons problem and the Spratly Islands dispute. Medium-term issues comprise the emergence of China as a near-superpower, the question of what sort of Asian policy the United States will pursue, the reemergence of Japan as a full-fledged military power, the terms of reintegration of Russia into a new Asian security system, and how to prevent an Asian arms race. Longer-term issues include the Northern Islands dispute, North Korean succession and Korean reunification, Taiwan as a security problem, the problem of Burma, and the Kashmiri problem and the related question of India-Pakistan nuclear arms rivalry. All these issues are analyzed at length, with the conclusion that, if the major powers can work together, none of them will engender a breakdown into a balance-of-power system and eventual war.

Two regionwide, medium-long term Asian security issues are

also considered. The first is alternative forms that a nonbalance of power Asian security system might take. Robinson favors a proto-collective security system, taking portions of the NATO and Rio pacts as models, using that as a framework to allow Japanese rearmament and containment of Chinese expansionism, basing its institutional expression on the regional military equality of the major powers, and linking it to the United Nations through Article 51 of the charter. It would also have to be established on the basis of subregional balances of power as well as an American commitment to regional security leadership and continued strong Asian military deployments. The second is the relationship between economics and security in Asia. Several propositions are advanced: security and economics are structurally similar; they interpenetrate through power, budgets, and economic and national security policies; the time factor, that is, economic development and military modernization, is critically important; differential rates of economic growth strongly configure security outcomes; and economic development and military strategy are related through technology. In all these instances, illustrations relevant to the 1990s are provided.

Robinson finally applies these notions to the prospects for Greater China. General trends and forces, global and regional, should pull the three components of Greater China together. The North Korean nuclear weapons and the Spratly Islands questions are not of great import to Greater China, nor (presuming they can be solved peacefully) will any of the medium-term security issues (except the Taiwan security question) affect relations among China, Hong Kong, and Taiwan. The most important determinants are not, therefore, developments within or among the three Chinese entities or solution of Asian security issues. Rather, the driving forces are to be found in how the major powers restructure their relations and how economic problems are addressed. Of these, how China and the United States work out their problems and how Beijing elects, in general, to address its international environment are critical. China could go either way: toward participation, interdependence, and internationalism or toward nationalism, isolationism, and belligerence. China and America stand at the crossroads of extended long-term friendship or emnity.

Huan on the Influence of Domestic Developments on International Relations

Guocang Huan addresses the way domestic developments in the three components of Greater China affect their relations with other

Asian nations and with nations outside of Asia. He asserts that the dynamics among China, Taiwan, and Hong Kong will be determined by internal developments in the three, by interactions among them, and by changes in the international environment. Huan contends that a reduction of political tension and an increase in contacts between Chinese on the mainland and on Taiwan, especially at the non- and semigovernmental levels, will be most conducive to maintaining a balanced relationship. He also foresees a less influential role of the international community, especially Washington, in Beijing-Taipei relations.

As for Hong Kong, the local authorities should speed up the democratic reform and increase the Hong Kong people's opportunities for political participation. Further, if Beijing wants a smooth transition in 1997, it will have to increase its credibility among the population of Hong Kong by establishing liberal economic and political policies in China and expanding its tolerance of Hong Kong's local opposition. A rational, stable, and peaceful relationship among China, Taiwan, and Hong Kong would foster the political and economic development of all three. It would also contribute to peace, stability, and economic prosperity in the Asia-Pacific region.

PART TWO

Politics

2
Playing to the Provinces— Deng Xiaoping's Political Strategy of Economic Reform

Susan L. Shirk

The classic problem in marketizing a Communist economy is how to create an effective political counterweight to the "center," the central Communist party and government bureaucracy that has a strong vested interest in perpetuating central planning and that dominates policy making in Communist states. In the Soviet Union, Gorbachev decided that the only way to create such a counterweight was to open up the political arena to mass participation and political competition. It was a high-risk gamble, but he believed he had no other choice. As he said in 1987,

> Restructuring will only spin its wheels unless the main actor—the people—is included in it in a thoroughgoing way. . . . In order to make restructuring irreversible and to prevent a repetition of what happened in the past, everything must be placed under the control—once again—of the people. There is only one way to accomplish these tasks—through the broad democratization of Soviet society.[1]

Deng's Approach to Reform

Although Deng Xiaoping never publicly articulated his political strategy of economic reform, it is clear from the actions he took that he made a very different strategic calculation. He believed that he could use local officials as an effective political counterweight to the center without changing the old political rules of the game. He opted to retain the traditional Communist bureaucratic polity, with only minor modifications such as the more frequent policy work conferences designed to enhance the voice of the provinces in bureaucratic policy making. Why did Deng and his reformist allies decide to stick with

23

the old authoritarian bureaucratic system? An important reason was that China's central bureaucracy was less strong and less entrenched than that of the Soviet Union.[2]

The Stalinist model of a centrally planned economy was transferred to China from the Soviet Union some forty years ago and was easier to uproot in China than in the land of its origin: forty years is a brief stretch of time from the perspective of 2,500 years of Chinese history. Moreover, during the period when the Soviet-style system reigned, central control over economic life was much less extensive and less effective than in the USSR itself. Particularly since the Great Leap Forward (1958–1959) and even more since the Cultural Revolution (1966–1976), local governments in China have played a stronger economic role than their counterparts in the Soviet Union. The central planning apparatus was also weaker. Chinese central planning was more primitive and less inclusive than Soviet central planning: even during periods with a relatively high degree of administrative centralization, the Chinese central bureaucracy controlled the production and allocation of fewer than 600 products, while the Soviets had central control over 5,500 products.[3] Under China's version of the command economy, a substantial share of economic activity went on outside the national plan, and much of it was administered at the provincial level.

China also had the "benefit" of the Cultural Revolution experience. During the Cultural Revolution decade, social life became highly politicized and unpredictable. Thousands of intellectuals, professionals, and officials were pilloried in public meetings, fired from their jobs, and imprisoned. Ordinary citizens had to worry about being criticized by their co-workers and neighbors. Political campaigns disrupted the economy so that living standards stagnated and China fell increasingly behind its East Asian neighbors. The Cultural Revolution had a genuinely traumatic effect on Chinese urban society, compared by some Chinese with the social trauma of fascism in Europe. Having experienced the irrationalities of the Communist system in such an extreme form, the Chinese, leaders and citizens alike, were more ready to consider changing the system.

In addition to creating a constituency for reform, the Cultural Revolution weakened central party and government institutions so that their resistance to the reform drive that followed was less strong than it would have been otherwise. The normal operations of central party and government bodies were severely disrupted during the Cultural Revolution, with thousands of officials transferred to lower-level jobs or sent to the countryside for reeducation. As a result, party and state bureaucracies were less daunting opponents to economic reform than they were in the Soviet Union and other Communist states where their reign had been uninterrupted. In fact, central bureaucracies became active proponents of reforms such as fiscal decentralization, which they believed would rationalize and preserve their limited domain.

The comparison between China and the Soviet Union illuminates the logic of Deng Xiaoping's political strategy of economic reform. In China, the central party-state bureaucracy was a less formidable obstacle to market reforms, and previous waves of administrative decentralization had created the possibility that provincial party and government politicians could become the reformist counterweight to the more conservative center. Although provincial politicians were the appointed agents of the central Communist party organization, they were expected to articulate local interests.[4] With the support of provincial politicians, Deng might be able to push his reform program through the bureaucratic decision-making process and thus avoid the risks of changing the political rules of the game.

The ramifications of Deng's crucial strategic decision to process economic reforms through the traditional Communist political system were momentous. Two features of Communist political institutions (characteristic of the prereform USSR as well as of China) were particularly significant for shaping reform policy outcomes.

Consensus Decision Making. Economic policy making was delegated by the Communist party to the government bureaucracy. Within the bureaucracy, decisions were made by consensus, not majority rule. Economic reform policies either achieved consensus through bureaucratic bargaining, were referred to higher levels in the hierarchy for resolution, or were indefinitely postponed. Government ministries or provinces that had strong objections to policy proposals could veto them or force them to be modified. Consensus decision making militated against redistributive policies; policies tended to protect the original positions of bureaucratic interests and shift resources only incrementally.

Reciprocal Accountability within the Communist Party. Communist party leaders were chosen by an elite "selectorate" composed of the Central Committee, the revolutionary elders, and top military leaders (fewer than 500 "selectors" in all). The largest blocs within the selectorate were local (provincial) party and government officials, central party and government officials, and People's Liberation Army officers. Officials in these categories were appointed to their posts by the top party leaders through the Organization Department, but they

25

also had the authority to choose the party leaders. The party leaders chose the officials and the officials chose the leaders. This pattern of reciprocal accountability between top party leaders and subordinate party, government, and military officials was called by Robert Vincent Daniels the "circular flow of power."[5] The aspirants to top party leadership "campaigned" by promoting policies that would enable them to claim credit and win support from members of the selectorate.

In this institutional context, the political consequences of Deng Xiaoping's strategic choice to "play to the provinces" were mixed. The strategy was very successful at enhancing the political clout of provincial officials and putting it behind the reform drive. A Communist party Central Committee in which the largest bloc was local officials strongly committed to dismantling the centralized command economy helped sustain the momentum of reforms.

But at the same time, local officials who enjoyed the rewards of partial reform became obstacles to carrying industrial reform through to complete marketization. As one Chinese account explained, because the financial system reform devolving funds and responsibilities to localities was one step ahead of other reforms, each new reform initiative threatened the financial interests of localities.[6] Local officials blocked important measures like the replacement of profits with taxes, which would have expanded the financial autonomy of factories while shrinking the financial control of local governments over them. Having taken advantage of their new financial authority to build political machines for themselves, the local politicians fought off any attempt by the center or the enterprises to change the rules of the game in either direction (that is, back to central control or forward to market freedom).

The economic consequences of creating a system that strengthened the financial incentives of provincial officials were also mixed. True, the officials responded to the new incentives with entrepreneurial zeal, promoting local industry like born-and-bred businessmen and -women. To observe provincial officials touting their local investment climate to foreign business people was to realize that over forty years of Communist rule had not eradicated the Chinese aptitude for commerce, even among Communist bureaucrats, a group generally thought to be sluggishly conservative.

In an economic environment still characterized by irrational prices and lack of risk, however, the revenue-maximizing behavior of local officials produced perverse results. For example, excessive local investment and construction, most of it to build profitable but wasteful processing plants, created supply shortages, inflation, and deficits, and local protectionism Balkanized the national market. Determined to protect what the Chinese call their "partial interests," local officials blocked or diluted crucial reform initiatives that would have improved the efficiency and self-regulation of state enterprises. And local bureaucratic entrepreneurs continued to stimulate economic overheating, causing inflation and other problems that discredited the reform drive and allowed conservative Communist party elders to subvert it. Yet even when the conservatives attained dominance within the party in 1988, they were unable to impose a new financial system on the provinces. To flout the wishes of provincial politicians would have been political suicide during a period of succession competition even for conservative leaders whose primary base of support was the central bureaucracy.

Fiscal Decentralization

One of the earliest and most important steps in China's economic reform drive was the devolution of financial revenue and authority to provincial governments. A Chinese account called fiscal reform "the breakthrough point for the entire economic reform."[7] Experiments with revenue-sharing contracts between the central government and provincial governments were introduced in Jiangsu and Sichuan in 1977, and the method was extended to all provinces beginning in 1980. The fiscal decentralization, popularly called "eating in separate kitchens," was the cornerstone of Deng Xiaoping's political strategy to build a coalition of support for the reform drive. A reform package including greater financial autonomy for provincial governments gave provincial officials a vested interest in promoting and sustaining the reform drive. Such a policy package was the best way to create a political counterweight to the central bureaucracy and achieve market reform without changing the political system.[8]

Fiscal decentralization was an attractive solution to the political challenge of economic reform in China because of the country's prior experience. The prereform financial and planning systems had been based on a sharing of resources between center and locality. Mao Zedong had pioneered the strategy of playing to the provinces to counterbalance the political weight of the central bureaucracy, building up the power of provincial leaders within the Communist party Central Committee. Moreover, the progressive diffusion of funds, especially over the Cultural Revolution decade, made the Ministry of Finance sympathetic to any fiscal scheme that would prevent the further deterioration of its control and shift responsibility along with resources to the local level.

27

The evolution of fiscal reforms after 1980 demonstrates the political clout of provincial officials and the interests of central party leaders in winning support for the reform drive and for themselves by negotiating good terms for the provinces. The form of fiscal decentralization policies, namely particularistic contracts negotiated by the center with each province, gave central politicians the opportunity to win the gratitude and the political support of officials from each province. Sharing formulas tilted toward the provinces left the central treasury short of funds. The solution was to close the central revenue gap by politically innocuous solutions that widely spread the costs, namely, making some industries central fiscal preserves under state corporations, extracting loans from all provinces, and shifting more budgetary responsibilities to all provinces. Chinese fiscal reform followed the winning formula of concentrated benefits and diffused costs. While the net effect of this fiscal reform formula on the relative financial positions of the central government and local governments as a whole is still being debated,[9] the formula undoubtedly created political rewards for central politicians and put local politicians solidly in the reformist camp.

This chapter describes why fiscal reform made sense in the Chinese historical context and goes on to describe the evolution of the fiscal system over the course of the reform decade, showing how it reflects the political value of provincial officials to central politicians. After a brief note on other reform policies aimed at enhancing the power of localities, I discuss the consequences of fiscal decentralization. The chapter concludes by showing that the political logic of fiscal giveaways to the provinces overpowered the centralizing instincts of Li Peng and his conservative party allies when they came to power in 1988.

The Prereform Financial Relationship between Center and Localities

In 1951, a mere two years after the Communist takeover, the basic shape of the fiscal system of the People's Republic of China (PRC) was laid down. Although subsequently subjected to frequent tinkering, it essentially persists to the present day.[10] The center monopolized formal financial authority and shared resources with lower levels. The form of the system was decentralized revenue sharing. The system was called "unified leadership, level-by-level management." "Unified leadership" meant that the central government determined provincial expenditure budgets and that provincial governments had little freedom to make their own spending decisions.[11]

Because there was no Chinese Internal Revenue Service, no national revenue collection bureaucracy, local officials collected profits and taxes as the agents of the central government.

"Level-by-level management" meant that the profits of enterprises run by central ministries went to the central government and the profits of locally run enterprises went to local governments.[12] Revenue flows were established by the quasi-ownership relations (what the Chinese call "subordination relations") between different levels of government bureaucracy and the enterprises. If a locality's revenues were insufficient to meet its expenditures as set by the center, then the locality was appropriated a share of the industrial-commercial tax and other taxes generated by local economic activity that were categorized as "shared" revenues. Or if revenues from local enterprises exceeded local expenditure needs, then the locality remitted a surplus to the center. Most provinces gave the center more than they received from it. Light industry, on which profits are high, was controlled mainly by local authorities, while centrally controlled enterprises were concentrated in less profitable heavy industry.[13]

The prereform fiscal system reflected China's tradition of centralized formal authority with a significant degree of de facto decentralization to the provincial level (although specific arrangements were not identical to earlier ones).[14] Influenced by this historical tradition, China's Communist leaders sought to strengthen central authority but in the end established an administrative structure that was more decentralized than that of the Soviet Union.[15] The horizontal authority of local governments was more on a par with the vertical authority of central ministries than was the case in the USSR. The bureaucratic rank of provincial governments was equal to the bureaucratic rank of ministries in the PRC, just as it had been in the Kuomintang's republican government.[16] The power of appointment was also less highly centralized in China than in the Soviet Union, with the party center responsible for filling only 13,000 posts on its *nomenklatura* list, as compared with 51,000 in the Soviet Union.[17] While the heads of provincial finance departments were appointed by the party authorities in Beijing (the central *nomenklatura* included all positions one and two steps down in the hierarchy), all lower-level financial officials were chosen by provincial party authorities.

The more prominent role of provincial officials in the PRC than in the USSR reflected not only Chinese tradition but also several contemporary factors. Because the technical capacity of Chinese central planners was inadequate to the task of planning the entire economy, Beijing's economic commands never had the scope that Moscow's did. Chinese central economic authorities from the beginning relied on local help for industrial planning, finance, and administration. Provincial officials also played a more prominent role in the Chinese Communist party than they did in the Communist party of the Soviet Union. Provincial-level Communist party organizations were stronger in China than in the Soviet Union, where they had been decimated by Stalin.[18]

The greater weight of Chinese provincial officials in the financial system also stemmed from differences in the Chinese and Soviet government-set price system. In the Soviet Union, the prices made heavy industry, which was under centralized administration, highly profitable. Chinese prices, in contrast, made heavy industry much less profitable and thereby forced the center to depend on revenues generated by light industrial plants, most of which were small and locally run.

On the expenditure side, the prereform PRC fiscal system was nearly as centralized as the Soviet one. Expenditures were decoupled from revenues. The fact that a province generated more funds did not mean it could spend them. Ministries handed down compulsory financial targets to provinces and had complete budgetary control over enterprise expenditures. If a province fulfilled its revenue collection targets and spent within the expenditure target, it was permitted to retain a small share of above-budget revenue, but its uses still had to be approved by the center.

Even on the revenue side, although the profits of locally run factories were earmarked as local revenues, the center was very much in command. Revenue-sharing contracts were renegotiated annually by central authorities. Year-by-year contracting caused haggling between center and provinces and made it impossible for provincial governments to accumulate funds for investment; whenever a province retained a substantial revenue surplus, the central government changed the terms to claim a larger share of it.[19] Annual contracts also enhanced central authority by forcing provinces to compete with one another to obtain a good deal from the center by demonstrating compliance with central instructions. By transferring funds through Beijing to backward regions, the center used the system to promote income redistribution and equalization of social services.[20]

Over time, however, the Chinese fiscal system evolved in the direction of greater decentralization. There were two reasons for this trend. First, given the center's essential dependence on the light industrial profits produced by local factories, it made economic sense for the center to create a system that was more "incentive compatible." Allowing provinces to retain a larger share of revenues, especially overtarget revenues, and granting them the discretion to spend them, would strengthen the motivation of provincial officials to promote profitable enterprises and conscientiously collect revenues from them. Deng Xiaoping, who when serving as minister of finance during the early 1950s, had laid down the basic principles for the financial system, stressed the incentive effect of allowing provincial governments to retain surplus revenues as a reserve fund.[21]

Second, in view of the political influence of provincial officials within the Communist party, it made political sense for party leaders to "play to the provinces." The way PRC institutions were structured made provincial officials a natural counterweight to central officials. Whenever Mao Zedong felt his political dominance threatened by rival party leaders and his policy initiatives obstructed by the central government planners and ministry officials who supported his rivals, he turned to provincial leaders for support. Mao's rhetoric of "playing to the provinces" linked the assertion of provincial authority to party leadership and politics in command, as pitted against the narrowly economic and partial interests of the ministries.[22] In two dramatic instances during the 1950s and 1960s, Mao Zedong used this strategy to overcome the resistance of central planners and ministry officials to his program for accelerating economic growth and social transformation and to defeat his party rivals.[23]

Mao sped the pace of agricultural cooperativization and launched the Great Leap Forward by mobilizing the support of provincial leaders at meetings in 1955–1957.[24] An integral part of the Great Leap Forward campaign to collectivize agriculture, industrialize the countryside, and speed up economic modernization was a package of policies delegating greater fiscal and administrative power to the provinces. Provinces were granted a larger share of their revenues, greater discretion over tax rates and expenditures, planning authority, and "ownership" of almost all central enterprises.[25] Theoretically, the new sharing arrangements were to be fixed for three years to enable provinces to make long-term plans, but when the Great Leap Forward turned into a national economic disaster, the arrangements were adjusted one year later in 1959. When economic failure caused Mao Zedong to lose prestige and the central economic organs to resurge, the fiscal system was recentralized. It was impossible to put the cat back into the bag, however. Funds and financial authority remained more dispersed than they had been before the Great Leap.

A second wave of decentralization was stirred up by Mao Zedong in the mid-1960s when he reclaimed power from central bureaucrats and Communist party moderates by launching the Cultural Revolution. In 1964, provinces were authorized to set aside a portion of their revenues as extrabudgetary funds, creating a financial cushion to win the support of provincial subordinates for Mao's national policy initiatives.[26] In 1968, enterprises were allowed to retain approximately 10 percent of their profits to use for local projects.[27] From 1965 to 1966 on, provinces regained authority over construction projects under a certain limit and were granted a share of their budget surplus for their own use.[28]

The fiscal system introduced in 1970 by Mao's radical supporters was even more tilted toward the provinces. A program of regional self-sufficiency, justified by the threat of war, was introduced, involving a massive transfer of central enterprises to provincial control and a shift of most revenue sources and expenditure categories to the provincial level.[29] Provincial governments were granted authority to set their own budgets and, after transferring a lump sum to the center according to contract, were able to keep and use all remaining revenues.[30] After Deng Xiaoping returned to power in 1975, he attempted to restore central control over budgetary authority and funds, provoking a political struggle in which the radical Gang of Four took the side of the provinces.[31] At the time of Mao's death in 1976, financial authority and resources were still highly dispersed, and provincial authorities, especially from the industrialized provinces that remitted a large proportion of their revenues to the center, were pressing for even more fiscal decentralization.[32]

The Initiation of Fiscal System Reforms

The history of the 1949–1976 fiscal system provides the context in which Deng Xiaoping and Zhao Ziyang decided to lead off the drive for fiscal reform. As one economic official said, "eating in separate kitchens" was the "result of history . . . there was no other rational solution."[33] The legacy of the prior system explains the political logic of fiscal reform.

A Tradition of Revenues Divided according to the Quasi-Ownership of Enterprises by Different Levels of Government. Centrally run enterprises provided revenues for the center, and locally run enterprises provided revenues for provinces. Different levels of government assumed proprietary financial rights over their own enterprises.[34]

A Trend of Dispersion of Financial Resources That Had Accelerated over the Decade of the Cultural Revolution. Provincial governments ran a large proportion of industrial enterprises, retained a substantial share of budgetary revenue, and controlled a sizable amount of extrabudgetary funds.[35] These resources and powers had come to be viewed by provincial officials as entitlements. The central treasury could not be supported by the taxes and profits of central enterprises and was dependent on profits and taxes generated by locally run (mostly light) industry.[36] As Donnithorne put it, the Chinese central government was in the position of a medieval king who was not able to live off his own funds and who therefore had to extract funds from feudatories.[37]

A Pattern of "Playing to the Provinces" in Elite Political Competition. Mao Zedong, by playing to the provinces during the Great Leap Forward and Cultural Revolution, had turned provincial officials into a key constituency within the party. After 1958, almost all the provincial party first secretaries were either full or alternate members of the Central Committee, and a significant number (approximately half) of Politburo members were concurrent or former provincial first secretaries.[38] Provincial leaders were important members of the "selectorate" that chose the party leader. To extend Donnithorne's metaphor, the feudatories had the power to select the king and could bring him down. The central government and Communist party had formal authority over provincial governments, but the political incentives of individual party leaders led them not to use this authority against provincial officials—to exercise self-restraint[39]—and to keep good relations with them instead.

No Division of Authority and Responsibility between Central and Local Governments. Funds had been decentralized, but fiscal responsibility had not. The system remained one of "eating from the big pot." The center was considered responsible for guaranteeing a given original level of local revenues even when the economic situation changed.[40] Whenever unexpected economic developments landed provinces in financial straits, the Ministry of Finance was expected to bail them out. According to the same principle, if the central budget was hard pressed, the Ministry of Finance could reclaim funds from the provinces by renegotiating the terms of annual sharing contracts. There was no institutionalized link between revenue and expenditure, between power and responsibility.

The initiative to expand fiscal autonomy with the eating-in-separate-kitchens reform came from both the bottom up and the top down. Several provinces proposed revenue-sharing experiments during 1976 and 1977. The boldest was Jiangsu, a highly developed coastal province that proposed a package of decentralizing reforms in planning, material allocation, and fiscal management. Jiangsu's proposed fiscal arrangement, the "fixed rate responsibility" system, was a variant of the "sharing total revenue" arrangement implemented nationally from 1959 to 1970 and in 1976. Total provincial revenues were to be split between center and province (Jiangsu's share was set at 42 percent), with the percentages remaining unchanged for four years. The province was to decide on its own expenditures (central ministries were to cease issuing spending targets to the province) and was to be responsible for balancing its own budget. Jiangsu's experiment was introduced in 1977, and by 1980 was judged a success in motivating the province to expand production and revenue and to contribute more revenue to the center.[41] Two other types of contractual sharing schemes that were tried out on an experimental basis in sixteen other provinces beginning in 1977 were suggested by the minister of finance, Zhang Jingfu.[42]

The move to popularize fiscal decentralization was proposed in 1979 by the Ministry of Finance, which was motivated by the desire to divest itself of sole responsibility for financial management.[43] The immediate context of the decision was the inability of the ministry to meet its revenue needs because the fiscal system had become so dispersed during the 1960s and 1970s. Provincial officials refused to listen to the center and pursued their own interests. When describing the position of the Ministry of Finance, officials often used the family metaphor: as family head, the Finance Ministry had a hard time managing the family without enough money. The children argued among themselves and complained that the family head mistreated them. In that situation, it is better for the family head to divide the family and put the children off on their own.[44]

From the viewpoint of the Ministry of Finance, the advantage of "eating in separate kitchens" was that it clarified the responsibilities as well as the resources of each tier of government and guaranteed central income at current levels. The reform would stem the progressive deterioration of central revenues and force localities to share financial risk with the center. Minister of Finance Zhang Jingfu diagnosed the problems with the previous system at the National People's Congress in June 1979:

> The current system of public finance administration, in terms of the relationship between central government finance and regional finance, is still in a state in which true "administration by separate levels" is unimplemented, the authority and duties of the various levels with regard to public finance are not clearly defined, what should be concentrated is not concentrated and what should be dispersed is not dispersed.[45]

Another official expressed the ministry viewpoint in more pointed language: "Financial power had become so dispersed during the Cultural Revolution that the eating-in-separate-kitchens system was the only way the Finance Ministry could fix its level of state revenue. After the Cultural Revolution, this was the only way the Finance Ministry could get its hands on the money."[46] When advocating the scheme to the bureaucracy, Ministry of Finance officials stressed its incentive advantages in arousing local economic activism, but in their own minds they viewed the scheme as a move in the direction of tightening up, not letting go.

The Communist party had instructed the Ministry of Finance to draft the 1979 fiscal reform.[47] According to a Ministry of Finance official, the decision to carry out fiscal decentralization was made by a small group of top party leaders including Zhao Ziyang, who had just come from Sichuan. As the ministry official put it, "They decided to give power and money to provincial leaders which made them happy and made them support reform." Others also attributed the initiative to Zhao, who, having just come from Sichuan, understood the perspective of provincial officials and convinced Deng Xiaoping to play to it.[48] The reformist leadership of the party promoted fiscal reform as a way to win the support of the provincial leaders for the reform drive.

The pressure from provincial officials for greater fiscal autonomy was palpable to central party and government officials. Some officials I interviewed said that the provinces left the Ministry of Finance little choice but to pursue fiscal decentralization. As one official said, "They couldn't *not* do it at that time; the provinces wouldn't have agreed." The provincial leaders "forced a showdown" with the center and insisted on a fiscal scheme that would be fixed for several years, that allowed them to decide how to spend their revenues, and that gave them a larger share of their revenues.[49] In the context of succession politics—Deng Xiaoping was fighting to get rid of Mao's chosen successor, Party Chairman Hua Guofeng, and place his reformist lieutenants Zhao Ziyang and Hu Yaobang in power—the provincial leaders could not be denied.

The meetings discussing the fiscal system reforms gave provincial leaders ample opportunities to voice their demands. At a central work conference in April 1979, fiscal decentralization was discussed and one form of decentralization chosen. A conference of provincial party secretaries in October 1979 decided to adopt a different form of decentralization.[50] The final formula and the timetable for implementation, as well as each province's sharing contract (including base figure, percentages to be remitted and retained, or amount of subsidy), were determined at a national planning conference attended by representatives of provinces and ministries in December 1979.[51]

The implementation of the reform was supposed to await the return of several thousand large enterprises[52] to direct central government subordination, but this condition was never met. Both the enterprises and the provinces objected.[53] Instead, at the December 1979 National Planning Conference, a sense of urgency, particularly on the part of provincial participants, compelled a decision to rush ahead to implementation without recentralizing the enterprises.[54] As Naughton observes, "Local governments got greater operational autonomy without having to sacrifice any of their revenue sources."[55]

At the time the "eating-in-separate-kitchens" reform was introduced, some critical voices were heard. A few economists identified the potential problems with the method at policy research conferences in 1979–1980.[56] A paper criticizing fiscal decentralization came out of the Economic Reform Small Group, the precursor of the Economic Reform Commission.[57] But the policy had such a compelling political logic from the perspectives of the reformist Communist party leadership, the Ministry of Finance, and provincial officials that any doubts about the wisdom of the policy were swept aside.[58]

"Eating in Separate Kitchens"

The fiscal reforms introduced in 1980 expanded the fiscal authority and resources of provinces. Although the contractual sharing form of the new fiscal arrangements resembled that of the past, the new arrangements were fundamentally different in three respects.[59] First, revenue shares were fixed for five years so that provinces could profit from increases in revenue and plan ahead. Second, provinces were responsible for balancing their own budgets by adjusting their expenditures to match their revenues. They could no longer rely on bailouts from the center. Third, provinces had budgetary authority to arrange the structure and amount of local spending. They ceased to receive mandatory fiscal targets from the central ministries.[60]

The new system was applied flexibly to the thirty provincial-level governments, establishing different specific arrangements for different regions. The reform included five separate arrangements.[61]

1. Guangdong and Fujian, the two provinces where national efforts to attract foreign investment were concentrated, were granted the most generous plan, "lump sum transfer." Almost all revenue sources were turned over to the provinces. Guangdong committed to contribute to the center 1 billion yuan per year and Fujian to receive

as subsidy 150 million yuan per year. The amounts were fixed for five years. The provinces could keep everything above these amounts.

2. The metropolises of Beijing, Tianjin, and Shanghai, which provided the lion's share of central revenues, were placed on the most restrictive plan despite their objections. Their plan, a version of the Jiangsu "sharing total revenue" arrangement, fixed a percentage of total revenue they were required to remit to the center each year.[62] Because the funds they generated were vitally necessary to the central government, their percentages were revised every year, in contrast with the Jiangsu scheme, which would have fixed them for four years.

3. Jiangsu continued its experiment in "sharing total revenue" with the percentages fixed for four years. With the exception of the profits and taxes of centrally controlled enterprises, which in all schemes continued to be channeled directly to the central treasury,[63] all taxes and profits were lumped together and then divided by percentage between center and province.

4. Sixteen provinces were put on a "sharing specific revenue" system that resembled the sharing arrangement in effect from 1951 to 1958. Revenue sources were divided into four categories: central fixed income, local fixed income, fixed-rate shared income, and income shared by adjustment. Central fixed income was obtained mainly from the profits and taxes of centrally run enterprises. Local fixed income was derived mainly from the profits of locally run enterprises. Fixed-rate shared income came mainly from those large enterprises that had been devolved to local management during the Cultural Revolution that the center wanted to reclaim (the center got 80 percent of their profits; the province 20 percent). The only revenue included in the category "income shared by adjustment" was the industrial commercial tax, the most important tax revenue. The contract fixed the sharing rate for shared income, adjustment-shared income, and the local remittance to the center for five years.

The "sharing specific revenue" system was chosen over the Jiangsu "sharing total revenue" system for the majority of provinces by provincial party secretaries at their October 1979 meeting.[64] The "sharing specific revenue" arrangement earmarked the profits of local enterprises for local revenues and thereby strengthened the local government's sense of proprietorship over the enterprises. During a period of economic expansion and optimism, most local officials preferred this form of revenue sharing.

5. Eight national minority provinces and autonomous regions that had previously received subsidies from the center to cover their chronic deficits were put on the "sharing specific revenue" system

with their subsidy fixed for five years and increasing annually by 10 percent. These provinces could retain the total amount of revenue collected above the budget.

The Evolution of Fiscal Sharing Systems, 1980–1987

The evolution of fiscal sharing schemes reveals the ability of provincial officials to win advantageous terms from the center because central party leaders needed their support for the reform drive and for their own political careers. Provincial officials could make a strong case to keep more revenues, because they were taking on more budgetary responsibilities and the reform environment created new uncertainties for their enterprises.

The terms of each revenue-sharing contract were set in bargaining between the provincial officials and the Budget Department of the Ministry of Finance. The agreement had to be approved by the Office of the Minister of Finance and by the State Council.[65] And if a province was dissatisfied with the terms of its contract, it appealed to the minister of finance or even higher to the State Council.[66] In effect, the responsibility for each contract was appropriated by the State Council, whose members were sensitive to political direction from the top levels of the Communist party. The revenue-sharing contract was a political document, and the politicians in the State Council wanted to claim credit for it.

When the new sharing rates between the center and various provinces were negotiated at the December 1979 Planning Conference, the provinces came out ahead of the center.[67] The Ministry of Finance agreed to lower its revenue targets and increase central appropriations by 3 billion yuan, reducing the provinces' expenditure burden by 10 percent and providing an additional several billion yuan as subsidies; it had to absorb a budget deficit of almost 13 billion yuan.[68] This pattern of fiscal bargaining between center and province, that is, setting initial sharing rates that were overly generous to the provinces and that left the center with insufficient funds, was observed by several officials I interviewed. It had occurred in the case of the Jiangsu experiment in 1977; after one year, the center's share was adjusted up from 57 percent to 61 percent.[69] One official explained that as a rule, the center gave in to provinces when negotiating base numbers and percentages. The center always felt it had to "take care of" the localities, especially because its reform policies were responsible for squeezing many local enterprises.

Although the original intention was for fiscal contracts to remain fixed for a period of five years, the economic and political environment interfered. On the economic side, the reform of other aspects of the economic system failed to keep pace with fiscal reform.[70] Prices were still administratively controlled, so whenever a product's price was revised, provinces whose revenues were affected demanded, and usually received, an adjustment in their fiscal sharing contract. When textile prices were changed, for example, textile-producing localities wanted the center to compensate them. And whenever the subordinate relations of an enterprise were altered by, for example, shifting a factory from local management to central management, there was a battle to get the center to redraw the revenue and expenditure sharing line.[71]

The environment was particularly perilous during the initial period of fiscal reform, which coincided with the 1981–1982 retrenchment. Especially hard hit were provinces like Liaoning that received most of their income from heavy industry, which bore the brunt of contractionary policies. In Liaoning's case, the center agreed to help by raising its revenue retention rate but made it wait a year because of heavy central deficits.[72]

In an uncertain economic environment, the system of fiscal contracting became a method for maintaining the center-provincial balance. One article from the Ministry of Finance praised fiscal reform for "in a period of change during the economic structural reforms . . . maintaining relative stability in the distribution relationship between the central administration and local administrations and reducing the pounding on the budget management system resulting from changes in economic factors."[73] In 1983, there was a major readjustment of contract terms to compensate provinces for the 1980–1982 changes in the subordinate relations of enterprises, changes in interest rates, changes in the prices of such items as soybeans and petroleum for agricultural use, and unexpected expenses to demobilize soldiers.[74] The provinces treated their original financial position as an entitlement that they expected the center to preserve by compensating for economic perturbations.

The central government was never able to shift fiscal responsibility to the provinces even though that had been the aim of the 1980 reform. After the reform was introduced, the kitchens were not entirely separate after all. Everyone still expected the center to feed them. As one Ministry of Finance assessment concluded, "While in name there is separate responsibility at different levels, this is not really implemented and the problem of 'eating from the big pot' has not been fundamentally resolved."[75] The provinces' financial dependence on the center had not been cured. A Ministry of Finance official complained in an interview that the reform system that was called a "guarantee for doing" (*baogan*, usually loosely translated as "contract") was in reality a "guarantee for not doing" (*bao bu gan*) system.[76]

The center's continuous solicitousness toward the provinces reflected China's institutional context. Policy making in the bureaucratic arena required consensus, which would have been impossible to obtain if provincial officials were alienated by tough fiscal treatment from the center. Keeping the provinces satisfied and on board the reform drive was an important consideration for reformist party leaders.

Another political consideration was succession politics. The eating-in-separate-kitchens reform was a set of particularistic deals for provincial officials designed to win their support for individual party leaders as well as for the reform drive. The only provinces that were clearly dissatisfied were the three metropolises, whose revenues were too crucial to the center to allow political considerations to dominate.[77] Zhao Ziyang tried to appease officials from the metropolises by periodically raising their revenue share.[78]

The fiscal giveaways served the collective interests of party leaders in building support for reform and their individual interests in building support for themselves but left the central treasury too poor to meet its obligations for providing price subsidies, infrastructure construction, and the like. Therefore, Beijing officials devised several politically innocuous approaches to meeting central revenue needs.

First, they appropriated the earnings of several of the most profitable industries by organizing them into national-state corporations. State corporations for automobiles, tobacco products, petrochemicals, nonferrous metals, and shipping were established during 1982–1983 to help solve the budget difficulties.[79] The creation of these corporations, which was urged on Zhao Ziyang by his adviser Ma Hong, was supported unanimously by the party leadership.[80] Central corporations were considered a matter of fiscal necessity even though they flew in the face of market reform principles. As monopolies they discouraged competition, and as bureaucratic entities they constrained the freedom of subordinate enterprises. Enterprises under these corporations chafed at the restrictions and often complained about them to the State Economic Commission, but there was little that commission could do. Beginning in 1984, the Reform Commission and State Council held meetings to discuss how to restore competition and enterprise autonomy to the sectors controlled by corporations, but no progress was made.[81] As of 1985, the revenues generated by these corporations, as well as by all enterprises under the ministries of petroleum, coal, and electric power, had become the preserve of the center.[82]

Most of the industries affected by the creation of central corporations were widely dispersed. To appease the provinces and ministries that lost revenues to the new corporations, Beijing offered them side payments, including a 20 percent share of the taxes and profits of the enterprises they gave up. Creating corporations was a more feasible way to increase central revenues than seeking revenue from particular provinces. Even so, central implementation of these corporations was lax. In the case of the tobacco corporation, for example, many localities refused to give up their cigarette factories, and no one forced them to do so. The automobile corporation also had less than a complete monopoly.[83]

Second, "temporary" shortfalls in central revenue were met by ad hoc extractions applied universally. Provincial governments lent the center 8 billion yuan in 1980 and another 4 billion in 1981; the center wrote off the loans in 1982.[84] In 1983, a 10 percent tax (later raised to 15 percent) on extrabudgetary funds was put on all provinces to generate central funds for infrastructure projects, and a 10 percent tax on construction projects financed by extrabudgetary funds was added at the end of 1983.[85] In 1987, all budgetary expenditures were cut by 10 percent, and local officials were required to lend this amount to the center.[86] Throughout the decade, local governments, enterprises, and individuals were pressured to purchase treasury bonds "voluntarily." Of course, these extractions proved that "eating from the big pot" worked both ways: the provinces were expected to bail out the center, just as the center was expected to bail out the provinces.

Finally, the central government shifted more budgetary responsibilities to all the provinces. The center handed over to provinces virtually all responsibility for price subsidies, housing and urban infrastructure construction, education, health, and many other budget items that were calculated according to uniform formulas.

The universal approach for generating central revenues was politically safer for party leaders than leaning hard on particular provinces. Everyone paid a little. No one felt the pinch too severely.[87] With the combination of particularistic sharing contracts tilted toward the provinces and a few sectoral preserves, uniform, universally applied extractions and uniform, formula-based expenditure obligations to pay back the center, party leaders had found a politically winning formula of concentrated benefits and diffuse costs.

The evolution of revenue-sharing arrangements after 1980 reflected central officials' continued deference toward provincial interests. The State Council sometimes justified policy modifications as measures to strengthen central financial control.[88] Party and government leaders did have worries about how to protect central revenues and key capital construction. And central budget deficits preoccupied conservative party elders and the central economic bureaucracies. But in fact, shifts in revenue-sharing arrangements were impelled more by changes in the situation at the lower levels than by the needs of the central treasury.

In 1982, two years after the reforms were introduced, ten of the sixteen provinces originally on the "sharing specific revenues" system shifted over to the Jiangsu "sharing total revenues" system, and by 1983, all provinces except the three metropolises and Guangdong and Fujian were on the Jiangsu system.[89] With the exception of centrally run enterprises whose profits and taxes still went directly to the center, the profits and taxes of all enterprises were pooled, with the center and province dividing the total.

The reason for the change was that readjustment, wage increases, and enterprise profit retention had reduced the remitted profits of local enterprises, and local governments were suffering.[90] Under the "sharing total revenue" system, local governments got a larger share of more stable industrial-commercial tax revenues in exchange for giving up a share of the profits of local enterprises. During a period of expansion, local governments preferred the "sharing specific revenue" system because local enterprise profits were growing and their claim on these profits was complete. The "sharing specific revenue" system also made their proprietorship of local factories more direct. But in a time when contraction and structural reform were threatening the profits of local factories, they preferred to spread their risk with a system that put their finances on a broader base. As one 1982 account explained, while the "sharing specific revenue" method seems attractive to localities, "as a matter of fact, when the local specific income increases slowly or even decreases because of various reasons, while the supplementary income from the revenue of industrial and commercial tax increases relatively sharply or does not decrease, the localities will be willing to accept the method of sharing total revenues."[91] In other words, provincial officials will opt for whatever sharing scheme will maximize their short-term return. In 1982–1983, the provinces obtained not only a beneficial change in the fiscal sharing method but also new sharing rates that were computed to compensate them for the loans they had provided to the center.[92]

The primacy of provincial interests was demonstrated once again when in 1982 Ministry of Finance officials and Zhao Ziyang's advisers proposed a radical transformation of China's financial system, the "replacement of profits with taxes." Instead of remitting profits, enterprises would pay a variety of taxes. Two objectives of this proposal were (1) to reduce the negotiability of enterprise and local government financial obligations by formalizing them in the form of taxes and (2) to weaken the financial link between enterprise "ownership" and budgetary revenues by creating local taxes and national taxes that all enterprises, regardless of their subordinate relations, would pay.[93]

Provincial officials resisted the effort to replace the easily manipulable and politically useful system of financial contracting with a uniform, legalized tax system. True, they wasted time and energy haggling over the terms of the financial contracts with the center above and the enterprises below, since their fiscal relations with both in the short term were zero-sum.[94] And the formal authority of the center gave it the upper hand in bargaining over fiscal sharing contracts with provinces so that provincial officials competed to win good terms from the center. Yet the center rarely used its leverage over the provinces, preferring to bend toward them for the reasons discussed above. And, most important to provincial leaders, the power to bargain profit retention contracts with local enterprises was politically valuable. It offered local officials opportunities to collect political rents and build local machines.[95]

Provincial officials also opposed a tax system to fund local governments from local taxes and national government from national taxes, to be paid by all enterprises, because they wanted to maintain their proprietary financial rights over local enterprises. The shift to the "sharing total revenue" Jiangsu system from the "sharing specific revenues" system in 1982–1983 had diffused but not broken the financial link between provincial governments and provincial enterprises. Provincial officials enjoyed the political and economic benefits of their role as corporate heads of the local economy and were loath to give them up.[96] One Ministry of Finance official said, "An objective of the replacement of profits with taxes reform was to break the administrative relationship of enterprises with localities, but it was not possible to do it. Some people's thought on this issue had not changed yet, and it was also a question of power."[97]

In a series of meetings to discuss replacing profits with taxes, provincial officials expressed their doubts and succeeded in modifying or delaying elements of the plan that they opposed.[98] The reform was introduced in two stages. The first, begun in 1983, required enterprises to pay only an income tax and allowed them to continue to retain and remit to local governments aftertax profits at the same level as 1982. The second stage, begun in 1984, converted all profits to taxes but did not eliminate negotiability or financial links based on the subordination relations of enterprises, although that had been the original intention. An adjustment tax was bargained out with individual enterprises in seven-year contracts granting one rate on current profit levels and another, lower rate for incremental profits.[99] Most important of all, because of the objections of provincial governments, the set of local taxes was never implemented, and the revenue base of center and provinces was never put on a firm legal footing. Instead, the State Council declared in 1985 that "temporarily" all provinces were to follow the system of "revenue sharing on the basis of dividing up tax revenues," which essentially replicated the Jiangsu "sharing total revenues" system.[100]

Thanks to an effective defense by provincial officials, provincial financial interests were left intact. Although all revenues from enterprises were called taxes instead of profits, little else had changed. As one official said, "It is the same regardless of whether we call it profits or tax; it's all revenue anyway."[101]

Not surprisingly, Communist party leaders did not intervene in the bureaucratic policy-making process to impose a thoroughgoing fiscal reform over the objections of provincial officials. The provincial officials were too important a bloc within the party to push around. Moreover, from the standpoint of individual leaders at the top levels of the party, replacement of profits with taxes would have impeded their career-building strategies. Party politicians took advantage of the particularism of fiscal contracting to win political support for themselves and therefore were not enthusiastic about abandoning it.

Even the Ministry of Finance, which was undoubtedly the agency most strongly committed to this reform, was basically satisfied with the current fiscal contracting system. Ministry of Finance officials acknowledged the unintended negative consequences of eating in separate kitchens—from their point of view the most serious of which was the central budget deficit—but they always defended it as an improvement over the pre-1980 system. They complained that the income of central authorities was only one-third of national financial income while central expenditure was two-thirds of national financial expenditures.[102] And it galled them that the center always ran deficits while provincial governments sat on surpluses.[103] Nevertheless, the combination of fiscal contracting with national state corporations and loans from local governments had increased the central share of budgetary income from 13.8 percent in 1972 and 14.3 percent in 1979, to over 20 percent in 1982, over 30 percent in 1985, and 35.3 percent in 1988.[104] The good thing about fiscal contracting, according to Ministry of Finance officials, was that "it could guarantee the center's financial income while at the same time arousing the activism of the localities."[105] Ministry officials were generally proud of their author- ship of the 1980 fiscal reform, claiming that it proved they were more reform minded and less conservative than everyone thought. One official said, "The Finance Ministry has to think about the interests of the localities as well as about the center. Some people who are not familiar with our work think we only care about the center, but it is not so." Another official said, "The Ministry of Finance supports reform. What we do not approve of is using money to buy reform from the lower levels."[106]

Officials at all levels in China were unanimous in their public commitment to introduce eventually the "system of divided taxes," whereby "on the basis of setting down the responsibility of central and local authorities, and in accordance with the principle of unifying responsibility and financial power, the income from different taxes is allocated to either the central administration or local administra- tions." They could agree on the advantages of the "system of divided taxes" over the system of "sharing total revenues" in breaking down localism, eliminating the constant wrangling between center and localities, and preventing the center and localities from having to bail out one another.[107] Yet because individual central and local officials had a political incentive to stick with the current system, nothing was done to change it.

Other Administrative Decentralization Policies

The eating-in-separate-kitchens fiscal reform was not the only policy designed to enhance the power of local governments. Over the course of the decade, the central government promulgated a number of different measures intended to improve the economic incentives of local governments and shift more responsibility to them in such matters as approving capital construction projects and foreign joint ventures, planning and material supply, retention of foreign ex- change earnings, and many others. The Central Committee declared its intention eventually to send down all industrial enterprises under ministry management to be run by local governments. The central government never abrogated its ultimate authority over the prov- inces; local budgets still had to be approved by the center, and the center could always reclaim control over capital construction or ma- terial supply as it did during the economic contraction of 1989–1990. Yet, because of various decentralization policies, provincial officials assumed day-to-day control of the local economy and took advantage of this control to build up local industry and local political machines.

One of the most significant decentralizing measures of the reform decade was the devolution of *nomenklatura* authority to Communist party officials in provinces and ministries in 1984. The Communist party retained its authority to appoint all government personnel, but the scope of each party committee's appointment authority was cut back to include only positions at the same level and one level down instead of two levels down. The effect was to cut the number of posts directly managed by the Central Committee from 13,000 to 5,000 and transfer two-thirds of the posts to province and ministry party committees. Provincial party committees in turn decentralized *nomenklatura* control to prefectural, city, and county party committees.[108] The reform did not reduce the total size of the *nomenklatura* but expanded the patronage opportunities of local party officials.

The "central cities" reform was another decentralizing measure that had far-reaching consequences. The idea of giving cities provincial-level economic power was favored by reformist party leaders as a method to improve the coordination of the economy. The eating-in-separate-kitchens fiscal decentralization (itself originally proposed as a method to improve coordination) had provoked conflict between central ministries and provinces because the provinces had become more powerful and more assertive. Many enterprises labored under the dual rule of ministry and province. Their managers complained about having "too many mothers-in-law" who interfered in their operations. Shifting power to cities seemed like a good way to free enterprises from the constant strife between ministries and provinces.

The central cities notion was first proposed in 1979 by Chongqing, a regional economic city that had long felt exploited by the Sichuan provincial government.[109] Zhao Ziyang took up the idea and promoted it at the Fifth Session of the Fifth National People's Congress in 1982. The best way to restore effective coordination of the economy, according to Zhao, was to put all enterprises except those important to military security under regions with cities as their center.[110]

Naturally the cities themselves, which had for years chafed at restrictions and extractions imposed by provincial governments, were wildly enthusiastic about the central cities idea. In contrast, the provinces hated to give up control over a major industrial city. Zhao Ziyang, who had only recently moved to Beijing from Sichuan, knew what he was doing when he made Chongqing the demonstration point for the central cities reform. The Sichuan authorities, who had benefited tremendously from Zhao's initiative making them the vanguard model of comprehensive reform, could hardly argue publicly with their patron. Other provinces had no choice but to follow suit.

And while Zhao Ziyang may have lost some popularity with the officials in provinces forced to give up power to central cities, he gained points with the officials in the cities themselves.

From 1983 to 1987, the Central Committee and the State Council extended provincial-level economic authority to nine cities—Chongqing, Wuhan, Shenyang, Dalian, Guangzhou, Xi'an, Harbin, Qingdao, and Ningbo.[111] While these cities were not granted the full authority of provinces—for one thing the provinces still managed personnel appointments in the cities—they were full-fledged entities under the national plan and the budget.[112] By 1988, national financial documents were discussing thirty-nine provincial-level units, ten more than the original twenty-nine.[113] The proliferation of subordinate units complicated the work of national planning and financial officials. Meanwhile, pressure from other cities jealous of the privileges of central cities forced central and provincial officials to extend special treatment, not as extensive as the powers granted to central cities but valuable nonetheless, to more and more so-called experimental cities.[114]

Special powers were granted to cities on a particularistic basis, enabling politicians to claim credit. The central cities reform, originally sold as a rationalizing measure, resulted in a proliferation of local government entities who engaged one another and the ministries in fierce competition. Many reformist economists and officials in Beijing who originally had been sympathetic to the central cities idea came to view it as simply a new form of localism.[115]

The competition among cities, provinces, and ministries was more bureaucratic than economic. Instead of ending jurisdictional conflicts, the central cities reform multiplied them. The Reform Bureau of the State Economic Commission was swamped with the many disputes that arose in the process of shifting enterprises and powers from provinces to central cities. Negotiations over the division of revenues and responsibilities between province and central city were as protracted and acrimonious as treaty negotiations between countries engaged in war. Provinces and central cities fought to keep profitable enterprises and divest themselves of unprofitable ones like coal mines.[116] Material supply issues were also relevant. When Wuhan became a central city, for example, the Ministry of Post and Telecommunications offered to send down to city jurisdiction its Wuhan factory producing telephone equipment; the city refused because it lacked the ability to provide the factory with the raw materials that the ministry could provide.[117] In another jurisdictional dispute, Wuhan wanted to take over several pharmaceutical plants that had previously been administered directly by the national Phar-

47

maceutical Bureau. Hubei Province and the Pharmaceutical Bureau both objected, arguing that medicines were special in character because their quality had to be maintained by unified management. The State Economic Commission ruled in favor of ministry-level management.[118]

The Effects of Fiscal Decentralization

The eating-in-separate-kitchens fiscal reform combined with other decentralizing measures gave provincial-level officials the incentive to develop their local economies and the wherewithal to do it. By 1986, the resources under local government budgets constituted half the total state budget, and local governments had significant amounts of extrabudgetary funds besides.[119] Local government and Communist party leaders responded to the new incentives with a burst of entrepreneurial energy. They founded new local industries and pitched the merits of their province to foreign investors. Stimulated by local initiatives, local and national growth rates skyrocketed.

Yet in the context of an only partially marketized command economy, local efforts to maximize revenues had numerous perverse results, most notably, economic overheating. One reformist economist defended fiscal decentralization by saying, "Often the reforms are good but the results are not necessarily good. If there are problems we cannot say the reform is no good. Maybe just the historical context is not right."[120]

Local decision makers acted rationally, but the economic signals in the environment were wrong. Because of irrational prices and lack of real financial risk, local government heads built new plants instead of improving the efficiency of existing plants. They invested in high-profit processing plants while neglecting infrastructure construction. It became impossible for the State Planning Commission to enforce the national plan. The locals diverted materials, manpower, and funds away from central capital construction projects to more profitable local activities.

This local construction drive created overheating and caused shortages, deficits, and inflation. The national media exhorted local officials not to ignore society's needs by producing only highly profitable products,[121] while from Beijing there was a call for subordination of local to national interest.[122] National policies, however, actually sent the opposite message.[123] Thus, although the shortages and inflation generated by the overheated economy harmed everyone collectively, under current policies the rapid growth was in the interest of provincial officials.

Ministry of Finance officials liked to portray provincial officials as enriching themselves at the expense of the central state, but in fact provincial revenues under the post-1980 system barely covered essential expenditures. Industrial revenues contributed three-quarters of provincial revenues, and the efficiency of factories had declined over the decade of reform. Therefore, the only way for local authorities to keep up with their budget obligations was to accelerate local industrial growth.[124] As one economist explained, "Local finances were propped up simply by the economic growth rate. . . . Had it not been for a 20 percent or even 30 percent industrial growth rate, some localities could not have made ends meet, and many localities would even find it impossible to pay workers and staff their wages."[125] Even with high growth rates, by 1985 four new provinces (Gansu, Jilin, Jiangxi, and Shaanxi) had entered the ranks of deficit provinces relying on central subsidies, and by 1987, two-thirds of all counties were operating in the red.[126]

While central authorities kept talking about coordinating the national economy like one big chessboard,[127] local authorities in pursuit of profit were dividing it up. Fiscal decentralization encouraged local officials to protect their local markets for their own factories by means of administrative blockades.[128] Especially in less-developed provinces, officials nurtured their infant consumer goods industries by excluding high-quality brand-name merchandise from Shanghai and other traditional manufacturing centers. To make matters worse, local infant industries robbed the brand-name factories of their usual sources of material inputs. Local energies were focused more on fighting bureaucratic battles (often at the State Economic Commission) to restrict competition than on competing in the national marketplace.[129] The Balkanization of the Chinese market, which had begun under Mao Zedong's policies of regional self-reliance, was exacerbated by the 1980 fiscal reforms.

Local officials were spurred by new revenue-sharing schemes to compete with one another in foreign investment and trade in ways central authorities viewed as detrimental to national interests. Provinces and cities tripped over one another to entice foreign investors by offering concessionary terms. Foreign joint ventures were sought after for their hard-currency export earnings, in which local governments could now share, as well as new technologies that could give localities the edge in domestic competition. In their eagerness to make a deal, local officials ignored the urgings of the center not to undercut the national interest by luring joint ventures with excessively low tax rates or promises of access to the domestic market.[130] (Once they locked in a foreign investor, however, local governments often imposed restrictions to protect local firms from the competition of the joint venture.) Central trade authorities were also upset about price gouging in Chinese exports, as local firms, hungry for hard currency, engaged in cutthroat international competition.

Another negative effect of fiscal decentralization was administrative interference in enterprise management. The eating-in-separate-kitchens financial system intensified local officials' sense of proprietorship over local enterprises, creating what the Chinese call "the local ownership system."[131] (The imperatives of building bureaucratic consensus forced authorities at all levels to promise special revenue-sharing arrangements to various departments as well, encouraging the "departmental ownership system.") The trend of strengthening the financial stake of bureaucratic entities in their subordinate enterprises, while motivating officials to support their enterprises, also encouraged them to interfere in enterprise operations. When a firm's bureaucratic masters were off in Beijing, the manager could easily ignore them; when they were close by, the manager was forced to listen to them. One reformist economist complained, "The central leaders, especially Zhao Ziyang, took too strong a line on fiscal decentralization and fundamentally confused the difference between economic and administrative reform. There is a contradiction between the two. Provincial officials meddle in local enterprises and stifle their economic autonomy."[132]

Local officials' interference in enterprise management might have played a positive role if the officials had promoted efficiency. But when local government officials stepped into factory decision making, it was rarely to enhance profitability by cutting costs or improving quality. Revenue maximization was not the sole objective of local officials. If revenue maximization had been the only or even the dominant interest of local officials, then the officials would have been more diligent at reducing losses in local firms during periods of economic contraction. As it was, local officials tolerated the inefficiency and losses of local plants because they needed the materials these plants produced and the employment opportunities they provided (as well as the politically useful gratitude of their managers). The managers of strong, profitable local firms frequently complained that local officials subverted them by appropriating their earnings to redistribute to weaker firms.

As Christine Wong points out, the local government had become both a player and a referee in local economic competition.[133] Administrative interventions in economic activity by and large were not conducive to enterprise autonomy or efficiency.[134] Local administrative interventions were designed to generate political resources for local officials instead.

After all, provincial officials had political interests at stake. Decentralizing reforms had granted them the authority to regulate access to the market and to redistribute fiscal benefits and burdens, investment funds, access to foreign investment and trade, and the like. These economic powers created new opportunities for local officials to collect rents from bureaucratic subordinates and enterprise managers. Naturally, like their counterparts in Beijing, local officials built up political capital by allocating benefits selectively and imposing costs uniformly.[135]

Provincial party and governmental authorities chose to collect rents in different forms and put them to different uses. One strategy was to build up an industrial empire by reinvesting funds in industrial expansion. A more populist strategy involved using the funds they collected to make dramatic improvements in roads, housing, and other public works projects.[136] The corruption strategy was to slip funds into their own pockets and those of their relatives and friends. Province and city heads were also expected to return a share of the rents in the form of political loyalty to the central party politicians who had been their benefactors in expanding their autonomy. And local party secretaries took at least some of the rents in the form of political loyalty from their own bureaucratic subordinates. They established local political machines by exchanging economic favors for political loyalty.[137] These machines, linking party leaders with government bureaucrats, bankers, and managers, then became the engine of local economic development.

Decentralizing reforms changed the career incentives of provincial officials. In the past, the focus of their ambitions had been the central party-state bureaucracy in Beijing. But after 1980, so much of the economic action occurred at the provincial level and provincial leaders exercised such national political influence that some politicians from the most dynamic regions chose to remain in the provinces instead of climbing the ladder to Beijing. One well-known example was Ye Xuanping, the governor of Guangdong Province, who turned down an offer to be a vice-premier of the State Council and decided to stay in Guangdong. (To the degree that the allure of national position faded, the center lost some leverage over the behavior of provincial officials.)

Under the post-1980 incentive structure, the political ambitions of individual local officials became closely identified with the economic accomplishments of their domains. As one press commentary noted, "Leaders one-sidedly consider and stress the partial interests of their departments, localities, and units in total disregard of overall interests. To show off their personal achievements in their official careers, they do not hesitate to infringe upon the fundamental interests of the state and the people."[138]

Whether an official aimed to climb the ladder of success to Beijing or to become a leading figure on the local scene, his or her reputation was enhanced by industrial growth and local building projects. A press commentator linked the local investment drive to the Chinese political structure: "Judging historically, those who dare not boldly build several more factories, enterprises, office buildings, auditoriums, and hotels will appear to be 'right,' will make only average achievements in their official career, and will have no capital to serve as officials and vie for leadership positions."[139] The center might preach local self-restraint in growth rates and construction, but in reality local officials in rapidly growing areas with a lot of construction were more likely to move up than those in sleepy backwater areas.

The cumulative effect of the economic and political incentives structured by post-1980 fiscal and administrative decentralization was dynamic economic growth distorted by shortages, inflation, and deficits, as well as by local protectionism and administrative meddling. These economic maladies provided ammunition for conservative Communist party leaders who wanted to stem the tide of marketization and restore central financial control. As the economic problems, inflation in particular, worsened over the course of the decade, the political strength of conservative party elites increased. The eating-in-separate-kitchens fiscal reform generated political support for the reform drive among the provincial officials who served in the Central Committee; yet its economic effects enabled conservative opponents of reform to win out over the reformers in succession politics at the top reaches of party power.

The Political Ramifications of "Playing to the Provinces"

Deng Xiaoping and Zhao Ziyang's strategy of playing to the provinces involved granting provincial and city officials greater freedom of action in their local arenas and encouraging them to play a greater leadership role in the national arena. The Thirteenth Communist Party Congress decided to reserve seats in the Politburo for the first secretaries or governors of the three metropolises, Beijing, Shanghai, and Tianjin. Provincial party secretaries constituted the largest bloc in the Central Committee, 43 percent of the full members of the Eleventh Central Committee (1977), 34 percent of the Twelfth Central Committee (1982), and 38 percent of the Thirteenth Central Committee (1987).[140] The presence of provincial advocates in these party bodies provided high-level support for sustaining economic reform, as Deng Xiaoping and Zhao Ziyang had intended it to. Government officials knew that the Central Committee would be reluctant to approve any policy rolling back reforms and retracting local authority. As one Beijing official complained, "Local officials used the slogans of reform such as 'enlivening the economy' to fight against financial recentralization."[141]

While local officials draped themselves in the mantle of market reform, what they really meant by reform was in fact the perpetuation of the hybrid, partially reformed system and not a genuine market economy. The objections of local officials to the reforms replacing profits with taxes and dividing taxes by levels showed that they preferred the current arrangements to more thorough market reform. They preferred to maintain their quasi-ownership rights over local factories and exploit these rights to collect rents for themselves to playing only the role of referee in market competition.

The evolution of fiscal system reforms after 1987, when the conservatives staged a comeback in elite politics (Hu Yaobang was purged, Zhao Ziyang replaced him as Communist party secretary, and Li Peng became premier), demonstrated the influence of provincial officials within the party. Even during a period of conservative resurgence at the top, fiscal policies were constrained by provincial preferences and the political incentives of national leaders to play to the provinces.

When they increased their influence at the top reaches of the party after 1987, older-generation conservative leaders like Chen Yun and Yao Yilin (Yao became head of the State Planning Commission and a member of the Standing Committee of the Politburo) wanted to change the fiscal rules to weaken the incentives for local construction and put more funds under central control. As Yao Yilin expressed this view,

> Our economy is now excessively decentralized and proper decentralization is called for. . . . The central finance suffers huge deficits every year; efforts must be exerted to cut deficits back each year until they are basically effaced. Under such circumstances, localities should contribute more to the central coffers in addition to the central finance's practice of economy.[142]

Chen Yun and Yao Yilin expected their protégé Li Peng, who had been elevated to the premiership and membership in the Standing Committee of the Politburo in 1987, to support fiscal recentralization by abolishing fiscal contracting and establishing a system of divided taxes (separate systems for central taxes and local taxes) as the tax-for-profit policy had originally proposed. Instead, they found that Li Peng was unwilling to impose unpopular financial policies on provincial officials.

The split in the conservative ranks was caused by differences in the political incentives operating on individuals from different generations. Chen and Yao were too old to be governed by political ambition; at the end of their political careers, they were free to promote their policy preference for financial centralization without regard to its appeal among members of the selectorate.

Li Peng, in contrast, was young enough to aspire to succeed Deng Xiaoping as China's top leader. When taking a policy stance, he had to take into consideration the views of the selectorate, including the members of the Central Committee as well as those of the elders.

Li Peng's reluctance to antagonize provincial leaders helps us understand the 1986 State Council decision to retain fiscal contracting and to renegotiate individual sharing deals with the provinces that left the central government with even less revenue than before. What Li Peng came up with was a package of particularistic giveaways that enabled him to claim credit with provincial officials. First, the State Council began to emphasize the contractual form of revenue-sharing arrangements. The term *contracting* had acquired great reformist cachet derived from the dramatic success of the agricultural reform and the introduction of the enterprise contract system in 1987.[143] Then the council asserted that according to these contracts, provinces would be fully responsible for their expenditures (except in the case of natural disasters).[144] Lastly, the council diversified the revenue-sharing system into at least six different arrangements, two of which were forms of "progressive contracting" that gave incentives for local governments to "have greater initiative to invigorate their economies."[145]

Li Peng made a point of sympathizing with the economically strongest regions that even under eating-in-separate-kitchens had been required to contribute a large share of their revenues to the center.[146] He had the State Council identify thirteen "high revenue areas which have to deliver a larger percentage of revenues to the state [and] have little enthusiasm for increasing revenues," a set of powerful localities including Jiangsu, Liaoning, Beijing, and Chongqing.[147] The State Council granted these localities three-year, revenue-progressive increase contracts that would rouse their enthusiasm by allowing them to retain a big chunk of the revenues they generated above the base level.[148] In another decision made at the same time, Li Peng and the State Council responded to the jealousy of the high-revenue, high-contribution provinces by changing the terms of Guangdong's easy deal. Beginning in 1988, for three years, Guangdong would increase its remittance to the center at a rate of 9 percent per year instead of keeping 100 percent of revenues above a very low base.[149] Li Peng also promoted plans for Pudong, a new special economic zone for Shanghai. Li challenged Zhao Ziyang, who had a base of support in the coastal areas of Guangdong, Fujian, and the Fourteen Open Cities, by building his own support base in the economically dynamic parts of China that had so far received less preferential treatment by the center, including Shanghai, Beijing, Chongqing, Jiangsu, and Liaoning.

Central authorities admitted that the 1988 version of fiscal contracting would reduce central revenues and cause short-term profit seeking on the part of the provinces.[150] In theory, they continued to advocate a system dividing taxes between levels as the best alternative. As one article put it, however, "The contract system is more readily acceptable to different circles,"[151] in other words, more politically feasible.

Li Peng's actions to give more financial authority and resources to provinces indicate that the influence of provincial officials within the Communist party had grown to the point that no contender to top leadership stood a chance of winning without the support of at least some provincial officials.

When the political balance within the party elite shifted even more to the conservative side after the Tiananmen crackdown and the purge of Zhao Ziyang in June 1989, the conservatives again proposed eliminating provincial revenue contracts and strengthening central financial authority. During the work conferences preceding the Fifth Plenum of the CCP Thirteenth Central Committee in November 1989, Yao Yilin spoke in favor of the recentralization proposal, but provincial party secretaries and governors argued vehemently against the proposal and in the end rejected it.[152] The minister of finance had to announce at the 1990 meeting of the National People's Congress that the system of fiscal contracting would continue, with only a few local experiments in divided taxation.[153]

The issue of financial recentralization was again hotly contested during the 1990 drafting of the Eighth Five-Year Plan and the Ten-Year Plan. At a November 1990 meeting of provincial leaders, Ye Xuanping, the governor of Guangdong, strongly articulated the provincial demand for continued financial autonomy.[154] The cleavage between the interests of center and localities was more out in the open than ever before. Provincial leaders were reported to have put aside their squabbling over relative gains to present a unified front against the center.[155] As a result of the conflict, the date for the Seventh Plenum of the Thirteenth Central Committee, originally planned for October 1990, was postponed several months until late December, and the enlarged Politburo meeting that usually precedes a Central Committee plenum failed to be held.[156]

The vehemence of the provincial opposition to fiscal recentralization impressed Li Peng, who came out for a compromise that would retain the fiscal contracting system for the entire five-year period and would introduce the system of dividing taxes only on an experimental basis. Li's position was adopted by the Central Committee and was incorporated in the long-term plans. By showing his sympathy with the local officials' views, Li could keep the support of at least some of these officials and prevent them from siding with one of his political rivals.

The provincial leaders within the Central Committee were successful in blocking the center from retracting its grant of financial authority to the provinces. Soon after he spoke out openly against the center's proposals in late 1990, however, Ye Xuanping was forced out of his position as Guangdong governor and given the purely ceremonial post as vice chairman of the Standing Committee of the Chinese People's Consultative Congress. At the same time, the head of the Communist Party Organization Department stressed the need for the center to reshuffle officials periodically from one place to another.[157] The message was clear: the center would defer to the views of the officials in the selectorate when making policy, but the center held the power to appoint officials, and any official who challenged party leaders by organizing a bloc would be dismissed.

The eating-in-separate-kitchens fiscal reform was a successful political strategy for building a coalition of support for the reform drive among provincial officials. Once provincial officials were the largest group within the Central Committee and were committed to the current situation of partial reform, it was unthinkable for ambitious central politicians like Hu Yaobang, Zhao Ziyang, or even Li Peng to attempt to roll back the reforms. Some of the economic problems produced by fiscal decentralization produced an elite conservative backlash against the reform drive and provided ammunition for the conservatives to strengthen their influence at the highest reaches of party leadership. But even when the conservatives strengthened their hand after 1987, the incentives produced by reciprocal accountability operated on the younger generation of conservative leaders, discouraging them from antagonizing the provincial representatives in the Central Committee by pushing recentralization.

3
Party and Army in Chinese Politics—Neither Alliance nor Opposition

Feng Shengbao

This chapter discusses some approaches that may illuminate the factors affecting the relationship between the Chinese Communist party (CCP) and the People's Liberation Army (PLA). China, as a Leninist-socialist society, has a closed system. The more dramatically Chinese politics changes, the more mysterious the process of these changes has become, especially those with the PLA. Luckily, the information based on publications and interviews with PLA officers and concerned civilians is still adequate for us to look into this army, to explore questions like the real relationship between the CCP and the PLA, and to obtain a fair picture of the political development in China. To that end, the first step is to understand Chinese terminologies. The second is to evaluate the real guide to the army, the party's ideology, which is public knowledge to all of our readers. The third is to search for elements of continuity. And the fourth is to evaluate the serious problems rooted in history and the June 4, 1989, tragedy of Tiananmen.

The PLA and Chinese Politics

Before June 4, 1989, Western observers were worried about a possible reversal of China's reform, but many of them tended to focus only on the probable swift changes of events in the post–Deng Xiaoping period. They favorably evaluated China's economic and military reforms and were quite optimistic about the future, despite the warnings from their Chinese counterparts that China's reforms might lead to a chaotic situation in which the government might proclaim martial law. According to the experience drawn from the Four Little Dragons—Taiwan, Hong Kong, South Korea, and Singapore—by the top Chinese leaders,[1] the use of military force was applicable to China. Chinese leaders made clear, long before the Tiananmen massacre, that it might be necessary to take military control in case of "chaos." Sadly, many U.S. experts admitted that they were taken by surprise with the June 4 tragedy. Why did they fail to foresee this outcome?

In late May 1989, when civilians blocked tanks as troops forced their way through the streets, many people were under the illusion that a civil society was in the making. All official statements announced solemnly and repeatedly that the PLA belonged to the people. Foreign newspapers were not surprised at reports that the PLA units refused orders from their commander. Chong-Pin Lin commented, "Such a view, prevalent among Western observers, seemed confirmed when the PLA soldiers who were ordered in late May 1989 to enforce martial law against the demonstrating masses in Beijing appeared passive and reluctant."[2] This army, however, consequently destroyed both its own image and that of Deng Xiaoping. Angry, sad, and upset, people were forced to view China and its army in a new perspective.

Meanwhile, certain Chinese specialists overseas (mostly from Taiwan) found their pessimism about China's reforms to be justified. They had been critical of Western Chinese specialists, yet because of their lack of connection to the mainland for forty years, these experts had nothing more convincing to offer.

Scholars and students from the mainland were also perplexed when they looked at Chinese politics, especially the military field. These scholars, including reform advocates and practitioners, seldom spent much time on studies of military reform in the past decade (primarily because this was taboo for them). The tragedy of Tiananmen impelled them to understand the PLA. China's scholars, particularly those from the PLA, can help the outside world obtain a better picture of basic facts about the PLA.

What is the relationship between the CCP and the PLA, alliance or opposition, as asked by some U.S. specialists? It is neither alliance nor opposition. When Western scholars view the PLA, they sometimes forget that this army functions in a Leninist-socialist society with a proletarian dictatorship.[3] This is how a PLA officer approached the same issue:

> In war times, we did not have any state power on which to rely. Our army got all its weapons and equipment from the enemy. Therefore, we had always regarded army building as a central task in safeguarding our own rank. . . . However, after we took power we could mobilize the whole country.

In this process we must consider the military issues as against the entire country as a whole, not something separate.[4]

In Leninist countries, ideology is not only a means for party control over the people but a guide for party action as well. According to Marxist-Leninist state theory, the state or the government is but an instrument of class dictatorship. "The army is the chief component of state power. Whoever wants to seize and retain state power must have a strong army."[5] Deng Xiaoping holds the same idea: the army is "a strong pillar of the people's democratic dictatorship."[6] According to Leninism, proletarian dictatorship is the reign by only one class: the proletariat, through the Communist party. It cannot be shared. And it means direct use of violence, mainly through the army, regardless of legal restraint.

The PLA is the instrument of the party's monopoly in China. There is a gentleman's agreement stipulating that any non-Communist party is banned from recruiting from the PLA. The CCP and the PLA, as two social organizations, overlap. One-third of the military officers and soldiers are party members.

China has not yet departed from its feudal tradition. All top commanders of the PLA grew up under wartime conditions. The whole army is controlled by a war-hardened partriarch, for whom the military is a personal instrument. When the old generation is gone, it is hoped that this phenomenon will fade away, too. The PLA is in the process of transition. Tradition has not yet been exterminated, and the new system is far from being established. But a close look and a full understanding of the changes are imperative.

The relationship between the army and the party is predicated on the army's subordination to the party. The PLA is not a neutral (as in the West) or an independent political unit (as in some developing countries) capable of making an alliance with the party or becoming a center of opposition to the party.

The Western distinction between civilian and military cannot be applied to the relationship between the party and the army in China. Even the term "civilian supremacy" is confusing when referring to China, where the party is an organization overriding the army, and not a civil servant. "Party supremacy over the military" is a more appropriate term in China.

The PLA officers cannot be clearly divided into two camps: political commissars and professional commanders. One person can be a commissar today and a commander tomorrow. Although some officers may place more emphasis on "red," whereas others focus more on "expert," there are no fundamental ideological differences among the officers. No individual officer can be independent from the party committee. "The doctrinal differences between the leadership and the officers [and between different officers too] should not be viewed in black and white terms; their divergence is basically a matter of degree."[7] Officers are purged because they are believed to challenge the supremacy of the party or Mao Zedong; that is, the factions of Peng Dehuai and Lin Biao were both purged as the outcome of political conflicts with Mao Zedong rather than because of their divergence on military policies within the army.

If we do not view the PLA from this broader angle, we may fail to understand many of its great changes. The term "professionalism," for example, must not be confused with Chinese military "modernization" or "regularization." In Chong-Pin Lin's exposition on this, he points out that Western perceptions of a professional and depoliticized Chinese army are wrong:

> Military professionalism requires non-participation in politics by the military officer who is politically neutral and where military loyalties undercut his primordial (ethnic, religious, parochial, and class) sentiments which otherwise often manifest in loyalties based on personal connections.[8]

By this definition, current Western interpretations will result in a serious misunderstanding of the military reform. Lin also reminds us that "in the *Selected Works of Deng Xiaoping* (1975–1982), at least nine of the total forty-seven speeches directly deal with military reforms. Yet, the term 'professionalization' (*zhiyehua*) appears nowhere in the collection."[9] Some Chinese military writers appeal for the establishment of a "professionalized" (*zhiyehua*) army.[10]

In January 1980, Deng Xiaoping for the first time used the terms *zhuanyehua* (specialization) and *zhuanye zhishi* (professional knowledge).[11] In the old days, military officers were just political cadres doing military jobs. Now the PLA devotes most of its time to military buildup. A professional contingent (*zhuanye duiwu*), an officer corps (*junguan tuan*), of a modernized army has already been formed. They are personnel with special skills or professional knowledge, and they have been gradually alienated from Marxist doctrine. Therefore, the development of the military has become their career interest, not just a political task. If they have any special interest, it is military development. They are becoming an independent interest group. During the summer of 1989, this trend of independence from the party became visible, as this chapter addresses later.

Irreversible Trend for Military Reform

After Tiananmen, Chinese political restructuring completely stopped. By comparison, what is the situation with military reform?

Before 1975, Deng Xiaoping's position was lower than that of Chen Yun both in the party and in the government. Deng's position was no higher than a marshal. He started to play a special role in the debate over the thesis that practice—as opposed to "two whatevers"[12]—is the sole criterion for testing truth. He challenged Mao's "established policy" (*jiding fangzhen*) and set up a new ideological, political, organizational, and military line. At this time his prestige began to increase greatly.

In 1975, Deng claimed that "the army needs to be consolidated"[13] since the army then was in considerable chaos. During the Cultural Revolution, the size of the armed forces had increased substantially, to more than 6 million, equal to that of the United States and the USSR combined.[14] A large proportion of the state budget went to military expenditures, with much of that for food and clothing. Deng was worried that the army was not combatworthy. In consolidating the army, five problems—bloating, laxity, conceit, extravagance, and inertia—had to be solved.[15]

In December 1977, when Deng reappeared as chairman of the Central Military Commission, he reconfirmed the tasks set up in 1975 and emphasized that the army should attach strategic importance to education and training. Later he planned to take up the problem of the army's technical equipment and the question of military strategy. This process, the consolidation of the PLA, was a precondition for military reform.

The most important prerequisite of reform was Deng's revision of China's global view of war and peace; based on his new theory, he pushed military reform. In 1977, he started by reviewing the possibility of a new world war and ended in denying the possibility of it in the near future; he formed his new theory between 1979 and 1985. At an enlarged meeting of the Central Military Commission in 1985, Deng said, "For many years we have been emphasizing the danger of war. However, there have been some changes in our views."[16] According to Yang Shangkun "the change in the outlook for war is a fundamental basis for making all important decisions."[17]

On December 31, 1987, Huan Xiang reported, "Deng Xiaoping said that nowadays the world is in an epoch of peace and development."[18] Up to 1988, however, many Chinese scholars and officials still suspected the "great changes of the epoch."[19] Some people emphasized that "the change does not mean the realization of peace and development. The current time is just an epoch to fight for peace and development."[20] Yet others felt:

> At the end of the 1980s the historical US-USSR Summit was held on two cruisers which were at anchor in the Malta sea. To this day, people generally have understood that the Cold War that had lasted for over forty years had ended. An unprecedented epoch of peace has come.[21]

Deng Xiaoping's statement in 1984 about world peace and development was different from all the other Communist leaders in the socialist countries.[22] He actually changed the paramount principle of the international Communist movement about the so-called epoch of war and revolution and transformed it into the epoch of peace and development. This is ignored by most people.

During World War I, Lenin pointed out that the twentieth century had entered an epoch of imperialism and proletarian revolution, with the fundamental characteristics that war was inevitable and imperialism was on the eve of proletarian revolution. Never had a Communist leader of socialist countries diverged from Lenin's doctrine until Deng Xiaoping did.

At the 1984 forum held by the Central Military Commission, Deng clearly remarked:

> We have asserted several times that a big war may not break out. . . . Now still the USA and the USSR have the capacity to initiate world war. Each of them is able to exterminate the world. Who will dare to act? . . . Now we should really and soberly make a new adjustment. It is very important that we can feel at ease to build and shift our focus on construction. Without this kind of adjustment how we can feel at ease to build in fear and trepidation? It is impossible to construct and reform. It is impossible to confirm the correct principles and direction of army building.[23]

Deng believed that a new world war was not inevitable and could be delayed or avoided. In February 1986 he said to former U.S. vice president Walter Mondale, "If we are doing well the war can be avoided."[24]

This change in thought led to a change in China's defense policy and army buildup. Fearing the possibility of a major war, China had pursued a mistaken military policy. Under the leadership of Mao Zedong, Lin Biao had actually stopped the army buildup and put China into a permanent state of war preparedness to deal with a possible war emergency (*linzhan yingji zhuangtai*). This had lasted for decades. China had not even started to build a regularized and modern defensive army during peacetime. "For meeting the possible war emergency, China retained a massive standing army for years. Over a hundred divisions were always kept at full strength and with full equipment. Lots of conventional weapons were ready for people's war. It resulted in serious troubles."[25]

The change of viewpoint toward war and peace under a new epoch is interpreted by the CCP as a development of Marxism-Leninism. The ideological breakthrough has never been this significant in economic reforms. The leftists were always critical of Western market economy theory, which was introduced to China as a guide to economic reform. No one, however, has dared to challenge the ideological base concerning military reform, which was made by Deng. This is one important reason for the continuity of military reform after June 4, 1989.

The second reason is that development of the military has been proceeding much more smoothly than that of the economy during the last decade. Chinese military reform has improved military development aimed at "building powerful, modern, and regularized revolutionary armed forces."[26] Under the leadership of Deng Xiaoping, the PLA has been carrying out the reforms in the following areas: (1) military and national development, (2) equipment development and equipping the army, (3) men and weapons, (4) change of the military structure, and (5) strategy and tactics.

Military and National Development. Lin Biao advocated that "combat ipso facto is proportion" and "war preparedness is planning" (analogous to a "proportional and planned economy"). During the Cultural Revolution, an excessively large proportion of GNP for the military budget resulted not only in a heavy burden for the country but harm to the army as well. Deng Xiaoping demanded that the army "excercise restraint." In 1984, Deng said: "The army should subordinate itself to the general interest, which is to develop the country. . . . Since the development of all our services is tied to national development, they should devise ways to assist and actively participate in it."[27] By this he combined the military with civil development. Therefore, both the defense industry and the army would offer more economic and social projects. Meanwhile, the army could get supplements to its budget from the state. Soldiers' living standards could be improved.

Equipment Development and Equipping the Army. Deng Xiaoping further said, "Without modern science and technology, it is impossi-

ble to build . . . a modern national defense."[28] Yang Shangkun held
that

> the modernization of equipment of the army should involve
> more research; more technological reserve and less produc-
> tion. We should equip a limited number of troops at one
> time with one focus and renew the equipment of the whole
> army by echelons, with the coexistence of new and old
> arms.[29]

This policy has sped the development of China's military technology
and equipment. As Chong-Pin Lin pointed out, now China has
successfully caught up with the advanced level of world technology.[30]

Men and Weapons. Adhering to the principle of "taking class struggle
as the key link" and having no knowledge of contemporary war, Lin
Biao said, "We should give rein to the soldier's mind replacing
material force."[31] He regarded the army buildup as political but not
military. Lin Biao ignored military training, especially regular military
education. At the time Lin Biao was in charge of the Military Commission, three-fourths of the military schools were closed and most
of their faculties were disbursed.[32]

Under the leadership of Deng Xiaoping, the goal of building the
army has been changed to "better troops, efficient organization,
flexible command, excellent equipment, effective training, fast response, high efficiency and strong combat skills."[33] How will the PLA
reach these goals? First, "in the past, we conducted training and
study while fighting." The PLA was sent to the Korean War and the
Sino-Vietnam border war in turn. "But now, even if there were a war
going on, the army could not become competent without first having
had training in school because military equipment is different from
what it was, and many kinds of knowledge are needed to direct
present-day operations."[34]

Second, "educating all officers, from platoon on up, in officers'
training school"[35] has become the rule. The PLA believes that military
education has strategic importance. "Three things are required of
schools. First, they should train, select and recommend cadres. . . .
Second, they should help the cadres to conscientiously study modern
warfare and combined operations involving various services and
arms. . . . Third, our schools should restore our army's traditional
style of work."[36] By 1985 the educational level and special skills of
army personnel had been raised to a higher degree than those of
civilian cadres. Eighty-two percent of the group army (*jituan jun*)
command units had some education higher than high school. Sixty

percent of command units of the three general headquarters, military regions, and headquarters of the various services had an education beyond college level. Seventy-five percent of the personnel were trained in colleges.

Change in the Military Structure. The principles of the reform of the military structure are carried out according to *jingbing, hecheng, pingzhan jiehe,* and *tigao xiaoneng.*[37] The first term in Chinese, *jingbing,* means a better army and the reduction of bloatedness. Military strength has been reduced by 3.5 million since 1975, including a reduction of 1 million men that was decided in 1985. After several years of more streamlined administration, the staff of the three headquarters has been reduced more than 47 percent. In 1985 the ten military regions were reduced to seven. Their average strength has been reduced 29.3 percent. The army as a whole was reduced by 31 units at a level higher than army regulars (*jun*) and more than 4,000 units at the division (*shi*) level. Since many officers have been retired, the proportion between military officers and men has changed from 1:2.45 to 1:4.[38] Yang Shangkun said that "in order to give the soldier modern technological equipment, the PLA should be scientifically organized and trained diligently."[39]

All ground forces were reorganized as twenty-four group armies. The proportion of specialized troops has increased to more than half of the total. The combining (*hechenghua*) of the army makes it easier to gear peacetime training to wartime needs and to conduct combined operations in emergencies (*pingzhan jiehe*).

The PLA now has two kinds of divisions: A (*jiazhong shi*) and B (*yizhong shi*). Type A is in full equipment and personnel numbers. Type B is not full in actual numbers of both but is ready for expansion in the event of war. A few small units had already been capable of a fast response to a limited war (*tigao xiaoneng*).[40] Meanwhile, adequate attention is being paid to changes in the nature of weapons and combat to develop further the military structure.

Strategy and Tactics. Chinese officers have actively debated traditional strategy and tactics and believed these needed to be changed. After heated arguments, they concluded that the Western military theories were acceptable and helpful. Works in this area have sprung up like mushrooms. This phenomenon is unprecedented. During the Cultural Revolution, Lin Biao repeatedly emphasized that "all battles are finally decided by hand-to-hand bloody fighting within 200 kilometers." Mao Zedong said, "If the USSR should invade, we will have to go back to *Jinggangshan*" (a mountain—as a nice place for guerrilla warfare—whose name symbolizes people's war). Deng changed this strategy of people's war to keeping the enemy out of the territory. Many young professional officers are engaged in the study of this field and have been successful.

The military reform so far is a great success under the leadership of the party and Deng Xiaoping. This was a principal reason why the party and Deng still held authority after the June 4 incident. Recently, several high-level commanders of military posts clearly stated that the PLA should support the reform to achieve a regular, modern, and revolutionary war.

In an interview with a military correspondent, Wan Hai, chief of the air force, talked about the situation with the Chinese air force. At that time, the number of Chinese military airplanes ranked third in the world. If the function of aircraft and quality of equipment were not continuously improved over time, however, many planes would be shot down and the air force would not finish a strategic task like a "sudden air attack, air support, air transportation, aerial reconnaissance, air defence, and support of military action in port or at sea." Every chief of a regiment, division, or army could now fly. All leaders of air divisions could lead troops into aerial combat. All pilots had a college-level education. Among them, a number knew English. The air force required every airman to be provided with not only "lofty ideals," "high morals," "broad-mindedness," and "strict discipline," but also "rich knowledge," "perfect skill," "indomitable style," and a "strong physique."[41]

Ding Henggao, minister in charge of the Commission of Science, Technology, and Industry for National Defense and an advocate of reform, wrote in "Review and Prospects of China's Science Technology and Industry for National Defense" that further evolution of the international situation and strategic changes in China's defense construction called for defense science, technology, and industry to switch, as soon as possible, to the path suitable for its sustained, stable, and coordinated development in peacetime.

To accomplish such changes, it would be necessary to make greater readjustments and to conduct further reforms, and, focusing on increasing comprehensive economic results, to make great efforts in many areas. He also believed that proper introduction of competition and market mechanisms would help extend the military reform. He argued for implementing integrated management in planning, programming, and budgeting; perfecting laws and regulations for defense research, testing, and production; and establishing new orders catering both to the requirements of a planned commodity economy and to the characteristics of defense science, technology, and industry. Ding also advocated strengthening and perfecting the decision-making system. Evidently he strongly supported Deng's "established policy" of military reform and wanted to introduce the experience of economic reform to the military. He also argued for opening up and broadening international cooperation and exchanges in military technology and appealed for an efficient introduction of competent personnel and intelligence and the selection of outstanding scientific and technical personnel to study and to be trained abroad.[42]

In brief, the guiding viewpoints and the main policies of military reform are not likely to be reversed. Those who dare to challenge the military development will soon fail. Besides, the military reform has been establishing a modern army with its own strong political culture. This will continue to weaken the party's supremacy in the army.

Political Evolution and Depression within the PLA

Where does political evolution within the PLA stand after a decade of reform? While military reform of the PLA has been under way, the political reforms within the army are just beginning. The goals, methodology, and policies of the political reform of the army are not yet clear. Compared with the political changes in civil life, the political changes in the PLA are insignificant.

Before and after the Third Plenary Session of the Eleventh Central Committee of the CCP, a process of emancipation of the mind had begun and has been continuously and spontaneously pushed forward by intellectuals since 1977. The emancipation in the PLA, however, was always under control. Even Deng himself said in March 1981:

> We should not overlook the lingering "left" influence in the army . . . quite a number of people between the ages of thirty and forty tend to look at things from a "left" angle. Some army cadres, including a number with long service behind them, haven't understood the policies applied since the Third Plenary Session of the Central Committee, which they regard as capitalist.[43]

In addition, while the Cultural Revolution was negated thoroughly (*chedi fouding wenhua dageming*), Deng said in the same speech:

> As for the "three support and two military" [a policy of the Cultural Revolution][44], . . . We must say two things. First, that at the time it was correct for the army to go to the civilian units and deal with the situations there, which were

otherwise uncontrollable. So the "three support and two military" [policy] did prove useful. But second, they also did great harm to the army, for in their wake they brought many bad things and detracted from the army's prestige.[45]

Obviously, Deng appreciated the use of the army during the Cultural Revolution and implied that he would not hesitate to use it again for "uncontrollable" situations whenever necessary. The passive factor, however, allows the army to retain its old tradition of being an instrument of dictatorship.

Many passive factors in the political life of the army need to be solved. As early as 1928, Mao Zedong talked about the Red Army's "practice of democracy": "The officers do not beat the men; officers and men receive equal treatment; soldiers are free to hold meetings and to speak out; trivial formalities have been done away with; and the accounts are open for all to inspect."[46] But this was totally forgotten for decades. The relationship between officers and soldiers has become more tense than ever. Many conflicts between officers and men have occurred.

Compared with rehabilitation in civilian life, some important issues have been slow in being resolved and have been kept from the mass media. Part of the party history relating to the Red Fourth Field Army, for example, was fabricated and brought about the unjustified treatment by its top leaders like Xu Xiangqian and Li Xiannian toward officers and soldiers of all levels. One fictitious story was about a special Zhang Guotao telegram.[47] Another big issue was the West Road Army (xilu jun).[48] In 1984, Historical Review, Marshal Xu's autobiographical work, was published. Few people realized from his book that his colleagues, including former state chairman Li Xiannian, needed to be rehabilitated, too. Unfortunately, rehabilitation had not played a special role for the emancipation of the mind within the army.

As a result, a great depression exists in the PLA. The June 4 incident deepened the depression of the army and many felt persecuted.

A Great Tragedy for the Party and the Army

The June 4 incident was a great tragedy for the Chinese people. It was also a great tragedy for the CCP and the PLA.

During the anti-Japanese war, Mao Zedong said: "In China, war is the main form of struggle and the army is the main form of organization . . . China's problem cannot be settled without armed force."[49] And, "Without armed struggle, the proletariat and the

Communist Party would have no standing at all in China."[50]

The enemy at that time was the Japanese army. The enemies now, in the eyes of those octogenarians, are those who actively took part in the peaceful democracy movement, and they still want to use guns to protect themselves and to extinguish the enemies. As a matter of fact, many of the demonstrators did support the CCP and genuinely hoped that it would change for the better. The Tiananmen massacre shattered their dreams.

Now people are talking about the fact that Chinese soldiers killed their fellow countrymen for the simple reason that they represented "vested interests." But the June 4 incident is a great tragedy for the PLA, too. The whole army felt extremely upset after the incident. Why? What are the troubles behind this?

This was the first time in history that the PLA took action without consensus. Deng Xiaoping's authority no longer seemed absolute. Before June 4, Xu Qinxian, the Thirty-Eighth Group Army commander, sacrificed his own freedom by refusing to bring troops into Beijing. He was only one of many officers who were secretly punished later. Deng Xiaoping reportedly said: "Whoever voiced dissent is not the most dangerous. Whoever hides his dissent is dangerous." How many officers dared to speak out? There must be many who dared not to speak out.

As early as late April, just a few days after the student rallies, Deng Xiaoping and some other octogenarians had already rashly made up their minds to crack down on the student movement by violence. This was echoed in the *People's Daily*'s editorial of April 26, 1989. Meanwhile, Deng himself left for Wuhan to mobilize the troops. Even the Standing Committee of the Central Military Commission (SCCMC), however, could not make a final decision instantly. Among members of the committee besides Zhao Ziyang, Qin Jiwei, Hong Xuezhi, and Chi Haotian also disagreed about using the army to deal with the student movement. Liu Huaqing and Yang Shangkun greatly hesitated. In retrospect, Deng Xiaoping probably left Beijing to test the loyalty of his subordinates and more important to avoid issuing orders himself.

Later, after martial law was finally issued, every unit was asked to make a statement supporting it. The SCCMC moved one or two divisions from each of the twelve group armies (*jituan jun*) into Beijing. Apparently, he could not trust any single group army to come into the capital and to crack down on the prodemocracy movement. He also wanted to get more troops into hot water (*tuo xia shui*) so that at least the military commanders of half of the total twenty-four group armies would be held responsible.

The military activities were far from being unified on June 4. According to *A Day in Beijing under Martial Law* (published and later banned by the PLA), written by soldiers and officers who participated in the crackdown, we learn that

> the troops' movements from midnight of June 3 to early morning of June 4 were in great disorder. Except for the troops moving from the western direction, officers carried all the bullets for their troops. Those troops who did get the order to shoot did so only after a whole day's hiding on June 4. Some troops never shot, some shot in the air, some intentionally shot at crowds.[51]

Moreover, many soldiers preferred to be beaten than shoot into the crowd. Some of them were badly injured and are still in military hospitals.

The situation in the army and its future role are complicated. The April 5, 1976, incident can be an example. Before and after the reversal of the verdict on it, many policemen could not justify what they did during and after the crackdown and suffered as victims twice. They have learned lessons from that experience. Many sources revealed after June 4 that policemen dealing with the democracy activists in jail often paid more attention to legal rights than the soldiers.

Now the CCP insisted that the crackdown was completely correct. No one, however, claimed responsibility for issuing the order to shoot. The PLA was made a scapegoat (*bei heiguo*). When the people went to visit those troops that enforced the martial law, every military unit denied that they actually fired. Before June 1989, a general warned his son, a commander, "not to be a hero shooting people." A majority of soldiers think of themselves as being taken advantage of.

Now most enlisted men feel that being a member of the PLA is no longer an honorable title. The civilian-military relationship has suffered immensely. Scholars and students had been less critical of the PLA's misdemeanor. After the June 4 incident, the image of Uncle Lei Feng (a soldier who represents the spirit of serving the people) was further damaged. The memory of the army shooting at its own people can hardly be erased.

The veteran generals of the PLA are concerned about the June 4 incident, for they know that the military's affinity with the people is the lifeline of the army. Many young officers were sympathetic with the students. Many officers were said to have given their weapons to students.

Now some top leaders are saying that when the democratic movement emerges next time, they will dispose of it much earlier and use appropriate weapons, such as rubber bullets. But the changes will be greater than that. The PLA might take an altogether different attitude in dealing with future student demonstrations.

Almost all available information indicates that many officers considered shooting the worst choice in trying to control the situation. Thus, the June 4 incident has already resulted in a further shaking of the party's supremacy over the PLA. In addition, after Deng dies, probably nobody will be in a position like his to control the PLA.

People studying the PLA rarely pay attention to the above-mentioned facts about the army. No wonder Western experts still focus on the potential for the Chinese army to continue intervening in politics, particularly during the post-Deng period.

No Longer a Work Team but a Shock Brigade

Does the PLA continue to be a special work team of the party? Many people are worried about that because the June 4 incident showed the possibility of military intervention in the transition from totalitarianism to democracy. In the opinion of some, this time "the gun commanded the Party" because the 1989 student demonstration was resolved by military power. In their opinion, Zhao Ziyang or the Central Committee or the Politburo of the CCP, in fact, represented the party. But they do not understand that, having no tie in the army, Zhao Ziyang could get nowhere. Deng Xiaoping is actually the top leader. He and his fellow octogenarian companions are able to manipulate both the CCP and the PLA. During the 1989 movement, Deng represented the party, issued military orders, and made political choices for everyone to obey. The party and the gun are identical.

There has also been confusion over the attitude of the PLA during the summer of 1989. It was hard for the army to accept the order to use weapons against civilians. The PLA's attitude about democracy was vague despite the fact that many young officers were prodemocracy. It was said that some officers in power made this remark: "The June 4 action may be a successful surgical operation at a small cost for China." Does this justify the June 4 crackdown? The answers could be different. One extreme point was that had the PLA stood idle on June 4, like its counterparts in Eastern Europe, the Communist party would already have lost its power. While the East European socialist countries suffered from disorders after the transformation of 1989, this extreme idea gained popularity within the army. A moderate opinion of some officers was that the hard-liners were not conservative. They felt that the government needed successful experiences of reform. If China's economy improved, China's situation would be stable. Another group viewed June 4 as a prelude for a hopeful future because, with the lesson of the tragedy, the PLA will play a positive role.

The PLA was passive regarding economic reform. As a reformist leader, Zhao Ziyang did not have close relations with the army. Zhao devoted most of his efforts to invigorating the economy. People welcomed economic growth but were angry about the inflation and corruption that came along with it. The corruption within the PLA was as rampant as anywhere else. This never received appropriate attention from the leadership.

The PLA was dissatisfied with China's dwindling military budget, which was cut from 5.47 percent to 2.16 percent of the GNP between 1976 and 1986. Some officers complained that

> not every citizen, Party member, cadre, or military man understands the significance of army building. People might all know that "without industry the people could not be rich," "without agriculture the situation could not be stable," and "without trade the economy could not be invigorated," but few people understand that "without defense the country would have no security."
>
> During war the troops are "the most beloved people" but after retirement they become the unwelcome ones.
>
> The quality of new recruits is deteriorating. Even some with criminal records are being recruited.[52]

The day Zhao Ziyang became the general secretary, he began to worry about opposition from the military. He knew well his delicate position. According to interviews with some members of his think tanks, Zhao Ziyang was concerned only about how to continue his reform. He had to ask Deng Xiaoping to stay in the post of chairman of the Central Military Commission when people were talking about the elder politicians' retirement. He relied on Deng to subdue the army "dragon" and made little effort himself. This was Zhao Ziyang's style: if he could not deal with something well, he would just as soon forget it. This made the PLA hostile to Zhao.

In 1986, before Hu Yaobang's ouster, I was told by an officer that "if China's situation goes on like this, nobody knows who will be sent to the guillotine." Zhao Ziyang could find no way out from his trouble with the army when he was in office. He did not make efforts to let the army understand the economic reform under his leadership. This partly explained why many officers blamed the misleading reform for the emergence of the student movement and accused Zhao of deliberately misleading the student movement for his own interests. In the opinion of some officers, it would have been excellent if students had not demanded that Deng leave his office but had supported him in firing the largest *guandao* ("official profiteer") Zhao Ziyang instead. Unfortunately, many officers did not understand the significance of Zhao Ziyang's inclination to the democracy movement. In fact, if Deng did favorably respond to the students' demands, as Zhao did in early May 1989, it might have resulted in China's smooth transition to democracy, and Deng's position would not have been challenged.

According to reliable sources, Zhao had some opportunities to launch troops against the gerontocracy but refused to take the risk. The latest rumor was that Qin Jiwei (minister of national defense) tried to unify seven military regions to end martial law. Why were these steps not possible? Going back in history, we find that in 1971 Zhou Enlai had complete control of the PLA. He could maneuver the ground army to occupy every military airport. But Lin Biao's military clique, including Huang Yongsheng, the chief of staff, Qiu Huizuo, the chief of the Logistics Department, Wu Faxian, the chief of the air force, and Li Zuopeng, the chief of the navy, could do nothing but wait helplessly for arrest after their conspiracy was exposed. Zhao Ziyang well knew that there was no comparison between Zhou Enlai and himself.

What about the rumor of civil war, which spread so widely a few days after June 4, 1989? Why did so many people believe, even hope for it? People greatly exaggerated the divergence within the PLA and did not understand there was neither a new paramount leader who could replace Deng nor a new political organization or a party that could win popular support.

In 1989, the PLA did not initially ask to move into Beijing, for it had no special interests of its own. If the PLA had had any special interests and had been interested in greater political participation, it would have pressured the CCP or the government to meet its demands. This, however, was not the case; that is, no single unit was put under military control after martial law, and no military person beyond Qin was appointed to the Politburo of the Thirteenth Central Committee of the CCP. Jiang Zemin, a "civilian" party's general secretary, replaced Deng Xiaoping at the Central Military Commission.

Before June 4, as many Western specialists noticed, many soldiers "withdrew" from civilian posts after the Cultural Revolution. Why did this happen? The first reason was that now both economic and cultural construction needs cadres with special skills other than political qualifications. This also explains why, when Deng Xiaoping talked about military training, he always suggested officers become "cadres able to serve both in the army and in civilian units."[53] The army's withdrawal from or participation in politics was always decided by the party, not the army. Therefore, the PLA, as the main instrument of the party and the mainstay of the dictatorship of the proletariat, cannot absolutely withdraw from politics in China. The only difference is that now the PLA, which is totally devoted to military development, is no longer a work team but a shock brigade. Hidden contradictions, however, will also cause political changes inside the main instrument of dictatorship.

Still the Party's Army

The Brothers Yang. The Yang brothers conspicuously entered the limelight after Tiananmen. There are two contradicting views on the elder brother, Yang Shangkun. One explained that Yang Shangkun would play a significant role in the post-Deng period. The second held that he was but a careerist.

In 1988, people were very surprised to learn that Yang Shangkun (born 1907) replaced Li Xiannian (born 1909) as the state chairman when the party was talking about elder politicians' retirement. In the meantime, Li Peng told his friends that China's future would depend on Chairman Yang after Deng's death. Li's remark was improper according to the party's discipline. But Yang surely had rich political experiences in military, party, local, and parliamentary arenas. It was reasonable for some faction of the CCP to trust Yang Shangkun to play a more important role in the future.

After June 4, many people believed that Yang and Li should both be responsible for the June 4 massacre, although Yang was reported to have hesitated in proclaiming martial law. It was also said that on May 20, 1989, he delayed forcing the troops into Beijing when Deng pressed them to do so immediately. Some officers regarded it to Yang's merit. Others said that on May 20 the army was not ready for shooting. Unfortunately, after many days of mistreatment by the demonstrators, many soldiers were so angry that they were no longer reluctant to shoot.

Deng's trust in Yang Shangkun peaked after Tiananmen. Many quotations from Yang Shangkun's speeches cited by military writers in their published works also tried to prove his merits in Chinese military reform.

But after June 4, the people, particularly the army officers, were suspicious that Yang abused his power by appointing several relatives as high-ranking officers. Thus came the term the "Yang family army." As a matter of fact, Yang Shangkun never had a chance during wartime to build up his own *shantou* (faction) in the army. Now, it was very difficult for him to find enough officers whom he could trust. Although he then appointed his half-brother, Yang Baibing, as the chief of the General Political Department of the PLA and some of his followers to key positions, he still could not depend on this small *shantou* to control the whole army. All these arrangements were insufficient to change the PLA into an army largely under the control of the Yangs. On the contrary, Yang would ultimately pay for what he had done. Let us take a close look at some of the details that might give a better idea of whether the Yang brothers were careerists or scapegoats-to-be.

Organizational Guarantees of Control. After June 4, the CCP began to reemphasize the organizational line. Before 1989, the PLA had just raised many old officers' ranks as an honor and planned to readjust the command units. The original personnel plan made before 1989 was readjusted because all officers underwent the rigorous test of the June 4 incident.

After the readjustment, the air force and the navy did not change much. Chi Haotian, the chief of the headquarters of general staff, retained his post. He also maintained ties with Song Shilun, who was said to be liberal and argued against martial law. The original plans before the incident to promote some young promising officers to be his assistants, however, were rejected because of the readjustment.

Some officers moved from the GPD to the General Logistic Department shortly after Yang Baibing was raised to his post as chief of the GPD. It is not clear, however, whether those men were Yang's followers.

The commanders and political commissars of seven military regions were reappointed in 1990. As the chief of the GPD, Yang Baibing preferred to go to every military region to arrange the personnel changes rather than doing it in a general meeting. Some writers emphasized that this was designed to avoid unnecessary meetings, which could provide a chance for the dissidents to get together. Is, however, the following fact coincidental? Altogether, there were seven members of the Central Committee, one alternate member of the CC of the CCP, and one member of the Central Commission for Inspecting Discipline among the fourteen highest officers of different regions. Their promotion was basically decided before the Thirteenth Congress of the CCP in the summer of 1987.

Certainly, there were also some changes owing totally to June 4. Zhang Gong, for instance, was promoted more than two grades at this time because of his role in the massacre. Only one among the fourteen was from the former Second Field Army. The 1989 readjustment of military personnel still maintained some balance between various factions among marshals like Xu Xiangqian, Nie Rongzhen, and military academies and regions.

What is important is which officers and how many were purged after this readjustment. According to information leaking out a year later, at the meeting of the political work of the army, Yang Baibing said that twenty-one officers above the division level, thirty-six of battalion and regiment levels, and fifty-four of company level "seriously violated the discipline during the crackdown of the reactionary riot." "More than 1,400 soldiers threw away their arms and ran away." The army commander of the Thirty-eighth Division, Xu Qinxian, refused to obey the order and was sentenced; his predecessor, Lieutenant General Li Jijun, was suspended by the CMC because of violating military discipline.[54]

Surprisingly, while Li Desheng, as political commissar, left his office at the Defense University, his colleague Zhang Zhen, the chancellor, remained in office, and nobody in Shenyang Military Region was purged (if we regard this region as his *shantou*). In fact, some officers of Shenyang Military Region moved to other regions and were even promoted to higher posts, but no one moved into this region as its leader. A point of reference might be Li Desheng's experience during the Cultural Revolution. In January 1975, he resigned from the post of vice chairman of the CCP and from the Standing Committee of the Politburo of the CCP. He may again want to distance himself from such turbulent conditions as he did before. More significantly, the party committees of several group armies were reorganized after June 4.

Setting Up Regulations and Emphasizing Discipline. The events of 1989 and their aftermath called for Yang Shangkun, number one at that time in the PLA, to contemplate how the party could efficiently command the gun. It became the key task for him and Yang Baibing, the chief of the General Political Department of the PLA. Now let us take a look at how Yang Baibing worked to stabilize the PLA from the top to the bottom.

On June 6, 1990, Jiang Zemin signed three regulations, including the Routine Service Regulation and Discipline Regulation. These documents, regarding exposed problems such as the violation of discipline and the "liberalization" during the summer of 1989, were prepared by the General Political Department under Yang Baibing. The main content stresses "insistence of the party's absolute leadership of the PLA," and "the army's highest discipline to be always ready to obey commands of the Central Committee of the CCP and the CMC." Besides, these regulations warn "against excessive democratization":

> What should be punished is a break with the Party's policies, and resistance against command; negative fighting, and anybody forfeiting a chance for combat or divulging secrets or departing from a correct policy line, or shielding, and winking at evildoers, or participating in any illegal organization, etc.[55]

Meanwhile, the General Political Department under Yang Baibing's direct control expanded its power. It gained the power of supervising discipline. The special commission formerly responsible for this was dissolved. Did Yang Baibing abuse his power in doing so, or would he abuse his power after it was expanded? Who is in a position to examine his work?

The Ideological Trend. Yang Baibing requested the political department to stress political study to ensure his control over the army, but he did not want to go so far that politics would undermine professional military work. Some fundamental principles were reviewed and some changes were made. Following the elder politicians, some high-ranking officers still emphasized a greater danger of war. They also wanted to change the new regulations that required officers of certain levels to be graduates of military academies. Another trend pursuing further emancipation of the mind, however, was also happening, whether the authorities liked it or not.

Some phenomena might be significant. Before June 4, many novels based on actual military events (*jishi xiaoshuo*) were published and formed a new type of military literature termed "literature of exposure," to parallel a similar civilian "literature of exposure" started earlier in 1977 and 1978. After Tiananmen, five of them were banned: *Black Snow*; *Misfortune*; *Snow Is White, Blood Is Red*; *Sino-Vietnam Border War's Secret Record*; and *A Day in Beijing under Martial Law*. In these books, the military writers cited historical documents and interviewed many persons concerned. *Snow Is White, Blood Is Red*, for example, exposes Mao's mistakes at the beginning of the liberation war in northeast China, and pointed out that Lin Biao corrected Mao's strategic instruction to the Fourth Field Liberation Army. Zhang Zhenrong, author of the novel, told us that the lives of hundreds of thousands of civilians were spared during the liberation war in northeast China.

Those books also touched on the issue of the ideal relationship between the PLA and the civilian population, including the minority nationalities during peace. After those five books were banned, people became even more interested in them. Nobody could point to any of the facts they exposed and say that they were not correct. These books set us thinking. But Yang Shangkun reportedly remarked that "the conclusion of any important issue should be made by the central leadership in the future, and not by you right now." However, Yang Baibing protected Zhang Zhenrong from any more charges. Although under duress, people could not say much in public. A new trend of emancipating the mind actually started, however, and would continue much more deeply and widely.

Whenever the CCP meets with troubles, it calls on the army to solve them. To some extent, stabilizing the PLA and strengthening party supremacy over the military decide how the party will deal with the inevitable troubles in the future.

Prospects of the PLA's Role in the Near Future

I will discuss the role of the PLA in these likely situations: (1) direct military control, (2) reversal of the verdict of the June 4 incident, and (3) military unification with Taiwan.

Direct Military Control. Jiang Zemin is acceptable in his current position for the simple reason that he cannot threaten any faction either within the party or within the army. Jiang was appointed CMC chairman for the same reason. He was not regarded as a competitor to control the army at a time when nobody could take Deng's place and the government was weak.

Under these circumstances, some trends of thought should receive attention. More and more party cadres and military officers have become interested in the experience of direct military rule in Indonesia. Comparing Indonesia with India, they consider the general situation in Indonesia no better than that of India. But military rule, they believe, helps Indonesia develop much faster than India, which is considered a democracy. Studying the case, many officers, including a few liberals, express the belief that the PLA was in need of a strongman.

The second trend of thought, which may be more important and popular, argues that China's economic development has to wait for a chance. China's reform needs experience that can be obtained from other socialist countries. No matter what will happen to Russia, a return to authoritarian rule or success in both political and economic reforms, the new Russian experience will influence China greatly either positively or negatively. To some extent, China's future depends on Russian perestroika.

Third, Chinese officers are traditionally self-confident, but after Tiananmen many of them have felt that the army might not yet be capable of playing a role like that in Indonesia. I heard such remarks as "if the PLA were mature, direct military rule might be wonderful," and "the army is only anxious for China's progress." Almost all officers said the army would not be likely to intervene in politics. The army should be a main factor for stability in every country, including the United States.

The nature of the PLA at present is still political and a machine for revolution and dictatorship. Transition to democracy, however, cannot be completed by military intervention or violence; rather it will demand many compromises. The neutrality of the army from any and all political forces will be helpful for pluralism in Chinese politics.

Reversal of June 4. If the CCP at some point chooses to reverse the verdict of the June 4 incident, several problems must be taken into consideration. The most obvious is whether it would cause unrest. The reversal of the verdict is a catalyst that probably would trigger many hidden contradictions.

Another important concern is what the army leadership's or most officers' first concern would be. Would they support a reversal? The possible impact on the army should be taken into serious consideration. But the most important factor is the attitude of the people toward the PLA. The military hopes that the Chinese people understand the army's tragedy and trust them as being a great army without selfishness, just as before. Zhao Wei, the author of Zhao Ziyang's biography, said,

> The fact [was] that the army's involvement in the crackdown was absolutely in executing the orders. A number of armymen had been punished because they did not seriously implement the orders. To execute orders is always the sacred duty of any army. The armymen are not accountable for their act in executing orders. . . . This should be a principle to deal with the Tiananmen incident in the future.[56]

Eventually, however, a thorough reversal of the verdict of the June 4 incident is inevitable and will cause further emancipation of the mind within the PLA. Possibly the emancipation will challenge and change the political role of the army and its relationship with the party.

Military Unification with Taiwan. As for the question of the unification of Taiwan with mainland China, some people hold that China's terrible difficulty in the near future might cause the octogenarians to act precipitously. Taiwan, however, is not Kuwait; the Taiwan Strait is not the Sino-Vietnam border. War preparation for this type of maneuver must be massive. The sacrifice could be tremendous. A civil war in any sense is not advisable. The PLA knows well that a civil war would mean the extermination of the whole nation. Even a small war or some kind of military conflict would result in the loss of most of what China has gained since 1978. The mainland has begun to benefit from economic exhange with Taiwan in only a few years. More investment and trade are expected. The party would not be able to order the PLA to do anything if the octogenarians were to act irresponsibly. Whoever made such a move would lose his authority in the army.

The PLA has been an army of the party. But both the people and the army are waiting for something to happen. Modernization is not a political evolution itself, but it can influence political alternatives of transition. When Mao Zedong said: "In China the army needs democracy as much as the people do. Democracy in our army is an important weapon for undermining the feudal mercenary army," he was concerned about the political atmosphere within the army but not the relationship between the party and the army and between the state and the army.[57] Unfortunately, up to now not even the prodemocracy officers understand the political neutrality of a state army. And the opening up is also important for the progress of the army. The PLA should learn from the West not only in advanced technology but in democractic military experience as well.

4
Marxism, Confucianism, and Cultural Nationalism

Zhang Shuqiang

It is generally agreed that ideology refers to a system of concepts and principles concerning human life in its entirety, including the physical, social, intellectual, and affective domains. In China, it is often used interchangeably with the term "worldview"—a cognitive paradigm by which individuals make sense of their existence. Put at its simplest, an ideology is a theory of reality that motivates the subjective ordering of reality into good and bad, right and wrong, them and us, true and false, and so on. This chapter does not address the totality of what may conveniently be termed the Chinese ideology. It will focus on only three major ideological components of the present-day Chinese political culture: Marxism, Confucianism, and cultural nationalism.

Although the three components do not constitute an exhaustive analysis of the Chinese mind, they provide a composite stress pattern within the Chinese ideological domain, presenting clues to future conflicts. This chapter makes the following arguments:

- Traditional Marxism will continue to lose its viability as a justification for the Communist party's exclusive control of state power.
- The party orthodoxy, so far partly sustained by Confucian conservatism, will be challenged by political-moral precepts of the same tradition to the extent that the traditional "mandate of heaven" is totally forfeited. Neither an enlightened autocracy nor Western liberal democracy, however, seems practicable in the near future.
- The contention between the official cultural nationalism and the cultural nationalism embraced by the people will intensify, to the disadvantage of party orthodoxy.

The chapter concludes that despite the massive ideological regimentation following the Tiananmen Square massacre, the current leadership in Beijing has not been and will not be able to extricate itself from the ideological predicaments brought about by its political dogmas; by the pervasive influence of China's cultural tradition; and by the Chinese people's urgent desire to eradicate any obstacles in their determined pursuit of prosperity and pride. The 1990s will witness further erosion of the remaining authority of the Communist party in the ideological domain.

The Party's Burden of Marxism

The rationale underlying communism is a prediction made by Karl Marx that the evil system of man's exploitation of man will eventually be overthrown and replaced by a classless society that guarantees unlimited public wealth.

Reassessment of Capitalism. As an ultimate idealization antithetical to real-life social injustice in his time, Marx's theory is beautiful and morally compelling, in the abstract. His economic determinism lends a scientific outlook to the essentially Utopian theory. It thus provides a seemingly logical basis for the glorious eventuality of communism, to be achieved first by the violent overthrow of capitalism and then through a transitional period of socialism under a proletarian dictatorship. This proposition has since received added immediacy from Vladimir Lenin's diagnosis, made in the early 1910s, that capitalism is already in its terminal stage, "monopoly capitalism."[1] Its days are numbered.

That is the standard Marxist "big picture": the worldview or paradigm that maps past history and explains what the party business is all about. In the final analysis, to become a Communist believer is to attain "the Way" in such Marxist terms. And it apparently stands to reason that the party that sees the Way should be entrusted with the exclusive mandate to lead. But unfortunately for party ideologues, one piece in the paradigm has been conspicuously out of place: capitalism simply refuses to die.

Adding to the embarrassment of orthodox Marxist-Leninists is the apparent stagnation and decline of the theoretically superior socialist system. For the party's very survival, unorthodox practical reforms often blatantly capitalistic in nature have to be carried out within the established Communist ideology. Those reform attempts have forced open the forbidden realm of orthodoxy, creating an exciting intellectual environment where a new ideology or ideologies may gradually coalesce while interacting with the old.

Foremost among the rush of fresh ideas after the late 1970s is a bold reexamination of the recalcitrant capitalism. At a conference sponsored by the Academies of Social Sciences of several provinces and by the newspaper *Guangming Ribao* in December 1988, for example, Yu Guangyuan, a longtime party ideologue with a matching reputation, submitted a written presentation containing quite a few intellectually provocative points.[2]

He argued against the conclusion of Marx and Lenin, who said that conflicts between the relations of production and the productive forces under capitalism would lead to the demise of the capitalist system. Capitalism, he maintains, as a form of production relations is capable of accommodating levels of productive forces even higher than the present level, which has already exceeded the expectation of Marx and Lenin. Therefore the current stage of "monopoly capitalism" is not likely to be a terminal stage, close to the brink of death. Even if economic crises occur, they pose no fundamental threat to the capitalist system as a whole.

His argument amounts to a total rebuttal of Marx's "scientific" prophecy of the death of capitalism as well as Lenin's famous thesis in *Imperialism: The Highest Stage of Capitalism*. According to the classic Marxist economic determinism, it is precisely the development of productive forces that is supposed to destroy the irrational relations of production we know as capitalism.[3]

The Marxist theory of proletarian revolution is predicated on the impoverishment of the working masses and the polarization of wealth and poverty under capitalism. Without such a dichotomy, no acute intensification of class antagonism would occur. Nor would a proletarian revolution be needed—still less a Communist party that exists to lead such a revolution. Yu points out that those assumptions concerning impoverishment and social polarization may not be valid today, considering the size and wealth of the expanding middle class, or the "techno-intelligentsia and the managerial staff," in Yu's words. Although he still maintains that "capitalism will necessarily be replaced by socialism and communism," he candidly admits that "the simple conclusions by Marx and Engels in and of themselves are inadequate" to justify the faith. "Many people are working on it, but none have so far produced any definitive scientific work as an answer to the problem."[4] In plain language, nobody knows. Marxism is, after all, not as scientific as it purported to be.

Sensible skepticism is also evident in Liu Weihua's reconsideration of capital in *The Trend in the Socialization of Capital and Surplus Value*.[5] Citing wide proliferation of stocks and credits as evidence of the socialization of capital, he argues that capitalist enterprises have evolved into "socialized enterprises as opposed to private enterprises." Consequently, those enterprises are free from any individual owner's personal greed; operational responsibilities are separated from ownership to ensure rational and democratic practices; and capitalism has thus acquired new vitality. Liu's analysis actually attacks the fundamental concept of "scientific communism"—the exploitation of the workers as evidenced in the proprietary possession of the "surplus value" created by labor. The socialization of capital, he says, results in the "socialization of surplus value," making it possible for members of society to share the wealth created by labor. Hence social capitalism.[6]

This social blueprint would bewilder a free marketeer like Margaret Thatcher. But coming from within an ideological tradition that extols socialism as the ultimate virtue, it is intended as a compliment to the market. It acknowledges that capitalism may be de facto socialism. It is what Marx had envisioned after all. In other words, although party ideologues may think they are entrusted with the mission of initiating and advancing socialism, this is only an illusion.

But Western capitalists are also wrong in thinking that they are champions of private property. Today's capitalism *is* socialism. Radical Chinese political economists seem eager to debunk the diagnosis of monopoly capitalism made by Marx and confirmed by Lenin, and to rename it social capitalism. The most radical of them have even started searching for a new *ism* to label the symbiosis of socialism and capitalism within the system of private ownership.[7] They are no longer sure whether Marx, Engels, and Lenin really knew what they were talking about while prophesying the inevitable, forcible overthrow of capitalism as a logical consequence of private property rights. Provided that all members of society can share the surplus value under social capitalism, communism as a guiding worldview has indeed lost both its theoretical relevance and its moral superiority in the contemporary context. In short, Marxism is in reality redundant and morally irrelevant.

Because of the classic Marxist preoccupation with the relationship between the "economic foundation" and the "superstructure," which includes the role of the state, some Chinese theorists have also ventured into a reinterpretation of the capitalist state. Hong Yunshan claims that the capitalist state has in many cases become "the largest owner, the largest investor, the largest buyer of commodities and services, and the largest creditor to provide financing." Even though the recent wave of privatization has somewhat reduced the economic role of the state, he writes, it is "absolutely impossible to cancel the important position of the state economy and its irreplaceable function in the capitalist society." He goes on, "This economic entity cannot be viewed as serving the interests of a minority of capitalists. . . . As far as it services the whole society and is available to all the people, [capitalist] state economy is an economy of public ownership."[8]

It should be noted that according to Marx, Lenin, and Mao Zedong, the capitalist state can only serve as the "executive committee" of the bourgeoisie. For this reason the capitalist state must be destroyed, rather than reformed. Hong obviously thinks otherwise. And that puts the necessity and legitimacy of a proletarian revolution in jeopardy.

Furthermore, Marxism has traditionally consolidated its position on the inevitability of a violent proletarian revolution by categorically denying that a sector of public or socialist economy may spring from an existing capitalist political-economic structure. The proletariat must seize the state power, establish a dictatorship—euphemistically known as a "people's democratic dictatorship," in the People's Republic of China—and then nationalize the private ownership of means of production.

Current economic thinking in China, however, is just the opposite. Monopoly capitalism, or more specifically "state monopoly capitalism," is believed to be capable of facilitating "a complete qualitative change" in the nature of capital in a "peaceful, gradual, civil, and democratic process."[9] In the process, it is transforming the nature of a bourgeois polity.[10] Anyone who has a rudimentary knowledge of the *Manifesto* can see that it would take an arduous exercise in semantics to characterize this type of reasoning as "enrichment and development of scientific socialism."

Although these debates must take place within the established ideological framework and all the authors profess a faith in communism and a desire to advance Marxism, their advanced version of Marxism has vitiated the most substantive of the Marxist doctrines. Capitalism seems to be "converging" with socialism naturally and peacefully, because modern capitalism has already been socialized and contains "social features."[11] In the rhetorical tradition of true Communist doctrinairism, one party theoretician even claims that "only by accepting this thesis can we truly adhere to and develop Marxism."[12]

The conflict between this modern-day Marxism and the traditional Marxism is so obvious that the continuity and cohesion of the ideology have to be stretched to the most tenuous degree. A representative attempt is Hong Zhaolong's essay "Learn from the Scientific Attitude of Marx and Engels toward the Manifesto," published in commemoration of the 140th anniversary of the publication of the *Manifesto*. Hong stresses the necessity to "revise" some of the conclusions by Marx, Engels, and Lenin by citing Marx's own revision of the *Manifesto* after the 1848 revolution in Europe. His rather oblique, if not esoteric, references are meant to support the conclusion that "the development of realistic socialism has demanded a qualitative leap in the development of Marxism."[13] But he does not elaborate on what is meant by a qualitative leap. Nor is it clear to the reader how there can be two qualitatively different Marxisms. It would not be far wrong to interpret the ambiguity as thinly disguised disillusionment with state-enforced ideological correctitude.

Redesign of Socialism. In the Marxist morality play, the existence of communism is justified by that of its evil foil, capitalism. Barring the alleged evil, the party would have no place in the plot; and pending the death of Evil, a flustered Virtue would have to postpone victory indefinitely. The intended morals thus fall apart. The revelation of the character of Evil, with its vengeful vibrancy and resilience, is only one side of the drama. What is the role of its nemesis, socialism, in the larger scheme of things?

It is common knowledge among Marxists and non-Marxists that Marx said much about capitalism—more precisely, nineteenth-century capitalism—and little about socialism. His *Manifesto* should be read as a mere statement of intent rather than as a workable social program. Most ideas for developing socialism politically and economically that have come to be regarded as orthodox socialism are attributable to Lenin and Joseph Stalin. These two men essentially equated the institutionalization of socialism with the concentration of power in the hands of the party elite. The monopoly of power is defended in the name of "class struggle" in the political domain and "socialization of production" in the economic domain. The political expression of socialism is thus the dictatorship of the proletariat. Its economic counterpart is central-command planning.

Neither policy has fared well in practice. The dictatorial model of government has caused enormous suffering among all walks of life, including a considerable number of those near the pinnacle of the party hierarchy. The Marxist advocacy of class hatred gave rise to ruthless despotism under Lenin and Stalin. By the mid-1960s, the Stalinistic social control copied by China from the Soviet Union had been replaced by a more fanatic form of patriarchal despotism, centered on the orchestration of a personality cult. The result of such a consistent campaign is, naturally, widespread resentment and hatred of the power source. The guiding idea of class struggle for social justice has proved in a typically Orwellian fashion to be a handy pretext under which social injustice is perpetuated.

Zbigniew Brzezinski has summarized the evolution of the so-called proletarian dictatorship:

> The original idea in communism was essentially Utopian in its claim that the working class would emancipate itself. But Leninism distorted the idea and turned the Communist party into a political group led by a small elite. The group led first the workers' movement and then the revolutionary government of workers and peasants. Next, Stalinism institutionalized the exclusive authority of the party and created a complete controlling system, which is the totalitarian Communist state of the twentieth century.[14]

The ideology started as a grand aspiration of public participation in political and economic affairs during the early period of industrialization. But its dictatorial model, as a necessary extension of its obsession with class struggle, could not but produce a rigid hierarchy that places obedience above initiative and promotes impersonal and ambiguous "class interests" at the expense of the individual. Any autocratic government is programmed to shut out public participation, no matter what ideologies are advocated. The noble tenet of public participation, as implied in the very terms "socialism" and "communism," clashes with such an oligarchical polity. The harder the party tries to sell the idea of socialism, the more obvious will be the crude duplicity perpetrated by the party apparatus. In that sense, the Chinese brand of socialism as we know it today has had defeat built into itself.

The predicament is the topic of an article that appeared on February 15, 1988, in *Guangming Ribao*. The author, Kong Lingdong, says,

> The democracy required by socialism is a genuine and sound socialist democracy. It is not the control of a country by a group of people in its society, but the management of that country by its whole society—by all the members of the society—and their participation in the country's political life.

He makes a distinction between state and society, the former referring to the seat of power, or government, and the latter to the public. "As a force over society, any state has the tendency to detach itself from and dominate society." So "special attention needs to be paid to the eradication of the traditional thinking that the socialist state is by its very nature a state in which the people are the masters."[15]

He goes on to stress the importance of freedom of thought, freedom of speech, and academic freedom in balancing the state and society, to prevent "public servants" from becoming "masters of the public." The unstated question is, Who constitutes the state? The answer is, The party. True socialism, according to Kong's argument, should never ensure the party's dominant position, because the party has the inherent tendency to "detach itself from and dominate" the people. The very idea of socialism has come back to haunt the party.

To party ideologues, Kong's idea is dangerous heresy. It questions the alleged identical interests of the party, the state, and the people—the very basis for the people's allowing the party to run the state. Applying the Marxist principle that "the political structure of a society is determined by its economic foundation," Kong maintains that, under socialism,

> Producers can only come into contact with means of production through the mediation of the state. Therefore the producing masses have to be economically dependent upon the state: this relationship determines their political status. . . . Under such circumstances, ubiquitous state domination assumes an inevitable nature. State organs can encroach upon and control every aspect of society without any restraint. The real basis for a political form of high centralization of power lies in inadequate democracy.[16]

It is noteworthy that the accusation of the dictatorial political format has stemmed from the seminal Marxist principle of economic determinism. At the same time it agrees perfectly with Brzezinski's conclusion that "unless the nature of the Communist party is changed or it fades out, the issue of participation will remain a source of contention within the Communist party as well as between the party and the society."[17] If Kong's argument is stretched a little, it implies that state ownership controlled by the party is necessarily a dictatorship!

Regarding the socialist legal system, Kong warns that "any law that is not backed up by power is no more than a piece of paper. . . . If the masses are left with no means or conditions to control or manage the state apparatus, all guarantees are pointless." In short, the state—including such instruments of dictatorship as the armed forces, the police, and the judiciary branch—must be brought under the supervision of society. The party, particularly its inner circles, must be held accountable to the public, according to Kong's explication of Marxism. That scenario can be the worst nightmare for the entrenched party elite, as was evident in the nationwide 1989 democracy movement.

Chinese political scientists, Su Zhaozhi for one, have even revived the term "new leviathan" as an oblique reference to the current dictatorial model.[18] Nikolai Bukharin used the term in the 1930s to alert the Soviet public to the totalitarian rule practiced by Stalin in the name of communism. Following his rehabilitation in the Soviet Union in February 1988, Bukharin's warning is often cited by reform-minded party ideologists as another criticism of the dictatorial form of governance defended by the hard-liners. Specifically, a new leviathan is characterized by (1) unlimited state ownership and forced collectivization; (2) a privileged class of bureaucrats; (3) "backward socialism" in a police state; and (4) extreme concentration of power in the hands of one individual. The parallels between Bukharin's new leviathan and the political reality of China are too obvious for anyone to miss. If Bukharin's thinking represents genuine Leninism, how would one describe the party ideology in today's China?

Political autocracy cannot survive without the central planning of the national economy as its support. On that front, the party finds itself again in an ideological predicament. Central planning is more than a management style. It relates directly to ownership. It is possible only when the state owns all or most of the means of production. In Marx's analysis, proprietors of private properties see each other as opposing entities—hence there is competition. And thus there is an anarchic state in production, and eventually the concentration of property is in only a few hands.

The concentration of property conflicts with social production. A proletarian revolution is thus born. Given Kong Lingdong's premise that the state has come to dominate society in the sense that "public servants have on occasion become masters of the people" and that "the state nominally managed by the people is in actuality incapable of materializing the rights of the people," the revolution intended to emancipate the productive forces does not.[19] Instead of resolving, it reinforces the conflict between social production and the high concentration of property, now in the hands of the party elite.

Once the identity of the interests of the power elite—the state— and of the people—society—has proved untenable, central planning must be viewed as subjugation of the welfare of the public to the vested interests of the power elite. To the great consternation of all Communist leaders, this is an obvious mockery of the original intent of communism.

The economic redesign of socialism in China started with the introduction of private ownership and market economy. In essence, the socialist economy has to be revitalized by an injection of capitalism. Although the private sector is still small in China, it is precisely this vigorous capitalist tail, part of it implanted from abroad, that is wagging the socialist dog. In his report to the Thirteenth National Party Congress in October 1987, Zhao Ziyang once again conceded the faulty design of socialism[20]—first officially acknowledged at the Third Plenary Session of the party's Twelfth Central Committee in October 1984:

> A structure of ownership evolved in which undue emphasis was placed on a single form of ownership, and a rigid economic structure took shape, along with a corresponding political structure based on over-concentralization [sic] of power. All this seriously hampers the development of the productive forces and a Socialist commodity economy.[21]

To rectify the design faults, two key measures are introduced: (1) "developing an economy with different types of ownership, with public ownership remaining predominant"; and (2) "adopting diverse forms of distribution, with distribution according to work remaining predominant."[22] The former is a reluctant approval of private ownership of the means of production—the antithesis of socialism; and the latter is an equally grudging approval of "exploitation of man by man" in the quintessential Marxist sense. The official rationalization of the ideological about-face is a convenient code phrase—"the primary stage of socialism."

This opens the ideological equivalent of a Pandora's box. On the one hand, party traditionalists try belatedly to stress that it is what the party has meant all along. Hitherto unpublished speeches by Mao Zedong, Liu Shaoqi, and Zhou Enlai from 1956 and 1957 are cited to lend some legitimacy to the reborn capitalism of socialist China.[23] On the other hand, more radical elements within the ideological circles demand explicit constitutional approval and protection of private ownership, claiming that capitalism should be as much, if not more, entitled to institutionalization than is socialism, within the present Chinese political structure.

One prominent spokesperson for the radical group has been Yan Jiaqi, who insists that "efforts to set up a market economy on the basis of public ownership must be completely abandoned. Provided that private property is protected, private enterprise ought to be vigorously developed and economic legislation strengthened."[24] A milder version of his position has since been written into the Declaration of the Federation of Democratic China. The declaration, however, refrains from calling for full-blown capitalism. Its language is ambiguous:

> Every citizen has the right to possess and control his or her means of production and fruits of labor. The main root of the economic stagnation and political despotism in Communist-ruled countries is the deprivation of the citizen's

91

right to property in the name of "the State." The only way to resolve the economic problems of China and realize modernization is to return the social wealth to the people and vigorously develop an economy owned by the people.[25]

The deprivation of the people of their right to the fruits of their labor is an accurate description of central planning, according to Yan. The history of the People's Republic of China has shown repeatedly that the party leadership never considers any price too high when it comes to consolidating its power base. Enormous economic and human resources have been sacrificed in order to sustain personal politics among a closed network of political insiders. The rigidity of central planning is only a symptom of the disease of dictatorship. When the party tries to redesign its economic model in the hope of prolonging its grip on power, one has to ask what constitutes the center—the state—that prioritizes economic concerns. Yan Jiaqi's "socialist" (populist?) accusation that the state has deprived the people of their rights, along with Kong Lingdong's "Marxist" analysis of the relationship between the state and society, offers solutions. The party bosses of China believe these solutions must be stopped at any cost—even by machine guns and tanks.

Although the Tiananmen Square massacre temporarily silenced radical calls for democracy in China, the question of how to justify a commodity economy under socialism remains. One much milder post–Tiananmen Square argument that does not offend the party is this: "Commodity economy has been a neutral and objective economic modus operandi" from the days of primitive society until those of socialism. It is not possible to "formulate a law of value unique to socialism, or a law of competition, or a law of supply and demand peculiar to socialism.[26] By assuming the neutrality and universality of commodity economy, the seemingly innocent argument has practically neutered Marxism, which considers the market to be the basic flaw of capitalism. As Carver and Li have noted:

> [Marx] argued that the introduction of money to facilitate exchange was a revolution in human history, in that it provided a workable scheme of incentives to promote production. But it also required individuals to see each other as isolated or separate entities whose interests were necessarily opposed because each is the proprietor of private property. It was precisely this historically created relation of isolation and mutual opposition that Marx's communism was supposed to remedy through a system of planned production— a system which never progressed, in Marx's hands, beyond a mere statement of intent. Thus in his work, and in the

Marxist heritage, there is a basic objection in principle to monetary exchange on the market, and that analysis of commodity-exchange is at the root of the Communist attack on the market and on capitalist societies.[27]

The continuing theoretical equivocation is bound to generate tension within the party mind—so much so that it should not be surprising that the party leadership will continue to exhibit bizarre political and economic behavior from time to time.

No Ideological Solutions in Sight. The reassessment of capitalism and the redesign of socialism are signs that the party mind is in a psychotic state, although its ideological coping mechanism is still trying to function to preserve its institutional existence. But the myth of the party's monopoly of truth has been shattered completely, even for some of the most loyal of the loyalists. For the majority of people with no vested interest in the party, its theoretical paradigm is wrong beyond any reasonable doubt.

What is even worse for the party is its utter inability to invoke Marxism for its rescue. Talking about exploitation and poverty under capitalism only embarrasses the Communists. Predictions of the death of capitalism sound like self-mockery. Not surprisingly, the utopian and populist specter once painted by Marxism horrifies the entrenched party inner circles. And scientific economic determinism can be turned conveniently around, as so many party ideologists have demonstrated, to pull the rug from under the party's feet by accusing the party-controlled state of hampering the development of the forces of social production. This very Marxist reasoning has kept alive the main argument in the famous dissident Wei Jingsheng's 1979 article, "Democracy or New Dictatorship?": "Only when the social system is changed will society develop and will the people's livelihood and production develop at a fast pace."[28]

In the past the party leadership derived its legitimacy from Marxism, but Marxism has turned out to be an equivocation, if not a total fallacy. The burden is now on the party to prove it is still a relevant, liberating force. But it is running out of convenient justifications that have worked in the past. Left with no presentable deities to provide spiritual immunity, the party leadership is losing both its confidence in intellectual invincibility and the appearance of a moral cause. This crisis of faith characterizes the cultural and political milieu of China today and will continue in the 1990s as a persistent undercurrent, washing away the remaining underpinnings of the Communist orthodoxy.

Confucianism—Ally or Enemy?

New Confucianism. Two distinctions may be necessary for a discussion of the role of Confucianism in sustaining communism in China. One is the distinction between what is meant in this chapter by "Sinification of Communist ideology" and the constant theme of "socialism with Chinese characteristics" in official propaganda.[29] Sinification here refers to the subtle yet all-pervasive and powerful influence of the Confucianist worldview on the Chinese brand of communism. Although the influence has not been so much political as moral in nature, it has contributed to political tension in the most immediate sense—particularly since the mid-1980s. The crossing of an indigenous and moralistic philosophy with an imported political theory has produced a Sinicized communism with more resemblance to the bloodline Chinese ancestors than to the European godfathers. The so-called socialism with Chinese characteristics, however, serves only as a handy catchall phrase to rationalize anything that does not fit into standard Marxism. It is nothing but a euphemism for ideological retreat, without acknowledging intellectual deficiency or political deception on the part of the party leadership.

The second distinction needs to be made between new Confucianism in China and new Confucianism outside mainland China. Chinese academia tends to view the Confucian tradition in three major stages: first, covering the pre-Qin period and the Qin-Han dynasties; second, often referred to as neo-Confucianism, covering the Song-Ming dynasties; and third, contemporary, new Confucianism.[30] The last concept was proposed by Confucian scholars outside the People's Republic of China—namely, Yu Yingshih and Tu Weiming—and has since reached Chinese academia amid the influx of Western ideas.

Because the third wave of Confucianism in China is emerging in the context of modernization, its major concern is the contemporary role of Confucianism in China's reform. The recent examination of Confucianism may well have been motivated more by a resentment of Marxism than by a purely academic interest in Confucianism. Interest in contemporary Confucianism subjects the party to the heavily moralistic criteria of a value system with a more powerful claim to legitimate, ideological orthodoxy than that of a blundering and lackadaisical socialism. This interest has also set the Chinese new Confucianism apart from the new Confucianism outside the People's Republic of China. The latter focuses on the self-concept, as did the neo-Confucianism of the Song and Ming dynasties.[31] It attempts to assess the value of Confucianism in relation to the intellectual, moral, and spiritual consequences of Western-type modernization. The third wave in China, however, is unambiguously oriented toward an ideological reconstruction in anticipation of the abandonment of communism. As the philosopher Chen Xuelu put it, "It has occurred in the form of self-reflection with the intention of saving ourselves from an ideological crisis."[32]

Offending No Superiors. The Confucian worldview sees an equilibrium among all the elements in the cosmos. All the parts in the universe, human and otherwise, belong to a hierarchy that obeys its internal dictates. These dictates are analogous to the cosmic function in the term "heaven." When asked once about governance, Confucius replied that government is when "the king is king, the minister is minister, the father is father, and the son is son" (12:11).[33] This harmony is perceived as cosmic and is therefore referred to as the will of Heaven.

Despite its mystic aura, the belief system as a whole does not wander off into the realm of the supernatural. "The subjects on which the Master does not talk are—the preternatural, the violent, the chaotic, and the mythical" (7:20). Confucianism espouses a fundamentally and preeminently worldly attitude rather than one concerned with what is beyond this world. This is evident in Confucius's famous rhetorical questions: "While one is yet unable to deal with men, how can one deal with ghosts?" and "While one does not yet know about life, how can one know about death?" (11:11).

Its emphasis on the worldly calls attention to the positive interpersonal relationships to be guided by benevolence and virtue. This ultimate ethic standard originates with Confucius's assumption of an innate cosmic balance between the human world and the planetary system—"He who exercises government by means of virtue is like the Polaris, which stays in its place, and all the stars gather around it" (2:1). Heaven watches the whole of the human world, from the individual and the family to the state, and it maintains orderliness. This heavenly, cosmic function manifests itself in the social order, thus legitimizing the familial and social hierarchies. Daniel Kwok explicates Heaven's mandate—the legitimate authority to rule—in the following words:

> When the human order went astray, it was a deviation from the way (*dao*) of heaven and might involve a loss or miscarriage of the *ming* (mandate). Here then is the ultimate meaning of the *tianming* (Heaven's mandate), an impartial cosmic order, or orderly process, for the human order to emulate.[34]

The traditional understanding of authority draws from this cosmology. Society is understood as a hierarchy of social roles, with each individual fitting into a specific slot to ensure harmony. Role reversal is unthinkable. The rationale of the hierarchy is never questioned. The man-made law never attains the absoluteness of authority as an entity separate from the ruler who is the lawmaker. After all, what is the use of a man-made law before the mandate of Heaven?

But rules of conduct or social rituals, as a harmonizing mechanism, are given the force of law in the applied sense. Consequently, human relations are viewed not from a political perspective but from a moralistic point of view, the first moral canon being, "To constrain oneself and restore propriety is virtue" (12:1). In plain language, one should know one's place in one's clan and in society.

Politics is considered only an extension of moral philosophy. Submission to authority is continuous with filial piety within the all-encompassing concept of decorum, or propriety. It is a serious character flaw not to stand in awe of the mandate of Heaven, one's superiors, or the words of the sages (16:8). Those who are filial and fraternal do not "offend their superiors" or "stir up turmoil" (1:2).

Such a conservative worldview lends itself easily to the support of a centralized, patriarchal government, in which expressed differences in status and power are sanctified by the mandate of Heaven, which translates into day-to-day orderliness and stability. This conservative view of human society perhaps has contributed far more to the tolerance of dictatorial rule in China than has the imported Leninist-Stalinist dogmas. Marx and Engels, after all, were never explicit on the operational procedures of a proletarian dictatorship. More traditional than they would admit, Chinese Communists have perpetuated the notion of feudal autocracy "imposed by historical and social conditions," as in the words of Zhao Ziyang.[35] He limited such "feudal, patriarchal practices," however, to "some departments and grass-roots units."[36]

Yan Jiaqi put it more bluntly: "Neither the Nationalist party nor the Communist party has effectively eliminated feudal autocracy in China."[37] A deeper level of ideology overrides the opposing political philosophies. In that respect, the centuries-old Confucian tradition of subjugating the individual to the institution in return for social stability has molded the monarchical, republican, and socialist polities in more or less the same fashion. Current rulers are not essentially different from their predecessors in their attitude toward the people and in their emphasis on stability or the status quo.

Shu Zhaozhi and Wang Yizhou pointed out that Communist governance and feudal autocracy follow the same heritage.[38] The revolutionists' "great uniformity," iron discipline, and monocratic leadership are "tools to maintain feudal autocracy." This heritage, to a large extent, is characterized by a Confucian willingness to impose the institution on the individual. Any monocracy, Communist or otherwise, can certainly use that willingness to its advantage.

Marxism does not teach moral philosophy or formal ethics per se.[39] In China, where politics has traditionally been perceived as an extension of moral philosophy and social adjustment is often effected through a sense of decorum rather than explicit law, this void in the imported theory of government has to be filled with what is intrinsic to the host culture. Without borrowing from Confucianism, communism could not have been operational in China. The Sinification of Marxism has occurred in the interaction between patriarchal Confucian ethics and scientific Marxist politics, resulting in a semblance of the mandate of Heaven that the party can present to the populace.

How eager the current leadership has been to refurbish its mandate of Heaven since the Tiananmen Square massacre is illustrated by an interesting article in the government's official mouthpiece, *People's Daily*.[40] It tells its readers that the Ya'nan spirit—the party's "spiritual weapon"—is the "continuation and sublimation" of Chinese traditional culture, including Confucianism. Since there is little in Marx's works that the party can quote nowadays, it has turned to Confucianism as an ally.

But the self-serving attempt is clumsy to the utmost. Quoted in the essay is the Confucian saying, "No determined scholar or virtuous person will seek to live at the expense of other people [sic]; he will choose to die in his pursuit of virtue" (15:8).[41] The author claims, perhaps satirically in view of the June 4 massacre of idealistic demonstrators, that this spirit has evolved into the common will of the party. This somewhat loaded reference to killing for an immoral survival shows that although the party may hope to extend its lease on life on the strength of the Confucian emphasis on not "offend[ing] superiors" or "stir[ring] up turmoil," it has to contend also with other Confucian ideas that may turn out to be ominous for it (1:2).

Withstanding the Ruler to His Face. Confucius, as a moralist, is clear that the ruler's prerogative to rule is contingent on his ability to ensure harmony between Heaven and earth and between himself and the people he rules. Critics have accused the philosopher of imposing a rigid power structure: the king is king, the minister is minister, the father is father, the son is son (12:11). But critics seldom acknowledge the moral conditions Confucius set for the hierarchy: "The king is virtuous, the minister is faithful, the father is benevolent, and the

son is filial."[42] The ruler is held personally responsible for the welfare \
of the ruled. Lin Yutang interpreted the relationship as follows:

> The theory of the right to revolt was perfected from the very
> earliest days. . . . This is based on the theory of the "man-
> date of Heaven," which is that the ruler ruled the people in
> trust from Heaven for the welfare of the people, and then
> when a ruler misruled, he automatically forfeited his right
> to rule.[43]

An emperor is expected to "lead by virtue and regulate by propriety" (2:3). "When the ruler is devoted to propriety, the people
respond readily to the call on them to serve" (14:44). The determining
factor, according to Confucius, is the moral rectitude of the emperor.
If he is immoral, he is not a legitimate ruler at all. The monarch is
absolute only if he can maintain harmonious relationships, which in
turn ensure peace and abundance for the people.

It is a simple theory of government, placing faith in the emperor's moral responsibility. "To govern is to rectify" (12:17). "When a
ruler's personal conduct is correct, things are right without his
issuing orders; if his personal conduct is not correct, people will not
follow even if he issues orders" (13:6). "If he cannot rectify himself,
what has he got to do with rectifying others?"(13:13). Disequilibrium
in economic, political, and ethical terms is considered as error—not
the necessary dynamics of governance. And error is human in origin,
presumably moralistic in nature, social in consequence, and retributory in political terms. Any ruler who fails to maintain harmonious
relationships must be immoral and therefore is not a ruler at all.

A more populist position can be found in the book *Mencius*,
which teaches that "he who violates virtue is called a thief. He who
violates righteousness is called a brute. Those who are brutes or
thieves are called the worthless. I have heard of the killing of a
worthless person Shou [a tyrant]; I have not heard of the killing of a
king" (1:8).

The orthodox Chinese morality does allow an honorable place
for a forcible overthrow of a tyrant. According to Mencius, the
commoner is even in communion with Heaven, as the book proclaims, "Heaven sees according as the people see; Heaven hears
according as the people hear" (5:5). The dignity of the commoner is
placed even above the king's. "The people are the most important,
the land and grain the second, and the sovereign the lightest" (7:14).
Moral absolutes thus supersede monarchical absolutes, the two being
combined in the moral restrictions placed upon the emperor by his
subjects: "To love the king is to restrain the king" (1:4).

The legitimacy of a rebellion thus rests with the righteousness of the ruler. When asked about how a ruler should be served, Confucius said, "Do not cheat him, and moreover, withstand him to the face" (14:23). This is the Chinese version of loyal opposition. As a form of dissension, it breaks tradition by challenging what is already established, be it feudal, capitalist, or socialist. Meanwhile, through the moralizing of politics, it is a form of protest within tradition.[44] The Confucian political morality in the empire building of the past and the socialist revolution of today account for the regenerative and reformative capacity of the Confucian tradition.

Chinese Communists have taken pride in being rebels against a totally undemocratic Confucianism, particularly "the king's absolute authority over the ministers" and "the father's absolute authority over the son."[45] Their political posture once appealed to the populace because it represented a moral force relevant to the circumstances and comprehensible to the nation—not because of Karl Marx's economics in *Das Kapital*, much of which does not apply to an agricultural China anyway. The popular notion of revolution—literally, in Chinese, change of the mandate—was logical to the Chinese mind because the ruler at that time committed errors that were human in origin, moralistic in nature, social in consequence, and retributory in political terms.[46]

The human order automatically followed the dictate of the cosmic order in amending the situation to restore orderliness. The traditional political-moral principle permits legitimate overthrow of a ruler, but does not venture into new systems of social roles. Communists enjoyed popular support in their seizure of state power and quickly assumed feudal characteristics common to all previous dynasties without encountering much opposition from the populace. This may well be attributable to the predominance of Confucian conservatism in the political thinking of the Chinese mind.

In the final analysis, moral outrage against the political practice of a despotic rule is far more inflammatory to the national psyche than is the dubious authenticity of Marxism-Leninism. The leaders of China, through blatant abuse of the public trust, wanton arrogance toward the will of the people, crude and often self-defeating trickery in mind control, and most important of all, failure to maintain equilibrium, put themselves outside a legitimate claim to leadership. When the order was given to open fire on unarmed demonstrators in June 1989, the stark error in governance proved unmistakably human in origin, indisputably moralistic in nature, painfully social in consequence; it will have to be retributory in political terms. The bloody massacre, as a most graphic episode of party dictatorship, has made

99

a mockery of Confucian political-moralism. The party has lost its mandate of Heaven. Mao Huaixin, a Chinese historian, once cited a foreign Sinologist's observation to make a subtle point concerning political reform in China: "It would not be correct if Confucianism were understood as an official ideology at the exclusive service of the government. On the contrary, it is a weapon often in the hands of the opposite side."[47]

Confucius said, "It is possible to seize the commander of three armies; it is not possible to seize the will of the common people" (9:25). Those people in China will continue to withstand Deng Xiaoping to his face. Their actions, recurrent through trials of disillusionment and disintegration, are interpretable through a strong sense of moral community that precedes and overwhelms the shoddy propaganda being engineererd by the feeble minds of the few octogenarians. The shots in Tiananmen Square cannot obliterate the content of the national character.

New Authoritarianism? Liberal Democracy? Given the Confucian tradition of naive trust in the moral rectitude of the ruler and ready acceptance of a patriarchal dominance, it is not difficult to understand a recent interest in new authoritarianism as a potential key to the success of reform. New authoritarianism means an "enlightened autocracy" or an "elite democracy"—that is, a strong leader adopts undemocratic measures to enforce economic development, typically in a third world country with a young parliamentary system.[48] Law and order are maintained, according to the will of the ruler, as a crucial condition for modernization and democratization. This political blueprint has been in part justified by the economic miracles of the four "little dragons" of East Asia, all of which may be said to profess a devotion to Confucianism.

This model looks acceptable to a large assortment of Chinese reformists because it fits the Confucian political-moral paradigm, although Confucius himself did not stress the "iron fist" aspect of politics. It is premised on the righteousness of the ruler. Maintaining a patriarchal power structure, it is didactic in interpreting social roles: "The virtue of a superior person is like the wind, that of the inferior person like the grass; the grass must bend when the wind blows" (12:19). It is candidly undemocratic, so much so that it reminds people of another Confucian adage: "People can be made to follow; they cannot be made to understand" (8:9).

Such a theory has more appeal to people already in power—such as Zhao Ziyang before his ouster, and Deng Xiaoping[49]—than to people who have been denied power, like Wei Jingsheng and Hu

Ping.[50] But it also attracts people who are willing to risk their rights for longer-term benefits, if they can be convinced that the leader is moral and enlightened.[51] Those people look upon new authoritarianism as a necessary evil.[52] The only catch in the scenario is that the party must convince a largely cynical population that it is the enlightened oligarchy to command the national destiny at this historical juncture.

How enlightened the leadership was willing to be was proved on June 4, 1989. Testimony to the "benevolence" of the new Communist authoritarianism has been written in blood on the slabs in Tiananmen Square. Just as Shao Gongqin and many others predicted before the massacre, new authoritarianism cannot take off in China because "whether in theoretical or practical terms, China does not have the background or conditions that have brought about new authoritarianism in those third world countries."[53]

The first and foremost element missing from the political blueprint is an enlightened monarch. The old authoritarianism—the party establishment—has no inclination to make room. Shao points out that the party establishment never has allowed and never will allow any social force independent of itself to emerge. The current reform program was never intended to bring about a middle class independent of the party. Without a sizable independent middle class to maintain an unpoliticized economy and counterbalance the political will of the leader for the well-being of the nation, there can be no "new" authoritarianism to speak of. Authoritarianism is by no means new; what makes it new is a counterbalancing yet not necessarily hostile or insubordinate middle class that owns capital, possesses expertise, enjoys social recognition, and most important, does not have to agree with the politics of the party.[54] This would be a vital yet independent social and economic force that the Communist party will not tolerate. Deng himself said in 1986 that his "policy will not give rise to the emergence of new bourgeoisie."[55] It should not be pure coincidence that none of the successful cases of new authoritarianism has a clause in its constitution that stipulates adherence to anything like the four cardinal principles of the Chinese Communist party.

The proposed new authoritarianism in China is fundamentally a Confucianist social design with one element missing—the righteousness of the ruler. In today's China, the ruler is immoral in the sense that it is "upholding the crooked to rectify the straight" (2:19). It does not have a rational program to lower into its proper place, to be morally responsible for its conduct, even by the standard of new authoritarian countries. It has failed to maintain popular trust. It is shamelessly adhering to naked, old authoritarianism by brutal force. So "the people will not submit" (2:19). Paradoxically, the appeal and curse of new authoritarianism lie in the same Confucian paradigm.

A special mention may be in order here of the causal relationship between Confucianism and economic success, based upon ex post facto rationalization. Huang Wansheng questions the "new Confucianist" claim that the four little dragons took off on the launching pad of the Confucianist tradition.[56] No credible research findings to that effect have been presented to date, and scholars in Taiwan, Japan, and Singapore are somewhat puzzled by the attribution of wealth to autocracy. Bao Zunxin cited various postwar economic factors to repudiate the exaggerated role of Confucianism in Asian development.[57]

The faulty logic in post hoc rationalization might as well pinpoint anticommunism or Buddhism or Westernization as the reason for success in East Asia. Mao Huaixin probably is more reasonable in his statement that "rather than saying that Confucianism can be used to guide production or push forward economic development, one may claim that it can mediate in human relations, improve human qualities, enhance human ideals, thereby facilitating all social endeavors."[58] The alleged moneymaking potential of Confucian ethics may be more wishful thinking than levelheaded judgment.

Another alternative for China is Western liberal, parliamentary democracy. Contrary to the Confucian model, this is premised on the ruler's being unworthy of the trust invested in the office. To protect the rights of the ruled, political and legal—constitutional—mechanisms are set up for checks and balances. The Confucian model merges morals and politics into "benevolent government," with moral harmony serving as the sole basis of political harmony.[59] Social behavior is expected to be aligned with virtue and adjusted through ritualistic propriety (2:3). A sense of shame is thought to be superior to, and more effective than, the confines of law.

While Western liberal democracy seeks institutional change through innovations of the political machinery irrespective of personal character, the Confucian teachings appeal to the sense of the proper on the part of the educable individual, for ruler and commoner alike. This faith in the positive nature of the individual places a naive yet reverent trust in the ruler. Social and political modifications are called for only when the ruler becomes immoral.

In short, Western liberal democracy seeks an error-proof system, whereas Confucianism seeks an error-proof leader. C. P. Fitzgerald offered a succinct summary of the differences: "All Chinese thinkers held that the moral character of the ruler was the factor which determined the value of his government; none ever advanced the view that a change in the form of government would help to establish the rule of virtue and benevolence."[60]

This may provide insight into the debate on the viability of Confucianism in China's modernization program. Some believe "Confucian culture may have a role to play in the modernization process; at least it does not obstruct the process";[61] others argue that it is not a "spiritual pillar for modernization."[62] Bao Zunxin, for one, has emphatically concluded that "when we say the Confucian tradition is not appropriate for modernization, we mean the core of the value system cannot provide the positive value orientation toward modern science and technology and economic development."[63]

Some people have faith in moralizing interpersonal relationships for modernization;[64] others call for impersonal, legalistic checks and balances.[65] Confusion on the topic suggests that Western democracy is still viewed with much ambivalence. The Occidental remains exotic, but the Oriental is immediate and real. The exotic tantalizes, but that within reach offers certainty. The real is what one knows, be it good or bad; the lure of the faraway is inherently dangerous. One is fascinated by the foreign yet needs reassurance from what is home-grown. A choice must be made in the deepest recess of the national consciousness, and the Chinese remain too Confucian to adapt wholeheartedly to the fascination of Western democracy.

The feasibility of a Western liberal democracy in China is better studied beyond the narrow domain of political science. In the Confucian worldview, is there adequate room to accommodate it? The party leaders, for their own survival, say no—only "socialism with Chinese characteristics" will save China. They appeal to "Chinese-ness" in their effort to offset the "spiritual pollution" from the West. Radical reformists also say no, claiming that tradition must make way for the new. The more tradition is shed, the better.[66] "Modernization is a historical trend difficult to reverse. The traditional culture can only pass with time in a negative sense, no matter how many justifications it may have. . . . Nothing will change the overall historical trend: 'The Oriental belongs to the Occidental.' "[67] In stressing the incompatibility between the two paradigms, radical reformists indirectly concede the unfeasibility of Western democracy, if the Chinese choose to remain Chinese.

Given the opposing political motives of the two camps and their strikingly similar assessments of the feasibility of incorporating Western liberal democracy into the Chinese cultural reality, the likelihood of Western liberal democracy in the 1990s is dim. Not that the Chinese do not yearn for democracy; but the uncertainty of the new and exotic threatens the Confucianist priority of equilibrium. Confucian censure will be a part of the political establishment, as it has been for centuries. But a newfangled democracy awaits the opportunity to test its efficacy and resilience in the culture informed by Confucianism and deformed by Marxism.

Cultural Nationalism—A Rallying Call against Whom?

A ready case study of China's cultural nationalism may be the television documentary series "River Elegy." Premiered in the summer of 1988, it immediately captured national attention with its profound concern for the destiny of China. In its epic-style narrative, the five authors of the script transformed a conventional river motif into a sweeping, controversial overview of the cultural identity of China. The project had been initially entitled "The Great Artery," suggesting the concept of a bloodline. As the project developed, the title was changed to "River Elegy," proposed by Wang Luxiang.[68] One of the authors, Su Xiaokang, has explicated its significance:

> "Shang" is death that occurs prematurely before adulthood. Tantamount to death is stagnation. To remain stagnant without the hope of ever being reinvigorated or undergoing metamorphosis is a most painful demise that inflicts agony upon all the descendants of Emperors Yan and Huang, upon all those who are born and brought up in this land.[69]

As a lament over the decline of a proud civilization, the series draws attention to the futility of a timeless pursuit of national glory in the barren yellow earth of the hinterland and the voiceless rocks on the Great Wall. Historical vicissitudes and contemporary dilemmas are symbolized by the loess plateau that presses a nation to its yellow bosom, and by the meandering Great Wall that confines the people who built it. China is presented as a nation shackled by its own past. To regain the joy of life, it must look toward the vast expanse of the ocean and beyond, like the perennial muddy torrents of the Yellow River—ever eastward, bound to join the serene blue.

Two Cultural Nationalisms. The television series shocked the nation by portraying the Yellow River, the revered cradle of Chinese civilization, and the Great Wall, a proud accomplishment of the ancestors, as ideological bondage. No frontal attack on the ruling Communist party is made in the series, but the impatient message of an iconoclast is clear and loud. Beneath the rebellious message against time-honored ancestral values throbs the impatient heart of a full-blooded new generation with an urgent sense of mission to reassert the pride of being Chinese.

Many Chinese and foreign commentators agree that "River Elegy" "remains at its heart deeply nationalist."[70] In his commentary, Shi Ren praised the television series for "stimulating the patriotic spirit" and "revealing a crisis" in the "psychological state of denying facts to ourselves as well as others." The denial is the "lullaby, anesthetic, or opium" that "glosses over our backwardness."[71] Even those critical of the authors' analysis of China's historical evolution have to acknowledge that "it has originated unmistakably from a fervent patriotism, no matter how many people will accuse it of practically denying the present-day worth of the traditional Chinese culture."[72] Controversies over its philosophy of history or culture notwithstanding, "River Elegy" has given voice to a cultural nationalism that is urgent, simplistic, idealistic, and refreshingly unethnocentric. It is keenly sensitive to this generation's responsibility to create, explore, and renew.

The television series met with fierce opposition from the political establishment. Wang Zhen, vice president of the People's Republic of China, sensing the danger in the orthodoxy being challenged, responded with statements like, "Intellectuals are the most dangerous."[73] In the crackdown following the Tiananmen Square massacre, the program was banned, and all remaining copies of the script and videotapes were destroyed. Most of the scriptwriters had to flee the country.[74]

The official version of cultural nationalism soon took over the media in an effort to offset the impact of the television series. Discussion on cultural nationalism became "a major ideological and political struggle." "River Elegy" is said to "serve . . . [the scriptwriters' and like-minded radical reformers'] political objective of crossing out the socialist system and the Communist party's leadership."[75] Jiang Zemin, the secretary general of the party, quickly set the keynote: "In contemporary China, patriotism essentially is synonymous with socialism."[76] Promotion of cultural nationalism is intended to "withstand all the pressure from the outside."[77] The series is accused of "beautifying capitalism" and "relegating new democratism and socialism to the domain of old culture."[78] In short, the party insists that its policies best represent the national spirit. Cultural nationalism, in essence, is the will of the party.

The campaign against the television program, however, betrays the real concern of the party. It is neither cultural identity nor national prosperity that concerns the party leadership. What frightens them is the surge of the popular will to search for the meaning of being

105

Chinese in Communist-controlled China. The very act of questioning the cultural identity threatens the party orthodoxy.

The cultural and national identity of China, the party claims, is subordinate to its own ideological values. To be Chinese is to embrace the party's role as teacher and leader; modern-day "national essentials" consist in solidarity with the party. To be Chinese is to accept socialism, to follow the party, to abide by its interpretation of Marxism, and, most important of all, to accept a Communist-controlled government. A politically correct cultural nationalism is defined by the four so-called cardinal principles. Striking indeed is the similarity between this definition of China's cultural nationalism by the party's Propaganda Department and the notorious Nazi interpretation of national character.

Cultural Symbiosis. The cultural and national identity imposed by the party is a parasitical growth on the host culture of traditional values, particularly the Confucian type of moralistic interpretation of politics.[79] A moralistic reading of harmonious social relations has been twisted into the political necessity of maintaining the party's predominance. Contention and opposition are looked upon as the unbalancing of a social order that would otherwise have guaranteed common welfare. Dynamic politics in checks and balances is rejected, for fear of a confusion of respective social roles suggesting lack of moral responsibility. Patriarchal political control is rationalized on the basis of the shared interests of the extended family, with authority vested in seniority. The not-so-moral political will of the ruler is once again allowed to assume an institutional orthodoxy and to arbitrate on all issues—cultural, ethical, legal, and economic. This grotesque cultural characteristic perpetuated by the Communist rulers sheds light on the conservative aspects of the host civilization.

Fortunately, China has not lost the other side of the Confucian tradition that the monarchical absolutes should be contingent upon moral absolutes. And Mencius's words still ring true: "If a king does not set his will on benevolence, all his days will be in sorrow and disgrace, and he will die. . . . How can you [the king] improve? You will only drown with your kingdom" (6:9). It is significant that the elegy is sung at this historical moment, calling on the nation to bid farewell to the past, to seek options hitherto untried, and to rejuvenate the nation with a new vision.

The authors of "River Elegy" are perhaps overenthusiastic about the West, partly because of their eagerness to reform China and partly because of their lack of knowledge about the West. It is highly questionable whether the literary symbolism of the yellow and the blue is meaningful in anthropological or sociological analysis. But as a piece of literary writing, it gives voice to this generation's painful yearning for a resurgence of national pride, for a new greatness. If one desire defines the cultural and national outlook of this decade, it is the heart-rending yearning for change. The potential of this yearning for mobilizing the population should not be underestimated by anyone who has witnessed the unprecedented, nationwide protests of May and June 1989.

The two cultural nationalisms are the rallying calls for two camps. On the one hand, the Chinese people are inspired by a real possibility to rejuvenate the nation, both economically and culturally, by assimilating nourishment from the West and by demanding an end to the exclusive control of the state by the party elite. Uncertain as the prospect of success may seem, the desire is sincere and overwhelming. On the other hand, the anxious totalitarian regime is trying to prolong its grip on power by appealing to a pseudonationalistic sense that the party is the nation. Past conflicts of interest between the nation and the party have left no question in the Chinese people's minds as to which side they must take to achieve national salvation. Thus the two politically loaded cultural nationalisms revolve around the legitimacy of rule by the party. After all, the most serious obstacle to China's rejuvenation, as the events in June 1989 have shown the whole world, is the party.

In the foreseeable future, the contention between the two cultural nationalisms will be restricted to domestic politics. The reform-minded section wants to keep the door open for more ideological impact from the outside; the party will have to tolerate Western influences in return for material or psychological benefits to pacify a dissatisfied citizenry. Given the current international scene, neither side in China sees any danger of encroachment on China's sovereignty, in spite of warnings about "imperialist foreign powers" in party propaganda.[80] Any real threat from the outside would most probably unite the two opposing camps, with the party establishment having the most to gain. Internationally, China is thus expected to maintain an amicable diplomatic posture for the time being.

Domestically, the contention between the party and the populace is primarily one between democracy and autocracy within China. Even though the party has occasionally and halfheartedly presented the issue of national identity as a conflict between a vulnerable China and annexationist, imperialist powers, its real objective is to be accepted as a bona fide representative of national interests, thereby discrediting any opposition to its totalitarianism. Given this analysis, China's nationalistic sentiments will have to be focused primarily on internal political conflicts. Like their East European counterparts, who successfully confronted the Communist parties in their own countries with unambiguous calls for national salvation in the autumn and winter of 1989, the Chinese people may find nationalism the greatest source of strength in their opposition to Communist totalitarianism.

Conclusion

In conclusion, the 1990s may witness the following ideological trends in the People's Republic of China:

• Marxism will be increasingly irrelevant to the People's Republic of China. The party will be forced to defend its revisionism while maintaining a token allegiance to the cause of Marxism. This ideological predicament will serve only to discredit the party orthodoxy further.

• The Confucianist acceptance of an established power structure has sustained the party in the past. But operating as it now does, without even a resemblance of "mandate," the party is up against the moral censure inherent in mainstream Chinese culture. This is an ideological force that will put the party on the defensive for years to come.

Neither new authoritarianism nor Western liberal, parliamentary democracy are viable options for the foreseeable future. The former may appeal to the Chinese because it seems to fit the Confucian political-moral paradigm, but it will only serve to perpetuate old authoritarianism in the form of the Communist party. The latter does not yet have a place in a culture informed by conservative Confucianism.

• For its political survival, the Communist party is trying to present itself as a bona fide champion of the Chinese cultural tradition. Its politically motivated appeal to the nationalist sentiment of the population will continue to be countered by the powerful resurgence of a national resolve to rid the nation of totalitarian shackles. Appeals to national pride are certainly not a moral asset for a regime that has shamelessly dragged the country into chaos and massacred its own people.

The 1990s will find the party trapped in ideological predicaments. The communiqué of the Seventh Plenum of the Thirteenth National Party Congress in December 1990 warns:

The years from 1991 to 2000 will be very pivotal. Success or failure in our efforts . . . will have a direct bearing on the rise or fall of the Chinese socialist system.[81]

The Chinese Communist party has admitted it is seriously contemplating its fall in the 1990s.

PART THREE
Society

5

The Size, Control, and Composition of China's Population

Judith Banister

In a broad overview of the population dynamics of the People's Republic of China (PRC), this chapter discusses the relations among demographic, economic, and political trends in the China mainland. Drawing on lessons from the experiences of the 1980s and previous decades, it focuses on what is likely to happen to the Chinese population during the 1990s. Cataclysmic events in China have shown many times that it is risky, even foolhardy, to make predictions about the PRC. Yet population levels and demographic continuities and changes have a built-in momentum that allows some confidence in projecting likely trends for the decade already begun. Longer-term predictions are indeed riskier.

The Size of China's Population

The PRC's nationwide census conducted at midyear 1990 counted a slightly larger population than that predictable from previous official data. Using data from its annual surveys of population change, for example, China's State Statistical Bureau (SSB) had estimated a total population (excluding Hong Kong and Taiwan) of 1,111,910,000 at year-end 1989. If the SSB's estimated 1989 rate of natural population increase for China (14.33 per thousand population) had continued in the first half of 1990, the mid-1990 population would have been about 1,119,910,000.[1] Yet the census counted 1,133,682,501 people, or 13.8 million more than expected.[2] Such a discrepancy is minor for such a huge population, an underestimate of only 1.2 percent. It does

The observations and opinions in this chapter are those of the author and do not reflect the policies of the U.S. government or the U.S. Bureau of the Census. The author greatly appreciates the able research assistance of Christina Wu Harbaugh and Andrea Miles.

113

suggest, however, that even the best surveys of fertility in China during the 1980s may have undercounted births.

Meanwhile, China's permanent population registration system has been losing track of some people, producing an undercount of the total population every year. Moreover, the birth registration system excludes so many "illegal" births that it remains hopeless for estimating the fertility level or the rate of population growth. According to the minister of the State Family Planning Commission, "The difference between the household registration figure and the calculated figure based on sample surveys is becoming bigger and bigger year by year. The total number of births shown in the family planning work report is approximately 30 percent less than the calculated number of births based on sample surveys."[3] Beginning with the year 1981, the State Statistical Bureau ceased using the birth registration system to derive China's official fertility estimates. In 1987, it stopped using the registration system for year-end population totals and adjusted upward all the previously reported totals for year-end 1982 through 1986.

The 1990 census count was a preliminary, hand-tabulated count. Entry of data from all questionnaires into the computers would give a final count in 1992 or 1993. Meanwhile, analysis of the single-year, age-sex structure of the population, based on a 10 percent sample of the questionnaires, indicates any detectable undercounting or over-counting of certain age-sex groups in the census. Until census data can be tested for completeness, the preliminary count is the most accurate figure available for the size of the PRC population.

What will happen to China's population size and growth during the 1990s? Population growth is determined by births, deaths, and international migration. In the case of the PRC, gross or net international migration is still negligible compared with the huge population of the country. Although immigrants into China and emigrants, including refugees, from China may be important in other contexts far beyond their numbers, for purposes of population projections international migration can safely be ignored.

Mortality

In general no striking trends are expected in China's level and pattern of mortality during the 1990s. There is little prospect of significant deterioration in health and mortality conditions unless China has a serious political breakdown, civil war, international war, or a major famine, none of which seems very likely. Although no epidemic is predictable, AIDS at least is not a problem in China. In the five years ending in 1990, 300,000 selected people were tested for exposure to the AIDS virus. Only 446 people tested positive, of whom 68 were foreigners and 368 were narcotics addicts in the mountainous boundary region of Yunnan province bordering the lawless drug-producing area of neighboring Burma.[4]

By the early 1980s, China had already achieved high life expectancies of around sixty-six years for males and sixty-nine for females, a longevity unusual among poor countries at China's stated level of development.[5] During the 1980s, there was some breakdown of the rural health delivery system as the people's communes were dismantled. Yet the evidence so far indicates that, under the period of economic reform in both urban and rural areas, survival chances improved for both sexes at most ages.[6] After the 1990 census data on mortality and age-sex structure from the 10 percent sample tabulation have been assessed, whether and how much mortality improved in China during 1982–1990 will be clearer.

Mortality conditions may improve further in the 1990s, especially if prosperity increases and the government continues to emphasize preventive public health strategies and to upgrade the quality of curative medical care. But even if mortality conditions improve at most ages and life expectancy rises further, China's crude death rate would probably not change much. China's current crude death rate of six or seven deaths per thousand population per year is low, both because the population's survival chances are good and because the population has a young age structure.[7] Continued progress in reducing mortality could lower the crude death rate a little, which would raise the rate of natural population increase only slightly, with only a small effect on population growth.[8] Therefore, for projection of China's population increase for the coming decade, mortality change does not have a significant effect. The main factors that will affect China's population growth in the 1990s are fertility—the average number of births per woman—and the ages of women at the onset of childbearing and the timing of subsequent children.

The Timing of Childbearing

Regarding the timing of births, if women have their children younger than was customary in the recent past, births are bunched, a pattern that contributes to an increase in the birth rate and the rate of natural population increase. Postponement of childbearing to progressively older ages spreads out births over more and later years, a pattern that tends to lower the birth and natural increase rates.

In China, the timing of childbearing is strongly affected by age

115

FIGURE 5–1
Pattern of Childbearing in China, 1979, 1982, and 1987

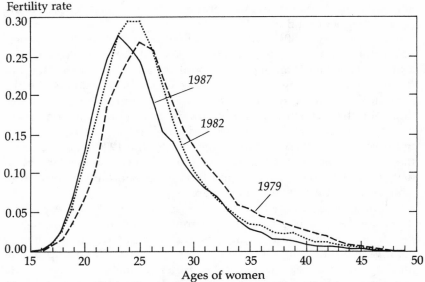

Fertility rate

Ages of women

NOTE: Age-specific fertility rates measure the number of women of a given age who bear a child in a given year. Based on reported, unadjusted fertility survey data.

SOURCES: *Fertility Survey* 1982, p. 161; *Fertility Survey* 1988, pp. 183, 193.

at marriage because few births occur outside marriage and almost all couples have a child as soon as possible after marriage. During the 1970s, a key component of China's family planning program was the required postponement of marriage, which successfully raised the mean age at first marriage by several years in both urban and rural areas. By 1979, the average age at marriage was 25.5 years for urban women and 22.6 years for rural women, considerably older than in previous decades. But the forced late marriage policy was unpopular, and after the death of Mao Zedong the government in 1980 reduced the required minimum marriage ages by several years, to age twenty for women and twenty-two for men.[9]

There was an immediate sharp drop in marriage ages. Figure 5-1 shows that between 1979 and 1982, the ages when women began to have children also declined. The whole curve of age-specific fertility shifted to younger ages of women, and births were bunched in the early 1980s, thus raising birthrates. Even though the government started encouraging later marriage once again, age at marriage and onset of childbearing dropped a little more before stabilizing.[10] As figure 5–1 shows, between 1982 and 1987, the ages when women began childbearing declined further and the age-specific fertility curve continued to shift toward younger ages.

What determines age at marriage in China today? In addition to government policies, strong cultural factors play a part. The financial arrangements surrounding marriage tend to postpone the wedding until the groom's family can scrape together the high bride price and the bride's family can accumulate her dowry. But people want to marry young in order to bear their child or children in early adulthood. Then the children will grow up soon enough to help their parents with farm work, household work, and other services and to support their parents financially whenever disability or age interferes with the older generation's ability to work.

What can be predicted about the timing of marriage and childbearing in the 1990s? China's government backed down on the rigid policies of the 1970s that required artificially high marriage ages. In the 1980s, people persisted in marrying younger and bearing children younger than the government wanted, in spite of renewed official efforts to encourage and sometimes impose later marriages. Therefore, it is unrealistic to assume, as some demographers have, that China's people can all be persuaded or forced to postpone marriage for women until their late twenties and to postpone first births until age twenty-seven or older. Rather, the likeliest scenario is a continuation of the tight concentration of childbearing when women are in their twenties, especially their early twenties, as shown in figure 5–1.

Eventually, with further economic development, age at marriage and age at onset of childbearing will probably rise gradually in the PRC as has happened in Japan, Taiwan, and South Korea. But no major rise is expected in the 1990s.

Figure 5–1 shows that the pattern of childbearing that has evolved in the PRC includes both early onset and early cessation of childbearing. Compared with 1979, the cessation of childbearing came at younger ages by 1982 and at even younger ages by 1987. The peak age of fertility declined from age twenty-five in 1979 to age twenty-three in 1987. We assume that the peak childbearing ages of women will continue to be ages twenty to twenty-nine as in 1987. Figure 5–2 shows that China is now experiencing a surge in the number of women in these fertile ages. The number of women in their twenties increased from 81 million in 1982 to about 112 million in 1990. Because the total number of women in their twenties will be at its maximum in the early 1990s, China's government is concerned

117

FIGURE 5–2

NUMBER OF WOMEN IN PEAK CHILDBEARING AGES IN CHINA, 1982–2000

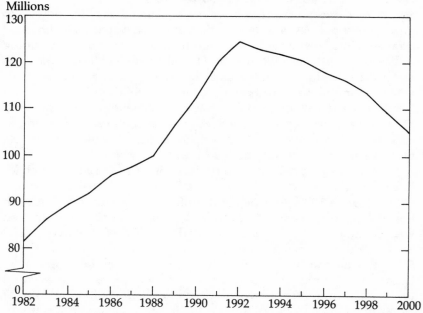

Millions

NOTE: Peak childbearing ages are twenty through twenty-nine. Women in these ages have single-year, age-specific fertility rates of 0.1 or above (meaning that each year 10 percent or more of the women bear a child), based on 1987 data.

SOURCE: Figure 5–1; modeled at the U.S. Bureau of the Census.

about an imminent "birth peak." This striking phenomenon will, however, be temporary and will ameliorate in the late 1990s.

Determinants of Fertility

As of 1989–1990, the fertility level in China was low, between two and three births per woman on average. China's nationwide fertility survey of 1988 reported a total fertility rate (TFR) of about 2.5–2.6 births per woman for 1987, dropping to around 2.2–2.3 for 1988.[11] The SSB's annual surveys of population change reported official annual crude birth rates of 20.78 births per thousand population in 1988 and 20.83 in 1989.[12] The 1990 census reported a crude birthrate of 20.98 for the year from mid-1989 to mid-1990.[13] The higher-than-expected count of total population in the 1990 census suggests that all these fertility estimates are slightly underreported. This information and the modeling from these data lead to a tentative estimate that China's total fertility rate has been steady during 1988–1990 at about 2.3 births per woman. It is interesting to note that as the TFR rose in 1986 and 1987, China's government responded by clamping down on unauthorized births and appears to have succeeded in reducing fertility in 1988 and subsequent years to below the 1987 TFR.[14] This hypothesis, however, cannot be confirmed until more detail from the 1990 census is available.

Such low fertility is unusual at China's level of development. What has brought this about? First, China's compulsory family planning program has successfully held down the number of births to fewer than most couples want. The program works because of the strong political control over people's personal lives in the PRC. Although government controls have diminished during the past decade of economic reforms, China's system of micromanaging people's daily lives is still a major factor keeping fertility down in both urban and rural areas. If the family planning program ever shifted to a voluntary one, the fertility level would probably rise closer to the average level of desired fertility.

In recent decades, some political and socioeconomic changes have encouraged attitudes favoring increased use of birth control. Illiteracy was reduced and educational attainment increased during the 1980s, according to 1990 census data.[15] In China as elsewhere, more years of education, especially to junior middle-school level or higher, tend to bring about a desire to limit childbearing. The Communist ideology of male-female equality and sustained efforts to employ women outside the home have enhanced the status of Chinese women in the economy and in daily life. Millions of women in China therefore perceive alternatives to additional childbearing and child rearing. Gradual urbanization and the movement of some rural workers into nonagricultural work have also encouraged low-fertility lifestyles. Finally, decades of family planning propaganda and education have convinced millions of China's people that the population is too large, that their own city or town or village is too crowded, that each couple's childbearing has effects on society outside the immediate family, and that people should have no more children than they really need or want. Even if China's compulsory family planning policy were lifted, the people who have internalized these attitudes would probably continue limiting their own childbearing, although perhaps not to the one or two children currently demanded.

Contributing to low fertility in the PRC as well is the comprehensive family planning delivery system. Almost all localities in China have either a specialized family planning clinic or at least a local family planning worker, a health worker or doctor, and a health station, clinic, or hospital to provide birth control supplies and operations. Contraceptives, intrauterine devices (IUDs), steriliza- tions, and abortions are available nearly everywhere and are free or very inexpensive. As long as the government commitment to provi- sion of these supplies and techniques continues, Chinese women and couples can prevent the conception or birth of a child they themselves do not want at the time.

Many other factors, however, tend to keep fertility from drop- ping further in China. Low agricultural mechanization and the recent fragmentation of communal fields into family plots mean that physi- cal labor is still important. Peasants perceive that they must have children, especially a son, to provide family labor, carry on the family name, and provide security in old age.[16] Analysts from China's State Planning Commission noted this effect of the agricultural reforms of the 1980s: "It has become a clear advantage to have a large family, especially one made up of male workers."[17] Chinese culture also mandates that nearly everyone have a child or children. China, unlike Western countries, traditionally had and still has a system of universal marriage and universal childbearing. By their early thirties, over 99 percent of China's women have married, and it is rare for a married couple to have no children.[18] Finally, levels of education and literacy are inversely correlated with numbers of children in China, and there were still 180 million illiterate adults in 1990.[19] The educational attain- ment of most rural couples is low, stopping at primary school level; this is not enough education to transform their attitudes toward fertility.

Current Family Planning Policies

Since 1979, the PRC government has been promoting a one-child policy. The policy has been very successful in the tightly controlled cities but much less successful in rural areas. In general, peasants have refused to yield in their determination to have at least one son.[20] The rural economic reforms have also weakened the government's ability to prevent unauthorized births, although China retains its distinction as having the world's most restrictive and effective family planning program. The constant tug of war between the government and the people has produced the current situation in which the one- child policy continues to be implemented where it is reasonably successful, while a one-and-a-half-, two-, or rarely a three-child policy is in effect in many rural areas.

The one-child policy prevails in almost all urban nonagricultural areas of China, whose total population was counted as 296.5 million in the 1990 census.[21] The military population of 3.2 million is also subject to the one-child policy.[22] The Han Chinese portion of the 1990 census, urban plus military population, is estimated at 284.0 million people, 25.1 percent of the PRC population.[23] In areas implementing the one-child policy, all married Han Chinese couples are restricted to one child, regardless of its sex, except for certain infrequent situations, such as if the firstborn child is handicapped, both members of the couple are themselves single children, or it is a second marriage in which only one partner has one child from the previous marriage.

The one-child policy also continues to be implemented in the rural areas of particular provinces and province-level municipalities: Beijing, Tianjin, Shanghai, Gansu, Jiangsu province next to Shanghai, Hebei province surrounding Beijing and Tianjin, and China's most populous province of Sichuan.[24] The rural areas of these provinces had a 1990 census total population of 215.4 million, of whom approximately 206.5 million were of the Han Chinese majority (and constituted 18.2 percent of the total PRC population).[25] Therefore, the population subject to the strict one-child policy (including the urban and military Han populations) in 1990 totaled approximately 490.5 million, or 43.3 percent of China's population.

Sixteen provinces have received permission from the central government to allow a second birth to rural Han Chinese couples whose firstborn child is a girl but to apply a one-child limit to those with a firstborn son. This one-and-a-half-child policy, to phrase it awkwardly, applies in rural areas of the three northeastern provinces of Heilongjiang, Jilin, and Liaoning; the northern provinces of Inner Mongolia, Shanxi, and Shaanxi; the east coast provinces of Shandong, Zhejiang, and Fujian; the central Chinese provinces of Anhui, Henan, Hubei, Hunan, and Jiangxi; and the southern provinces of Guizhou and Guangxi. Rural populations in these provinces as of 1990 totaled 523.4 million, of whom about 480.7 million were Han Chinese. Therefore, the one-and-a-half-child policy applies to a Han population constituting approximately 42.4 percent of the total PRC population.

Only six provinces have received permission to announce a rural two-child policy, in which rural Han Chinese couples are typically allowed to have two children. They are the southern coastal provinces of Guangdong and Hainan; the southwestern province of Yunnan;

and the northwestern provinces of Xinjiang, Qinghai, and Ningxia. The rural populations of these provinces total 93.3 million, of whom about 23.2 million belong to minority groups. A two-child policy applies, then, to a rural Han population of about 70.1 million, constituting 6.2 percent of China's total population.

Much fragmentary information suggests that minority group couples are usually allowed two children in a one-child-policy area and three children in a two-child-policy area.[26] In the absence of more detailed data, we assume that in each category of place, the minority group residents are allowed one more child than the Han Chinese residents. In provinces where the rural Han population is subject to a one-and-a-half-child policy, the piecemeal evidence suggests that rural minorities are generally allowed two.[27] On these assumptions, 490.5 million people are subjected to the one-child policy, 498.3 million to the one-and-a-half-child policy, 116.1 million to the two-child policy, and 28.8 million to the three-child policy. If every couple complied with the birth restrictions applied to them and bore the number of children allowed but no more, the PRC population would have a total fertility rate of approximately 1.5 births per woman.[28]

The fact that the TFR is still about 2.3 births per woman suggests the extent to which the family planning policies are violated by couples determined to have another child. Common stratagems for having an unapproved child include securing an illegal IUD removal, placing the IUD inside the underclothes during the required abdominal X-ray to check that the IUD is in place, hiding from family planning workers during pregnancy, leaving home for the duration of the pregnancy and returning with the child, trading or adopting children of relatives and claiming that the children were orphaned or abandoned, and attempting to change an ethnic status from Han to a minority.[29] In many of China's villages, couples cannot succeed in carrying an unapproved pregnancy to term against the harassment of the local leadership unless they leave the village. Since the reforms of the 1980s, greater worker mobility has been allowed to speed economic development. Among this "floating population" are many couples who take advantage of the opportunity to have one or more unauthorized births; these couples are called the "excess birth guerrillas." They succeed whenever the family planning workers of their home village cannot keep track of them and when their births are not the problem of the authorities where they "temporarily" live.

Some slippage also occurs between China's compulsory family planning policies as stated at the national and provincial levels and the ways policies are implemented at the local level. Local cadres charged with enforcing these unpopular policies get caught between a powerful hierarchy demanding success in holding down fertility and their neighbors, friends, and especially relatives who often want another child. Although most cadres in China find it necessary to appear to try to implement the policies—to avoid reprimands, fines, job loss, expulsion from the Communist party, or other penalties— many cases of complicity between peasants and cadres to violate the rigid birth restrictions have been reported.

Fertility in the 1990s

For the 1990s, China's momentum for population growth remains great. The national, provincial, and in some places the lower levels of government will thus continue trying to hold down fertility as much as politically feasible. "Stabilizing" the policy has been a guiding concept in recent years. Such a policy requires family planning authorities to resist any further loosening of the one-child or two-child policy in each area and prevent the peasants from believing that the number of births allowed might change in their favor. The most likely scenario for fertility in the 1990s is a continuation of the current unstable equilibrium between millions of couples seizing every opportunity to have another child and coercive pressure from all levels of government trying to prevent each unauthorized birth. The government is walking a fine line in the face of changing economic, cultural, and political conditions. Any relaxation of government restrictions can allow fertility to rise. Greater economic independence can give more families the option to flout the tight fertility policies. Yet if the government reacts to popular resistance with increased coercion (as in 1983), a backlash (as in 1984) could force the government to ease up, also causing births to increase.[30]

A slight reduction in the TFR from 2.3 births per woman in 1990 to perhaps 2.1 in the year 2000 seems likely, reflecting two factors. First, gradual urbanization will probably continue in China; and after rural couples transfer their registration to urban places, they may be subjected to tighter fertility limitations. Second, a continuation of the fertility decline of the 1980s among China's minority population appears likely. The family planning program was applied to most minority groups for the first time in the 1980s, with significant results. Minority women had a total fertility rate of four to five births per woman at the beginning of the 1980s.[31] By 1986, the TFR of minority group women was calculated as 3.40 births per woman, which was 1.12 births higher than the Han figure of 2.28 that year.[32] The fertility of certain minority groups remains much higher than Han fertility, which suggests a potential for further fertility decline among part of

123

the minority population, which constitutes 8 percent of China's total.

Could China's fertility drop even further than assumed by the turn of the century? Neighboring South Korea calculated that it had a 1988 total fertility rate of only 1.6 births per woman, and Taiwan's TFR was reported to be 1.7 births per woman by 1986.[33] Such a low level seems possible for China only if the PRC experiences a booming economy in the coming decade, combined with no diminution of the government's comparatively effective political micromanagement of the number of births each couple has. But events of the 1980s suggested that these two requirements are to some extent contradictory—perhaps not mutually exclusive but at least competing.

Really vigorous economic progress in the 1990s would require further dismantling of the stifling structure of Communist political control of the economy or at least some basic reorganization of political guidance over economic matters. In the 1980s, the easing of political power over economic decisions facilitated great economic progress but also led to less control in social life, including a weakening of the systems of tight fertility control in the countryside.[34] The same contradiction would probably operate in the 1990s.

Another impediment is that China's crisis of succession may take years to resolve, and bold economic initiatives by the national government appear to be on hold until it is over. Unfortunately, half the 1990s could be lost while the question of who shall succeed Deng Xiaoping is decided. China's economic progress in the 1990s is therefore unlikely to create conditions that usually lead to spontaneous reduction of fertility to very low levels.

Since fertility in China is currently held artificially low by restrictive policies, any fertility decline that might accompany economic improvements is unlikely to offset the fertility increase expected to result from greater social freedom. Besides, the PRC has not yet achieved the per capita income or living standards characteristic of Taiwan and South Korea a decade ago, and it is therefore not poised to achieve by voluntary means today's low fertility level in Taiwan or South Korea by ten years from now. Could such low fertility be achieved in the PRC by force? The government has tried hard to do so since the one-child policy was introduced in 1979 and has encountered enough peasant resistance to back off to a partly one, partly two child policy. If the government attempted to reintroduce a blitz campaign of required sterilization of all couples with two children and forced abortion of all pregnancies outside the official birth plan, as was done in 1983, another backlash is predictable. This time, perhaps the backlash would be fiercer, because now the glow of the early economic reform period in the countryside is past and the government has less political capital to draw on than it did then. Thus it is unlikely that China's government could bring about a low total fertility rate of 1.6 or 1.7 births per woman by the year 2000 through either voluntary or coercive means.

Alternatively, will fertility rise in the 1990s? If political chaos reigns, or if there is significant democratization of China's government, then an increase in fertility is likely. But perhaps it is more realistic to assume that some cautious Asian version of democracy will evolve very slowly out of authoritarianism in China, on the model of South Korea, Taiwan, Thailand, or Singapore. Meanwhile, members of China's elite are so convinced that China is overpopulated and that China's population growth and size must be contained that compulsory family planning is likely to continue with any authoritarian government.

If China's fertility level drops gradually to 2.1 births per woman in the year 2000 but no lower, then the country will have a population of about 1.30 billion at that time. If the current fertility level (TFR estimated at 2.32) holds steady from 1990 to 2000, then the population in the year 2000 would be about 1.32 billion. A slight rise in fertility to a TFR of 2.5 births per woman in 2000, a level surpassed more than once in the 1980s, would produce a total population of about 1.33 billion at the turn of the century.

Under these scenarios, which by no means exhaust the whole range of possibilities, China's average population growth rate for the 1990s decade would be 1.4–1.6 percent a year. This population growth will require a proportionate expansion of the available supplies of food, clothing, housing, transport, and services.

Age Composition

The age composition of China's population is shifting rapidly. This is not alarming or unexpected—it is a natural part of and sequel to the demographic transition from high mortality and fertility to the low mortality and fertility that China has now. China achieved a steep drop in mortality in the 1950s and, once past the devastating famine of the Great Leap Forward, experienced continuing improvements in life expectancy thereafter. The fertility level of China's city nonagricultural population dropped in the mid-1960s to about half its previous level, and the same thing happened to the fertility of the rural population from 1970 to 1977. The huge cohorts of children born in China in the 1960s and the very beginning of the 1970s flooded the primary school system in those decades. Then they reached labor force ages in the 1980s, straining China's ability to provide entry-

FIGURE 5–3

CHINA'S POPULATION PYRAMID, 1990

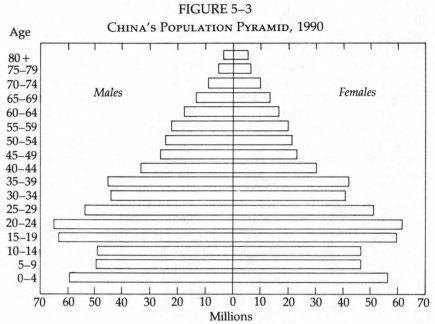

SOURCE: Modeled at the Center for International Research, U.S. Bureau of the Census.

level jobs. Figure 5-3 shows that China's age structure in 1990 had a big bulge in the age groups fifteen to nineteen and twenty to twenty-four. These same large birth cohorts will be in their peak childbearing ages during the 1990s. This situation could cause the "birth peak" feared by the family planning leadership of the PRC.

The cohorts of people born in the late 1970s and early 1980s are considerably smaller than those born in the prior decade (see figure 5-3). The comparatively small cohort born in 1975, for example, reached primary school age in about 1981, which started to lift pressure on the system of primary education. These children reached junior middle school age in the late 1980s. This relatively small cohort of all those born in 1975 reached age sixteen (working age) in 1991. Therefore, throughout the 1990s as successive small cohorts enter working ages, the problem of providing enough entry-level jobs will gradually diminish. Women of the same small 1975 birth cohort will be in their peak childbearing ages of twenty to twenty-nine in the years 1995–2004. As subsequently born cohorts reach their peak childbearing ages in the first decade of the coming century, the

FIGURE 5–4

CHINA'S POPULATION PYRAMID, 2000

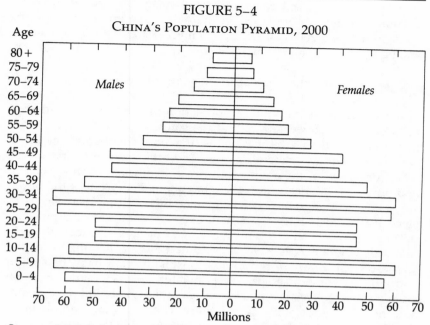

SOURCE: Modeled at the Center for International Research, U.S. Bureau of the Census.

demographic momentum driving rapid population growth will diminish. Figure 5-4 shows that by the turn of the century, the huge cohorts will already be in their late twenties and early thirties, while much smaller groups will be in the ages fifteen to nineteen and twenty to twenty-four. Note, however, that the year 2000 age structure contains an "echo effect" of the older population bulge, their children, who will also grow up and move up the age pyramid.

Throughout the 1990s and the first quarter of the coming century, the PRC will enjoy what has been called its "golden age" with regard to the age composition of the population.[35] Continuation of rather low fertility is expected to keep the population growth rate low, minimizing the burden of child dependency. The proportion of the population in the elderly ages will increase only gradually, keeping the aged dependency burden low or moderate throughout the coming several decades. The age structure of the population will be concentrated in the prime working ages. The low dependency ratio during these decades could contribute to increased savings and investment. The medical needs and health problems of the people

127

are expected to remain comparatively manageable because the proportion of China's population in the oldest age groups will not be high. In the year 2000, for example, only 1 percent of the population will be aged eighty and above.

Population Distribution and Movement

The geographic distribution of population in the China mainland is uneven. The northwestern half of the country has around 5 percent of the people, if an arbitrary line is drawn on the map at the angle customary for such generalizations. The other half of China's territory, composed of the south, southwest, southeast, central, coastal, and northeast (Manchurian) areas, has about 95 percent of the population. This situation has been bemoaned by the Chinese government since 1949, and heroic efforts have been expended to distribute the population much more evenly, to almost no avail. In fact, though, the areas where people have concentrated during the long history of Chinese civilization are those most hospitable to human habitation and crop growing. The sparsely populated areas can support some people through livestock grazing or mineral exploitation or trade but are not suitable for dense populations. The historically uninhabited areas were and are almost uninhabitable. As China's population has doubled in the Communist period, population density in most areas has also approximately doubled, leaving China's population distribution relatively unchanged. This pattern reflects China's geography: the enormous variations in climate, topography, water supply, soil, and other natural conditions strongly determine where people choose to live and can live.

This said, the distribution of China's population has shifted marginally in recent decades. Migration to China's frontier areas of the northwest, north, and northeast has increased population faster in those provinces than elsewhere. Differential rates of natural population increase have caused the populations of some areas to grow more than others. In the past two decades, for example, Han Chinese fertility dropped to a low level, while the fertility of most minority groups remained higher. The populations in minority regions have therefore been growing faster than those in Han areas.

China's gradual urbanization has also redistributed the population somewhat. Nationwide censuses have reported that, of China's total population, 13 percent was urban in 1953, 18 percent in 1964, 21 percent in 1982, and 26 percent in 1990.[36] These figures should be used only as general orders of magnitude because the census definitions of "urban" have differed slightly over time. The movement of people into cities and towns has created greater urban population concentration than was the case in the early Communist period or even in the prereform period around 1977. Yet three-quarters of China's population is still rural. Most rural people continue to till the land and live near their farming plots. As a result, the population is rather evenly distributed over the arable, habitable plains, deltas, and river valleys of the country.

The geographic immobility of the PRC population in the 1960s and 1970s was largely a result of the deliberate government policy to tie people to their place of permanent population registration through location-specific food rationing and legal restrictions on movement. The exceptions were government-sponsored and government-ordered campaigns that sent youth to the countryside or migrants to border areas. The policy was highly successful in keeping people in their village or city of origin and in preventing the futher urbanization that would otherwise have occurred. While the blocking of free movement to urban areas prevented explosive growth of China's city populations and the overurbanization seen in many other developing countries, it also hampered the economic transformation of the countryside and depressed rural incomes.

As part of the economic reform program starting in the late 1970s, however, the government began allowing workers to move in order to increase their earnings.[37] In the 1980s, millions of people were allowed to migrate permanently to a (usually nearby) city or town. In addition, by the late 1980s, an estimated 50–80 million people were away from their permanent residence locations, most employed at jobs that could not be done or did not pay adequately in their home villages.[38] Skilled and unskilled workers were allowed to leave their homes, where they had no work or their productivity and income were low, to go where opportunities were greater. This policy change contributed to more sensible allocation of labor in rural and urban areas, a more vibrant system of wholesale and retail markets, the absorption of millions of surplus agricultural workers into non-agricultural jobs, and the rapid economic growth of the reform period.[39]

Greater population movement has other implications, in addition to the economic benefits. People on the move are much harder to control than people who live out their whole lives in one village or neighborhood. Chinese sources report that increased crime in cities has been caused by elements of the floating population from rural areas. Millions of couples and individual women—the excess birth guerrillas—have borne children outside the official birth plan while away from the prying eyes of their designated family planning workers. Mobile people, who naturally see more of the country than those who rarely go anywhere, may develop wider social and political perspectives and experience more of a "revolution of rising expectations" than they might have done had they never left home.

China's government is trying to control these manifestations of population migration, which officials see as negative, while retaining the basic concept that worker migration can be economically beneficial to all concerned. In 1989 and 1990, the authorities did send some migrants back to their home villages, but fragmentary evidence suggests that the total numbers of permanent migrants and floating population have not diminished. As some Chinese migration experts have commented, once the peasants have experienced urban life, they are generally not willing to return to a rural agricultural existence; instead they search until they find other work opportunities, and they leave home again.

Demographic Impacts and Responses in the 1990s

In summary, in the 1990s China's population is likely to continue growing at 1.4 percent a year or more, record numbers of women will be in their peak childbearing ages, the numbers of entry-level workers will decline, urbanization will progress further, and geographical movement of workers will continue. During the coming decade, the population in labor force ages (using the international standard age group fifteen to sixty-four) will grow a little more slowly than the total population, because of the small cohorts reaching age fifteen who were ages five to nine and ten to fourteen in 1990 (see figure 5-3). This slowdown will be a relief after the situation in the 1980s when the labor force age group increased much faster than the population.[40] The PRC succeeded in increasing the number of jobs faster than the growth of population in labor force ages but only by keeping many surplus laborers in agriculture and retaining great redundancy in urban enterprises.

How will population developments in the PRC affect the general stability and success of a post-Deng regime? Basically, population growth and change are not the central determinants of the viability of the Chinese government. Economic, political, and military factors will have the greatest effect on the ability of a post-Deng regime to survive at all or to develop legitimacy and the support of the people. A continuing population growth rate of 1½ percent a year will be a strain if the economy is nearly stagnant and the political system in turmoil. But if the succession is swiftly completed, the leaders move aggressively to get the economy moving again, provincial and national leaders once again cooperate in pursuit of their common goals, and the military keeps out of the way, this level of population growth can be dealt with successfully in the 1990s.

While the predictable population trends of the 1990s are manageable for a reasonably well-functioning government, certain political and economic shifts could strongly affect demographic trends. A serious social breakdown, for example, or tragic political mistakes could cause a rise in mortality, as happened during the famine of the Great Leap Forward. But this is not very likely. It takes a major disaster like the Great Leap famine to raise China's death rate significantly. The Cultural Revolution, although it was a traumatic experience for millions of people, had no perceptible effect on China's level of mortality.

The fertility level in the 1990s might be very responsive to political or economic changes. Further weakening of Chinese communism or strengthening of democratic forces could lead to the discrediting and rejection of compulsory family planning, followed by a sudden rise in the birthrate. In China's agricultural areas, further loosening of economic controls and an increase in prosperity could enable millions to ignore or overcome official restrictions on their childbearing, thus raising rural fertility. In China's urban areas, however, and in some relatively prosperous rural areas increased incomes from nonagricultural jobs mean that people have more to lose if they violate rigid rules on the number of births allowed. Penalties are often severe, including paying large portions of their incomes in fines or losing their jobs altogether. Therefore, in the 1990s, increased urbanization and transfer of farm workers into nonagricultural enterprises may prevent the affected workers and households from having more children than allowed. Those members of the floating population who move to urban areas yet get away with ignoring birth restrictions probably succeed because they have not transferred their legal registration to the urban place and because their nonagricultural work is in the informal sector of the economy.

The population of China, already the world's most populous country, will continue growing in the 1990s, even though fertility is not much above replacement level, because of the bulge in the age structure at the peak childbearing ages. At the turn of the century, there will be 1.3 billion or more people living on the China mainland. To raise living standards in the 1990s will require increasing per capita income while the population is still growing. Although China and many other countries have shown that this can be done, it is not an easy task.

Nevertheless, China is beginning to reap the benefits of its largely completed demographic transition. Death rates at all ages are low for a developing country. The people of China experience better health and longer life than the population in most other countries at China's level of economic development.

China's fertility, also unusually low for a country as poor as the PRC, will continue to have both negative and positive effects on the quality of life. Most of the deleterious effects of China's low fertility flow from the fact that it is achieved partly through required family planning. The negative effects of China's low fertility include frequent harassment of women and couples in childbearing ages; disruption of personal and family life when women flee their homes to bear a child; health problems caused by dangerous, illegal IUD removals or required abortions late in pregnancy; female infanticide or severe neglect of girls; and the social and economic discrimination meted out to the children who do not happen to be an only child, especially those children born outside the official birth plan.

China's low fertility will also bring considerable benefits in the 1990s. A population growing at 1½ percent a year causes far less social dislocation than a population growing at 2.5 or 3 percent a year. China is no longer up against the very rapid population growth rates still faced by most south Asian, Middle Eastern, African, and Latin American countries.

Because China's fertility decline came mostly in the 1970s, the children of the smaller birth cohorts are now almost grown. China's economy has begun reaping the benefits of the low fertility of the past decade and a half. The resource costs of providing enough places in primary and middle schools have eased in the 1980s, and these benefits continue. The struggle to provide entry-level jobs in an economy already overburdened with too many unproductive workers will diminish considerably in the 1990s. Many other developing countries are plagued with growing unemployment and underemployment as their labor force age groups inexorably continue to increase rapidly.

China's controlled and directed urbanization will also continue to have both negative and positive effects. China has moved so slowly in loosening its controls over migration that optimal distribution of labor power and skills has certainly not been achieved. Rural men and women who could provide urgently needed urban services have too often been pointlessly hampered or prevented from moving to a city or town. So far it does not appear that this will change in the near future. The positive side of China's measured pace of urbanization is that overurbanization has been avoided. Vast fetid urban slums of the unemployed who have moved from the villages, a common sight in the developing world, are rare in China. Although urban areas feel crowded because of inadequate investment in urban housing and transport systems, the PRC's urbanization policies of the reform period have been successful enough that the national government of the 1990s will probably want to stay the course. It is also possible that a more liberal faction might further loosen the restrictions on rural-to-urban migration.

In conclusion, compared with most poor developing countries, China is in an enviable demographic position. The PRC shares with Taiwan and Hong Kong the benefits of low mortality, low fertility, and low natural population increase. In these three places, the dependency burden—consisting of both child dependency and aged dependency—is currently low and will remain so for the next decade. The age structure of the PRC population in the 1990s will promote productivity and saving, because of the low dependency ratio and concentration of the labor force in their twenties and thirties just beyond entry-level ages. China's population in the 1990s, regarded by China's elite as one of its biggest headaches, also contains important elements that are part of the solution rather than part of the problem.

6

Traditional, Modernist, and "Party" Culture in Contemporary Chinese Society

Zhiling Lin

Contemporary Chinese society represents the combination of three cultural currents. One, the traditional cultural orientation stemming from the country's 5,000-year history, continues to exert a strong hold over most Chinese but has been significantly weakened as a consequence of the influence of the Chinese Communist party. It has, however, experienced a renaissance in recent years, especially in the countryside, where the party's control has been relatively less tight. Traditional ideas such as self-sufficiency, individual development, self-respect, respect for knowledge, and reward for virtue were rapidly and widely reestablished as soon as it was possible. The second cultural current, the modernist impetus resulting from the impact of the West, is some 250 years old. Because of the concentration of industrialization and modern education in cities, especially in big cities, its impact is most strongly felt in urban areas. It does, however, increasingly penetrate the countryside as well. The third, the "party" culture, is only four decades old, but it superimposes its Marxist-Leninist orientation on the other two currents first by attempting to overcome some elements of traditional culture and second by clothing itself falsely in traditional garb and using other elements of the tradition for its own purposes.

Traditional culture, although severely warped by party culture, has survived in important measure. Moreover, as a result of the "open door" era after 1978, people have recognized that it is party culture, not the traditional orientation, that has weakened China. They have also recognized that traditional and modernist currents, far from opposing each other as the party claims, in fact can and will combine to save the country. Thus it is party culture itself that is one of the problems for China. In order to preserve the best in the

Chinese traditional outlook amid modernization, party culture must be transformed. And that transformation will, in the end, lead to the end of Communist party rule in China.

These ideas are well illustrated by the response to the Chinese television series "River Elegy" in the late 1980s.[1] Using the Yellow River, the cradle of traditional Chinese culture, as a symbol, the series suggested that the traditional culture, just like the Yellow River itself, brought disaster to China and its people. The series taught that if China is to modernize, the time has come to do away entirely with old Chinese traditions; they are a leftover influence from the past and a fetter upon modern society. China must look to the blue water of the "ocean"—the West—and not to the muddy water of the Yellow River. But the series had a second message: it is party culture, attempting to clothe itself in traditional cultural garb, that is the real obstacle to progress. Therefore party culture must also be modified and even replaced.

"River Elegy" engendered a storm of criticism throughout the country. The party clearly received the message of criticism and reacted strongly; it wished to maintain its disguise, the identification in the popular mind of traditional and party culture. At the same time many Chinese were incensed that the cultural tradition was so thoroughly and unfairly attacked, feeling that "River Elegy" sought to deny the greatness of Chinese history and thus to call into question the basic idea of Chinese nationalism itself.

Thus even before the Tiananmen Square incident of 1989, "River Elegy" caused people's attention to focus on the role traditional culture should play in the modernization of China, to the interaction between traditional and modern culture, and to the manner in which party culture plays upon both for its own benefit.

Interaction of Tradition and Modernization

The essence of traditional culture derives mainly from the traditional philosophies of Confucianism and neo-Confucianism and from the religions of Taoism and Buddhism. Over the course of thousands of years, they amassed an enormous storehouse of human wisdom and basic scientific knowledge. Traditional culture also includes the kernel of such ideas as civil rights and guidance about people's livelihoods and morality. This culture has been accepted generation after generation and has taken deep root among the people.

But ruling groups have always tried to make use of the cultural heritage for their own purposes. For example, neo-Confucianism, originating more than a thousand years ago, teaches that everything in the world has its own rules and must develop accordingly. One interpretation of this concept is that capable people should be able to discover, learn, and apply those rules. Therefore, the future could be put into the people's hands. This is indeed early science. The rulers established a different and false interpretation, however, according to which everything has been prearranged by some unknown force; human beings can only obey the commands this force has prescribed for them and therefore should accept their fate. This distorted concept helped feudal emperors and lords exercise their dictatorship, for they could claim to be representatives of the heavens, of a god, or of the unknown force. Lorded over by the establishment, the people were forced to become passive and patient. This passive acceptance was then given the fine-sounding name of "Chinese traditional culture."

As a result of such distortions, many Chinese and outsiders have historically believed that there is an inevitable clash between Chinese tradition and new, largely Western ideas. Accordingly, they believe that to modernize, China would have to give up its traditional orientation. Alternatively, some traditionalists have concluded that if the conflict is indeed irreconcilable, then China must forgo modernization and preserve its traditions—or at least must modernize slowly and carefully, seeking to preserve the most important aspects of tradition at every point.[2]

But in light of recent events in China and elsewhere, this conflict appears to be both unnecessary and artificial. China must reevaluate its institutional heritage and then "decide to what extent it can be converted to the requirements of the modern era."[3] No absolute clash exists between tradition and new ideas. They are not life-and-death opponents. Under certain conditions they not only can coexist but can work together to beget a new, modern China that still retains its traditions.

This potential has been demonstrated—not in China, but within the Sino-Confucian cultural tradition—in Hong Kong, Singapore, Taiwan, and South Korea (and even in Japan, although the Sino-Confucian element there was early overlaid with other philosophical traditions).[4] And in China itself, traditional and modern ideas have successfully complemented each other. Thus, during the anti-Japanese resistance war of the 1930s and 1940s, deliberate emphasis on such traditions as nationalism and strong family ties helped keep the country together sufficiently to allow a highly underdeveloped nation to wear down and overcome a modern imperialist invader. Almost all Chinese know the song *"Song-hua-jiang Shang,"* or "On the Song-hua River," famous during and after the anti-Japanese resistance. This song combined the Confucian emphasis on the integrity of the family with nationalism—the integrity of the nation. Mutual dependence within the family has always been regarded as a Chinese virtue. Reliance on that quality enabled large numbers of Chinese to live successfully through such disasters as the Great Leap Forward and the Cultural Revolution. The Chinese cultural tradition encourages people to be kind to each other and asserts that people everywhere are brothers.[5] This is consistent with the central idea of the French Revolution: liberty, equality, and fraternity. The May Fourth movement, which since 1919 has formed the basis of the Chinese emphasis on modernization, took this phrase over completely.[6]

Communist Party Work Unit Culture

The trouble has been that a third element was introduced into the equation with the coming to power in 1949 of the Chinese Communist party. The party rules through "unit culture": that is, all party authority is exercised through the work unit and its directing party branch.[7] Culture means, among other things, social structure, styles of living, modes of thinking, concepts of values and morals, art and literature, interpersonal relations, and currents of intellectual thought. Through the work unit, the party controls each of these areas of life and thereby creates its own "unit," or party, culture.

For instance, salaries, the basis of economic life for the individual, are entirely controlled by the party. Consequently, the party is in a position to decide both the individual's style of living and the structure of society as a whole. Similarly, by controlling housing, the party-governed work unit can easily control such socially vital activities as marriage, reproduction, personal activities, and speech. Because the party assigns all jobs, the individual can choose only between accepting an assignment or having no job at all. Job change becomes impossibly difficult, families are broken apart for long periods, and travel is generally possible only with work unit permission.[8]

To survive under such tight work unit control, the individual must divorce inner life from its outward expression and restrict outward behavior to whatever the party demands, however much it clashes with basic personal desires and hopes. Individualism is thus accursed. Ambition is evil. People are "the masses," not individuals. Each should fulfill his or her role as a tiny cog in a huge machine. Hence the negative side of traditional culture is blown out of all proportion: "Fat pigs will be slaughtered first"; "It is the tall tree that subjects itself to the wind"; "The exposed section of a rafter decays first."[9] These and many other traditional Chinese sayings are constantly used by the party to convince the "masses" that individualism has no place in party-led unit culture. It follows that individuals have no choice other than to accept what is given to or imposed upon them. What follows is learned, outward passivity and, through the process of cognitive dissonance, an inner disrespect of self and fear even of thinking one's own thoughts.[10] A kind of twisted mentality results: everyone must beware of everyone else; people must be doubtful about everything; each person must be prepared to turn anyone else into the party—and to be turned in—during the endless political campaigns, movements, political study sessions, and struggle and criticism sessions that make up the very center of party-controlled unit culture.

This mentality exacts a second cost upon the Chinese people and their society. They are reluctant to accept new ideas and new ways of thinking lest they risk punishment from the party, even though such ideas and thoughts might be desirable and might well contribute to the modernization of the country. Passivity—outward and inward—thus in the end opposes even modernization, since the latter by its nature means to explore new fields and to encourage changing the old. One must therefore "carry out one's daily duty," whether it makes sense or not, just as the monk every day is expected to toll the morning bell.[11] One does only the least that is expected, no more, and one takes a passive attitude toward one's work, even though the party encourages more than that. With no rewards offered for hard work, for creativity, or for performing in an outstanding manner—and with high risks incurred for standing out—one learns to do no more than is minimally expected.

Chinese tradition, on the contrary, stresses other virtues. It encourages people to be outstanding, to advance to the limit of their ability, so as to "bring honor and glory to one's family and ancestors." It emphasizes that "in order to be outstanding"—a person above others—"one must be prepared to undergo hardship and experience bitterness." And it expects that "the high-ranking official," having gone through much hardship and suffering to attain his rank, "will dress accordingly when returning to visit his native village" and will thus bring honor upon his family.[12]

The party's twisting of culture is reflected as well in the fields of literature and art. The party early defined its policy of absolute control of these fields in the well-known *zheng-feng* movement in 1944, usually referred to as the Yenan Forum.[13] After 1949, when the party controlled the whole country, writers and artists were required to take on a completely Communist point of view if they wished to publish or perform. They had to go through "ideological remolding."

They were forced to "sink themselves" into the lives of the workers, peasants, and soldiers, "the only real life," in order to write and produce "what workers, peasants, and soldiers [were] pleased to see and hear."[14] But by being forced to serve the people in terms of party policy and outlook instead of looking at life through their own viewpoint, they were in fact constrained to stop writing and producing what they really wanted to say. They feared to create in a manner different from what the party expected. The party prescribed certain literary and artistic themes and proscribed others. "Petty bourgeois self-expression" was forbidden. Only topics that reflected the party's interpretation of the bright side of society were permitted. Literature and art were in that manner reduced to propaganda, writers and artists being expected to act as mere party-directed educators of the people.[15]

In turn, "the people" were expected to follow the examples established by party-approved artistic and literary works. Such works generally glorified examples of the "best" of the approved classes (workers, peasants, soldiers), to use them to construct a society that, in the end, would be leveled down to a classless configuration. The trouble was that even during this relatively early period of party rule—the 1950s—the changing nature of Chinese society did not fit this image. It was relatively easy for the party to suppress or even physically to eliminate certain components of traditional society such as landlords, petty bourgeois urbanites, capitalists, and the like. But the persistence of traditional values and attitudes combined with the growing impact of modernization increasingly conflicted with the party's image of what Chinese society should look like. Indeed, the party's attempts to "modernize" the country on the basis of its own principles led consistently to disaster, as in the Great Leap Forward and the Cultural Revolution.[16] By way of reaction, the party more and more frontally opposed modernization as well as tradition. The Great Leap Forward at least was advertised as a means by which China would overcome the fetters of tradition and in one move bring the country economically into the modern world. The Cultural Revolution, on the other hand, was an out-and-out attack not only on Chinese tradition but on the social and economic consequences of modernization as well. Thus the party drew a clear distinction between the culture that it hoped to create—and was succeeding in creating, by virtue of its totalist control of society—and that represented by the combination of the Chinese tradition and the impetus to modernize.

Moreover, the Maoist concept of social organization increasingly conflicted with that evolving from modernization. Mao's idea was to

139

bring forth, through party-led "modernization," a classless society according to the Communist ideal.[17] But Chinese society did not move toward that end, for Mao artificially set class against class as a putative engine of social progress. Modernization, on the other hand, strives toward both class harmony and an ever-more finely differentiated society in order to achieve social progress. And the Chinese tradition is squarely in line with this pursuit, for it too advocates compromise, harmony, the Confucian Golden Mean, and coexistence among various elements of society.

Communist Party Reforms

Until the Cultural Revolution, as well as Mao's own life, ended in 1976, the party more or less had its way with how Chinese society was organized. Tradition was either suppressed or exploited by the party for its own purposes. And modernization in the true sense—democratization, marketization, freedom of individual expression—was not allowed to make an undue impact on society, even though much industrialization and other aspects of that process were allowed to proceed.

But after 1976 the party knew that in order to save itself in the eyes of the Chinese people, it would have to change its image by conducting "reforms." It therefore made important internal economic changes, mostly in agriculture but later also in industry, and it opened the country widely to the winds of foreign influence and new ideas.[18]

The reformist impetus was reflected in the cultural sphere as well. There the party permitted a resurgence of traditional values, orientations, and practices, while simultaneously opening the country widely to the winds of new ideas from abroad.[19] During the post-1978 "Deng decade of reform," traditional and modernist cultures reinforced each other, demonstrating that China could rapidly modernize, could use traditional ideals and values for that purpose, and could at the same time preserve the best of the Chinese tradition. As a result, the party's image of society and of the culture it had created sharply contradicted the reality of an increasingly close combination of tradition and modernization.

Once again, developments in the literary and artistic spheres illustrated these relationships. During the post-Mao period, beginning with the publication in 1977 of "Scar," a short story attacking the Cultural Revolution,[20] writers and artists were able to express themselves with increasing, although limited, freedom. This was a phenomenon nearly unprecedented since 1949.

For instance, the female writer Dai Houying was able to publish the novel *People, People!* stressing the value of the individual in society as a person of innate value rather than merely as a contributor to the whole.[21] The novel also urged that interpersonal relations be based on emotions, true feelings, and honesty instead of party principles and the double standard of behavior—private versus public—that party culture imposed. Traditional ethics as well as modernist individualism were thus united and stood opposed to the party's ethic of collectivism.

Another example is the reception accorded the script of the movie *Unrequited Love*, written by the well-known writer Bai Hua.[22] Its famous theme, "You love your country, but does your country love you?" indicates that China's shortcomings will cause it always to betray even the best, most well meaning of its citizens. Such people have no place in China, the film suggests; like the film's hero, they will be forced to flee and to lose their very lives despite their total devotion to their motherland. But in reality the trouble is not China as a country and a culture; it is the manner in which the party has misruled the people and has corrupted within them even feelings of simple patriotism.

It is also important to understand the role played by new ideas imported from outside China during the post-1978 decade. These ideas helped change the popular image of the relationship between traditional culture and party culture. For the first time since the late 1940s, the "open door" permitted foreign influence to penetrate the country without being seen as threatening. That influence entered China through many means: the media, translation, the arts, tourists, trade, businesspeople, exchanges of scientists, and the sending of students and scholars abroad.[23] In combination, they demonstrated that there was literally a world of difference between China's internal situation and that of many other nations; that the difference in standards of living and behavior now so obvious did not have to be that way; and that through reforms, China could also modernize rapidly.

These newly perceived facts and ideas were catalysts that caused the Chinese people to wake up. The new attitudes infected many in the party as well, including its leader, Deng Xiaoping. He received a kind of mandate—and the party received at least a temporary reprieve from the wholesale rejection of its rule as a result of the Cultural Revolution, the Great Leap, and the very nature of its system—to modernize the country by whatever means were found to work best.[24]

For much of the decade the party was highly successful in this

141

venture, leading the country through by far the most productive period in the century. But an unintended consequence emerged in the popular mind. The new policies applied in a reformist manner enhanced people's appreciation of modern social structures, morality, values, lifestyles, and ways of thinking. Interest in these aspects of modernization in fact boomed; yet people discovered that current, party-created Chinese culture stood opposed to these new ways of thinking and living. People therefore began to criticize current culture—and they thought, mistakenly, that the newly perceived negative aspects of current culture were merely a reflection of traditional culture. Thus, for instance, Bo Yang's book of essays *Ugly Chinese*, which denigrated the negative aspects of traditional culture, was widely cheered.[25]

The conclusion drawn was that China needed to get rid of traditional culture once and for all in order to modernize. All old traditions should be thrown out; Bo argued that the very nature of the Chinese people is passive, lazy, and unwilling to be individually assertive. Some even went so far as to claim that China had no hope of modernization at all, because traditional culture had poisoned people so deeply and for so long.

But while traditional Chinese culture does contain some negative elements standing at times opposed to modernization, in fact these are minor. By contrast, traditional culture almost entirely supports modernization, and the two are quite compatible. Modernization—in the sense of such outcomes of the process as democratization, marketization, and the emergence of a complex and differentiated society—is the friend of traditional Chinese culture. There are many examples, of which only a few need be cited.

Mencius, who lived from 372 to 289 B.C., was far ahead of his time in advocating democracy and the pursuit of material benefit. He believed that respecting, protecting, educating, helping, and enriching people would be the best way to develop the country. If people were allowed to pursue their own goals, he reasoned, a stable, peaceful, and developing society would follow.[26] The party, however, criticized Mencius on the grounds that progress can take place only through class struggle, not through intergroup harmony.[27] In the opinion of the party, a stable society only perpetuates the ruling class in power and thus thwarts progress. Mencius wrote that if the rulers and the people are in harmony, progress can and will take place— precisely what modernization emphasizes. His doctrine boiled down to the suggestion that class struggle destroys both social harmony and economic progress.

In advocating a differentiated society, Mencius was thoroughly modern: people's station in society would depend on their talents, their experience, and their education. This idea is diametrically opposed to the party's policy of establishing a person's position in society according to the party's own judgment of a person's class.

The ancient sages Confucius, Mencius, Mozi, and Xunzi all conveyed ideas that accord well with the modern ideas of popular rule and effective government. Confucius opined twenty-five hundred years ago that if a ruler is virtuous, he will be supported by those around him: that is, a government cannot rule for long through dictatorship and suppression. Mencius said that the uncaring ruler will not keep his reign for long. Mozi advised that a ruler should encourage things that do people good and eliminate those that harm people. Xunzi taught that the ruler should make full use of the resources that the natural environment provides.[28]

While one cannot entirely equate these ideas with the modern notions of democracy, human rights, and environmentalism, enough correspondence exists to have prepared the Chinese people to be receptive to these notions when they were introduced as "new" ideas from the West. The party constantly criticizes these ideas, however, fearing their corrosive impact on its own exclusive rule. It accordingly tries to convince the Chinese people that such ideas are "feudal remnants" best cast aside, "poisonous weeds" that must be pulled up and thrown away.

Let us inspect the content of current party culture more thoroughly. It consists of two parts. The first is what the party has imposed on the people. It has suppressed expressions of individual personality, it has forced people to hide their true feelings, and it has made people adopt a double standard of public versus private beliefs and behavior. It has leveled society economically by forcing everyone to work for very low wages, which until quite recently vary little whether one works hard or not.

The second part of current party culture is a corruption, a twisting, of certain aspects of traditional culture. For instance, it has amplified the Confucian principle of obedience of lower social groups to higher and of children to parents to suggest that the Chinese people should unquestioningly obey the party as children obey their parents. Because the party is presented as the mother of the Chinese people, everyone must listen to and obey that party without question.[29]

Tragically, the party has succeeded in convincing the Chinese people that the practices and beliefs it has imposed on them *are* traditional Chinese culture. For example, traditional culture teaches that people should work hard and not necessarily expect a reward.

143

Hence, the party reasons, an economically leveled society is good. In instances where it is difficult to twist traditional culture to party ends, the party has merely conducted frontal attacks. For instance, traditional culture emphasizes the high value of education and knowledge. Unable to overcome this element through deliberate misinterpretation, the party has constantly criticized and imprisoned intellectuals, has deemphasized learning for its own sake, and has structured the educational system to provide higher education to only a tiny minority, coming mostly from "correct" class backgrounds. When education threatened to produce groups outside of total party control, the party shut down the whole educational system and physically attacked those who had the misfortune of having attained a higher level of learning.[30]

Indeed, the party tried with all its might to extirpate traditional culture, and it nearly succeeded. For the ten years of the Cultural Revolution, no expression of traditional culture was possible. The party falsely attempted to identify itself with traditional culture in order to replace it with party culture. Through such false identification, of course, the party could argue that modernization and party culture were natural partners—indeed that the two were coming to be one and the same—and that party culture was at least partly the product of the incorporation into Marxism-Leninism of the best elements of traditional Chinese culture. Thus the party attempted to convince people, through a historically and factually distorted analysis, that some elements of traditional culture were inherently bad and should be replaced, while other elements possessed positive features that composed the Sinic content of Marxism-Leninism. If it could successfully convince people, the party could look forward to redeeming itself in their eyes and could continue in power without fear of the kind of massive popular opposition that previously had periodically welled to the surface.

But it was not traditional culture that conflicted with modernization and that held China back. The two are quite compatible, and traditional culture clearly encourages modernization. It is party culture that is the enemy of both.

Growing Recognition by Intellectuals of Party Distortions

The entire sequence of events leading to the Tiananmen Square incident of June 1989 and the events that followed illustrate this thesis. During the late 1980s, thanks mostly to the "open door," it became increasingly clear to some Chinese that traditional culture and party culture were not the same. They came to see that the obstacle to modernization was therefore not traditional culture but party culture. They concluded that traditional culture could combine with modernization to change dramatically the face of the country while at the same time preserving the best of that culture. That made it possible for some Chinese for the first time to reevaluate party culture. They understood that party culture was not only unnecessary for modernization but actually was undermining it.[31]

These people were precisely those who had, first, received a higher education of sufficient quality to see things as they were and who had, second, been influenced by the winds of change blowing into China during the 1980s. They composed a small portion of the total population, however—most were students, faculty, and other intellectuals. Other sectors of society—workers and peasants in particular—could not make that perceptual breakthrough, because the party prevented their attaining a sufficient educational level.

That goes far to explain why the Tiananmen demonstrations occurred in the first place and why they did not produce what the movement organizers and participants desired. The participants were mostly students. They were young and enthusiastic, the most sensitive and active part of the society. Besides, they had more access to modernist ideas and developments. They therefore became more open to new ideas and influences from the outside world and more willing to accept them. At the same time they lacked experience and had not yet been thoroughly suppressed by party culture. Hence they were prone to impulsiveness. Toward the spring of 1989, when economic reform had reached the point where political reform was also needed, the students wanted to seize the opportunity to impel China forward. But they did not know how. Their marches, demonstrations, and hunger strikes were all well organized, but they lacked clear goals, programs, and principles.

Faculty on the campuses were the first to be influenced by the students and to ally with them. Intellectuals at large followed. But they acted cautiously. They could have implemented the modernist ideas coming from abroad directly and completely, but they hesitated because their experience under party culture had taught them to be cautious. Numerous party campaigns and postcampaign persecution had made them afraid. They had already suffered too much to believe that they could change things overnight, and they knew that without the whole society's awakening, such changes were not likely to take place. So they vacillated. They accurately perceived the country's problems, and they saw the trend of the future, but they were too repressed by party culture to evince enthusiasm, much less impulsiveness. The best they could do, therefore, was to sympathize rather than actively to participate.

The other groups in society involved in the protest movement—some workers, a few peasants, but mostly persons or households engaged in newly permitted private-sector production or enterprises—were relatively small in number and made up an even smaller proportion of society as a whole. They harbored resentments deep in their hearts against the party, and the student movement provided them an opportunity to express these sentiments openly. But basically the workers were the beneficiaries of the current system and the party culture it produced, which is to say they were conquered by party culture. They were too used to the "iron rice bowl" and the "big pot meal" system to desire basic change. In the end, therefore, they came down on the side of the authorities.

Only private enterprise owners, who vigorously hoped for more economic freedom so that they could develop their businesses further, were interested in thorough, systemic change. Only they sided with the students and the intellectuals in protests for political changes. Many more people in the big cities sympathized with the students, especially in Beijing after the hunger strike took place. The government's indifferent attitude angered them even more. When they finally saw tanks and troops enter the city and approach the student demonstrators, they became so angry that they accepted the unshirkable duty of trying to stop the military threat. They entered into the streets and fought with the troops more for basic humanity than for political reasons.[32]

The rest of Chinese society was either too far away from the events in Beijing and other large cities—both geographically and mentally (in the case of peasants) or too much a part of the system itself (in the case of bureaucrats) or too afraid to turn the tools of their trade against their leaders lest they lose their own lives (in the case of soldiers). They could therefore have only a partial understanding of the degree to which party culture distorted society, suppressed and twisted traditional culture, and prevented the natural union of modernist and traditional orientations to develop the country rapidly. Like the workers, they did not desire a thorough change. So they did not join the protest movement.

The Tiananmen suppression was therefore inevitable, even though it took direct, brutal, and wanton use of military force to accomplish it.

The students, intellectuals, and individual private enterprise owners were severely punished. Students and most intellectuals were concentrated on the campuses and therefore were easily controlled—

arrested, criticized, exiled to the countryside as punishment, disciplined by being sent to military camps, or killed. The party blamed "Western influence" for the people's awakening and discontent with the establishment, and it once again started a campaign against "Western liberalization" and "wholesale Westernization" while propagandizing what it called "Chinese traditions" such as blind obedience, self-restraint, and patience. Here again, as it had done whenever it wanted to oppose new ideas and nonparty ideological influences, the party used its own twisted version of the cultural tradition to force students and society in general to reject modernist ideas entering China from the outside.

That is why the so-called Learn from Lei Feng movement was resurrected after twenty-five years. Lei Feng, a common soldier who died on duty in 1964, supposedly left a diary that stressed extreme, unthinking obedience to the party, and shortly after his death, the party launched a nationwide movement to learn from him. The party, arguing that such obedience stems directly from traditional culture, thereby tried to persuade people that they should not only blindly obey the party but should also reject foreign influences. In this way the Chinese tradition would supposedly be preserved.

As for workers, they went back to the "big pot meal" way of living. Their relatively low level of education and the material benefits bestowed upon them by the regime made them believe that obedience to the authorities and patience were the best and most rewarding virtues—another party distortion of traditional culture. Peasants did not overly care about the political movement. Their greatest concerns were family and harvest. But even here the party made sure they continued to believe that way, by tightening its control at the local level and by denying them most opportunities for a better education.[33]

Individual entrepreneurs, who had reemerged in Chinese society after 1978, were a negligible threat for three reasons. First, they were small in number and highly visible. Second, four decades of party propaganda had convinced much of the population that merchants and the commercial culture they represented, actually a part of modernist culture, were bad; and forty years of excessive egalitarianism had taken away from the people any interest in competing. The Chinese people by this time greatly disliked to compete; if everyone is paid the same, why work harder? And so even though individual entrepreneurship was obviously making a difference during the post-1978 decade, the population was primed to reject such efforts. Third, because of their relatively low educational level, many entrepreneurs had difficulty in distinguishing good from evil, and they absorbed some of the bad as well as the good of the new external influences entering the country from abroad. Among the foreign imports were new lifestyles, an emphasis on acquisition of material goods, and such practices otherwise not entirely unknown to China as gambling, prostitution, group violence, and sharp business practices.

Party propaganda exaggerated the evil side effects of these influences and tried to convince people that such effects were inseparable from the original foreign influences as a whole. Thus, for a time, many in society were convinced by this logic, however faulty it was, and they therefore rejected not only private entrepreneurs as conduits for the importation of external influences but also the orientation toward a market economy that they represented. The party was thus able both to punish the entrepreneurs and to convince people that a free economy was not good.

China's Future

What of the future? Three conclusions seem apparent from the above analysis. First, it is impossible for party culture to continue to dominate China overwhelmingly. For one thing, the post-Mao door to the outside world has been open for a dozen years, and most Chinese have had a chance to view the outside, however restrictedly. But so long as the people perceive bigger and bigger differences between themselves and people in other countries, they will be more and more doubtful about what they have been told by the party. Finally, however, they will understand, accept, and approve of the main trends of development throughout the globe and demand to be a part of them. Further, the intellectuals are once again a step ahead and will continue to lead the way. For some time they have been reevaluating the official explanation of traditional philosophy. In Shanghai, scholars are reexamining Confucianism and reinterpreting Mencius— for example, a conference was recently held by the Mencius Society in Zhou Xian, Mencius's home town.[34] To the extent that this evaluation is allowed to proceed, the gulf between party culture and its false propagation of tradition on the one hand and true traditional culture on the other hand will grow even wider.

But second, it is equally impossible for new ideas, the modernist concept from Western democratic countries, and the culture this concept represents to take over in the near future. The party's twisting of traditional culture causes people to hesitate to accept, and sometimes actually to resist, new ideas. Moreover, the Chinese people generally are not yet at a sufficiently high educational level to understand many of the new ideas. These ideas are not only new but

148

also complex. Such novelties as a democratic constitution, a market economy, and the paradox that inflation can sometimes accentuate economic growth are all contrary to what people have experienced and have been told over a long period. It will therefore take another period—not necessarily as long, but not short—to bring them to an understanding, acceptance, and finally approval of such ideas. Finally, the party has tried to equate economic reform with modernization itself. But because these reforms for political reasons are as yet incomplete and because the party deliberately exaggerated some of the negative side effects of economic reforms, the people—especially the workers, the main element in Chinese society and the main supporters of the party—will retain doubts about the reforms. They want to wait and see.

Third, beyond doubt party culture is nonetheless being slowly undermined. This does not mean that China will in the end undergo total modernization. Nor does it mean that some kind of exclusive "Middle Kingdom" distortion of traditional culture will emerge. Both are impossible. Eventually, party culture will be replaced by a combination of genuine traditional culture and modernization. There will be many doubts, much conflict, and even painful and tragic battles along the way. In the end, however, party culture will finally be overcome and traditional-plus-modern culture will be established. It is this new and viable combination that will finally enable China to restore its greatness in every sense and still to take its place alongside other advanced nations as being both fully modern and culturally unique.

During this long period that China is just entering, it is extremely important for the door to the flow of outside influence to be kept as wide open as possible. That influence will not corrode the Chinese tradition. It will merely help people to approach new ideas, thoughts, and practices with open minds, and it will therefore enhance prospects for tradition-backed modernization. But even a partially opened door—one limited to the import of technology and an increase in trade—is better than none. For cultural influences will invariably enter along with science and business. Moreover, technology and business can and will promote higher levels of, and more widespread, education, because they demand knowledge. And education and knowledge, both traditional and modernist, are China's hope.

PART FOUR
Economy

7

Chinese Agriculture—
Modernization, but at What Costs?

Jean C. Oi

At the beginning of the decade of reform in 1980, Deng Xiaoping offered much hope for tackling the incentive problem plaguing Chinese agriculture.[1] He dared to dismantle the hallmarks of the Maoist system by decollectivizing agriculture and abolishing communes to break the "iron rice bowl," reinstitute household farming, and reopen markets. Peasants enthusiastically responded to calls to "dare to stand out" and "get rich first." By 1984, production and procurements reached an all-time historical high. State granaries were so full that grain lay rotting on the roadside for lack of adequate storage facilities.[2]

A decade after Deng's agricultural reforms began, however, the future of China's agricultural sector was uncertain. Will the family responsibility system continue? Will it ensure continued production increases? Or will an agricultural crisis occur? What are peasants' attitudes toward the regime? Is China moving toward marketization of its economy? Can China's agriculture be "modernized" and, if so, at what economic, political, and social costs?

This uncertainty is prompted in part by the crackdown in the Tiananmen incident in 1989, but primarily by the disappointing performance of the grain sector in the rural economy since the mid-1980s.[3] After steady increases in the first half of the decade and the record-breaking harvest of 1984, grain production decreased (see figure 7-1). The acreage sown to grain (see figure 7-2) decreased dramatically, and yields continue to stagnate (see figure 7-3).[4] The 1989 and 1990 harvests were good; but even the approximately 412.5 million tons produced in 1990 did not meet the state-set target of 425 million tons for grain production.[5]

This chapter examines the reasons for grain production problems and the issues that must be resolved if China is to modernize its agricultural sector in the 1990s. Because many of the problems stem

153

FIGURE 7–1
GRAIN PRODUCTION IN CHINA, 1979–1991
(10,000 metric tons)

SOURCE: *Zhong Guo Tong Ji Nian Jian* (Chinese statistical yearbook), 1992, p. 357.

from the broader context in which grain production takes place, much of the discussion will necessarily be on nonagricultural aspects of the rural economy. Increasingly higher returns from alternative employment opportunities, particularly work in the fast-growing rural industrial sector, make grain production unattractive to China's peasants.

The Incentive Problem

The key issue is not so much the structure of agricultural production but sufficient incentives for peasants to increase grain production. The failure of Deng's agricultural reforms to provide a lasting solution to the incentive problem, which plagues China's agriculture, is clear

FIGURE 7–2

AVERAGE ACREAGE SOWN TO GRAIN IN CHINA, 1979–1991
(10,000 mu)

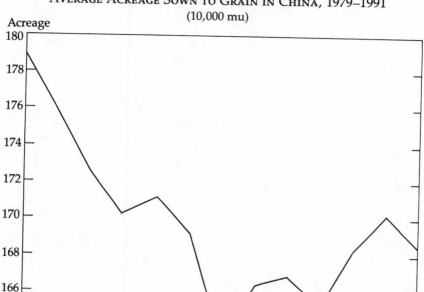

NOTE: One mu equals about 0.16 acres.
SOURCE: *Zhong Guo Tong Ji Nian Jian* (Chinese statistical yearbook), 1992, pp. 192, 352.

in hindsight. The reasons for the tremendous increases in grain production go beyond the household responsibility system. Certainly the institution of the responsibility system provided some of the needed incentives to spur production, but it alone would not have been enough. The combination of the household responsibility system and other *material* incentives provided the necessary conditions for increased production and sales in the early 1980s.[6]

The fate of the responsibility system alone is unlikely to determine whether increases in production or an agricultural crisis will occur in the 1990s. The more important question is, How does the state accommodate the changes that have taken place in the rural economy and make returns from growing grain competitive? Since

FIGURE 7–3
GRAIN YIELDS IN CHINA, 1979–1991
(kilograms per mu)

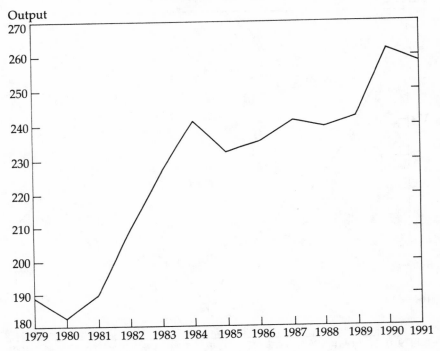

NOTE: One mu equals about 0.16 acres.
SOURCE: *Zhong Guo Tong Ji Nian Jian* (Chinese statistical yearbook), 1992, pp. 205, 352, 357.

1985 the institutional structure of agricultural production has remained the same, but the economic incentives that accompanied it are no longer sufficient to motivate peasants to grow and sell grain to the state. Peasants have had an increasing number of income opportunities outside of grain production.

Temporary Solutions, 1979–1984. Peasants have always been rational economic actors. But only after the 1978 Third Plenum reforms did peasants gain the necessary freedom to choose economic activities that would bring the greatest return, and only after a number of years of reform did opportunities appear that allowed peasants to exercise their new freedom. The economic and political context of the early

156

years of reform was such that peasants had few viable alternatives to growing grain and selling it to the state.

In the early 1980s, when decollectivization was just beginning, many peasants were going it alone for the first time as producers. After almost three decades of collective production, when peasants were told when, how, and what to do each day, not all peasants knew how to be good farmers. Not all peasants had the necessary skill to grow cash crops or engage in animal husbandry. Peasants often remarked that growing the more lucrative crops, such as watermelon, or raising chickens and rabbits, takes special skill. It was also a time when few nonagricultural jobs, other than construction, were available. The growth of most nonagricultural opportunities, such as work in rural industrial enterprises, did not appear until about 1984.

During the early years of reform, the free markets were still undeveloped, and peasants had neither the information nor the transport facilities to stray far from their local markets. Markets were legalized after the Third Plenum reforms, but the free market was not necessarily the peasants' first choice. During the early 1980s, when peasants had few known outlets, selling to the state was a secure and desirable market opportunity. In 1984, the market price of grain was lower than the state-offered, overquota prices, for example. In such situations, when grain was difficult to sell, peasants vied to sell it to the state because of both the price and the security.[7]

During the first few years of reform, moreover, the price increases of 1979 made growing as much grain as possible and selling it to the state worthwhile. Peasant incomes increased substantially. Whereas peasant income increased only 0.5 percent per year between 1957 and 1977, the rate of income increase adjusted for inflation from 1980 to 1985 was 14 percent. An increase in both the amount of peasant grain rations and the consumption of fine grains, that is, wheat and rice, accompanied this. Peasants had something to buy with their newly earned income and that was, perhaps, equally important. In a strategic move, the reformers reconfigured the economy and provided more consumer goods. Production of most consumer items increased by at least 100 percent. Rural spending (adjusted for inflation) on consumer goods increased by over 50 percent from 1978 to 1981.[8]

Reemerging Discontent, 1985 to the Present. The period between 1979 and 1984 was, unfortunately, only a period of transition between the collapse of the Maoist system and the institutionalization of the Dengist system. In retrospect it was only a honeymoon. Fairly quickly, the economic context changed. A survey of 13,000 peasant households in 155 villages reveals that between 1984 and 1988 the net income from grain production (income from products less production costs) declined 15.6 percent.[9] Grain production dropped 25 million tons in 1985 and failed to surpass the 1984 level until 1989, and even then at lower yields. The reasons for these declines include the following:

Pricing structure. In 1985, the state indirectly reduced the incentive for peasants to grow and sell more to the state by abolishing the unified procurement system and changing the price structure. Ironically, even though the unified procurement system was a dreaded burden on the peasants, it offered peasants a higher total return for grain sales to the state. This was particularly true in 1983 and 1984 when harvests were abundant. The state was obligated to pay the peasants a high, over-quota price for all grain above the basic quota amount. As suggested above, at times this price was higher than the market price. When for the first time it had more grain than it knew what to do with, the state decided to relieve itself of a financial burden and limit the amount of grain it would buy at a set price from the peasants. In doing this, it also restructured the price ratio for quota and overquota grain sales—the institution of an arrangement known as *daosanqi* (reversing the 30:70 ratio).

The net results of *daosanqi* have been an issue of controversy, but a study done by a research group under the State Council has shown that many peasants received, on the whole, less income for selling their increased output.[10] It paid peasants the higher price for more of the sale: the amount paid at the higher over-quota price was changed to 70 percent, while the low basic-price grain equaled only 30 percent. But peasants no longer have the guarantee of getting the high over-quota price for all grain above the base quota. Consequently, once the contracted amount is met, the price for the surplus will depend on the market. If the price is low, then the peasants will receive the lower price. No longer is a higher return guaranteed.[11]

Scissors effect. The rapidly rising costs of production inputs account for the largest decrease in the profitability of growing grain. The "price scissors" for agricultural products have widened faster than the increase in procurement prices. According to one study, the price scissors between industrial and agricultural goods were 77.1 billion yuan in 1984 and by 1987, 114 billion yuan. This means that if the prices of industrial goods had not risen, keeping the price scissors at the 1984 level, the peasants would have received an additional 40 billion yuan in sales to the state of agricultural goods. The state would need to increase prices between 15 percent and 20 percent to bring the price scissors back to the 1984 level.[12]

In theory, the input and price problems are compensated for by state provision of scarce and expensive inputs, such as fertilizer and diesel fuel, at low rationed prices. These are given as a bonus for selling to the state. This prospect made the state contracts more attractive than the low state-set price would itself suggest. The attractiveness of state sales, however, was quickly diminished in many areas when the state failed to hold up its part of the bargain.[13] Peasants sold the grain to the state, but then failed to get the promised inputs from the state.[14]

The increased costs along with the lower returns have led to the decreased use of certain inputs, which contribute significantly to the lower yields. While there has been no appreciable decrease in the use of chemical fertilizer, the use of manure has decreased. Manure is more burdensome to apply, but has greater benefit to the long-term health of the soil. The use of the expensive plastic mulch and pesticide has also decreased.[15] To get increases in production, the state had to mandate an increase in the acreage sown to grain.[16]

IOUs. On top of the structural problems that have already been described, the state compounded an already bad situation by failing to pay peasants for their grain in 1988 and 1989. I am referring here to the practice of issuing "white slips"—that is, IOUs instead of cash upon delivery. This only further reduced the incentive for peasants to sell to the state. Peasants were required to deliver their grain as usual, but they had to wait before they could get cash for their sales.

The state realized the anger this was causing and issued a ban on issuing white slips. This, however, only forced some places to stop buying grain until there were more funds. Peasants were still left in the situation of being stuck with their grain and needing money. Other places bought grain but tried to get around the white slips by crediting the savings accounts of those peasants selling the grain. The catch was that peasants had to wait three months to use the money.[17] The problem of IOUs was fairly widespread, although some local officials are reluctant to admit that such problems occurred in their area.[18] Not surprisingly, such problems have caused extreme discontent among China's peasants and have resulted in further declines in grain production. The use of IOUs continued into the 1990s.

Markets and alternative sources of income. The reemergence of the market has had the greatest impact on peasant enthusiasm for selling grain to the state. By the mid-1980s, peasants could sell their grain in an increasing number of markets. For the first time in decades, the state faced real competition for the peasants' grain.[19] With the rapid development of rural enterprises that began in 1984, an increasing number of feed companies, oil-processing companies, and cornstarch factories needed to procure substantial amounts of grain as raw material. These new enterprises established procurement stations at their factories within the villages, or they went to surrounding areas to directly procure grain from the peasants. Under such circumstances the peasants were not hampered by lack of transport. The market came to the peasants with prices that were generally higher than the state-set price.[20] According to a state council survey, by 1988 the gap between the state procurement price and the market prices continued to widen, resulting in a difference of 11.8 yuan per 50 kilograms of grain.[21]

Competition took not only the form of markets for grain but also the form of alternative employment opportunities for peasants' labor. Peasants freed from dependence on the collective increasingly have chosen to pursue other, more lucrative sources of employment, such as growing cash crops, forestry, animal husbandry and fishing, and working in nonagricultural industry. The disparity between the relative returns from growing grain and these activities is substantial. During the period between 1984 and 1988, for example, the return (in terms of net income per workday) increased only 15.1 percent for grain, but the return from cash crops increased 96.5 percent.[22]

Thus, no longer is it simply a matter of returns on grain production or returns on grain sales to the state; it is a matter of the profitability of relative returns as compared with other income sources and sales opportunities. These opportunities are key in explaining why peasants increasingly are moving away from grain production and why local governments increasingly are putting resources into nonagricultural activity. Again, this trend has continued into the 1990s.

Township Enterprises and Declining Investment in Agriculture

The fastest-growing alternative income opportunity is rural industry. In contrast to the disappointing performance in grain production, rural industry has been a success story. Growing by leaps and bounds since the mid-1980s, rural enterprises[23] have become the most profitable sector of the rural economy. Income from these enterprises increasingly has kept many local governments afloat. By 1987, industry had already surpassed agriculture as the dominant source of total rural income.[24] In 1987 alone, it produced close to 300 billion yuan in income, over 35 percent of total rural output, and 16 billion yuan in taxes—twice as much as the agricultural tax. The total gross value of output generated by rural enterprises rose almost ninefold from 49 billion yuan in 1980 to 474 billion yuan in 1987.[25] In 1988, the total output value rose another 36 percent and constituted well over 50 percent of total agricultural output and almost a quarter of total national output. Revenues rose over 40 percent from 1987, and taxes alone increased 44 percent from 1987, with net profits increasing 35.6 percent.

Rural enterprises, in addition, have absorbed most of the increasing surplus labor created by decollectivization.[26] In 1988 alone, the number of workers employed rose almost 8.5 percent, constituting almost 18 percent of the total labor force and almost a quarter of the agricultural labor force.[27] The percentage of the rural labor force engaged in town and township enterprises rose from 9.5 percent to 23.83 percent.[28]

Rural industry provides not only jobs but one of the most lucrative employment opportunities. During the period from 1984 to 1988 the return, in terms of net income per workday, increased 45.9 percent for participation in nonagricultural industries, compared with 15.1 percent for grain.[29] Many jobs in rural enterprises also have another advantage: peasants need not have any special skills to undertake such work, unlike the skill needed to engage in cash cropping.[30]

The rapid and profitable development of rural enterprises has affected the behavior of both individual peasants and local governments. Increasing opportunities in rural industry have allowed peasants to act on their predisposition against grain production by making their reliance on land—as the major means of livelihood—unnecessary. In highly industrialized areas some peasants began returning the land leased to them almost as soon as the responsibility system was instituted. They did not want the burdens attached to contracting land, and they had sufficient income to buy grain on the free market—not only for consumption but, if necessary, to meet their grain responsibilities to the state. In some areas peasants were allowed to give some or all of their land back to the collective, which then appointed a small number of peasants to serve as specialized large-scale farmers.

Most peasant households have adopted a less radical position. A large number of peasant households keep their land, but leave only the women or the elderly of the family to work the land. In such a situation, for one or two people to work the land and grow grain for the family is fairly profitable. The earned total income from grain is comparable to the income of the family member who works in the factory.[31] The entire family, therefore, does not need to work the land.[32] In those villages that have mechanization and unified management of agriculture, a woman or older man can more than manage all of a family's contracted land.[33]

Peasants have adopted a household strategy to maximize the family's income possibilities and to secure the cheapest available grain. This household strategy is a problem for the state because it makes farming a sideline enterprise for an increasing number of peasants. Studies show that the number of peasants engaging mainly in grain production is decreasing significantly. A survey of 13,000 households found a 16 percent decrease. The largest increases were in animal husbandry and in rural industrial enterprises.[34]

Local government investment also evidences the increasing abandonment of agriculture. Despite the growing rural collective economy, collective investment of capital in agriculture, as a percentage of total collective investment in fixed assets, declined from 39.6 percent in 1982 to 9.4 percent in 1988.[35] The decline in the use of rural enterprise funds has been particularly sharp. The amount used declined 71.6 percent from 1979 to 1988. Breaking that figure down from 1979 to 1983, when communes still existed, the amount of subsidy averaged about 3.3 billion yuan each year. But from 1984 to 1988, after communes were disbanded and township enterprises developed rapidly, subsidies averaged only 1.54 billion yuan per year.[36]

A lack of sustained capital investment is widely recognized as a main factor in the agricultural stagnation and the lack of sustained growth. The problem is not new. Since 1949, agriculture has almost always received a small share of central capital expenditures. The trend, however, has worsened since the beginning of the reforms. Official statistics clearly show that central level investment in agriculture has declined significantly from the beginning of the 1980s. In 1980, for example, it constituted over 9 percent of total investments; by 1988 it was only 3 percent of total investments (see figure 7–4).[37]

The center's strategy has been to shift the burden of aiding agriculture to the localities. The persistence of this thinking is evident in a recent Ministry of Agriculture study that points to the great increase of collective funds at the local level and advocates the use of these funds as the solution to agricultural stagnation.[38] The problem, as suggested above, is the increasing failure of localities to follow the center's wishes.

The local governments' rationale for decreasing investment in agriculture is similar to individual peasants' rationale: agriculture is

FIGURE 7–4

AGRICULTURAL INVESTMENT AS PERCENTAGE OF TOTAL INVESTMENT IN CHINA, 1952–1991

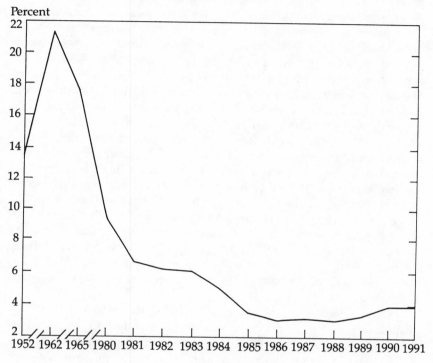

SOURCE: *Nong Ye Nian Jian* (Agriculture yearbook), 1992, p. 9; *Zhong Guo Tong Ji Nian Jian* (Chinese statistical yearbook), 1992, p. 158.

the least effective use of existing capital; it produces the least return, especially in grain production. The bottom line is that agriculture, in sharp contrast to rural industry, generates almost no direct income for local governments.[39] Unlike the land, which also belongs to the collective, those factories that are contracted out to individuals to manage pay rent as well as various fees and taxes to the local authorities. The term "cash registers" of local governments sums up nicely the relationship of local governments to their rural enterprises.[40]

Whenever possible, local authorities have invested, not surprisingly, in the further development of rural enterprises. Until the latter half of 1988, this did not create major problems. The center expected the localities to invest in agriculture, but took no direct actions that would channel funds from industry to agriculture. The localities merely were encouraged to develop agriculture and use those funds to support agriculture under various policies such as "using industry to support agriculture." The situation changed dramatically in the latter half of 1988. The central state proclaimed that more funds should be allocated for procurements, in particular, and for the agricultural sector, in general. It widely publicized its decision that the key task of 1988 and 1989 was to stabilize agriculture and ensure that funds be made available to pay the peasants. This was part of a general retrenchment program to slow inflation but, more specifically, was a policy to deal with the discontent over the lack of payment and the consequent drop in grain production and sales. The central authorities knew that the IOUs had to be dealt with immediately and resolutely. But, unlike previous announcements that more support should be given to agriculture, this time the state took steps to ensure that more funds would be earmarked for this purpose. It did not simply leave it to the localities. The state cut loans to other sectors of the rural economy to free funds in this period of fiscal austerity. The chosen target was the rural enterprises. Extra funds were allocated for procurements, while credit to the rural industrial sector was severely curtailed.

One outcome of the conflict between the center wanting to reallocate credit to agriculture and procurements and the localities needing to protect their local enterprises was the phenomenon of IOUs.[41] The local grain bureaus are expected to pay peasants for their grain sales. The grain bureaus get their money from the local agricultural banks. The problem is that the local banks do not always have the funds on hand. Money earmarked for agricultural procurement is spent elsewhere, namely, given as loans to rural enterprises, and cannot be recalled in time for the procurement.[42]

The practice is not sanctioned, but, from the perspective of the local banks and local officials, to use these procurement funds makes economic sense. Local governments want and need to keep rural industry going and developing because it is a major source of tax revenue and the major source from which the local government can extract income. In times of fiscal austerity, it is imperative for local government officials to use whatever funds are available for the development of income-generating enterprises. Unfortunately, support for agriculture continues to fall victim to this conflict of interest.

The Costs of "Modernization"

The future of the agricultural sector depends on whether China will be willing to pay the political and economic costs of complete and successful reform. Many of the problems I have described require that the leadership make difficult political as well as economic choices that will threaten to undermine the very essence of a socialist system. The question is whether the leadership can go beyond partial reform to implement far-reaching systemic changes. Many of the problems plaguing the agricultural sector are due to the partial nature of the reforms, that is, to China's inability or unwillingness to get out from between the plan and the market.[43]

Price Reform. The dilemma that the Chinese leadership faces with regard to procurement prices is one of the best examples of this. The obvious solution would be to raise the procurement price for grain. But such a solution assumes that consumer prices for grain would also be raised to absorb the new costs of procurement. This is, of course, where China is stalled and where a political decision will have to be made.

Price reform (the prices of grain being only one of many commodities affected) is badly needed but is one of the most complex reforms and carries the heaviest political price in Communist systems—the possible alienation of the mass of the population, which has been accustomed to low-priced subsidized commodities.[44] The central Chinese state is burdened by the billions of *yuan* that it spends each year on grain subsidies for urban residents who pay less for their grain than the government spends on procurement.[45] Yet, it has been very slow to institute price reforms that would eliminate the subsidies and raise the price of the basic commodity of its urban residents for fear of the political turmoil and discontent likely to follow. There were signs that Beijing was moving in the direction of price reform in 1988, but fear of political instability and discontent in the urban areas proved, in the end, stronger than the will for reform. In 1990, the state tried to ease the grain subsidy problem by reducing the rations of urban residents in certain areas of the country.[46] In 1991, a general grain price increase was instituted, but so were subsidies to urban workers. Finally, in 1992 central authorities announced that rationing would eventually be phased out. So far this has taken place only in a few areas.

Marketization. A related but discrete problem is the extent to which the central state wants to give up control of the distribution of goods to the market. There has been much talk about market reform, but if one looks closely at the operation of the economy, the market has never been allowed to play fully its heralded role of regulating supply and demand. China did deregulate the prices of certain commodities and production inputs and allowed these goods to be circulated on the free market. The problem is that it concurrently retained the rationing system and allowed it to be vulnerable to corruption.[47]

During most of the 1980s, the same items have had both market and state prices—not only in agriculture, but in the industrial sector as well. The existence of both has created a hierarchy of prices, or what the Chinese call the "double track" system for goods.[48] The state continued to offer low-priced centrally distributed inputs to protect state enterprises and to sweeten the contracting system in agriculture. But doing so undermined the state's attempts to let the market play an increasing role in the distribution of these same inputs. The state continued to buy at the low state-set prices the same inputs that were being sold on the open market at higher prices.

Moreover, the existence of both plan and market has become a source of corruption, a problem that plagues the system. Those charged with the distribution of goods or the coupons needed to redeem goods are given a valuable resource with which to trade favors or profit. The goods from the central distribution system are sold on the market at high market prices, while the shelves of the state supply and marketing cooperative where peasants are supposed to get their rationed goods are empty.[49] Peasants receive coupons for their centrally allocated fertilizer or diesel fuel, but when they go to the sales and marketing cooperative to redeem their coupons, they are told that supplies have run out.

The costs of inputs, which determine profit margins, depend on how one gets inputs, which in China is often translated as who one knows in the system, that is, *guanxi*.[50] The situation has only gotten worse since the early days of the contract system. Low-priced inputs remain in short supply, and the list of inputs affected is growing.[51] The market has become not the first but the last choice for the procurement of inputs. The market has become, in practice, the last alternative when all other avenues for procuring the low-priced, rationed goods have been exhausted, and getting negotiated price goods that are supplied by the state is often hopeless. Studies show that in 1988, after ten years of reform, peasants buy only 30 percent to 40 percent of their inputs on the open market.[52] The amounts now are much lower.

In 1989, in the wake of the worsening situation in the distribution of inputs, the Central Committee and the State Council issued a directive that recentralized distribution of certain goods to the supply and marketing cooperatives. This response to the input problem suggests that the more conservative elements within the leadership, at least for the time being, had won the day. This, however, did not resolve the problem: Nonlicensed agents are still managing to get and distribute supplies of agricultural inputs.[53] Peasants continue to face shortages and high prices in the early 1990s.

Property Rights. The means of production is another problem fraught with political implications. Deng Xiaoping and the economic reformers went to great lengths to stress that the contracting system would not change the socialist nature of the system. They insisted that the peasants' relation to the means of production was the same: it was still collective ownership. Individual peasants were only leasing the land from the collective. This may be good from an ideological standpoint, but in practice causes problems. The lack of ownership of the means of production increasingly is seen as the root of why peasants fail to invest in their land. The contracts were extended to at least fifteen years, but even so the fact remains that the land is not theirs; it can be taken away at a moment's notice. Recent developments suggest that the time has come for the leadership to rethink whether the contracting system, as it currently exists, should be retained in the 1990s.

The once-lauded solution to the incentive problem, the land-contracting system, has become a source of peasant discontent and seems increasingly unviable. The system in itself does not ensure increases in production, as mentioned above. The case could be made that the system has become a hindrance to increases in production. The problems are complex and differ in different areas of China. In the most industrialized areas, it was problematic almost from the beginning. In those areas, peasants were content to leave farming and work in the rapidly developing and lucrative factory jobs. The land was turned over to specialized farmers or to those who work the land for the collective. Others who decided to keep their land or were forced to accept responsibility for a piece of land hired poorer peasants to work the land, or, in some cases, left their fields fallow if they earned enough from other occupations to buy grain on the free market.

The major problem with the system as it exists in most of China, where peasants still work the land, is too many peasants and too little land. The plots assigned to a household are extremely small and scattered. Studies show that an average family has about nine scattered plots. This problem has resulted from increasing population pressure and the constant need to reallocate land contracts as households change size.[54] The small size of the plots prevents the use of mechanization, which most would define as the modernization of agricultural production.

The land-contracting system has become a particular source of anxiety in the wake of the Tiananmen crackdown in 1989. This is one of the most salient effects of the crackdown on democracy. Peasants again have become increasingly nervous, fearing that the hard-liners will pull back from reform and recollectivize agriculture. Rampant rumors that production will be recollectivized have further inclined peasants to stop investing in their land.

The solution to the land problem, like other solutions discussed in this chapter, encompasses a significant political component. China's leaders must accept the fact that the structure of China's rural economy is changing. Fewer and fewer people will be engaged in the production of grain, especially because of the way the incentive system is structured. The trend toward rural industrialization is unlikely to be reversed. Attacking individual entrepreneurs and clipping the growth of rural enterprises will not ensure the growth of agriculture in the long run. The continued growth of the nonstate sector, especially the rural enterprises (in spite of the immediate post-Tiananmen cutbacks), raises the question whether it even works in the short run.[55] China's countryside is moving toward diversity, toward a modern rural economy. Some of China's leaders, however, seem intent on keeping peasants in their traditional status.

It is imperative that China's leaders rethink whether expecting all rural households to work the land, grow grain, and sell grain to the state is feasible. The transition to a modern economy would probably be easier if the central state abandoned the idea that all areas must be grain-sufficient. Grain production should not nor need not be the prime occupation of all rural residents in China.

If China is willing to adopt a new view of what the rural economy should look like, then it can choose one of two courses to deal with the land problem. The less radical, more realistic approach to China's current land-contracting system is to allow a smaller number of peasants to grow the grain for the rest of society. This approach would be the equivalent of the grain-specialized households that exist in the most industrialized villages in China.[56] In Da Qiuzhuang outside Tianjin, for example, which is one of the richest villages in all of China, nine peasants produce enough grain for the entire village and enough to sell large amounts to the state, while the other peasants work in the villages' many rural industries. Because these peasants are engaging in economies of scale and have the support of the local community, which subsidizes various costs, they make a profitable living growing grain.[57] This is not an isolated example. Other villages that are the most industrially developed and, therefore, the wealthiest often have few, if any, peasants engaged in agricultural production. In these situations, directly investing and subsidizing those in agriculture is in the interests of the local authorities.

This course of action would dramatically change the structure of the rural economy and the relationship of individual households to the major means of production. It would not necessarily threaten, however, what can loosely be called the collective or socialist nature of rural villages, that is, the redistribution of income.[58] Redistribution of income continues and, if anything, has increased in those villages that have gone the route of industrialization and specialized farmers. These are the villages that have the best welfare benefits, the best collective services, and the highest standard of living.

There are indications that the state wants to move in this direction. Some areas have tried to concentrate the size of holdings and expand the number of large-scale farms to achieve an economy of scale.[59] The problem in the wake of the Tiananmen crackdown was that these indications were fuel for the recollectivization rumors. In one county that tried to move to economy-of-scale farming, a special office had to be set up to resolve land-related problems, including concerted efforts to calm peasant anxiety over recollectivization.[60]

Not all villages have the resources to provide employment for the bulk of the population, however, nor the resources to have only a few engage in profitable large-scale grain production and subsidize those that choose to do agriculture. In the meantime, the regime is trying to help peasants by having local governments increase services to the peasants through the unified management system or what it calls the double guarantee contracts.[61] Again, it seems likely that only the well-managed and already wealthy villages will be able to provide the needed services.

The more radical step is for China to institute private ownership of land, which would require a fundamental redefinition of the basic principles that underlie China's system. China would be forced to admit that the means of production is not the defining characteristic of its political and social system. Although there has been some movement in that direction, there are great reservations about undertaking such a step, particularly given the pre-1949 experience. The state needs to protect against land speculation and provide the incentives that come with private ownership to invest in one's own property.

A note of caution. Privatization of land ownership would alleviate fears about the responsibility system. Privatization will encourage them to invest in their property, but will *not* take care of the larger incentive problem. The central state still must find a way to pay peasants more for grain and make it a profitable enterprise for those who remain in agriculture. The leadership can continue to rely on additional mandatory quotas to obtain more grain from the peasants,[62] but the political costs are likely to increase. Increasing procurements will alienate not only peasants, but local governments that are short of cash.[63] The central state must ensure that increased investment is made in the rural infrastructure. That will require the center either to intervene directly with substantially larger investments in the agricultural sector or to devise incentives to ensure that local governments will themselves invest in agricultural production.

Prospects

China will not likely suffer an agricultural crisis, but the prospects for Chinese agriculture in the 1990s are not good if China continues on its present course. The system can probably continue to limp along, but advances will not be made. The state can continue to rely on administrative measures to get larger grain sales from the countryside; but the costs, especially the political ones, will become increasingly high. Contrary to popular press reports, peasant attitudes toward the center's agricultural policies are increasingly those of discontent. The discontent of local officials, whose interests have been hurt by the center's demand for more procurements and curbs on rural industry under the recent retrenchment policy, is perhaps more worrisome for the center in the long run. The reported rebellion of provincial officials at a meeting in Beijing over attempts to take more local revenues may indicate a growing rift between the center and the localities.

The center continues to dictate economic policies that directly affect the localities' abilities to develop their own local economies, but it now expects localities to pay for these policies, even if they go against local interests. The IOUs and other forms of creative financing localities resorted to during the retrenchment and later in the 1990s reveal the widening gap between the interests of the central state and local levels of Chinese government.[64]

This conflict has contributed to peasant discontent. To squeeze credit and curb revenue-generating rural industry have caused local cadres to press local peasants for additional funds. This underlies much of the increasing peasant burdens.[65] Local officials are "investing" in agriculture by collecting fees and levying various surcharges on peasants.

What will be the future form of agricultural production? Some reports suggest that conservatives, such as Chen Yun, are on the rise.[66] But developments in China's rural economy suggest that Deng's successor will have difficulty rolling back the reforms and reinstating central planning. Large-scale farms may be developed, village and township governments may be pressed into providing more services to individual households—the spread of unified management or "double contracting." But peasants or the local officials are unlikely to return to Maoist forms of communal production that required everyone to engage in agricultural production.

China's peasants and local officials responded to Deng's initial call to develop a diversified economy. They have progressed significantly, taken every opportunity to develop a modern rural economy, and relied on rural industrialization to generate wealth and absorb the surplus labor resulting from decollectivization. Now, to modernize its agricultural sector, China's leadership must relinquish its desire to keep the countryside in the traditional subordinate role of producing grain only for the urban areas.

8

The Retreat to Central Planning in China after Tiananmen

Ellen Salem

Confronted with an economy in shambles, increasingly obdurate economic regionalism, massive unemployment, and the ever-present specter of social instability, China's leadership in the year and a half after Tiananmen chose to revive outdated policies to deal with the challenges of a new era.

Symbolic of that retreat to the past was a reliance on slogans to prompt the populace to follow the party line, a hallmark of the Mao years. There was a new twist, however. Rather than follow the lead of the self-sacrificing Lei Feng of pre–Cultural Revolution fame—or fabrication as many claim—industrial workers were exhorted to find their inspiration to produce more steel in the new heroes of the Chinese Revolution: the athletes who won gold medals at the Asian Games. "Seeing our athletes winning medal after gold medal, inspires our workers," an employee at the Anyang Steel Mill told television viewers. "While the athletes compete in the games, our workers compete at the furnaces, winning gold medals through achieving higher output."[1]

The return to the tried, but hardly true, was accompanied by an unexpectedly strong resurgence of economic regionalism. Local rights replaced political reform as the rallying cry, particularly in the southern provinces. Indeed, the repeated postponements of the Seventh Plenum of the Central Committee appeared to be due as much to the struggle between those who ascribed to Chen Yun's "bird cage" economics and those who advocated quickened moves toward a market economy as to the efforts by the provinces to stave off interference from the center, primarily in the form of increased taxes.

Nonetheless, the Eighth Five-Year Plan (1991–1995), rubber stamped at the Party Congress on December 25, 1991, advocated strengthening the mechanisms of central planning, or, in the words of Prime Minister Li Peng, China will stick to a program to "cure and restructure" the economy—Li-speak for recentralization. Market-oriented reforms, and more specifically price reform, were ruled out for the while by Li on grounds that "local price adjustments are often related to the people's livelihood directly and must be controlled strictly." As a sop to the more liberal, market forces and central planning were to be "synthesized." This course of action would serve only to exacerbate the country's economic and social problems.[2]

All efforts were to be made to rescue the state industrial sector, which, funded by ever-increasing state subsidies and loans, produces a very high percentage of unsalable goods, setting the stage for another round of hyperinflation. By propping up the state sector, China put in place a policy of survival of the unfit and inhibiting the development of the institutions needed for a market system to function: namely, competition, further price liberalization, and property rights.[3]

At the same time, the general regulatory environment was tightened to bolster the authority of the state over the provincial economies. If not relaxed, this move would be counterproductive. To retain a degree of local autonomy and prevent the center from bankrupting the localities, provincial, regional, and village authorities would have to devise increasingly ingenious ploys to keep wealth at home. In the process, they would strengthen the economic satrapies that are coming to dominate the economic map of China.[4]

In sum, immediately after Tiananmen China again chose to rule out genuine economic reform. If continued, such a course could lead only to instability, greater inequalities in the supply-demand equation, and the intensification of the beggar-thy-neighbor policy that has long characterized periods of political and economic disintegration.

To compound the problem, a change in leadership was imminent. A prolonged leadership crisis could plunge China into an economic and political abyss. The paralysis in decision making that followed Tiananmen might therefore recur, and the center's hold on the provinces could become increasingly tenuous—a recipe for years of economic chaos.

The Road to Retreat

Since the mid-1980s, China's attempts to reform its economy have suffered from a glutton's illusion: that you can have your cake and eat it too. This illusion culminated in the Tiananmen massacre— fundamentally a result of the pressure for political reform and the creation of competing, but complementary, centers of power generated by the economic changes of the open-door policy. Once again, China's leadership refused to come to terms with the truism that lasting economic and political reform go hand in hand.

The response was a temporary retreat to a command economy, accompanied by tightening of political control. Stability, not economic reform, determined all policy decisions.

The Challenge of Tiananmen. To understand the rationale behind China's political and economic policies, we must examine the conflicts that climaxed in the Tiananmen massacre. In his address to the People's Liberation Army (PLA) in the wake of June 4, Deng Xiaoping remarked that "what had happened was bound to have happened." It was far better, he commented, that the problem had come to the fore so that the situation could be attacked sooner rather than later.[5]

The "situation" mentioned by Deng was not just the challenge to the Chinese Communist party posed by the students demonstrating in the capital's central square. Rather, he was saying that the "open door policy" and economic liberalization had spawned alternative centers of power. Equally pernicious was that democracy, a deviant ideology, was threatening the primacy of the Communist party.

The Communist party, Deng recognized, had ceased to be the sole possessor and dispenser of wealth and power. Membership in the party was no longer seen as the only means of economic advancement. The manager of a prosperous collective was not necessarily a cadre. In many a small town, particularly in the coastal regions, party officials had become increasingly prone to collude with local businessmen to enhance their influence and would work in tandem with the entrepreneur to obtain access to foreign exchange and foreign travel. Consequently, the allegiance of many cadre to the center diminished and local party officials were often heavily involved in protecting local interests at the expense of Beijing.[6]

Equally disturbing, sought-after jobs were in the marketplace—and particularly foreign joint ventures—and party membership was fast losing its appeal. This is hardly surprising, since the party itself was viewed as venal, with cadre corruption the norm and ideology proven to be a litany of meaningless phrases. It was all too clear to the leadership in Beijing that for them to retain power, only a purge, followed by a tightening of the power of the center, would suffice.

The Response to Tiananmen. A year before the Tiananmen massacre, the party's general secretary, Zhao Ziyang, had told the party leadership that the implementation of price reform—which he strongly advocated—could well require the declaration of martial law. The old guard would have none of this and began a piecemeal campaign to derail the reforms that had been initiated under Zhao's aegis.

Tiananmen gave the conservatives the excuse they were looking for to make a head-on assault on economic and political reform. The effort to rectify the "situation" resulted in an almost total, if temporary, dismantling of the political prerequisites for the shift from a command economy to a market economy. Such a change in economic policy should have required that the party

- give up running the economy and end its arbitrary exercise of political power
- permit the selection of leaders mainly on the basis of merit rather than party connections
- loosen control on the individual to allow the operation of a labor market to encourage individual entrepreneurial initiative

Zhao had set in motion all these reforms. They were taken up most readily in those provinces where local interests did not have to contend with the overwhelming power of the state industrial enterprises, particularly coastal Guangdong, Zhejiang, and Jiangsu. Not coincidentally, growth rates in these provinces had far surpassed the national average in the years since the initiation of the open-door policy in 1978.[7]

On the political front, Zhao had instigated changes that dovetailed with the economic reforms and were designed to hasten the implementation of a market economy. These were the separation of the functions of party and government; the removal of the party from the direct management of state-owned firms; the implementation of the responsibility system under which all firms, whether in the state, collective, or private sectors, were responsible for their own profits and losses; the institution of a bankruptcy law; and the abolition of the iron rice bowl, or lifetime guaranteed employment.

But the Fifth Plenum, held in October 1989, put the nails in the coffin of economic and political reform. Essentially, the programs espoused were designed to brook no interference in the party's efforts to regain ground lost under the Zhao regime.

First and foremost, the plenum legislated to halt the movement toward price reform. A recentralization of power and authority was stressed, while a shift from the "regional inclination policy," or one that gave special privileges to the special economic zones and the coastal provinces, was replaced by the "industrial inclination policy." In effect, the state industrial sector was accorded highly preferential treatment, at the expense of the collective and private sectors, in terms of cash and raw materials. A decision was also made to abolish provincial authority to approve significant investment, while the provinces were required to increase their contributions to Beijing. Finally, there was a reemphasis on increasing agricultural production. "Comprehensive" agricultural programs, which would require more state control of the agricultural sector, were propounded.[8]

Digging Up the Foundations. Events have borne witness to the deleterious effect of these dictates. The separation of party and government both in the bureaucracy and on the factory floor, which was called for by Deng and implemented as much as possible by Zhao, was reversed after Tiananmen. Zhao, moreover, was dubbed a subversive for his efforts.[9]

Political concerns, not economic concerns, determined all government policy. Under the guise of central planning, the party now attempted to run the economy. Zhao's think tanks were either disbanded or downgraded. The dynamic and productive tension that existed when the conservatives, reformers, and radicals were slugging it out in print, public forums, and behind closed doors was no more.

The party once again became more arbitrary and dogmatic, while systematic efforts to control intellectual life were undertaken. Concomitant to this, political criteria once again took precedence over competence, and classes in political indoctrination were reintroduced.

In the economic sphere, the management responsibility system was modified. The factory director once again came under the thumb of the party representative and "democratic management"—a euphemism for party trade union control—was on the rise again. In addition, the cornerstone of the management responsibility system, that enterprises should be responsible for their own profits and losses, was no more, if only for a while. The bankruptcy law, in practice, became a dead letter, with the state bailing out unprofitable state-owned enterprises.[10]

Ironically, the worst of the Zhao regime was retained wherein major economic decisions were made without any thought of the broader ramifications of specific policies. Under Zhao, this knee-jerk approach to strategic planning all too often resulted from reckless enthusiasm. In contrast, decision making after Tiananmen was prompted by fear. The leadership was acutely aware that it had lost the mandate of Heaven. Economic decisions, then, were aimed at bolstering political power and, as much as possible, buying off the populace, principally through subsidies to the state industrial sector. In addition, there was a general perception that a major change in the leadership would occur once Deng Xiaoping died. As a result, many economists were loath to stick their necks out for fear of offending the new—and as yet unidentified—lineup. On the one hand, cosmetic changes for fundamental structural defects in the state sector were all the vogue. On the other hand, a grandiose and costly attempt to remake the economic map of China, with Shanghai as the linchpin, began.[11]

To complicate the situation, the government lacked both the managerial skills and the authority at the local level to implement recentralization. Even its ability to deflate or inflate the economy selectively by printing money was in doubt.

A story carried in the official *People's Daily* illustrates this dearth of management skill and local influence. According to the paper, a certain province received renminbi (Rmb) 480 million from the central government to come to the rescue of 18 bankrupt large and medium-scale state enterprises. But once the funds were in the hands of local officials, the money was given to 168 large, medium, and small enterprises. As a result, the 18 enterprises selected by the central government were left with only Rmb 75.6 million to share among themselves.[12]

From Bad to Worse

"China can be viewed as an economy in cold storage" or so said the American Central Intelligence Agency in its annual assessment of the Chinese economy. According to the report entitled "The Chinese Economy in 1989 and 1990: Trying to Revive Growth While Maintaining Social Stability," by the end of 1989 nearly two-thirds of China's urban factories were closed or operating below capacity, while more than a million locally run enterprises were shut down as a result of the austerity program. In addition, urban unemployment was at its highest in more than a decade. These economic problems threatened the country's social stability.[13]

In essence, China embarked on a path that could increase the unpredictability and shorten the periods between abrupt changes in economic policy. This situation evolved because the austerity program did not redirect funds to infrastructural development, nor did it address the problem of the debt-ridden state industrial sector. Massive inequalities between supply and demand remained. Reinflation then got under way, and before long China could yet again have to cope with hyperinflation in a deteriorating economic, social, and political environment.

Profligate Austerity. Conventional wisdom in Hong Kong in the early 1990s held that China's austerity program had come to an end, that Western economic sanctions fostered the emergence of a kinder, gentler China, and that the reemphasis on the open-door policy would, in time, offer highly profitable opportunities for the foreign investor. These assumptions could turn out to be wishful thinking. The austerity program—a misnomer if ever there was one—was conceded by the Chinese to be a failure. China in 1991 was in the throes of an economic crisis. For the first time since 1978, real rural incomes declined. Unemployment, in a country where the iron rice bowl is sacrosanct, was nearing 20 percent, not including the countless numbers thrown out of work by the closure of rural factories throughout China. More important, many of these rural workers could no longer return to the fields since an improvement in agricultural techniques rendered their labor unnecessary.[14]

At the end of 1990, the economy as a whole had been in recession for almost a year, despite marginal gains in productivity toward the end of the year. Deficit spending and huge subsidies to the state industrial sector beggared the central government. In an effort to remedy the situation and preserve domestic stability, a regime that has lost the mandate of Heaven embraced an economic program that would suffer sudden policy fluctuations for the foreseeable future.[15]

Band-Aids for Fractures. China's 1989–1991 austerity program, it must be emphasized, accomplished only two of its six stated aims. It reduced inflation and, to a degree, reinstated rigid central planning. But the underlying goal of the program was to address the inequalities in supply and demand that were, in the main, exacerbated by a woefully inadequate physical infrastructure. Funds that were to have been spent on infrastructure instead increased subsidies to the state industrial sector and urban centers to stave off the threat of social instability.[16] The cancellation of soft loans that followed the Tiananmen massacre further cut spending on infrastructure, while foreign investment plummeted as well. At the same time, price reform and the chance to step toward a market economy became history.

Ominous Statistics. Efforts to stimulate the economy, which started at the beginning of 1990, initially met with scant success. To meet the targeted 6 percent annual growth in industrial production, the economy would have had to have grown 8 percent in the last quarter of the year—a task of Herculean proportions. Consider the following. In the first seven months of 1990, industrial output edged ahead by a mere 2 percent to Rmb 763 billion, with foreign-funded as well as rural enterprises accounting for much of the increase. State-owned enterprises continued to stand still, just as the collectively owned enterprises did. In contrast, rural industries grew by 6 percent, while foreign-funded and private firms registered an impressive 39 percent rise over the same period in 1989.

Alarmed at these statistics, the government pumped massive infusions of cash into the economy. As a result, those who received the least performed the best. In the first ten months of 1990, industrial output gained 4.1 percent over the same period in 1989. Industrial output by state-owned enterprises, however, rose a mere 1.4 percent, while collectively owned enterprises recorded a surprisingly high increase of 8.5 percent. Foreign-funded enterprises and private firms were the star performers, with production up 44.7 percent over the same period in 1989.

Early in September 1990, Zou Jiahua, the head of the State Planning Commission, said that the number of loss-making state-owned enterprises was on the rise—and now comprised 34 percent of the total—and these could survive only with the help of the state. In the first seven months of 1990, total losses by state-owned enterprises doubled. As a result, state revenue, most of which was derived from taxes on state-owned enterprises, was only marginally better than the same period in 1989, far below the targeted growth of 10 percent set in the central government's budget for 1990. Moreover, the enterprises owed the state Rmb 11 billion in tax for the first six months of 1990, nearly double the figure at the beginning of the year.

These numbers tell of a drop in the efficiency of the state-owned industrial sector, which made up an overwhelming proportion of the country's industrial output. Thus the austerity program failed in one of its major goals, to improve industrial efficiency. Zou Jiahua also noted that progress toward yet another goal of the program—to adjust the country's industrial structure—"is slow."[17]

All things considered, the first two years of the Eighth Five-Year Plan, with its emphasis on the state sector, were going against the tide. Those sectors where competition was given free rein performed the best. Indeed, consistent encouragement of the nonstate sector, accompanied by a quickening of the pace of price reform, would be the optimum choice of a government once again faced with the specter of hyperinflation and massive unemployment. That is, indeed, what happened after 1991.

Survival of the Unfit. The economic structure of China had undergone substantial changes since 1978. At the end of 1989, the state industrial sector accounted for 56 percent of total industrial output value compared with 78 percent in 1978. By the same token, government-run commerce accounted for 39 percent of 1989 gross retail sales, down from 55 percent in 1978. In part, this shift was the result of the collapse of the people's communes and the establishment of the household contract system, which led to an improvement in agricultural productivity (the profit motive, of course) and the movement of the surplus agricultural labor force into rural industry.

By the end of 1989, there were 1.5 million township enterprises, accounting for 28 percent of gross industrial production in 1989. In the cities, moreover, small government-owned enterprises were turned into collectively run enterprises. These accounted for 36 percent of total industrial output, a 13 percent rise over 1978. In addition, collectively run enterprises accounted for 33 percent of total retail sales in 1989. At the same time, the private sector increased in importance. In total output, the private sector's contribution to total output value leaped from nothing in 1978 to 5 percent in 1989. By June 1990, the number of private enterprises had risen to 88,636 and had created 1.4 million jobs.

On the whole, rural industry, township enterprises, and the private sector succeeded with little help from the central government and have demonstrated remarkable entrepreneurial skills. More important, they quickly grasped a major reality of the market place: to survive, the business must produce goods that the market wants. The state sector, in contrast, led a charmed life, with the government footing the ever-mounting bill. In 1989, the government spent an estimated Rmb 60 billion subsidizing loss-making enterprises, or about 20 percent of state revenue. In the first half of 1990, government expenditure—almost all of it to subsidize state enterprises—rose 16.4 percent against a budgeted 9.7 percent rise, while the enterprises owed the state Rmb 10.8 billion in taxes.

Even with this massive influx of funds, 60 percent of production ends up in warehouses. Moreover, about 30 million state factory workers, or one-third of the state factory work force, were redundant. Added to that, an estimated one in three of all state-owned factories was operating in the red.[18] Yet, China could ill afford to let these enterprises fail: the cost would be in social stability. In addition, the leadership's tenuous control of the provinces would be further eroded. Thus, the government had no choice but to pour funds down a bottomless pit if it wanted to preserve stability and maintain itself in power. To a certain degree, the state enterprises will continue to toe the official line, since Beijing foots the bills.

Inflation Down, but Not for Long. In August 1990, China's inflation fell to its lowest level of the year, while consumer demand showed some signs of revival. According to the State Statistical Bureau, prices in thirty-five cities rose 2.7 percent in August 1990 over August 1989. Partly as a result of a deluge of credit, retail sales in August rose 1.9 percent from a year earlier. From January through August, however, retail sales totaled Rmb 534 billion, roughly on a par with the same period in 1989. Total industrial production for the same period inched up a mere 2 percent, despite efforts to stimulate the economy.

This situation threw the authorities into something of a tailspin. They began efforts to prime the pump more vigorously, while simultaneously increasing the price of some commodities: specificially sugar, cotton goods, and some household products. In October 1990, for example, industrial output surged to 12.7 percent, fueled by state credits. By November, domestic prices rose 5.3 percent over the same month in 1989. In thirty-five cities, however, fuel prices jumped by 50 percent over the same period, and services rose by 18 percent. In addition, retail sales broke out of their long period of sluggishness and increased by 10.3 percent. Loans to ailing industries during the year through November surged, from Rmb 102 billion ($19.7 billion in U.S. dollars) in 1989 to Rmb 248.6 billion ($47.8 billion in U.S. dollars).

This pump priming was slated to continue under the Eighth Five-Year Plan. Add to this the fact that Rmb 663 billion ($127.5 billion U.S. dollars)—the equivalent of one-half of 1989's national income—was held in savings deposits. Moreover, one presumes that substantial funds were secreted in safe-deposit boxes, since savings accounts are taxed, to say nothing of being stashed away under the proverbial pillow. Should the populace be spooked by fears of hyperinflation, as it was in 1988, and withdraws its funds from the banks, runaway inflation would be all but inevitable. (Fear of instability at the top prompted many an individual to save for a rainy day.)

At mid-1990, Wang Bingquan, state counselor and minister of finance, said that the national financial situation was still fairly grim and that it would be necessary to tighten both financing practices and credit. Economists at the State Council Development Research Centre expected total lending in 1990 to exceed Rmb 200 billion.[19]

Clearly, the People's Bank of China decided that it would pay no heed to the warning of the minister of finance. According to the bank's planning director, the government planned to offset the surge in loans by printing money. About Rmb 40 billion was printed in 1990, or more than double that printed the year before.[20]

Compounding the problem, Beijing lost its grip on the fiscal reins. First of all, the contract responsibility system, whereby enterprises agree to hand over a specified amount to Beijing, meant that those enterprises that did well did not hand over an increased percentage of their profits: conversely, those that were in the red simply did not pay taxes. In addition, local government agents were responsible for collecting 70 percent of China's tax revenue. According to the World Bank, "The delegation to local governments of the responsibility for tax administration . . . has put local governments in the position of setting tax policy. . . . There are strong forces at work in the decentralised fiscal system against collecting tax revenues, particularly those that must be shared with the centre at a high rate."

To make matters worse, corruption was endemic, tax evasion was a national sport, and tax collectors were public enemy number one to many peasants. (One unfortunate tax collector was beaten to death in 1989.) Beijing could do little to turn the situation around without the active assistance of the localities. Granted, their refusal to pay up was partly attributable to greed, but local officials also needed funds to take care of the local populace, hard hit by unemployment, to ensure a modicum of social stability.

Too Many People, Too Few Jobs. Most threatening to social stability was the rapid rise in unemployment. During 1992–1996, China's already oversaturated labor market was expected to be flooded with 92 million new workers as the population comes of age, about 76 million of whom were in the countryside. Already, China's employment outlook was at its bleakest since 1949, the year of the Communist takeover. The new peak, according to the Chinese press, "will hit our country as job opportunities are narrowing."[21]

Figures on unemployment or "those waiting for jobs" varied widely. For 1991, China had a labor force of an estimated 543 million, of which 60 percent were employed in the agricultural sector.[22] The New China News Agency (NCNA) said that out of China's 1.1 billion population, about 11 million were unemployed in the urban areas, up by 0.5 million from 1989. Some Chinese economists, however, believed that these figures grossly understated reality and posited that joblessness was anywhere between 20 million and 30 million in the cities and up to 120 million in the countryside.[23] These figures appeared to be more accurate than those released by the NCNA, since nearly two-thirds of all urban factories were closed or operating below capacity at year-end 1989. In addition, more than a million locally run enterprises, primarily in the countryside, were shut down, throwing some 3 million out of work.[24]

This wide-scale forced closure resulted from the government's belief that the rural enterprises were profiting at the expense of the state sector by diverting scarce resources to themselves. Rural enterprises were also blamed for increasing inflation, promoting corruption, and evading taxes, as were private enterprises. The rural areas had to absorb one-third more workers who were required to work the land, as well as millions of construction workers sent back to the countryside since the construction boom was halted. Many of these newly unemployed swelled the ranks of the some 70 million "floating population," or itinerant workers.

In a striking reversal of policy, plans were afoot to revamp China's rural industries, of which about 800,000 were closed or forced out of business in the wake of Tiananmen. According to the *China Daily*, "Leading government planners have stressed that enormous economic and social benefits would be created by absorbing rural surplus labour, estimated at 100m, into developing the township's industrial sector." Consistency was hardly a hallmark of Chinese economic planning.[25]

Clearly, the authorities had a time bomb on their hands. The growing pool of idle workers led to an increase in crime, and municipal authorities were very hard pressed to deal with the problem. They were already overburdened by the necessity to provide housing, health care, and food for the unemployed.

Beggar Thy Neighbor. Provincial and local protectionism in China was reborn with the declaration of the open-door policy in 1978. The first wave of protectionism occurred in 1980–1981, when provinces started to develop their own processing industries. The second took place between 1985 and 1988, with provinces competing—sometimes with the aid of arms and military vehicles—for scarce raw materials and foreign exchange export earnings.

Unlike the first two waves, the post-1989 wave was taking place during economic downturn, flagging markets, and tightened political control. The combination of old and new barriers was frustrating government attempts to redirect resources to state factories and prompting the surreptitious establishment of small, inefficient factories. The case of cotton was a good example. All cotton was supposed to be sold to the state. In fact, in 1990, the state managed to control only 60 percent of production. What happened was that the cotton-producing areas set up their own mills, with the compliance of local officials. This phenomenon of setting up local factories in commodity-producing areas, which began in 1985, was a direct result of the distorted price system that favors processed goods over commodities.

New types of market barriers were emerging as well. These

barriers were set up through a set of administrative and economic schemes and well-concealed tricks. Local governments manipulated prices and provided sales commissions. They also raised taxes, imposed extra levies or higher retail prices, and lowered the gross margin rates of sales departments. Finally, they gave orders to banks' credit departments.

In many instances, these barriers were a response to Beijing's insistence that priority be given to medium- and large-scale state industries. Local officials had to pay heed to the central government, but at the same time they could not allow small local industries to go under since these industries played an important role in providing employment and constituted a significant source of tax revenue, especially at the county and village level.[26] These practices combined to prevent the functioning of macroeconomic regulations. Likewise, they countered efforts by Beijing to restrict the money supply.

Thus, China's leadership was in no position to regain control over the country's myriad local fiefdoms. It lost the ability to institute fiscal, monetary, and many regulatory policies.

The Yellow River Chorus. Well aware that Hong Kong and Guangdong could become China's economic powerhouse after 1997, China took steps aimed at moving economic power from the south to the center of the country.[27] Political concerns were a major determinant in the decision to revive Shanghai and redirect foreign investment from Guangdong to the once thriving commercial center. The leadership believes that Hong Kong and Guangdong were bases of political subversion.

What better way to deal with this situation than to build up Shanghai and its hinterland—areas where the dictates of the central government generally held more sway? At the same time, this effort to redirect investment to the center would, to some degree, assuage the poorer central provinces, since the resuscitation of Shanghai through the development of the Pudong economic zone was the linchpin of a plan to boost the economies of central and north China.[28]

Moves in this direction included the abolition of special treatment for the special economic zones (SEZs). In theory, Beijing was to scrap all export subsidies to the regional governments but would allow them to retain 80 percent of their export earnings. This plan would put the SEZs on equal footing with export firms throughout China, with one important difference. The SEZs would not receive any new incentives from Beijing in the coming years and would have to rely on their own resources for future economic development. Moreover, Guangdong would have to foot some of the bill—in the form of additional taxes—for the development of Pudong.[29]

There was scant likelihood, however, that this grandiose scheme for a renaissance in Shanghai would come to fruition easily. Investment incentives were no better than those offered by the country's five special economic zones. In point of fact, the announcement of the incentives provoked little initial enthusiasm among foreign investors, who believe it would be difficult for Shanghai to compete with the long-established centers, primarily in Guangdong. In addition, Shanghai's transport nightmare could discourage even the most patriotic overseas Chinese investor. It could take decades to unsnarl the traffic jams on Shanghai's roads and in the ports. Pudong, on the eastern shore of the Huangpu River, was accessible only by ferry or through two narrow and congested road tunnels, although the new, high-level bridge completed in 1992, did alleviate congestion somewhat. Shanghai's dream of challenging Hong Kong and Guangdong would be a long time coming.

Dwindling Funds from Abroad. The World Bank warned that prolonged difficulties in the world economy could hamper reforms in China. The country might find itself facing problems raising overseas capital and overcoming trade barriers. Foreign investment could dwindle as well. According to a 1990 World Bank report, these developments may, in turn, hamper Beijing's willingness and ability to institute reforms. The 1991 decision by the bank to step up lending could mitigate the problem. The bank said, however, that high oil prices could undermine its efforts to cushion the shock on the world economy.[30]

In addition, in 1991 the global economy was on the verge of a global crunch coupled with rising inflation. The conflicting demands of Europe, the United States, and even Japan for increasingly scarce capital, together with the spiraling U.S. dollar, the cost of oil, and the mounting indebtedness of third world countries, collectively contributed to the credit crunch. In such an environment, China could find it difficult to get the necessary amounts of soft and commercial loans to fund development.

Foreign investment could fall off as well. After posting an average growth rate of 30 percent a year since 1980, new foreign investment contracts increased a mere 8 percent in 1989. That year, foreign investment commitments reached $5.6 billion, slightly exceeding the $5.2 billion recorded in 1988. This increase was due primarily to the boundless and ill-advised enthusiasm foreigners had for investment in China before the Tiananmen massacre. Booming investments from Taiwan in subsequent years, according to Chinese statistics, exceeded

$1 billion.[31] This figure overstated reality, however. Taiwanese investment very often consisted of fully depreciated plant and equipment, which was recorded on the books at replacement cost.

Back to the Future

The contents of the Eighth Five-Year Plan for 1991–1995 indicated that the Seventh Plenum of the Central Committee could provide the stage on which contending members of the old guard shout their last, great hurrahs. Evidence indicated archconservative Chen Yun had the edge over the more moderate Deng Xiaoping. In addition, shackles of sorts might be snapped on by the restive provincial governments.[32] Whatever the case, the direction of decision making over the next several years would be determined by the order in which the powerful veterans of the Long March retired from the scene. The longer the moderates retained their tenuous hold on power, the slower the pace of retreat from reform and the higher the probability that the Deng-era reform could weather the storm.

Indeed, however, the host of economic and social problems facing China left the leadership—whoever they may be—with little room to maneuver. Instituting full-scale price reform at this juncture would be political suicide and would almost certainly result in massive social unrest. Was China then caught in an endless cycle of boom and bust? Not necessarily. What China needed was a charismatic and effective leader who could garner popular support for a period of genuine austerity during which price reform would be implemented and infrastructural problems addressed. At the end of the Deng era, no one among the second and third generation of leaders appeared equal to the task, but that did not preclude the possibility that a suitable candidate was waiting in the wings.

More Than Mere Rhetoric. In November 1990, the Chinese press featured speeches by the members of the old guard ominously reminiscent of the rhetoric of the Cultural Revolution. In a speech printed in the official *People's Daily*, Peng Zhen, for example, waxed eloquent on the "inevitability of the fall of capitalism." In another article in the *People's Daily*, the vice-president of the Chinese Academy of Sciences praised Chen Yun's precepts as the ultimate in economic thought. Chen, the Central Advisory Commission chairman, was the "grandfather" of central planning. In yet another indication that the tide was then turning, if temporarily, against the reformers, Prime Minister Li Peng told members of a high-level academic conference that the "synthesis of state plans and market adjustment"—code words for rigid central planning—had been accepted by more and more people as the cure for China's economic ills.

Just how far the leftists were able to dominate the drafting of the Eighth Five-Year Plan was evident from an article in the *People's Daily* by Yuan Mu, the spokesman for the Chinese cabinet and the director of its research unit. The article in the party mouthpiece defended the austerity program, saying it should continue for two more years. In a preview of the Eighth Five-Year Plan, Yuan said that only a few new projects would be undertaken during the 1991–1995 period. He stressed that the development of the economy should be "persistent, stable, and coordinated." In other words, policies favored by Chen Yun should be followed.[33] The conservatives appear determined to overlook the fact that many of the elements of the austerity program that began in 1988 brought on the post-Tiananmen economic crisis.

Price controls and more administrative controls, for example, prompted the growth of regionalism, or "economic warlordism." Massive subsidies to the state industrial sector were matched by just as massive increases in stockpiles, a clear indication that the maintenance of production was then almost entirely dependent on an increase in capital from the government. Yuan also called for a major adjustment to the open-door system, brought on by fear of the vulnerability of the Chinese leadership to external pressures. This vulnerability was first brought home by the economic sanctions imposed in the wake of the June 1989 massacre in Beijing. In 1991, it was reinforced by events in the Soviet Union and Eastern Europe, as China saw itself as the last, beleaguered bastion of socialism.

Yuan wrote, "While maintaining our policy of opening to the outside world for the next ten years, I am afraid that we must reconsider how we can better place the Chinese economy on the basis of self-reliance, or how to better integrate opening to the outside world and self-reliance. It is still as Chairman Mao once said: 'Self-reliance is the basis and external assistance must be secondary.' " Yuan's prescription for rural development called for "perfecting" the rural responsibility system, "developing and expanding the collective [rural] economy," and "positively, but carefully developing management on a moderately large scale." In other words, Yuan called for a return to partial collectivization.[34]

In response to the upsurge in the power of the arch-conservatives, Deng Xiaoping gathered his strength to dilute the power of the extreme conservatives by early 1992. But a political victory alone could not guarantee economic reform. China's leaders, whatever their ideological bent, would have to grapple with the problem of massive unemployment and the myriad problems of the state industrial sector before they could institute price reforms. This prerequisite suggested that genuine price reform would be postponed for the foreseeable future.

A Genuine Turnaround?

A genuine turnaround in the Chinese economy may be a long time coming. The condition of the state industrial sector may continue to deteriorate, while any genuine efforts to return the sector as a whole to profitability would threaten social stability. Policies that look set to be put in place could only worsen problems. Regionalism may intensify and could come to drive China's economy as a whole; there may be intermittent bouts of high inflation; and massive unemployment would go hand in hand with low inflation. Conversely, efforts to find jobs for the jobless would result in high inflation or a huge increase in state subsidies and thus hidden inflation. Finally, the budget deficit might reach alarming proportions.

The best one could hope for is that a new leadership would emerge with the courage and capability of separating party from government, abolishing central planning, and instituting price reform. Above all, that leadership must realize that economic reform could not proceed without political reform. It was most likely that this leadership would be a product of the "fourth generation" trained mostly in the West, unlike its cohorts in the "second and third generations," technocrats educated in the Soviet Union. This fourth generation, however, would not hold the reins of power until the beginning of the twenty-first century.

The Millstone Grows Heavier

In the wake of Tiananmen, China's unexpectedly rapid shift in the post-1991 period from global pariah to prodigal to favored son served to obscure those elements in the economy that portended an increasingly unstable future. The ramifications of this instability may be considerable, as China appeared to be set on a course that would make it a major player on the East Asian economic and political stage. Before examining some key elements that seemed certain to contribute to problematical and uneven economic development, we must highlight a congeries of factors that played a key role in China's emergence as a potential economic powerhouse.

From Retrenchment to Pragmatism. First and foremost was the speed with which China reversed a policy calling for a renewed emphasis on central planning to one stressing economic pragmatism. This change was prompted by the recognition that the maintenance of power by a regime that had lost its political legitimacy necessitated the creation of wealth. It was all too clear that the most efficient instruments of wealth creation lay outside the state industrial sector.

Equally important was the consensus that massive technology transfer was necessary if China were to improve its competitiveness and assume a major role in the global economy. It was obvious that the hasty reform of the state industrial sector would have a destabilizing impact on China as a whole.

In the author's conversations with Shanghai's former mayor Zhu Rongji in March 1991, Zhu noted that the complexity of the reform of Shanghai's state industrial sector and the large-scale unemployment that would result from meaningful reform ruled out a fundamental overhaul of that sector. A far better solution, he believed, was to build up Pudong's industrial plant, primarily with foreign investment, which could then siphon off workers from the state industrial sector. Reform would then be a far easier proposition. Yet, time and tide were not on the side of the gradualists.

The Lure of the Motherland. Almost in tandem with China's decision to loosen the reins on the development of the collective and private sector, Hong Kong's major industrial and commercial conglomerates, which hitherto had eschewed large-scale investment in the mainland, began to invest heavily in a range of Chinese ventures, ranging from large infrastructural projects to major retail outlets. In 1992 and 1993, hardly a day went by without some important Hong Kong company announcing yet another major investment in China. The overseas Chinese from Malaysia, Thailand, and Indonesia, once minor investors, joined in the act as well. Taiwan's economy was fast being intertwined with that of China, and Singapore was constantly on the lookout for major projects to invest in. Korea, too, rapidly became one of China's major trade partners and was set to expand its presence further in China. In sum, a combination of a revitalized collective and private sector and massive foreign investment resulted in economic growth that in 1992 was the highest in the world.

Disruptive Continuities. Yet, this success story was marred by many of the same problems that saw China retreat to central planning in the wake of Tiananmen. These contradictions inherent in the economy could only be exacerbated by high economic growth.

The first of these legacies from the past was the persistent underperformance of the state industrial sector. Little had changed since 1989, and claims that the problems of triangular debt had been solved were, in main, a gross exaggeration. Stockpiling continued, while unauthorized credit to the state industrial sector was largely responsible for bank lending exceeding the state-set target by about 50 percent.

The extension of unauthorized credit was merely a part of a larger problem—in Beijing's eyes—that would only intensify as economic expansion deepened: the continued weakening of the power of the central government, save at gunpoint, and the parallel strengthening of provincial and local power. This decline, in turn, would lead once again to the creation of alternative centers of political and economic power that the authorities were intent on stamping out in the wake of Tiananmen. For despite some progress in the dismantling of the political prerequisites for the move from a command economy to a market economy, Beijing remained firm in its determination to hold the monopoly on political power. Conflict seemed inevitable as increased provincial economic strength and independence would bring with it real political power. It could be argued that Guangdong, despite its economic strength and independence, managed to stave off, through a variety of stratagems, the ire of Beijing. Nonetheless, the seeds of conflict between provincial economic powerhouses and the central government were planted in fertile soil.

Bottlenecks Proliferate. For the near term, other ramifications of economic reform were more problematic. China's social and physical infrastructure was simply not up to the task of supplying the needs of an economy that, in 1992 and 1993, was growing at double digits. Major infrastructural projects could not be built overnight. Thus, energy shortages and transportation bottlenecks, already severe, would accelerate unless industrial production was very sharply curtailed—a highly unlikely event.

Equally problematic was the dearth of individuals with the training to cope with the scope and increasing sophistication of industrial expansion, the airline industry being a case in point. As noted in the *Far Eastern Economic Review*, "The proliferation of new airlines has created more senior positions than there are qualified people to fill them. Some pilots barely adequate as first officers have been promoted to captain."[35]

Shanghai and Beijing led the country in percentage of population enrolled in institutions of higher learning (including technical schools), but these percentages were hardly adequate given China's pressing developmental needs. As of 1989, 1.42 percent of the population of Beijing was enrolled in postsecondary institutions, followed by 1.05 percent in Shanghai. This figure compared with 0.17 percent in Guangdong, which, though low, was still above the national average. These percentages compared with Hong Kong's 6 percent, Singapore's 5 percent, and Japan's 19 percent.

While ever-increasing influxes of migrant laborers waited outside factory gates for jobs, particularly in the Pearl River Delta, factories throughout the delta faced a shortage of skilled workers. With only two universities in the province, joint ventures recruit from the north but as investment increased in cities such as Shanghai and the northern coastal and major interior cities, this source would dry up. Returned students from abroad would mitigate, but hardly solve, the problem. Moreover, this dearth of highly skilled labor would make China's ambitious plans to upgrade its industrial base difficult to realize and, at the same time, would contribute to the uneven development of China as a whole. This, in turn, would lead to increasing tension between the rich provinces and the poor provinces.

Inflationary Pressures. Another ramification of infrastructural shortages—in this instance, the physical—was that they would add to the inflationary pressures that were once again surfacing. While the consumer price index (CPI) escaped relatively unscathed from the price reforms put in place in the previous several years, the producer price index was showing signs of strain. This, in time, would feed into the CPI. As a result of heavy pressure from investment and industrial demand, steel prices, for example, at year end 1992 rose 70 percent from the beginning of the year, while production material prices in 1992 jumped 134.4 percent over 1991. This increase in the CPI would affect the urban areas in tandem with the removal or reduction of subsidies, which for many covered everything from haircuts to housing. Coupled with increasing unemployment, prospects of social instability remained high.

The Day of Reckoning. Efforts at reforming the state industrial sector during 1992 and 1993, as in the past, proceeded at a snail's pace because of the dangers inherent in adding yet more unemployed to millions displaced by the advances in the agricultural sector. Some efforts at restructuring did take place, but the dimensions of the problem were such that the managerial skills available in China were still not equal to the task.

Efforts at reform at Beijing's Capital Iron and Steel, dubbed a "model enterprise" by Deng Xiaoping, made a travesty of industrial relations. The company instituted a 365-day work policy and employees were, not surprisingly, angry and complained of being treated like animals. A report in the *South China Morning Post* noted that Capital Iron implemented a new wage policy as well. The policy was intended to base workers' wage increases on skills. But, said the workers, the policy was flawed: "How is a worker who has never used and never had access to a computer supposed to pass a computer test?" queried one worker.[36]

The latest in the saga of China's "model enterprise" took place before the gates of the Zhongnanhai compound in Beijing, which is home and office for China's senior leaders. Some 200 elderly women who were retired from Capital Iron staged a protest and demanded pensions. This could well be a portent of future instability if the pace of retrenchment were to accelerate.

In the past, China could afford its huge investment in inefficient enterprises, thanks to its high savings and investment ratio: both ran at about 35 percent of gross domestic product (GDP). Had this state of affairs continued, a gradualist approach that assumed increased employment prospects in the private-collective sector, more efficiency spurred by increased competition from the private sector, and technology transfer resulting from foreign investment and the like would have merit. It seemed likely that a gap between savings and investment was imminent. Both subsidies and a plethora of goods no one wanted to buy were instrumental in creating the Chinese propensity to save. But the size and scope of subsidies were diminishing, and the Chinese would have to pay market prices for about 80 percent of retail goods by the end of 1993. At the same time, the flood of quality retail goods was gradually creating a consumer society.

Faced with a potential savings and investment deficit, a growing government deficit, a diminishing ability to control credit growth, and pressing needs for massive infrastructural projects, Beijing would find funding unproductive enterprises increasingly unattractive. Including domestic and foreign debt, the 1992 deficit was forecast to be about Rmb 58.7 billion. Subsidies to the state industrial sector—with about two-thirds of the enterprises losing money—were about Rmb 50 billion. To put it another way, in 1991, the state industrial sector generated Rmb 1.1 trillion, but subsidies and other funds spent to support that sector accounted for 83 percent of total output.

China's entry into the General Agreement on Tariffs and Trade (GATT) could hasten the day of reckoning for much of the state industrial sector. Although one could not rule out exaggeration from the Chinese as part of the GATT negotiating process, Chinese officials said that 20 million people could lose their jobs in the three years after China reenters GATT. Even efficient operations within the state industrial sector would find it increasingly difficult to sell their products in the face of lower tariffs and increased competition. Thus, the cost of supporting the state industrial sector as a whole would increase. In addition, many township and collective enterprises could go bankrupt because of competition from imported products. One indication of the precariousness of many segments of China's industry came from the textile industry, which stated early in February 1993 that one-third of its work force of 7.5 million nationwide was "redundant."

The Development Conundrum. Provided China stayed its course, its transition from a centrally controlled to a market economy could be remarkably difficult. Simply put, the goals of the Chinese leadership were incompatible with many of the policies that would have to be implemented to achieve those aims. In essence, China's leaders wanted the following:

- first, to stay in power
- second, to maintain stability and stave off chaos
- third, to create a strong and prosperous China that will play a major role in Asian and global affairs

To achieve the third, China would have to create a competitive industrial base by fostering competition and attracting foreign investment in high-tech industries. It would, in addition, have to upgrade its vastly inadequate social and physical infrastructure and enter GATT. Last, and most problematical, it would have to overhaul totally the state industrial sector.

Were China allowed the luxury of time, a gradualist approach might work, but at a price: spiraling budget deficits and a stop-and-go approach to industrial expansion so as to stifle hyperinflation. Unless China could somehow turn back the clock, even this gradualist approach could be unmanageable unless a workable system of credit control could be put in place. Beyond that, the Chinese agreement to broaden the market access of foreign firms already began to take its toll, not only on the savings and investment ratio but also on factories that were producing substandard goods. To restrict market access would be counterproductive, since China's ability to upgrade its industrial base relied heavily on foreign inputs. Moreover, its entry into GATT would be threatened.

The list of either-or scenarios was extensive, and all pointed to increasing social instability. How China would deal with the potential of chaos, or *luan*, remained to be seen. At best, expect abrupt but short-lived changes in policy (band-aids for fractures, really)—at worst, a futile attempt to turn back the clock and once again retreat to central planning. Ironically, the state industrial sector, which once served as an effective means of bolstering the power of the central government, had become a millstone, which, at the very least, posed a severe threat to that power.

9
Greater China and the Development of Science and Technology

Richard P. Suttmeier

"Greater China" has entered our vocabulary as a credible concept in a way that would have been unimaginable just a few years ago. When we speak of the Chinese and their future, it is no longer necessary in some cases to qualify "which Chinese?" The challenge now is to identify the reasons why the qualifier is still relevant. This chapter will explore whether the identifying qualifier still matters in the areas of science and technology.

At the first science and technology task force symposium of the Pacific Economic Cooperation Conference (PECC), which was held in November 1990 in Seoul, Korea, the mainland was represented as "China" and Taiwan as "China, Taipei." There, one could get a sense of the potential weight of a future Greater Chinese presence in science and technology in the Asia-Pacific region. With Hong Kong, Taiwan, and the mainland all represented, the "Chinese" delegation was one of the largest.

One of the symposium's keynote speakers was Taiwan's Dr. Li Kwoh-ting, who has contributed so much to Taiwan's industrial, educational, and scientific development. Introducing him, Vice Minister Zhu Lilan of the State Science and Technology Commission of the People's Republic of China (PRC) recounted his many accomplishments in Taiwan's development. Li in turn noted how remarkable it was for an old, American-trained male scientist from Taiwan to be introduced by a young, Soviet-trained woman scientist from Beijing. That would have been unimaginable just a few years earlier.

The credibility of the Greater China concept is, of course, a function of the important changes in the two Chinese political entities during the past decade.[1] These, however, have not been independent of the broader context of change in the Asia-Pacific region and in the

195

international political economy. In considering the Chinese and their future, therefore, we should attend to factors that either facilitate or retard new forms of Chinese integration, both endogenous and exogenous to the Chinese communities. The domestic and international dynamics of scientific and technological development powerfully influence both the mainland and Taiwan.

Background

In both Chinese communities, the quest to institutionalize scientific research and technological innovation has been conditioned by a strong desire to maintain an essential "Chineseness." This quest has produced variegated patterns of scientific and political development, characterized by a complex interplay of nationalism and cosmopolitanism.[2] A vigorous Chinese nationalism has provided the backdrop for much of modern Chinese politics; struggles over who can legitimately claim the mantle of nationalism constitute the main cleavages in the polity.

All claimants have also seen it as their nationalist responsibility to foster the development of science and technology as a means for achieving national wealth and power. But in doing so they have also unleashed forces of cosmopolitanism, which have had an uneasy relationship with nationalism. Indeed, at times cosmopolitanism has been antithetical to some forms of nationalist expression.

The problems of reconciling nationalism and cosmopolitanism, science and politics, have continuously bedeviled China's efforts to institutionalize modern science and technology. Many of China's best and brightest youth have entered careers in science and engineering out of nationalistic impulses, only to find the conditions of Chinese politics at odds with the realization of their professional aspirations. Nationalism, thus, has been both a spur and an obstacle to scientific and technological development. While significant scientific communities have appeared in the service of Chinese political entities, both before and after 1949, some within those communities have shown significant dissatisfaction with the political formulas imposed by those who claim legitimacy through Chinese nationalism.

Since the late 1940s, this dissatisfaction within the technical community—one of the more cosmopolitan segments of the population—has led to an exodus from the Chinese polity by many who sought careers in science and engineering elsewhere. The concept of the Chinese technical community is thus inherently ambiguous. It normally refers to one of the national communities of scientists and engineers working within one of the two Chinese political entities. It can also be applied to the remarkable transpolity group of technical personnel—a product of inhospitable politics—whose membership is determined by race and ethnicity rather than place of employment.

In recent years this group has provided technical personnel from the national communities of the mainland and Taiwan with opportunities to cooperate. Our understanding of the Chinese and their future, in the areas of science and technology, must, therefore, be sensitive both to the conflict and cooperation between the national communities, and to the meaning and significance of a tradition of Chinese science that transcends political boundaries. Our understanding must also consider the radically different international context in which the Chinese will find their future.

The Global and Regional Context

The past decade has been one of remarkable changes for these two Chinese communities. Many of the international political factors that conditioned Chinese politics for much of the twentieth century have faded in significance. The political importance of international economic factors, however, has increased. These factors are subject to rapid technological change and institutional innovation and during the past decade have been highly dynamic. International commercial competitiveness, for instance, is increasingly a function of the ability to link innovative technologies to new manufacturing and marketing strategies. New technologies have altered the structure of costs of manufacturing—by reducing the labor costs of manufacturing, for instance—and thus the comparative advantages of nations. These changes have placed more of a premium on the availability of technical resources such as R&D manpower and facilities rather than on inexpensive labor in foreign investment and plant location decisions. Along with the globalization of markets has come a globalization of technology.[3]

As the value of technical capabilities for competitiveness has become more widely recognized, those in possession of technology have become more guarded in sharing it. To get technology, one must have technology—as the new forms of international corporate relations and strategic alliances demonstrate. These changes in the international economy condition the patterns of economic and technological transformation that have occurred in the two Chinese communities.

For Taiwan and Hong Kong, like the other Asian Newly Industrialized Economies (NIEs) of Singapore and South Korea, the very success of their export-oriented industrialization based on low factor costs has forced a series of economic reorientations. The first has been to imitate the old industrialized nations by moving manufacturing offshore. As practiced by firms from Hong Kong and Taiwan, this shift has opened possibilities for greater economic integration with the PRC.

But while the search for offshore manufacturing sites has been the most visible response to the challenges of economic transformation, decisions to enhance indigenous science and technology capabilities and to ensure access to advanced technology from the countries of the Organization for Economic Cooperation and Development (OECD) are perhaps of greater long-term significance. These decisions are expected to position the economies of the NIEs for higher value-added production (based on increased knowledge inputs) and thus permit them to stay in the world's high-technology competition.

A distinctive East Asian NIE strategy (which the PRC seeks to emulate) has emerged as a response to these new challenges. With reference to Taiwan's experience, the strategy has five major goals:[4]

1. *To search for new technical links and strategic alliances with companies from the OECD world.* To facilitate these links and alliances, the NIEs have established science parks and high-technology industrial zones as a strategic task. The science park is thus replacing the export processing zone as the distinctive signature of East Asian industrialization.

One of the more successful of them is Taiwan's Hsinchu Science and Industry Park. Ten years after its establishment in 1980, Hsinchu has begun to realize the desired synergies coming from the interactions of foreign high-technology investment and technology transfer, energetic domestic R&D and higher educational sectors serving both domestic and foreign clients, and a new domestic technological entrepreneurship.[5]

2. *To accelerate investments in domestic R&D and advanced domestic education.* Until the late 1970s, Taiwan's investment in R&D was extremely modest, approximately only 0.5 percent of GNP in 1978. Over the course of a decade, however, it grew at an average annual rate of about 12 percent (in contrast to Korea's 14 percent and Japan's 4 percent).[6] Excluding defense, the ratio of gross expenditures on R&D to gross national product (GERD/GNP) had increased to approximately 1.2 percent by 1987. It is scheduled to grow to 2 percent by the mid-1990s.[7] Including defense-related expenditures, the GERD/GNP for 1987 was probably closer to 2 percent.

While R&D investment and manpower development have been growing rapidly in all the countries, these enhancements of national

TABLE 9–1

COUNTRIES WITH THE LARGEST NUMBER OF STUDENTS
IN THE UNITED STATES, 1987–1990

	1989–90	1988–89	1987–88
China, PRC	33,390	29,040	n.a.
Taiwan	30,960	28,760	23,770
Japan	29,840	24,000	13,360
India	26,240	23,350	16,070
Korea	21,710	20,610	18,660
Canada	17,870	16,030˙	15,410
Malaysia	14,110	16,170	23,020
Hong Kong	11,230	10,560	10,710
Indonesia	9,390	8,720	n.a.
Iran	7,440	8,940	14,210

n.a. = not available.
SOURCE: Institute of International Education.

capabilities are also being focused on areas of high technology and infrastructure, which have been given high priority. Taiwan's ten–year science and technology development plan, for instance, targets energy, materials, information, automation, biotechnology, hepatitis-B control, electro-optics, food technology, disaster prevention, environmental science and technology, synchrotron radiation, and ocean technology.[8]

3. *To increase the numbers of students going abroad—especially to the United States—for advanced education.* Although table 9–1 does not allow us to gauge with precision the disciplinary preferences of foreign students, we can assume that the major share of those from East Asia are studying science and engineering. More notable is how the East Asian region has come to dominate the placement of students within U.S. universities, and how, within that regional representation, students from Greater China are by far the most numerous.

4. *To induce a "reverse brain drain," which will bring well-trained and experienced technical personnel back from the United States.* Much of the success of Hsinchu is due to the interest shown by seasoned Chinese technical personnel in the United States in returning to Taiwan and starting their own high-technology firms.

5. *To establish technical outposts in countries like the United States to monitor and, where possible, capture new technologies.* These outposts can be companies that would be in centers of high technology such as

Silicon Valley, or they can be equity positions taken in companies already established in such locations. Investments of this sort from Taiwan reached $1.5 billion in 1991. Alternatively, outposting can take the form of imaginative and conscientious staffing of diplomatic offices, as Taiwan has done in posting of representatives from the National Research Council at quasi-diplomatic offices around the United States.

While Taiwan and the other NIEs have shown that they are adept at making this five-point strategy work, the international conditions in which the strategy is employed continue to change rapidly.

The globalization of technology implies a diffusion of scientific and technological (S&T) capabilities beyond the boundaries of the old industrial countries into other areas of the world. While the measurement of this change is both difficult and controversial, certain standard indicators of scientific and technological development, such as numbers of scientists and engineers, numbers of research facilities, and levels of R&D expenditures, are unavoidable. These measures do not automatically translate into efficient or effective performance, but they do reflect levels of effort.

The relative positions of the Asian NIEs with regard to GERD/GNP and the numbers of scientists and engineers in R&D is shown in table 9–2. As table 9–2 indicates, a cross-national comparative look at such indicators reveals that the wealthiest countries of the OECD world still dominate world science and technology. Major efforts have been made elsewhere, however, to change that dominance. Taiwan and South Korea, for example, have made gains over the past decade. Nevertheless, by themselves, the Asian NIEs would find it difficult to match the mobilization of resources found in the countries of Europe.

The regional dimensions of Asian science and technology change dramatically, however, with the inclusion of data from Japan and from the PRC. With this addition, we see a concentration of resources in one regional techno-system that could be exceeded only in Europe by augmenting Western European strengths with Eastern European and Russian strengths. A broader Asia-Pacific accounting, including data from the United States, Canada, and Australia, would produce an S&T region having a combined annual R&D expenditure of $200 billion, with more than half the world's R&D scientists and engineers.[9]

Scientific creativity and technological innovativeness are not simply additive functions of manpower and expenditure figures. The more germane questions are how well technical resources are used and how effectively research and development organizations cooper-

TABLE 9–2

NUMBERS OF SCIENTISTS AND ENGINEERS IN RESEARCH AND
DEVELOPMENT AND GROSS EXPENDITURES FOR R&D AS A PERCENTAGE
OF GROSS NATIONAL PRODUCT IN SELECTED COUNTRIES, 1986–1988

	S&Es in R&D	GERD/GNP
Korea (1988)	47,213	1.90
Taiwan (1987)	23,541	1.16
Singapore (1988)	5,876	.90
Indonesia (1988)	32,038	.12[a]
China, PRC (1988)	450,000	1.50
Japan (1987)	418,300	2.90
United States (1987)	806,200	2.70
India (1986)	85,309	.90
W. Germany (1987)	151,500	2.80
France (1987)	108,200	2.30
United Kingdom (1986)	98,700	2.40

a. 1987.
SOURCE: For Japan, the United States, India, Germany, France, and the United Kingdom, U.S. National Science Foundation; for Korea, Taiwan, Singapore, Indonesia, and China, Pacific Economic Cooperation Conference; for high China, author's estimate based on various sources.

ate across political borders. The numbers do provide a base, however, against which questions of managerial effectiveness and cross-border cooperation can be posed.

For East Asia, a central question is, To what extent should Japanese technical resources be counted as part of the regional system? This question involves Japan's willingness to transfer advanced technology, the openness of Japanese universities to science and engineering students from Asia, the accessibility of the Japanese research system (especially its corporate labs), and the willingness of Japanese corporations to cooperate with other Asian companies in the development of technology.

Until recently, Japanese engagement in the Asian techno-system was questionable at best. Now, however, things may be changing. Japanese universities are becoming more accessible to the Asian student, and Japanese companies have begun to see that transferring technology and engaging in cooperative technological development with others are in their interest. Although such developments are welcomed by Japan's Asian neighbors, they also raise concerns that Japanese cooperation initiatives may promote and, simultaneously, mask a deepening Japanese economic domination of the region.

Asian countries therefore seek ways to position themselves to elude Japanese techno-economic hegemony. Until recently they could rely on the United States while also diversifying technical links with countries of Western Europe. This approach is still used, but with less certainty of success. U.S. interests in maintaining a presence in East Asia have changed. At both the corporate and the governmental levels, furthermore, attitudes toward technology transfer and scientific cooperation are undergoing reconsideration. Prominence is given now, for instance, to the protection of intellectual property in state policy and corporate behavior. Similarly, the challenges and opportunities of European integration—with reference to the European Economic Community (EEC) and to the changes in Eastern Europe—are causing European governments and corporations to focus their energy and attention more on Europe itself.

Such changes argue powerfully for greater intra-Asian scientific and technological cooperation. The terms of cooperation, however, must be settled first, and profitable complementarities must be found. The latter may be difficult with regard to the NIEs. All are trying to master many of the same technologies from a position of rough technological parity. The costs of developing new technologies are often staggering, and the basic science required often exceeds capabilities. The preferred model of Asian cooperation would be for the NIEs to serve as a bridge between the needs of the latecomer NIEs such as Thailand, Malaysia, and Indonesia and the advanced countries. But for reasons noted above, the reliability of the advanced countries is less clear than one might hope.

The PRC Factor

In this context, the PRC's role becomes intriguing. As we consider the PRC's presence in a new Asian techno-system, we cannot ignore the legacy of scientific and technological development it brings and how it differs from Taiwan's role.

In the West, successful scientific and technological development has long been recognized as a systemic phenomenon. Research and development are linked with education, with the economy, and principally with public policy. For the system to cohere, the presence of complementary assets is required.[10] In relations between R&D and the economy, for instance, these include managerial, manufacturing, financial, and marketing capabilities.

Scientific and technological development on the mainland appears to have left a legacy of an extensive R&D system but few complementary assets. This is the result of both the autarkic themes of Maoism and the developmental distortions inherent in socialist systems, all of which have undervalued the cultivation of complementary assets. Taiwan's active participation in the international capitalist political economy, in contrast, has left a legacy of reasonably well-developed complementary assets. Yet, because so many of its technical needs in the past could be efficiently met by technology transfer, its R&D system was slower to develop and, arguably, can be considered suboptimal in size in the face of new techno-economic challenges it now faces.

Scientific and technological development on the mainland and on Taiwan have many common origins in such pre-1949 institutions as the Academia Sinica, the National Resources Commission, universities, and professional societies.[11] Two similarities in scientific and technological development after 1949 are also notable. One is the close relationship between science and national defense. Thus, while often shrouded in secrecy, Taiwan's Chung Shan complex has been a major center for R&D for some time. On the mainland, especially after 1958, more and more of China's resources became committed to national security missions, a trend now recognized as a serious distortion of developmental priorities. In both places, military research and industrialization have been quite insulated from the civilian economy. There is now in both a strong interest in redeploying technical resources from the defense sector to serve commercial purposes, as indicated by the efforts on both sides of the Taiwan Strait to develop the aircraft and space industries.[12]

In spite of major differences in the economic systems, both communities have neglected R&D at the enterprise level. While explanations for this neglect differ (the prevalence of small firms in Taiwan; the failures of socialist incentives on the mainland), the result has been the same: in both systems the state has served as the main patron for R&D; in both, the problem of linking research to production has been an important policy issue.

Such similarities, however, should not be allowed to mask the many important differences in how research has been organized and in how science has been linked to the economy. On the mainland, the Chinese decided to follow Soviet patterns of organization. They accepted the logic of innovation implied by that organization, a logic that is perhaps best described as an extreme version of a supply-push approach.[13] As the mainland Chinese invested heavily in the accumulation of resources throughout the 1950s, the numbers of scientists, engineers, and R&D institutes grew rapidly. The positive environment created for this approach to scientific and technological development during the early 1950s did not last; it fell victim to

Maoist radicalism beginning in 1957.

In Taiwan, by contrast, heavy investments in research were slow in coming, in part, one suspects, because of the prevalence of a demand-pull approach to innovation. In the absence of a demand for original research (in most fields), Taiwan's technical needs were readily met by the acquisition of technology from abroad. This was part of Taiwan's strategy of economic development. Taiwan's system of education, in comparison, received careful attention at all levels. While higher education improved and expanded, it did so without sacrificing other parts of the system and without the high-priority programs to produce as many scientists and engineers as possible that characterized the approach on the mainland, at least until the beginning of the Cultural Revolution.

Thus, Taiwan, unlike the mainland, did not have an identifiable, separate science policy until recently. Its strategy, instead, was to concentrate on human resource development appropriate to its economic needs, which, until the 1970s, were understood in terms of supporting agricultural productivity, technical infrastructure development, and labor-intensive, export-oriented industrialization. Although the mainland has clearly had a more explicit science policy, the faults of its institutional design and the frequent interventions of radical politics have stopped investments in science and technology from being used efficiently and from serving the cause of economic development.

The PRC, therefore, entered the post-Mao era as a poor, underdeveloped country whose R&D system had many weaknesses. While this remains the case, it is not the whole story. For all its problems, the PRC's legacy of development also includes the establishment of excellent centers of research and a very large R&D establishment. In the context of this discussion, the latter can be seen as an enormous potential resource for regional cooperation. Recall that Shanghai and Beijing, for example, have more scientists and engineers than does all of Taiwan or Korea.

Much of this talent is now being redeployed to take advantage of commercial opportunities within China and in cooperative ventures with parties from the Asian region and beyond. This talent is seen in the formation of a large number of new technology companies by ministerial institutes, by universities, and by institutes of the Chinese Academy of Sciences (CAS). During the past decade, evidence of a larger PRC technological presence in the regional economy includes the appearance of the Legend computer (produced by a Hong Kong–CAS joint venture) and the Kexin Company (a Singaporean–academy joint venture to market CAS-developed technologies and products internationally). Korean firms such as Daewoo have held discussions with Chinese high-technology companies such as San Huan (which has world-class technology for producing supermagnets), and the Chinese have emerged as a competitive presence for the supply of satellite launch services. Such instances will probably increase dramatically during the 1990s, and Taiwan will be represented in many of them.

The PRC's ability to further participate in, and perhaps shape, the future of a new Asian techno-system is closely related to the future of its reform program. As illustrated by the slogan "Economic development must depend on science and technology, and science and technology must serve economic development," hopes for a close link between science and technology and economic expansion underlie the "four modernizations" policy. The experience of the 1980s, however, was that both the science and technology system and the economic system need reform. Failures to reform the economic system placed an upper limit on reform in the science and technology system. Both, arguably, are now dependent on political reform.

In spite of the dilemmas of reform, mainland China has seen remarkable change in its scientific and technological development over the past decade. It has spent large sums on foreign technology; it has sent large numbers of students abroad for study; it has reestablished the university system and added graduate programs and enhanced university-based research; it has initiated major changes in the funding of research and in science policy and management structures; and, most recently, it has taken a series of measures designed to ensure that China will be a player in the international game of high technology. Among these is a national, high-technology research program, which targets research in biotechnology, space, information, automation, lasers, energy, and materials. China has developed policies to encourage the defense sector, with its high-technology capabilities, to enter the civilian economy.[14] China has also launched programs to encourage high-technology industrialization and special science and industry parks. Some twenty-seven high-tech development zones have been established so far. In an effort to appeal to Taiwan interests, the State Science and Technology Commission has joined with the Xiamen city government to establish a high-tech development zone and to build an "international scientific and technological town" in Xiamen.

Beneath the surface of these developments, however, lies an ambiguity about China's role in the Asia-Pacific region and in the global order. While all would agree that a return to the isolation of the Maoist period is both undesirable and probably impossible, they would not agree on the degree and mode of involvement with the international capitalist order and its flow of science and technology.

It can be argued, for instance, that a high-technology future is conceivable only with a thorough internationalization of the science and technology system and of the economy.[15] Such internationalization is required for access to a scientific and engineering education, to R&D opportunities not available at home, and to advanced technology that it will need. But, as important as access to foreign science and technology is, foreign interactions are of greatest significance in furthering the institutional reform that China so desperately needs.

This need is exemplified by comparing the mainland's effort to stimulate high-technology entrepreneurship within the institutional context of a science park with Taiwan's. One key to success for Taiwan's Hsinchu has been the ability of researchers at the government-operated Industrial Technology Research Institute (ITRI) to use their knowledge and experience to spin off new companies. Such success has depended on a knowledge of the market, the availability of venture capital and managerial talent, and a clear sense of property rights.

While the PRC has had some success in spinning off new companies from its research institutes, the enormous potential for success is far from being realized because of the persistence of unreformed institutions. Property rights remain opaque, obligations to the work force continue to have many of the worst features of socialism, and the unreliability of capital and labor markets means that these inputs must be acquired administratively through wasteful, politicized bargaining.

That all the necessary resources for reform can be found within China is unlikely; only challenges offered by a foreign presence will effect real change. These challenges could come as easily from the Asian NIEs, including Taiwan, as from the countries of the OECD; indeed, given linguistic and cultural similarities, challenges from the former may be more efficacious.

It is the external presence, however, that engenders fear among some of the political elite about the future of Chinese socialism. They are therefore reserved about the internationalization needed for scientific and technological development. In their cautious view, China must take from the international environment what it needs, while enhancing its technical resources by its own efforts. Global interdependence over the long term is not inevitable in this view. The tension in mainland thinking and policy development between the need for internationalization and the anxiety it produces will probably be a major factor in the kind of future the Chinese face. A powerful, virtually inescapable—though by no means a determining—influence on the management of this tension will be the continuing dynamism of the region.

Therefore, in spite of the fears of internationalization, the PRC will probably see its future tied increasingly to the Asia-Pacific region. The trends of the past decade, which are leading to a more pronounced Chinese mainland science and technology presence in the region, are therefore likely to continue. New forms of Asian regional cooperation—some featuring the PRC—can be expected. As the PRC continues to need a wide range of production and managerial technologies, the NIEs may supply them in more appropriate forms than the OECD does.

At the same time, China's own high-technology initiatives will continue. The PRC has incurred the costs of establishing an extensive R&D system. Only the commercialization of high technology will yield returns. The Chinese realize that the PRC economy is not ready for the best that its research institutes can turn out; thus they see an export orientation as essential for high-technology development.[16] Chances for success in such development will be greatly enhanced by experience in operating in the world economy, experience that Taiwan and the other NIEs have accumulated over the past three decades.

It was clear by mid-1992 that prospects for cooperation between the PRC and Taiwan in science and technology were no longer hypothetical. Scientific and technological contacts expanded quietly following the 1987 Taiwan policy changes to allow family visits to the mainland. Interest in recruiting scientists from the mainland who were studying in foreign countries was announced by Taiwan in June 1991, and by November of that year, the National Science Council had received twenty-five applications. Two prominent mainland scientists now engaged in collaborative work in Taiwan are Guan Weiyan (who, following student prodemocracy demonstrations, was removed from his post as president of the University of Science and Technology in 1987) and Qian Kunxi. Physicist Guan, an early leader in mainland superconductivity research, is working on a superconductivity project at National Tsing Hua University, while Qian, a cardiologist, has joined National Taiwan University to work on an artificial heart project.

By the first half of 1992, evidence of improving PRC-Taiwan cooperation in science and technology became more abundant. According to a mainland source, the areas of exchange had expanded from fields such as agriculture, aquaculture, forestry, and traditional

Chinese medicine to oceanography, automobiles, computers, textiles, machine-building, electronics, chemical engineering, aviation, nuclear power, and meteorology.[17] Important visits were made to the mainland in May 1992 by Chao Yao-tung, former minister of Economic Affairs, and by Wu Ta-yu, president of the Academia Sinica. Both came away impressed with selected areas of mainland science and technology and returned home with calls for expanded cooperation, which would allow PRC personnel to visit Taiwan.

Wu extended an invitation to twelve senior PRC scientists to visit Taiwan, the first seven of whom (five being Communist party members) visited the island in June amid extensive media coverage. Also in June, the Ministry of Economic Affairs drafted guidelines for importing technology from the mainland, which provided for mainland technical personnel to come to Taiwan as part of the transfer process. Exploratory discussions on cooperation on nuclear fuel cycle issues were reported. Concerns about land and labor costs on Taiwan, the value of the Taiwanese dollar, shortages of high-level technical manpower, and apprehensions about the China strategies of Korean and Japanese companies produced new interest in investing on the mainland among Taiwan's computer manufacturers.

Political differences between the two Chinese entities are still major impediments to improved economic ties and continue to influence scientific and technological relations as well. As of this writing, it is still too early to gauge the implications from the establishment of formal diplomatic relations between Beijing and Seoul for cross-straits science and technology cooperation, but one suspects it will alter the patterns of cooperation and the assumptions used in approaching expanded exchanges. Uncertainties about China's military intentions in the region have highlighted the continuing importance of defense technology on both sides of the strait and serve as reminders of the close relationship between high technology capabilities and security.

Yet, without minimizing the persistence of political obstacles, the dramatic changes in the international environment require us to see China's political divisions in a new light. New common interests among the Chinese communities (especially with reference to Japan) may be emerging, and attractive scientific and technological complementarities are being discovered.

Science and technology are increasingly major factors in an age when economic and environmental issues seem to be vying with military security issues for international attention. Science and technology are seen as the foundations of economic security and of wise management of the global commons. In the Asia-Pacific region, where virtually all of the nations have redoubled their efforts to enhance scientific and technological resources, this view is especially strong. The focus has been on the activities of the nation-state, and successful national policies have been those that discern the patterns and flows of international forces. The importance of such forces is recognized now more than ever. Yet, the challenge of discerning these patterns has become more formidable—in large part because of the ambiguous tensions between global and regional tendencies.

The two Chinese political entities seem to be hedging their bets in the face of new international uncertainties. In so doing, they have altered the ways in which their political differences are perceived. New patterns of Asian scientific and technological cooperation that involve the mainland, Taiwan, and Hong Kong are likely to enhance the relative position of the Chinese in a new Asian techno-system. At the same time, the transpolity Chinese technical community noted earlier ensures a Chinese role in global processes.

The strong historic pulls of Chinese nationalism and of the vigorous competition over who can claim its mantle are still there. But the scientific and technological imperatives of the changing world order could well bring forward in the Chinese communities those sometimes suppressed, more cosmopolitan visions of the Chinese and their future. If so, the Chinese may be especially well positioned to face the new, twenty-first century world of regional and global uncertainty.

PART FIVE
Taiwan

10
The Effects of Democratization, Unification, and Elite Conflict on Taiwan's Future

Yung Wei

Transition from an authoritative to a more competitive political system has never been an easy process. Maintaining a balance between the enhancement of political participation on the one hand and the preservation of sociopolitical stability on the other is a challenge to the leaders of all countries caught up in the process of democratization. Since democratization means giving people more autonomy to decide their own future, it frequently leads to internal political cleavages and even separatist movements in the name of self-determination. Consequently, the process of democratization is often beset by the problem of national unification, which may lead to serious problems of elite conflict in any society moving toward a more open political system.

The experience of the Republic of China on Taiwan (ROC) in the past forty years testifies to the problems confronting a country caught up in both democratization and national unification. How can the government and people of the ROC deal with the problem of political democratization without affecting social stability and economic development? How can the ROC handle relations with mainland China so as to pursue formalities with other countries yet avoid a military confrontation with the mainland? Is national unification with mainland China feasible in the foreseeable future, or is the preservation of the status quo, without declaring formal separation or independence, a more realistic way of "solving" the unification-separation issue?

What factors have contributed to the conflicts between the ruling party, the Kuomintang (KMT), and the major opposition party, the Democratic Progressive party? Will the KMT stay in power, or might the DPP take over the government through elections? What have been the reasons for the intraparty elite conflicts within the KMT and

213

the DPP, and how will these conflicts affect the future policies and strengths of these parties? If internal political struggles intensify, might there be a military takeover? How will internal political developments affect the relationship between the ROC and other nations and political systems, especially the United States and mainland China? These questions have frequently been raised by observers concerned with the future of Taiwan.

The purpose of this chapter is to provide relevant analysis, if not answers, to these questions. It will start with a discussion of socioeconomic development in Taiwan and its impact on the political process. This will be followed by a more extensive analysis of the process of political democratization initiated by President Chiang Ching-kuo and its influence on national unification and on the external relations of the ROC. It will conclude with an exploratory analysis of the relationship between democratization, unification, and elite conflict, along with some cautious predictions of what may happen to Taiwan under different scenarios.

Socioeconomic Development and Its Impact on Political Participation in Taiwan

Any analysis of the political future of Taiwan must include an examination of economic growth and the resultant social change, the two key factors affecting political development on the island. In fact, the ROC's experience in developing Taiwan from a rural society with some light industries into a sophisticated, export-oriented economy has been viewed as a "deviant" case to the "dependency theory" and world-system analyses.[1] Taiwan also defies categorization into the much circulated conceptual model of bureaucratic authoritarianism that has been widely applied to the analysis of politics in the third world, particularly in Latin America.[2]

By and large, Taiwan has evaded the predictions that economic development in a non-Communist, third world country accepting foreign aid and loans from developed countries leads to long-term dependency; that the gap between the rich and the poor sectors of the population widens in the process of economic growth;[3] and that economic development does not always bring about democratization, but may lead to an unholy alliance among the bureaucrats, businessmen, and the military. Thus far, none of these seems to have happened in Taiwan.

Various factors may have contributed to the exceptional development experience of the ROC on Taiwan. Two of these are the maintenance of a high level of cohesion among the ruling elite and the emphasis by the ROC government (GRC) on both growth and equity in its development efforts. As for the high level of elite cohesion in Taiwan, it became a major goal of the government of the ROC and the ruling party after the defeat suffered at the hands of the Chinese Communists on the mainland. The transplantation of the bureaucratic, educational, and technocratic elite from mainland China to Taiwan and their successful integration with the local Taiwanese elite not only served to replace the administrative and technocratic personnel among the 480,000 repatriated Japanese, but also contributed to political integration on the island.[4]

Growth with Equity—Sun Yat-sen's Goals for Development

The idea of growth with equity is rooted in the teaching of Dr. Sun Yat-sen, the founding father of the Republic of China. Two features are unique: first, his strong emphasis on the correlations between political democratization, social equality, and economic development and, second, his conviction that constitutional democracy cannot be reached overnight, but must be achieved through several stages. Influenced by both the humanist thought of traditional China and the democratic-socialist ideology of nineteenth-century Europe, Sun Yat-sen strongly advocated that political democracy is meaningful only when accompanied by social justice through equitable distribution of the benefits of economic development. This emphasis on egalitarianism in the process of social, political, and economic development has been largely incorporated in the constitution of the ROC, the guideline for formation of policies in relevant areas.

In addition to his emphasis on egalitarian approaches to national development, Sun Yat-sen contributed a three-stage theory of political development to China's modernization process. In the earlier stage of his revolutionary career, Sun Yat-sen believed in a more direct and immediate transplantation of Western constitutional democracy to China. This was after the success of the republican revolution in 1911. But following a series of setbacks after the establishment of the republic, he came to realize that political democratization must be a gradual and well-planned process. Sun Yat-sen theorized that a non-Western country moving toward democracy must go through three stages: first, national unification through military rule; second, political socialization and organization through tutelage; and third, constitutional democracy through the promotion of self-government at the local level and of parliamentary and party politics at the national level.[5]

215

The Strategies and Results of the ROC's Modernization Efforts

In accordance with the teachings of Sun Yat-sen, the basic strategy employed by the ROC government in its modernization efforts in Taiwan was first to improve the rural sector through land reform and then to support the development of the industrial sector by the expanded rural sector. Finally, after the improvement of living standards and the elevation of the educational level of the people, came full-fledged programs toward democratization.

The result of the ROC's economic development is a well-known story. Between 1952 and 1989, the gross national product increased by 2,334.4 percent; industrial production increased by 7,092.3 percent; exports by 118,876.4 percent; and imports by 54,689 percent. In 1989, the Republic of China became one of the leading trading nations of the world, with a GNP of $150.3 billion and a per capita GNP exceeding $7,509. In 1952, the ROC ranked sixty-first worldwide with respect to the total value of its two-way trade. In 1989, the ROC became one of the thirteen leading trading nations of the world. This rapid economic expansion made the ROC, with its effective control of a territory comparable in size to Switzerland, one of the major newly industrialized countries enjoying sustained growth.

As a result of accelerated growth, significant changes have occurred in the structure of the Taiwanese economy. Agricultural production decreased from 35.9 percent of the total economy in 1952 to 5.0 percent in 1989. In the same period, industrial production increased from 18.0 percent to 43.6 percent. Following economic growth, social and cultural indicators also posted substantial gains. For instance, the average life expectancy of the people of Taiwan increased by more than 14.9 years between 1952 and 1989: that of males from 56.5 to 71.7, and that of females from 60.7 to 76.5. School-aged children attending primary schools climbed from 84 percent to 99.9 percent of those eligible; and senior high school graduates enrolled in institutions of higher learning increased from 26.3 percent to 44.4 percent. The number of college graduates increased from 86,000 in 1952 to 1,910,000 in 1989, making the ROC on Taiwan one of the most educated non-Western countries. All these figures testify to the dramatic improvement in the quality of life on Taiwan as a result of sustained social and economic progress.

Efforts toward Equal Distribution for the Benefits of Development

It ought to be pointed out, however, that the pursuit of economic growth and the improvement of social conditions in Taiwan are not

216

the only concerns of the government of the ROC. While growth has always been an important goal, equalized distribution of the benefits of economic growth and social progress has also been a primary concern of the leaders of the ROC.[6]

Owing to its conscientious efforts toward a more equal society, the government of the Republic of China (GRC) has made significant progress toward equality in land ownership, income distribution, educational opportunities, and political participation. First, let us examine the case of land ownership. Through a series of policy measures such as the reduction of land rent, sale of public land to the peasants, and ownership of the land by former tenants, the ROC has achieved its goal of equalization of land ownership on Taiwan.[7]

Land reform on Taiwan has not only brought about a significant improvement in the livelihood of the people on rural Taiwan; it also has led to an increasing interest among farmers in participation in community affairs, as well as a rising expectation among the children of farmers to pursue a higher level of education. The former landlords, who have been compensated by the government for their land with bonds and stocks, have become increasingly interested in economic pursuits in the urban centers, thus losing interest in politics in the rural community. Their previously dominant role in local politics was gradually replaced by the self-tilling farmers. Consequently, political power has been redistributed in the countryside and in small towns on the island.[8]

The increment of educational opportunities for the children of farmers was particularly impressive. According to data provided me by the Land Reform Institute during a 1971 research trip to Taiwan, the number of former tenant farmers' children attending primary schools increased 257 percent between 1948 and 1971; those attending middle schools, 2,827 percent; and those enrolling in college, 16,820 percent. These facts are especially significant because between 1952 and 1971, the population employed in agricultural activities on Taiwan increased only by 128.4 percent.

Land reform and equal opportunities for education have led to a high degree of social mobility on Taiwan. According to a survey conducted by the Research, Development, and Evaluation Commission (RDEC) of the Executive Yuan (cabinet) in 1986, the children of workers and farmers have experienced the highest level of upward social mobility in the past decades. Using intergenerational occupation change as the measurement, it was discovered that 37.7 percent of the children of skilled and unskilled workers have become either professionals or civil servants. As for the children of farmers, 28.9 percent have been able to do the same. These data fully illustrate the dynamism of the modernization process on Taiwan (see table 10–1).

Income distribution is another important measurement of social and economic equality.[9] The rapid economic growth and the rising level of income in the Republic of China have been accompanied by a steady improvement in income distribution. In 1952, the family income of the wealthiest 20 percent of Taiwan's households was approximately fifteen times that of the poorest 20 percent; by 1987, the gap had narrowed to 4.85 to 1. This ratio reflected a general downward trend. But a slight increase in income disparity occurred after 1984, causing some concern among officials and scholars in the ROC (see figure 10–1).

Political Participation and Social Integration

Now let us turn to opportunities for political participation. During the Japanese occupation of Taiwan from 1895 to 1945, the Chinese on Taiwan had limited opportunity for anything remotely related to political activities. The Japanese monopolized all administrative positions, from the governor-general of the colonial government to the headmasters of village schools. As previously stated in this chapter, after the 480,000 Japanese departed at the end of World War II, their political and occupational positions were assumed by the Taiwanese, especially those in the smaller cities and villages.[10]

Since 1951, provincial elections have been held on Taiwan. Many Taiwanese found avenues into politics by participating in political activities at the county and provincial levels. Today the overwhelming majority of the provincial assemblymen are Taiwanese, as are all the city mayors and country magistrates. The president, the premier, more than 40 percent of the members of the Executive Yuan, the mayors of the special municipalities of Taipei and Kao-hsiung, and more than 48 percent of the members of the standing committee of the KMT are all Taiwanese.[11]

Elections at the national level had been suspended since the ROC government moved to Taiwan in 1949. In 1969, the deadlock of political participation at the national level was broken. With the holding of supplementary elections in 1969, 1972, 1975, 1980, 1983, 1985, 1986, 1989, and 1992, a sizable number of new members were added to the three branches of the representative bodies at the national level: the National Assembly, the Legislative Yuan, and the Control Yuan.

Efforts made by the ROC government to increase political participation have contributed to the decline of provincial feeling and an increase in social and political integration (see figure 10–2). According

TABLE 10-1
INTERGENERATIONAL OCCUPATION CHANGE AMONG VOTERS IN TAIWAN, 1986
(percent)

Father's Occupation	Respondent's Occupation						
	Professional & business	Civil servants	Farmers	Skilled & unskilled workers	Unemployed & retired	Other	Total
Professional & business	51.9	18.4	1.9	15.4	8.5	3.8	100 (366)
Civil servants	42.6	31.5	2.0	12.2	7.6	4.1	100 (198)
Farmers	23.4	5.5	27.3	31.3	8.6	4.0	100 (877)
Skilled & unskilled workers	31.1	6.6	3.9	44.4	8.2	5.8	100 (257)
Unemployed & retired	34.1	14.7	7.9	30.8	9.4	3.2	100 (598)
Other	15.8	10.7	17.4	21.9	25.7	8.6	100 (375)
Total	29.4 (856)	11.5 (336)	14.4 (419)	27.2 (793)	12.7 (370)	4.5 (130)	100 (2915)

SOURCE: Yung Wei, "Sociopolitical Development in the Republic of China: Analysis and Projections," paper delivered at the American Management Association Executive Round Table, "Toward Improving U.S.-Taiwan Economic Relations: Opportunities and Pathways," Plaza Hotel, New York City, June 15, 1987.

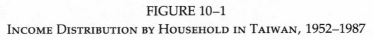

FIGURE 10–1

INCOME DISTRIBUTION BY HOUSEHOLD IN TAIWAN, 1952–1987

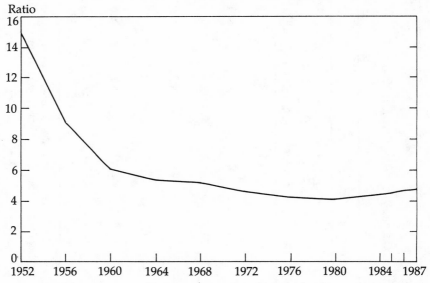

NOTE: The ratio equals the income of the wealthiest 20 percent divided by that of the poorest 20 percent.
SOURCE: *Economic Development, Taiwan, Republic of China* (Taipei: Council for Economic Planning & Development, June 1988).

to consecutive surveys conducted by the RDEC in the 1985–1991 period, both the government and the ruling party enjoyed steady majority support among all sectors of the population, although the extent of support varied from election to election. Generally, the KMT fared better at elections for representative bodies. From this kind of election the KMT received between 65 percent and 75 percent of the vote. In elections for magistrates, the support fell to barely 50 percent.

Correlating the social background of the voters and party support revealed that the ruling party, the KMT, received more support from the male voters, the more highly educated, the upper-income, and the upper and upper-middle class. The non-KMT candidates received more support from the female voters, the less highly educated, the lower income, lower-middle, and working classes (see figures 10–3, 10–4, 10–5, and 10–6).

Another indication of social and political integration on Taiwan is the increase of intermarriages between Taiwanese and mainlanders.

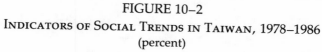

FIGURE 10–2
INDICATORS OF SOCIAL TRENDS IN TAIWAN, 1978–1986
(percent)

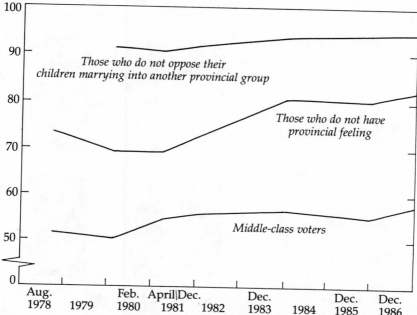

SOURCE: Yung Wei, "Sociopolitical Development in the Republic of China: Analysis and Projections," prepared for delivery at the American Management Association Executive Round Table, "Toward Improving U.S.-Taiwan Economic Relations: Opportunities and Pathways," Plaza Hotel, New York City, June 15, 1987.

According to a recent survey conducted by the RDEC, more than 25.2 percent of the voters have close kin (parents, siblings, or children) or are themselves married to the other provincial group. Another 17.8 percent reported intermarriages between other kinds of relatives. These two figures indicate that four of every ten voters on Taiwan have some relative married to another provincial group.

Democratization under Chiang Ching-kuo— From Gradual Reform to Radical Change

Despite the conscientious efforts made by the GRC toward political democratization, several obstacles continue to hinder a smooth transition from a less competitive political structure to a more open one.

221

FIGURE 10–3

Profile of Voters by Gender in Legislative Elections in Taiwan, December 1986

(percent)

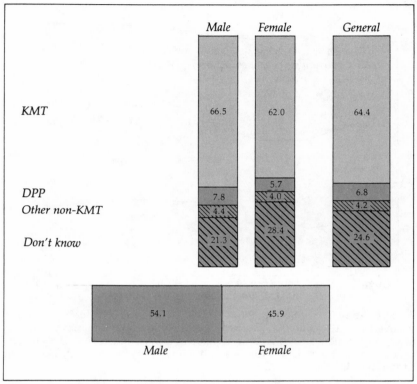

Source: Same as for figure 10–2.

These obstacles no longer include martial law and the restriction on the formation of new political parties, which were eliminated in 1991, but still include the lack of a general election and of membership of the representative bodies at the national level, the existence of the Formosan Independence Movement, the threat from mainland China, and the gradual but persistent decline of the international status of the ROC.

The withdrawal of the ROC from the United Nations led to the emergence of a more active and critical opposition movement on Taiwan. The election in 1972 saw fifteen non-KMT members win seats in the Provincial Assembly and four in the Legislative Yuan. With the

FIGURE 10-4

PROFILE OF VOTERS BY EDUCATIONAL LEVEL IN LEGISLATIVE ELECTIONS IN TAIWAN, DECEMBER 1986

(percent)

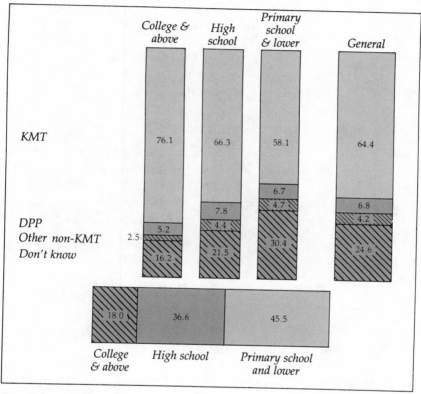

SOURCE: Same as for figure 10-2.

passing of Chiang Kai-shek in 1975, politics in Taiwan entered the Chiang Ching-kuo era. To cope with economic stagflation amid the oil crisis, Chiang Ching-kuo launched the far-reaching Ten Big Projects. To meet the rising expectation among Taiwanese for more participation in the political affairs of the nation, he sped up the recruitment of young talent into higher echelons of the government. He also implemented an elaborate program to enhance administrative efficiency and deliver service to the people with vigor and determination. Yet the opposition still felt unsatisfied.

In the local elections held in November 1977, the KMT suffered

FIGURE 10–5

PROFILE OF VOTERS BY FAMILY INCOME IN LEGISLATIVE ELECTIONS IN
TAIWAN, DECEMBER 1986

(percent)

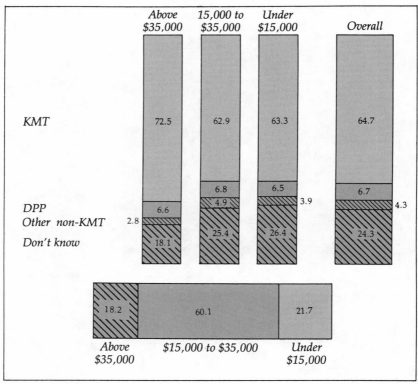

SOURCE: Same as for figure 10–2.

unprecedented losses. Not only did the KMT lose five mayoralties and magistracies, twenty-one seats in the Provincial Assembly, and six seats in the Taipei city council to the opposition; the election also brought about a major riot at Chung-li in Tao-yuan county.

In January 1979, there was supposed to be an election on the membership of the representative bodies. Yet owing to the withdrawal of recognition of the ROC by the United States, the election was postponed. In one way or another, the postponement of the election led to the occurrence of the Kao-hsiung incident, which led to the arrest of many of the opposition leaders by the GRC.

In June 1980, the GRC announced the resumption of the election

FIGURE 10–6
PROFILE OF VOTERS BY CLASS IDENTIFICATION IN LEGISLATIVE ELECTIONS IN TAIWAN, DECEMBER 1986
(percent)

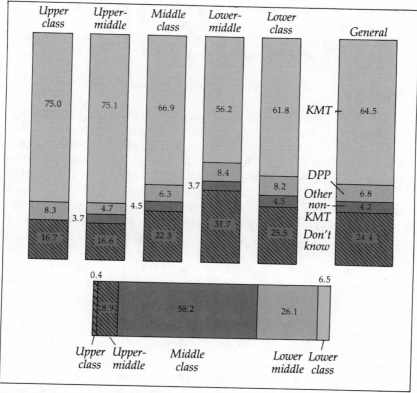

SOURCE: Same as for figure 10–2.

of the representatives at the national level. The result of the election showed no significant change of the basic alignment between the KMT and the Dang-wai (outside-the-party). Both parties claimed victory, with the KMT receiving 73 percent of the votes and the opposition claiming one-fourth of the newly elected seats.

From 1980 onward, the opposition continued mounting its pressure upon the GRC for more political participation. Meanwhile, however, internal dissension was already present among the leaders and followers of the opposition movement. A "criticizing K'ang Ning-hsiang [a moderate wing of the Dang-wai] movement" was launched

225

by the more radical wing of the opposition, which might have contributed to the defeat suffered by K'ang's group in the election of 1983.

In April 1984, the opposition established the Public Policy Research Association as a focal point of organizational activities. In the election of 1985, the candidates supported by the association were successful in their bids for various positions in the local election. Encouraged by the result of this election, the opposition completed the formation of a formal political party.

The GRC's Conciliatory Approach toward the Opposition

Facing all the international challenges and domestic turmoil, the government of the ROC decided that a conciliatory rather than confrontational strategy should be applied. Under the personal guidance of President Chiang Ching-kuo, a task force composed of twelve members of the standing committee of the KMT was formed to deliberate an all-encompassing program for reform in the government and in the ruling party. Among the subjects under planning and review were: (1) reinforcing the membership of the central representative bodies; (2) legalizing the structure of the provincial and local government in Taiwan; (3) drafting a national security law (for the preparation of the lifting of martial law); (4) revising the law on civic organization, to pave the way for the formation of new political parties; (5) improving law and order; and (6) reforming the ruling party.[12]

To gain insight into the planning process for this unprecedented political reform, four study groups composed of government officials and scholars were sent to the United States, the United Kingdom, the Federal Republic of Germany, and Japan to examine the process of democratization as well as party politics in these countries. Reports resulting from these study tours were used for the drafting of various proposals for the enactment of the national security law, the revision of the law on assembly and parade, and the revision of the law on election and recall.[13]

By August 1986, all preparations for the lifting of martial law had been completed pending approval through the internal procedures by the government and the ruling party. Yet, sensing what was coming, the Dang-wai made a preemptive move by announcing the formation of the Democratic Progressive party (DPP) on September 28, 1986. On October 8, 1986, in an interview with Katharine Graham, publisher of the *Washington Post*, President Chiang Ching-kuo formally declared the intention of the ROC's government to lift martial law and to permit the formation of new political parties. Following this announcement by President Chiang, new legislation was passed that paved the way for the coming of a new era of party competition in Taiwan. By the end of 1990, more than fifty political parties had been registered with the Ministry of Interior Affairs.

Beyond the lifting of martial law and the permission for the formation of new political parties, the announcement by President Chiang Ching-kuo to permit retired servicemen, and later the people on Taiwan in general, to visit their relatives on mainland China has had lasting effects on the political development on Taiwan, relations with mainland China, and the external relations of the ROC with the rest of the world.

Intraparty Elite Conflict and Readjustment in the Post–Chiang Ching-kuo Period

The passing of President Chiang Ching-kuo on January 13, 1988, ushered in a new period in political development on Taiwan. In accordance with the constitution, Dr. Lee Teng-hui, the vice president, was sworn in as the successor of Chiang as president of the republic. But his succession to the chairmanship of the ruling party was not as smooth as the presidency. It took a two-step effort for the supporters of Lee Teng-hui to gain the acting chairmanship of the party through a meeting of the Standing Committee and then through a standing ovation in the Thirteenth Party Congress. In both cases, there was hidden and overt resistance to his assumption of the chairmanship of the ruling party.[14]

President Lee Teng-hui demonstrated during the period of the Thirteenth Party Congress that he was not content to be merely a titular head of state, but actually aimed at becoming a substantive leader with strong opinions on personnel matters, both in the party and in the government. Many domestic and international observers of Taiwan politics believe that President Lee Teng-hui's actions, coupled with an unprecedented demonstration of the independent will of the delegates to the Thirteenth Party Congress in selecting members of the Central Committee of the ruling party, might have sown the seeds for later conflicts within the ruling party.[15]

The story of the Special (Provisional) Meeting of the Central Committee of the KMT held on February 11, 1990, was covered extensively by news reports and political analyses on Taiwan and abroad and does not need reiteration here. What should be pointed out, however, is the surfacing of covert resistance to Lee Teng-hui's leadership among a significant portion of the existing power structure

227

within the ruling party. Another salient fact became clear during the debates over the method of selecting the KMT candidate for the presidency of the republic. There was a lack of clear rules and procedures that would have allowed all the leaders legitimately to declare their interest in gaining the nomination of the party for the presidency of the republic and for the members of the Central Committee to openly express their wish in this matter.[16]

The majority of the political analysts in Taiwan believed that Lee Teng-hui managed to succeed to the presidency as well as to the chairmanship left by Chiang Ching-kuo, yet he "did not inherit the authority of Chiang Ching-kuo."[17] Had he chosen a Yen Chai-ken type of leadership, playing the role of nominal head of state, it would have been well received; or if Lee Teng-hui had preferred to be a substantive leader but was willing to go through a more open process of democratic competition within the party, he still would have been supported. What the leaders and the rank and file of the ruling party could not accept was the attempt to become a new strongman by using the procedures generally regarded as appropriate only for the late Chiang Kai-shek and for Chiang Ching-kuo, who in the opinion of many political observers on Taiwan had acquired party and government leadership through a prolonged period of sacrifice and dedication.[18]

Controversies within the Special Meeting of the Central Committee of the KMT were carried over to the meeting of the National Assembly in March. Lee Teng-hui and Lee Yuan-tsu were elected president and vice president of the republic, but only after much oral and physical confrontation in the National Assembly, a difficult and complicated process of mediation by senior statesmen among contending presidential and vice-presidential candidates, and a large-scale student demonstration for constitutional reform.

The so-called Kuo-Shih Hui-yi (National Affairs Conference) may or may not have resulted from the student demonstration. Some observers believe the conference was held to deal with the side effects of the meeting of the National Assembly.[19] Divided into sections on parliament reform, local government, central government, constitutional reform, and mainland China policy, the conference arrived at many far-reaching conclusions. These included the retirement of all senior members of national representative bodies by the end of 1991; the curtailing of the recruitment of members of the national representative body from overseas Chinese and from occupational groups; the popular election of the governor of Taiwan and the mayors of Taipei and Kao-hsiung municipalities; the end of the period of mobilization and the suppression of rebellion; and the treating of both sides of the

Taiwan Strait as political entities (Cheng-chih Shih-ti) and enacting laws to deal with relations between them.[20]

National Affairs Conference and Its Aftermath

During the course of the National Affairs Conference, substantive differences between the KMT delegates and the majority of the independent participants became clear. The KMT delegates favored broadening the popular base of the ROC government on Taiwan yet still preserving the essence of a national government on Taiwan, pending eventual reunification with mainland China. The DPP participants sought a much more drastic change of the nature and the structure of the political system on Taiwan, including a total overhaul of the membership of the parliament and the drafting of a completely new constitution by a special constitutional convention and through a referendum by the people in Taiwan. If all these recommendations were accepted and implemented, it would be tantamount to the establishment of a new Republic of Taiwan.[21]

Discussions within the National Affairs Conference, and particularly views voiced by members of the DPP, caused considerable concern among the members of the more orthodox wing of the ruling party. Partly to offset the separatist flavor of the National Affairs Conference and partially to gain a dominant role in deciding policy regarding national reunification, a National Unification Council was established under the aegis of the president's office.[22] The main purpose of the board is to study problems relating to national reunification and to develop broad general guidelines on this important policy area.[23]

The chairman of the National Unification Board is President Lee. In 1992, the three vice chairmen were Vice President Lee Yuan-tsu, Premier Hau Po-tsun, and the senior adviser to the president, Kao Yu-shu. Members of the board include top-ranking officials of the ROC government, leaders of various sectors of society, leading scholars, and major newspaper publishers. A guideline for national unification has recently been adopted by the council. In addition to reiterating the basic position of the GRC toward national reunification, it sets clear stages for a gradual development toward unification.

The first stage is for mutually beneficial interchanges. During this stage, the GRC would gradually loosen all restrictions on exchanges between the two sides of the Taiwan Strait. It would also establish a nongovernmental intermediate agency to deal with the rights and privileges of the people involved in the exchange process. In addition, it would seek to establish the principle of mutual noninterference between mainland China and the ROC regarding each other's external relations with other countries.

In the second stage, official channels of communication between mainland China and Taiwan would be established, following the reduction of tension and hostility. Cooperation would be achieved in the development of the Yangtse River, the Ming Chiang River, and the Yueh Chiang River Delta. The gap between the living standard of the people on mainland China and those on Taiwan would narrow and pave the way for eventual national reunification. Finally, in the third stage, the mechanism for deliberation (*shieh-shang*) of national unification would be established between the two sides. Unification could thus be achieved under the principle of political democracy, nationalization of the armed forces, privatization of property ownership, and social pluralism.[24]

Until recently, mainland China was steadfast in its policy toward Taiwan. Mainland China maintained that it is the sole government of all China, that it will not rule out the use of force in settling the Taiwan problem, and that it is firmly opposed to any international arrangement for the GRC that could create an impression of "two Chinas" or "one China, one Taiwan." It also strongly advocated the solution of the unification issue under its "one country, two systems" model.

Yet with the establishment of the Commission on Mainland Affairs and the Foundation for Exchanges across the Taiwan Straits by the GRC, the regime of mainland China seemed to be softening its position. The communique issued by the Chinese Communist party (CCP) at the end of the Seventh Session of the Thirteenth Party Congress stated that the party would treat the questions of Hong Kong and Taiwan separately; that Hong Kong and Macau would be restored to the PRC through the "one country, two systems" scheme by the end of the 1990s; and that efforts would be made to promote interchanges across the Taiwan Strait so as to facilitate a peaceful reunification between mainland China and Taiwan.[25]

Although the language used by the Chinese Communist authority is vague, political observers in Taiwan sensed a slight change in the tone used for discussion of the Taiwan issue. No longer does anyone mention a timetable for the unification of Taiwan, as Teng Hsiao-ping and other CCP leaders often did in the past. Furthermore, there is more emphasis on peaceful means and processes for achieving the goals of reunification. Nevertheless, Taiwan must be careful not to overestimate this and infer that the CCP has renounced the use of force as a strategy for completing the task of national unification.[26]

Following the April 1993 meeting in Singapore between Koo Chen-fu, chairman of Hai chi-Hui Foundation for Exchanges across the Taiwan Straits in Taiwan, and Wang Daohan, president of Hai-hsieh-hui (Strait Coordination Associations) of mainland China, relations between the two sides entered a new era. The fact that the new secretary-general of the Strait Exchange Foundation in Taipei, Cheyne Chin, was until February 1993 the deputy secretary-general in President Lee's office, testifies to the importance the GRC places on relations with mainland China.

There exists, nevertheless, a host of problems between Taipei and Peking. The PRC government insists on the "one China" principle and refuses to recognize the international personality of the ROC. It also denies the GRC's request for "equal footing" between the two Chinese political systems. The GRC, conversely, has decided to launch a diplomatic offensive toward membership in the United Nations, despite strong opposition voiced by Peking. These are but a few examples of the existing differences between Taipei and Peking. Only time can tell, therefore, whether the meeting between Koo and Wang is the beginning of the melting of the iceberg of mutual distrust and resistance between Taipei and Peking, or merely a temporary appearance of the sun in a sky full of clouds.

Democratization, Unification, and Elite Conflict in Taiwan Politics in the 1990s

Having discussed the process of democratization and the development of unification policy under President Lee Teng-hui, we may turn to the analysis of current problems and future trends. First, let us examine the political situation in Taiwan. After the debacles at the party congress in February 1992 and at the National Assembly in March, the ruling party recuperated somewhat from the intraparty struggle among leaders at the highest echelon. Attention focused on when the new meeting of the Central Committee would be held. According to the party constitution, the meeting should be held on an annual basis. But widespread sentiment among members of the Central Committee to elect members of the Standing Committee by secret ballot created a concern in the party headquarters. The wounds resulting from the last Central Committee meeting had not yet fully mended.

Another issue was the election of a party chairman by secret ballot—an issue that took the central stage in the special party meeting held in February 1992. This would not have to be dealt with until the Fourteenth Party Congress; hence there would still be enough time for the party headquarters to deliberate the methods and processes to choose the congress delegates who would be voting for the membership of the Central Committee, and for the latter then to vote for party chairman and members of the Standing Committee of the party.

As a political party with a Leninist heritage, the KMT is confronting all kinds of challenges. Among the more obvious ones are decision-making processes that are too centralized; a full-time party staff that is too large; a budget to support the full-time employees and party activities that is necessarily too large; decreasing support for party policies and positions among members of the parliament; and declining interest in joining the party among the educated youth. Thus far, the existing plan for party reform focuses more on the structural aspects than on the actual functioning of the party; even less attention is given to a reevaluation of the basic nature of the party. Consequently, younger party members, especially intellectuals, hold a prevailing opinion favoring an extensive review and overhaul of the structure and operation of the party.[27]

Among the suggestions made frequently by party workers and members are election of the party chairman by ballot; nomination of party candidates and party delegates by votes and through primaries; election of members of the Central Committee and Standing Committee by secret vote; reduction of full-time party employees and party budgets; separation of the party from the government, but strengthening of the coordination between the administrative and legislative branches of the government through the mediation of the ruling party; and enhanced policy research within the party, to serve as a national and objective foundation for policy formation within the ruling party. Despite assertions to the contrary, these recommendations are shared by many party leaders and followers irrespective of whether they are dubbed as "mainstream" or "nonmainstream" factions.[28]

Although expectation among members of the party for reform is rising and differences among party leaders did emerge during the 1993 meeting of the Central Committee, there is no immediate danger of a large-scale split among the rank and file within the KMT. One of the major factors contributing to party solidarity is the feeling that "We have done it together!"—meaning the various achievements of the KMT in Taiwan during the past forty-five years. According to various opinion surveys, members of the KMT feel a strong identification with the party at the voting booth. More than 80 percent of the KMT members consistently voted for KMT candidates. The KMT members also demonstrated strong identification with the basic positions of the ruling party.[29] A word of warning, however: if the "mainstream" faction of the KMT were to fail to achieve a rapprochement with the "nonmainstream" faction in the Fourteenth Party Congress in August 1993, intraparty cohesion and voter support in the November 1993 local election could suffer.

The Opposition Parties

The opposition party, the DPP, is still facing the problem of intraparty conflict. The Mei-li-dao (Formosa) faction and the Hsin-tsao Liu (New Wave) faction within the DPP are frequently at odds on various issues and positions, including different stands on the question of Formosan independence, participation in the National Affairs Conference and the National Unification Board, and their response toward the arrest of Huang Hua, an advocate and activist of the Independence movement, by the GRC. Generally, the Formosa faction is willing to play the role of an opposition party, avoiding confrontation with the ruling party on basic issues that may induce strong response from the government. They are more inclined to participate in activities sponsored by the GRC or the KMT, whereby they believe they will have an adequate chance to voice their opinion and exert influence, such as in the National Affairs Conference.

The New Wave faction of the DPP, however, seems to distrust and disregard most of the opportunities for communication and reconciliation provided to them by the GRC or KMT. They are much more open and vehement in their position for an independent Taiwan; they are also more inclined to use street demonstrations as an instrument either for the proclamation of their beliefs or as a method to obstruct government policies.[30]

Among leaders in the opposition parties, K'ang Ning-hsiang and Chu Kao-cheng deserve some analysis. Long regarded by the more radical wing of the DPP as being too soft toward the KMT, K'ang Ning-hsiang still commands some influence among both liberal intellectuals and urban residents who prefer some checks and balances for the KMT. After the cessation of the publication of the daily newspaper, *Capital Morning Paper*, K'ang was experiencing a temporary setback. But after becoming a member of the National Unification Council and of the Control Yuan, K'ang Ning-hsiang seemed to have recovered from his political downfall.

As for Chu Kao-cheng, the well-known "activist" legislator, he has formed a "third party": the Chinese Social Democratic party. The basic ideological position of the party is similar to that of the Social Democratic parties in Europe and Japan, but it has also incorporated

233

FIGURE 10–7

Voters' Self-Identification as to Class in Taiwan, August 1978–December 1986

(percent)

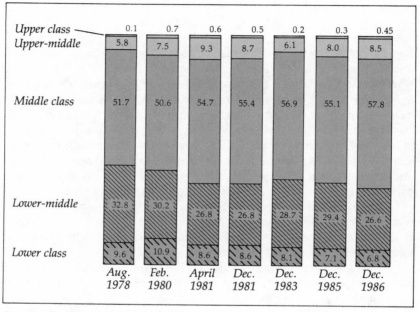

SOURCE: Same as for figure 10–2.

aspects of the ideas on the liberty of human beings contained in the philosophical thinking of Immanuel Kant. Whether this party will emerge as the major third party in Taiwan is still not clear, although various opinion polls show that a section of the people in Taiwan prefer that there be a third political force in addition to the KMT and the DPP.[31]

Aspirations of the Middle Class

Two salient elements of the social and political life of Taiwan have functioned to prevent large and fundamental sociopolitical cleavages and have contributed to cohesion and stability in the society: the emergence of a strong middle class and the existence of a moderate consensual opinion structure among the voters of Taiwan. According to my own opinion surveys and those conducted by many other scholars, there is without question a strong middle class in Taiwan.

As the data in figure 10–7 clearly demonstrate, more than 50 percent of the voters in Taiwan identify themselves as middle class. These voters have shown a high level of consistency in their political attitude and voting behavior. Their basic inclination favors social and political reform, but not at the cost of stability and economic growth. Consequently, the majority of the middle class voted for the ruling party, the KMT, which is generally regarded as a party for moderate social reform and steady economic growth.[32]

In addition to the middle-class identification of most of the voters in Taiwan, a stabilizing element in Taiwan politics is the persistent demonstration of a moderate consensual opinion structure. The majority of the voters tend to be in the "slight approval" and "approval" categories in a six-category scale ranging from strongly approving to strongly disapproving. A paper of the writer presented to the Chinese Association of Political Science postulated six ideal types of opinion structure in a competitive political system. Consecutive opinion surveys clearly demonstrated a strong tendency among voters in Taiwan to choose a right-of-center position in favor of the government policy and position (see figures 10–8 and 10–9). This opinion structure may help explain the high level of consistency of the percentages of the votes received by the ruling party.[33] Unless the KMT makes serious mistakes in its domestic and foreign policies and the economic situation of the country deteriorates substantially, there is little possibility of a takeover of the government through election by either the DPP or other opposition parties.

As for relations among the political elite, a complex picture emerged after the departure of Premier Hau from the cabinet in January 1993. Despite the rather high level of popularity enjoyed by former premier Hau as revealed by various opinion polls,[34] Hau was more or less forced to resign by pressure originating directly or indirectly from the president's office. The new premier, Dr. Lien Chan, is widely known to have close relations with President Lee, as are most new members of Lien's cabinet. Consequently, the previously existing tension between the cabinet and the office of the president has evaporated. Yet intensified frictions have surfaced in the central Standing Committee of the ruling party. Whether these frictions will subside or grow will depend on the outcome of the Fourteenth Party Congress in August 1993.

New Issues in the ROC's External Relations

Having discussed the issues concerning both democratization and unification, we may now turn to the question of the external relations

235

FIGURE 10–8

A Theoretical Construct of Public Opinion on Government Policy in Taiwan

(percent)

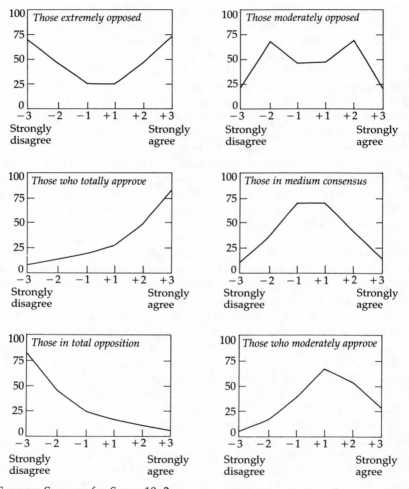

Source: Same as for figure 10–2.

of the ROC. Until President Lee Teng-hui assumed office, the foreign policy of the ROC had been a steadfast attitude of noncoexistence with mainland China in terms of diplomatic relations with other countries. Although various suggestions have been made to develop

FIGURE 10–9

ATTITUDES OF ROC VOTERS TOWARD HOUSE REGISTRARS, 1978–1986

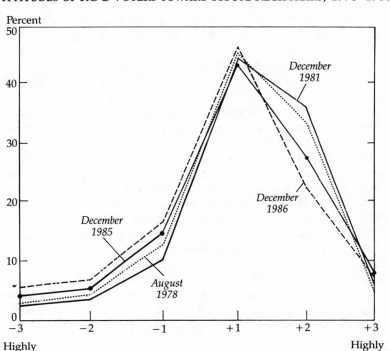

SOURCE: Same as for figure 10–2.

a more flexible posture toward unification and diplomatic recognition,[35] no significant change resulted.

Yet after Dr. Lee Teng-hui became president, things did start to change. First of all, in the Thirteenth KMT Party Congress, President Lee made the policy statement that "we must have more confidence and take more practical, more flexible, more forward-looking measures to elevate and to bring about a breakthrough in substantive diplomacy." In the second session of the Thirteenth Party Congress President Lee went further, stating, "We believe that there is only one China and that China must be reunified. But we must have the courage to face the reality that we do not exercise effective control of mainland China. . . . Only with this kind of realization may we develop a pragmatic approach to create the conditions for new opportunities, so as to strive for the fulfillment of our final goals."[36]

With these new policy postures advanced by President Lee himself, external relations of the Republic of China entered a new era of "pragmatic diplomacy" and "dual recognition."[37] Although there are still debates as to the meaning of "pragmatic diplomacy" and its relations with "dual recognition," the underlying principles of the new policy are quite clear. First, the ROC is willing to establish formal diplomatic ties with all friendly countries, regardless of whether they have ties with mainland China. Second, the GRC will be willing to participate in and become a member of any international organization wherein mainland China is already or may soon become a member, so long as the principles of equality, parallelism, and mutual non-subordination are observed.

As a result of these more flexible and practical policy postures, the ROC was able to establish or restore ties with a number of small to medium-size countries, such as Grenada, Liberia, the Bahama Islands, Belize, Lesotho, Guinea Bissau, and Nicaragua. The loss of formal ties with Saudi Arabia and with South Korea and the establishment of diplomatic relations between mainland China and Singapore, as well as reestablishment of ties between mainland China and Indonesia, have been setbacks for the ROC. Yet with the democratization process continuing in Russia and Eastern Europe, and with many countries in the third world highly interested in the economic strength as well as the technological know-how of the ROC, we may be cautiously optimistic for further expansion of external relations of the ROC.[38]

As for relations between the ROC and the United States, there is no outstanding issue between the two countries. Although the people of the ROC are somewhat disappointed with the U.S. relationship with mainland China after the Tiananmen incident, substantive relations between the ROC and the United States remain cordial and close. Given the trade, scientific cooperation, and cultural exchange between the two countries, as well as the increasing investment by Taiwanese businessmen in the United States, it is reasonable to believe there will be stable and close relations based on mutual interests between the ROC and the United States.

Conclusions

Having examined the ROC's responses to such challenges as national unification, diplomatic isolation, and conflict among the elite, we come to several conclusions. First, the KMT must try hard to resolve intraparty conflict among top-level leaders. The KMT still enjoys substantive support in Taiwan, yet it is faced with a genuine threat from the DPP to remain the ruling party on the island.

Second, in the December 1992 election, the DPP gained fifty-two seats out of a total of one hundred sixty-one in the Legislative Yuan. As a result, the DPP has evolved into a credible force for checks and balances against the KMT. If the DPP manages to capture more than half the counties and cities in November 1993, it would greatly enhance its influence and prestige in Taiwan. Many top leaders in the KMT have started to worry about what might happen in a direct presidential election if the KMT failed to heal the wounds of intra-party conflict.

Third, the major political issues facing the ROC on Taiwan will be: constitutional reform, reform in the ruling party, debates over a cabinet versus presidential system of government, maintenance of law and order, social welfare, environmental protection, labor problems, relations with mainland China, and the expansion of external relations. Advocacy of Formosan independence has gained more acceptance among the people on Taiwan, but legal separation of Taiwan from mainland China is still unlikely to grow into a mainstream political movement.

Fourth, the ruling and the opposition parties will have overt and covert factions. It is not unlikely for the KMT to develop into a party similar to that of the pre-breakup Liberal Democratic party of Japan, with clear, identifiable factions in both the party structure and the legislative branch of the government. Factions in the legislative branch have already become prominent in recent years. With the mushrooming of various think tanks, foundations, and funds in Taiwan, the linkage among knowledge, money, and power has increasingly become a political reality in Taiwan. It is still too early, however, to assess the real impact of these new organizations and activities on practical political matters.

Fifth, the issues of democratization on Taiwan, national unification, and the ROC's foreign relations have a three-way impact on each other. If the process of democratization in Taiwan leads to the formal separation of Taiwan from mainland China, it would cause grave concern to the PRC and would increase the tension in the Taiwan Strait. Conversely, if interactions between mainland China and Taiwan proceed at a much quicker pace and at higher levels than the people of Taiwan are prepared for, and particularly if they are conducted through direct government-to-government channels, the Taiwanese people would be gravely concerned and might find separatist movements more appealing.

The best approach for the GRC is to adhere firmly to the one-

China principle and to the eventual unification of China under the principles of democracy, liberty, and respect for the free will of the people on both sides of the Taiwan Strait. Furthermore, the ROC should handle its relations with mainland China with caution and through an evolutionary, step-by-step process. The ROC should also try to expand its foreign ties, but not at the cost of completely separating Taiwan from China or of alienating mainland China to the point of leading to possible military confrontation in the Taiwan Strait.

Sixth, mainland China does not seem to pose any serious threats against Taiwan in the foreseeable future. Leaders in Peking are busily engaged in an effort to upgrade the living standards of the people. They have repeatedly said that they need a peaceful international environment to allow them to devote themselves fully to domestic developments. This does not mean, however, that the ROC should rest its security solely upon the goodwill of the mainland regime. It should enhance its defense capability by overhauling its outdated air-and-sea defense capability. Only by gaining an edge in quality can the ROC compensate for its deficiency in quantity when compared with the mainland.

Finally, the development process of Taiwan is a precious experience that should be shared with other countries, and with mainland China in particular. Already experts from Eastern Europe and Latin America have come to Taiwan to learn more about the process of privatization and land reform. Agricultural teams have already gone to mainland China from Taiwan to offer technical assistance to Chinese farmers. This constructive interaction, based on concrete need and practical experience, may prove not only a useful instrument for external relations but also a vehicle for the peaceful reunification of China.

11
Toward Taiwan's Full Participation in the Global System

Chi-ming Hou

In this chapter I speculate on what Taiwan's economy will look like in the 1990s and beyond. My contention is that Taiwan's economy is likely to remain strong in this period and will be further integrated into the world economy. I will first identify the underlying factors that have contributed to the outstanding economic performance in the past—factors that I believe are deep-rooted in the Chinese tradition and hence should not disappear overnight. I will also argue that there are no inherent economic reasons why Taiwan's current economic ills, which are described by some as the symptoms of stagflation, should not vanish in a short time. Finally, I discuss the forces that could further internationalize or globalize Taiwan's economy.

Economic Performance

Taiwan's record of economic growth has been phenomenal, and the fruits of economic growth have been widely shared by all income groups on the island. Furthermore, the improvement of the material well-being of the people was accomplished in a climate of high consumer sovereignty without undue government control, high economic stability without serious inflation or unemployment, and financial solvency without foreign debt. Much structural transformation also took place, causing a shift from primary to secondary industries. Other countries have done as well as Taiwan in some of these areas, but few, if any, have done as well as Taiwan in all of them:

- For the entire period 1953 to 1989, GNP grew at an average rate of 9.0 percent a year.
- Per capita GNP grew at 6.3 percent a year from 1953 to 1988.
- As a measure of stability, consumer prices rose over the period

241

1953–1988 at a rate of 6.8 percent a year.

• Wholesale prices increased at a slower rate, averaging 5.3 percent a year from 1953 to 1988. It should be noted, however, that from 1953 to 1988 in only seven years did consumer prices go up by more than 10 percent a year and in nineteen years consumer prices went up by less than 4 percent a year. The sharp price increases in 1974 and 1980–1981 were brought about primarily by worldwide oil crises.

• The rate of unemployment for the entire period averaged just 2.7 percent.

Other economic data further illustrate the growing strength of Taiwan's economy:

• As for income distribution, the share of the top 20 percent declined from 41.1 percent to 38.2 percent in 1988.

• The ratio of average disposable income per household of the top quintile to that of the bottom declined from 5.33:1 in 1964 to 4.17:1 in 1980, and then it went up to 4.50:1 in 1985 and 4.85:1 in 1988.

• The Gini coefficient, as a measurement of income inequality, declined from 0.321 in 1964 to 0.294 in 1970, and then to 0.277 in 1980. It gradually grew to 0.299 in 1987.

Data on income distribution in the 1950s are scarce and probably less reliable than more recent data. According to one estimate, based on rather limited data, the family income of the wealthiest 20 percent of the households was about fifteen times that of the poorest 20 percent.

• In industrial transformation, the share of agriculture in net domestic product declined from 38.3 percent in 1953 to 6.1 percent in 1988. The corresponding share accounted for by industry (manufacturing, construction, electricity, gas, and water) increased over the period from 17.7 percent to 46.2 percent in 1988.

• In employment, the share of agriculture declined from 55.6 percent in 1953 to 13.7 percent in 1988, while the corresponding share of industry increased from 17.6 percent to 42.6 percent.

• In both production and employment, the shares accounted for by manufacturing rose sharply, from 11.3 to 38.7 percent over the period in net domestic product and from 12.8 to 34.5 percent for employment.

• As for financial solvency, Taiwan has changed status from debtor to creditor. As most know, Taiwan has accumulated, for better or worse, a foreign exchange reserve of over U.S.$80 billion under the control of the Central Bank.

It is not our intention, however, merely to propagandize Taiwan's good performance. Many undesirable developments have obviously occurred concomitantly with the accomplishments. Any visitor to Taiwan can quickly notice how bad the traffic is, how bad the air is, and how bad the housing situation is—and the lack of recreational facilities. What is worse than all this but less noticeable to visitors is the serious deterioration of social ethics and law and order. In a nutshell, whether the quality of life, when both material and non-material aspects are considered, has improved at all despite the marvelous economic performance is questionable.

The Contributing Factors

How did Taiwan achieve its "economic miracle"? Economists may never sort out and agree upon the complicated causes and effects of economic change in Taiwan. In our view, the early adoption of an export-expansion strategy by the government was the most important factor in Taiwan's success. Other policies or factors, of course, were important. Indeed, government policies designed to improve the quality of labor and the savings ratio were essential in making the export-expansion strategy effective. What is suggested here is that unleashing the power of the potential productive resources—especially labor—through this strategy made the accelerated modern economic growth in Taiwan possible. The measures adopted for export expansion may be briefly summarized.

In July 1955, the government issued Regulations for the Rebate of Taxes on Export Products, probably the beginning of the adoption of an export-expansion strategy. The regulations provided for the rebate of import duties, defense surtaxes, and commodity taxes to encourage the processing of imported materials for exports. Another big push for export expansion was made in 1958 when the Program for the Improvement of Foreign Exchange and Trade Control was initiated.

This program, together with subsequent regulations, promoted export expansion in the following ways:

• There was a significant devaluation of the currency. At the same time a dual exchange rate was adopted, with one rate as the basic official exchange rate and the other applied to export proceeds and inward remittances. A single exchange-rate regime was adopted in place of the earlier dual-rate system in 1961.

243

- Tariffs were reduced, and strict import controls were eased, especially for imports of materials and equipment to be used in the production of exports.
- The scheme of export incentives was expanded to include not only rebates of customs duties on imported raw materials but also exemption from business and related stamp taxes, a lower taxable income base, special low-interest loans, direct subsidies, and government-financed export-promotion facilities and market research.
- Tax-and-duty-free export processing zones were created (one in Kaohsiung in 1966 and one each in Nantze and Taichung in 1969), which were designed, by and large, for the purpose of attracting foreign investment. As it turned out, a great deal of foreign capital did come in, primarily directed toward export-oriented activities.

A word may be added here on exchange-rate policy. Before 1955 the New Taiwan (NT) dollar was grossly overvalued. The basic exchange rate of NT$15.55 to U.S.$1 had been in force since 1953. In 1955 the government allowed exporters a higher exchange rate (through the device of "exchange surrender certificates," which were given to exporters and could be sold freely on the market to importers). In 1961, a single uniform exchange rate was introduced at NT$40 to U.S.$1. This rate remained unchanged until 1973.

According to a calculation by Kuo-shu Liang and Ching-hou Liang, the official exchange rate was quite favorable to exports during the years 1956–1960, 1969–1973, and 1975–1980. It was only slightly unfavorable in two years, 1964 and 1974. After 1980, the NT dollar continued to be undervalued. From the fourth quarter of 1980 to the fourth quarter of 1985, for example, the NT dollar was undervalued in relation to the U.S. dollar by as much as 26 percent. (The extent of the undervaluation is calculated on the basis of nominal exchange rates, adjusted for relative changes in the price levels of the two countries.)

The export-promotion policies have had a profound effect on Taiwan's exports. Export trade, which had grown by 11.6 percent a year in 1953–1962, rose at a rate of 28 percent a year in 1963–1972. In 1952, the total value of merchandise exports was U.S.$0.1 billion. By 1980, it had risen to U.S.$19.8 billion. It continued to rise to U.S.$30.7 billion in 1985 and U.S.$66.2 billion in 1989.

The ratio of exports of goods and services to gross domestic product (GDP) rose from 8.0 percent in 1954–1956 to 20 percent in 1964–1966, 43.4 percent in 1974–1976, 56.2 percent in 1984–1986, and 50.0 percent in 1989. Thus, it is clear that the rate of growth of exports exceeded that of the rest of the economy by a wide margin.

The measures for export expansion undoubtedly paved the way for Taiwan to mobilize its resources to exploit the rapidly growing world market from about 1950 to the mid-1970s. But external demand alone does not necessarily guarantee an increase in exports; there also has to be a change in domestic supply. Fortunately, several key government policies were adopted that improved domestic supply. First, the government promoted agricultural development. A land reform program was carried out in 1949–1953. The government also played a crucial role in introducing new crops, improving irrigation and drainage, and strengthening and coordinating the rural organizations essential to dissemination of new technology. The Joint Commission on Rural Reconstruction, established in 1948 as a joint Sino-American organization and aided by American funds and technical knowledge, was instrumental in carrying out the government's agricultural policy.

The impressive increase in agricultural production made enormous contributions to industrial development and export expansion. It kept food prices relatively low, making it possible for the industrial sector to enjoy an abundant labor supply at a relatively low wage rate. It also provided an important source of foreign exchange as agricultural exports financed more than half of all imports in 1951–1964. Furthermore, by compulsory purchases, land taxes, and the rice-fertilizer barter system, the government transferred a considerable amount of capital (the so-called agricultural surplus) from the agricultural sector to the industrial sector. All rice collections were obtained at government purchasing prices that were much lower than market prices, whereas chemical fertilizers were supplied to farmers at prices above world prices by a government-owned enterprise. The government collected as much as 73 percent of the rice marketed in 1954 and about 50 percent marketed in 1966–1968. In net terms, the proportion of total agricultural production transferred to the rest of the economy was estimated as high as 22 percent in 1950–1955 and around 15 percent in 1956–1969.

Second, the government encouraged savings that made possible the high capital formation rates. The ratio of gross national savings to GNP averaged 14.5 in 1952–1959, rising to 33.6 in 1980–1989. In net terms, the average ratio of net savings to national income rose from 10.6 in 1952–1959 to 31.4 in 1980–1989. Aside from emphasizing the Confucian virtue of thriftiness in general, the government adopted two policies that aimed at increasing savings, namely, a relatively realistic or reasonable interest-rate policy and a tax-incentive policy.

The interest-rate policy was successfully adopted in the early

1950s as a weapon to combat inflation. The rationale was that a reasonable interest rate (that is, a positive inflation-adjusted interest rate) was necessary to attract savings. Thus, in March 1950, a special system of savings deposits was introduced that offered a nominal interest rate of 7 percent per month or 125 percent a year. At that time, the inflation rate (as measured by wholesale prices) was 10.3 percent per month. The public responded promptly; total time and savings deposits jumped up sharply and inflation was brought to a halt. As S. C. Tsiang has demonstrated very convincingly, the flow of savings into the banking system was very sensitive to interest rates.

A relatively realistic high interest rate has been largely maintained. From the middle of 1951 to 1986, the nominal interest rate on one-year time deposits was below the inflation rate only in 1973–1974 and in 1979–1980, when prices increased drastically as a result of the oil crises. For most years in this period the real interest rate was between 7 and 10 percent.

These interest rates pertain to the formal financial sector, that is, the banking system, which consists primarily of government-owned banks under the government's direct control. Lending and borrowing outside the banking system have been and still are very substantial. It is estimated that for 1964–1985 no less than 37 percent of the borrowing of medium and small business came from the "black" or "gray" credit markets. The interest rates in these markets (known as the "curb market interest rates") were much higher (often by more than 100 percent) than the bank interest rates.

The high curb market rates, which were free from government control, seem to indicate that the bank rates, as high as they were, were probably below the natural rate that would clear the market. But the official interest-rate policy has to be commended. Many developing countries adopt policies that result in interest rates substantially lower than those determined by market forces, hence badly distorting the allocation of resources. A detailed study on the relations between interest rates and savings in Taiwan has yet to be done. It is reasonable to assume that the government's interest-rate policy must have been an important factor contributing to the high savings rate in Taiwan.

With respect to the use of tax policy to encourage savings, the government allowed, for a long time before 1981, tax exemptions on interest income earned from time deposits of a duration longer than two years. Since 1981, for each person, interest income up to NT$360,000 per year (U.S.$14,423 according to 1992 exchange rate) has been exempt from income taxation. Ninety percent of all taxpayers are estimated to have taken advantage of this exemption. As for interest income resulting from the curb market, no tax is paid at all. The tax exemption on interest income is probably an important factor in the high savings rate in Taiwan, along with tax evasion in the case of interest income derived from the curb market.

Third, the government's strong educational policy greatly improved the quality of the labor force and hence contributed to industrial development. Aside from its decisive role in shaping the entire educational system, the government also has devoted substantial amounts of money to education. Public expenditure on education rose from 1.7 percent of GNP in 1951–1953 to 5.1 percent in 1986.

In 1952, 42 percent of the population aged six or older were illiterate. The proportion had dropped to 15 precent by 1970 and to 8.4 percent by 1985. The proportion of the population six years of age or older with a secondary education was about 9 percent before 1957, rising to 42 percent in 1985. The portion of the population with a higher education also increased greatly during this period. The skills developed by education have contributed to improvement in labor productivity, have increased the labor force participation rate of women, and have facilitated labor mobility. All of these changes have contributed to industrial development.

The Significance of Export Expansion

The export-expansion strategy was clearly catalytic and instrumental in Taiwan's success. It is not just that export expansion overwhelmed the import-substitution policy, which was not dismantled until very recently. The real significance of export-expansion policies is that they freed the economy in large measure from government control and allowed market forces to function. The population's energy was thus unleashed to exploit the world market.

Since export-promotion policies were by and large directed at all industries without special favor to any particularly selected or targeted industries, entrepreneurs were essentially left alone to develop those industries whose products they could sell profitably in foreign markets. As one would expect, they invested in those industries that the theory of comparative advantage predicted as profitable. In the early phase of its development, Taiwan exported primarily labor-intensive products.

As labor became more expensive relative to capital, however, capital intensity (as measured by the capital-labor ratio) in the export sector gradually deepened. The ratio of industrial exports to total exports has gradually gone up. In the early 1950s, Taiwan's exports were mainly agricultural and processed agricultural products, with industrial products accounting for less than 10 percent of total exports. After 1955, the share of industrial products rose by leaps and bounds: 50 percent in 1962, 80 percent in 1971, 90 percent in 1980, and 94 percent in 1985.

In 1952, sugar and rice were the leading exports. By 1966, textile products had become the leading exports, but bananas, canned food, and sugar were still more important than any other products. In 1976, textile products remained the leading exports, followed by electrical machinery and apparatus and plastic articles. By 1986, electrical machinery and apparatus had become the leading exports. Furthermore, the combined total of plastic articles, metal manufactures, machinery, and chemicals exceeded that of textile products. This pattern indicates that export expansion has brought about structural change and industrial upgrading. Taiwan's economy has not remained static at a particular level.

A particular feature of export expansion in Taiwan is that small and medium enterprises (roughly, those with fewer than 100 employees) have played an important role in developing foreign markets. For the period 1978–1985, export earnings of small and medium enterprises constituted about 65 percent of the total export earnings in Taiwan. The ratio was probably much higher in the early years. Furthermore, these small and medium enterprises depend very heavily on foreign markets. More than 70 percent of their total sales came from exports in 1981–1985, and their dependence on exports has increased steadily since 1972.

The fact that Taiwan's exports have consisted primarily of labor-intensive products and that most of the export trade has been done by small and medium enterprises has enormous implications. First, this pattern of export expansion has created a great number of jobs. According to one estimate, the proportion of the total increase in employment attributable to the increase in the production of exports went from 20 percent in 1961–1966 to 27 percent in 1971–1976. The share of employment in export industries in total employment went up from 12 percent in 1961 to 34 percent in 1976. Another estimate indicates that employment generated directly and indirectly by exports accounted for 56 percent of total employment in manufacturing (excluding beverages and tobacco) in 1966 and 54 percent in 1971. Thus, export expansion has clearly been the key factor in employment growth and in the full-employment situation in Taiwan, which has been maintained over the past three decades.

Second, while export expansion has reduced income inequality, employment expansion has reduced the share of farm employment in total employment and hence the degree of income inequality between the agricultural and the nonagricultural sectors. But more important, the expansion of labor-intensive industries has increased the demand for unskilled and low-income workers both in the agricultural and in the nonagricultural sectors. According to data in the Industrial and Commerical Census, in 1961, 54 percent of all nonagricultural workers and employees were employed in industries with an average wage of 75 percent or less of the average wage of all nonagricultural workers and employees. That portion was reduced to 32 percent in 1966 and 18 percent in 1971. With 50 percent of the average wage of all nonagricultural workers as the dividing line for determining low-income workers, 25 percent of all nonagricultural workers were employed in low-wage industries in 1961, 2 percent in 1966, and 0.1 percent in 1971.

Evidently the rapid development of labor-intensive industries provided opportunities for new entrants into the labor force who would otherwise have been absorbed primarily in agriculture and other low-wage industries, thus deepening the level of poverty. The newly developed industries not only absorbed recent entrants and stole workers from low-pay industries but also created demand for unskilled workers as various linking effects permeated the entire economy. This increase in demand, when coupled with an improvement in the worker's knowledge and skills resulting from better education, must have contributed to the increase in labor productivity and wages in low-wage industries.

Third, export expansion has contributed to the high savings ratio. A recent study suggests that the savings ratio in Taiwan is positively and significantly related to the exports ratio, which is the ratio of exports to the sum of exports and domestic consumption expenditures. It stands to reason that when the exports ratio goes up, profits from exports will rise. It is likely that the propensity of the proprietors of small and medium enterprises to save is very high as these enterprises are usually family businesses. But this issue remains to be studied.

Persistent Stagflation?

Recent economic indicators have given rise to pessimism about the vitality of Taiwan's economy. The economy is often said to be undergoing stagflation—recession and inflation at the same time, with no end in sight. Some fear that there is something fundamentally wrong with the economy.

There is no question that the economy has slowed. The annual growth rate of GNP, having been in double digits for all of 1986 and most of 1987, slowed to 7.3 percent by the end of 1987 and registered 7.4 percent in 1989. It contracted steadily throughout 1990, declining from 6.82 percent in the first quarter to 4.70 percent in the fourth quarter. For 1990 as a whole, the growth rate turned out to be 5.3 percent. While such a growth rate is by no means small by world standards, for Taiwan, it must be considered so. In all the years since 1953, only three (1974, 1975, and 1982) have seen a growth rate lower than 5 percent.

For manufacturing, the picture is even darker. The annual growth rate of production in manufacturing began to slow down in 1988, when it was only 3.6 percent, far below its long-term average. (It averaged 15.3 percent in 1970–1979 and 16.5 percent in 1960–1969.) It was not much higher in 1989, when it was 3.7 percent. It got worse in 1990. There was not only no increase but actually a decline by 1.9 percent. In 1991, however, the annual growth rate went back to an increase at 7.3 percent.

Private investment, which includes fixed-capital formation and increases in stocks, grew at 11 percent in 1989, already very low in comparison with previous years' marks. In the fourth quarter of 1989, it grew by only 5.7 percent. In 1990, private investment declined 7.5 percent in comparison with the 1989 level. Gross capital formation, as a proportion of GNP, was maintained at 22 percent in 1990, roughly the same as in 1989 and 1988, but this amount was largely due to a sharp increase in government investment and the investment of public enterprises. Furthermore, a gross capital formation rate of 22 percent is rather low, when compared with the average of 30 percent in 1970–1980.

On the inflation front, wholesale prices did not increase from 1982 to 1989, except in 1984 when there was an increase of 0.5 percent. For all other years, wholesale prices actually declined. In 1990, it continued to decline at 0.6 percent. But the index of wholesale prices began to go up modestly in 1991 at 0.17 percent. Consumer prices rose by less than 1 percent in 1986 and 1987 and by 1.3 percent in 1988. In 1989, the rate of increase was 4.4 percent. In 1990, it was 4.1 percent, and it was 3.6 percent in 1991.

Consumer prices, then, have not gone up beyond 5 percent a year. But the figures on the volume of the money supply are astonishing. The money supply, which includes currency, checking accounts, and passbook deposits, increased 51.4 percent in 1986, 37.8 percent in 1987, and 24.4 percent in 1988. These rates far exceeded the growth rates of GNP (11.6 percent in 1986, 12.3 percent in 1987, 7.3 percent in 1988). In 1989, even with a relatively tight policy in effect, the money supply still increased at 6.1 percent, not much lower than the rate of increase in GNP, which was 7.4 percent. The money supply declined in 1990 at 6.6 percent, but the volume of money (as defined above) stood at NT$1.9 billion in 1990 in comparison with NT$751 billion at the end of 1985. And in 1991, the increase rate jumped again to 12.1 percent, with the volume of money reaching NT$2.2 billion.

As for the costs of production in the manufacturing sector, wages went up by 10.1 percent in 1986, 9.9 percent in 1987, and 10.9 percent in 1988. In 1989, they went up by 14.6 percent. Since labor productivity did not go up as fast as wages, unit labor costs went up by 11.7 percent from 1986 to 1989. During the same period, the index of wholesale prices dropped from 100 in 1986 to 94.9 in 1989; and the index of consumer prices increased by 6.3 percent. These numbers suggest that profit margins in manufacturing were reduced.

Pessimists often cite these data to support the stagflation thesis. They claim that the drop in private investment, the rise in unit labor costs, the decline in the output of manufacturing, and the slow growth of GNP all indicate economic stagnation. They therefore also believe that the recent rise in consumer prices coupled with the enormous size of the money supply constitutes a time bomb that could result in serious inflation.

The crucial element of the stagflation thesis is, of course, the loss of vigor of private investment. Several factors may have contributed to the decline of private investment.

The large appreciation of the currency (from U.S.$1 = NT$40 in 1985 to roughly U.S.$1 = NT$26 in 1989, or 54 percent) has undoubtedly hurt exports—the dependent industries. Their profit margins and investments must have been greatly reduced, if they can still make any profits and investments at all. The social unrest caused by labor-management confrontations and strong environmental protests have also made many enterprises hesitant to invest. The uncertainty created by domestic political struggles and the rising crime rate can hardly inspire businesses to expand either. In short, the investment climate has deteriorated enough to create a crisis of confidence—a loss of confidence in the vitality of the economy. This anxiety is also reflected in the violent fluctuations of the stock market. The index of the stock prices reached about 12,680 points in February 1990, only to drop to about 2,560 points in the first half of October in the same year. Concomitantly, the deterioration of the domestic investment climate has been accompanied by a considerable outflow of capital. That is, people have transferred their money out of the country to other places for various uses including investment abroad.

251

Without question, there is a certain degree of truth in the pessimistic stagflation thesis as described. But in our view, it is exaggerated. Given a growth rate of GNP above 5 percent, an inflation rate below 5 percent, and an unemployment rate around 2 percent, it is highly doubtful that the term *stagflation* is appropriate. At any rate, the economic slowdown of the early 1990s was short-lived. Much of the slowdown was attributable to the persistent trade imbalance. As the trade imbalance continued to be reduced, a fundamental cause of Taiwan's current economic ills was removed. Furthermore, the sharp currency appreciation that started in 1985 apparently halted in September 1989. Thereafter, the currency depreciated, a development undoubtedly favorable for exports. The newly adopted Six-Year National Development Plan put into effect in 1991 is a strong stimulus for a speedy recovery from the current economic slowdown; it may even propel the economy into a course of high growth for a long time to come.

The Trade Imbalance

Before 1971, Taiwan had a trade deficit, with respect to merchandise trade, every year except 1965. Beginning with 1971, Taiwan has had a trade surplus every year except 1974 and 1975 when the price of imported oil sharply increased. But before 1981, the trade surplus as a proportion of GNP (the trade surplus ratio) was not very large, reaching 6 percent only in 1972 and 1978. In other years, it was around 4 or 5 percent. After 1980, the trade surplus rose dramatically. The trade surplus ratio reached 20.0 percent in 1986. Since the surplus in merchandise trade was not offset by trade in services and items in the capital account, foreign exchange reserves piled up quickly. They amounted to only U.S.$0.9 billion in 1972, but by the end of 1986, they had gone up to U.S.$46.3 billion, or 61 percent of GNP. In November 1990, they amounted to some U.S.$72 billion, or 44 percent of GNP. Growth continued in 1991 and 1992. What contributed to this development?

First, for fear of hurting exports, the NT dollar was allowed to depreciate. From the fourth quarter of 1980 to the fourth quarter of 1985, the NT dollar was undervalued in relation to the U.S. dollar by as much as 26 percent. Interest rates were kept high in order not to stimulate domestic demand and imports, because of the fear that inflation would be incubated by the trade surplus. In real terms, bank interest rates were kept as high as 10 percent every year from 1981 to 1985.

Tariff and nontariff barriers were left virtually unchanged from

1980 to 1986. The ratio of tariff revenues to imports actually went up from 7.46 percent in 1981 to 7.89 percent in 1985 and remained at 7.67 percent in 1986. It did not begin to decline drastically until after the second half of 1987. The maintenance of high tariff protection in the face of the rising trade deficit was only a reflection of the deep-rooted philosophy of import substitution, without due consideration to the costs of such a policy.

Export-expansion policy was justified to the extent that it offset or neutralized the bias against exports, such as the policy of tax rebates on imported materials. But measures biased in favor of exports, such as undervaluation of the currency or loans at low interest rates, were certainly beyond what "free trade" requires. Moreover, certain social costs like those related to environmental protection were not adequately shared by export industries, resulting in the selling of goods to foreigners at less than "true" cost. The inadequacy of Taiwan's environmental protection policy has created serious social tensions and public demand for higher standards of such protection, which, in turn, became a major deterrent to domestic investment.

The huge size of the trade surplus and of the amount of foreign exchange reserves is very harmful to the economy, since the accumulation of these reserves represents an outflow of capital. In the judgment of many, Taiwan has an urgent need to upgrade its economy (that is, to make it more capital intensive and technology intensive), to protect the environment (especially the air and water), and to improve the quality of life (transportation, parks, and the like). For this, Taiwan needs all the funds and foreign exchange it can get. Taiwan is still a developing country, and its per capita income is still very modest. It makes no sense to export capital, more than 20 percent of GNP a year.

Furthermore, the trade surplus has resulted in an excessive supply of money in the economy, which undoubtedly constitutes a serious inflationary threat. Thanks to imports, prices have not generally gone up, but excess liquidity has certainly helped convert the stock market into a casino and has caused real estate prices to skyrocket. The sharp rise in land prices and speculation in the stock market by workers have also hindered domestic investment.

The widespread indulgence in speculative activities has encouraged some people to avoid ordinary work and withdraw from the labor force. The soaring land prices have also made some landowners, quite a large number, feel rich, encouraging them to retire early. These factors have contributed to a decline in the participation rate of the labor force. As a result, wages have risen sharply, a labor shortage has developed, and employment in the manufacturing sector has declined. Such conditions have hindered domestic investment.

The huge trade surplus has resulted in serious trade negotiations with the United States—as the trade surplus is primarily with the United States. Of course, the American trade deficits have largely been a result of that country's own making: prolonged budgetary deficits and an inability to produce enough goods and services to sustain its level of consumption and investment. From the U.S. point of view, Taiwan has created the trade surplus, so Taiwan has to take steps to reduce it. Unfortunately, under American pressure, or rather the threat of deadly "301" action, Taiwan has relied unduly on the use of currency appreciation to reduce the trade surplus. As a result, many export industries, which are largely labor intensive, have been seriously hurt. Some of them have moved to Southeast Asia or the Chinese mainland.

The trade imbalance will remain a problem for Taiwan to deal with for a long time to come, but indications are that it has become much less troublesome. The ratio of the trade surplus to GNP was down to 9 percent in 1988 and 1989, in comparison with 18 percent in 1987 and 20 percent in 1986. In 1990, it continued to go down to 7 percent.

This substantial reduction of the trade surplus has eased pressure to increase the value of the currency and the money supply. It will do much to solve the problems associated with stagflation.

The Six-Year National Development Plan, 1991–1996

The government has officially adopted a national development plan for 1991–1996, which was drafted by the Council of Economic Planning and Development (CEPD). The fundamental objectives of the plan are: (1) to increase national income; (2) to upgrade the industrial structure; (3) to reduce regional inequalities; and (4) to improve the quality of life.

The specific targets of the plan include, among others, the following:

- an annual growth rate of 7 percent for GNP
- per capita GNP of U.S.$13,975 in 1996
- an unemployment rate of 2.1 percent for 1991 and an average of 2.3 percent in 1992–1996
- an inflation rate of 5 percent for 1991 and an average of 3.5 percent in 1992–1996
- a total of U.S.$103 billion worth of merchandise exports in 1996

(or an increase of 53 percent over the 1990 amount), and a total of U.S.$95.6 billion worth of merchandise imports for 1996 (or an increase of 74 percent over the 1990 amount)
- a reduction in the trade surplus of goods and services to U.S.$1.4 billion, or 0.47 percent of GNP, in 1996
- a projected exchange rate of U.S.$1 = NT$27.3
- total government expenditure of U.S.$301.8 billion (or NT$8,238.2 billion) for carrying out the plan

To improve the quality of life and achieve regional balance, specific blueprints have been prepared for the geographical distribution of the construction of new transportation networks, industrial sites, harbors, reservoirs, public housing, recreational facilities, and the like. To make the economic structure more capital and technology intensive, the government has selected ten industries to be "star" industries. The government will help them develop, especially by acquiring new technologies. A manpower plan has also been developed to ensure the availability of the necessary technicians and workers.

It is still hard to evaluate this ambitious plan with the limited details published so far. But since it is known that most of the government expenditures for the plan would be for public investment, the economic impact should be enormous. The total government expenditure for the plan is estimated at 21.7 percent of the projected total GNP for the six-year period. Fixed capital formation as projected in the plan would constitute 18.2 percent of projected GNP.

While no one yet knows how a public investment of this magnitude would affect the economy in general and private investment in particular, one thing seems clear. If the early 1990s economic situation needs stimulus, the public investment entailed in the new Six-Year National Development Plan will provide it.

Prospects for the 1990s

In 1986 a long-term economic projection for 1986–2000 was made and published by the CEPD. A picture of Taiwan's economy in the year 2000 was painted in some detail. Since no revision of this projection has been made, it seems useful to review briefly what the projection entails. In many ways, the new six-year economic reconstruction plan has incorporated much of the general philosophy and many of the guidelines of the long-term projection.

For 1986–2000, the average growth rate is projected at 6.5 percent for GNP and 4.1 percent for per capita GNP (the average growth rate of the population is 1.1 percent). By the year 2000, per capita GNP is projected to increase to NT$522,570 at current prices, or U.S.$19,140 (at the exchange rate U.S.$1 = NT$27.3). There will be no serious inflation, since the annual inflation rate, as measured by wholesale prices, is projected to be 3.5 percent. The unemployment rate will be kept below 3 percent. Thus, the objective of growth with stability is to be maintained.

Industry and services will continue to be the main pillars of the economy, as the role of agriculture will continue to decline. For 1986–2000, industrial production will grow at 6.0 percent a year, services at 7.4 percent a year, and agricultural production at 1.5 percent a year. By the year 2000, services will account for 50.5 percent of gross domestic production, with industrial production accounting for 46.5 percent and agricultural production for 3.0 percent.

The economy will continue to be outward oriented. For 1986–2000, exports of goods and services will grow annually at 6.1 percent and imports of goods and services at 7.9 percent. In the year 2000, the combined total of exports and imports of goods and services will be 102.8 percent of GNP. (The proportion for exports of goods and services will be 51.6 percent, and for imports of goods and services, 51.2 percent.)

The driving force behind economic growth will be the increase in labor productivity. Since the proportion of the working-age population (fifteen to sixty-four) to total population will increase from 65.2 percent in 1985 to 68.9 percent in 2000 and since the unemployment rate will remain low, the average annual rate of increase of total employment as well as the labor force is projected to be 1.9 percent for 1986–2000. With such a rate of increase in the labor force and employment, an increase in labor productivity of 4.5 percent a year is projected to achieve an annual GNP growth rate of 6.5 percent.

To improve labor productivity, fixed capital is projected to increase at 8.7 percent a year for the period. In the year 2000 the gross capital formation rate will be 28 percent. These, then, are the prospects for Taiwan's economy in the 1990s as projected by the government. How realistic are these projections?

To illustrate whether the official projections are achievable, we may make use of the relationship between the rate of growth of national income on the one hand and the savings ratio and marginal capital-output ratio on the other. If the marginal capital-output ratio is 3, a $3 investment will produce $1 of national income. Thus, if the savings ratio is 30 percent and the marginal capital-output ratio is 3, then the annual rate of growth of national income will be 10 percent.

Or, given a savings ratio of 30 percent and a marginal capital-output ratio of 4, the growth rate of national income will be 7.5 percent.

For the twenty years from 1970 to 1989, the ratio of gross national savings to GNP averaged 32.4 percent, whereas the ratio of net savings to national income averaged 30.8 percent. For the same period, the marginal capital-output ratio averaged 3.5. If these ratios should hold for the next ten years, the growth rate of GNP would be considerably higher than the projected 6.5 percent.

Of course, as wages go up and labor-intensive industries lose their competitiveness in the world market, the economy will undergo structural change and become more capital intensive. As a result, the marginal capital-output ratio will be higher. But economic upgrading or structural change is a slow process, and, unless the government artificially intervenes, capital intensity will not jump overnight, as the past has demonstrated.

The same is true with savings. While a great deal of research is still needed to explain why the savings ratio in Taiwan has been so high, it is generally believed that such patterns are deeply rooted in Chinese traditions and values. Parents, for example, always try to save for their children, and thrift is regarded as a virtue in and of itself. To be sure, these traditions and values are changing, but they do not die suddenly. Similarly, the vitality, ingenuity, and industry of the entrepreneurs and workers, who have channeled savings into efficient and profitable investment in the past, will not disappear instantly.

Thus, all the basic ingredients of economic success in the past should continue for some time, making a prosperous economy possible in the future. If the growth rate of GNP is smaller than in the past, the reason is primarily that the savings ratio will probably not climb any higher. But the economy will be more technologically advanced and capital intensive, with more infrastructure and environmental protection to improve the quality of life.

We should make it clear, however, that this rosy picture is based upon certain preconditions. First of all, political and social stability must be maintained to create a favorable domestic investment climate and to avoid massive capital flight. Second, labor-management relations have to be relatively harmonious to keep wage increases compatible with productivity increases. In the past forty years, labor markets have in general been highly competitive; there does not seem to have existed any exploitation of one side by the other. Now collective bargaining is being introduced, and efforts have to be made to avoid all the pitfalls associated with this mode of labor-management relations, such as those frequently found in other countries.

Third, as a multiparty system continues to expand and influence politics, political parties may be strongly tempted to establish a social welfare program designed to win votes. Such a system is likely to discourage savings, adversely affect work incentives, and destroy the traditional family structure and virtues, as demonstrated by the experiences of many countries.

Fourth, the government should speed up the privatization of public enterprises to maintain effective competition in the markets. It should refrain from interfering with economic activities except in cases of genuine market failure. Public investment should not overwhelm private investment, and the direction and structure of the economy should be determined by market forces.

Fifth, Taiwan should continue its economic internationalization policy as publicly announced. These conditions for economic prosperity are recognized by many. Let us hope they will be met.

Toward Further Economic Internationalization

Economic internationalization in its purest form allows complete freedom of movement of goods, capital, and labor among nations. In the real world no country has tried to achieve this. Taiwan is no exception. All Taiwan wants to achieve, in external trade and investment, is to make its market as accessible as those of the economically advanced countries. Taiwan wants a trading system based on free multilateralism consistent with the basic principles of the General Agreement on Tariffs and Trade.

Taiwan has made significant progress toward import liberalization. The average nominal tariff rate was 55.7 percent in 1974, 39.1 percent in 1978, and 30.8 percent in 1984, falling to 12.6 percent in 1988. The effective tariff rate (that is, the ratio of total tariff revenue to total imports) fell from 11.6 percent in 1979 to 5.66 percent in 1988.

Tremendous progress in removing nontariff restrictions has also been made, especially since 1983. Import restrictions have been loosened on a wide variety of commodities. At present, nearly all categories of imports may be brought in without restriction. Import procedures have also been simplified.

In addition, efforts have been made to loosen restrictions on foreign investments to open domestic markets further to foreign investment. Foreign banks, for example, are allowed to conduct business in much the same way as Chinese banks. Foreign firms can also operate in more service areas such as insurance, transportation, and leasing, among others. Since the deregulation of exchange controls in July 1987, there has been virtually free movement of capital.

Looking ahead, we see that Taiwan will be more and more integrated with the world economy. Further import liberalization has occurred; in 1992 the average nominal tariff rate was reduced to 7 percent (tariffs on agricultural products fell to 19.8 percent and tariffs on industrial products to 5 percent). The average effective tariff rate was reduced to 3.5 percent in 1992, about the same level as in many Western developed countries.

Japan and the United States have been, and still are, Taiwan's largest trading partners. In 1989, 30.7 percent of Taiwan's total imports were from, and 13.7 percent of its exports went to, Japan. (The corresponding percentages were 40 percent and 18 percent in 1967.) In 1989, 36.2 percent of Taiwan's exports went to, and 23.0 percent of is imports were from, the United States. (The corresponding percentages were 26 percent and 31 percent in 1967.)

Taiwan has tried hard to diversify its markets for exports and sources of imports, by increasing its trade with Europe and Southeast Asian countries. It has met with some success, especially in Southeast Asia.

Some Concluding Remarks

The picture of the economy of Taiwan in the 1990s presented here is very promising, even though the growth rate of GNP will not be 8 or 9 percent a year, as in the past forty years. If the underlying economic forces are allowed to work, however, a growth rate of 7 percent is not only achievable but very likely.

The international economic environment will probably not be as favorable in the 1990s as in the 1960s and 1970s, when world trade expanded greatly in part because of the liberal trade policy of the United States. Now the world economy is fast dividing into economic blocs. In addition to the Free Trade Agreement (FTA) between the United States and Canada, an FTA between the United States and Mexico was reached in August 1992. With these FTAs and the close American ties with Latin American nations, the countries in the Americas will likely form an economic bloc.

As for Europe, many fear that Europe under the Maastricht Treaty will become a "fortress Europe" with strong protectionist tendencies. This fear is strengthened by recent developments such as the economic and monetary integration of fifteen European countries. Given the political change after 1989 in Eastern European countries, they may someday be absorbed into the single market of Europe.

There have been talks about forming some sort of economic bloc in East and Southeast Asia, but the cultural and political differences in these countries, as well as the unpleasant memories of World War II, are difficult obstacles to overcome.

Taiwan's economy is outward oriented, as we all know. Past experiences have shown that the ingenuity, flexibility, and adaptability of the people in Taiwan can survive and prosper in the most difficult of circumstances. The world economy in the 1990s may not be as liberal as one would like, but it is growing and changing. With growth comes change, and new opportunities will always be there to exploit.

Here we should note the recent changes in relations between the two sides of the Taiwan Strait. Both trade and investment between Taiwan and mainland China have risen sharply, and continue to grow. Accurate estimates are hard to come by, because a considerable part of Taiwan investment has not been officially registered. According to the official report, total Taiwan investment in the mainland was about U.S.$3 billion in 1989, while the total volume of trade (through Hong Kong) was estimated at U.S.$3.5 billion in 1989. Taiwan investment in the mainland rose to U.S.$4 billion in 1990, U.S.$5.8 billion in 1991, and U.S.$5.5 billion in 1992. Parallel to that, the total volume of indirect trade (through Hong Kong) between Taiwan and the mainland increased to U.S.$4 billion in 1990 and U.S.$5.8 billion in 1991.

There should be a great potential for trade and investment between Taiwan and the mainland, since the assets of the two areas are complementary: Taiwan is relatively rich in technology, capital, and management, whereas the mainland is rich in labor and natural resources. Both would lose if this potential cannot be realized because of political obstacles.

Bibliography

Council for Economic Planning and Development. *Long-Term Prospects for Economic Reconstruction in the Republic of China on Taiwan 1986–2000*. May 1986.

———. *The Six-Year National Development Plan 1991–1996*. January 1991.

———. *Taiwan Statistical Data Book 1990*.

Directorate-General of Budget, Accounting and Statistics, Executive Yuan, Republic of China. Quarterly National Economic Trends Taiwan Area, The Republic of China, August 1990.

Hou Chi-ming. "Relevance of the Taiwan Model of Development." *Industry of Free China*. February 1989.

Hou Chi-ming and Chen Tain-jy. "The Taiwan Economy: Problems and Prospects." *Asia Club Papers No. 1*. Tokyo Club Foundation for Global Studies, April 1990.

12
Reconciling Confucianism and Pluralism during the Transition of Taiwan's Society

Hei-yuan Chiu

In the near future Taiwan will be an open, pluralistic, and democratic society, unless the continuing reforms are seriously set back. Taiwanese society today is experiencing a broad range of changes. It has been achieving unusual economic growth. It is instituting reform in a conservative and passive way. It has gathered scattered social movements under political and social control. It has increasingly granted autonomy to associations or groups. It is changing its values and attitudes without abandoning tradition. It has a heightening problem of anomie, or alienation. It is facing the process of secularization and religious revival. Finally, it is being trapped by an identity crisis.

In the first three sections of this chapter I examine social attitudes, alienation, and the quality of life. In the final part I analyze the interesting contrast between secularization and religious revival.

Satisfaction with Personal Life

According to the September 1990 Social Attitude-Opinion Survey, 79 percent of Taiwan's adults express satisfaction with their personal life in general, while 15 percent of them show dissatisfaction. For lack of a reference point of comparison, it is difficult to evaluate the level of satisfaction. By taking satisfaction with personal life in general as a reference point for different aspects of personal living conditions, however, we can get a picture of people's quality of life that is clear and meaningful.

As the results of the survey show, the overwhelming majority of Taiwan's adults are very satisfied with their parent-child relationships (94 percent), friendships (93 percent), and marriages (92 percent). Fewer are satisfied with their own educational achievements (38 percent), their leisure (51 percent), and their financial conditions (58 percent). Thus, people in Taiwan are satisfied with their social life but are less satisfied or are even dissatisfied with their living standard. The average level of satisfaction with all items relevant to social life, or interpersonal relations, is 89 percent—much higher than with personal life in general. The average for all items regarding the living standard is only 61 percent.

Compared with the results from a survey conducted in 1985 that had the same set of items, the total change was slight.[1] Personal satisfaction with leisure activity decreased by 16 percent, but there was only a 3 to 6 percent decrease for the rest of the items. For example, 3 percent fewer of respondents in 1990 showed satisfaction with their own educational achievement; 4 percent fewer were satisfied with financial conditions; and 6 percent fewer were pleased with their neighborhoods and friendships. Thus the decreasing satisfaction with leisure activity is a significant and substantial change. As the subjective indicator shows a bad feeling about leisure, so the objective figures for the variety of leisure resources also demonstrate worsening conditions and declining quality.

Although the residents of Taiwan spend more and more money on leisure and entertainment, the quality of leisure has seriously declined. As the official statistics show, a total of 2.2 percent of per capita income was spent for leisure and entertainment in 1974, 4.5 percent in 1980, 5.3 percent in 1985, and 7.0 percent in 1988.[2] The government records also show an increasing number of people traveling around the world. For example, twelve persons per thousand went abroad in 1980, seventeen persons in 1985, and thirty-four persons in 1988. The domestic resources for leisure activities are limited and worsening, though. The playground area for a population of 10,000 decreased from 27.35 hectares in 1981 to 23.65 hectares in 1988. Although four national parks were set up in the mid-1980s, people still do not have enough outdoor space for leisure activities. From subjective and objective indicators, we see that people's need for a better leisure life has become stronger but that their resources have become more limited. Thus people are dissatisfied. In the future, leisure will be an important part of life—not just for killing time, but as a potential source of power for a change in lifestyle and even the development of the culture.

Although the changes for other aspects of the quality of life are slight, the tendency is clear and meaningful. Some are statistically significant. Table 12–1 shows that people in 1990 were slightly more satisfied with parent-child relationships and marriage, but not significantly so. For parent-child relationships, there was a 2.5 percent

TABLE 12–1

Satisfaction of Respondents with Quality of Life in Taiwan, 1985 and 1990

	Percentage Satisfied in 1990	Percentage More Satisfied than in 1985	Percentage Less Satisfied than in 1985	Percentage Other	G^a	df	p-value
Parent-child relationships	94.9	+ 2.5	− 1.5	− 2.2	.6	2	.729
Marriage	92.6	+ 1.9	− 1.6	− .4	3.8	2	.149
Relationships with relatives	86.4	− 7.9	+ 2.1	+ 5.8	158.4	2	.000
Neighborhood relationships	82.5	− 8.0	+ .5	+ 7.4	188.8	2	.000
Health	77.0	− 2.5	− 1.0	+ 3.5	147.2	2	.000
Housing	71.8	− 2.8	− 1.4	+ 4.1	109.2	2	.000
Work	68.0	− 4.3	− 4.2	+ 8.5	170.0	2	.000
Finances	58.4	− 6.6	− .7	+ 5.9	103.9	2	.000
Leisure	52.1	− 16.7	+ 7.6	+ 9.1	195.7	2	.000
Education	37.6	− 4.4	− 2.8	+ 7.2	161.4	2	.000

a. G-square shows the maximum likelihood estimates of partial association by controlling for sex, age, education, and marital status.

SOURCE: Data are taken from the General Survey on Social Change (1985) and the Social Opinion Survey (1990).

increase, which is not statistically significant according to the result of loglinear analysis: the G-square is 0.6, p-value is .729. The same unchanged situation is also found for marriage. Thus we can tentatively expect that people's satisfaction with the familial relationship may be maintained, or at least it will not change rapidly.

From the same analyses we can see that other interpersonal relationships have become worse. People are less satisfied with their relationships with relatives and neighbors. For these two relationships roughly the same percentage of difference is found between 1985 and 1990—a 7.9 percent decrease for the relationships with relatives and an 8.0 percent difference for relations with the neighborhood. These differences are statistically significant. People are less satisfied with the relationships outside the family: a meaningful trend in terms of alienation. In the future, this tendency will continue.

A consistent decline holds for the rest of the items regarding the standard of living. All the differences between 1985 and 1990 are negative and significant. In other words, people in 1990 are less satisfied with their education, work, housing, health, and financial situations. All the G-square figures showing the changes are statistically significant. The largest difference occurs for satisfaction with financial condition—6.6 percent; the smallest occurs for health—2.5 percent. It is reasonable to predict that people will remain unsatisfied with their education, financial situation, and other aspects of living. In the near future conditions of leisure will hardly be improved, and people's need for quality leisure activities will be heightened.

Changing Social Attitudes

A structural transformation took place in Taiwan in the late 1980s. People's social attitudes are likely to be affected by this great transformation. Changing social attitudes in turn influence the path and magnitude of structural change. For instance, the continuing process of liberalization and democratization has significant impact on people's attitudes and values. They become more open-minded, more tolerant of different political opinions, and more interested in political reform. These changing attitudes are the foundation of further democratization.

Other social attitudes might be similarly linked. Using two waves of survey data that have the same attitude items, we can identify changes in different social attitudes. Sex, age, education, and marital status are introduced in the loglinear analysis. Only for five attitude items is there no significant difference between the surveys. For the other twenty-nine items the responses are statistically different. Although the changes are expected, the results are still surprising. Many people maintain a conservative attitude, however. The changes are large, but they are not large enough to reverse the direction.

Liberalization and Changing Attitudes. The continuing reforms and political changes are the focus of the changing phenomena of Taiwan. The respondents of two waves of surveys show the changing political attitudes (see table 12–2). Generally speaking, liberalization becomes the main theme in the process of political reform. This process affects individuals' attitudes significantly. For instance, fewer people agree with such statements as "It is better to have older men make political decisions" (23 percent fewer); "Government should decide whether an opinion can be circulated or not" (13 percent fewer); "National affairs should be decided by the head of the government" (9 percent fewer); and "Too many different thoughts result in social chaos" (8 percent fewer).

All these attitude changes demonstrate that the people of Taiwan are becoming more liberal in the process of structural liberalization. Although a few citizens were liberal before the political reforms, more people became liberal after the structural changes occurred. Nevertheless, when more people have become liberal, structural transformation will be accelerated.

But the acceleration is slowed by a politically oversocialized people who insist on retaining their conservative ideology. Although 8 percent fewer of the respondents of 1990, compared with 1985, agree that too many different thoughts result in social chaos, for example, 63 percent still agree with the statement. In other words, the majority of Taiwanese people seem not to be pluralistic even now. They are afraid of having many different thoughts; they like stability. For a similar reason, the majority of people still believe that an increased number of social groups might hurt social stability. In the 1990 survey, 58 percent of the respondents agreed with the conservative argument. Thus, freedom of speech is not grounded firmly in Taiwanese society. The authoritarian government limits freedom and many people accept this in the interest of stability.

Some bigger changes clearly derive from absurd politics. The so-called senior people's representatives, who were elected almost forty years ago, still control three organs of the parliament. They are so old and so loyal to the ruling party that they do not take responsibility. Under the greater control and influence of the ruling party, 39 percent of respondents in 1985 agreed with the statement that political decisions should be made by the old; 38 percent disagreed with the statement, because more and more people are convinced that the old representatives have to retire. Thus, only 16 percent of respondents in 1990 agreed with the same statement, while 66 percent said no. The retirement of the old representatives, however, has still not materialized. The changing attitude of the people would have played a significant role if the situation had not improved before 1992, the deadline promised by Kuomintang.

In conclusion, although significant changes in political attitudes can be empirically detected and statistically tested, freedom of speech and freedom of forming associations cannot be taken for granted. Under the shadow of possible instability and chaos, the majority of people do not support the liberal position. Although 15 percent of the people disapprove of the government's authority to decide whether an opinion can be circulated, one third of the people approve of the role of the government as investigator.

Alienation. Eight items are identical in the two waves of social surveys. By controlling for the effects of age, sex, education, and marital status, changes from 1985 to 1990 can be observed on six items. Only on the items regarding feelings of meaninglessness and feelings of alienation from one's neighbors do the respondents of the two-wave survey not show the difference. Almost all the items demonstrate a growing tendency for people to feel more alienated.

More people feel powerless and disoriented. Compared with the responses of 1985, in 1990 6 percent fewer people thought an ordinary citizen could influence public policy, and 4 percent fewer believed in the possibility of influencing social development by frequently presenting opinions. Of greater importance, 12 percent more people advocated not caring about public affairs. In 1985, 28 percent thought that way; in 1990 it was 39 percent. From these three categories—especially the third—we can see an increasing tendency to feel powerless. This tendency should be carefully examined in the light of political liberalization and democratization, because the results seem to contradict the need for political reform.

The main purpose of political reform is to enforce the people's power by liberalizing and democratizing; yet more people now feel they are powerless. Perhaps this contradiction shows the difficulties for any kind of expected reform. When rising expectations remain unsatisfied for a long time and the establishment tightly holds power, the people may become disappointed but inactive. In practice, despite rapid and tremendous change, the progress of reform could not meet the expectations of the people. Furthermore, in recent years the government and its public policies became more ineffective under the pressure of released social and political forces.

TABLE 12–2
CHANGES IN SOCIAL ATTITUDES IN TAIWAN, 1985 AND 1990

Statement	Agree in 1990	% Difference between 1985 and 1990			G^a	df	p-Value
		Agree	Disagree	Percentage Other			
Bearing hardship leads to success.	78.3	− 12.5	+ 6.9	+ 5.6	324.9	2	.000
When the rich earn more, it is good for all.	21.4	− 10.1	+ 9.5	+ .6	63.5	2	.000
The rich should always be respected.	21.9	+ 5.3	− 6.1	+ 1.3	30.0	2	.000
Political decisions should be made by the elders.	15.8	− 23.1	+27.7	− 4.7	488.2	2	.000
National affairs should be decided by the government head.	32.9	− 9.2	+10.6	− 1.4	43.2	2	.000
Violent criminals should be punished immediately.	62.4	− 0.1	+ 0.0	+ 0.0	4.6	2	.099
Different thoughts result in social chaos.	62.7	− 7.7	+10.1	− 2.4	56.0	2	.000
Government should control circulation of an opinion.	32.8	− 13.1	+14.7	− 1.6	122.0	2	.000

More interest groups mean less stability.	57.9	− 8.8	+10.4	− 1.7	59.1	2	.000
Parliament's interference leads to poor administration.	28.9	+ 3.3	+ 2.0	− 5.4	12.0	2	.003
It is wrong to ask congressmen to vote for or against an act.	42.3	+ 0.6	− 0.9	+ 0.4	12.9	2	.002
Officials should obey orders rather than serve the people enthusiastically.	16.1	+ 3.3	− 0.6	− 2.7	22.8	2	.000
People should be allowed to change their minds at all times.	49.7	+ 6.5	− 1.1	+ 5.3	13.0	2	.000
Too much red tape is necessary to do anything.	56.9	− 3.8	+ 3.0	+ .8	15.1	2	.000
There is no trust among people.	24.8	+ 2.8	− 4.6	+ 1.8	33.2	2	.000
Common people should be able to influence public policy.	51.4	− 6.2	+ 4.6	+ 1.6	44.0	2	.000
Life has no meaning.	10.7	− 1.3	+ 2.8	− 1.6	5.8	2	.055
I do not care about public affairs.	39.4	+11.8	−14.0	+ 2.2	192.3	2	.000
Less contact with neighbors avoids trouble.	10.3	− 0.3	+ 0.2	+ 0.3	0.7	2	.691
One should influence social development by presenting opinions frequently.	55.3	− 4.0	+ 2.4	+ 1.7	18.3	2	.000
The spirit exists after death.	53.3	− 5.5	− 5.0	+10.4	83.4	2	.000

(Table continues)

269

TABLE 12-2 (continued)

Statement	Agree in 1990	% Difference between 1985 and 1990			G^a	df	p-Value
		Agree	Disagree	Percentage Other			
More people believing in God leads to a more stable society.	47.0	− 9.1	+ 0.1	+ 8.0	76.6	2	.000
One should work hard rather than depend on God.	83.1	− 3.4	− 0.5	+ 3.9	36.7	2	.000
Madness comes from offending a god or a ghost.	12.9	− 1.3	− 5.7	+ 7.0	112.3	2	.000
No criminal charge should be made against a mentally ill person.	32.3	−13.1	+ 0.2	+ 6.9	135.1	2	.000
The more strict the discipline, the more the achievement.	18.1	−17.5	+ 4.1	+13.4	658.1	2	.000
Sufficient freedom is necessary for good childhood development.	25.5	−15.0	+ 2.5	+12.4	543.3	2	.000
I would like to increase my knowledge.	80.3	− 6.8	+ 1.7	+ 5.1	151.4	2	.000

I would feel the importance of family if I left it.	83.2	− 7.7	+ 2.7	+ 4.9	133.4	2	.000
I would like a quiet life with less change.	86.4	+ 0.9	− 0.5	− 0.4	1.6	2	442
I like having a relationship with my family.	81.4	− 7.4	+ 2.8	+ 4.6	109.0	2	.000
I would like to be self-actualized.	70.4	− 10.4	+ 0.9	+ 9.5	224.3	2	.000
Protection is more important than promotion.	70.7	− 12.8	+ 2.8	+ 10.0	235.5	2	.000
I would like to experience varieties of living.	79.8	− 13.5	+ 4.1	+ 9.4	344.9	2	.000

a. G-square shows the maximum likelihood estimates of partial association by controlling for sex, age, education, and marital status.

SOURCE: Data are taken from the General Survey on Social Change (1985) and the Social Opinion Survey (1990).

271

In a rapidly changing society with a weakening authoritarian regime, the norms in different areas are transforming or collapsing. In the political sphere, fundamental laws and the bases of institutions are in a process of slow reform. Newly emerged party politics and social movements forcefully challenge the old norms and values, but they establish a dilemma between maintaining power and creating a new set of norms.

Liberalization and internationalization of the economy are the main policies of the government. The economic strength of the private sector is so energetic that the related regulations cannot effectively control it. Many businessmen and industrialists violate the regulations or public policies. Thus the underground economy booms domestically, and investments from Taiwan to mainland China grow fast.

The social order and norms are also in a confusing condition. The crime rate increased around 1986, and various types of gambling have become popular. In general, people emphasize deregulation in various domains. The government and the conservatives try to emphasize and restore the social order. In sum, social norms and values are changing and confusing because of the serious impact of the structural transformation. More important, the people feel the continuing change and they seem to be confused.

Work Ethic and Social Control. A few items in the surveys pertain to the work ethic, child rearing, and social control. The results are meaningful in pinpointing the uniqueness of the social changes taking place in Taiwan. As some sociologists and economists have suggested, the work ethic of Taiwanese and other East Asian people is an important factor in the facilitation of Asian economic growth. The majority of Taiwanese people greatly emphasize the necessity of hard work. In 1985, 91 percent of the survey respondents agreed with the statement that bearing hardship leads to success. Obviously, the emphasis on hard work is accepted by an overwhelming consensus. Nevertheless, only 78 percent of the 1990 respondents confirmed the statement. The 13 percent discrepancy shows the critical change in the work ethic. Although the percentage is still very large, the difference between the two waves of surveys is statistically significant. The consensus is not overwhelming now.

The changing attitude regarding hard work and success might be the result of the "bubble economy"—one of unsustainable expansion—and the so-called money game. After the bubble economy has ended, however, some people may change their attitude, while others may continue to deemphasize hard work. In other words, the effect of the changing work ethic may have a complicated impact on social and economic development.

Since 1989, the president and the premiers of Taiwan have emphasized the seriousness of the problem of public security. The majority of people are willing to support an authoritarian regime to execute a more repressive policy. According to the results of the two waves of surveys, people have retained their strong belief in immediate punishment for violent criminals. In 1985, the percentage in agreement with this was 62.5 percent; in 1990 it was 62.4 percent—showing a difference of only one-tenth of a percentage point. The unchanged attitude shows a conservative orientation for the strategy of social control. Even in another survey conducted in 1990, two-thirds of the respondents favored executing the criminal in public. In addition, fewer people agreed with waiving criminal charges against the mentally ill. The unchanged and the changing attitudes all demonstrate the persistence of traditional ideas about legal justice.

Social Problems

According to a survey conducted in 1990, the following were considered the top ten social problems. The percentages indicate respondents who rated the problem as very serious or serious.

(1) juvenile delinquency, 83 percent
(2) transportation, 82 percent
(3) public security, 79 percent
(4) environment pollution, 77 percent
(5) vice and prostitution, 73 percent
(6) bribery in elections, 72 percent
(7) speculation, 70 percent
(8) discrepancy between poor and rich, 69 percent
(9) rising prices, 69 percent
(10) gambling, 66 percent

At least two-thirds of the respondents rate the above social problems as serious. In addition, seven other problems are rated as serious by more than half the respondents. These are moral degeneracy (63 percent), corruption (60 percent), collusion between politicians and the rich (58 percent), economic crime (58 percent), providing for the aged (56 percent), social welfare (55 percent), and consumer protection (54 percent). These problems obviously cannot be ignored, because the majority of people believe they are serious. By using another criterion—that is, the amount by which the percentage considering the problem serious exceeds the percentage considering it not serious—we could identify five other potentially serious problems. These include getting a higher education (49 percent vs. 33 percent); overpopulation (45 percent vs. 38 percent); workers' rights (43 percent vs. 34 percent); divorce (43 percent vs. 33 percent); and judiciary injustice (38 percent vs. 22 percent).

As a result, almost all the problems listed in the questionnaire except one are rated as serious. The seriousness of each, however, is unique. Three major categories can be identified. The social impacts of these problems result in different effects on the changing socio-political situation of Taiwan. For example, since the problem of public security is considered serious by almost 80 percent of the adult population, the government is supported by the majority of people in adopting forceful measures to improve the situation. In another example, although 43 percent of the people rate as serious the lack of protection of workers' rights, 34 percent rate the problem as not serious. Thus when the workers' movements have been repressed by the government, workers cannot get support from the masses. The majority of people accept the argument that frequent social movements hurt public security and then hurt the economy.

The Five Most Serious Social Problems. Juvenile delinquency is the most visible and serious social problem. People's subjective feelings can be matched with the objective situation shown by the official statistics. Although the fluctuation in the number of juvenile criminal cases since 1985 does not show a consistent trend in terms of proportion to the total number of criminal cases, juvenile crime does increase in proportion to the population under eighteen. For instance, eighteen young men were arrested for every ten thousand under eighteen in 1985, but twenty-eight in 1988.

Since 1985 the number of registered motor vehicles, especially passenger cars, has skyrocketed. There were 698 cars for every 10,000 people in 1985, but 1,057 in 1988. Traffic has been the most significant and popular topic and excuse among the residents of metropolitan Taipei. A rapid transit system is being constructed. An increasingly chaotic transportation situation is expected by both government officials and residents. Thus, the people in Taiwan rate transportation as the second most serious problem: 82 percent of respondents indicate this. Again, the subjective rating corresponds to the objective situation.

Since August 1989, President Lee and Premier Hau repeatedly decried the worsening public security. In May 1991, President Lee unexpectedly nominated a military general to be premier. The reason given by the president for the surprising nomination was to restore and enforce public security. The media frequently report on information relevant to public security and give it enormous publicity. Under intensive media influence, the people of Taiwan have become more nervous about public security. No crime statistics show a worsening in public security, however, since 1989.

In actuality, the worst period was around 1986, and it improved in the middle of 1989, before the president acknowledged the seriousness of the problem. The crime rate in 1985 was thirty-two cases per 10,000 persons, and it increased rapidly to forty-nine cases in 1986. Nevertheless, the crime rate has declined slightly but continuously. In 1988 the rate became forty-five per 10,000 in the population. Ironically, the monthly figures showed an improving condition in early 1989.

In 1989, sixty-three convicted criminals were executed. More people were sentenced to death in 1990. The total number of death sentences issued from 1979 to 1988 was lower than the number issued in 1989. Between 1979 and 1990, 156 men were executed, but the total number for 1989 and 1990 was 137. It is clear that the judiciary system cooperated with the administration very well. Both of them were determined to reduce the crime rate by severe punishment.

The bubble economy that included speculating on the stock exchange, skyrocketing real estate prices, and collective gambling came to an end in the middle of 1990. The whole economy then seemed to be depressed. Public security became a decoy issue to deflect attention from economic troubles, both for government officials and for capitalists. In addition, after the government was forced to lift martial law, the high-ranking officials of the regime could not tolerate so many protests and blamed them as an important cause of public security problems.

For instance, the National Police Administration announced the ten important causes of the worsening situation of public security. Among these, social protest was identified as the second most important. Therefore, restoring public order became a practical and important policy to enforce the capitalists' confidence. In order to achieve this political goal, the government suppressed the people and businesses that might be suspected of hurting public security on the one hand, and repressed social protest and social movements on the other. A new authoritarian regime appeared to be emerging.

In recent years, the environmental movement has grown fast. Relevant protests and other collective actions have occurred frequently. Although environmental pollution has not lessened, the new cabinet, headed by an army officer, has been friendly toward the industrialists and hostile toward the environmental movement. The people do feel that environmental pollution is a very serious problem, however; 77 percent of respondents showed their dissatisfaction. This percentage is slightly lower than that concerned with public security (79 percent). But the policy and the attitude of the government toward these two problems are totally different.

The Bureau of Environmental Protection was established in 1987, but the environment is still seriously polluted. The number of days when the pollutant standard indices (PSI) value was above 100 was 13.75 in 1986, then increased to 17.33 in 1987, and declined to 15.09 in 1988. The air pollution problem has not improved consistently, and water pollution has become worse. The proportion of unpolluted rivers has decreased from 73.7 percent in 1986 to 71.6 percent in 1987 to 67.3 percent in 1988. Despite these unfavorable conditions, until 1993 the government appeared unwilling to adjust economic policies to reduce the size of industry with high pollution. By emphasizing economic growth during a depression, the government suppressed the environmental movement.

The problem of prostitution has been troublesome both to the government and to ordinary people. After the mid-1970s, the national government executed several policies to try to solve the problem. But prostitution and related social ills have remained serious problems. Such problems as pornographic books, magazines, and videotapes and prostitution in massage parlors, hotels, and other places are almost out of control. In the late 1970s, the famous Peit'ou prostitution district was closed, and the government raised special fees from several businesses in order to weaken prostitution-related activities. The businesses continued to prosper in terms of growing size and increasing profit, however, although the majority of them "went underground." Consequently, the problem has become more serious and complicated, but the government cannot resolve it effectively.

According to official statistics about sex offenses, especially pornography and prostitution, the situation has been worsening since 1970. In 1971, 298 persons were charged with crimes relating to pornography and prostitution. The number increased to 682 in 1979 and 2,088 in 1987. The figures reflect only a small part of a serious problem. People in recent years have begun to feel that pornography and prostitution invade or influence their private lives. Various neighborhood organizations and women's groups have protested and engaged in activities to protect themselves or the victims. The survey showed that 73 percent of the respondents rated the problem as serious; only 14 percent suggested it was not serious.

The Five Most Progressively Deteriorating Social Problems. In the late 1980s and early 1990s, Taiwanese society experienced tremendous and dramatic changes. These changes might have meaningful implications for social problems, both objectively and subjectively. Fortunately, we have another data set. The social survey of 1985 has the same set of questions about sixteen social problems. Compared with the data of 1985, seven problems are rated more serious in the 1990 survey (see table 12–3). The criterion for selecting these seven problems is that at least 10 percent more of the respondents in 1990 rated the problem as serious than did in 1985. The problem perceived to have intensified most is rising prices. Only 30.5 percent of respondents rated this problem as serious in the first survey in 1985, while 69.2 percent rated it so in 1990. The increase is almost 39 percent. Close behind this problem in escalation is the discrepancy between rich and poor, which shows a 27 percent increase. Next is environmental pollution, showing a 25 percent increase. The problem of public officials being elected through bribery is of serious concern to 18 percent of respondents, public security to 15 percent, transportation to 14 percent, and caring for the elderly to 13 percent.

Changes in the respondents' ratings between the two waves of surveys are meaningful because they can be correlated with the corresponding changes that occurred in the objective situation. Inflation occurs in the last half of 1990, and therefore people will feel the rise in the prices of commodities. Similarly, actual income inequality has increased in recent years, such that people feel the widening discrepancy between the rich and the poor. The Gini concentration coefficient for 1980 is .277; it then increases continuously, to .283 for 1982, .287 for 1984, .296 for 1986, and .303 for 1988. Furthermore, in the late 1980s, because of an increase in currency, many more people were involved in various money games of speculation, such as the illegal private lottery, overspeculation on the stock exchange, and illegal investment companies. It is likely that the discrepancy between the rich and the poor is much bigger than the official Gini coefficients show. When actual income and wealth distribution become more unequal and people feel the inequality subjectively, social stability and other social problems might be influenced. In other words, inflation and inequality might contribute to the dissatisfaction of people.

Third in deterioration is the problem of environmental pollution. Because of the 1990 economic crisis, the government tried to promote some large-scale industries that are environmentally controversial. This policy added to the complicated environmental problem. It is likely that environmental pollution will be a big issue in the 1990s. The environmental movement will be suppressed by the government,

277

TABLE 12-3

JUDGMENTS OF RESPONDENTS ON THE SERIOUSNESS OF SOCIAL PROBLEMS IN TAIWAN, 1985 AND 1990

	Percentage Rating Problem as Serious in 1990	Percentage Increase from 1985	Point Percentage Decrease since 1985	Percentage Other	G^a	df	p-Value
Juvenile deliquency	83.4	+ 2.1	− 3.5	+ 1.3	19.7	2	.000
Transportation	81.7	+12.9	−13.2	+ 0.3	102.2	2	.000
Public security	79.1	+15.0	−15.4	+ 0.5	151.0	2	.000
Environment	77.0	+25.1	−24.3	− 0.8	297.2	2	.000
Vice and prostitution	73.2	+ 5.3	− 4.5	− 0.8	14.5	2	.001
Politicians getting elected by bribery	72.3	+17.8	−11.2	− 6.6	125.6	2	.000
Rich-poor discrepancy	69.3	+26.9	−26.6	− 0.3	412.8	2	.000
Prices	69.2	+38.7	−38.2	− 0.5	809.9	2	.000
Moral degeneracy	62.8	+ 6.7	− 7.9	+ 0.7	36.3	2	000

					G^2	df	p
Corruption	59.9	+ 1.5	− 4.4	+ 2.9	28.5	2	.000
White-collar crime	58.1	− 10.1	0.0	+ 10.0	127.6	2	.000
Care for the elderly	55.9	+ 12.5	− 17.9	+ 5.5	188.8	2	.000
Difficulty in entering a higher school	49.3	− 9.7	+ 2.6	+ 7.0	105.4	2	.000
Overpopulation	44.4	− 26.3	+ 18.0	+ 8.4	392.2	2	.000
Divorce	43.2	+ 3.1	− 9.4	+ 6.1	65.3	2	.000
Employment	35.0	− 33.4	+ 22.4	+ 9.0	536.5	2	.000

a. G-square shows the maximum likelihood estimates of partial association by controlling for sex, age, education, and marital status.

SOURCE: Data are taken from the General Survey on Social Change (1985) and the Social Opinion Survey (1990).

especially under the Hau administration.

Being elected through bribery is the fourth serious problem. In 1985, 54 percent of respondents called it serious; in 1990, 72 percent rated it so, representing an 18 percent increase. Although being elected through bribery has been a serious problem for a long time, the Kuomintang (KMT), the ruling party, usually has sufficient financial resources to win the elections. Having faced a strong challenge from the opposition in the past decade, the KMT has tried to stay in power by winning the elections. Many of its candidates spent a lot of money to be elected. Numerous rumors about bribery were spread in the election of 1989. Since the KMT will continue to decline as democratic reform continues, the situation will not be improved. By losing its hegemony of power, however, the KMT will be under stronger pressure to give up the unjust and illegal strategy.

Public security, which is considered to be the number one problem by the government, ranks only as fifth to the survey respondents. The misplaced emphasis results in conservative enforcement by the establishment. Public security becomes an important excuse for the government to enforce its authoritarian rule.

Secularization and Religious Revival

The majority of people in Taiwan are believers in folk religion. Although it has been negatively affected by modern education and other social institutions, folk religion is still persistent. In the late 1980s and early 1990s, however, secularization has taken place. Fewer people believe that the spirit exists after death. In 1985, 53 percent of the adult population agreed with a statement asserting the existence of the spirit, but only 48 percent agreed in 1990. And 9 percent fewer agreed to the statement, The more people who believe in God, the more stable the society.

In spite of the significant movement toward secularization, however, the majority of people still maintain their religious beliefs. After all, 48 percent do believe that the spirit exists after death, while only 20 percent positively disbelieve that. Again, 47 percent insist that society is stable if more people believe in God, and only 31 percent do not think so. On the basis of the persistent religious beliefs of the people, then, religious organizations, government control over folk religion, large and increasing contributions to religious groups and temples, and large-scale religious activities can be supported.

The strong utilitarian orientation of folk religiosity motivates people to accumulate wealth as fast as they can. When structural conditions are favorable to the development of a capitalistic economy, this utilitarian orientation is enforced and leads to the accumulation of wealth. Furthermore, the continuing economic prosperity, due to the high economic growth rate, enriches the temples because of the reciprocal transactions between people and the gods they worship. In turn, the enriched temples, with their new or renovated buildings and great festivals, reinforce people's commitment to folk religion with a utilitarian orientation.

The persistent solidarity for hundreds of years of the local religious organizations remains a major force to maintain local group identity and to motivate group action. Furthermore, the sophisticated tolerance and control of the state over folk religion has led to a stable and desirable political situation that facilitates the capitalistic development of Taiwan. Usually temples and other religious organizations are integrated with the dominant or even monopolistic local political power of the KMT. In addition, the contributions of entrepreneurs and local leaders to the local religious organizations, especially to the major temples, elicit local people's respect and approval and also obscure the boundary and conflict between classes. Frequent religious activities, especially those collective gatherings for festivals, distract people from involvement in political and social protests. Thus, repressive measures of political and economic deprivation are ignored.

Despite the strong impact of popular secular humanism represented by modern education, folk religion is still the most popular religion in Taiwan. Although the number of believers has decreased, the number of temples, the property of the temples, and large-scale religious activities have increased. Even if folk religion in Taiwan does not revive strongly, it will influence Taiwanese society in the future because of the people's beliefs and local solidarity.

Buddhism is an influential religion in the society of Taiwan. But the number of orthodox Buddhists is not large. According to our surveys, 10 to 15 percent of the adult population can be identified as Buddhists. The figures provided by the government reports and the Chinese Buddhist Association are much overestimated, because there are no objective records or nationwide surveys. The influence of Chinese Buddhism, however, is very important for the believers of the syncretic folk religion. In Taiwan, Buddhism developed with continuous growth from 1950 to 1980. In recent years it seems to have had a revival.[3] Although reliable data about membership are limited, the population of orthodox Buddhists has expanded significantly. Frequent Buddhist activities are promoted by monks known as Sanghas, and secular Buddhist devotees are visible.

Because of the malaise among the people during the recent

period of rapid transition, a few Taiwanese Buddhist groups have successfully played an active role in coping with the worsening social situation. Most famous is the emergence and development of a huge Buddhist organization initiated by a nun called Cheng-yen. A huge hospital and a nurses' school have been set up in Hualien for serving the people of remote eastern areas, and the fame of the nun and her organization is so great that tremendous results have occurred.

In addition to Cheng-yen's achievement, other Buddhist organizations also contribute substantially to the development of Buddhism and society. Many well-educated Buddhists have joined these programs and activities. Obviously, Taiwanese Buddhism is in the process of a hopeful revival. In the future, Taiwanese Buddhism will be a vital force in the changing society and culture.

After a decade of nearly stagnant development, Taiwan's Christianity seems to be in a crisis with limited hope.[4] An interdenominational committee was formed to promote Christianity in Taiwan.[5] The committee's target has been to double the size of Taiwan's Christian population. According to the plan, a 23 percent annual growth rate is expected; realistically, that is exaggerated and almost impossible. Although the growth rates of some Protestant denominations are larger than the growth rate of the total population of Taiwan, they still are not large or stable. Furthermore, many other denominations have smaller and even negative growth rates. Subjective expectation could be a motivation for the church leaders, but objective conditions might not be favorable to church growth. From 1950 to the mid-1960s, the Christian churches, both Catholic and Protestant, experienced a wave of great awakening. The annual growth rates exceeded the growth rates of the whole population. Unfortunately, after the mid-1960s many churches faced a decline.

In the late 1980s, a few churches developed quite well, but not all. The main figures for the promotion program come mainly from the church with the high growth rate, and thus the projection is optimistic. The Christian churches, however, are influential in the society, culture, and politics of Taiwan. Among the high-ranking officials of the government, the proportion of Christians is much higher than that of the general population. President Lee is pious and frankly reveals that he prays every night and has had revelations for solving his political problems. The Christian organizations of Taiwan are very active in education, medical services, social welfare, and other charitable and sociocultural activities. The impact from the Christian church has been impressive and substantial, and it will continue.

In the 1980s, the people of Taiwan faced a rapidly changing polity and society. The changes, including political liberalization, economic growth, and social pluralization, are continuing in the 1990s. But the conservative nature of Taiwan and the complexity of the problems of reform greatly hinder progress. With rising expectations, people feel more powerless and disoriented when reforms are hindered. Religiosity is found to be correlated with powerlessness and insecurity. Religion helps these people to cope with the stress of rapid change. Furthermore, some religious organizations are so active that they attract many people. Some convert and become believers, while others merely affiliate with religious organizations or participate in religious and charitable programs.

Cheng-yen's Buddhist Tsu-chi Charity Enterprise Foundation reflects the religious revival that is responding to the changing social situation. The number of members of the organization is quickly increasing. At the end of 1990, 1 million members—almost 10 percent of the adult population of Taiwan—were participating in the programs of the foundation. The foundation is powerful and influential, its members enthusiastic and pious. One commentator said:

> A big transformation began in the 1980s, with better economic and educational achievements. People have gratitude and compassion in their hearts because of the Tzu-chi. They begin to contribute to the society silently. . . . This is the conscience of Taiwan. . . . Of course, the problematic social institutions, the imperfect politics, and the gloomy and inadequate standard of living also nourish the Tzu-chi's charity enterprise.[6]

In the future, religion will continue to grow and become a more influential force in the changing society. Christianity, growing Buddhism, and some newly emerged religions not only provide shelter but also cultivate conscience and morality for society. Folk religion will decline but will maintain its strength.

Bibliography

Chiu, Hei-yuan. "How to Use the Data from the Survey on Social Change in Taiwan, 1985." National Science Council Monthly 17(1): 1–9.

———. "Report on the Survey on Social Change in Taiwan, 1990" [in Chinese]. Taipei: Institute of Ethnology, Academia Sinica, 1990.

———. "Report on Social Problems in 1990." A Project Report of the Social Opinion Survey to National Science Council, 1991.

Chiu, Hei-yuan, and Li-shiang Yau. "On Religious Changes in Taiwanese Society." In Hei-yuan Chiu and Ying-hwa Chang, eds., *Social and Cultural Change in Taiwan*. Taipei: Institute of Ethnology, Academia Sinica, 1986, pp. 655–86.

Directorate-General of Budget, Accounting, and Statistics. "Social Indicators in the Taiwan Area of the Republic of China, 1989."

Kao, Hsin-chiang, ed. *Buddhist Priestess Cheng Yen's Meditations* [in Chinese]. Taipei: Chiu-ko, 1989.

Strickler, Rahn, and Chung-chien Hsia. *The Church in Taiwan: Present Situations and Projections* [in Chinese]. Taipei: Gospel Movement for the Year 2000, 1990.

Yang, Kuo-shu, and Chi-cheng Yeh, eds. *Social Problems of Taiwanese Society* [2nd edition, in Chinese]. Taipei: Chiu-Liu Books, 1984.

Yang, Kuo-shu, and Hei-yuan Chiu, eds. *Taiwanese Society in Transition* [in Chinese]. Taipei: Institute of Ethnology, Academia Sinica, 1988.

Yau, Li-shiang. "An Exploratory Study of the Changes in Buddhism in Taiwan since 1950" [in Chinese]. Unpublished manuscript, 1988.

PART SIX
Hong Kong

13

Hong Kong's "Ungovernability" in the Twilight of Colonial Rule

Siu-kai Lau

Until the 1997 issue erupted, spelling the scheduled termination of colonial rule, Britain had been able to maintain stable and effective governance in Hong Kong. What is most extraordinary is that colonial rule was not disturbed even amid the feverish worldwide anticolonial torrent immediately after World War II. The tenacity and endurance of colonial rule in Hong Kong can be attributed only partially to the political ability and adaptability of the colonial administrators.[1] In fact, a fortuitous constellation of favorable conditions alone could have made effective colonial governance possible, especially in the postwar period. Together these conditions have endowed the colonial government with a reasonable degree of political legitimacy, making colonial rule generally acceptable to the people of Hong Kong. The "popularity" of colonial rule can be gauged by the fact that the Hong Kong Chinese prefer it to rule by their socialist motherland.

Although China will inevitably resume sovereignty over Hong Kong in 1997, the people of the territory have just now realized that as a consequence Britain will quit the place in due course and will no longer act as buffer between themselves and China. The political environment in Hong Kong has all at once become extremely complicated. Politically speaking, the 1997 issue means the intrusion of new actors into the local political scene, the spawning of new social and economic problems, the appearance of new political conflicts, and the erosion of the authority and legitimacy of the colonial regime. On top of all this are problems arising from changes in the international economy and questions generated by Hong Kong's own socioeconomic transformations. These problems and issues have in turn been accentuated by the malaise over 1997.

As a result of all these momentous changes directly or indirectly related to the 1997 issue, the favorable conditions that have all along facilitated effective colonial governance have weakened. While Hong

Kong is far from ungovernable, the maintenance of effective control in the remaining years of colonial rule has become problematic. Although the Hong Kong government is not totally oblivious to its worsening predicament, it has been slow in reacting to it. In groping for a way out, it has tried different tacks singly or in combination but without settling upon any. In its desperate effort to develop a formula for effective rule, the government is caught in a mass of complications. Nevertheless, the closer 1997 approaches, the more limited the government's options will become. In all likelihood, the remaining options will narrow down to some forms of power sharing, authority consolidation, and consensus building by the government, which would end its monopoly on political power.

Conditions of Effective Colonial Governance in the Postwar Era

Notwithstanding the colonial status of Hong Kong, Britain rarely justified its rule on ideological grounds. Tenets such as "the white man's burden," "manifest destiny," or the civilizing mission of imperialism were rarely deployed explicitly to articulate a doctrine of colonial rule centering on the redemptive function of colonial domination.[2] This deemphasis on the ideological basis of colonial legitimacy stemmed apparently from the pragmatic economic motive that drove Britain to wrest Hong Kong from the moribund Manchu China in the first place. It also reflected the peculiar context wherein Hong Kong had been preserved as a British colony for more than a century and a half. Until the early 1980s, colonial rule was never seriously challenged (except for the brief period of Japanese occupation during World War II). What underlay this remarkable political enterprise of Britain was a fortuitous convergence of conditions that made prolonged colonial rule possible. These conditions over time endowed the colonial government with a veneer of political legitimacy, enabling it to boast of benign rule and rule by consent. In another sense, the concurrence of these conditions also delineated the uniqueness of Hong Kong as a colony. These conditions can be briefly described.

The Absence of the Option of Political Independence. Irrespective of the preference of the people, the possibility that Hong Kong could declare independence did not exist. China had always been firmly opposed to an independent Hong Kong, and this was a position common to the Manchu and the Kuomintang governments, which were too weak to recover Hong Kong, and the Communist government, which was strong enough to do so but chose to tolerate British occupation. To the Hong Kong Chinese, the departure of Britain would mean reversion to Chinese rule, which was perceived as a worse alternative.

Moreover, despite the antipathy of the people of Hong Kong toward the socialist government of China and the impending sovereignty transfer, they were still ambivalent about the issue of independence.[3] This ambivalence obviously attested to the lingering nationalist sentiments among the Hong Kong Chinese.

The impracticality of independence left subordination to colonial rule the only viable option available to the Hong Kong Chinese. Fearful of a Chinese takeover, particularly after the Communist regime was established in China, the residents of Hong Kong were not in a position to challenge colonial rule. Not surprisingly, then, throughout the history of Hong Kong no serious nationalist movement had been launched against the colonial regime. Consequently, colonial rule sustained itself because of its irreplaceability and indispensability in the eyes of the Hong Kong Chinese.

Autonomy of the Colonial Government. A notable feature of British colonial policy was to devolve power to the colonial authorities, who were enjoined to achieve financial self-sufficiency. Metropolitan trade unions, parties, and other political organizations were not dominant in the colonies.[4] Accordingly, the Hong Kong government enjoyed a great deal of political autonomy in administering the territory. The degree of autonomy had increased since the end of World War II, when British colonial policy shifted to a more "humanitarian" and developmental approach. As a solid indicator of enhanced autonomy, the British government turned over financial authority of the colony to the Hong Kong government in 1958. In the postwar period, the metropolitan government rarely interfered in Hong Kong's internal affairs. The other side of the coin is that the people of Hong Kong seldom sought the intervention of London in dealing with the colonial government.

China also largely left Hong Kong alone. Except for the riots in 1967, when hot-headed leftists in Hong Kong stirred up anticolonial disturbances as a counterpart to the Cultural Revolution in China, the involvement of China in local affairs was minimal and highly restrained. This restraint also discouraged the people of Hong Kong from bringing their grievances against the Hong Kong government to the Chinese authorities.

The autonomy of the Hong Kong government *vis-à-vis* both the British and the Chinese governments was critical to the assertion of its authority in the territory. This status helped create its image as the ultimate power holder, which in turn inspired awe and respect in the colonial subjects and made for effective colonial governance.

Monopoly of Political Power. As a colonial government, the government of Hong Kong naturally had a monopoly on political power, a monopoly enshrined in the constitutional documents of the colony—the Letters Patent and the Royal Instructions. What distinguishes Hong Kong from other British colonies is that until recently Hong Kong had not undergone any meaningful transfer of power to the colonial subjects, in contrast with various power transfers in many other nonwhite British colonies since the turn of the twentieth century.[5]

Because the government monopolized political power, the Hong Kong Chinese saw co-optation by the colonizers as the only means to obtain political status. In fact, the colonial government had over time instituted a structure of political mobility for the colonial subjects based on political sponsorship from above.[6] Through political co-optation, the Hong Kong government enlisted the collaboration of the Chinese elite in colonial rule. Given the depoliticization of the Chinese community and its freedom from serious social conflicts, the acquiescence of the Chinese elites in colonial domination went a long way to ensure effective colonial rule.

General Consensus on the Political System and Public Policies. The public has generally accepted the political system and the major policies formulated and implemented by the Hong Kong government,[7] so much so that the Hong Kong people vociferously demanded their preservation in the post-1997 arrangements. In particular, government by consultation, limited involvement of government in social and economic affairs, a moderate welfare role of government, an untrammeled capitalist market system, the rule of law, independence of the judiciary, political elitism, consensus politics, and political moderation had become common precepts in Hong Kong. In such a context, political radicalism was difficult to nourish. In fact, it was difficult to muster serious challenge to colonial rule.

Integrity and Performance of the Civil Service. The Hong Kong government was in essence a bureaucratic government, or a government by career civil servants. Because it was intrinsically difficult for a colonial government to justify itself in ideological or moral terms, particularly in the postwar period, it was essential for the colonial bureaucracy to demonstrate that its efficiency, competence, solicitude toward the public, incorruptibility, dedication to common interests, and capability of delivering services and benefits to the people. In short, the colonial government had to legitimize its rule primarily on the basis of performance.[8] And in fact it was granted a certain measure of legitimacy by the Hong Kong people, who gave it credit particularly for the postwar economic takeoff, even though the Hong Kong government, unlike governments in other successful developing countries, did not assume leadership for economic development.[9]

Depoliticization of Society. The preclusion of independence meant that the colonial government was immune from overthrow by its subjects. Acceptance of the colonial government thus constituted a solid foundation for effective governance. It was, however, not a sufficient condition, for the government could still be incessantly challenged by different political and social forces for a variety of reasons. As a depoliticized society, Hong Kong nevertheless was incapable of mounting sustained and organized political actions against the government, even if there were pervasive popular discontent and grievances.

The Chinese community in Hong Kong was basically atomistic, comprising numerous loosely related familial groups and their extensions. Strong "national" political and social organizations capable of mass mobilization were nonexistent. The low degree of social and political organization of Hong Kong reflected its basic character as a society of recent immigrants from China who had fled their homeland to submit themselves voluntarily to colonial rule. These people had low political aspirations and were deferential to political authority. Because they could resort to social ties to meet their needs, their reliance on the government was correspondingly reduced, thus further reinforcing their apolitical or even antipolitical tendencies.

The colonial government also contributed to the depoliticization of society by its abstention from involvement in social and economic affairs. The practices of laissez faire and social noninterventionism by the government insulated the society and the polity from each other, in effect isolating the government from the social and economic conflicts in society.[10]

Low Level of Social Conflict. Even though Hong Kong was a society characterized by social inequalities, it had been generally free from serious social conflicts. The strength of family ties, the "trickle down" effects of the miraculous economic growth in the postwar period, the service and welfare provisions of the government, and the muted ethnic discrimination were major explanatory factors. The general abhorrence of conflict in Chinese political culture also played a role.[11] Social conflict was also reduced by the general expectation of abundant opportunities in society and the prevailing assumption that individual efforts could uplift one's socioeconomic standing, even though in reality Hong Kong was far from an open society.[12]

Most pertinent, though, was the popular belief in the supremacy, fairness, and justice of the market mechanism in the allocation of resources and the distribution of income. As a result of this belief, many conflicts were channeled into the marketplace, thus reducing the chance of their conversion into political conflicts. The general acceptance of the impersonal law established by the colonial regime also guided conflicts into the legal system and resolved them there, sparing the government many political troubles.[13]

Economic Growth. The economic resurgence of the West and the establishment of the liberal international economic order dominated by the United States in the postwar period provided Hong Kong with a hospitable environment for economic development. The gigantic progress made by the Hong Kong economy in the postwar period not only bolstered the government's claim to legitimacy on the basis of performance, but also was the key solvent of potential social and political conflicts. It was easier to distribute more economic goods to the people when the economic pie was expanding. Moreover, economic growth swelled the revenue of the government, enabling it to fulfill its increasing welfare and service commitments to society. A prospering economy also diverted people's energy to the economic realm, thus further ensuring political peace.

In all, while there is no denying the politico-administrative adeptness of the colonial government, the favorable factors that followed World War II largely account for effective colonial governance in Hong Kong in the period. Nevertheless, sustained development is bound to bring about problems of various kinds, and the sudden emergence of the 1997 issue has substantially changed the situation faced by the government. The conditions underlying effective governance have eroded, with the process of erosion continuing unabated. The halcyon days now at an end, the colonial government finds itself in a turbulent political environment: against such a background, the problem of ungovernability arises.[14]

Erosion of the Conditions for Effective Governance

Since the 1970s, socioeconomic changes in Hong Kong have gradually transformed the relation between government and the people. In fact, the way Hong Kong is governed has to be modified if effective governance is to be maintained. In spite of the government's efforts to cope with the changing situation through administrative reforms—expanding governmental functions and creating intermediary structures to enlist popular support—it has been only moderately successful. Indeed, the increase in political demands from the public and the rise in organized political activities geared to procure concessions from the government have palpably overloaded the political system.[15]

In a drastic alteration of the sociopolitical context wherein the government functions, the 1997 issue has rendered the existing method of governance obsolete, created serious problems of adaptation for the government, and made it difficult for it alone to exercise effective rule. Exacerbating the predicament of the government, the economic prospect of Hong Kong has become clouded, as the 1997 malaise overlaps with a looming worldwide economic recession and an increase in protectionist sentiments in Hong Kong's major overseas markets.

All these changes have affected the conditions that sustained colonial governance in the past, although they suffer from varying degrees of erosion. To appraise the new political environment engulfing the Hong Kong government, we must scrutinize the extent to which the conditions discussed earlier have been eroded.

Independence. Even though the option of independence is foreclosed by the Sino-British Joint Declaration, which stipulates the reversion of sovereignty to China in 1997, the short life of the colonial government is an inordinately important political fact in itself. Whereas to deter political challenge in the past, the government could exploit its indispensability and irreplaceability in the minds of the people, its scheduled departure undermines its political authority. Inasmuch as the Hong Kong Chinese take an instrumental and utilitarian stance toward the colonial regime, the loss of its right to rule is bound to invite nondeferential political actions against it. As the myth of the longevity of the colonial government is shattered and the people of Hong Kong have to face apprehensively an uncertain political future that they abhor, they will gradually see their interests as different from those of the colonial government. The gap between them and the government has already widened and is likely to widen further as 1997 approaches. It will lead them increasingly to assert their interests against what they perceive as the government's own self-interests.[16] As a result, public pressure on the government will inexorably escalate.

Declining Government Autonomy. Since the Sino-British negotiation over the political future of Hong Kong in 1982, the autonomy of the colonial government has suffered an irreversible decline. The signing of Joint Declaration by China and Britain has in effect brought the two superior governments to the center stage of local politics, as they are ultimately responsible for the implementation of the process of the transfer of sovereignty. To make matters worse for the colonial government, China always prefers to deal directly with the British government with regard to local affairs simply because British officials have long-term stakes in a cordial Sino-British relationship, whereas local colonial officials might harbor more negative feelings against China as their own careers have been adversely affected by the termination of colonial rule.

As Hong Kong enters the transitional period, an increasing number of problems can be dealt with only by the British and the Chinese governments jointly. A glance at the issues under the jurisdiction of the Sino-British Joint Liaison Group illustrates this point. Moreover, both Britain and China have reversed themselves by taking an increasing interest in local affairs, and they (notably China) frequently make themselves felt in the decision-making process of the Hong Kong government. The autonomy of the government is further constricted by the fact that the Sino-British Agreement—and for that matter the Basic Law promulgated in early 1990—has basically frozen the status quo and hence has circumscribed the policy-making sphere of the government. Under these circumstances, policy innovations are difficult to make and might even be met with suspicion from China. Moreover, as a result of the greater prominence of the two superior governments in local policy making, residents of Hong Kong have a growing tendency to direct their lobbying activities to them. Those with grievances against the colonial government find it expedient to solicit the support of either China or Britain with the expectation that the government will be forced to concede to their demands. The government has been frustrated by its fading autonomy. Moreover, a government suffering from declining autonomy does not have a strong will to govern, which is essential to the exercise of effective rule.

Political Reforms. To entice the British Parliament to accept the Sino-British Joint Declaration and to muster popular support for the colonial government in the remaining years of its rule, the Hong Kong government has introduced some power-sharing political reforms since the early 1980s. Nevertheless, because of the hesitancy of the British government, the opposition of China and the established interests, the lukewarm attitude of the people to institutional reforms, and the weakness of the prodemocratic forces, only a modicum of democratic reform has been implemented.[17] Even though the incorporation of elective elements into the political system does not alter its executive-centered nature, it has subjected the government to more political constraints. The increased political participation by the people has created moderate public opinion pressure on the government, which it has to take into account. The appearance of many small-scale political groups, all claiming to speak for the people, also adds to the political pressure on the government. The same can be said of a more outspoken and representative legislature and the increasing politicization of many socioeconomic groups. Most important of all, the government's monopoly over the opportunities for political mobility has ended.

Though far from dominant, the electoral channel provides an alternative outlet for those with political aspirations. The competing co-optative offensive of the Chinese government not only lures away some members of the colonial establishment but also creates an even more promising ladder of political success. Therefore, the co-optative tactics that the government had so successfully employed in the past to build up its ruling coalition have become less and less effective at mobilizing the support of the established elites. In fact, this ruling coalition is plagued by centrifugal tendencies within itself, and it is also more vulnerable to challenge from the outside. As the government can depend less on the support of the established elites, its control over the political situation is loosened.

Popular Support. While the maintenance of effective colonial rule is becoming an ordeal to the government, public support of the political system and the major policies of Hong Kong remains basically intact, although people would like the government to play a more active economic and welfarist role.[18] In my 1988 survey, I found that 70.5 percent of respondents agreed or very much agreed with the view that even though the political system of Hong Kong was not perfect, it was the best under existing circumstances. In addition, the survey findings show that a plurality of respondents define a government willing to consult public opinion as *democratic*, an indication that the consultative practices of the government continue to be endorsed.

The acceptance of the basic character of the political system and the key existing public policies should not, however, be exaggerated or automatically presumed for the future. Even this crucial condition could experience long-term erosion. The momentum of electoral politics could, for example, foster second thoughts about the existing system. The decline in governmental authority and performance could diminish public support for the political system. Public debates about the appropriate types of political reform for Hong Kong and alternative public policy agendas will probably have some pedagogical effects, alerting people to the deficiencies of the system and the inadequacies of current policies. Once the system falters or public policies fail, people will be more prepared to contemplate alternatives. As a result, consensus at present rests on a less solid foundation than in the past.

The Bureaucracy. The opening up of the political system and the imminent termination of colonial rule have dealt the civil servants—particularly the Chinese civil servants—a severe blow. Being largely anti-Communist and immersed in the British administrative tradition, civil servants generally feel betrayed by Britain. Although China is keen to woo them, civil servants by and large do not have confidence in the future, nor do they trust the Chinese government. At the same time, they also harbor increasing mistrust of the British government as the interests of Britain and Hong Kong are perceived to diverge.[19]

Political reforms, though moderate, threaten the political dominance of civil servants, generating among them a growing sense of unease and frustration. Although they give verbal support to democracy, they lack confidence that democratic government is likely to be achieved in Hong Kong. They are not committed to adapting themselves to a more open mode of political operation. As a result, they lament the decline of their political supremacy and have difficulties in dealing with the new political challenge.[20] It is thus not surprising that "to the extent that these senior public administrators supported democratic government, they also demonstrated a stronger inclination to leave the territory by 1997."[21]

The demoralization of the civil servants is inimical to the integrity and performance of the civil service. It is also part and parcel of the problem of ungovernability that afflicts Hong Kong in the transitional stage. The jitteriness of the civil servants has weakened the government. The weakened government, in turn, has invited aggressive demands from the civil servants, obsessed with their own short-term self-interests. The recent spate of pay disputes, industrial actions, and demands for pension guarantees and British nationality attests to the erosion of the influence of the government, which can no longer rely on hierarchical authority to keep its own house in order. The recalcitrance and unruliness of the civil servants thus weaken the authority of the government and its ability to deal with the escalating public needs. Because the government is still the only organized political force in Hong Kong, its own disorganization is bound to have ominous political reverberations. The collective actions of the civil servants are received with hostility by the public. At a time when the people have increased their moral demands on public officials to exercise leadership, the self-seeking behavior of these officials only erodes public trust in and support for the government.

Lackluster Economy. The problem of ungovernability is worsened by the recent lackluster economic performance of Hong Kong. Until the past few years, Hong Kong had recorded impressive growth in its real gross domestic product (GDP). The average annual growth rate of GDP between 1961 and 1973 was 9.5 percent, moderating to 8.9 percent between 1974 and 1983. In 1984–1988, GDP rose by 8.1 percent a year.[22] Since then, the growth rate has plummeted. GDP grew by 5 percent in 1992.[23] At the same time, the rate of inflation has jumped to around 10 percent per year. Thus, Hong Kong finds itself in stagflation at a most inopportune time.

At Hong Kong's present stage of development, its economy must be propelled by more capital- and technology-intensive industries that produce higher value-added commodities for it to remain competitive. Furthermore, its service sector has to be enlarged and upgraded.[24] To achieve these ends, Hong Kong needs long-term investments. Nevertheless, the 1997 problem has deterred local capitalists from long-term and large-scale capital commitment. In any case, because most of Hong Kong's entrepreneurs—traders or small manufacturers—find it difficult to take on the economic challenge of the future single-handedly, Hong Kong's economic competitiveness has declined. Moreover, capital outflow has weakened the economy, whose difficulties are accentuated by the downturn of the Western economies, international protectionism, and the rise of competitors in the Asian-Pacific region who can exploit cheaper labor. Admittedly, the use of cheap labor in China by Hong Kong's manufacturers and the benefits reaped from China's economic reforms have alleviated some difficulties, but not enough—at least in the short run—to solve Hong Kong's problems.

Further complicating its economic difficulties, inflation was high in 1989–1991 in Hong Kong and is expected to hover at a high level in the near future. Both the brain drain and the shortage of labor contribute to high inflation. The gradual devaluation of the Hong Kong dollar, which is linked to the weakening U.S. dollar, has also fueled the inflationary pressure in an economy highly dependent on imports both for production and for consumption.

The implications of the economic slowdown for a government whose political legitimacy derives mainly from economic performance are adverse. If poor economic performance continues for a long time,

297

the myth that colonial governance and the economic miracle of Hong Kong are organically linked will be broken, and the value of the government to the people will diminish.

Politicization of Society and Proliferation of Social Conflicts

Social change in Hong Kong in the postwar period has weakened the family and the traditional organizations in the Chinese community. The increasing complexity of society has generated public needs and social problems that can be effectively dealt with only at the governmental level. People increasingly depend on the government to solve not only collective problems but also their family and personal problems.[25] The political overload is obvious, a problem aggravated by escalating public criticism of governmental performance. In fact, the growing politicization of Hong Kong in the past two decades has been quite closely related to the expanding role of the government in meeting social needs and the delivery of public services.

The 1997 issue has heightened the problems stemming from modernization in Hong Kong. A major impact of the 1997 issue on society, for example, is the abrupt interruption of the identity-building process and the corollary process of community formation. At the same time, social authority, never really strong in the first place, has eroded.

As a society of immigrants and sojourners, Hong Kong has had a weak sense of community from the very beginning. In the 1960s, an inchoate sense of community identification appeared, particularly among the younger generation, who considered Hong Kong as their homeland. Even so, it can still be said that this sense of community commitment is only weakly developed. The sudden intrusion of the 1997 problem not only exposes the fragility of this sense of community but also undermines it. Faced with a future sovereign that is widely perceived as overwhelmingly powerful and uncontrollably arbitrary, and an inalterable situation dictated by history, Hong Kong Chinese have become fatalistic, frustrated, fearful, jittery, and pessimistic. They are gripped by a paralyzing sense of powerlessness. Like others who lack a sense of security, the citizens of Hong Kong have turned inward. Self-regarding behavior has become rampant, amply reflected in large-scale emigration in recent years. Personal trust has declined, along with public morality, even among officials. People are increasingly guided by short-term considerations and utilitarian calculations. More and more people feel no qualms about resorting to dubious or downright illegal means to achieve their goals. Overwhelmed by anxieties and diffuse fear, many think and act irrationally. The community formation process, begun in the 1960s, has been interrupted, and the social fabric, frayed. As a breeding ground of social conflict, Hong Kong's weakened community has suffered a rise in violent and organized crime, corruption, personal conflict, and social problems recently.

As both an integral part of the weakened social fabric and a cause of that weakness, the authority of social leaders and organizations has suffered from further decline. Compared with political authorities, social authorities enjoy less public trust.[26] This pattern reflects the lingering hold of traditional political culture among Hong Kong Chinese, for in traditional China government officials were expected to be the repository of public interests whereas social leaders were seen largely as upholders of sectional concerns. Public trust in social leaders has never been high in Hong Kong.[27] The rapacious self-regarding orientation of the social elites and their minimal commitment to society have been vividly demonstrated since the onset of the 1997 issue. Such comportment on the part of the elites is hardly conducive to public trust in them. As a result, public cynicism and even contempt toward social authorities are on the increase. The degradation of social authority in turn speeds up the unraveling of the social fabric.

As mentioned before, all along Hong Kong has been free from conflicts springing from serious social cleavages, in spite of the ethnic inequality that is an inherent feature of a colonial society and the staggering economic inequalities produced by an unfettered capitalist society where the government plays only a limited redistributive role. Nevertheless, because of the favorable conditions that sustained effective governance in the past, the great potential for social conflict had been largely unrealized.

With the intrusion of the 1997 issue and the disappearance of the economic miracle, Hong Kong can no longer remain a low-conflict society. At least three major types of social conflict are emerging, although all of them are still in the early stage of formation: class conflict, conflict of identities, and the conflict between Hong Kong and China.

Class Conflict. The factors accounting for the gradual increase in class consciousness in recent years are legion. In the first place, the continuous decrease in income inequality in the first three decades of the postwar period was interrupted in the mid-1970s; since then income inequality has widened. The Gini Index (used to measure income inequality) was .49 in 1960; it fell to .43 in 1971. Between 1971 and 1976 it remained at .43, gradually rising to .45 in 1981.[28] It appears that income inequality in the 1980s continued to widen, and the prospect in the 1990s is not encouraging.

The widening income gap is related to the growing significance of the service sector and large-scale organizations in the economy. The exodus of professional and managerial talent triggered by the 1997 issue has driven up the salaries of employees in the modern service sectors, particularly those holding upper-middle-class jobs. The organized actions of the civil servants have also led to substantial pay hikes for employees in the public sector. The decline in the importance of the traditional manufacturing industries and their relocation in China to take advantage of the cheap labor there have put a brake on the improvement of the wages of the workers. Under these circumstances, the decision in 1990 of the government to allow the import of foreign labor brings out into the open the strained relations between capital and labor.

Changes in the structure of the economy have resulted in the domination of large corporations in many sectors. The Hong Kong dream that a hard-working and frugal person might eventually become a prosperous entrepreneur has increasingly become just a dream. The slowdown of the economy will further dampen people's hopes about their chances for economic success. The gradual appearance of a layer of the superrich addicted to conspicuous consumption and crass materialism constantly reminds those in other economic divisions in society of their lower status. As a result, manifestations of class consciousness and discontent with the gap between the rich and the poor are inevitable.

The findings from the 1988 survey by Thomas Wong provide some evidence of incipient class consciousness in Hong Kong.[29] While the majority of respondents explained poverty by personal fault or reasons rather than social causes, most perceived conflicts between the rich and the poor in society. More ominously, they considered conflict between them as inevitable.[30]

Wong's respondents also saw many opportunities for upward mobility in society, perceiving Hong Kong as open enough to reward individual endeavor and effort. Nevertheless, beneath these sanguine views are more realistic and even pessimistic assessments of an individual's chance for success. Three-quarters of the respondents, for example, saw the likelihood of job mobility (changing to a better job) for themselves as either none or very little. The gap between general expectation and personal reality is likely to engender feelings of failure and dissatisfaction.

In Hong Kong, class conflict is most likely to express itself in political actions. Except for the employees in the public sector and large corporations, the workers in Hong Kong are faced with numerous small employers; hence they can hardly organize on a large scale and use market tactics (such as strikes) to force employers to make concessions. The weakness of the trade unions further cripples the workers' bargaining position *vis-à-vis* their employers. These are precisely the reasons why it is the government itself that has acted since the late 1960s as the surrogate guardian of the interests of the workers by enacting legislation to provide them with minimal protection. Because market power has not been available and the government has been the salient channel of redress, political action has been the major means for the pursuit of class interests by the workers of Hong Kong.[31]

Economic stagflation is bound to aggravate class conflict in Hong Kong. On the one hand, economic demands from the workers will increase. On the other hand, the advantaged sectors are also more ready to defend their interests in a zero-sum economic game, whether against the lower strata or the government.

Conflict of Identities. The fear of 1997 has spurred a large number of Hong Kong residents, notably those in the higher social classes, to acquire foreign passports to safeguard their freedom of movement after 1997. The decision of Britain to grant British nationality to 50,000 elite families, with the proclaimed goal of keeping them in Hong Kong, is a prominent example of the way the Hong Kong population will be "internationalized."

Although it is difficult to estimate how many Hong Kong Chinese will hold foreign passports after 1997, there may be more than half a million of them by then. As those with and those without foreign passports are in categorically different situations, they will likely develop separate identities and mentalities over time. The relationship between them is not likely to be cozy.

Several factors are important in strengthening the sense of identity among Hong Kong Chinese without foreign passports. For one thing, the "threat" from China is prone to foster a stronger sense of common fate among those with no way to leave. Their interests in Hong Kong will probably be more real than the interests of those who can easily exercise their right to leave the territory. The eventual return of Hong Kong to China, the increasing economic ties between the two places, and China's escalating appeal to nationalistic sentiments as a means to narrow the social distance between itself and capitalistic Hong Kong, however, may little by little sharpen a Chinese identity among those who can claim only a Chinese nationality.

With time, there will be subtle changes in the mentality of both the Chinese nationals (the "stayers") and the "sojourners" (those with foreign nationalities or rights of residence in other countries as well as those with serious intentions about leaving Hong Kong eventually). Differences in the orientation and outlook of these two categories will progressively widen, particularly in the way they perceive the needs of Hong Kong, the future prospect of the place, and the desirable kind of relationship between Hong Kong and China. To put it crudely, the "stayers" are more likely to paint a rosier picture of the future of Hong Kong to allay psychological insecurity and to boost self-confidence. They will also be more inclined to take an accommodating stance toward China because they cannot afford the detrimental consequences of a confrontation between Hong Kong and China. I also expect the "stayers," out of jealousy, self-righteousness, or economic self-interest, to cast the "sojourners" in a negative light, castigating their lack of moral commitment to their community and their preoccupation with the material exploitation of their former fellow citizens. That the "sojourners" will perhaps take a more pessimistic view of Hong Kong's future and a more uncompromising attitude toward China will pit them against the "stayers." Moreover, because most of the "sojourners" belong to the privileged social strata, the conflict of identities between them and the "stayers" will be reinforced by the rising class conflict.

It is thus not accidental that in my 1988 survey, 68.2 percent of the respondents declared that they would not trust people with foreign passports or rights of residence as their political leaders (only 17.7 percent thought otherwise). It can further be inferred that the colonial government will gradually be seen from a racial perspective and its interests increasingly defined as conflicting with those of the "stayers."

Thus, as the result of self-righteousness, material interests, feelings of ethnic injustice, nationalistic appeals, and fear of China, the formation of a new identity among the "stayers" (the identities of the "sojourners" might not be recognizable) is likely to drive them into conflict with others, though in the meantime there is no way to determine the intensity and scope of conflict. Nevertheless, as 1997 draws closer, those who have yet to join the ranks of the "stayers" or the "sojourners" will shrink in number, and the distinction between the two groups, like the lines of conflict, will be sharpened. In the beginning of the conflict, the "stayers" might demand equal treatment with the "sojourners" both economically and socially and oppose public policies that gave preferential treatment to the "sojourners." It is not impossible that eventually they might demand preferential treatment for themselves. The fact that Chinese nationals are already guaranteed a privileged political status by the Basic Law (only those Chinese nationals without foreign passports or rights of abode elsewhere can fill top governmental posts after 1997) would mean that the "stayers" will be well disposed and well placed to use political means to achieve their social and economic ends. Incidentally, the conflict between identities might even spill over into the conflict between the "stayers" and the colonial government, as the foreign nature of that government will become ever more evident in the eyes of those staying.

Hong Kong–China Conflict. To the Hong Kong Chinese, the reversion of sovereignty to China in 1997 is perceived as an abrupt decision imposed on them against their will by the Chinese government. Their attitude toward China is a combination of fear, hostility, condescension, and aversion. This view can easily be explained by the fact that many Chinese have fled to Hong Kong to escape from Communist rule, the vastly divergent paths of development of Hong Kong and China since World War II, and the staggering disparity in living standards and way of thinking between the people in the two societies.

Objectively speaking, China and Hong Kong have all along shared many complementary interests, allowing capitalistic Hong Kong and socialist China to coexist harmoniously for more than four decades. China, moreover, is willing to allow Hong Kong to maintain its capitalistic system after 1997 under the formula of "one country, two systems." After the conclusion of the Sino-British Joint Declaration, the ties between Hong Kong and China have strengthened. Economic interdependence has in fact increased. Nevertheless, Hong Kong Chinese often emphasize the incompatibility of interests between China and Hong Kong and are prone to define the relationship in terms of conflict. In my 1988 survey, for example, 56.3 percent of the respondents believed that China's interests conflicted with those of Hong Kong (only 27.8 percent thought differently). Such an a priori definition of the relationship between Hong Kong Chinese and their future political sovereign is certainly not conducive to a cordial encounter between them. Actions taken by China that benefit Hong Kong are taken for granted and soon forgotten, whereas those that are seen as contrary to Hong Kong's interests immediately become issues pitting the two entities.

The most serious confrontation was the Daya Bay nuclear plant controversy in 1986, which left behind bitter feelings on both sides. Because China's participation in local affairs will inexorably increase, these conflicts will remain a troublesome issue in the short term. Not surprisingly, the Tiananmen Square incident of June 4, 1989, aggravated the turbulent relationship between China and Hong Kong. Although such conflicts will probably become more muted as 1997 approaches, they could be quite intense sporadically. The increasingly large component of "sojourners" in Hong Kong and their more uncompromising stance toward China will very likely complicate the relationship between China and Hong Kong. The exploitation of the conflict for partisan political purposes by local politicians has been and will continue to be an important factor in heightening the conflict.

The conflict between Hong Kong and China has ominous implications for effective governance in Hong Kong. It will involve China in opposition to both the British and the colonial governments, as China's accusation after the Tiananmen Square incident that Britain subtly encouraged Hong Kong as a base of subversion vividly demonstrates. The Hong Kong government is constantly under public pressure to take a hard-line position toward China to defend local interests. Public disappointment with the colonial government on that score is an important cause of its decline in authority. The conflict between Hong Kong and China also expresses itself internally in the contention between the pro-China and the anti-China forces on the one hand and between people who choose different strategies to deal with China on the other.

The weakening of the social fabric, the erosion of social authority, and the appearance of social conflicts are bound to manifest themselves politically. Hong Kong will become more and more politicized and conflict ridden. The partial opening up of the political system and the introduction of popular elections will inevitably stimulate further politicization and intensify political conflict. As the incumbent government, the colonial government cannot avoid the rising political temperature in the remaining years of its rule. It will be burdened with more strident political demands, not amenable to easy accommodation.

The Problem of Ungovernability

When a government whose basis of effective rule has eroded is simultaneously overloaded with political demands and overcharged with political responsibilities, the problem of governability naturally surfaces. Even though the colonial government bitterly resents the label of "lame duck," its image as a lame-duck government has in fact been widely popularized. As a generic concept, ungovernability is a problem whose substance and seriousness can be understood only in specific political contexts, for its manifestations differ greatly across societies.[32]

In Hong Kong, despite the weakening of the conditions for effective governance, the government does not face the imminent danger of breakdown in authority and serious ungovernability. Nonetheless, signs are still growing that maintaining effective governance in the final years of colonial rule will become increasingly difficult. One of the indicators of ungovernability is the diminished will of the officials to govern. Although hard evidence is difficult to come by (because officials plagued by a threatening political environment tend to become more secretive), impressionistic data seem to show a governing bureaucracy suffering from demoralization, a numbing sense of uncertainty, and defeatist sentiments. The will to govern is particularly weakened with respect to the expatriate officials, whose political future in Hong Kong is clouded. It would be hard for them to overcome the enervating passivity and resignation as well as a disruptive frustration. This would have serious implications for the way Hong Kong is governed in the next few years. Moreover, such a disposition on the part of expatriate officials and their local colleagues who have similar attitudes or who plan to quit before the Chinese takeover would pit them against local officials who see a career beyond 1997 or who are committed to the place. If such is the case, internal conflicts within the government will increase and further hamper its ability to govern effectively.

In face of the turbulent political environment, the dearth of political skills on the part of government officials has been eminently exposed in the past few years. They have a predisposition to react nervously and occasionally in a paranoid way to external criticisms. The government frequently takes unnecessarily strong stands or resorts to inappropriately draconian measures to demonstrate its control of a situation. Compared with the past, the government today is less able to maintain composure and exude self-confidence. It tends instead to exhibit a siege mentality, which leads to overreactions at some times and to undue secretiveness at others. As a result, there appear to be random shifts in the positions the government adopts, projecting a damaging public image of indecisiveness and incompetence. A government widely perceived to succumb to pressures despite its originally proclaimed firmness of position is bound to lack public confidence.

Another indicator of the problem of ungovernability is the worsening public evaluation of the performance of the government and the concomitant erosion of public trust. To a government that bases so much of its legitimacy on performance, being rated by the people as increasingly incompetent is a very serious matter. The depreciation of the performance ratings of the government can be easily corroborated. In my 1985 survey of the Kwun Tong (a local community) residents, 61.2 percent of the respondents agreed or strongly agreed that the Hong Kong government was a good government. Likewise, in my 1986 survey of Kwun Tong residents, 43.6 percent of the respondents rated the performance of the government as good or very good, while 46.6 percent considered it about average.[33] In a Hong Kong–wide survey I conducted in 1988, 41.2 percent considered the performance of the government good and 0.8 percent as very good. In a January 1990 telephone survey commissioned by the City and New Territories Administration of the government, 43 percent and 33 percent of the respondents respectively rated the performance of the government and the work attitude of civil servants as good. But these figures dropped to 35 percent and 29 percent, respectively, in March 1990.[34] The favorable ratings in July, September, and November 1990 were 37, 36, and 35 percent, respectively.[35] In an October 1990 poll commissioned by a major newspaper in Hong Kong, the results "indicate[d] some disenchantment with the Hong Kong Government, the Governor, and British Government representatives" in Hong Kong.[36] Compared with many other societies, public evaluation of government performance is still quite high. Nevertheless, there seems to be a downward trend of public ratings of government performance, reflecting the increasing public disappointment with the government's competence in resolving problems.

Well aware of the decline in authority of the Hong Kong government, the people tend to attribute it to the intrusion of China into the local political scene. China's presence has unraveled the myth of the omnipotence of the colonial government. In my 1988 survey, 54.3 percent of the respondents held that, compared with three years before, the authority of the Hong Kong government had become weaker. Among those who claimed that the government had suffered from declining authority, 82.9 percent thought that it was the Chinese government that had weakened its authority, while 42.5 percent were of the opinion that the democratic "fighters" in Hong Kong had done so. Of all the respondents, 64.9 percent were afraid that Hong Kong's prosperity and stability would be endangered if the government's authority weakened. In fact, 47.7 percent of them were worried about political turmoil in Hong Kong before 1997. As a result, it is no surprise that among those who perceived a decline in governmental authority, 42.6 percent would like to see the government reinvigorate its authority by extreme measures.

Moreover, people are more ready to take actions against the

government to influence public policies and decisions. More important, unconventional collective actions are increasingly used to pressure the government, despite the fact that many Hong Kong Chinese still have reservations about such actions.[37] Scanning newspaper reports, Cheung and Louie found an increasing tendency for people to use agitational and confrontational tactics against the government to improve their quality of life and to assert their political and civil rights.[38] The number of street protests, for example, increased six times in the period 1984–1990.[39]

A battered government also invites the rise of criminal activities, which have already led to an alarming deterioration in public order and a drop in public confidence in the police. The sudden recent surge of violent and organized crime constitutes a serious and embarrassing challenge to government authority, in addition to the discovery of corrupt and immoral behavior among a number of senior officials and public figures.

Finally, people are less deferential to governmental authority than before. Officials are constantly lambasted and ridiculed in the mass media and on public occasions. Even the governor is not immune from public disapprobation, a drastic change from the past when governors inspired tremendous respect and even awe among the colonial subjects. In my 1988 survey, when I asked about attitudes toward those who constantly criticized the government, I was somewhat surprised that 37.4 percent had a favorable attitude. Only 27.5 percent of respondents did not like the government critics. If people begin to derive satisfaction from public criticism of the government, their support for that government may have waned.

What all these signs of ungovernability reflect is a strained relationship between the government and the people, as escalating demands for governmental actions increasingly overburden an enfeebled and disintegrating government. Naturally, an intensified conflict like this will inevitably reinforce the social conflicts mentioned earlier. Furthermore, this conflict could possibly even take on an anti-British and anticolonial coloration, for the weakened Hong Kong government will quite likely come to be perceived as self-serving, catering primarily to its own interests or the interests of Britain or selling out Hong Kong's interests to China. The appearance of anti-British and anticolonial sentiments would unavoidably further erode the government's ability to rule.

Nevertheless, despite all the negative factors detracting from the government's capability to rule, in the short run I do not foresee any possibility of a collapse of governmental authority, because the conditions relevant to effective governance, though eroded, still remain

307

moderately strong. Most important, the economy of Hong Kong, despite stagflation, is still vibrant. Not only does Hong Kong enjoy full employment, but it in fact suffers from a labor shortage. Hong Kong is likely to continue to benefit from the growth of the economies in the Asian-Pacific region. Its economic link with China will also prove enormously valuable both in the short run and in the long run. Another factor is the obsession of the Hong Kong Chinese with stability and their abhorrence of confusion. They know very well the indispensability of the colonial authority in maintaining social order. As already noted, some would even like to see the government take stern measures to reassert its authority, probably considering such extremes as a means to guarantee stability in Hong Kong. The general endorsement of the existing institutional structure, which owes its origin to colonial tutelage, is of great help to the government in maintaining its rule.

In addition, as the government is publicly credited with the modernizing success of Hong Kong, it has probably accumulated substantial political support. This stock of political goodwill from the people is likely to have been depleted quite a bit, but the balance should enable the government to sustain itself for some while. The general satisfaction with colonial rule in the past and the reluctance of the people to face the future might even produce some measure of nostalgic political support for the government. When people think that the future government is unlikely to be better than the departing one, they will probably deal more magnanimously with the outgoing one.

Another factor contributing to stability is that the emigration from the higher occupational strata creates vacancies for those staying behind. Opportunities for upward occupational mobility for the young and better educated have multiplied. At least in the short term, as many people are lured by suddenly brightened career prospects, their support of the government and their opposition to instability will help maintain governability. Moreover, the public still respects and supports the economic, social, and judiciary institutions of Hong Kong. These institutions are separate from the government, and their relationship with it is nonantagonistic. As a result of the limited role of the government in society, these institutions are of enormous importance in the maintenance of the social order. The independent stabilizing functions performed by these institutions should alleviate the difficulties of the government to a certain degree. Finally, even China is worried by the possibility of the breakdown of colonial authority. Simply out of self-interest, China is likely to come forth to help the colonial government if it is caught in great difficulties.

Despite these ameliorating factors, the conditions for effective colonial governance will likely erode more quickly as 1997 approaches, and the difficulties faced by the government will continue to mount. Unlike decolonization elsewhere, Britain cannot quit Hong Kong at any time it deems expedient. The Sino-British Joint Declaration has already fixed a date for British departure, and for Britain to quit Hong Kong before 1997 is unthinkable. Therefore, Britain has no choice other than to strive to maintain effective governance in Hong Kong in the remaining years before 1997, even though to do so is increasingly taxing.

To maintain effective governance in the twilight of colonial rule, the colonial government must strengthen its political authority, for the erosion of the favorable conditions for effective colonial rule undermines colonial authority directly or indirectly. A critical condition for effective rule in the last years of the transitional period is the establishment of a strong political authority that can command respect from the public, can formulate and implement public policies with long-term considerations and impact, and is publicly perceived to have longevity (that is, it will not be completely replaced in 1997). With the decline in its authority and the inevitable end of colonial rule, the colonial government has absolutely no chance to rebuild a strong authority all by itself in the next few years. Even though the government is highly jealous of its political autonomy and is extremely reluctant to share power with others, future development in Hong Kong is bound to lead to the formation of a combined or allied authority structure in which the colonial government constitutes only one of the components, albeit a very important one.

Nevertheless, a government that has monopolized power for so long and that had in the past rarely experienced political challenges can hardly be expected to recognize the need to share power to maintain effective rule. As a matter of fact, even though faced with current and future difficulties, the Hong Kong government still adopts a public posture of self-confidence, complacency, and arrogance. To a certain extent, this might represent an overreaction to the "lame duck" image laid upon it by the public. In any case, the government tends to dismiss all problems as immaterial and incessantly reiterates its ability to grapple with Hong Kong's problems single-handedly. It tends to rebuff and snub those it believes are encroaching on its prerogative to make public decisions. In response, the people of Hong Kong and China and foreign investors are increasingly incredulous. Too keen to project decisiveness and competence even when objective conditions counsel otherwise, the colonial government is intransigent, itself part and parcel of ungovernability.

Objectively speaking, two categories of options are available to the government in the remaining years of its rule. In the first category, the government would rely solely on itself to exercise authority. The second category comprises those strategies it can use to expand the authority it can practically exercise by allying itself with other political authorities, particularly China. Since the signing of the Sino-British Joint Declaration, the government has tried various options or a mixture of them but does not appear to follow a consistent line of action. One thing, however, is clear: as far as possible the government favors an option or a combination of options that give it the most decision-making autonomy.

Unlike decolonization in other British colonies, the colonial government will not transfer power to the local people. Nor have the people of Hong Kong strongly demanded the devolution of power to them. Under the Sino-British agreement, Britain is to maintain its rule over Hong Kong up to 1997; then the territory will revert to China. China opposes any attempt of the British to transfer power to the local people for fear that it will deprive Chinese sovereignty over Hong Kong of any real substance. In contrast, despite some clumsy moves to influence local affairs, China is loath to see the colonial government undermined since such weakening would imperil the stability and prosperity of Hong Kong. Accordingly, Britain is ultimately responsible and is held responsible by China for the administration of Hong Kong until 1997. Hence, there is a strong temptation for the colonial government to hold on to power as far as possible.

As a result of the deterioration of the conditions for effective governance, however, such a do-it-alone approach is inadequate to the task. On the surface this approach is a feasible option as the colonial government is not and will not be under any threat of overthrow by the people or restoration of Chinese sovereignty in advance of 1997. There are two types of do-it-alone approaches: the active and the passive.

In the active do-it-alone approach, the colonial government would pursue a positive course of action to tackle Hong Kong's problems, to counter any political challenge from China or from within the territory with gusto, and to enlarge its power base. In view of the problems hindering effective governance, however, this is hard to achieve. The minimal coercive capacity at the disposal of the government, its declining ability to expand the colonial ruling coalition through co-opting the local elites,[40] the increasing fiscal constraints,[41] the limited professional expertise of an administration headed by generalist civil servants, and the emergence of China as the alternative power center together make this approach an ineffective one.

In the passive do-it-alone option, the colonial government can always manage to preserve its monopoly over power by pursuing lethargic governance. If it refrains from making difficult decisions and withdraws from taking policy initiatives, the need to share power with others will be minimized. This approach, however, would be tantamount to relinquishing the responsibility to govern effectively a place embroiled in drastic and difficult changes. This option would seriously jeopardize Hong Kong's future prospects, create problems that would make life extremely difficult for the colonial officials themselves, severely impair the Sino-British relationship, place Britain under international censure, make Hong Kong a controversial issue in British domestic politics, and render it impossible for Britain to exit in glory in 1997. Therefore, if the colonial government is to follow such a course of action, both it and Britain are bound to pay a huge political price for it.

If the colonial government is to choose a power-sharing approach so that an expanded authority structure can be built, it has to make the important decision on whom it should ally itself with. Theoretically speaking, the natural choice must be the future sovereign of Hong Kong, that is, China. In fact, some form of Sino-British cooperation has been ordained by the Joint Declaration, particularly in the latter part of the transitional period.[42] Since the signing of the Joint Declaration, Sino-British cooperation has indeed achieved quite substantial results, which include the participation of Hong Kong in GATT as an independent member and the setting up of a new pension scheme for civil servants.

There is, however, much friction between the countries. The Tiananmen Square event and the involvement of Britain in the retaliatory actions of the West against China have strained the Sino-British relationship to the breaking point. On the part of Britain, cooperation with China in the transitional period is hampered by several factors. In the first place, British mistrust of China is deep rooted. Working with China might impede the pursuit of British national interests in Hong Kong in the last years of colonial rule. Because of different national needs and perceptions of the situation, the two governments' notion of their own interests and the interests of Hong Kong will inevitably diverge. Given the antipathy of the residents of Hong Kong to the Chinese government in general and to Chinese "meddling" in local affairs in particular, collaboration between Britain and

311

China might further confirm the "lame duck" image of the colonial government in the public mind. Because many civil servants in Hong Kong harbor extremely negative attitudes toward China, closer cooperation between the two governments is also likely to divide the civil service and demoralize part of it. In short, to enlist the support of China in the expansion of the political authority in Hong Kong, Britain might eventually have to run the risk of playing second fiddle to China in governing Hong Kong in the transitional period. Unless the situation is desperate, the colonial government is expected to be only lukewarm toward the formation of an allied Sino-British political authority to bolster the declining authority of the colonial government.

Britain, of course, can choose to ally with other political forces to buttress its political capability. To win the support of a foreign government or a number of foreign governments is obviously an option. But in an age when colonialism is widely seen as an anachronism, the chance of obtaining the support of a foreign government for colonial rule is minimal. Although out of self-interest or because of anti-Communist motives, foreign governments might adopt a "sympathetic" stance toward Hong Kong, none of them (not even the U.S. government) has been willing to play an explicit role in undergirding colonial rule. Apparently the intense animus of China to any foreign intervention is enough to deter active foreign involvement in local affairs.

Britain's attempt to arrest the decline of colonial authority has also met with limited success. The lack of political leaders and strong political organization in Hong Kong in the first place prevents the colonial government from expanding its authority through power sharing. The existence of China as an alternative power center inhibits the efforts of Britain to cultivate local leaders as its supporters. Attempts to mobilize support for the government in its last days through the provision of popular elections and representative government have been impeded as a result of China's opposition, the resistance of the established interests in Hong Kong, and the government's own reservations about the loss of political autonomy and its apprehension about inability to control the political situation. The political groups in Hong Kong are quite fragmented, and the government has in fact reinforced the fragmentation by expediently seeking the support of different groups in various times for different political purposes. In the end, the internal support base of the government remains shaky.

In the past half-decade or so, the government had wavered among various options to strengthen its authority. It has not yet settled upon a consistent line of action, although the government has tried very hard to avoid power sharing with either China or the other political forces in Hong Kong. The government has recentralized power at the top of the administrative apparatus and appeased the civil servants through exorbitant pay raises, improved fringe benefits, and partial capitulation to their pension demands. The increased reliance on the staunch supporters of colonial rule to fend off political challenges from both Hong Kong and China is another indication of a government desperately holding onto power. In the future, this inconsistent and unstable strategy will undermine the government's efforts to maintain effective rule, and alternative options have to be sought.

Even though the colonial government is quite jealous of its autonomy and finds any possible interference from China wholly unpalatable, it will gradually have to seek China's support to bolster its weakening authority. As a matter of fact, China is increasing its demand for a larger say in local affairs. Before an allied Sino-British authority can appear, the two countries should first be able to agree on the types of policies to be adopted in Hong Kong and to reconcile their different interests. The process of developing Sino-British cooperation is bound to be difficult, conflict ridden, and messy. Nevertheless, in view of the fact that the governments share a fundamental interest in the stability and prosperity of Hong Kong, cooperation or joint actions between them on at least an ad hoc basis are quite likely in the future. And China's support is crucial if the colonial government is to formulate and implement policies with post-1997 implications and applicability. As 1997 draws near, the ability of the colonial government to make decisions alone will be severely constrained. Another favorable factor for increasing Sino-British collaboration is the growing demand of the people of Hong Kong for an improved relationship between the two governments, which is perceived to be of paramount importance to the future of the place.[43] The closer 1997 approaches, the less reluctant Britain will be to share power with China, and the opposition of the "pro-British" elements to Sino-British cooperation will also soften. As soon as a basic *modus vivendi* between China and Britain can be established, a decent form of allied authority can take shape.

Once China and Britain establish a collaborative relationship, political authority in Hong Kong can develop through the joint efforts of the two governments to groom and promote political leaders and through the inclusion of these leaders in the authority thus forged. Again, this collaboration is not easy to achieve, involving, as it does, a lot of give and take between two governments with very different views on the desirable qualities of the future leaders of Hong Kong, particularly with respect to their allegiances. As a matter of fact, the complicated and multiple channels of leader recruitment established by the two governments as a result of their tussle over the future political system of Hong Kong leave much room to identify and choose the future leaders of the territory. Nonetheless, these can be mitigated to some extent since both governments tend to prefer leaders with a moderate-to-conservative inclination. And, given the moderate-to-conservative, pragmatic orientation of the Hong Kong people and their realization that only leaders with the blessing of both governments can function effectively during the transition, such leaders should be able to garner a fair level of popular support.

Ultimately, if the allied authority comprising Britain, China, and the moderate-to-conservative leaders is to enjoy popular support, it must be able to formulate and implement short- and especially long-term policies that directly address the needs of Hong Kong. It should also be capable of withstanding political challenges within the territory, dealing with serious problems, and tackling tough issues. All this would alleviate the problem of ungovernability in the latter part of the transitional period and lay the necessary (though not sufficient) foundation for possible progress in the future.

Conclusion

Dealing effectively with the problem of ungovernability in Hong Kong in the twilight of colonial rule requires two conditions: the consolidation of an allied, albeit messy, political authority in Hong Kong and the formulation and implementation of policies that address the major problems plaguing the territory before and even after 1997. The two requisites are closely related since long-term policy objectives can be devised and implemented only by a strengthened and expanded political authority. Compared with the policy program, the consolidation of political authority is much more important and urgent. Because the conditions for effective governance by the colonial government have diminished, that government does not have the means to enhance its authority. More likely is an expanded political authority comprising the Hong Kong government, the Chinese government, and the moderate-to-conservative leaders. As political authority coalesces, the autonomy of the colonial government will decline, China will become more involved in local affairs, and the two governments will develop local leaders. Any allied authority is bound to bear the difficulties and strains among the three parties, however, and such an alliance might even occasionally aggravate the conflicts already existent in Hong Kong.

14

The Hong Kong Economy—To the 1997 Barrier and Beyond

Yun-wing Sung

Since the advent of Sino-British talks over the future of Hong Kong in 1982, the Hong Kong economy has undergone a series of economic crises, including a collapse of the stock and real estate markets in 1982, a crisis of confidence in the Hong Kong currency in September 1983, and a second collapse of the stock and real estate markets during the Tiananmen incident in 1989. Although the Hong Kong economy has so far been able to recover from all these shocks, the hemorrhage in the form of brain drain and capital outflow has accelerated since the Tiananmen crisis. Since 1982, there have been frequent predictions that the Hong Kong economy would soon disintegrate because of this hemorrhage; the Tiananmen incident aggravated the crisis.

Paradoxically, despite the Tiananmen incident and the Gulf War, the Hong Kong economy is still relatively vibrant. Although the real estate markets collapsed in Canada, the United States, and Japan in 1990, real estate prices in Hong Kong rose beyond their pre-Tiananmen peaks. Despite economic recession in North America, Hong Kong still experienced moderate economic growth: 3.9 percent in 1991 and the official forecast for 1992 was 5 percent. For an economy that has grown for many years at close to double-digit range, such rates appear slow. Hong Kong, though, has a long-term labor shortage, and the unemployment rate has been less than 2 percent since the beginning of 1987. Given the extreme tightness in the labor market, growth rates in the 4–5 percent range are quite satisfactory. Rising unemployment in North America and the strong demand for labor in Hong Kong explain the recent signs of an increase in the return of overseas Hong Kong migrants.

The paradox of the future of Hong Kong is that the political picture looks gloomy while the economic picture looks bright. Although Hong Kong has very little leverage over the unpredictable political events in Beijing, events that have cast a long shadow over its future, its economy is extremely dynamic and resilient: situated on the eastern Pacific rim, Hong Kong is in the center of the fastest growing region in the world.

This chapter dwells on the bright side of the picture, concentrating on economics instead of politics. The continued economic development of Hong Kong, however, is conditional on the preservation of political stability and the efficient administration of law and order. Because these preconditions cannot be guaranteed, the risk of investing in Hong Kong is quite real. For many investors, though, the returns of investing in Hong Kong appear to be high enough to compensate for the risks.

The attitudes toward political risks in Hong Kong of the residents and those of multinational investors are quite different. The citizens, who tend to have most of their assets in Hong Kong, do not want to put all their eggs in the Hong Kong basket. Their reaction to 1997 is to diversify out of Hong Kong. Because international investors have only a small part of their portfolios in Hong Kong, they tend to move into the vacuum left by indigenous Hong Kong capital. Thus, the outflow of human and financial capital from Hong Kong is partly balanced by an inflow, and this inflow has enabled the Hong Kong economy to remain strong. Although the picture of Hong Kong often presented in the press is uncompensated hemorrhage of skills and capital, the true picture is of the internationalization of Hong Kong's economy: an outflow of native skills and capital to establish international links and connections and an inflow of international skills and capital that strengthen its international links. The internationalization of the Hong Kong economy is the key to the survival of Hong Kong as a distinct entity under Chinese sovereignty.

The Brain Drain

The exodus of skilled people from Hong Kong is well known. What is not well known is that the outflow has been exceeded by an inflow: in 1989, for instance, emigrants totaled 42,000, and immigrants totaled 77,300, making a net inflow of 35,300.

While the outflow of skilled people from Hong Kong is alarming, it is far less catastrophic than the outflow from East Germany in 1989. In 1989, the rate of exodus (the number of emigrants per capita) from East Germany was 5 percent, and that of Hong Kong was 0.74 percent. The East German rate was clearly unsustainable: in a few years' time, the majority of the young and able-bodied population would have been gone. The number of Hong Kong emigrants stayed around 20,000 per year from 1980 to 1986. It rose to 30,000, 45,800, and 42,000 in 1987, 1988, and 1989, respectively, and then rose further to 62,000 in 1990. The Hong Kong rate of exodus in 1990 was about 1 percent per year, possibly a sustainable rate, especially when the outflow is more than balanced by the inflow.

The rising trend is clearly due to anxiety over 1997 and over the Tiananmen incident in particular. In 1987 and 1988, about 24 percent of all emigrants were professionals, managers, and administrators. Since emigrants include children and dependents of professionals, a more meaningful ratio is the proportion of emigrant families headed by professionals. The ratio is estimated to be 62 percent.[1]

Paul K. C. Kwong estimated "depletion ratios" (the portion of people who emigrated in 1987 and 1988 in a given profession) to gauge the impact of emigration on several professions. In 1987–1988, he found that "some 10 percent of the 1986 stock of engineers; 11 percent of the nurses and midwives; 13 percent of the lawyers, judges, medical doctors, and dentists; 22 percent of the accountants and auditors; and 35 percent of the programmers and system analysts had been lost."[2] The figures appear catastrophic. It must be remembered, however, that the loss was alleviated by immigration as well as by new graduates.

Students studying abroad are potential migrants. The total number of student visas issued by major countries (Australia, Canada, the United Kingdom, and the United States) stayed at around 11,000 per year from 1981 to 1986 but jumped up to 13,404, 15,026 and 19,168 in 1987, 1988, and 1989, respectively.

The government estimates that the number of emigrants will stay at around the 1990 level of 62,000 in 1991–1992. Thereafter, emigration will likely rise as Hong Kong approaches the psychological barrier of 1997. It appears likely that more than a half-million people will leave between 1990 and 1997.

As for the inflow of 77,300 immigrants into Hong Kong in 1989, 27,300 were legal immigrants from China, and 50,000 came from other countries. Any Chinese has the right to enter Hong Kong by international treaty concluded between Britain and the Manchus, but China has exercised "voluntary export restraint." China unilaterally halved the quota of emigrants from 150 to 75 per day as a gesture of goodwill during the Sino-British talks over the future of Hong Kong in 1982. The Chinese legal immigrants were mostly wives and children of Hong Kong residents admitted for family reunion, and their skill level is low. Anecdotal evidence suggests, though, that the children of these immigrants were very hardworking and upwardly mobile, as would be expected of most first-generation immigrants.

317

The other immigrants come from a variety of sources. Because of the severe labor shortage in Hong Kong, the government announced a program in 1990 to allow firms to import 3,700 skilled workers and 10,000 experienced operatives under contract. Among professionals, a prominent group is the Chinese from Southeast Asia, who came to fill the vacancies left by local emigrants. Chinese from Southeast Asia often face discrimination at home and are relatively willing to migrate to Hong Kong. People from Macau often have Hong Kong ties, providing another source of immigration. And finally, the increase in investment from multinational companies has brought about an increase in expatriate staff.

Official statistics are likely to understate both emigration and immigration. There appear to be a considerable number of people who left Hong Kong as nonemigrants but switched their status upon arriving at their destinations. Moreover, students going overseas for studies are not regarded as emigrants, although most of them may not return because of concern over 1997. Immigrants are also understated because illegal immigration from China is still considerable. These immigrants are unskilled and tend to work on construction sites. Returning émigrés have the right to enter Hong Kong as long as they possess a Hong Kong identity card. Their exact numbers are unknown, and they are not regarded as immigrants.

Despite considerable immigration, those who emigrate are usually the cream of the crop. Indeed, Hong Kong is experiencing a major loss of skill and knowledge. If Hong Kong can maintain its prosperity in the 1990s, however, a significant proportion of the emigrants may return to work in Hong Kong after they have obtained their foreign passports. The international exposure and experience of returning emigrants would be a valuable asset for the Hong Kong economy. Of course, the returnees are likely to be in the minority, but the overseas connections of the nonreturnees are part of an international network that also benefits Hong Kong. The great majority of Taiwanese overseas students, for instance, do not return to Taiwan after graduation, but, together with the returnees, their skills and connections have formed an international network that has contributed tremendously to the success of Taiwan's personal computer industry. For Hong Kong, the present net loss may turn out to be a net gain in the long run.

As far as the accumulation of human capital is concerned, 1997 may turn out to be a blessing in disguise. Knowledge and skill are often valuable assets or a qualification for emigration: the 1997 crisis has thus increased the incentive of the citizens of Hong Kong to acquire the right skills. Middle-aged executives and professionals with little interest in further training in the past are now eager to learn new skills to qualify for emigration. Hong Kong's students are likewise working and studying harder to get the right qualifications.

The Hong Kong government has planned to double the enrollment in Hong Kong's tertiary educational institutions by 1995. The rapid expansion in tertiary education is, in part, a response to the brain drain. Whether the response is adequate is difficult to tell. Two-thirds of the holders of university degrees in Hong Kong were educated overseas. As a result of the 1997 crisis, many Hong Kong students are in overseas institutions, and how many of them will return is very uncertain.

At present, returning emigrants are not particularly numerous because it takes a few years to obtain foreign passports and the number of Hong Kong emigrants who have already obtained their foreign passports is not very large. Their number will increase rapidly in the coming few years, though, and there may be many more returning emigrants. With the recent economic recession in Canada, there are signs of a significant increase in returnees, not only of middle-aged emigrants but also of their children who have graduated overseas. According to a 1990 government sample survey of 12,000 households, the number of heads of households in Hong Kong who have acquired residential status overseas has doubled in comparison with a similar survey in 1989.[3] The commitment of returning emigrants to Hong Kong will hinge on China. If pragmatism prevails in Beijing, returning emigrants are likely to stay on. Otherwise, they will leave again.

To combat the brain drain, the Hong Kong government can relax the present stringent controls on immigration, especially immigrants from China. In the fall of 1990, the government announced that mainland Chinese who have stayed overseas for two or more years can work in Hong Kong. While this is a step in the right direction, much more can be done. The Hong Kong government, for example, can negotiate a program with Beijing to admit skilled manpower into Hong Kong.

The Capital Outflow

Although capital moves freely into and out of Hong Kong, there is no official record of such movements. It is therefore very difficult to estimate the size of the capital outflow.

Although the outflow is very large, the inflow is also considerable. According to a press report, the outflow in 1990 was HK$33 billion and the inflow was HK$26.2 billion.[4] Japan, China, and the

United States are respectively the first, second, and third largest investors in Hong Kong. Japan invested HK$7 billion in 1990, accounting for 27 percent of total foreign investment for the year. Hong Kong is the first choice in Asia after Indonesia for Japanese investment. Recently, Taiwanese, South Korean, and ASEAN investors have also been active in Hong Kong.

We know definitely that the size of outflow is much larger than the size of the inflow and that the net outflow of capital is considerable. Hong Kong has developed a large surplus on the current account, which must be offset by a deficit on the capital account. In 1989, the net outflow was nearly US$5 billion or 8.0 percent of Hong Kong's gross domestic product (GDP). Historically, Hong Kong has had net inflows during periods of prosperity and outflows during political crisis (figure 14–1). The huge capital inflows of the early and mid-1960s turned into an outflow in 1967, the year that the Cultural Revolution in China spilled into Hong Kong, leading to riots and terrorist acts. The net outflow increased to nearly 5 percent of GDP by 1969 but declined thereafter as stability returned to China. The mid-1970s were also years of capital outflow, in response to the struggle between Deng Xiaoping and the "Gang of Four" as Zhou Enlai and Mao Zedong passed away in 1975 and 1976, respectively. The net outflow in 1976 increased to a record of 7 percent of GDP but declined rapidly thereafter. Huge net inflows emerged after the inauguration of economic reforms in China in 1978, increasing to 6.5 percent of GDP in 1981, a record since 1967. The net inflow declined rapidly after 1982, however, reflecting anxiety over the future of Hong Kong, turning into a net outflow in 1984. In 1989, net outflow increased from 6 percent to a record of 8 percent of GDP, in reaction to the Tiananmen incident.

Net capital outflow has abated as Hong Kong rapidly recovered from the shock of the Tiananmen incident. In March 1990, the Hong Kong financial secretary forecast in his budget speech that net capital outflow in 1990 would reach U.S.$6 billion, or 8.4 percent of GDP. Net capital outflow in 1990, however, turned out to be only $3.5 billion or 5.0 percent of GDP. Net capital outflow in 1991 further declined to U.S.$2.5 billion, or 3.1 percent of GDP.

Although net capital outflows broke all historical records in 1989, the implication is not entirely negative. Capital outflow may represent capital flight, but it may also represent productive investment overseas. Statistically, it is very difficult to distinguish between the two. As Hong Kong is in no immediate danger of a Communist takeover and the Hong Kong currency is very stable, most of the capital outflow probably represents diversification of investment. The huge

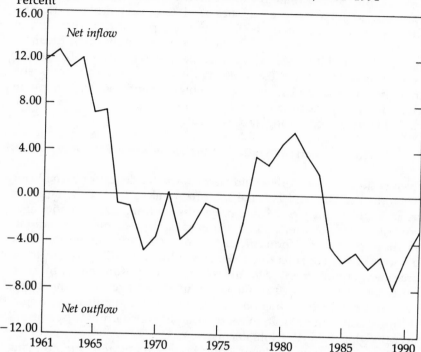

FIGURE 14–1

Hong Kong's Net Capital Inflow and Net Capital Outflow as Percentage of Gross Domestic Product, 1961–1991

Source: Hong Kong Census and Statistics Department, Estimates of Gross Domestic Product, various issues.

net capital outflow indicates that Hong Kong is investing overseas on an unprecedented scale, building up a network of international links and connections. Such links are invaluable for the survival of Hong Kong in the uncertain 1990s.

Press reports that investment in Hong Kong has dropped sharply because of concern over 1997 are numerous. Such reports are very misleading. Although investment in plant and equipment in Hong Kong has dropped, other forms of investment by Hong Kong residents in and outside of Hong Kong have risen. First, there is massive Hong Kong investment overseas, building up Hong Kong's international links. Second, Hong Kong citizens have invested heavily in human capital, both in and outside Hong Kong. Expenditures (both public and private) on education are classified as consumption rather than investment in national income statistics, a grossly misleading label. Moreover, a significant part of private investment in human capital is the forgone earnings of the people who have to devote their time to study rather than to work, and these forgone earnings do not appear in national income statistics at all. Given political uncertainty, the shift from investment in plant and equipment to investment in human capital is entirely predictable. Human capital is difficult to nationalize, and it is easier for skilled people to emigrate. The reality is that investment by Hong Kong has increased tremendously, though it has shifted from investment in plant and equipment in Hong Kong to investment overseas, and also to investment in human capital both in Hong Kong and overseas.

The Internationalization of the Hong Kong Economy

Even without 1997, there would be a natural tendency for Hong Kong firms to diversify and become multinational as they grow larger, a trend hastened by 1997. Some pressures on firms to internationalize are arguably desirable. Though firms naturally become multinational as they grow, indigenous firms are often slow to internationalize because of the considerable risks and difficulties of operating in an unknown environment. The pressure on Hong Kong firms to internationalize may well turn out to be an advantage as multinational firms can conduct production, financing, sourcing, and marketing at the most convenient locations and the ability to coordinate operations over the globe is a very valuable asset.

The international links of Hong Kong are not only vital to Hong Kong's prosperity but also essential to its role as the gateway of China. Moreover, they also significantly constrain China in its policy toward Hong Kong. Hong Kong's population is becoming internationalized as more and more local residents have acquired foreign passports or immigration visas. The British nationality package will grant 50,000 full British passports to heads of households, of which 36,200 will go to important professionals, 13,300 to government employees, and 500 to key entrepreneurs. Including family members, the total number of British passports will not exceed 225,000. The United States will increase its Hong Kong immigration quota for family reunion from 5,000 in 1990 to 20,000 in 1994, and for 1991–1993, there is an additional immigration quota of 36,000 for employees of American firms in Hong Kong. The immigration visa holders will be allowed to enter the United States until the year 2002. Singapore has granted around 50,000 immigration visas to Hong Kong professionals, who can wait for up to five years to enter Singapore. All these measures will help keep key people in Hong Kong. By the year 2,000, around 1 million Hong Kong citizens will have acquired foreign passports or immigrant visas, and perhaps another million can apply for immigration because of family connections. The large number of people with a right to exit will be a severe constraint on the future government of Hong Kong.

Two contending strategies have helped Hong Kong survive the 1997 crisis. The first strategy centers on the development of representative government: some have argued that a representative government will be able to stand up to intervention from Beijing. The second strategy centers on the internationalization of the Hong Kong economy and the right to exit. Although the two strategies are not mutually exclusive, they conflict because the building of representative government in Hong Kong demands allegiance and commitment to China and Hong Kong instead of allegiance to foreign governments. The Tiananmen incident tipped the scale in favor of the second strategy.

There are signs that the scramble for foreign passports is abating in Hong Kong, as normality has returned to China and the portion of Hong Kong's population most eager to obtain foreign passports have already done so. In the first stage of the British nationality package, in which 43,000 British passports were to be granted to heads of households, the Hong Kong government expected 300,000 applications. There were, however, only around 63,600 applications, including an unknown but probably substantial number of marginally qualified or unqualified applicants induced to apply by an intensive government publicity campaign.

Hong Kong had been a place where civil liberties thrived despite the absence of democratic institutions. Colonial rulers in Hong Kong were held in check by the British Parliament as well as by the influence of China. After 1997, it is possible that the internationalization of Hong Kong's economy and the right to exit can preserve civil liberties there.

Hong Kong as the Key to China's Open Door

The economic value of Hong Kong to China is the main factor in China's tolerance of capitalism in Hong Kong. The Chinese view Hong Kong as a window of China or a bridge to the outside world. Capitalist and free-wheeling Hong Kong is the key to the opening of the Socialist and rigidly regimented Chinese economy.

Hong Kong is China's foremost partner in commodity trade, tourist trade, direct foreign investment, and loan syndication. Since

323

1979, Hong Kong has contributed 59 percent of all direct foreign investment to China and 70 percent of China's tourist earnings. In 1990, China's exports to Hong Kong were 43 percent of total Chinese exports; China's imports from Hong Kong were 38 percent of total imports. Hong Kong also plays an important role in transshipment.

In examining the role of Hong Kong in China's trade, we must distinguish among transshipment, entrepôt trade, and direct trade. In transshipment, goods are consigned directly from the exporting country to a buyer in the importing country, although the goods are transported via an entrepôt and may be temporarily stored at the entrepôt for onward shipment. Transshipped goods may change their mode of transportation at the entrepôt: Chinese goods, for example, are carried by train or coastal vessels to Hong Kong where they are consolidated into containers. Transshipped goods are not usually regarded as part of the trade of the entrepôt, and they do not clear customs because they represent only goods in transit.

Unlike transshipment, entrepôt trade is included in the trade statistics of the entrepôt, since imports for reexports are consigned to a buyer in the entrepôt and the buyer takes legal possession of the goods after clearing customs. These imports may then be processed before being reexported: processing may include packaging, sorting, grading, bottling, drying, assembling, decorating, diluting, or even minor manufacturing processes such as the preshrinking of gray cloth. According to Hong Kong's official definition, any manufacturing process that permanently changes the shape, nature, form, or utility of the basic materials used in manufacture turns the product into a domestic export—that is, an export manufactured in Hong Kong—qualifies the good for classification as Hong Kong origin.

Direct trade includes domestic exports and retained imports. Retained imports are the difference between total imports and imports for reexports. The role of Hong Kong in China's open-door policy can be summarized under four main functions: Hong Kong as financier, trading partner, middleman, and facilitator (figure 14–2).

Hong Kong as Financier. Hong Kong accounted for 59 percent of contracted direct foreign investment in China from 1979 to 1990. The share of Hong Kong in China's external loans was smaller because Hong Kong did not extend soft loans to China. The Hong Kong share rose from 0.6 percent in 1983 to 9.4 percent in 1989, however.

Hong Kong plays a leading role in syndicating loans to China. The share of China's external loans syndicated in Hong Kong rose from 16 percent in the 1979–1982 period to 31 percent in 1987 (table 14–1).

FIGURE 14–2

THE ROLE OF HONG KONG IN CHINA'S OPEN-DOOR POLICY

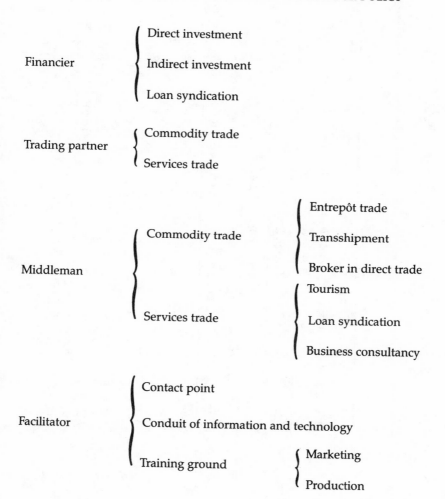

SOURCE: Author.

Hong Kong as Trading Partner. Hong Kong's role as trading partner refers to direct trade only. Entrepôt trade is covered under the middleman function. Table 14-2 shows that Hong Kong was an important entrepôt for China until 1951, but the entrepôt trade of Hong Kong withered in the early 1950s as a result of, first, the

325

TABLE 14-1

HONG KONG'S CONTRIBUTION TO FOREIGN INVESTMENT (CONTRACTED) IN CHINA, 1979–1990
(millions of U.S. dollars)

| | Direct Foreign Investment | | Foreign Loans[a,d] | | | | | | |
| | Total | From Hong Kong[b,c] | Total | Hong Kong as[a,d] | | | Total | From Hong Kong[e] |
				Lender	Center of syndication	Subtotal		
1979–82 average	1384	919 (66)	1,240	19 (1.5)	75 (6.0)	94 (7.6)	2,624	1013 (38.6)
1983	1917	642 (34)	1,513	9 (0.6)	104 (6.9)	113 (7.5)	3,430	755 (22.0)
1984	2875	2,175 (76)	1,916	51 (2.7)	250 (13.0)	301 (15.7)	4,791	2476 (51.7)
1985	6333	4,134 (65)	3,534	73 (2.1)	513 (14.5)	586 (16.6)	9,867	4720 (47.8)
1986	3330	1,449 (51)	8,401	244 (2.9)	1538 (18.3)	1782 (21.2)	11,737	3231 (27.5)
1987	3680	2,466 (67)	7,817	401 (5.1)	2400 (30.7)	2801 (35.8)	12,136	5132 (42.3)

1988	6189	4,033 (65)	9,814	580 (5.9)	1945 (19.8)	2525 (25.7)	16,002	6558 (41.0)
1989	6294	3,645 (58)	5,185	488 (9.4)	718 (13.8)	1205 (23.2)	11,479	4851 (42.3)
1990	6986	4,258 (61)	—	—	—	—	—	—

a. Foreign loans exclude foreign currency loans from the Bank of China.
b. Including Macao (most are from Hong Kong).
c. Figures in parenthesis represent percentage share of total direct foreign investment in China.
d. Figures in parenthesis represent percentage share of total foreign loans to China.
e. Figures in parenthesis represent percentage share of China's total utilization of foreign capital.

SOURCES: Syndicated loans, *Asian Finance* and *Asian Banking*; other data, Almanac of China's Foreign Relations and Trade, various issues.

TABLE 14-2
CHINA–HONG KONG TRADE, VARIOUS YEARS, 1931–1991
(millions of U.S. dollars)

	China's Exports to Hong Kong			China's Imports from Hong Kong		
	Total	Retained in Hong Kong	Reexported elsewhere	Total	Hong Kong goods	Hong Kong reexports
1931–38 average	87 (31.5)	16 (6.3)	70 (25.2)	87 (21.3)	9 (2.1)	79 (19.2)
1950	137 (24.8)	—	—	221 (37.8)	—	—
1951	151 (20.0)	—	—	281 (23.4)	—	—
1952	145 (17.6)	—	—	91 (8.1)	—	—
1955	157 (11.1)	—	—	32 (1.8)	—	—
1960	207 (11.2)	—	—	21 (1.1)	2 (0.1)	19 (1.0)
1965[a]	487 (20.5)	397 (16.8)	88 (3.7)	13 (0.6)	3 (0.2)	10 (0.5)
1970	467 (20.7)	376 (16.6)	91 (4.0)	11 (0.5)	5 (0.21)	6 (0.2)
1975	1378 (19.0)	1096 (15.1)	282 (3.9)	33 (0.5)	6 (0.08)	28 (0.4)
1977	1734 (22.8)	1306 (17.2)	428 (5.6)	44 (0.6)	7 (0.09)	38 (0.5)

Year						
1979	3044	2139	905	383	121	263
	(22.3)	(15.7)	(6.6)	(2.5)	(0.8)	(1.7)
1981	5293	3465	1828	1961	523	1438
	(24.1)	(15.7)	(8.3)	(8.9)	(2.4)	(6.5)
1983	5818	3680	2139	2531	856	1675
	(26.2)	(16.6)	(9.6)	(11.8)	(4.0)	(7.8)
1984	6689	3979	2709	5033	1443	3590
	(25.6)	(15.3)	(10.4)	(18.4)	(5.3)	(13.1)
1985	7168	3746	3422	7857	1950	5907
	(26.2)	(13.7)	(12.5)	(18.6)	(4.6)	(14.0)
1986	9778	4734	5045	7550	2310	5241
	(31.6)	(15.3)	(16.3)	(17.6)	(5.4)	(12.2)
1987	13762	5710	8052	11290	3574	7716
	(34.8)	(14.4)	(20.4)	(26.1)	(8.3)	(17.9)
1988	18269	5579	12690	17030	4874	12157
	(38.4)	(11.8)	(26.7)	(30.8)	(8.8)	(22.4)
1989	21916	4599	17323	18816	5548	13268
	(41.7)	(8.8)	(32.9)	(31.8)	(9.4)	(22.4)
1990	26650	4361	22287	20305	6086	14219
	(42.9)	(7.1)	(35.9)	(38.1)	(11.4)	(26.6)
1991	32137	3687	28450	26631	6975	19656
	(44.7)	(5.1)	(39.6)	(41.7)	(10.9)	(30.8)

NOTE: Figures in parenthesis represent percentage share of China's total exports (imports).

a. Export figures are for the year 1966.

SOURCES: Hong Kong data: 1931–1938, C. F. Tom, *Entrepot Trade and the Monetary Standards of Hong Kong* (Chicago, Univ. of Chicago Press, 1957); 1948 and after, *Hong Kong Trade Statistics*; 1966 and after, *Review of Overseas Trade*, Census and Statistics Department, Hong Kong. Chinese data: 1931–1948, UN Statistical Office, *Yearbook of International Trade Statistics*; 1950–1979, *China Statistical Yearbook*; 1981 and after, *China Customs Statistics*

centralization of trade in the hands of state trading companies and the reorientation of China's trade to the Comecon bloc after the 1949 Communist takeover and, second, the UN trade embargo on China and the U.S. ban on all imports from China following China's entry into the Korean War in 1951. China's imports from Hong Kong dwindled to negligible amounts. China's exports to Hong Kong also declined, but the amount of exports was still substantial because of China's need to earn hard currency, particularly after the Sino-Soviet rift of the late 1950s. Before 1979, however, only one-quarter to one-third of China's exports to Hong Kong was reexported, and the rest was retained in Hong Kong for internal use. Since 1979, the picture has changed dramatically. Of China's exports to Hong Kong, the reexported portion grew rapidly and exceeded the retained portion by 1986. From 1977 to 1990, China's imports via Hong Kong and imports of Hong Kong origin grew 374 and 869 times, respectively. Hong Kong reemerged as a major entrepôt for China, and China also became a major market for Hong Kong products.

Hong Kong was the largest final market (that is, excluding Chinese exports via Hong Kong) for Chinese exports in the late 1960s and early 1970s, but the Hong Kong market was overtaken by the Japanese market and the U.S. market in 1973 and 1987, respectively. The Hong Kong market, however, still accounted for 7 percent of China's exports in 1990. China continues to regard Hong Kong as its largest market, as Chinese trade statistics disregard the substantial reexports of Chinese products via Hong Kong. Domestic exports of Hong Kong to China grew from negligible amounts to U.S.$6.1 million in 1990. In 1984 Hong Kong became the third largest supplier of goods to China after Japan and the United States. Part of the reason for the rapid growth of Hong Kong's domestic export is due to Hong Kong's investment in processing and assembling operations in China. Hong Kong firms supply such operations with the required raw materials and components, parts of which are made in Hong Kong. It should be noted that China has regarded Hong Kong as its largest supplier from 1987 onward, as Chinese trade statistics count a substantial part of the reexports of Hong Kong to China as imports from Hong Kong.

China's exports retained in Hong Kong have been stagnating since 1984, and their share of China's total exports has declined sharply. China has been unable to capture the higher end of the Hong Kong market, which was dominated by Japan. Given the increasing affluence of Hong Kong and the Japanese dominance in vehicles, capital goods, and quality consumer durables and consumer goods, the future of Chinese products in Hong Kong is not very bright.

Service trade, mostly tourism, is also important. Table 14–3 shows that Hong Kong accounts for around 60 percent of tourist arrivals and 70 percent of tourist expenditures in China. Numbers of Chinese tourists visiting Hong Kong have also increased rapidly. Such trips, however, are usually paid for by the Hong Kong relatives of the Chinese tourists.

Hong Kong as Middleman. Hong Kong plays the role of middleman both in commodity trade and in services trade, including tourism, financial services, and business consultancy. A middleman creates opportunities for trade and investment by lowering transaction costs. In commodity trade, Hong Kong is an important entrepôt as well as center of transshipment for China. The value of transshipped goods is not available as they do not go through customs, but their weight is known. In 1990, transshipment of goods to (from) China weighed as much as 9 percent of China's imports (exports) from (to) Hong Kong. This implies that a significant portion of China's trade is transshipped via Hong Kong. Hong Kong trading firms also appear to perform an important brokerage role for China's direct trade, amounting to U.S.$15 billion or 7 percent of China's total trade in 1988. As for tourist trade, Hong Kong is the foremost gateway for China tourists. Many foreigners also join package tours of China organized in Hong Kong, and the percentage of foreign tourists leaving (visiting) China via Hong Kong has been increasing since 1982, rising to over 55(44) percent in 1987 (table 14–3). Loan syndication, discussed under the financier function, can also be viewed as a middleman activity performed by Hong Kong. Hong Kong has been the center for raising 80 percent of China's syndicated loans (excluding soft loans and nonsyndicated loans) during the past several years. Hong Kong is also the principal center for China's consultancy services.

Since the inauguration of the open-door policy, China has established numerous direct links with the rest of the world, including diplomatic, commercial, and transportation links. Paradoxically, the middleman role of Hong Kong is becoming more prominent, and an increasing share of China's commodity trade, tourist trade, and loan syndication is handled through Hong Kong (tables 14–1 to 14–3). It is worthwhile to construct a theory of intermediation to explain this paradox.

The usual explanation of entrepôt trade in terms of transportation cost is faulty because it ignores the importance of transaction

TABLE 14-3
Hong Kong's Contribution to China's Tourism, 1978–1990
(thousands of tourists)

	Hong Kong Residents			Foreigners			Total Tourists
	Number	Tourist arrivals[a]	Tourist spending[b]	Number	Hong Kong exit[c]	Hong Kong entrance[d]	
1978	1,501	(83)	(74)	248	NA	NA	1,809
1979	3,526	(84)	(80)	383	NA	NA	4,204
1980	4,324	(76)	(74)	564	NA	NA	5,703
1981	5,065	(65)	(68)	714	(46)	(40)	7,767
1982	5,287	(67)	(68)	807	(40)	(34)	7,924
1983	6,476	(68)	(69)	913	(40)	(34)	9,477
1984	8,916	(69)	(70)	1,182	(40)	(36)	12,852
1985	11,983	(67)	(70)	1,455	(45)	(39)	17,833
1986	12,990	(57)	(64)	1,550	(50)	(43)	22,819
1987	15,559	(58)	(65)	1,815	(55)	(44)	26,902
1988	18,092	(61)	(65)	1,922	—	—	31,695
1989	16,843	(69)	(73)	1,530	—	—	24,501
1990	18,000	(66)	(71)	1,740	—	—	27,460

NA = not available; percentages in parentheses.

a. Percentage share of Hong Kong visitors in China's total tourist arrivals.

b. Percentage share of Hong Kong visitor's expenditure in total tourist expenditure in China.

c. Percentage share of foreign visitors who leave China via Hong Kong.

d. Percentage share of foreign visitors who enter China via Hong Kong.

SOURCES: For expenditures of Hong Kong tourists, Sung (1985: 57); for foreigners leaving and entering China via Hong Kong, Hong Kong Census and Statistics Department; for other data, *Chinese Statistical Yearbook*, various issues.

costs. It is useful to classify reexports into processed reexports and pure reexports. Processed reexports have been physically treated (packaged, sorted, and so on), whereas pure reexports have not been changed in any physical way.

Pure reexports are difficult to account for theoretically because they involve higher costs than transshipment (other things being equal), owing to two factors: one, reexports have to clear the customs of an entrepôt twice, whereas transshipped goods do not have to clear the customs of the entrepôt at all, so fewer delays and lower storage costs for transshipment are involved; and two, transshipped goods are insured and financed just once, whereas reexports have to be insured and financed twice—first when they are imported into the entrepôt and second when they are reexported. While transportation costs determine transshipment, pure reexports are determined by both transportation costs and transaction costs, and processed reexports involve processing costs as well.

Since China's adoption of an open-door policy in 1979, it has been easier to trade directly with China. The transaction cost of establishing a direct trade link has gone down, and this should lead to a rise in direct trade relative to indirect trade. China started to decentralize its foreign trade system in 1979, however, replacing vertical channels of command by horizontal links. The number of trading partners and trade links multiplied rapidly, creating a huge demand for intermediation. Before 1979, establishing trade links with ten trading corporations would have ensured a complete coverage of China trade. The number of trading corporations increased to over a thousand by 1984, and it is prohibitively costly for an individual firm to establish trade links with all Chinese trading corporations. Intermediation emerged to economize on the cost of establishing trade links, and this demand for intermediation was channeled to Hong Kong because of its comparative advantage in trading. China's foreign trade decentralization came in three waves: 1979, 1984, and 1988. The share of China's trade through Hong Kong jumped after each wave of decentralization (table 14-2).

The rapid jump of the share of China's loans syndicated in Hong Kong in 1987 (table 14-1) appears to be related to the decentralization of China's financial system. Starting in 1986, selected provincial governments and enterprises were allowed to raise foreign loans without central approval. Decentralization appears to have a determining effect on intermediation.

As for tourism, the China Travel Service used to have a monopoly in organizing tours for foreign tourists, but in 1984 the management of the tourist trade was partially decentralized to provincial and local governments. It is noteworthy that the percentage of foreign tourists going to and departing from China via Hong Kong increased in 1984–1985. This development is consistent with the theory of intermediation. Hong Kong tour operators organize many tours to China, including one-day tours of Shenzhen. Data on foreign tourists leaving or entering China via Hong Kong after 1987 are not shown in table 14-3 because Taiwan lifted its ban on travel to the mainland in late 1987. This of course led to another jump in the number of foreigners visiting China via Hong Kong.

Hong Kong as Facilitator. Besides the functions of financier, trading partner, and middleman, Hong Hong facilitates the open-door policy in many intangible ways. It serves as a contact point, being the main base for China's trade and investment for both foreign and Chinese companies. Hong Kong is an important conduit of market information and technology transfer. Hong Kong also provides a market and production training ground for China: some skills can be learned only through practice in a free market environment, and Hong Kong affords a dynamic and convenient training ground. To use Hong Kong as a market and production training ground, China has invested heavily in Hong Kong, and the assets owned by Chinese enterprises and government agencies in Hong Kong in 1992 were valued at U.S. $20 billion in press reports.[5]

Since China plans to decentralize its exports further, the prospect of Hong Kong as an entrepôt is very bright. There are significant economies of scale and economies of agglomeration in trading activity, and other cities such as Singapore or Shanghai would find it very difficult to compete with Hong Kong because it is the established center for China's trade.[6] The existence of economies of scale in intermediation would enhance the demand for the middleman as small firms will not be able to trade efficiently. Kozo Yamamura argues that significant economies of scale exist in the production of trading services, as the production of these services usually involves large fixed costs and small or declining marginal costs.[7] In the production of market information, which is part and parcel of intermediation, he argues that considerable costs are involved, and the same market information is useful in many transactions. Moreover, trading firms can also consolidate small orders to use warehouse and shipping capacities efficiently to achieve economy of scale.

Traders tend to agglomerate in a city, suggesting that there are significant external economies involved. Once a city acquires a comparative advantage in trade, the advantage appears to feed upon itself, and more trading firms will come to the city, making the city even more efficient in trade.

There are in fact external economies on both the demand and the supply sides in trade. External economy on the demand side operates through search: an increase in the number of potential trading partners makes trade easier. Economic theory suggests that agglomeration should be most prevalent in the trading of heterogeneous goods under conditions of low search and travel cost.[8] A rise in heterogeneity increases the need to search in a marketplace with many sellers. A decline in travel cost will shrink cost differentials between marketplaces and will lead some buyers to shift from small (local) marketplaces to larger (more distant) ones.

External economies on the production side are also important in trade. John Hicks observed that an increase in the number of merchants in the trading center will permit specialization and division of labor, not only by lowering costs but also by lowering risks.[9] The larger the number of traders, the easier it is to acquire information, and the easier it is to arrange multilateral contracts or to develop specialized contracts such as insurance and hedging.

Robert Lucas stressed the importance of agglomeration, especially in service industries, because people in the same trade can interact and learn from one another.[10] He called this "externality of human capital."

Our theory predicts that a decline in travel and communication costs will lower the transaction cost of establishing a trade link, and the fraction of world trade handled through intermediation will thus decline. Declining travel costs, however, also raise the attractiveness of large trading centers relative to small ones, and the fraction of world trade handled through large trading centers may not decline. The secular decline of the fraction of world trade handled through intermediation is quite evident. Before the modern era, for instance, goods usually changed hands many times in long distance trading. Chinese-European trade was usually handled by Indian and Arab middlemen, but these middlemen lost their livelihood with the advent of modern communications. Large entrepôts, though, including Hong Kong, Singapore, Gibraltar, Bahrain, and Puerto Rico, continued to thrive. The large Japanese trading companies, which handle a substantial portion of Japan's foreign trade, are also prospering.[11] Empirical analysis shows that an increasing share of the trade among market economies is handled through Hong Kong in the form of entrepôt trade, confirming our theory on the efficiency of large trading centers.[12]

Even in the very long run, Shanghai is likely to be the only

Chinese city capable of challenging the position of Hong Kong in intermediation, but Shanghai's transport and communication facilities lag considerably behind Hong Kong's and its service industries are rudimentary. China's commodity trade will shift toward less bulky and more heterogeneous goods, enhancing the demand for intermediation. The open-door policy has led to the development of services trade and investment besides the traditional commodity trade, and this will also create the need for intermediation as the "products" of services tend to be more heterogeneous. Moreover, the secular decline in travel costs and transportation costs will imply that the locational advantage of Shanghai will be less important, while proficiency in trading skills will be more important.

The Chinese themselves are establishing many trading companies in Hong Kong, showing that they recognize the established efficiency of Hong Kong in trading. Some Hong Kong traders fear competition from Chinese trading companies in Hong Kong. The situation, however, is not a zero-sum game because of economies of agglomeration; the arrival of Chinese trading companies further strengthens the position of Hong Kong as a trading center.

The Impact of the Tiananmen Incident on the Hong Kong–China Economic Nexus

The effects of the Tiananmen incident on brain drain, capital outflow, and the internationalization of the Hong Kong economy have been examined. This section will concentrate on its influence on the economic relationship between Hong Kong and China.

Since the fall of 1988, China had pursued a policy of retrenchment and recentralization to combat inflation. The policy was strengthened after the Tiananmen incident and was reversed only in mid-1991. The Tiananmen incident and economic retrenchment led to a decline in the volume of China-related business, but China has also become more dependent on Hong Kong since the incident. For instance, Hong Kong's loans to China declined from U.S.$580 million in 1988 to U.S.$488 million in 1989 (table 14–1); Hong Kong's share as a lender of foreign loans to China jumped from 5.9 percent in 1988 to 9.4 percent in 1989. The total number of foreigners visiting China also declined significantly in 1989 (table 14-3), but the share of foreign visitors leaving China via Hong Kong jumped to a record high of 75 percent and of entering China via Hong Kong to 67 percent.

Such tendencies are easy to explain. After the Tiananmen incident, soft loans to China dried up. Hong Kong's loans to China were all commercial loans, and the increase in China's dependence on

Hong Kong loans was expected. In the case of foreign investment, Hong Kong's investment in China tends to be for strictly commercial operations, whereas part of the investment of other countries is supported by official loans. The adverse effect of the suspension of official loans for foreign investment in China will be much greater for countries other than Hong Kong. Moreover, Hong Kong's share in foreign investment is particularly high in Guangdong. As Guangdong has remained relatively stable in the recent political turmoil, Guangdong's share in national total foreign investment is likely to rise, and this tendency will lead to a higher share for Hong Kong in total foreign investment in China. The same regional factors operate for tourism. As foreign tourists shift from the north to the more stable south, Hong Kong's share in tourism will rise.

As for shipping and transshipment, the plans of Japan and other countries to build ports in Shenzhen and other coastal cities will be held up, if temporarily, by the Tiananmen incident, and China will be even more dependent on Hong Kong for shipping and transshipment. China's increased dependence on Hong Kong was predictable.

Contrary to our expectation, Hong Kong's share of China's direct foreign investment declined in 1989 (table 14–1), a decline due to the sudden emergence of Taiwan as a significant investor in 1989. As part of the retrenchment program, China drastically recentralized the power to borrow from foreign lenders in 1988. According to our theory, this change would lead to a fall in the share of China's foreign loans syndicated in Hong Kong, and this was exactly what happened (table 14–1).

After the cutting off of soft loans following the Tiananmen incident, China was under great pressure to expand its exports to pay off its foreign debt. As a result, China devalued the Renminbi against the U.S. dollar in December 1989 and in November 1990 by 21 percent and 9.6 percent, respectively. China's exports continued to grow at double-digit rates, and the growth rates in terms of the U.S. dollar for 1989 and 1990 were 10.5 percent and 18.3 percent, respectively, 16 percent in 1991, and 18.2 percent in 1992.

Despite the retrenchment of the reform program on many fronts, reform of the external sector has been little affected, and there has been no marked recentralization of foreign trade. The share of China's imports via Hong Kong in the form of entrepôt trade stayed at 22.4 percent from 1988 to 1989 (table 14-2). The share of China's exports reexported via Hong Kong rose from 27 percent in 1988 to 33 percent in 1989. This increase was related to Hong Kong's investment in processing and assembling operations in China, mainly in Guangdong. Most of the output of these operations is transported to Hong

Kong for packaging or finishing before being reexported. They constitute processed reexports.

China further liberalized its external sector in January 1991.[13] Provincial governments and export enterprises were allowed to retain 80 percent of their foreign exchange earnings, and subsidies on exports were abolished. The number of commodities that could be exported only with licenses decreased from 185 categories in 1990 to roughly 90 categories. The further decentralization of China's trade again led to a greater intermediary role for Hong Kong. The share of China's exports reexported via Hong Kong rose from 36 percent in 1990 to 40 percent in 1991, and the share of China's imports imported via Hong Kong rose from 27 percent in 1990 to 31 percent in 1991.

One important impact of the Tiananmen incident has been the increasing regionalization of the Chinese economy. The prestige and authority of the central government and the party have suffered severely, while the role of the army has been enhanced. The Chinese army is divided into seven military regions, and there have been obvious signs of conflict between military regions since the Tiananmen incident. Southern China, especially Guangdong, stands to benefit from the further regionalization of the Chinese economy, and the important role of Hong Kong in the regional development of the coastal provinces is likely to be heightened further.

Although the Tiananmen incident had led to a fall in China-related business in 1989, China became more dependent on Hong Kong because of its isolation. It should be noted that, after the incident, Beijing was quick to reemphasize the strategic role of Hong Kong in China's open-door policy. The heads of China's trading companies in Hong Kong met Zheng Tuobin, China's foreign trade minister, in mid-June 1989, who stressed that the importance of Hong Kong to China has grown as China's foreign economic relations have come under severe stress since June 1989. He emphasized that tourism, foreign loans, and commodity exports were the three major sources of China's foreign exchange earnings, and the first two sources had dwindled after the Tiananmen incident. China has to rely mainly on commodity exports, and Hong Kong is one of the major channels for these exports. He also stressed that China would not punish the employees of China's companies in Hong Kong even though many of them openly supported the prodemocracy movement.[14]

In 1991, the absolute volume of China-related business in Hong Kong rose beyond the pre-Tiananmen peak. Although Hong Kong manufacturers had secured Southeast Asia for alternative production sites, China still offered the best offshore site because of its proximity and cultural affinity. There has been a revival of Hong Kong investment in China since the second quarter of 1990. Hong Kong's share of China's direct foreign investment increased from 56.5 percent in 1989 to 63.4 percent in the first half of 1990 and remained at these levels in 1991 and 1992.[15]

Hong Kong's China-related entrepôt trade grew by 20 percent in 1990 and 33 percent in 1991. The only China-related business that had not recovered was syndicated loans, owing to the worldwide decrease in the supply of bank loans as well as to China's drastic recentralization of the power to make foreign loans. It should be noted that China launched another reform drive in the spring of 1992 after Deng Xiaoping's Shenzhen tour, and Hong Kong's China-related business in 1992 was at a record pace.

Port and Airport Development

The dramatic increase in China-related entrepôt trade, transshipment, and tourism has strained the port and airport facilities in Hong Kong. Hong Kong became the world's busiest container port in 1987, surpassing New York and Rotterdam in 1986 and 1987, respectively. All indications are that China-related traffic will continue to rise, and the Kai Tak Airport is forecast to be operating at absolute capacity by 1997.

Four months after the Tiananmen incident, the Hong Kong government announced a decision to spend HK$127 billion (U.S.$16.3 billion) on a new airport and other port facilities. This amount is in addition to substantial public works already committed, and the total infrastructure spending for the period 1990–2006 is estimated to be about HK$227 billion at 1989 prices.

It is clear that the new airport and port facilities will further strengthen the position of Hong Kong as the gateway to China, and the project is of tremendous benefit to both China and Hong Kong. Although the site of the airport was controversial, China has agreed to the need for a new airport. China, however, has been extremely concerned about the financial implications, since the project may consume most of Hong Kong's fiscal reserves. While the Hong Kong government wants a big and modern airport that would meet its needs well into the twenty-first century, for financial considerations China prefers a more economical airport.

The discussions of economies of agglomeration and economies of scale in trading activities make clear that a big and modern airport will benefit both Hong Kong and China. Moreover, the financial strength of the Hong Kong government is sufficient to build the proposed airport. The cost of the project was revised upward to HK$140 billion,[16] and 55 percent would be borne by the private sector, leaving 45 percent or HK$63 billion for the government. The fiscal reserves of the Hong Kong government stood at $91.8 billion at the end of March 1992, not including the land fund of the future SAR (Special Administrative Region) of Hong Kong, which is projected to reach $40–70 billion by 1997. Moreover, the new airport will release vast amounts of extremely valuable land in the city for redevelopment. The government can also raise loans to finance part of the expenses since the airport will produce a steady stream of revenue. The financial position of the government is sufficient to accommodate moderate cost overruns or revenue shortfalls. China's support of the project will make it easier for the Hong Kong government to invite private participation and raise loans to ease the financial burden.

China also intervened in the membership of the new Airport Authority, which was set up in 1992.[17] The term of office of the Airport Authority will straddle 1997. Membership in the authority will affect decisions over matters of grave economic interests, including awarding tenders to construct the airport and allocation of flight time slots.

The huge port and airport project implies substantial capital spending, which will have an expansionary effect on the economy. It was estimated that the project would raise real GDP by about 1 percent every year and generate some 10,000 new jobs every year during the construction.[18] The government plans to import construction workers to facilitate completion of the project.

After a year of deadlock, China and Britain signed an agreement over the airport on July 4, 1991. It was agreed that the Hong Kong government will complete the airport before mid-1997. Hong Kong is required to leave the future SAR government fiscal reserves not less than HK$25 billion. The Hong Kong government will appoint someone from the Bank of China Group to sit as a full member of the board of the Airport Authority. Moreover, the Hong Kong government will listen to Chinese views before deciding on the appointments of the Airport Authority.

The airport agreement has further strengthened the confidence in Hong Kong's future. According to a quarterly survey, those who want to emigrate fell by 2 percentage points from August 1990 to May 1991, and fell further by 7 percentage points from May 1991 to August 1991. On the other hand, those who did not want to emigrate increased by 3.8 percentage points from August 1990 to May 1991, and increased further by 6.2 percentage points from May 1991 to

August 1991. In August 1991, a total of 69.4 percent of the interviewees had no desire to emigrate.

The Political Economy of 1997

The paradox of the future of Hong Kong is that the political picture looks gloomy but the economic picture looks bright. If Beijing is bent on self-destruction, Hong Kong will, of course, be doomed. If pragmatism prevails and Beijing continues its policy of economic reforms and open door, the present outflow of skills and knowledge and capital from Hong Kong can turn out to be a valuable asset in the long run. The two greatest assets of Hong Kong are its cosmopolitanism and its resilience. Hong Kong's cosmopolitanism contributes to its entrepôt trade, its status as the gateway to China, and its role as an international financial center. Hong Kong's resilience enables it to adapt and exploit new opportunities in vicissitudes. The outflow of expertise and capital enables Hong Kong to build up its international links and strengthens its sophistication and resilience. Hong Kong is now investing massively in infrastructure, in human capital, and in international links. If pragmatism should prevail in Beijing, Hong Kong will stand to benefit tremendously from its investments. The future of Hong Kong depends first and foremost on what happens in Beijing rather than in Hong Kong itself. By investing massively in international links, human capital, and infrastructure, however, Hong Kong has significantly increased its chances for survival and prosperity to 1997 and beyond.

The risks of 1997 are very real, but the stakes are also high. In the past, Hong Kong had no lack of entrepreneurs who had invested wisely in times of uncertainty and prospered greatly afterward. One can only hope that the present generation of entrepreneurs facing the 1997 barrier will fare as well.

PART SEVEN

Relations among the Three Chinese Entities

15

The Evolution of a Divided China

Byron S. J. Weng

In this chapter, a divided nation is defined as a modern nation-state that has been divided into two or more distinct and functionally independent competing successors, but legally remaining an international actor by virtue of the policies of one or more of her competing successors.[1]

Some Theoretical Observations on Divided Nations

The term "competing successor" is used here for want of a commonly accepted one. It is used as an abstract designation of a political entity with its own distinctive territory, people, and government that claims to be sovereign, but remains a component unit of a divided nation. It is meant to convey the notion that such political entities are by nature competitive aspirants to the exclusive status of successor to the divided nation.

The Concept of Divided Nations. Divided nations and competing successors are products of the cold war era, and as such they are unique subjects of international law. They bring to international society a set of problems not known in the past. Terms such as "multisystem nation" help to bring out their complex nature but do not thoroughly describe them.[2] The very existence of the competing successors reflects the inadequacy of existing international law.

Examples of divided nations are limited to Germany, China, Korea, Vietnam, and Cambodia.[3] They result from civil war or international agreement, but their division is invariably artificial in that it is externally imposed, as with Korea, or prolonged, as with China. Each of these nations is (or was, until reunification) composed of two or more competing successors.

International Status of Competing Successors. The international status of competing successors differs considerably, depending on

345

their sovereign claims, the recognition they grant each other, the international recognition they receive, and the status of their membership in international organizations. The known status levels are summarized in table 15–1.

In China and Cambodia and in Vietnam before 1975, sovereign claims were made internally over the whole territory of the divided nation by all competing successors. In 1990, however, Taipei implied that it would not insist it is the government of the mainland. In Germany, international occupation agreements determined the status of the competing successors. The two Germanys ratified a series of agreements signed between 1970 and 1972, agreeing to the division into East Germany, West Germany, and Berlin.[4] But the events of 1989 and 1990 changed all that. For Korea, the Armistice Agreement of 1953 left the two competing successors quarreling endlessly.[5] Since September 1990, however, several rounds of direct negotiations between the two Koreas have led to improvement in relations. On September 17, 1991, the Forty-sixth Session of the General Assembly voted to admit them both into the United Nations as members. On December 13, 1991, Seoul and Pyongyang signed an Agreement of Reconciliation, Nonaggression, Exchange, and Cooperation.

Externally, the German competing successors accepted dual recognition from other countries and cross-recognition from each other. Before December 1991, the two Koreas accepted dual recognition but not cross-recognition. Mainland China and Taiwan accepted neither, although Taiwan has released a number of feelers for cross-recognition recently.

To offer a deeper understanding of the concept of divided nations, the dual nature of their competing successors and the stages in their evolution are examined below.

The Dual Nature of Competing Successors. Any theory about divided nations must recognize that under present international law, the status of competing successors has a dual nature. One competitor may consider its rival as illegitimate and therefore without the authority to engage in any official international relations. If the two engage each other, the bilateral affair is considered an internal matter and free from external interference. But when a third country enters a transaction with one of the competing successors, it is clearly a matter of international relations.

Even bilateral affairs have a nebulous and difficult nature. It is seldom clear whether they constitute a central-local (vertical) relationship as one side may aver or a rival (horizontal) relationship between equals.[6] Certainly, they differ from matters between component

TABLE 15–1

INTERNATIONAL STATUS OF COMPETING SUCCESSORS TO DIVIDED NATIONS, 1990

Competing Successor Governments	Sovereign Claims	Cross-Recognition	International Formal, Substantive Recognition[a]		UN Membership
PRC: Beijing	Whole of China	No	140+	150+	Permanent member, Security Council
ROC: Taipei[b]	Whole of China[b]	Offered	27	140+	Excluded
FRG: Bonn[b]	W. Germany	Yes	Both generally recognized		Member
DRG: E. Berlin[c]	E. Germany	Yes	Both generally recognized		Member
ROK: Seoul	S. Korea	Talking	Dual recognition		Observer[d]
DRK: Pyongyang	N. Korea	Talking	Accepted		Excluded[d]
Cambodia: Phnom Penh[e]	Whole of Cambodia	No	Uncertain		Member

a. "Formal" means formal diplomatic recognition. "Substantive" means substantive relations in the absence of formal diplomatic recognition. The numbers refer to countries granting recognition to or maintaining substantive relations with the competing successor.

b. In the Asian Development Bank, the ROC membership is based on its effective domain. On January 1, 1990, Taipei applied formally to the GATT for membership in the name of "Taiwan, Pescadores, Quemoy and Matsu."

c. The two Germanys merged economically on July 2 and officially reunified into one on October 3, 1990.

d. The two Koreas were admitted into the UN as members on September 17, 1991.

e. In Cambodia (Kampuchea), the United Nations is endeavoring to help end the power struggle among the fighting parties by setting up a Supreme National Council.

SOURCE: Author.

provinces, cantons, or states within a normal country.

Mutually Influential Relations. The competing successors are often mutually "penetrated," or influential. By definition they compete for the rulership of a unified country. In time they will interact and eventually settle their differences in one way or another. It stands to reason that they try to influence each other by all means, including penetration of each other's decision-making process. According to James N. Rosenau,

> A penetrated political system is one in which nonmembers of a national society participate directly and authoritatively, through actions taken jointly with the society's members, in either the allocation of its values or the mobilization of support on behalf of its goals.[7]

To speak of the competing successors of divided nations as penetrated systems is to suggest that the relationships between them are more sensitive and more tense than what is normal between two independent political entities. Generally, the competitors are still tied together by common patriotic sentiments. Like siblings of a family, their instinct is to identify with each other, to interact, and amidst rivalries and feuds to assist and compliment each other. Even while they quarrel, a glorious achievement or an incident of national shame in one is cause for celebration or condemnation in the other. They pay greater attention to each other than to outsiders. In a skewed fashion, they give one another special favors in safe areas or impose tighter controls and regulations in threatened areas. There are linkages of all kinds that cannot be severed by political decisions alone.

The Evolution Process of Divided Nations. Finally, this chapter examines in detail the life cycle of divided nations. In December 1985, I proposed a framework for analyzing and projecting the development of relations between mainland China and Taiwan on the basis of the Henderson-Lebow paradigm and on the familiar patterns of international confrontation, competition, and collaboration.[8] According to this model, five sets of variables would determine the unfolding relationship between the parties. They are:

- the attitudes and policies of the parties toward each other
- the relative merits of their respective systems as seen in the results of their competition, both in internal development and foreign relations
- superpower politics, with special reference to their respective China policies

TABLE 15–2

A Paradigm of the Evolution of Divided Nations

Stage	Relationship	Phase
I	Hostility	Hot war, cold war
II	Stalemate	Tense, relaxed
III	Competition	Closed, open
IV	Cooperation	Limited, comprehensive
V	Negotiation	Informal, formal
VI	Settlement	
	A. Partition: Transitional, indefinite	
	B. Unification: Nominal, substantive	

Source: Author.

- the example set by, and the lessons to be drawn from, the Hong Kong model under Beijing's "one country–two systems" policy
- developments in the international environment, especially the Asia-Pacific region

The patterns of relations were theoretically projected to evolve in four stages, from hostility to competition to cooperation to unification. Each of the stages was further divided into two substages, making eight phases. Thus, a division process that starts with a civil war may progress in a zigzag through cold war, closed and open competition, and partial and general cooperation to nominal and eventually substantive national unification.

Looking back, the aforementioned framework has indeed been a helpful tool for analyzing, interpreting, and even predicting developments of relations between mainland China and Taiwan. But we also see some shortcomings in its formulations. Based on what we have learned from later developments, we may propose a new paradigm with earlier gaps filled in. As shown in table 15–2, there are six instead of four stages and two possible outcomes instead of one.[9]

Hostility implies the expression of enmity through words and deeds. It entails mutual nonrecognition and competing claims to successor status. It also implies a zero-sum game and an intolerance in the mind of the players. In the beginning, it is likely to be characterized by a hot war: that is, it involves military conflict. At its extreme, it means not stopping the fighting until one side is totally annihilated. Normally, it ceases when one side surrenders or is

349

defeated. The wise and skillful would use force only to effectuate a victory without any killing. When, for external or internal reasons, the two sides are prevented from resorting to force or become reluctant to do so, a hot war may turn into a cold war. In this situation the state of war is sustained and victory is sought by means other than military. The parties may engage in destructive ideological and psychological warfare, employing deceptive schemes and distorting truth even at great cost to themselves. A milder form of cold war may only require keeping a hostile posture while allowing natural developments to take their course.

A stalemate here denotes a situation in which at least one of the contending parties finds itself unable to move without courting an undesirable outcome, but the other party is not prepared to force the issue. The nuclear stalemate in the global cold war is well known. The local cold war of a divided nation may also develop into a stalemate sooner or later. The stalemate stage, a refinement of my earlier analytical framework, is the missing link between the hostility and competition stages. A stalemate is a clear incentive for change and therefore a potential turning point in the relationship between hostile rivals. For, when a stalemate results, a previously unwanted change in one's basic posture may become highly desirable. Without a stalemate, a cold war may drag on indefinitely.

There are two phases of stalemate, tense and relaxed. At first, the realization that a stalemate exists may make the player nervous. He may attempt to fortify and close the border and introduce more oppressive internal measures for fear of penetration by the enemy. He may be tempted to arm further. If the other side is able to force his hand, there may be a regression to hot war. In a true stalemate, however, when a player realizes that the other side is not in a position to take advantage of his weakness, he is likely to relax. Hostile exchanges become more routinized and mechanical. While attempts to subvert and supplant the opponent regime may continue, desirable changes may be contemplated as well.

Competition is distinguished from confrontation in that it implies an objective judgment. To be in competition is to set aside hostility, accept a peaceful coexistence, and let oneself be judged by performance records *vis-à-vis* those of the opponent. Typically a long drawn-out cold war may be replaced by a less vitriolic competition stage after a perceived stalemate and a lessened threat. Such a competition is normally systemic—that is, it is an effort to prove the superiority of one's system over the opponent's. The system can be economic, social, political, or all three. The competition may be endless and impossible to judge, but claims and counterclaims of superiority and constant comparison of each other's successes and failures are its unmistakable signs.

Initially the competition is closed, not open. Closed competition is carried out while the rivals are still separated from each other on all fronts. Attention will gradually shift to nonconfrontational areas. Each side goes about its own business, and no exchanges of persons or goods take place between the two domains. Open competition indicates at least unofficial contacts and interflows across borders. The process and means of competition can be quite vicious, although a convincing victory is achieved by peaceful and fair methods. Usually a decline in subversive activities is observable. Controlled exchange of ideas and goods and limited visitation of persons are permitted. Intense competition in the international arena is to be expected.

Cooperation represents another stage of evolution, when the contending parties actually decide to live with their differences and work together in areas of mutual interest without altering their existing standings. Since open competition involves contact, a decision to enter it is itself conducive to cooperation. Some of the inherent reasons for cooperation in most divided nations include family reunions, economic growth, political benefits, common security interests, and cultural betterment. As hostilities subside, meetings in third countries between scientists and artists of the two territories may be followed by official endorsements for sports events and other nonpolitical contacts. For humanitarian reasons, borders may be opened for visitations by members of long-separated families. Inevitably, problems arise that cannot be solved without the cooperation of the rival regimes.

Ad hoc, limited, and experimental acts of cooperation may lead to regular, ambitious, and comprehensive ventures. Overtures from one side for limited exchanges in nonpolitical areas can set the ball rolling, even if the immediate response from the other side is not positive. Such overtures may include unilateral legislation or establishment of special institutions. Expanded linkages for increased tourism, trade, investment, and cultural interflow are more than likely. This may require acknowledgment of coexistence and informal negotiations. If they are successful, semiofficial agreements may be concluded regarding such issues as exchanges of criminals and refugees. Dual membership in nongovernmental international organizations and certain nonpolitical, intergovernmental organizations may be worked out under special conditions. Even intermediate bodies or joint administrative apparatus with the blessing of both may not be out of the question. Should the conditions for a serious settlement appear ripe to leaders of both sides, they may attempt negotiations.

Negotiation means meeting and bargaining to surmount difficulties standing in the way of a settlement. It is only natural that numerous internal and external barriers to settlement will exist, and overcoming them requires time and effort. Many long, drawn-out negotiations at several levels are unavoidable, both before and after an agreement to settle. Hence a negotiation stage is added in this paradigm.

Internally, the negotiators must deal with the divergent ideologies, values, and procedures built up over decades. Drastically different ownership systems and uneven stages of development are complicated knots that cannot be untied quickly. Unification, for instance, will reduce two central governments to one. That means a loss of power for some leaders and redundancy and unemployment for many bureaucrats. The parochial power considerations and vested interests may not yield to a reunification proposal. Externally, alliance systems and treaty obligations will be affected. Contradictory foreign commitments must be ironed out. Some external forces may oppose or sabotage a settlement for their own interests.

The process of negotiation may take some doing. Leaders who have been enemies do not easily get together. Formal talks can be arranged only after successful informal negotiations. Any exchange of visits between leaders will probably be preceded by those between their messengers and proxies. Preparatory meetings can be as difficult as plenary procedures. Board room conversations and corridor diplomacy may be more important than formal sessions. The negotiators may be "brothers" and colleagues or friends of old, whose past entanglement can be an advantage or a disadvantage. Something can go wrong at any point.

If all goes well, the final settlement stage may be reached. Settlement here signifies an adjustment agreed to by the contending parties. Divided nations remain divided because they are ready neither to settle their differences nor to accept a permanent and legal separation. That is to say, if one side or a controlling outsider refuses to compromise, there can be no settlement.

Alternative scenarios can be constructed for a given case. In broad terms, a settlement can be unification or partition. Either way, there are various possible arrangements. Unification means the acceptance of one central government and a common foreign and defense policy. It also means the merger of two systems and two ways of life. It may be nominal or substantive. Often it involves more than one phase and may lead to a confederative, federal, or unitary state. Under a unitary system, the subordinate units may enjoy different degrees of autonomy. Partition means the legal and permanent separation of one country with a common historical tradition into two or more sovereign units. It can be transitional or indefinite. If transitional, the country may later be unified. An indefinite partition will probably mean the normalization of the status quo, with or without adjustments. The more logical partition arrangements along natural frontiers or ethnic lines are possible but hard to materialize in the real world.

It must be pointed out, however, that progression through the six stages and twelve phases is not necessarily linear and gradual. More than likely, regressions will occur at some point and the actual course will have a zigzag pattern. Presumably, under exceptional circumstances, one or more stages may be leapt over. An extraordinary event such as a successful coup d'état in one capital by the sympathizer of the rival regime or a compelling need to fend off a common enemy may change the picture overnight. Furthermore, the stages may be overlapping rather than clearly demarcated. Conceivably, some hostile exchanges may still take place during negotiations. There may be pockets of cooperation even during a hostile stage. In the long run, however, this six-stage process may have to run its course before a divided nation can be peacefully united.

Generally speaking, the scope and content of interactions can be economic, social, cultural, political, legal, military, or a combination of these. The strategy employed by each can be offensive or defensive, active or reactive, positive or negative. The linkages can be direct or indirect, official or unofficial, limited or extensive. The traffic can be ad hoc or regular, frequent or sparse, one-way or two-way, smooth or troublesome. The patterns of relations thus developed can be hostile or amicable, competitive or complementary, cooperative or confrontational, stalemated or progressive, adamant or conciliatory, divisive or integrative.

The status quo will prevail when conditions for change are absent. As changes in the various factors accumulate over time, the thinking and attitudes of the players also change. At some point the scale is tipped and a qualitative change results. The relationship then shifts from one to another stage.

These observations about divided nations are perhaps inadequate to constitute a general theory. To the extent they are sound, they provide a pretheory of divided nations, a framework within which we can better analyze and evaluate the China case.

The Evolution of a Divided China

China was divided into two parts in 1949, when the People's Republic of China (PRC) was established on the mainland by the Communists and the government of the Republic of China (ROC) retreated to Taiwan.

The Past Five Stages. Over the past forty-some years, the relationship between the PRC and the ROC has undergone five stages of development.[10] Briefly, these are:

- tense cold war, 1949–1958
- relaxed, stalemated cold war, 1959–1971
- closed competition in a state of nominal cold war, 1971–1978
- unilateral overtures for negotiation and open competition, 1979–1987
- open competition and partial cooperation, 1987–present

The initial division was a result of the 1946–1949 civil war, but the stalemate that followed was due at least in part to Soviet and U.S. interventions. At first, the hostility was very pronounced. The Communists wanted to "liberate" Taiwan by force, and the Nationalists swore they would "recover" the mainland by a counterattack. Then a state of cold war persisted for three decades because of the Taiwan Strait, the Korean War, and the American Seventh Fleet.

The local cold war between Beijing and Taipei might have flared up were it not for superpower restraints. During 1955 and 1958, the Taiwan Strait was tense with skirmishes in the air and on the sea that threatened to involve both the USSR and the United States. Fortunately, neither of the superpowers was keen on a fight. Following the second Taiwan Strait crisis, realizing that China's divided-nation question would probably not be solvable until the global cold war had given way to a new situation, both Beijing and Taipei began to tone down their hostile exchanges. During the 1960s, Beijing was preoccupied with internal power struggles, and Taipei turned its attention to economic development. Gradually, hostile exchanges became routinized and ritualistic.

To be sure, the local cold war did not end even when there clearly was a stalemate. Attempts to subvert and supplant the opponent regime continued. Taipei prosecuted real or imagined Communist spies periodically, while Beijing persecuted anyone who had Taiwan or Kuomintang (KMT) connections, especially during the Cultural Revolution years. One's traitors were the other's heroes. Huge rewards of gold were offered by both governments to pilots who defected. Each side went to great lengths to isolate the other from international recognition. In both societies, rights and wrongs were warped and values distorted, owing to the local cold war.

In late 1971, the PRC and the ROC experienced a fundamental change in their relative international standing. Apparently Mao Zedong concluded that the Soviet Union was a real threat, following the 1968 invasion of Czechoslovakia and the 1969 Zhenbao Island incident. Beijing and Washington began to warm up to each other because of perceived common strategic needs. In November 1971, the PRC replaced the ROC at the United Nations and in other international organizations with Washington's tacit support. By the end of 1972, ping-pong diplomacy, the Nixon visit, and the Shanghai Communiqué were parts of history. Needless to say, Beijing's confidence was boosted, while Taipei felt betrayed and jolted.

Interestingly, the Taiwan Strait stalemate became less tense after 1971. Taipei and Beijing changed their policies toward each other in the 1970s. In retrospect, one may say that the UN shock awakened Taipei to its own unrealistic, larger-than-life posture over the previous three decades. In international politics, a protector is not dependable over the long run. For reasons of domestic power politics, the KMT regime would continue to claim it was the sole legitimate government of the whole of China. But anti-Soviet propaganda was stopped, and its slogan themes were quietly changed from counterattack to anti-communism. Having reexamined its position, the KMT regime decided its strength lay in the economic arena. Hence, Taipei shifted its strategy toward a new game of economic competition with Beijing. By this time, Taiwan was already on its way to becoming one of the four Asian dragons.

For its part, Beijing too had a new outlook across the Taiwan Strait. The Great Leap Forward and the Cultural Revolution had wrought serious internal disorder and disaster in the mainland. There was much to do to regain strength. To improve relations with Washington, it was unwise to continue accusing the Americans of "occupying" Taiwan. Accordingly, the policy of "liberating" Taiwan was dropped in favor of a more neutral policy of "unification." As long as Taipei subscribed to the one-country principle, for Beijing it was agreeable and in fact preferable to postpone the question of unification with Taiwan. Thus Beijing was inclined to engage in peaceful competition with Taipei rather than to fight a military battle.

The situation between 1971 and 1978 was therefore one of relaxed, stalemated, nominal cold war and of mutual acquiescence in or tacit agreement on peaceful competition. Each side tried to prove the superiority of its system over that of the other through performance. There was a decline in the intensity of ideological confrontation as well as in the frequency of subversive activities. Instead, Taipei said that Beijing should "learn from Taipei" in economics, while Beijing did all it could to squeeze the ROC out of international organizations and forums.

Until the end of 1978, the competition was peaceful but closed. Neither side had ceased its basic hostility toward the other completely. An enemy sympathizer was still liable to criminal prosecution. Neither side opened its borders to people from the other or allowed its people to set foot on the other's territory without special permission. Even contacts in a third country were strictly controlled. Then, in 1979, Beijing took the lead in guiding mainland-Taiwan relations toward another stage.

The victory of Deng Xiaoping and his supporters at the Third Plenum of the Eleventh Central Committee of the Communist party of China (CPC) in December 1978 was a watershed for the PRC in more than one way. It started the PRC's far-reaching economic reform. It signaled Beijing's readiness to pursue a new course in foreign policy. And it ushered in a new approach to Taiwan and brought the "Hong Kong 1997" issue onto Beijing's national agenda.

On New Year's Day, 1979, Beijing made the first of its détente overtures and invitations to unification talks. It offered to end hostility and to stop the ritual bombardment of offshore islands, and it called for "three links and four flows": that is, postal, commercial, and communication and transportation links in the fields of sports, scholarship, culture and arts, and science and technology, as well as visitation for separated families. The three links and four flows would help pave the way for open competition and mutual cooperation between the two sides. This "smile offensive" was perceived as deceptive and dangerous by the KMT leaders. Hence Taipei responded with a "no contact, no negotiation, no compromise" policy.

But Beijing persisted. In September 1982, Marshall Ye Jianying issued a nine-point proposal in his capacity as chairman of the National People's Congress. It outlined general terms for Taipei after unification and promised to establish a "special administrative region" (SAR) under the formula later to be known as "one country, two systems." In 1984, the formula was used in connection with Hong Kong. Beijing signed the Sino-British Joint Declaration with London and proposed using the Hong Kong model for Taiwan, with even more concessions.

Meanwhile the opposition, the Democratic Progressive party (DPP), had gathered force inside Taiwan. Its demands for localization and democratization were supported by many in the KMT ranks. An enlightened leader, President Chiang Ching-kuo, responded to the pressure positively. There was a marked liberalization amid continuing calls for political reforms and economic transition. Businessmen, the displaced, and the ambitious took advantage of the new freedom and explored the mainland market for opportunities. Soldiers who had left families on the mainland forty years earlier cried out for visitation rights before they died. Suddenly the overtures from across the Taiwan Strait were no longer just deceptive and dangerous. In November 1987, the invisible "bamboo curtain" was set ajar by a new policy.

At first, Taipei permitted only limited, unofficial, indirect, unidirectional, and controlled interchanges. Within the first twelve months some 400,000 Taiwan residents traveled to the mainland for family visits, tours, trade, and investments. This placed even more pressure on Taipei for a more open policy toward the mainland.

For its part, Beijing used carrots and sticks that were appropriate for the situation. On the one hand, it sweetened the deals for Taiwan visitors with exemptions, privileges, and favors. On the other hand, it squeezed the ROC even harder in the international arena. "It's a 'tiger's mouth trap,'" some alarmists in Taiwan were heard shouting, but to no avail. Established policies rejected Beijing's "three links" call. In fact, there were mail exchanges but not mutual postal service, goods trading but not business linkage; and effective shipping and aviation but not transport connections. Taipei's policy of "three nos" became something like "no contact unless it is unofficial and approved first, no negotiation except when necessary for settling an urgent problem, and no compromise unless it is judged harmless and profitable."

The new developments in relations between mainland China and Taiwan after late 1987 have been so rapid that an observer finds little time to digest the unfolding events. For a time there was "mainland fever" on the island and "Taiwan fever" on the mainland. The two parties have improved relations so much that it is now possible to speak of partial cooperation between them.

Isolated, issue-specific cooperation followed before long. In order to control illegal immigrants, gun smuggling, and crime, to regulate marriages and inheritance, and to deal with the conflict of laws arising from the interflows of persons and goods, the two sides were soon talking by proxy through such intermediaries as the Red Cross societies. Agreements were signed and procedures established to handle repatriation of boat people and refugee criminals. The 1989 annual meeting in Beijing of the Asian Development Bank was an occasion for Taipei to launch a new mainland policy. The 1990 Asian Olympic Games, also held in Beijing, became an opportunity for testing the air as well as cultivating brotherhood.

Partly to wrest power from the mainlander-dominated KMT and partly in fear of a sellout to the Communists, the opposition in Taiwan, the DPP, reacted to the fast-moving situation with some

357

drastic moves. Many of its leaders were veterans of political imprisonment. It is not surprising that they sided with the independence movement. In the fall of 1990, the DPP formally adopted a resolution stating that the ROC's sovereignty did not extend to Mongolia and mainland China. Soon afterward an affiliated body, the Taiwan Sovereign Independence Movement committee, was established. During the 1991 National Assembly elections, the party actually made the issue of Taiwan's independent sovereign status a part of its platform.

So far the independence movement had not been a real force to contend with. Public polls show that its popular base has not exceeded 30 percent of the adult population. Nonetheless, Beijing keeps a close watch on the movement and has never failed to threaten it with force. The KMT leaders in power have reasons for condemning it also. Huang Hua, one of the most outspoken workers for the movement who had already spent twenty-one years in prison, was sentenced to a further ten-year term in December 1990.

In the meantime, both Beijing and Taipei have planned more positive things. Anticipating new developments to come, both have reorganized and strengthened their institutions and leadership for cross-straits affairs and made corresponding policy adjustments. The stage is set for a new round.

Beijing is hoping in the 1990s not only to bring the two sides closer but to determine the future status of Taiwan as well. And Taipei has begun making its own countermoves. Will there be further, more comprehensive cooperation between them? Will there be serious negotiations? Will the question of a divided China be settled? So that we may have an overview of the divided-China question, we shall examine next the determinants of relations among competing successors, focusing especially on their internal changes.

Relevance of Internal Changes. All five sets of determinants that I examined in 1985 appear still to be the key variables for evaluating the prospects of a divided China in the 1990s. In each category, significant developments have occurred during the past several years.

Key determinants of the divided-China question. First, developments in the international environment have been dramatic. The cold war has finally ended. A global regrouping is taking place. Whether or not Gorbachev was responsible, as Beijing says, the Communist world has largely collapsed. In Eastern Europe, most countries are now going through a systemic transformation and face some tremendously difficult tasks. The Berlin Wall is down and the two Germanys have merged into one. The Soviet Union is no more. The European

Community promises to become a more formidable competitor for the United States and Japan. The United Nations may have its second spring. When Iraqi troops occupied Kuwait, the United States was able to assemble an international force with the blessing of the Security Council to sanction Saddam Hussein.

In the Asia-Pacific region, Beijing has pledged not to export revolution or to give military support to Southeast Asian national liberation movements. Both PRC-ASEAN and ROC-ASEAN relations have improved. The two Koreas have improved their relations greatly. Moscow and Beijing have established formal diplomatic relations with Seoul. The United States has led in the establishment of a Supreme National Council in place of the anti-Vietnam coalition that represented Cambodia at the United Nations. To do so, Washington engaged in direct talks with Hanoi and supported the Hanoi-backed Phnom Penh government.

In short, the global air is one of change and reconciliation, the Gulf war of 1991 notwithstanding. With the two Germanys reunited and the two Koreas seemingly on their way, some may say the time for settling the divided-China question is also drawing near.

Second, major-power relations have altered so much that it is meaningless to speak of a "China card" now. Before its disintegration, the Soviet Union fulfilled China's conditions for normalization of relations—withdrawal of Soviet troops from Afghanistan and from Sino-Soviet borders and removal of Vietnamese troops from Cambodia. As a gesture of goodwill, Moscow handed Zhenbao (Damansky) Island over to Beijing in 1988 without first signing a border treaty. The Deng-Gorbachev summit of May 1989 did not overly worry the U.S. strategists. American sanctions against Beijing over the Tiananmen suppression of June 4, 1989 brought their bilateral relations to a low ebb. But such sanctions lasted only about a year. The June 4 bloodshed was forgotten quickly in other capitals as the Iraqi-Kuwait situation took over the headlines.

Third, with regard to the relative merits of mainland China and Taiwan, Taiwan has outperformed the mainland in both economic development and political democratization. Perhaps the mainland excelled in sports, foreign relations, and the space industry. But, from the people's point of view, Taiwan is clearly favored. Taiwan inhabitants have come to enjoy increasingly more economic prosperity and political freedom. Taiwanese society is said to suffer from the "maladies of too much money and too much freedom too soon." In contrast, mainland residents had to go through yet one more round of political rectification in the aftermath of the Tiananmen episode. Their economic future is improved but still uncertain as the regime continues to experiment with haphazard and sometimes confusing reforms. Talk of emulating Taiwan has surfaced in both the mainland and Taiwan, but not even the Communist leaders speak of Taiwan emulating the mainland. Quite understandably, the current leadership in Beijing is not eager to acknowledge this fact.

Fourth, the competing successors' attitudes and policies toward each other have improved significantly. Taipei has tacitly accepted coexistence with the mainland and abandoned its exclusive claim to successor status. It has proceeded unilaterally toward the establishment of institutions for contacts and the enactment of pertinent legislation. In May 1991, it annulled the laws that treated the CPC as a rebellious group. Beijing's Taiwan policy has remained unchanged since 1979, but it has welcomed Taipei's new moves and responded with favorable policies. Its primary target for united front work has been expanded to include not only the KMT leadership but also the people of Taiwan.

Finally, the Basic Law of the Hong Kong special administrative region and the politics associated with its drafting have already offered many lessons for Taiwan. Interpretations in Hong Kong range from the most optimistic to the most pessimistic. The optimists project a bright future not only for the Hong Kong SAR but also for the mainland itself, partly because of the contributions that the SAR is expected to make. Believers are eager to seize the opportunities such a prospect will bring. The pessimists see an impending disaster similar to Shanghai's after 1949. Such pessimists cannot wait to leave the territory and seek a safer, even if unfamiliar, pasture.

Judging by the waves of emigration over the past several years, apparently the majority of Hong Kong people lean toward the pessimistic. The reasons are numerous and complicated. Mistrust of the Communist system and the corrupt ways of Chinese bureaucracy are central. The propensity of the Chinese authorities to interfere, especially when contrasted with the laissez-faire style of the British colonial government, must be a heavy factor. Beijing has taken pains to make clear that the Hong Kong SAR's autonomy is authorized by the Central People's Government and not based on the sovereign rights of the Hong Kong people. The Basic Law gives the future SAR a high degree of autonomy but reserves the central government's absolute right to take it away. Beijing seems to want the Hong Kong people to accept its "river water, well water" philosophy, like it or not. The two waters are supposed to maintain their separate characters. Yet the expectation, in both Beijing and Hong Kong, is that the river (the mainland) may flood the well (Hong Kong), but not the reverse.[11]

Internal changes as key variables. The five sets of variables analyzed above provide a useful way to see the past, know the present, and think about the future of mainland-Taiwan relations. An examination of the internal changes in the three territories—the mainland, Taiwan, and Hong Kong—may yield a silhouette of the picture, with all the essential features.

For our purpose, an internal change denotes any variation of conditions in a legally defined, exclusive, sovereign domain over time. By international law, internal affairs are not to be interfered with by outsiders or international organizations. Of course, external powers may in actuality penetrate what are supposedly internal affairs and get away with it. Variation means here any apparent or perceived differences in the conditions of a political society. It may come from artificial alteration, replacement, conversion, or natural transformation.

Changes in one competing successor's direct policy toward another—for example, Taipei's mainland policy, Hong Kong's Taiwan policy, or Beijing's policies toward Taiwan and Hong Kong—are not internal changes by our definition. The same is true regarding the foreign policy and relations of the competing successors. Changes relating to the conduct of such policies and relations are, however, internal changes—for example, the establishment in Taipei of an intermediary institution charged with semiofficial functions involving the mainland, such as the Straits Exchange Foundation, or the enactment of a law such as "regulations on relations between the two shores."

Not all internal changes are of equal significance. We may identify certain categories or items of internal changes as more pertinent. Without actually constructing a hierarchical taxonomy, we may observe that a number of specific internal changes have been or will be salient determinants in the configuration of relations among the competing successors where the future of a divided nation is concerned. Some changes are common to all competing successors: for example, system performance in terms of economic growth and development, political stability, and foreign policy and relations. Others may have something to do with the peculiar characteristics of each. If we can successfully identify the key items to watch, we can project the direction of change and the pattern of relations among the competing successors in the period to come. A chronology of selected events showing the interactive nature of internal changes among the three competitive successors is presented in appendix 15–A.

It would not be wrong to say that the Deng victory in Beijing in

1978 was the key factor that caused the chain of events leading to the Taipei decision to allow its citizens to visit relatives on the mainland. The visitation in turn would trigger further developments between mainland China and Taiwan. Hong Kong became deeply involved. Meanwhile, with Lee Teng-hui, a native son, taking the helm in Taipei, the DPP, largely Taiwanese in composition, gained more room to navigate. The interactions among the competing successors continued at a steady pace.

In the Henderson and Lebow study, it was hypothesized that

> As divided nations develop internal strength and hostility between their respective superpower backers decreases, they are likely to possess greater freedom of action and seek improved relations with each other.[12]

The China case appears to prove that hypothesis. Superpower interference in China's internal affairs has no doubt diminished because some of the incentives to interfere have disappeared in the post–cold war setting. The Chinese competing successors have certainly taken more assertive postures. Taiwan's economic strength and the mainland's political status have helped boost their egos and confidence. Even if the superpowers still take an interest in the China-Taiwan tangle, they may no longer be able to stop or sway the decisions of Beijing and Taipei, which in turn determine their mutual relations.

As mainland-Taiwan relations move into the cooperation-negotiation stage, the relative weight of domestic sources may further increase. A mutually fed inertia is likely to emerge.

Configuration of Relationships. In this section I examine the relationships among the competing successors and their prospects for the future.

China's competing successors. For a divided China, there are in fact only two competing successors. Hong Kong is but a piece of lost territory that China, represented by whatever government, would want to recover. Technically, it does not fit into the picture of a divided China. The people of Hong Kong are predominantly Chinese, but the Hong Kong government is not a Chinese government. It does not aspire to succeed to the legitimate rulership of China. Come 1997, the territory is destined to become a special administrative region under the PRC. All that Hong Kong people can hope for is an effective, autonomous status, relatively free from central interference.

I have treated Hong Kong as a quasi-competing successor, however, and examined Hong Kong's internal changes in this chapter. I did so from two considerations. First, the PRC has not only chosen to deal with the Hong Kong question on the same footing as the Taiwan question—that is, to deal with both as territories to be united under its policy of one country, two systems—but it has also declared the Hong Kong formula a model for Taiwan. Second, Hong Kong is a significant Chinese territory with some status in the international community in its own right. I will therefore continue to speak of three competing successors in the remainder of this chapter.

Of the three, mainland China is the large, poor, Communist, reforming, and hegemonic actor. Its sheer size in population and in territory makes it so weighty in international politics that every other international actor thinks twice before defying Beijing's claims or demands. Aside from its direct policies toward Taiwan and Hong Kong, events inside the mainland that will probably be most carefully watched by concerned governments are its system reform, its leadership change, and its democratic movements. Ideological campaigns and revolutionary convulsions are more in the background now but still of concern, as shown in appendix 15–B.

Taiwan is an island country—small, capitalistic, newly rich, democratizing, and relatively isolated. Although small in territory, in other respects it is not a country the world can easily ignore. As of the end of 1991, its population of more than 20 million ranked it above some 130 of the 166 members of the United Nations. Its economic prowess is well known. It is the world's thirteenth largest trading nation and possesses the second-largest foreign currency reserves in the world. Nevertheless, Taiwan is now politically overshadowed by its rival, the mainland. Complicated historical reasons account for this, and Taipei's own past policies may have been responsible in part. The developments to note in Taiwan are those in its mainland policy, the leadership struggle inside the KMT, constitutional reform, and the DPP's association with the Taiwan independence movement and its implications for party politics. Economic transformation continues to be of fundamental importance to the island. Social stability may also be a concern, however, because sudden wealth and sudden freedom may have combined to cause a situation that threatens governability. See appendix 15–C.

Hong Kong is a bustling free port, rich, capitalistic, decolonizing, and deeply "penetrated" by the mainland. Hong Kong possesses important economic know-how as well as wealth and charms, so its future development will have a significant impact on the future of China as a whole. And if Beijing wants to make Hong Kong an example of the second system under its one country–two systems policy, the ups and downs of this place will no doubt have an important influence on the future course of mainland China–Taiwan relations. Destined to return to the fold of the PRC in 1997, the territory is in the latter part of its transition period. The mainlanders and the Taiwanese will be watching Hong Kong's new election politics, activities of PRC elements, and the effectiveness of schemes designed to safeguard the stability and prosperity of the future SAR. Erosion of government authority and trends in emigration also make some people ("Not us," Beijing says) quite nervous. See appendix 15–D.

As examined earlier, the competing successors have made significant progress in their interrelations. The hostility is largely gone. There is now significant cooperation in many areas. Channels of communication are increasing and becoming more direct all the time. Traffic volume has become significant. Of course, the pessimists in all three places are leaving for other countries. But the optimists and the gamblers are staying on and looking forward to new opportunities precisely because of the changes.

A triangle of mutually penetrated systems. The Rosenau concept of penetration introduced earlier clearly applies to Hong Kong, where Beijing is authoritatively participating in the mobilization of support on behalf of the territory's goals. In fact, the territory is being prevented from having goals not acceptable to Beijing. To either mainland China or Taiwan, the penetration concept in its strict sense does not generally apply. Rosenau notes further, however, that there are "penetrated systems with respect to types of issues or issues areas," and that "the functioning of any type of political system can vary significantly from one issue-area to another."[13]

It may be meaningful, then, to speak of mainland China, Taiwan, and Hong Kong as examples of penetrated vertical systems in the issue area of national integration, with different degrees of penetration. Hong Kong, as noted, is deeply penetrated by the mainland. Between Hong Kong and Taiwan, for decades the relationship has been confined to the nonpolitical and has remained awkward and distant, partly because of Beijing's pressure on the British Hong Kong authorities.[14] Across the Taiwan Strait, the seesaw over the years has come out in favor of the mainland. This is not just because of the size of the land and population. It is also because it is easier to penetrate Taiwan, a relatively open system, than mainland China, a hitherto closed system.[15]

In any case, a triangular relationship is arising among China's competing successors and may stabilize during the 1990s. In this triangle the mainland acts as tone setter and protector, Taiwan as opposer and challenger. The two are like estranged lovers or brothers, except that some DPP members would prefer them to become just neighbors. As for Hong Kong, it has never claimed or wanted to be a sovereign actor. Its primary role is that of bridge and facilitator.

Prospects for a Settlement. The chronology of events presented in appendix 15–A shows the relevance of internal changes in the affairs of a divided China. It also points to the direction in which China's competing successors may be going during the 1990s.

Will China's competing successors enter a new stage of comprehensive cooperation? In due course, yes. Increasing cooperation among China's competing successors is no longer in doubt.

Between the mainland and Hong Kong, traffic has been busy during the past decades. Friction does occur. Beijing's outspoken sensitivity over such issues as the British offer of the right of abode to 50,000 families, the selection of the new airport site, the use of Hong Kong's reserves, the composition of the final court of appeal, Governor Patten's democratization proposals, and the internationalization of Hong Kong have caused waves of nervous reaction among the Hong Kong people. Hong Kong's mass demonstrations in support of the democracy movement in the mainland and the continuing anti-Communist activities of the liberal organizations have caused Li Hou, the former deputy head of Beijing's Hong Kong and Macao Affairs Office, and Zhou Nan, the New China News Agency chief in Hong Kong, to blurt out condemnations of those who use Hong Kong as "a base for toppling" the Beijing government and "a forward base" of the Front for Democracy based in Paris. Nonetheless, Hong Kong and the mainland have become economically interdependent. Soon they will be politically so as well. Like it or not, Hong Kong is already deeply penetrated and destined to be even further integrated with the mainland.

In the next rounds of interactions between Taiwan and mainland China we may look forward to special laws for regulating cross-straits relations, first promulgated by Taipei and possibly to be followed by Beijing; formal mutual acceptance of conditional coexistence; and arrangements for common membership in more intergovernmental international organizations.[16] There will be exchanges of visits by proxies and later by key officials. Future disputes with neighboring countries over the South China Sea Islands and the Diaoyutai Islands will no doubt find the two shores coming together more than before. Intermediary institutions will become more and more official. They will be replaced, in due course, by joint administrative apparatus for certain issues. The next time Taipei proposes sponsoring an Asian

Olympics, Beijing will probably not stand in its way. The possibility of an alliance or mutual security arrangement too has been mentioned, but this is more uncertain. Perhaps the two sides will cooperate in defense matters against a common threat without a formal pact.

All this is based on the assumption that Taiwan does not declare independence or otherwise provoke Beijing into a drastic change of policy. In this regard, the DPP's moves following its impressive 1992 election victory are worth a close watch.

As for Taiwan–Hong Kong relations, the situation will improve along with Taiwan-mainland relations. The Hong Kong government has already relaxed its political and immigration control over Taiwan elements in recent years. Taipei may follow suit. The Hong Kong example will be cited more often by Taiwan authorities and commentators as they think about their own future. More Hong Kong people will realize that Hong Kong's promised autonomy is guaranteed in an important way by the existence of a separate Taiwan. The yearly 1.3 million-plus visitors from Taiwan have been very good business. Beijing wants them, as does Hong Kong. One can expect trade and tourism between Hong Kong and Taiwan to rise further. Concurrently, Taiwan sources in Hong Kong will surface and engage in more nonpolitical activities. This will give rise to fewer disruptions than before. In short, the existence of a strong and prosperous Taiwan is good for Hong Kong and vice versa.

Negotiations across the Taiwan Strait will undoubtedly take place, and the unofficial Koo-Wang talks in Singapore in April 1993 are probably a harbinger of things to come. Unofficial negotiations will surely take place in the decade to come. Official negotiations will be harder to come by. The obstacles to official negotiations are both political and technical.

Politically the two sides are still far apart. Beijing's Taiwan policy has been basically unchanged since 1979: that is, CPC-KMT party (not government) talks for unification under one country–two systems; and use of force only if certain conditions apply. With regard to the unification talks, Beijing's overtures are now extended to and focused on the traders, investors, and even moderate elements of the DPP. As to the potential use of force, Qian Weichang, a spokesman for Beijing's Committee for the Promotion of China's Peaceful Unification, said that force may be used if Taiwan is invaded by another country, if Taiwan declares independence, or if Taipei fails to come to negotiations for a settlement after a long time. This last condition seems to be new. Previously, the third condition was "serious internal disorder in Taiwan."

366

Across the straits, President Lee Teng-hui spelled out three conditions for talks in his 1990 inaugural message: first, that the mainland develop a system of democracy and free economy; second, that Beijing denounce the use of force regarding Taiwan; and third, that Beijing stop obstructing Taiwan's effort to establish external relations and expand its international space. On the basis of such conditions, the Presidential National Unification Council (NUC) has put forward a set of guidelines for national unification (hereafter, NUC guidelines).[17] The guidelines set short, middle, and long-term objectives and propose to move toward unification under the principles of reason, equality, and security, through peaceful and graduated avenues, in three stages.

At the end of 1991, there was a standoff. Taipei rejected the one country–two systems formula because that would mean lowering its own status to that of a local government and, worse, leaving the people on the mainland to the mercy of communism. Beijing, in turn, criticized President Lee's three conditions, saying they were no different from all other suggestions from Taiwan so far: excuses to perpetuate the unsatisfactory status quo. Beijing seemed to want to talk first and work out the differences later, but Taipei insisted that cooperation is the order of the day.

Technically there are problems of who should talk with whom. Beijing suggests party-to-party talks, but Taipei says Taiwan is a democracy and the KMT cannot represent the whole people. Besides, the DPP would certainly object to and criticize any agreement arrived at as a sellout. Should Beijing offer to hold multiparty talks to which the DPP and the so-called democratic parties on the mainland were also invited, Taipei would still object, because the KMT cannot control the DPP but the CPC can tell the so-called democratic parties what to do. Taipei proposes government-to-government talks but Beijing says no, for these talks would imply that Taipei has an equal status with Beijing. If Beijing were to treat Taipei as a local government and turn the talks into a central-local negotiation, Taipei would have to reject them.[18]

The internal conditions of the competing successors have to change further so that a time comes when serious, official negotiations can take place. Perhaps Beijing is fully aware of this. A paragraph in the communique of the Seventh Central Committee Plenum released on December 30, 1990, reads as follows:[19]

> The plenary meeting indicated that, during the 1990s, in accordance with the principle of "one country, two systems," the return of Hong Kong and Macao to the motherland shall be realized while exchanges between the two

TABLE 15–3

POSSIBLE OUTCOMES OF NEGOTIATED SETTLEMENT BETWEEN CHINA
AND TAIWAN

Partition	Unification
Two Chinas (German model)	Confederative arrangement
One China, one Taiwan	Federation
(DPP-preferred)	Unitary state: three formulas
	One country, two systems
	(CPC proposal)
	One China, two regions
	(KMT proposal)
	Condominium, national or
	regional

SOURCE: Author.

shores of the straits shall be positively developed and peaceful unification of the motherland promoted. All comrades of the Party and people of all nationalities in the country, including compatriots of Hong Kong, Macao, and Taiwan and overseas Chinese, should actively join in the great task of promoting the motherland's unification and advancing China's status.

This is interesting. The tone of the statement is that no realization of unification with Taiwan is expected during the coming decade. Can it be that Beijing has neither the confidence that Taiwan can be enticed into the fold nor the intention of forcing the issue? Is it an indirect reply to Taipei's NUC guidelines?

Possible outcomes of a negotiated settlement. Judging by the analyses of the previous section, it is premature to speak of a negotiated settlement. However, ten years can be a long time, and history is full of surprises. It may not be out of order, however, to hedge about the possible outcome of a negotiated settlement between mainland China and Taiwan, which is likely to be one of those specified in table 15–3.

Partition, whether transitional or indefinite, still appears unacceptable to Beijing at this point. Indeed, the official position of the KMT also rejects the idea. This option, however, may not be out of the question. Many analysts in Taiwan have pointed to the German model and argued for a stable, transitional partition before unification. If Beijing can see that final settlement of the question is not likely for the 1990s, a more satisfactory arrangement, one that is beneficial to both, may be worked out. There have been two de facto Chinas for four decades. Travelers to the two shores and traders who do business in both must apply to two separate governments for their purposes. With a new generation, rational thinking may prevail. This is all the more plausible because of the NUC's three-stage proposal for unification.

The initiative for a partition would probably come from Taiwan. The KMT and the DPP seem to differ because the former insists on the one-China principle while the latter prefers a separate, sovereign Taiwan, but their positions are not irreconcilable. In substance the mainstream KMT thinking is an independent government over "the Taiwan region" with all the powers of a sovereign. If the time for unification were not yet ripe and the choices were between (1) unification under Beijing's terms, (2) one China, one Taiwan, or (3) two Chinas for a transitional period, like the two Germanys, the third alternative would probably be chosen. The difference between the KMT and the DPP positions then becomes one between two Chinas and one China, one Taiwan. Ultimately, these options would each produce a different result. But for the period of transition, they are different only in nomenclature.

Should there be unification, broadly the options are confederation, federation, or a unitary system. A confederation is nominal unification involving only a few units—the mainland, Taiwan, and maybe Tibet. It is the easier to bring about, Beijing willing. Federation is the ideal, given China's vast size, regional variations, and history of despotic centralism. All the provinces and autonomous regions of the PRC and Taiwan would have to be involved. Hong Kong and Macao are too small to become equal component units; they might remain SARs. This is a difficult option, good for some future date, rather than for early unification. The most likely solution is still a unitary system, simply because Beijing insists on it and the KMT government in Taipei does not object to it.

There are three formulas for a unitary system: one country, two systems; one country, two regions; and some sort of condominium. The first two have been offered by Beijing and Taipei respectively. The third is a logical possibility and can be applied nationally or regionally. The idea is to have the country or parts of it ruled somehow by the two governments jointly. Taipei's NUC guidelines incorporate a suggestion that during the second stage, "the two shores shall develop Fujian, Guangdong, and the Yangzijiang delta jointly, and extend this to other regions gradually."[20]

If the statement from the year-end CPC Central Committee Communiqué quoted above actually is an answer from Beijing to the

NUC guidelines, even this idea of a condominium may have its round. With time and changed conditions, we may have reason to look forward to other formulas in the years to come.

Conclusion. Interesting questions are sometimes raised about the Chinese. Why did China not develop into a major naval power before the twentieth century? Why have the Chinese not built a colonial empire overseas? Why have they always seemed timid subjects when residing in other countries? Why are they so cultured and so backward at the same time? Why do they appear so inscrutable?

Until 1911, China was a continental, inward-looking, and self-conscious "middle kingdom." Traditionally, Chinese people live off the land. They strive for harmony and are peace-loving. For millenniums they have embraced the idea that politics and administration are the business of the emperor and his officials, not the common people, and that it is better to stay away from officialdom. The family or clan is the source of one's life, past, present, and future. Hard work and thriftiness are virtues wherever one goes. The paradox of culture and backwardness is explained in terms of the two worlds in Confucianism: that of the noblemen (*junzi*) and that of the commoners (*xiaoren*). The fine culture applies primarily, if not exclusively, to the world of noblemen. No, the Chinese are not inscrutable. They are just different.

Nevertheless, the Chinese, especially the Hans, generally subscribe to the notion that all Chinese belong to one nation and that there should be only one sovereign state of China. *The Romance of the Three Kingdoms* is a story of one nation divided, not of three nations. To the Chinese, mainland China and Taiwan, too, are one nation and should be one state, even though Taiwan was ceded to the Japanese in 1895 and has been separated from the mainland ever since. Likewise, Hong Kong is a Chinese territory, notwithstanding that it has been a British colony for 148 years. "With regard to important affairs in the land under Heaven, unity comes after a long period of separation and separation comes after a long period of unity"—so goes the opening statement of *The Romance of the Three Kingdoms*. But there is no clue as to how long is long. If Chinese history is the guide, the times of national division have been as long as or longer than the times of national unity. Furthermore, a long period of separation can last hundreds of years. Forty or fifty years is relatively short. The question of a divided China is not a matter to be settled at will by anyone.

Perhaps a bit of caution is in order. In the 1990s, the evidence suggests that all the positive possibilities suggested in this chapter will probably occur. But setbacks and unforeseen developments may render logical, theoretical projections senseless and irrelevant. The complicated process of negotiations may not always lead to agreements, and unification or partition may not mean a real improvement. The key is inside mainland China, where real changes must come before a peaceful unification of the two shores can occur. The Chinese may see their future as one, but the people on the two shores have had very different political and economic experiences. As the new decade dawns, China's open door policy continues. The stoic regime has been restrained, in deeds if not in words, in responding to international pressures after the Tiananmen suppression. It has accommodated, if only reluctantly, reasonable international demands. Its foreign policy line continues to favor "a peaceful and stable international environment" and the "five principles of peaceful coexistence." But who can say that the system reform in China will work or that there will be no more intervening historical "accidents," such as the Tiananmen tragedy?

After all is said and done, there remains one final question: Is it good for the people if the status quo is ended in favor of an agreed unification or separation?

The lists in appendixes 15–B, 15–C, and 15–D may be useful as a quick reference on key aspects of internal changes in mainland China, Taiwan, and Hong Kong. They are pertinent to the question of a divided China during the 1990s. Each item is potentially a trigger of chain reactions among the competing successors. Some supporting background information has been provided for each category. The lists are in no way meant to be final or exhaustive. Rather, they can be and should be improved and updated as new situations develop.

APPENDIX 15–A
Chronology of Interactive Changes in Mainland China, Taiwan, and Hong Kong, 1978–1992

December 1978: A moderate faction led by Deng Xiaoping emerges victorious in Beijing's power struggle. Beijing turns sharply away from the Leftist line after the Third Plenum of the Eleventh CPC Central Committee.

New Year's Day 1979: Message to Taiwan compatriots spells out a new Taiwan policy. The CPC establishes Taiwan Affairs Leadership group, with Yang Shangkun in actual charge.

1979–1989: Deng's modernization diplomacy leads to improvement

371

of Sino-American and Sino-Soviet relations.

1979: Taipei responds with a defensive Three Nos policy.

1980–1990s: Economic reforms in the mainland attract Hong Kong trade and investment.

SEPTEMBER 1981: Ye Jianying stipulates conditions for settlement of Taiwan question in a nine-point policy statement.

1982: Article 31 of the PRC Constitution provides for the establishment of Special Administrative Regions.

1982–1984: Sino-British negotiations on the future of Hong Kong. Britain, the United States, and Japan endorse Beijing's one country–two systems policy on Hong Kong, 1983, 1984.

JUNE 1983: Deng Xiaoping establishes six points regarding Taiwan in conversation with Winston Yang.

1983: The State Council establishes Office of Hong Kong-Macao Affairs.

1983–1990s: Taiwan residents respond to Beijing overtures. Hong Kong's entrepôt trade facilitates rapid, indirect trade expansion.

SEPTEMBER 1984: Sino-British Joint Declaration signed.

SEPTEMBER–OCTOBER 1984: Taipei issues new but timid Hong Kong policy.

1985: First Legislative Council elections are held in Hong Kong.

DECEMBER 1985: Public opinion in Taiwan presses for internal reform and change in mainland policy. Chiang Ching-kuo signals new policy line.

1985–1990: The Hong Kong SAR Basic Law is drafted and enacted.

1985–1991: Middle-class emigration from Hong Kong rapidly rises.

SEPTEMBER 1986: The DPP is established.

JULY 1987: Martial law is lifted in Taiwan. The DPP openly asserts "the right to advocate Taiwan independence" in the summer of 1987.

OCTOBER 1987: The ROC Ministry of Interior approves limited visitation policy on "humanitarian grounds." About 1.3 million Taiwanese residents a year have visited the mainland since then. They contribute more than U.S.$1 billion worth of foreign exchange to mainland China per year.

January 1988: Chiang Ching-kuo dies. CPC General-Secretary Zhao Ziyang sends condolence message.

July 1988: Lee Teng-hui is elected KMT chairman.

July 1988: Beijing makes substantial concessions to Taiwanese traders and investors by law. By the end of 1989, 1,600 Taiwan enterprises had invested U.S.$1.2 billion; indirect trade volume for 1990 amounted to U.S.$3.5 billion.

August 1988: Taipei's Executive Yuan establishes the Joint Conference on Mainland Work and the KMT-Mainland Work Guiding group.

September 1988: Beijing launches the Committee for the Promotion of Peaceful Unification of China. Hu Ch'iu-yuan, a Legislative Yuan member, visits Beijing against KMT advice in his capacity as honorary chairman of a new League for China's Unification.

1985–1989: Taipei gradually lifts control over one-way traffic to the mainland. There is "Taiwan fever" in the mainland and "mainland fever" in Taiwan.

April 1989: Taipei releases trial balloon for "one country, two governments." Shirley Kuo, finance minister, leads Taipei-China delegation to the annual Asian Development Bank meeting in Beijing, May 1989.

1989: The State Council establishes an Office of Taiwan Affairs.

April–June 1989: A major democracy movement is active on the mainland. There is lukewarm support from Taiwan.

May–June 1989: There are massive Hong Kong demonstrations and other support for Tiananmen students.

June 4, 1989: Tiananmen demonstrators bloodily suppressed. Instant and unreserved protests occur in Hong Kong and there are extended international sanctions, but only half-hearted condemnation from Taipei. Most people expected that the bloody June 4 suppression would halt whatever momentum had been building up across the Taiwan Strait, at least temporarily. But on the contrary, the pace seems to have accelerated since then.

March 1990: Plastics tycoon Wang Yong-ching signs agreement of intention with Fujian authorities to move a multibillion dollar investment to Haichang. The plan folds after disclosure and heavy pressure in Taiwan. Deng Xiaoping ordered green-light treatment and priority development of Haichang.

April 1990: The Basic Law of the Hong Kong SAR is promulgated.

June–July 1990: President Lee Teng-hui convenes a special National Affairs Conference.

September 1990: Asian Olympic Games are held in Beijing. Chinese people in all competing successors cheer for the PRC's gold medals. Taiwan and Hong Kong both send large delegations.

September 1990: The DPP adopts a resolution that Taiwan's sovereignty "does not extend over Mongolia and mainland China."

September 1990: Red Cross societies of mainland China and Taiwan sign an agreement on the repatriation of refugees and criminals, following serious incidents of alleged maltreatment and deaths of refugees being repatriated; 6,081 illegal entrants from mainland China were repatriated by Taiwan between July 1989 and September 1990.

October–November 1990: Taipei establishes the following three-tier structure for dealing with mainland affairs: the presidential National Unification Council for decision making; the Mainland Affairs Council under the Executive Yuan for coordination and for Hong Kong affairs; and the Straits Exchange Foundation, a semiofficial, intermediary institution, for implementation.

December 1990: The CPC Leadership Group on Taiwan Affairs reorganized with more military leaders as members.

December 1990: The National Unification Council discloses draft guidelines for national unification.

December 1990: President Lee announces the intention to terminate the Period of Mobilization for Suppression of the Communist Rebellion by May 1991.

December 1990: The Hong Kong government decides to issue two-year multiple entry visas to Taiwanese passport holders, as visitors from Taiwan exceeded 1.2 million for 1990.

December 1990: Beijing holds a major conference on Taiwan work.

February 1991: Taipei relaxes regulations prohibiting mainland visits by civil servants.

March 11, 1991: The Guidelines for National Unification, passed by the NUC on December 18 and the MAC on February 23, are proclaimed in Taipei.

April 1991: Taipei relaxes regulations preventing the return of former Taiwanese students from the mainland.

APRIL 29, 1991: SEF delegation visits Beijing's Taiwan Affairs Office. Tang Shubei of Beijing's Taiwan Affairs Office stipulates five principles on relations with Taiwan.

MAY 1, 1991: ROC President Lee Teng-hui proclaims the end of the Period of National Mobilization for the Suppression of Communist Rebellion. The PRC becomes a "political entity" instead of a "rebellious group" in Taipei's official language.

MAY 22, 1991: Taipei abolishes the special law dealing with rebellion.

JUNE 3, 1991: Taipei abolishes the special law on ferreting out Communist spies.

JUNE 7, 1991: Responsible person in the CPC Taiwan Affairs Office makes a three-point proposal to Taipei.

AUGUST 22, 1991: Two mainland Red Cross officials, accompanied by two journalists, arrive in Taiwan at the invitation of the Taiwan Red Cross.

SEPTEMBER 1991: The United Democrats of Hong Kong win a landslide victory in the partial elections of Legislative Council members in Hong Kong. Pro-Beijing forces suffer a devastating defeat.

OCTOBER 9, 1991: PRC President Yang Shangkun issues warning to Taiwan independence advocates that "Those who play with fire will be burned to ashes."

OCTOBER 13, 1991: The DPP adopts a new charter and commits itself to build "a Taiwanese republic with independent sovereignty."

OCTOBER 30, 1991: Beijing issues internal instructions on cross-straits activities (twenty-three articles). "International" conferences held in Taiwan were to be shunned.

DECEMBER 9, 1991: Taipei issues rules regarding the handling of mainlanders' applications for residence in Taiwan.

DECEMBER 16, 1991: Beijing establishes the Association for Relations across the Taiwan Straits (ARATS).

DECEMBER 31, 1991: London announces that Governor David Wilson will leave his job soon without naming a successor.

JANUARY 7, 1992: Beijing issues rules governing Chinese citizens traveling to and from the Taiwan region.

JANUARY–MARCH 1992: Taipei issues further notes on handling applications for various purposes by residents going across the Taiwan Strait. Further relaxation of regulations on visitation, trade, and cultural exchange.

FEBRUARY 25, 1992: The Standing Committee of the NPC passes the law on territorial waters and contiguous zones, which enables the PRC to exercise control over the waters surrounding Taiwan and its offshore islands.

MARCH 10, 1992: Beijing formally appoints forty-four Hong Kong Affairs Advisors.

MARCH 20–MAY 28, 1992: The second ROC National Assembly completes constitutional amendments in Taipei.

MARCH 23, 1992: The SEF and the ARATS delegations meet in Beijing to discuss the authentication of documents and handling of registered mails but meeting ends in failure because of disagreement on whether to incorporate the "one China" principle.

END OF MARCH 1992: Beijing rejects Hong Kong Government's new airport financing scheme. The Port and Airport Development Scheme is delayed.

SPRING 1992: Deng Xiaoping makes tour of southern China, stirring up debates over reform inside the mainland and new optimism in Hong Kong.

MAY–AUGUST 1992: Semiofficial delegations led by former economy minister, Zhao Yaodong, president of the Academia Sinica, Wu Dayiu, and president of the Taiwan Institute of Economics, Liu Taiying, visit mainland China and receive red-carpet treatment from Beijing.

MAY 10, 1992: Taipei's spokesman for the President's Office, Chiu Jinyi, suggests that the two shores conclude a non-aggression pact. On May 29, Yang Shangkun rejects the suggestion.

MAY 30, 1992: Wang Zhaoguo, head of the State Council Taiwan Affairs Office, reiterates Beijing's three-point proposal of June 7, 1991.

JULY 3, 1992: Governor Wilson leaves Hong Kong. The new governor, Chris Patten, arrives July 9, 1992, and gains wide approval with his populist appeal.

AUGUST 1, 1992: Taipei proclaims the Law on Relations between the People of Taiwan and Mainland Regions. Beijing's response: Taipei has no authority to enact such a law.

AUGUST 4, 1992: ARATS head Wang Daohan proposes a meeting with

SEF head Koo Cheng-fu and receives an affirmative answer from the latter by mail on August 22.

SEPTEMBER 5, 1992: Eighteen reporters visit Taiwan at the invitation of the SEF, followed by delegations of mainland scientists, legal scholars, economists, etc., for the first time since 1949.

OCTOBER 7, 1992: Governor Chris Patten proposes a political reform package for Hong Kong. Beijing reacts strongly. Sino-British relations enter a period of tension and stalemate.

OCTOBER 12–18, 1992: The 14th CPC Congress adopts Deng Xiaoping's reform line and formally endorses the doctrine of Socialist Market Economy.

DECEMBER 19, 1992: The DPP scores a relative victory in the elections of the Second Legislative Yuan members in Taiwan at the expense of the ruling KMT. Beijing is alarmed by the surge of mass support for the "one China, one Taiwan" campaign.

DECEMBER 28, 1992: Delegations of the SEF and the ARATS meet in Hong Kong to renew talks on document authentication but fail again.

APPENDIX 15–B
KEY ASPECTS OF INTERNAL CHANGES IN CHINA'S COMPETING SUCCESSORS

Mainland China

CONDUCT OF NATIONAL-INTEGRATION POLICY

- Adoption of new policies about Taiwan and Hong Kong
- Modifications of terms of negotiation or unification with Taiwan
- Military preparations or exercises aimed at Taiwan and Hong Kong
- Reorganizations of party and government institutions in charge of Taiwan and Hong Kong affairs
- Activities of the Chinese People's Political Consultative Conference, the "democratic parties," and other united front organs
- Flexibility regarding border control
- New interpretations of the Hong Kong SAR Basic Law

Background
- *New Taiwan policies pronounced by Ye Jianying, Deng Xiaoping, Yang Shangkun, and other leaders since 1979*

- *New Hong Kong policies pronounced by Deng Xiaoping, Ji Pengfei, Lu Ping, and other leaders*
- *CPC Taiwan Affairs Leadership group*
- *State Council Office on Hong Kong–Macao Affairs, 1983*
- *Committee for the Promotion of Peaceful Unification of China, 1988*
- *State Council Office on Taiwan Affairs, 1989*
- *Hong Kong's repatriation of refugees to the mainland with Beijing's cooperation*

Conduct of Foreign Policy and Relations

- Flexibility regarding the Taiwanese question in bilateral relations
- Flexibility regarding Taiwan's membership in international organizations, especially the General Agreement on Tariffs and Trade, the Asia Pacific Economic Conference, the Organization for Economic Cooperation and Development, and the United Nations Economic and Social Committee for Asia and the Pacific
- Modifications of the basic stand regarding Hong Kong's international position
- Interpretation of relevant provisions of the Basic Law

Background
- *UN resolution to replace the ROC with the PRC, 1971*
- *U.S.-PRC Shanghai Communiqué, 1972, and other similar communiqués with many countries since then*
- *Taiwan Relations Act, 1979, passed in United States*
- *Asian Development Bank resolution on the membership of Taiwan, 1986*
- *Applications for memberships in international organizations from both PRC and ROC*
- *Hong Kong's membership in GATT and other UN specialized agencies*

Changes in Leadership

- Outcome of the Deng Xiaoping–Chen Yun debate
- Which of the elders dies when
- Military leadership reshuffle after Deng Xiaoping
- Rise of an administrative, not revolutionary, generation
- Ups and downs of Soviet-oriented generation
- Further development of factions and cliques

Background
- *Purge of Gao Gang and Rao Shushi, 1955*
- *Purge of Peng Dehuai and others, 1959*
- *Purge of Liu Shaoqi and others, 1966*

- *Lin Biao affair, 1971*
- *Gang of Four, 1971–1976*
- *Return of Deng Xiaoping, 1977*
- *Removal of Hu Yaobang, 1986*
- *Removal of Zhao Ziyang, 1989*

ECONOMIC SYSTEM REFORMS

- Development of private ownership system
- Pace of price and wage reform
- Autonomy of special economic zones and coastal areas
- Autonomy of enterprises from party interference
- Substantiation of responsibility system
- Balance between planning and market mechanism
- Implementation of the Eighth Five-Year Plan and the Ten-Year Program

POLITICAL AND ADMINISTRATIVE SYSTEM REFORMS

- Effective separation of party and government
- Improvement in the legal system
- Governability, effective dialogue with the people
- Establishment of a civil service system
- Election reforms and relevant manipulations
- New policy on autonomous regions and national minorities

Background
- *Land reform, 1950*
- *Socialist reforms, 1950–present, of marriage, religion, judiciary, etc.*
- *Three-anti and five-anti campaigns, 1951–1953*
- *Socialist transformation, 1953–1965*
- *People's communes, 1958*
- *Cultural Revolution, 1966–1969*
- *Deng Xiaoping's reform, 1979–present*

POPULAR, DEMOCRATIC MOVEMENT

- Continuing development of student movement
- Regime's policy on human rights issue; key cases include Wei Jingsheng, Wang Dan, Liu Xiaobo
- Reversals of verdicts on June 4–related cases
- Activities of returnees from the United States, Japan, Europe
- Linkage between democratic elements in PRC and outside world

Background
- *Ming Fang movement, 1957*
- *April 5 movement, 1976*
- *Beijing Spring, 1978–1979*
- *Student demonstration, 1985*
- *1989 Democracy movement*
- *Democratic Front, Paris, 1989–present*

IDEOLOGICAL CAMPAIGNS AND POLITICAL RECTIFICATIONS

- Personnel changes in propaganda field
- New evaluation and use of Mao Zedong thought
- New debates in arts, philosophy, literature
- Contradictions: for example, the Four Principles versus the open door policy and social pluralization
- Education policy and control of university students

Background
- *Thought reform campaign, 1950–present*
- *Campaign to suppress counterrevolutionaries, 1950*
- *Campagn to weed out counterrevolutionaries, 1955–1957*
- *Antirightist campaign, 1957*
- *Campaign against rightist tendencies, 1959*
- *Socialist education movement, 1962–1966*
- *Cultural Revolution, 1966–1976*
- *Antispiritual pollution campaign, 1983*
- *Antibourgeois liberalization campaign, 1987*

REVOLUTIONARY CONVULSION

- Rise of fanatic personalities
- Any new mass movement or campaign

Background
- *Establishment of the PRC, 1949*
- *Great Leap Forward, 1958*
- *Cultural Revolution, 1966–1969*
- *Tiananmen suppression, June 4, 1989*
- *Developments in the Communist world, 1989–1991*

APPENDIX 15–C
INTERNAL CHANGES

Taiwan

CONDUCT OF MAINLAND POLICY

- Implementation of the National Unification Council guidelines for national unification
- Modifications of terms of negotiation or unification with the mainland
- Pronouncements on mainland policy by government officials
- Activities of government institutions in charge of mainland and Hong Kong affairs
- Activities of the semiofficial, intermediary institutions
- Modifications of Hong Kong policy

Background
- *Temporary provisions during the period of Communist rebellion, 1948*
- *Three Nos policy, 1979*
- *Visitation policy, 1987*
- *Agreement on refugee and criminal repatriation, 1990*
- *The presidential National Unification Council, 1990; the Mainland Affairs Council under the Executive Yuan, also in charge of Hong Kong affairs, 1990; the Straits Exchange Foundation, 1990*
- *Adoption of the guidelines for national unification, 1991*

CHANGES IN CONDUCT OF FOREIGN POLICY AND RELATIONS

- Flexibility regarding names and dual recognition
- New formulas for pragmatic diplomacy
- Strategy for reentry into international organizations
- Adoption of new Hong Kong policy

Background
- *Efforts to exclude the PRC from international arena before 1971*
- *Setback at the United Nations, 1971, and in bilateral relations since*
- *United States passes Taiwan Relations Act, 1979*
- *ABD resolution on the membership of Taiwan, 1986*
- *Application for GATT membership in the name of "Taiwan, Pescadores, Quemoy, and Matsu," 1989*

- *Hong Kong's membership in GATT and other UN specialized agencies*

Changes in Leadership

- New leaders after the constitutional reform
- Outcome of mainstream and antimainstream contest inside the KMT
- Charismatic dark horses after elections
- Successor to Hao Pei-t'sun in the military

Background
- *Death of Chiang Kai-shek, 1985*
- *Death of Chiang Ching-kuo, 1988*
- *Election of Lee Teng-hui as head of both the state and the party, 1990*
- *Appointment of Hao Pei-t'sun as premier, 1990*
- *Launching of the Democracy Foundation by Kuan Chung, 1990*

Constitutional Reform

- Termination of the Period of National Mobilization for Suppression of the Communist Rebellion, May 1991
- Elections of deputies to the parliamentary bodies, 1991 and 1992; new composition arises after retirements of twenty-five octogenarian stalwarts
- Amendment of the constitution begins, 1992
- New electoral system for the presidency
- Establishment of new provinces and municipalities under the central government

Background
- *Temporary provisions effective during the period of Communist rebellion, 1948–present*
- *Martial law, 1948–1987*
- *The Twelve Man Committee, 1986*
- *National Affairs Conference, 1990*

Party Politics and Independence Movement

- Election of new KMT chief
- New leadership of the DPP
- Direct link between independence movement and election results
- Linkage between independence movements inside and outside Taiwan

- KMT's self-designation as a "revolutionary" party

Background
- *February 28 incident, 1947*
- Free China Fortnightly *and the Chinese Democracy party incident, 1960*
- *Democracy movement by magazine publications, 1961–1979*
- *Chung-li incident, 1977*
- *Kaohsiung incident, 1979*
- *Rise of an opposition (Tang Wai) movement, 1979–1986*
- *Birth of the DPP, 1986*
- *Independence movement surfaces, 1990*

ECONOMIC TRANSFORMATION

- Upgrading of industry
- Internationalization of banking system
- Diversification of markets
- Investment overseas, movement of key enterprises
- New foreign investments in Taiwan
- Strength of labor and ecology movements
- Appreciation of Taiwan dollar

Background
- *High investment in education*
- *Massive U.S. aid before 1965*
- *Land reform and privatization, 1950s*
- *Export-oriented, labor-intensive industries and export processing zone, 1960s and 1970s*
- *Public construction projects, 1970s*
- *The Ten-Year Plan, 1980–1989*
- *Rapid appreciation of Taiwan dollar, late 1980s*

SOCIAL STABILITY AND MOBILITY

- Control of crime and triad societies
- Pluralization, social movements, and governability
    - Industrialization and urbanization
    - Martial law, 1948–1987
    - Economic miracle, creating sudden wealth
    - Liberalization since 1987, creating sudden freedom

APPENDIX 15–D
INTERNAL CHANGES IN HONG KONG AND THEIR BACKGROUND, 1949–PRESENT

Hong Kong

ELECTION POLITICS

- 1991 and 1995 results
- Formation of parties and groups jostling to fill the power vacuum following British departure
- Emerging personalities

Background
- *Positive noninterventionism before 1980*
- *First district board elections*
- *White Paper on the further development of representative government in Hong Kong, 1984*
- *First Legislative Council elections, 1985: functional constituencies*
- *White Paper on the development of representative government, 1988*

MOVEMENTS OF PRC ELEMENTS

- Frequency and areas of interference
- New border policies
- Change in nature and size of investment in Hong Kong
- Open recruitment of CPC members in Hong Kong
- Areas of disagreement, such as the new airport and SS Tamar site
- Use of Chinese and English in official communications

Background
- *Sino-British negotiations, 1982–1984*
- *Drafting process of the Hong Kong SAR Basic Law, 1985–1990*
- *Hong Kong's extraordinary reaction to the democracy movement in Beijing and the June 4 massacre, 1989*
- *Hong Kong's dependence on the mainland for water, food, and refugee control*
- *Presence of the NCNA, PRC banking institutions, and various front organizations in Hong Kong*
- *Hong Kong as China's golden goose*
- *Appointment of advisers begins, 1992*

SCHEMES FOR SAFEGUARDING STABILITY AND PROSPERITY

- New airport and related "rose garden" projects
- Settlement of Vietnamese boat people issue
- Alteration of the Hong Kong currency reserve system
- Intertwining relations between Hong Kong and Shenzhen
- Internationalization of Hong Kong

Background
- *Provisions of the Sino-British Joint Declaration, 1984*
- *Provisions of the Hong Kong SAR Basic Law, 1990*
- *Continuing Sino-British talks through Joint Liaison Group and the Land Commission, 1984–present*
- *Hong Kong experience under British colonialism*

THE PEOPLE'S CHOICE

- Governability decreases with erosion of government authority
- Movement of multinational enterprises
- Emigration trends
- Type and nature of investment overseas
- Trade and investment relations with Shenzhen and Guangdong
- Stock exchange and real estate market fluctuations

Background
- *1967 upheaval*
- *Endless flow of illegal immigrants from the mainland, 1949–present*
- *Rapid rise of middle class emigration since 1985*
- *Increasing waves of corruption, crime, and unreasonable demands, 1989 and 1990*

SOURCE: Author.

16

Post–Cold War Security in the Asia-Pacific Region

Thomas W. Robinson

Well into the 1990s, the shape of global and regional security arrangements in Asia and the rest of the post–cold war world ought to be reasonably apparent. But with a few exceptions, they are not. While obvious trends and forces even now significantly alter security, diplomatic, and economic relations among Asian states, so far little has changed internationally. With the cold war overlay removed, Asia is being further transformed by economic development, and only a few security issues are on the table for more or less immediate solution. With the exception of the question of North Korean nuclear weapons (and the possibility of renewed conflict on the Korean peninsula), Asia is a zone of relative peace. None of the major powers has any interest in confronting any of the others on the battlefield. And no middle power has any interest in settling security or other problems with its neighbors by force, with the possible exceptions of Kashmir and Korea. Only the Spratly Islands question stands on the agenda of non-Korean security issues that could, in the near future, engender conflict, and the probability of violence there is small.

Nonetheless, unless the major powers grasp the opportunity presented by the present calm to construct a new, higher-order Asian security system and to address a series of subregional security issues, the probability of conflict could rise dramatically and the smoothness of regional relations could be replaced by serious major power rivalry and breakdown into a war-inducing balance-of-power system. It is useful, therefore, indeed mandatory, to try to understand what the future might bring by way of Asian security arrangements in general and of solution to specific security issues. This analysis will first indicate how post–cold war global and regional trends and forces will configure the Asian security future, then inspect short-term subregional and regionwide security issues, and finally consider specific medium-term issues and possible shapes of the system that will evolve.

Global and Regional Trends

Global and regional trends and forces are comparatively easy to understand:[1] multipolarity; the triple revolution of democratization, marketization, and interdependence; the universal primacy of domestic problems; the rise of technology as the major force propelling economic and military development; and the emergence of global issues, especially environmental questions. In Asia, this means:

- relative equality among the major powers (America, China, Japan, and Russia)
- the further spread and deepening of the drives toward democracy and market economics
- the breakdown of national boundaries, engulfing the remaining socialist states and stimulating modernization even in the least-developed nations
- the likelihood of continued peace among the major Asian powers, as none can afford to divert significant resources from domestic economic construction or political reordering
- revision of the regional "pecking order" according to technology-induced rates of growth
- the need to invent international institutions to grapple with increasingly serious environmental issues

Multipolarity further implies the absence of any organized Asian security system, at least as yet. The triple revolution, together with domestic primacy, supplies sufficient time—perhaps until the end of the decade—wherein the relevant nations can work together, if they are wise enough, to construct a new and better security system. Technology further provides an essential element in solving the many problems that will emerge during the search for a system acceptable to all. And the environmental question challenges the parties to work together for common ends. If Asian and trans-Pacific politicians could seize the opportunities thus presented by these positive indications of the future, they could solve specific security issues and create a system that could lead to long-term peace and stability in the region.

But reality is never so kind, not only because vision and leadership are often lacking but also because the path to such a felicitous future is always blocked by the obstacles of rapidly changing relations of power; of the uncooperative, chance, and often threatening concatenation of events; and the emergence, usually because of domestic changes, of security issues that demand immediate solution. The path is thus tortuous, and the probability of peace, stability, enhancement of regional international organizations, and solution of security problems before they become threats remains low. The prospect of undesired outcomes must therefore be faced. Indeed, preparation for unpalatable futures must be made, while learning from the terrible losses incurred earlier in the twentieth century. The trick is to confront constructively and solve security issues, using each such occasion to build a security framework that will prevent the emergence of, or cope peacefully with, new issues.

This may sound too idealistic to be workable, with so many apparent threats and pitfalls during the early 1990s or just over the horizon. Yet the present juncture is the first time in the twentieth century, at least since the end of World War I, that Asia has the opportunity to seek its own security future in relative freedom. Statesmen and scholars alike can therefore seize the opportunity therefore to move to something better before being overwhelmed, once again, with the details of daily events and crises. The early 1990s have already witnessed cries and proposals, official and not, for "common security," "cooperative security," "cooperative engagement," "comprehensive security," and (much more faintly) "collective security." Most of these come from the western shores of the Pacific: Malaysia, Singapore, Japan, and South Korea have all forwarded proposals or called for serious dialogue on the future of Asian security, and other nations (India and Indonesia) have entered a creative debate.[2] There are voices even in China and Vietnam that evidence full understanding of the opportunities of these early years, although they do not yet inform official policy.[3] At least officially, the Americans have unfortunately lacked or deliberately eschewed new thoughts, apparently assuming that the situation does not require new initiatives and that other regions are more important to global and American security. An American policy of laissez faire, ad hockery, muddling through, benign neglect, and dependence on leftovers from the cold war (the so-called hubs and spokes policy) has thus emerged willy-nilly. (To be fair, early Clinton administration statements suggest a more enlightened approach. And there is a growing nongovernmental movement in the United States to fill the gap that opened during the Bush administration.[4] But even there, despite the emergence of an abundant if preliminary literature, no idea so far has had sweeping appeal. The Canadians, however, are to be commended for seeing more clearly the need and convening a series of helpful meetings.)[5]

Subregional Issues. In the early 1990s, only two subregional, short-term issues threaten security: the North Korean nuclear weapons question and the Spratly Islands issue. If not handled carefully, both could tempt or force the states in question to use force in attempted resolution, causing systemic changes of such magnitude that the nascent drive to construct a better security future would be side-tracked.

North Korean nuclear weapons. The North Korean nuclear weapons problem is more serious and immediate.[6] If not solved very soon by denying such instruments to Pyongyang, it could lead to a sundering of the Nuclear Non-Proliferation Treaty, an enhanced prospect of war on the peninsula, and the possession of nuclear weapons by several new states, principally Japan. The North Korean situation, and Pyongyang's strategy of desperation, is well known, as are its several motives for acquisition. The fact of North Korea's weapons program is also not in doubt. It appears clear that nothing save the use of force by the United States will stop Kim Il Sung from carrying his plans through to successful completion. Efforts by the international community—the International Atomic Energy Agency, the five states most directly affected, and the United Nations—however well intentioned, do not have the teeth to be effective. Nor is there any catalog of material and diplomatic temptations yet offered (or, I aver, offerable) to dissuade Kim from persisting. The Americans, in the throes of putting the new Clinton-led government into place that pledges, rightly, to put domestic problems first, will not move militarily. (If the Bush administration drew back in 1991 from an Iraq-like policy of threat and escalation, the Clinton administration is much less likely to go even to that point.) And a new government in Seoul, led by Kim Young Sam, is, rightly, afraid to test Kim Il Sung's threat to start a new war if his nuclear sites are attacked, is equally afraid of what might happen if there is any externally induced rocking of the succession boat in the north, and is overly mindful of the Korean parallel to the economic consequence of German reunification. South Korea thus cautions the Americans even more.

China, which has very little residual influence in Pyongyang, behaves as if it is the only conduit for the outside world's appeals to Kim and thus hopes to retain the initiative in its hands. And since Washington deceives itself in this regard (just as it did in the Vietnam War, when it hoped the Kremlin would somehow deliver Hanoi to the negotiating table), the United States has no real freedom of action. Kim Il Sung thus has a winning strategy and will soon, if he does not already, possess the bomb.

There is, however, a concerted South Korean–American strategy that might work, if only the Chinese would cooperate in the Security Council: to bring the nuclear issue to a head, deliberately and immediately, by swift Security Council–led action and parallel American preparations, in earnest, for strikes at North Korean nuclear sites. Kim Il Sung's bluff would thus be called. Concomitantly, the north would be offered full global recognition (particularly by the United States and South Korea), massive economic assistance would be tendered—thereby saving the Kim dynasty from inevitable economic bankruptcy and political destruction—and the north would enter the same path of rapid economic development through marketization and interdependence that China is traversing. That route would, it is true, also lead to the eventual destruction of Kim's rule but through an evolutionary process that would minimize the probability of war and maximize the prospects for peaceful, negotiated reunification. Even to write down such a strategy, though, however reasonable it seems, is to indicate its futility. None of the states in question has the fortitude to face the issue, particularly the United States and China, and the probability of such cooperation by South Korea—which could, obviously, lose the most if the strategy failed—is very low.

Since the outside states are unwilling to bring the matter to a head, and presuming that internal North Korean events do not intervene, it is best to prepare for a nuclear North Korea. In that instance, the south will have to be shored up militarily by an explicit American nuclear guarantee, with sale or transfer of the most up-to-date American equipment, thorough modernization of South Korean–American military cooperation, and by ensuring that Seoul continues to grow so rapidly that the north will be left even more distantly in the dust. Some sort of arms embargo will have to be thrown around the north to prevent it from spreading nuclear weapons, the accompanying technology, and other weapons of mass destruction around the globe. North Korea will have to be isolated economically as well—not so difficult a task with Pyongyang's policy of self-isolation. Such isolation will hasten North Korea's economic breakdown and make it harder to produce each new nuclear weapon. The world will have to wait out the rest of the Kim regime and hope that the eventual succession will be relatively peaceful and that, afterward, the reunification process will not be too messy.

The Spratly Islands dispute. The Spratly Islands dispute is the only other subregional Asian security issue that threatens outbreak of war in the early 1990s.[7] The facts of this matter are also well known. While several members of the Association of Southeast Asian Nations (ASEAN) claim portions of the island group and while the consequent complication militates against outbreak of violence, the dispute reduces to a contest between China and Vietnam. It is true that China is building up its military capabilities in the South China Sea so that by the mid-1990s it can, if it wishes, seize the Spratly Islands against even the most determined Vietnamese opposition. The military capabilities of Vietnam, while not negligible, by that time will not be able to stand up to those deployable by China. But even to attempt military seizure would be a disaster for China. Its entire approach to Southeast Asia, Indochina and ASEAN alike, is predicated on a verbal policy of peace. To throw its word away in the context of universal suspicion of Chinese intentions and Southeast Asian readiness to find the Chinese guilty of a Janus-faced policy would be to guarantee the rapid creation of a coalition against it, the conversion of ASEAN into an anti-Chinese security community, the reintroduction of American naval power and security commitments in the region, and the beginning of an earnest American effort to create an all-Asian, anti-Chinese containment system. Given Beijing's dependence on good economic relations with the rest of Asia and with the United States and its need to develop economically without the threat of major foreign military involvement, the last thing China wants is a war. Particularly unwelcome would be a war against a united Southeast Asia supported by the United States. Moreover, for several years China has been actively pursuing a diplomatic policy of reconciliation with Vietnam and of downplaying its problems with ASEAN nations stemming from its general military buildup and the security implications of its rapid economic growth. Wars do not grow out of such circumstances, at least not immediately. It is true that China has claimed all the Spratly Islands belong to China alone, and it is true that, if diplomatic circumstances were to change and present Beijing with the opportunity to seize the islands without unacceptable consequences, it would probably strike—but not in the immediate future.

The only other candidate for subregional conflict in the near future is Kashmir. But the near-term outbreak of a new Indo-Pakistani war over that territory is not likely. The subject will be explored later under medium-term subregional security issues.

Regionwide Issues. At least five security issues will demand attention in the near future.

China's economic growth. First is the security implication of China's continued high economic growth.[8] While double-digit increases in gross national product (GNP) are not likely to continue throughout the 1990s, even a 5 percent annual increase will double that nation's wealth within a decade, allow it to outdistance Japan decisively somewhat later, and even to rival the United States as the world's largest economy in the twenty-first century. In per capita income, China will not be so well off, but the centuries of poverty and backwardness are over forever, barring ecological or political disaster. This change should, of course, be regarded as a major victory for the human race and an example for the remaining socialist states of what the transition to a market economy and economic interdependence can accomplish.

But the nations surrounding China are, quite properly, fearful of what security posture a superpower China will adopt and already worry that massive additions to national power will inevitably lead to significant changes in Beijing's military capabilities and in national interests. In Asian eyes, China has been arming itself much beyond its legitimate defensive needs and has progressively involved itself in situations and disputes farther and farther from its political frontiers. It will continue to do that, without any doubt. The only question is whether its projection of military power will be benign, under an international flag, and carried forth by a government much less Communist or whether it will use its new power to create an Asia that is, in effect, its own preserve. If China wants hegemony, it will need containment and deterrence, and that implies a concentrated effort to organize substantial power against it and to draw in extraregional military power and commitments, principally American, as insurance.

The trouble is that China, on the one hand, and the surrounding Asian nations and the United States, on the other hand, have already begun to enter a vicious circle. China cannot be dissuaded from modernizing its military, providing itself with a viable projection force, enlarging and perfecting that force, and constructing a military machine that will become Asia's largest and most effective. It is already well down that road. Furthermore, China cannot be dissuaded from finding interests to go along with that force. At some point, therefore, China will be tempted to employ or test its new force. Sensing this, the surrounding nations and the United States have three choices. Either they will, separately or together, try to engage Beijing in constructing some variant of a higher-order regional security system. Or they will, again separately or together, elect to appease Beijing by policies of selective delay, retreat, or compromise in the face of vastly superior power. Or they will band together to oppose China through a cooperative arrangement, however loose or tight (that is, from security talks, coordinated maneuvers, and the like to a formal alliance similar to NATO).

If concerned nations try to construct a regional security system that includes China, it may be possible to avoid a split on security issues between China (and perhaps one or two others that would become Chinese satellites) and all the rest. Such a choice would best enhance the probability of an outcome favorable to all. The second choice, appeasement, is a recipe for disaster, unless the affected states use the time gained to improve their own military power and China proceeds, through internal evolution, significantly farther toward an interdependent market democracy. The history of appeasement policies elsewhere indicates that disaster is much more likely. Even if successful, appeasement would undoubtedly grow over into the third choice, for no Asian state—even a heavily rearmed Japan—could cope with the new Chinese power by itself. And a NATO-like plan is also fraught with danger, for any anti-Chinese cooperative arrangement would spell the return of a balance-of-power system to Asia and thus the prospect of war itself, which is almost always the outcome of such a system. Building a higher-order system would have to wait until the Chinese threat had passed, and that could entail delay until well into the next century. It will take much effort and a great deal of statesmanship on all sides to avoid the less desirable choices. And the history of international relations is not supportive either: whenever a new major power arrives on the scene, the disturbance caused thereby is so severe that systemic break-down—war—is the usual outcome. With a China possessing such enormous power and with a nation that has a history of making life difficult for its neighbors, trouble ahead is likely, and much time, organizational effort, and material investment will be required before China is successfully integrated into the Asian and global security systems.

U.S. policy. The China problem is directly related to the second regionwide, short-term concern, the policy of the United States.[9] Given the long and highly intense involvement of America in Asia, it is astonishing that Washington's security policy is seen, within the region, as a problem. But it is. Fresh from its (and the free world's) victory in the cold war and its impressive victory in the Gulf War, the United States is already sampling the sour and unnecessary fruit of its post–cold war policy of relative neglect of Asia. An economic crisis with Japan has emerged and approaches a climax, with incessant Japan bashing taking on national security overtones. Not surprisingly, some talk of a fundamental split. After Tiananmen, Washington also decided—not without reason and not without much initial international support—to draw a line between itself and China. This response is quite natural, given the events in China, the contrast between the survival of the Beijing regime and the downfall of Communist governments almost everywhere else, and American moralism. But the people also demand that the Beijing regime be punished continuously for its transgression and ignore the post-Tiananmen domestic transformation, while the American government discovers a wide range of perfidious Chinese acts in the economic and security realms. And so a crisis there too has emerged, a crisis America deliberately prolongs and worsens.

Toward its former enemy, Vietnam, which now much needs American economic investment and which must face China alone, Washington has turned a near-deaf ear—not without reason, once again, for Hanoi has many sins to live down and is hardly angelic in its international behavior. Instead of taking advantage of the situation to make a historic reconciliation with Vietnam and also serve its Southeast Asian policy well, America has continued to put overly moralistic obstacles in its own path. And when Asian states of whatever political or economic orientation practically beg the United States first to remain in the region in strength and then to lead the way to a better security future in the region, Washington responds with threats of economic investigation and new tariff barriers, takes such important states as South Korea for granted, mostly ignores others like India that approach Washington anew, declares that America never had it so good in Asia, and avers that no major amendments to security arrangements are necessary for the foreseeable future. But most important, Washington has begun to reduce its forces in Asia and to talk of the desirability of much larger withdrawals to follow. That, again, is a natural inclination in a post–cold war world, but it opens a gap between American commitments and capabilities in Asia. Regional states can thus be excused for questioning American avowals of maintaining a strong security presence in Asia, for beginning to arm themselves as never before, and for initiating discussions and proposals that, given its function as natural leader, the United States ought to be making itself.

Many Asians are worried that America may prove unreliable in Asia. It is thought to shirk its duty as leader; it appears to be denying its own interests (which if anything, are enlarging in the post–cold war world) in Asia. And it risks opening a gap between its stated policies and the power with which it actually supports them. It is in fact perceived to be looking the other way at the very moment when its authority is greatest, when its power could most efficiently break through to a new era, and when the opportunity is there to take the combined positive, moral, and realistic initiatives that America has, more than once, been known to launch. Historically, when Washington has pulled back from Asia, as it has before, it has done so primarily in response to domestic demands to reduce commitments abroad and attend to problems at home. Such is also the case in the early 1990s. But in this instance, fortunately, both the citizenry and the political leadership appear to understand that the retreat cannot go too far, that America is forever tied to Asia, that to let go now courts disaster, and that Asia as a whole is changing so fast that it requires a hands-on, fully engaged policy.

The question is how far the American force drawdown will proceed, how long it will be before the country reinvigorates its Asian policy, and whether Asia will tire of waiting for Washington in the meantime. Moreover, security-related events in the region could arise, forcing America to reenter Asia under unpalatable and otherwise avoidable circumstances. It would not be best, for instance, if Japan, plagued by American backbiting and increasing worries about North Korean nuclear weapons and the Chinese military buildup, were to nullify the Security Treaty and rearm in earnest. It would not be desirable for the North Koreans, in their desperation, to decide to take a final chance and launch a new attack against the south. Nor would it be helpful if China, increasingly concerned about political trends on Taiwan and perceiving an America consumed with domestic problems, were to invade the island. Many other circumstances (Burmese implosion, Kashmiri uprising, and Khmer Rouge resurgence, to name a few) could also drag the United States back into active participation in an Asian conflict on very unfavorable terms. These problems are probably some years off before they force themselves onto the American television screens and the Oval Office desk. Yet the concern is immediate, for what America does—or, more likely, does not do—in the near future will determine later efforts to cope with these issues.

Japan's security future. The third regionwide issue is how Japan will address its security future.[10] Like the first two issues, decisions made in the early 1990s will influence the shape of late twentieth century and early twenty-first century security in Asia. And assumptions, accurate or not, about what Tokyo will do later will affect other countries' security policies now. National security policies are like stock markets: the future is heavily discounted. Japan would strongly prefer to do nothing, making no alterations in its security policy. Relying so completely on the United States has paid off handsomely for the Japanese Foreign Ministry for many years, and it cannot be blamed for being reluctant to change. And, of course, the Japanese people, still under the shock of World War II and the occupation and for long having enjoyed the economic benefits of the American security guarantee, are as a whole strongly opposed to any major alteration in the status quo. Yet government and populace alike know that the stability of the past half century cannot last much longer.

Life in post–cold war Asia threatens to be difficult indeed. It is not just the White House that presses the Japanese to take on a more active security role, the Congress that threatens them with severe economic punishment unless major changes are made in domestic Japanese society, and the many analysts that talk about modification or even abolition of the Security Treaty and Article 9 of the Japanese Constitution. It is also the problem of North Korean nuclear weapons, impending Korean reunification and possible war, the growing perceived threat of China, the problem of Russia and the Northern Islands, the defense of Japanese business interests and personnel when the Americans can no longer provide it, and the form and extent of Japanese participation in international peace-keeping operations. Japan must also confront the host of demands from states across the globe that the Japanese link their wealth with responsibility.

So Japan must change. The only question is how, at what pace, and in what direction. Tokyo's preference is not much, very slowly, and only hand in hand with the Americans. But since at least the first two are no longer possible, the question becomes whether the country will take the present as an opportunity to exercise responsible leadership or merely be pushed by events and other states' policies into reactive responses. Many in Japan would like to see their government take on leadership. That would mean careful modification of Article 9 of the Constitution to enable participation in UN and perhaps other joint security operations, negotiations with the United States on modernization of the Security Treaty, a historic compromise with Russia over the Northern Islands (that would, finally, open up a new era of Japanese-Russian economic and security cooperation), and a committed attempt to work out an arms control arrangement with China before it is too late. But Japan will probably not act without further external pressure, allowing the opportunity to slip away without addressing its foreign policy and national security future in a holistic manner. Tokyo will thus continue to be subject to American broadsides, fail to demonstrate statesmanship, and be subject to piecemeal erosions of its security position. In the end, therefore, Japan is likely to be forced into a corner: if it is cast adrift by the Americans and threatened by the Chinese, if it loses the Russian opportunity, and if it faces Korean nuclear weapons and reunification as a *fait accompli*, Japan could eventually be forced to go it alone in Asia. Indeed, many other Asians have already gone through the same reasoning process and have concluded that Japan will reemerge onto the regional security scene in a manner not in accord with their desires. That being so, they have begun to introduce a Japanese factor in their own security calculations. Hence, the same vicious circle met in American-Chinese relations may be emerging with Japan.

Post-Communist Russia. The fourth short-term regionwide Asian security issue is what to do about post-Communist Russia.[11] The two aspects of this problem are how to keep Russia afloat economically and prevent political backsliding, and in what manner to involve Russia and the other states of the Commonwealth of Independent States in Asian security affairs. Like the previous three, this is a long-run problem but one that must be addressed sooner. Russia's economic future is a question of the content and amount of economic assistance, how to implement a new trade and investment regime, how to integrate the emerging Russian market economy into the greater Asian-Pacific interdependent economic arena, and how, through these economic instruments, to add weight to those progressive forces in Russia and the central Asian states that favor democracy and marketization. The involvement of Russia in Asian security affairs concerns Russian arms sales in Asia and the role that Moscow and central Asia should play in immediate issues (such as Korea) and in whatever post–cold war regional security system might arise.

The economic question is complicated by the nature of Siberian-Russian Far Eastern geography and by the legacy of Soviet economic isolationism. The most important issue is how to maximize the probability of successful economic transition and hence minimize chances of political reversion. With such high stakes, a lot of money, technological transfer, business advice, and investment initiatives are necessary. International economic institutions, direct government-aid agencies, and private business must combine their efforts to provide this support. Some of this has already been done, but much more remains. The only large supply of untapped financial and personnel wherewithal is Japan (South Korea, Taiwan, and the United States can and should do more, it is true). But a Russo-Japanese economic breakthrough awaits solution of the Northern Islands question, which may not come in time. If sufficient time and resources can be found, however, a Russian Siberia and Far East might, for the first time, participate in Asian economic affairs as relative equals, opening new vistas for international economic relations.

The Asian security implications of a marketized, democratic Russia are profound. That country would add such enormous weight to the group of Asian, European, and North American market democracies that any military force now imaginable could be countered. In Asia, this goal means making Russia a full, equal, and universally accepted player in regional security affairs for the first time since before World War II. It means close American-Japanese-Russian cooperation in regional security institution building. It means, therefore, having the means, when and if it were to become necessary, to counter China. And it means that America and Japan could work out their differences on security policy without the threat that Japan would be forced into unhappy choices. Thus, prospects for a better security future throughout Asia would be greatly enhanced.

But immediate security issues stand in the way. With Boris Yeltsin's leadership in the Kremlin under desperate pressure, Moscow elected, unfortunately, first to sell high-technology military hardware to China and India and second to try to protect a residual Russian position in Asia by signing a series of questionable security agreements with those same two countries. Russia understandably feels the need for hard currency and also desires to continue the progress, made under Gorbachev, toward restored relations with China. It is less understandable, however, for the Kremlin to sign agreements with the Chinese leadership that point directly against the United States and its Asian allies and that associate Russia with China in a new strategic, alliance-like relationship. Russia's sale of missile technology to India, violative of the Missile Technology Control Regime (MTCR), and its signing of a new security treaty with India are likewise questionable. If such moves were part of a general strategy of making friends everywhere in Asia (that is, settling with Japan over the Northern Islands and with the United States regarding nuclear weapons control and mutual reduction of Siberian-based missiles and bombers and Pacific Ocean–based missile submarines), it would be understandable and acceptable. But that does not seem to be the case, although both Japan and the United States are also to blame for not moving more quickly to solve their respective problems with Russia in Asia. Rather, the Yeltsin government appears to be grasping at straws in its Asian policy without considering the implications of its moves. Although Moscow's moves in the security realm stem from the urgent domestic situation (to improve the economic situation would alleviate the security problems), the Yeltsin government does not appear to be making similar mistakes in Europe.

An Asian arms race. The fifth immediate regionwide Asian security issue is the emerging Asian arms race.[12] Here again, the facts are fully known. With the possible exception of Bangladesh, Mongolia, and Nepal, all regional states are well along in programs to produce, purchase, or otherwise acquire large quantities of expensive, high-technology military equipment. The motives are equally obvious. First, most Asian military establishments, noting from the Gulf War what is necessary to wage modern war successfully, pressed their civilian counterparts to embark on thorough, long-term modernization programs. Many are already well under way.

Second, many nations have allowed their traditional fears of the putatively predatory policies of other nations to reemerge, now that the overarching limitations of the cold war are no longer present. Third, the well-known action-reaction mechanism of the arms race is at work. Even if every single state were entirely justified in its military acquisition program for "defensive" reasons alone, its neighbors would tend to regard such activity as threatening and react accordingly: India arms to defend itself against China and Pakistan, Pakistan against India, and South and North Korea against each other. The list is expandable indefinitely. Fourth, a general and undifferentiated fear and suspicion of China has emerged, the product of the very success of the Chinese economic expansion and the potential that country is perceived to possess to dominate all Asia. Fifth, supplier nations are hungry for the hard currency that military sales bring, justifying their sales efforts by pointing to the necessity of keeping people employed at home. Sixth, many Asian nations have the additional money at hand for such purchases, the product of their successful economic programs of the 1970s–1990s. And last, there is no arms control leadership present now, in contrast to the cold war era.

The unfortunate result is not merely the spending of a lot of money for little added security, if any. When the early 1990s round of purchases is over, military commanders will again approach their civilian counterparts with the request for even more, on grounds that their neighbors have also procured modern equipment and pose a threat at least as great as they did previously. That would be tragic enough: huge efforts by large numbers of people and equally immense expenditures of resources will have gone for nought. More tragic is the systemic consequence: all the other short-term issues noted above relate to state-to-state national security-related differences. The nations in question justify their arms acquisitions on the need to prepare for resolving their security problems, by force if necessary. That means the strong likelihood that the incipient Asian arms race will take on a momentum of its own; what theorists term a

"Richardson process" will take hold. The unavoidable outcome will be the emergence of an alliance-versus-alliance, balance-of-power system. And the inevitable end of most every balance-of-power system is war. If so, the sole remaining question is, What can be done to stop this murderous process before it takes on too much momentum?

The answer is easy in theory and almost impossible in practice. If the security issues in question were addressed directly and solved in reasonable time and without conflict, the arms race could be stopped in its tracks or at least greatly slowed. But that would take a combination of enormous sacrifices on the part of practically every Asian nation, an unprecedented degree of statesmanship and understanding, and the enlightened leadership of the one nation, the United States, that could—through example and diplomacy—indicate the way ahead. Just to list these conditions shows how improbable the avoidance of a war-creating arms race is. That does not mean, however, that the effort should not be made. And the burden falls directly on the United States, not only as the most powerful participant but also as the one nation that can exercise acceptable leadership. Equally important, Washington has not yet committed itself to that leadership, so the way is open for it to do so. And it is not too late.

The Clinton administration professes to remain fully involved in Asian security affairs and seems to understand, albeit in a still nascent manner, that new initiatives are required. But this means, to use a basketball analogy, a "full court press," that is, strong measures, taken now, in several arenas:

- *Dispute settlement.* The North Korean nuclear question, the Northern Islands issue, and Kashmir are the obvious candidates.
- *Bold new arms control initiatives.* American and Russian nuclear drawdowns of missiles and bombers in northeast Asia, full compliance with the MTCR in south Asia by all parties, and a new American-Chinese arms agreement regarding Taiwan are examples.
- *American-led talks.* These talks would address subregional Asian security arrangements, a more formal trans-Pacific security institution, and new plans for eventual creation of higher-order security structures that would include all relevant states.

It is idealistic to think that if only the Americans would come to their senses, knock a few heads together, and come forth with the realistic and moralistic syntheses for which they are justly famous, the Asian security millenium would come. But without U.S. leadership, there will be no way to avoid eventual war. And, given the burgeoning strength of Asia as a whole, America risks being dealt out of whatever system does emerge and then having to fight conflicts there on terms it had no hand in arranging.

The Future Asian Security System

The short-term issues just cataloged lead to the conclusion that what is or is not done now will strongly condition longer-term outcomes. But other matters will also influence a new Asian security system. These, too, can be divided into subregional and regionwide matters.

Subregional Issues. Subregional security issues are five, the first being the Northern Islands question.[13]

The Northern Islands. This matter has been an important element in Japanese–Soviet (Russian) relations since 1945. In 1954, Moscow first hinted at the return of at least some of them, and in 1991, Russian Premier Boris Yeltsin stated the Kremlin's desire to reopen the case. In the absence of the August 1991 events in Red Square, it would probably have been solved within a few years. But Russian popular opinion, an important factor for the first time, complicates negotiations. Nonetheless, the way is open—and has always been open—to compromise. And now that the Russian need for the largest two islands for protection of the Sea of Okhotsk and Russian missile submarines and bases is lessened and the need for Japanese economic assistance and international support has been accepted in Tokyo as well as in Moscow, the way ought to be open for settlement. Japan insists on return of all four islands, with no possibility of compromise. But because serious negotiations have not as yet taken place, that proposition is untested. Moreover, the Japanese legal case, while strong, is not airtight. Finally, the Japanese Foreign Ministry knows that a historic opportunity is at hand to turn a long-term relationship of enmity into mutual advantage if not full-blown friendship. It is thus a question of specific terms and of how to arrive at an agreed-upon end. The terms involve which islands and how much money. The obvious bottom line regarding territory is the return of three of the four islands to Japan, with Russian retention of the largest, Iturup. The negotiating process needs some lubrication, however, which is where the Americans might possibly come in. The United States, now being a "friend" of both Japan and Russia, with high stakes in a successful outcome of the negotiations, and *persona grata* to both Tokyo and Moscow, could well engage in a mediation process.

There is, after all, a precedent in the Japanese-Russian Treaty of 1905 as well as in the Camp David process. The way seems open to an American-sponsored solution. Indeed, it is surprising that Washington has not already taken such an initiative. But whether or not America becomes formally involved, the way is open to settlement, if not now, then within a few years.

North Korean succession and Korean reunification. The second issue is the process and outcome of the North Korean succession and Korean reunification.[14] While one cannot speak of known facts about something that has not yet taken place, some things are probable. First, there is no guarantee that the succession in North Korea will be smooth. Indeed, some kind of struggle in Pyongyang once Kim Il Sung is gone is likely. His son, Kim Jong Il, is not destined to succeed him, at least for long. His personal characteristics, the accumulated popular resentments against the Kim dynasty by many people hurt by the regime, the absence of the authority and charisma of the father, and the fact that no Communist ruler has yet been able to arrange a succession all favor removal of Kim Jong Il from power. That will undoubtedly engender a struggle among other contenders, probably military factions, termed the royalists and the revisionists. Given the lack of institutionalization of authority in the north, plus the well-known Korean cultural tendency to see things in black and white and to fight first and compromise if forced to only later, violence seems inevitable. This conflict could very well spill over into a north-south fight. While a new Korean war would be a disaster for both parts of Korea, the eventual outcome is a given: victory of the south—supported by the United States and perhaps others—and reunification on southern terms, that is, by conquest. The other path to reunification is by means of economic collapse of the north and emergence of a new, liberal leadership willing to negotiate reunification as the trade-off for saving the North Korean people from starvation and the successor regime from being overthrown like the East German government. That scenario would not entail a new war, at least, but it would be messy and highly risky for all.

Once Kim Il Sung is gone, the days of the northern kingdom will be short, and a reunited Korea will emerge, either from the rubble of war or from the smoke-filled negotiating room. A country with 5,000 years of recorded history, culturally the most highly integrated people on the face of the earth, and surely one of the most proud and nationalistic, cannot be kept apart for much longer, especially when the cold war reasons for their artificial separation are no longer in place. Of course, if one wishes to avoid the prospect of conflict, the best way is to address the North Korean problem immediately: force the nuclear weapons question and solve it, open the north to rapid and full-scale economic development and interdependence, and transform the society and the polity so that, when the succession crisis comes, the struggle will not be between two sides, each of which has everything to lose, but between a multiplicity of forces, many of which will want internal, peninsular, and international peace.

Taiwan. Taiwan will, in all probability, become a major security issue sometime in the 1990s, more likely in the last few years of the decade than in the next several.[15] The reasons why the matter is likely to come to a head but not before about 1997 are several. First, since 1992 with the populace in control of their government, political trends on the island favor the gradual emergence of forces for Taiwanese independence. It appears only a matter of time until the Democratic Progressive party comes to power. Seeing that, the mainland is not likely to sit idly by until the island is on the verge of a declaration of independence. It could convince itself it had no choice but to move militarily (presuming the Americans are, in Beijing's estimate, unlikely or unwilling to defend Taipei by force), even though the cost, in martial and diplomatic terms, would be very high. Second, despite the military modernization program now under way in Taiwan, mainland Chinese military modernization will eventually far outdistance the island's. Qualitative superiority may remain in Taipei's hands, but against the numbers that Beijing could bring to bear, even a highly superior but much smaller force would soon be overcome. And Beijing too is moving ahead rapidly in the qualitative sense. Third, it is not clear that, if called on *in extremis* by Taiwan, the United States would be able to respond effectively. Although America has an additional interest in Taiwan's autonomy stemming from the emergence of democracy there and the U.S. interest in Taiwan's role in the global economy has been strengthened, the United States may be reluctant to get into a direct conflict with a strong China. Of equal importance, Washington has tacitly amended its military strategy with the proposition: Do not enter conflicts unless you expect to win quickly and with comparatively little bloodshed. A new Taiwan crisis, given this and the expected continued retreat of American military power from Asia during the 1990s, might therefore be expected to favor the mainland and not the island.

Much will depend, of course, on the status of American-Chinese relations at the time of crisis. If the two nations will, in the meantime, join to solve outstanding differences, if Washington will deliberately seek a security partnership with Beijing, or if the growth in Chinese military power is not as rapid as projected, a peaceful outcome might eventuate. But if, in contrast, as is likelier, Washington and Beijing find more issues on which to differ, grow ever-more suspicious of each other, and begin to plan and configure their forces taking the other as putative enemy, Taiwan could become an early test case of what will be termed Chinese expansionism and of the American drive to organize the region against the mainland. Obviously, it would be better if Washington and Beijing try to work together concerning Taiwan. Indeed, it is no longer practical for the United States to aver that Taiwan-mainland relations are for the two Chinese parties to work out between themselves, so long as the process and the result are peaceful. Perhaps it would be better to use the period before 1997, when Hong Kong reverts to mainland rule and when Beijing will be on reasonably good behavior toward Taipei—presuming no declaration of independence, or incipient declaration of independence, in the meanwhile—to address the issue directly. That suggestion does not imply American negotiations with Beijing on Taiwan's future behind Taipei's back, but it does mean encouragement of Beijing-Taipei talks as begun in early 1993 in Singapore, three-sided talks on admitting both Chinese parties to the General Agreement on Tariffs and Trade (GATT), and discouraging Taipei from thinking that its policy of seeking readmission to international organizations will take it all the way back to the United Nations. Moreover, the Pentagon should take into consideration, when figuring out the staging and levels of Asian-deployed and -configured force reductions, the possible need to support the defense of Taiwan directly, how to do so within the cultural requisites of American military policy, and what kinds of actions, budgetary outlays, deployments, and training ought to be taken.

Burma. The fourth eventual subregional security concern is Burma.[16] For most of the post–World War II period, Burma has been of little interest to anyone. But with the Rangoon repression of 1988, the end of the cold war, the drive almost everywhere else toward democracy, the refusal of the Burmese military authorities to recognize the election of 1990, and the rise of a serious armed opposition in many parts of the country, Burma is emerging, if still slowly, as a security issue.

The problems are several. First, the internal situation of the country is very tentative, and the concerns of the international community are increasing. The government rules only through force, its nonmilitary domestic support is almost nil, Burma is the source of much of the world's heroin, an ecological disaster is in the making from the cutting and selling abroad of the country's forests, and the regime is propped up, militarily, by Chinese arms transfers. Second, Burma could implode. Given the many ethnic groups and tribes in that nation and the desperation of the Rangoon government, the possibility of civil war and "ethnic cleansing" is increasing. Third, although Burma has not been a security concern of its neighbors (indeed, a kind of unwritten Chinese-Indian agreement not to intervene in Burma has been in existence for decades), that period may soon come to an end. If China or India were to intervene for its own security reasons, the other might feel compelled to do the same. Competitive intervention spells international conflict.

Thailand also has important economic and security interests in Burma that could lead it to take a more direct role in internal Burmese developments. And if there were another slaughter of Burmese citizens in the streets of Rangoon or if Nobel Prize winner Aung San Suu Kyi or others of her entourage were to be further harmed, American democratic and human rights sensitivities might become fully engaged. Finally, the impending establishment of the Burmese section of the American-sponsored Radio Free Asia could, in its attempt to convey the message of freedom and hope to the Burmese people, tip a very precarious situation into violent internal conflict.

What needs to be done? For one, the external powers can no longer ignore the Burmese situation. It would be best if they consulted about it. Second, steps should be taken to shear away international support for the military government by stopping the flow of Chinese military supplies and mounting a major, cooperative international effort to stem the stream of heroin into and through China and Thailand and on to Europe and North America. Third, official contact should be initiated with the formally established opposition Burmese government in exile and decisions made whether to supply it with military and other forms of assistance. Care must be taken, however, not to precipitate the downfall of the military regime prematurely, leaving nothing but chaos in its wake. Engagement must be the watchword regarding Burma, lest Asia find itself host to a regional Bosnia, or India and China find themselves in an unwanted and unexpected confrontation over a country where neither has any major interest.

Kashmir. The last subregional security issue is the Kashmir question[17] and the related India-Pakistan nuclear arms question.[18] Under present circumstances, there appears no way to resolve the Kashmir problem to the satisfaction of all concerned. The sides are irreconcilable: India will not allow Pakistan to take back what Pakistan considers its own nor does Pakistan have the power to alter the situation unilaterally. It is an emerging security issue for two reasons. First, domestic events in the two countries may change so that India can no longer hold its portion of Kashmir, Pakistan may believe it must bring the matter to a head no matter what, or India may believe it is able to take advantage of Pakistan and extend its rule over the whole region. But despite its democratic government and its large and marketizing economy, India is none too stable. The long British-induced domestic peace in the country may be challenged, if not soon ended. If so, India may find itself weak enough to tempt Pakistan to move. The same can be said of the internal Pakistan situation and India's desire to put an end to the Kashmir problem through conquest. Second, both nations possess nuclear weapons, and confrontation over Kashmir could take on nuclear dimensions. It apparently did so once before, in 1988, and could well do so again. If either New Delhi or Islamabad experienced great internal pressure, the possibility of nuclear conflict could rise rapidly.

What, if anything, can be done about the matter? Failing peaceful solution by the two nations, the best that can be hoped for is encouragement of several departures. First, a viable nonnuclear balance of military power needs to be maintained between India and Pakistan. This should normally mean international support of Pakistan as the weaker party. But in the context of an uncertain domestic situation in both countries, perhaps India should be supported as well. At a minimum, responding to the Indian economic opening with foreign investment and to Pakistani good behavior in the nuclear realm with limited arms sales and transfers is called for. It is impossible, however, to cut into the problem of Indian and Pakistani tensions without addressing most other issues of the subcontinent and even the regionwide question of China's security relations with other Asian states. But if America, China, and the Soviet Union joined in 1988 to help stop escalation to the nuclear level of the Kashmir scare, perhaps the three can work together again, on a more permanent basis, for assurances against renewed confrontation and escalation.

Regional Issues. Finally, we consider regionwide Asian security questions for the medium term. Perhaps the most important of these is the forms that a non–balance-of-power post–cold war Asian security system might take.[19]

Form of a security system. Some initial propositions are in order.

First, any such system, both by definition and for workability, must include all the major powers—America, China, Japan, Russia, and probably India as well. Second, a system cannot spring into being without extended and difficult negotiations among these four or five and without prior solution of most of the bilateral issues now dividing them. Third, a new regionwide system can probably coexist with subregional systems or arrangements of the kinds under preliminary discussion in the early 1990s. In fact, the creation of a general Asian security system, and the international institutional apparatus that would go along with it, would likely follow from subregional arrangements. Fourth, the new arrangement would have to supersede existing alliances, guarantees, and agreements. But these existing arrangements would be phased out only gradually, so that there would not be a gap between the present cold war leftover orientations and the new system. Fifth, the effort to avoid a new regionwide balance-of-power system would have to be based, paradoxically, on establishment or maintenance of a series of subregional local balances of power. Sixth, if the major powers all agreed to sponsor the new arrangement, most of the other powers should be asked to join; that is, the system should be all-inclusive.

If these propositions were to bear a reasonable relationship to what actually emerged, the result would probably be close to a collective security system. For success, it could not be directed against any of its Asian or trans-Pacific members. It could, in theory, be a NATO-like alliance, with definite geographic boundaries and operational only within those boundaries. But if it were all-inclusive, it would be much like the Rio Pact (the collective security treaty of the Western Hemisphere). Probably some combination of NATO and the Rio Pact would be best: a regional collective security organization with a strong institutional structure. It would not necessarily include all NATO's apparatus—a council, a secretariat, and the like—nor would it necessarily train, equip, maintain, or deploy forces under its flag. Perhaps a closer analogy would be a regional rapid deployment force with national units earmarked for use under a relatively loose command structure and mobilizable only in agreed-on time of need. Not only would national forces therefore remain in being, but those of the major powers would all be stronger than that force under the alliance's flag. Defined in this way, the new system would have some collective security characteristics, some collective defense characteristics, and some that stemmed from continued maintenance of national forces.

One evidently necessary condition for success would be the relative military equality, at least in Asia, of all the major powers. If so, Japan would be allowed to rearm rather strongly and rapidly, so long as that process took place in accordance with the initial agreement, that is, with the permission and participation of America, China, and Russia. The system would have to be linked with the UN system as a regional defense arrangement under Article 51 of the charter. Institutions brought into being by the initial agreement would surely have to balance their power and staffing between the demands of each of the major powers for equality with each other and the needs of the middle and minor powers for guarantees of their security.

Much more could be said about such a regime, but perhaps this description indicates the range of possibilities. It should be emphasized that if this set of arrangements is to emerge eventually and a balance-of-power system thereby to be avoided, work will have to begin very soon, before the current vague ideas about common, cooperative, and comprehensive security become focused. It would also not do to wait for resolution of all the short- and medium-term Asian security issues discussed here. Their solution may, and probably will, require the simultaneous bringing into being of many of the characteristics of the new system. International security systems rise, and exhibit characteristics, out of the necessity of the times. The Washington Naval Disarmament Treaty system of 1921 was a response to the needs of its time, the "spokes and hubs" alliances put together by the United States were an adjunct of the cold war, and the orientations of the members of the Strategic Triangle (the United States, the Soviet Union, and the People's Republic of China) were a response to the demands in Asia of the nuclear age.

So it will also be in this case. But in all instances, an essential ingredient is leadership, usually by one nation, led by people of vision, acting in response to a clearly perceived need, and securing the initial consent of at least most of the other participants. These ingredients are present in the Asia of the early 1990s, in the interval of relative calm after the end of the cold war and before the emergence of something new. That something will surely come. It is only a question of time and, largely, of initiative. If initiative is lacking, then Asia is in great danger of being forced back into another replay of the balance of power. And although it is surely possible for a balance to keep the peace for a time, in the end it would have to break down into conflict. And the region cannot risk, again, any new major conflict; the destruction would be too great and the damage to the encouraging economic and political progress of the 1970s–1990s would be unacceptable. There is therefore little choice but to begin building a new regional security institution now.

Security and Economics. The second regionwide security issue for the long term is the relation between security and economics.[20] There are many facets to this important but still poorly understood question. The matter has existed from the beginning of the modern era, of course, but only in recent years has it become an explicit part of policy. Among many relevant topics are structural similarities between the two fields, the relation between economic and military power, the link between national security and economic policies, the reciprocal influences of economic development and military modernization, and the mediating role of technology between economic development and military strategy.

Structural similarities. Security and economics share structural characteristics. Each has explicit assumptions, principal elements, goals, units of analysis, and empirically based ideas and propositions. Economics holds that the relative scarcity of the basic elements of land, labor, capital, and technology orders human economic activity, usually through production, prices, and a supply-demand market equilibrating mechanism. The economy is the totality of such activity at various levels of production and consumption for purposes of survival, profit, growth, and conservation. Government is an intervening variable, either adjusting market inequities and setting general economic goals or substituting itself for the market and administering the economy directly.

National security affairs stem from the scarcity of security and the human desire to maximize physical safety. The principal elements of national security are intellectual (tactics and strategy), material (equipment and environment), and human (organization, morale, and command), and they relate to each other at various levels, from the individual soldier through ever-larger and more complex units to a nation's total military force. The goal is victory through war, deterrence of war, or appeasement of a more powerful enemy, achieved through some combination of plans, equipment, training, and field operations. All governments use the military instrument—some, like democracies, less and others, like authoritarian or totalitarian polities, more. Economics and national security are united through competition of buyer and seller through the market or opposing military units through war. The two fields intellectually part company in game theory terms: economics is a cooperative, non–zero-sum game to establish a compromise, while military affairs are noncooperative, a zero-sum activity fought literally to the death.

These ideas find ample illustration in Asia, as witness the different approaches to trade and military strategies of the democratic polity par excellence, Japan, and its totalitarian opposite, North Korea. Japan stresses capital and technology, orders its economy through the market mechanism, looks to private property and trade to achieve high individual standards of living and rapid growth, trusts to others (for example, the United States) critical elements of its national security, deliberately deemphasizes military activity and organization, and thinks not of victory through war but of avoiding war through deterrence or economic appeasement. So long as Japan can thus substitute economic activity for military prowess, it can prosper. Conversely, if, as is becoming increasingly so in the 1990s, the security and economic assumptions underpinning that activity are called into question, Japan will have to reorder its economic priorities, provide itself with a viable military policy and a corresponding military force, and possibly even have to change many of the details, if not the very nature, of its polity.

North Korea is completely different. It emphasizes labor as the source of all value, disallows any market-oriented activity, forbids any holding or use of private property, is as completely autarkic as can be imagined, depends for its security on its own efforts alone, fields a very large military equipped almost entirely with domestically produced weaponry, seeks its security through threatening conquest of its opponent, and totally subordinates its domestic economy to the demands of military strategy. Such a regime brought North Korea much of what it wanted, until the 1990s began to show that such priorities could not provide further security and that the associated economic, political, and diplomatic costs threatened the entire political and security edifice. Pyongyang will have to change in the direction of marketization, interdependence, and economic opening as well as decrease the size of its military, pull back from its threatening military posture, change its military strategy from victory to deterrence, and depend for security more on compromise and positive participation in regional military affairs. Failing these changes, either civil war or revolution is likely in North Korea, probably associated with the Kim Il Sung succession. No such outcome is possible in Japan, although major political changes in that country are surely likely.

Economic and military power. Economic and security affairs interpenetrate through power.[21] Power, whether measured by gross national product or destructive potential, is the universal solvent, converting inputs in one field into the output of the other, either by coercion or through cooperation. By coercion, for example, Japan converted its economic power in the 1930s into military power so successfully that it was able to conquer all the rest of Asia, particularly China, which lacked the economic base to compete militarily with Japan. Through cooperation, the United States after World War II elected to restore Japanese economic power but took care to disallow its conversion once again into military capability. Thereby, both gained—Japan economically and the United States militarily. That points up another aspect of power: economic and security goods can be exchanged to enhance mutual well-being. The history of the American-Japanese Security Treaty, for instance, is the history of the changing economic and security balance between the two countries. When, in the 1990s, the Japanese economy grew so large that it competes in size and dynamism with that of the United States, the security component of the relationship has to be changed accordingly. Economic and security trade-offs will no longer suffice, since, for equality in the relationship, Japan will have to play a larger security role and the Security Treaty will have to be revised to reflect such changes or be supplemented by new agreements.

Similar changes may be in store for American relations with South Korea, Taiwan, Thailand, and the Philippines. All of these have prospered economically under the American security umbrella for four decades, while the United States gained major security benefits during the cold war. But with the end of that conflict and the economic maturity of at least South Korea, Taiwan, and Thailand, the time has come to renegotiate both security and economic relations. Economic relations have been changing for some years, since such ties are easily changed by their very nature, but security relations will also have to be modified. The result, if the two transitions are successful, ought to be a stronger relationship of economic and security interdependence and equality. But that is easier said than done. The future is fraught with pitfalls, not the least of which is that both decision makers and analysts are unsure of the reciprocal nature of the security and economic trade-off, to say nothing of what the details of the changes ought to be when both aspects are in rapid and simultaneous transition. But throughout this process, economic power and military power will increasingly be seen as exchangeable qualities.

The relationship between economic and military power is seen through two further ties. One is the economic effects of military budgets. It appears that, so long as war has not actually broken out, military budgets of less than about 6 percent of GNP are economically tolerable, even beneficial, because of their stimulative industry-creating and technological effects. Beyond that point, however, military budgets become a drag on the economy. The beneficial effects are

411

illustrated in the cases of Japan and South Korea and the negative effects in the instances of North Korea and, during the 1960s and 1970s, of Vietnam. China supplies an interesting case: during the 1960s and early 1970s, its military budget was high and its economic growth correspondingly low, whereas, in the era of economic reform after 1978, the military budget was lowered, growth rates rose, and the country could afford higher military budgets in absolute terms.

The second illustration of the relationship between economic and military power is the mediating factor of the economic cycle. During a downturn, an economic stimulus can be supplied by increased military spending and thus mitigate negative economic effects, so long as the stimulus is not too pronounced. During an economic upswing, care must be taken not to spend too much on the military, lest the economy be overstimulated, inflation set in, and a downturn become inevitable. America and the Soviet Union during the cold war supply examples of both dangers, while Japan, with a comparatively small military budget in percentage terms, could not use a budgetary stimulus through military outlays. Interestingly, with generally high growth during the early 1990s in Asia, few if any regional states stand in such dangers. The significant exception is, once again, North Korea.

National security and economic policies. A further general approach to how economics and security are related is by inspecting economic and national security policies.[22] Generally, security policies tend to come first in national priority. This is obviously the case in wartime, when more than 50 percent of GNP goes to the military effort. But it is also seen in the case of arms races. These are of two kinds: deliberate and inadvertent. One nation might consciously attempt to bankrupt the economy of a rival by a military spending race. That is a dangerous game, since both may lose. But in the case of the United States versus the Soviet Union, the long-term result was the economic collapse of the Soviet Union after it attempted, for more than three decades, to compete with the United States and dedicated its perpetually smaller economy mostly to military production. (The economic effects on the United States were also pronounced, of course, and America will have to spend a portion of the 1990s restructuring its economy.)

The Asian regional examples are two: South and North Korea, and India and Pakistan. In both instances, the larger economies—South Korea and India—forced so much military spending on their opponents that they endangered the basic economic stability of their rivals. The danger of economic collapse is therefore acute in the case of North Korea, perhaps less so (because of the mitigating effects of foreign military assistance from the United States and China) for Pakistan. In nondeliberately induced arms races, all lose, since no more military security is obtained even though military budgets constantly rise. Asia in the 1990s has not yet entered into such a situation, although if military budgets continue to rise, that danger may appear.

The test, when national security policy is made to be more important than economic policy, is whether security is maximized through minimum outlays. That is very difficult to achieve. Once again, the North Korean instance is a case in point. For four decades, it has attempted to subordinate its economic policy to military goals through the so-called *ju-che* policy of deliberate economic self-isolation. The consequence has been economic disaster in the north. Although the obvious remedy is to open the economy to international influences, to do so would be to destroy the Pyongyang regime as now constituted. In very few instances does economic policy prevail over national security goals. Only when security is ensured can nations afford the luxury of economic goals. Postwar Japan is the only Asian instance of the priority of economics over security. If and when the umbrella of American security is removed, Japan will have to increase its military outlays drastically, thereby ceasing to be the only exception to the rule.

Economic development and military modernization. A fourth general relationship between economics and security is through the time factor, that is, how economic development relates to military modernization.[23] There are two categories of analysis. The first is the path nations adopt to foster economic growth. Generally, in later stages of economic modernization, export-led growth leads to faster growth and, hence, to stronger economies, higher possible military outlays, and greater security. South Korea, Japan, and Taiwan are obvious examples, as is China after 1978. If import substitution is the chosen path, a country can do well fostering economic growth at early stages; indeed, it can often do better than export-led economies as long as the level of technology is not high. But eventually the lack of inventiveness of such economies, together with the impossibility of producing all necessary goods within national boundaries, dooms such economies to fall increasingly behind. That is the case with North Korea and was the case with China, until it was forced to switch economic strategies in 1978. It also appears to be the case in India, which in the early 1990s was forced to admit that import substitution had failed and began to open its economy, with good results. The way a nation chooses to develop economically thus has important implications for national security.

The second characteristic of the time factor concerns the security implications of imbalances in growth rates. If one nation grows significantly faster than others or begins its modernization drive significantly earlier than others, the result is almost always imperialism and war, or at least dependence on another nation for security. Japan after 1868, *vis-à-vis* China, is a good example of the security consequences of higher differentiated growth rates. Japan simply outran China and, finally, subdued it, for all intents and purposes, through conquest. Burma, which has not modernized at all, now places its security fate in the hands of its neighbors. Thailand entered economic modernization late and had to become a security ward first of America and then of America and China. Only when it achieved export-led high growth rates could it breathe somewhat easier. India has grown slowly in comparison with China: hence, the menace New Delhi feels from Beijing.

The converse of imperialism or security threat is security guarantee. If one nation is much larger than another economically, the consequence can be security guarantorship. The United States extended such guarantorship over a number of weaker Asian nations at crucial security junctures for the Asian countries: South Korea, Thailand, and Pakistan are examples. The Soviet Union did the same: North Korea and North Vietnam are examples as, during the 1950s, was China. Security guarantorships last only as long as they are needed, and they are not needed once the rate of economic development picks up in the states guaranteed. To the extent, then, that rates of growth in Asian countries remain high, the need for American security guarantorship will decline, and with it the need for security treaties.

Technology, economics, and military strategy. A final aspect of the security-economic nexus is the complex triple relationship among technology, economic development, and military strategy.[24] Surprisingly little thought has been given to the mediating role of technology between development and strategy. There is evidence, in some instances, that technology leads strategy, in other instances that strategy determines technology, and in still others that strategy and technology are independent. One important issue for economic development is whether it is useful to be a modernization latecomer. If the rate of change of technology is exponential (which in some cases, such as jet engine technology, seems to be the case) and if military technology strongly influences military strategy, the modernization latecomer can never catch up with the technological and military leaders. During the cold war, that was, with good reason, thought to be the case between the two superpowers and the many smaller states in Asia, even China. But if the rate of technological change is logistical, then not only is there an "advantage" in being a latecomer but it will be increasingly easy for latecomers to catch up with the technological and military leaders. Pakistan can more easily provide itself with nuclear weapons in the 1990s to defend itself against India than India could in the 1970s against China. Moreover, the influence of high technology on military strategy appears to be dual. Since acquisition of high technology is easier for export-led latecomers, their rates of growth will be higher than otherwise, and their security threats the more easily addressed.

Such differences imply the use of different military strategies for different nations at various stages of technology-induced economic modernization. China had to adopt delaying tactics and guerrilla warfare against Japan in the 1930s but could emphasize combined arms force projection in the 1990s *vis-à-vis* its Asian neighbors. In general, military strategies useful at one level of technology, and hence of economic modernization, are not necessarily of equal utility at another. Nations must be quick to understand when to discard one strategy and adopt another, lest their security be threatened. China did poorly against Vietnam in 1979 because, among other things, its military leaders thought they could use the same kind of strategy they had, with reasonable success, used against the UN forces in Korea some thirty years before. But technology had changed, and China, attempting to "punish" Vietnam, found itself suffering enormous losses instead. The principle seems to be that military strategies must be economically efficient and also appropriate to the technological level of the country in question. Strategy must be matched to the kind of economic development model most suited to the country, and hence to the level of technology possible. Rapid economic development and technological changes in the Asia of the 1990s demand corresponding changes in military strategy.

Conclusion

All the topics discussed here—the general trends and forces, the short- and medium-term subregional issues, and the regionwide implications for security and economics—carry direct implications for the Chinese and their future. General trends and forces will tend to pull the three components of Greater China together, both in their relations with each other and in their domestic developments. In contrast, the two short-term subregional concerns—the North Korean nuclear issue and the Spratly Islands question—would seem, on balance, not to affect greatly inter-Chinese relations or domestic changes in mainland China, Hong Kong, or Taiwan. Nor will the larger number of medium- to longer-term security issues overly influence the three Chinese futures, at least while there is a concerted attempt to prevent any of them from breaking down into domestic violence and to diminish the threat of cross-border conflict or war itself—particularly regarding the Taiwan question. As of the early 1990s, such a breakdown seems unlikely.

If the domestic peace holds, the influence on the three Chinese entities of international developments depends on how the four major regional powers choose to revamp their security policies, whether as a group they will cooperate in striving to create a higher-order regional security system, and what kinds of relations between economics and security evolve during the twentieth century's last decade. Answers cannot be advanced with any reasonable degree of confidence, however: the range of possibilities is too great. Nonetheless, the most important variables are the degree of success the Americans and the Chinese in Beijing achieve in working out their problems and whether the many economic and security links and concomitant challenges can be addressed successfully by the relevant Asian nations. The probabilities of success may be higher here, merely because economic issues are more easily compromised than strictly security questions. It is the general security future of Asia that is so worrisome: history tells us that security crises are usually handled poorly by the major powers in question. Moreover, with no agreed-on system to help absorb the shock of the many impending changes in the power relations among America, China, Japan, and Russia—and with so many new middle powers rising to prominence nearly simultaneously—the probability that a higher-order security system will be created is relatively small. If so, the powers may, however unwisely, sink back into a balance-of-power system, with all the frightful consequences that that would eventually convey.

In that regard, much again depends on how the Chinese in Beijing relate to their international environment and to the other two Chinese entities discussed in this volume. If they elect to be participatory, interdependent, and internationally minded, Asia's future and the Chinese futures all have a reasonable chance of evolving in a relatively peaceful and constructive manner. If, however, Beijing takes a highly nationalistic, zero-sum, and pugnacious attitude, the futures will be problematic. In the past, this would have been more likely. With all the recent modernizing and transforming international forces bearing so directly on mainland China, however, the probability of a peaceful future is stronger.

17
Changing China-Taiwan Relations
Guocang Huan

In September 1991, the Democratic Progressive party (DPP), Taiwan's leading opposition party, passed a resolution to include the demand for Taiwan's independence in its party constitution. The DPP strategists believed that this move would increase the party's popularity and help it to gain more votes in the general election of the National Assembly in December of that year.

In the election, however, the DPP obtained only 23.9 percent of the total votes, much less than its 27.3 percent of the legislative election two years earlier. Meanwhile, the ruling Nationalist party (Kuomintang, or KMT) received 71.2 percent of the total votes; as a result, it now has 318 seats in the National Assembly, more than 75 percent of the total seats needed to revise the Taiwanese constitution in its favor. While observers are still debating how to interpret the election results, many have agreed that the DPP demand for independence alienated the middle class and business community, which has rapidly expanded its commercial operations across the Taiwan Strait during the past several years.[1]

In fact, relations between Beijing and Taipei have undergone some major changes since the fall of 1989. Before then, commercial ties between the two sides of the Taiwan Strait had already expanded. Nevertheless, under its three-nos policy (no contacts, no negotiation, and no compromises with Beijing), the KMT government officially banned any direct trade and investment between the two sides. It allowed only its citizens who were not government employees to visit the mainland. No Chinese citizens were permitted to visit Taiwan. The two governments had no direct contacts. Officially, Taiwan was still at war with China. In May 1990, Taipei ended its formal state of war with Beijing.[2] In December 1991, Beijing announced that the goal of relations between the two sides of the Taiwan Strait before the end

The author wishes to thank the Center of International Studies, Princeton University, and the Pacific Cultural Foundation for support for this study.

of the twentieth century should be "reduction of tensions and expansion of economic cooperation and cultural exchanges," rather than reunification.[3]

After establishing the official National Council for Reunification, chaired by President Lee Teng-hui, to promote reunification with the mainland, in March 1991 the Taiwanese government published the "Guidelines to the Country's Reunification," setting three steps toward the reunification of China and calling for further expansion of ties between the two sides.[4] Nevertheless, the government has made it clear that the precondition for reunification is the democratization of the single-party political system on the mainland and that negotiations must proceed with the two governments on an equal basis.[5]

The two sides have developed direct semiofficial dialogue. Since spring 1991, top officials of the Taiwan Red Cross and Foundation for Exchange between the Two Sides of the Taiwan Strait visited China several times and met senior Chinese officials in charge of Taiwan affairs. In August 1991, two senior Chinese Red Cross officials visited seven Chinese sailors who were held in Taiwan on the charge of attacking a Taiwanese ship; this was the first visit of Chinese officials to Taiwan since 1990.[6] In 1990, to negotiate the procedure of deporting illegal Chinese immigrants to Taiwan, two Chinese officials visited Quemoy. The two sides have also expanded their negotiations on many functional policy issues such as the deportation of China's illegal immigrants to Taiwan and cooperation against crimes and sea pirates in the Taiwan Strait.[7]

Under strong pressure from the business community, Taipei has further loosened its restrictions on business activities between the two sides, and it may soon allow direct commercial flight and shipping across the Taiwan Strait. It has allowed Chinese journalists to visit Taiwan, extended the length of visits for Chinese, and begun to allow actors, actresses, and artists to perform and to hold exhibitions in Taiwan.[8] Restrictions against government employees visiting the mainland were also lifted.

Beijing has continued to put political pressure on Taipei, demanding direct dialogue between the two ruling parties, the Chinese Communist party and the Kuomintang. The People's Republic of China has nevertheless rejected Taipei's proposal of negotiations between the two governments.[9] In July 1991, Beijing announced the ten points of its policy toward Taipei, among which it insisted on "no commitment to not use force."[10] Beijing has reacted favorably to Taiwan's recent election. With the exception of military exercises, however, Beijing has not increased its direct military pressure on Taipei. Rather, it has stated that Beijing does not oppose Taipei's purchasing weapons for defense purposes. The Taiwan Strait has remained peaceful.

In the international community, the competition between the two sides has heightened. Having established and restored diplomatic relations with Saudi Arabia, Singapore, Indonesia, and Brunei, Beijing reached an agreement with Seoul that both countries would upgrade the trade office in each other's capital to a trade mission with full diplomatic functions. The PRC established diplomatic ties with Seoul in 1992, which further isolated Taipei. Beijing has continued its efforts to delay Taipei's application for joining the General Agreement on Tariffs and Trade and other governmental international organizations. In November 1991, however, the Asian Pacific Economic Council, an organization involving mainly governments around the Pacific, accepted all "three Chinas" (Beijing, Taipei, and Hong Kong) as formal members.[11]

Meanwhile, under the new policy of flexible diplomacy, a policy designed to increase Taipei's international participation and de facto relations with other countries, Taipei has continued its efforts to expand foreign relations. It has set up a new International Development Fund, providing economic aid to East European countries, former Soviet republics, and developing nations and aiming to develop semiofficial or even official relations with them. In January 1992, Latvia, which has full diplomatic ties with Beijing, decided to establish consulate relations with Taipei: the first time a country had "official" diplomatic relations with both sides of the Taiwan Strait.[12] Beijing protested by not sending its ambassador to Riga but nevertheless decided not to cut off diplomatic ties with Latvia.

Three related factors will determine the dynamics of China-Taiwan relations in the next few years: internal development in both China and Taiwan, their policies toward one another, and the dynamics of the international environment. This chapter examines each of these factors and then discusses the possible developments of China-Taiwan relations in the next few years.

A Changing China and Its Policies

Over the past ten years, Beijing's Taiwan policy has undergone some major changes. In 1979, the Chinese government announced the shift in its policy toward Taiwan from the "liberation of Taiwan" to "a peaceful reunification with Taiwan." Since then, Beijing has made strong efforts to reduce tensions and to increase contacts with Taipei. It stopped political propaganda against the KMT government and significantly reduced the number of troops deployed along the southeast coast. At the same time, Beijing began to rehabilitate former KMT officials who had been purged during the first three decades since the founding of the PRC in 1949.[13] Nevertheless, in the international community, Beijing continued to compete against Taipei for diplomatic recognition.

In September 1984, Beijing signed an agreement with London on Hong Kong's return to China in 1997 under the format of "one country, two systems." Deng Xiaoping immediately began to use the same model to apply to China-Taiwan relations. Since then, Beijing has increased its efforts to approach Taipei about reunification. Chinese leaders have frequently issued statements and sent letters to senior leaders in Taipei, demanding the opening of dialogues and negotiations between the two sides. The PRC has begun to provide business opportunities to Taiwanese companies and to encourage Taiwanese citizens to visit their families on the mainland. In the international community, while continuing its competition against Taipei under the principle of one China, Beijing has become more flexible about coexisting with Taipei in more than six hundred nongovernmental organizations. Chinese diplomats have taken more initiatives to approach their Taiwanese counterparts. It abolished the Fuzhou Military Region, the military headquarters in charge of security affairs against Taiwan. These efforts have significantly reduced tensions and expanded nonofficial contacts between the two sides.[14]

Causes of the Shift. A few factors explain the major shift in Beijing's Taiwan policy. First, it is a result of China's reform and open-door policy. After the Cultural Revolution, a reform-minded leadership led by Deng came to power. This leadership was determined to reform China's economic and political system and to restructure China's relations with other countries. To do so, China had to create a relatively peaceful international environment, especially in the Asian-Pacific region. To reduce tensions with Taiwan was a part of China's comprehensive foreign policy. Moreover, China's economic growth needs overseas investment, technology, and market shares. Improving relations with Taiwan can encourage overseas Chinese to play an intermediate role between China and other countries, especially the nations of the Organization for Economic Cooperation and Development (OECD).

Second, having survived the Cultural Revolution, the reform-minded leadership was disillusioned ideologically. It was impressed with the successful economic development in the newly industrialized countries of Asia: Taiwan, Hong Kong, South Korea, and Singapore. The development models and experiences of these countries were widely introduced in China when the reform leadership was seeking an alternative development strategy to Maoism. As a result, the previous ideological and political conflicts with Taipei declined sharply. These changes made it possible for Beijing to readjust its political policy toward Taiwan.

Third, improving relations with Taiwan can increase Beijing's credibility in Hong Kong not only because a rational Taiwan policy and improved China-Taiwan relations can increase the confidence in Beijing of Hong Kong citizens but also because reduced tensions with Taipei can contribute to the stability of the Asian-Pacific region. Because of Hong Kong's high dependence on the OECD market, capital investment, and political support, improved Beijing-Taipei relations are regarded as one of the key indicators of Beijing's relations with OECD nations, especially with the United States.

Fourth, during the first half of the 1980s, China's foreign relations, especially those with the OECD nations, developed rapidly. Beijing established formal diplomatic ties with most countries in the world, while more and more countries cut off their diplomatic relations with Taipei. The PRC joined most governmental international organizations. Strategically and politically, Beijing and Washington were cooperating on a number of international issues in the Asian-Pacific region. Meanwhile, Beijing was able to secure economic aid and government loans with low interest rates from Tokyo. The Chinese leadership thus felt much more confident in dealing with Taipei. It apparently believed that the international environment was favorable to its strategy toward Taipei and that peaceful reunification with Taiwan was possible in the foreseeable future.

Complications. The Tiananmen Square incident in June 1989 was a temporary setback for Beijing's approach to Taipei. The Chinese troops' bloody suppression of peaceful prodemocracy demonstrators in Beijing shocked the people of Taiwan. The KMT government strongly criticized Beijing. It also provided financial and political support to China's democrats who managed to escape from the Beijing government.[15] In the international community, most OECD nations reacted to the Tiananmen suppression strongly: having condemned the Chinese government, they imposed economic sanctions on Beijing and distanced themselves from it. At the same time, some of them began to reconsider their relations with Taipei and expanded their cultural and commercial ties with it. Such a new international environment encouraged Taipei to adopt a new foreign policy: to emphasize the development of de facto foreign relations with any country that was willing to move closer to Taipei. The KMT government defined this policy as "flexible" or "pragmatic" foreign policy.[16]

Beijing has reacted strongly to Taipei's flexible diplomacy. It has accused Taipei of trying to create "one China, one Taiwan" or "two Chinas" or of "seeking independence." It has also repeated that if Taipei claims independence, Beijing will have no choice but to use force. After five small countries reestablished diplomatic ties with Taipei, Beijing immediately cut off its ties with them in a move to prevent dual recognition of both Beijing and Taipei. In early September 1991, Taipei took the initiative to recognize the three Baltic states. Beijing immediately followed suit. To date, Beijing has established full diplomatic ties with most republics of the former Soviet Union.[17] Having joined the United Nations in September 1991, Pyongyang and Seoul signed a nonaggression treaty in December 1991. Tensions between them have declined. These developments created the opportunity for Beijing to recognize Seoul in 1992. As a result, Taipei-Seoul relations were downgraded. As mentioned, in January 1992 Latvia, which has full diplomatic ties with Beijing, established general consulate relations with Taipei. Beijing immediately protested but did not cut diplomatic ties with Riga.

In other areas, however, having passed the period of crisis management (the second half of 1989), Beijing has become increasingly flexible in its dealings with Taipei. It has provided more economic incentives (low income-tax rates, greater market share, cheap labor and raw materials, and loans with low interest rates) to those Taiwanese companies that are interested in relocating their labor-intensive manufacturing operations to the Chinese coast. This is particularly important because Taiwan is under strong pressure to upgrade its economic structure and during 1989 and 1990 most OECD countries imposed economic sanctions on China. Chinese leaders have frequently received business elites and important scholars from Taiwan, encouraging them to expand further the relations between the two sides. The Chinese government has also given more favorable treatment to those Chinese citizens who have relatives in Taiwan. More business and academic conferences have been held on the mainland, involving experts from China, Taiwan, and overseas and focusing on Beijing-Taipei relations. Meanwhile, local authorities, especially those on the coast, have become more active in developing their own relations with Taiwan.

Anticipated Changes. In the next few years, Beijing's policy toward Taipei will continue to undergo many important changes. China's domestic development and its foreign policy in general will continue to reshape its Taiwan policy. Chinese politics has gradually entered the process of political and generational succession. Chinese politics will remain tense, unstable, and uncertain in the next few years. The forthcoming succession is most likely to provoke another power struggle within the central leadership. The central government's ability to govern is likely to decline further. The deepened power struggle and ongoing political instability may continue to discourage bureaucrats, especially those at local levels, from committing themselves to the policies of the central government. The recent collapse of the Communist system in the former Soviet Union and Eastern Europe has further challenged the legitimacy and stability of the political system.

Continuing political tensions and economic instability have intensified the antagonism between the state and society. Many people, especially urban residents, have distanced themselves from the government, refusing to acquiesce in political campaigns. Others have lost all their interest in official ideology and politics. The government is also facing increasingly determined defiance from oppressed ethnic minorities, who have been strongly encouraged by the collapse of the former Soviet Union.

These developments are likely to have strong effects on China's foreign and security policies in general and its policy toward Taiwan in particular. First, because of China's domestic political uncertainties and economic instability, Beijing will most likely concentrate on dealing with domestic issues. Its bargaining position *vis-à-vis* the OECD nations will remain relatively weak. Unless some sudden international crisis takes place, Beijing is likely to continue its current foreign and security policies. In fact, for the first time since 1949, China does not face any major direct security threat. The fundamental objective of Beijing's foreign and security policies will most likely remain creating a relatively stable and peaceful international environment while obtaining the maximum possible economic resources from abroad.

The hard-liners in Beijing will remain hostile to Western countries; political conflicts will continue between China and the OECD nations, especially the United States, over the issues of human rights and arms control. Nevertheless, repairing its relations with the OECD nations, especially the United States and Japan, will continue to be Beijing's top foreign policy priority because China needs foreign technology, capital investment, and markets, which are crucial to solving its economic instability and helping to stabilize the domestic political situation. At the same time, because of the collapse of the Soviet empire, China's strategic value to the West has declined sharply. Beijing's leverage in dealing with the OECD nations over the Taiwan issue will remain weak.

Second, political trends on the mainland may reduce Beijing's credibility in dealing with Taipei, while the gap in the pace of political development between the two sides will remain wide. As for Taipei, the key policy issue is how to deal with the high degree of political uncertainty in the Chinese mainland's political development during and soon after the succession process. In fact, Taipei has little influence on China's internal political and economic development. Unless Beijing's political succession produces a more stable, effective, and open-minded government, Taipei will continue a wait-and-see attitude toward the mainland. At the same time, to pursue economic interests and to avoid political tensions with Beijing, it will continue to loosen its restrictions against further expansion of cultural and economic ties with the mainland.

Third, given the high degree of uncertainty surrounding the leadership in China, Beijing's Taiwan policy must be regarded as a transitional one. More important, the Taiwan policy may play a role in Beijing's succession politics. In the summer of 1989, when the Chinese government was faced with the strong political challenge of crisis management, the conservatives within the government were highly critical of Taipei, accusing it of "sponsoring" the "counterrevolutionary rebellion" in Tiananmen Square. If political tensions in China rise again, especially during the succession process, the conservatives in Beijing may use Taipei as a weapon to attack their opposition within the government and in society. Thus, the mainland may provoke conflicts against the island.

Fourth, in the near future, Beijing will continue to offer favorable terms to Taiwanese investors, including low tax rates, import duty concessions, cheap land, low-cost labor, and cheap energy and raw materials. It will also make concessions on environmental protection controls to Taiwanese companies, which have increasing difficulty in building new plants in Taiwan because of the island's strong environmental protection movement. Moreover, local governments, especially those on the Chinese coast, will surely compete against each other in attracting Taiwanese investors. China's slowed economic growth may improve the supply of labor and natural resources somewhat.

The strengthened economic ties with the Taiwanese business community, whose majority are native Taiwanese, will continue to discourage the demand for independence on the island. More important, commercial activities across the Taiwan Strait can gradually reduce political tensions, improve mutual understanding, and create common interests between the two sides. China's southern coastal area, which receives most of the Taiwanese investment, may become a buffer zone between the Chinese central government and Taipei.

Nevertheless, some constraints act against a further rapid increase in Taiwanese investment in China. China's political uncertainties will discourage Taiwanese corporations from undertaking long-term, large-scale industrial projects in China. The shortage of hard currency, heavy burden of foreign debt, and difficulty in raising low-interest loans on the international financial market may weaken Beijing's ability to offer a greater share of the domestic market to Taiwanese companies. Because of the early 1990s economic recession and its huge fiscal deficit, Beijing will continue to have difficulty in increasing its investment in the infrastructure in areas that might attract Taiwan investors. If the inflation rate rises again, China may be unable to compete with other Asian countries in attracting Taiwanese manufacturers, despite its cultural advantages.

Moreover, because of the widening institutional gap with other market economies, China's competitiveness in the international market may not increase significantly. The heightened international protectionism in both North America and Western Europe will complicate China's efforts to expand its trade ties with these nations. Given this, Beijing probably will not be prepared to offer Taiwanese investors much broader access to China's internal markets. Rather, its basic strategy will remain to develop export-oriented processing industries.

Taken as a whole, Beijing's policy toward Taiwan is in transition. Over the next several years, Beijing will try to steer the relationship in the direction of formal negotiation with Taipei on reunification. Given the rapidly changed internal development of Taiwan and the international environment, such an expectation may not meet reality. Rather, the more realistic policy objective is likely to be further reduction in tensions, creation of more common interests with Taipei, and discouragement of the latter from moving to independence. On the issue of Taipei's access to participation in the international community, Beijing will have to be more flexible, moving away from a zero-sum approach to coexistence under the principle of one China.

A Changing Taiwan and Its Policies

Over the past two years, Taiwan's process of political democratization and economic development, which has become increasingly important in determining Taiwan's attitude toward China, has accelerated, forcing the KMT to adjust its policy toward Beijing. The changed international environment in both Europe and Asia has provided new opportunities for Taipei to increase its participation in the international community and to compete against Beijing. At the same time, Beijing's influence on Taiwan's internal politics remains weak.

Democratization. Taiwan's political system has become increasingly more liberal and democratic during the past several years. The KMT government has made strong efforts to encourage the development of the middle class and to develop its ties with local interest groups. It has also emphasized the Taiwanization of government, military, and party bureaucrats, a policy designed to reduce tensions between the mainlanders and Taiwanese and to recruit Taiwanese into the ruling circle. Despite the government's manipulation and suppression, however, since the early 1980s, the opposition has managed to obtain about one-fourth of the total votes during the island's local (county-level) elections. The demand for liberalization and democratization has increased significantly.

Under such increasingly strong popular pressure, the government lifted martial law on October 15, 1986, and restrictions on the press in January 1989. It then made strong efforts to reform the political system further. With a few exceptions, most political dissidents have been allowed to return to Taiwan and even to run for office. The role of official ideology has diminished quickly, and the KMT has speeded up its reform to wage election campaigns effectively. Although it maintains its monopoly over radio and TV stations, more private broadcasting operations have sprung up since the election campaign of December 1989. In December 1991, all old representatives of the National Assembly and Legislative Yuan, who were elected on the mainland in 1948, retired. As a result, native Taiwanese are becoming the majority in both institutions.

The political scene has diversified. Since September 1986, many opposition parties have been formed, and a good foundation has been laid for an effective multiparty political system. Tolerance of political expression has increased. With its official status, the opposition has gradually begun to shift its main strategy from street demonstrations to parliamentary competition. Taiwanese society is becoming accustomed to party politics. The labor movement, women's movement, environmental protection movement, and consumer movement have become more vocal and influential.[18]

This activity reflects the spread of democracy in society as a whole. During the past few years, the opposition has increased its political influence and now shares power with the KMT, particularly at the county-city level.[19] In the December 1989 elections, the DPP

427

and independent candidates won twenty-one seats in the legislative body, just enough to sponsor legislation. They also took six of twenty-one mayorships (one was taken by an independent politician), giving them jurisdiction over 40 percent of the island's total population. As a result, the opposition is now in control of more than 40 percent of the total local government budget and can directly influence public policy. Following the election in December 1991, during which the DPP gained only sixty-six seats (or 20.3 percent of the total number of seats to be elected) of the National Assembly, further constitutional reform was most likely in 1992.

Nevertheless, the opposition has been facing a fundamental internal crisis. During the past few years, the DPP has devoted most of its energy to competition for political power with the ruling KMT. With few exceptions, most of its cadres are not knowledgeable about public policy issues. Moreover, within the DPP, the demand for independence has increased, and the pro-independence faction is now the party's mainstream. On February 22, 1990, eleven DPP representatives of the National Assembly demanded revision of Taiwan's constitution and a change in the country's official name from the Republic of China to the Republic of Taiwan. In October 1990, some opposition politicians demanded that the government give up its sovereign rights over the mainland. In November 1991, the DPP passed a resolution to put the demand for Taiwan independence into its party constitution.[20] This development, in turn, has caused splits in the party, weakening its support from the business community and from the second- and third-generation mainlanders who may politically have sympathy with the opposition.[21]

Independence, however, does not have the support of the majority of the population. During the 1991 election campaign, the DPP failed to reach its goal of gaining 40 percent of the total vote. This was largely because the DPP's use of Taiwan independence as its key campaign slogan alienated many middle-class voters and businessmen who feared that a sudden jump toward independence would jeopardize the island's political stability, create chaos, and provoke a military confrontation with Beijing. In addition, over the past few years, commercial ties between the two sides of the Taiwan Strait have expanded rapidly. The Taiwanese corporations have sharply increased their trade with and investment in the Chinese mainland. Any political tensions with Beijing would surely hurt Taiwanese business interests in China.

Under pressure from other factions within the KMT, President Lee repeated the government's policy of opposing Taiwan's independence. During his time in office, Premier Hao Pei-tsun took a tough stance against the Taiwan Independence Movement (TIM). A few TIM leaders have been put on trial for advocating independence. Nevertheless, given the ongoing progress of Taiwan's political development, the TIM is increasingly likely to become a major political force capable of mobilizing some popular support and influencing Taiwan's internal politics and foreign policy.[22]

Social Changes. Meanwhile, the influence of native Taiwanese in the military, government, and KMT organization has increased significantly. In middle-level government organizations, more and more native Taiwanese have begun to replace mainlanders as heads of departments or bureaus. More native Taiwanese have been promoted to top government positions, and they now make up the majority of the central Standing Committee of the KMT and the cabinet. This development, in turn, has revived virulent tensions between native Taiwanese and mainlanders within the party-government-military institutions. In the general society, native Taiwanese are particularly influential in the business community and in local politics. Among the younger generation, however, tensions between Taiwanese and mainlanders have continued to decline, and intermarriage between the two groups has increased. These trends will restructure Taiwan's political system and redistribute power between the mainlanders and Taiwanese within the KMT and between the KMT and the opposition.[23]

Taiwan's rapid political, economic, and social transformation has brought some instability. The income gap has widened, and social tensions between various interest groups have increased. Legal institutions, which are not yet totally independent of the KMT, have not always been respected by various interest groups, and the authority of the government itself is now being challenged by a variety of social and political forces. But crime and corruption have increased, and political violence against public order, some politicians, and ordinary citizens has risen significantly. Existing progress toward a more liberal, pluralist, and democratic society needs to be consolidated and institutionalized.

The Economy. In the economic sphere, Taiwan has been undergoing a fundamental transition from a labor-intensive economy, highly dependent on the international market, to a semitechnological and capital-intensive economy with a rapidly growing domestic market. Overseas investment is also playing an increasingly important role in economic growth. During the past few years, Taiwan's economic growth has been unstable. The growth rate of real GNP fell from 11.8

percent in 1987 to 7.8 percent and 7.6 percent in 1988 and 1989, respectively, while the inflation rate edged up to 4.7 percent in 1989 from 0.52 percent in 1987 and 1.3 percent in 1988. In 1990, largely because of the recession in many OECD nations, real GNP grew 5.6 percent, and the inflation rate reached 6.5 percent. The government's monetary and fiscal policies have been cautious and conservative. The slowed economic growth has hurt Taiwan's export-oriented economy. According to government estimates, real GNP grew 7.0 percent in 1991.[24]

Structurally, Taiwan's economy has undergone some important changes. The government has encouraged the upgrading of the economy and the expansion of the domestic market. It has set up a science and industry zone and has provided information services, financial support, and tax concessions to research and industrial projects that will strengthen Taiwan's international competitiveness and improve the infrastructure. Its newly implemented six-year economic construction plan includes ten major infrastructure projects. It has also encouraged the business community to reduce its dependence on the U.S. market and to diversify its exports to other overseas markets, including the countries of the former Soviet Union and Eastern Europe. The United States now accounts for only about 33 percent of Taiwan's total exports, compared with 48 percent seven years ago. After the transfer of Taiwan's labor-intensive industries overseas, especially to the Chinese mainland and Southeast Asia, its service sector and machine-building and electrical production have grown rapidly.[25]

At this time, however, Taiwan faces a number of economic challenges. International competition for the manufactured goods market has heightened and will continue to do so. Both OECD nations, which have advanced technology and high capital investment, and developing countries in Asia such as China, Thailand, Indonesia, Malaysia, and the Philippines, which have abundant natural resources and cheap labor, are challenging Taiwan's position in the international market. While the Taiwan trade deficit with Japan has continued to widen, protectionism in North America and preparations for the unification of the European market in 1992 complicated the entry of Taiwanese goods into OECD markets, and this trend will continue. During the past few years, Washington has put strong political pressure on Taipei to appreciate the new Taiwan dollar further, to open up its domestic market, to reduce its trade surplus with the United States "voluntarily," and to internationalize its financial markets.[26]

Meanwhile, the business community has been calling on the

government to improve the investment environment, particularly by privatizing the banking industry and updating the infrastructure. Rapidly increasing labor cost, expensive land, the labor shortage, and the burgeoning labor movement have encouraged the business community to import illegal workers from China and discouraged its investment in labor-intensive operations. Taiwan's vocal environmental protection movement has forced certain industries to increase spending on antipollution devices. As a result, many companies, especially those that are labor-intensive or engaged in the manufacture of chemicals, have been actively looking for opportunities to move their operations overseas, especially to China's southern coast.

Trade across the Taiwan Strait has grown rapidly, reaching $3.7 billion in 1989 and $5 billion in 1990. Trade in 1991 and 1992 is estimated at $6.5 billion and $9.8 billion, respectively. China now is Taiwan's fifth-ranked trading partner, accounting for about 5 percent of its total foreign trade. More important, Taiwan has generated a substantial trade surplus against China. Taiwan's trade surplus against China in 1992 reached more than U.S. $6 billion.[27] In the next few years, Taiwan is likely to continue importing a large amount of raw materials and energy products from China. It will also increase its exports of parts and semicompleted products to China, but it may be more difficult to increase significantly its exports of manufactured goods to China, partly because of China's tough restrictions against imported consumer goods.

A few thousand Taiwanese manufacturers have set up processing facilities along the Chinese coast, particularly in Fujian and Guangdong provinces, and their operations were not stopped by the events of June 4, 1989. Rather, in an attempt to repair the damage to its Taiwan policy caused by the political crisis, Beijing has stepped up its efforts to attract Taiwanese investors to China. It has provided, or promised to provide, Taiwanese companies with cheaper land and labor, greater shares of the market, more tax concessions, and better supplies of raw materials and energy. In addition, China has no tough restrictions against industrial pollution. These incentives have led many Taiwanese companies to consider investing in China. Total Taiwanese investment in China by the end of 1992 was estimated to reach more than U.S. $11 billion.[28]

Certain political barriers in Taiwan continue to block investment in China. Taipei's current regulations do not permit direct investment in the mainland. Taiwanese industrialists may channel their investment through overseas subsidiaries or form joint ventures with foreign companies and then invest through them, but it is difficult for big corporations to do so without attracting the government's attention. More important, big companies in Taiwan are usually quite dependent on the government. In short, Taiwanese investment in China may come mainly from small and medium-sized, labor-intensive, and low-technology companies or those companies whose production costs have been driven up by the rising cost of labor, land, and environmental protection measures in Taiwan.

Flexible Diplomacy. During the past two years, Taipei's foreign policy has also undergone significant changes. Flexible diplomacy or pragmatic foreign policy has indeed improved, upgraded, and expanded Taiwan's relations with other parts of the world. A number of OECD countries have opened consulates or cultural and economic offices in Taipei. The Bahamas, Liberia, Grenada, Belize, and the Republic of Central Africa reestablished diplomatic relations with Taipei and severed their ties with Beijing. Taipei has begun to provide huge amounts of economic aid to these countries. Since spring 1990, Taipei has approached republics in the former Soviet Union and East European nations to expand commercial and even political ties between them.[29]

By using its increasingly strong economic power, Taipei has been actively competing with Beijing to join international organizations in which neither is yet a member or in which Beijing is not qualified for membership, such as GATT and OECD. In those international organizations in which both Beijing and Taipei are members, Taipei has been actively participating in their professional activities; in those organizations in which only Beijing has membership, Taipei has tried to enter or reenter by accepting more flexible formats such as Chinese Taipei or Taipei, China.[30]

Flexible diplomacy, however, has been challenged domestically. Some members of the legislature have questioned the necessity of "buying off" five small countries to persuade them to establish relations with Taipei. The TIM has continued to put strong pressure on the KMT government to move further toward independence. Recently, some politicians have begun to demand that Taipei apply for UN membership.[31] Yet, the issue of independence also reflects the power balance between various interest groups within Taiwanese society. Both inside and outside the establishment, the feeling against independence has remained strong, because a rapid move toward independence might provoke sharp conflicts or even confrontation between various social groups and undermine the current political stability.

On the international scene, too, flexible diplomacy has its limitations. Since June 1989, Beijing's political relations with most OECD nations have been strained, and the recent warm-up is still uncertain. But this resentment toward Beijing has not been fully translated into support for Taipei. Most OECD nations effectively separated their policy toward Taipei from their policy toward Beijing many years ago and would be unwilling to choose between the two unless another dramatic political crisis in China were to damage further their relations with the mainland. In the U.S. Congress, the demand for supporting Taiwan's bid to join GATT has increased. The Bush administration also showed its willingness to support Taiwan's application, although it did not actively lobby other OECD nations for Taipei on this issue.[32]

Most republics of the former Soviet Union and East European countries would like access to Taiwan's economic resources, especially consumer goods and loans. Nevertheless, they lack hard currency to pay for the imports from Taiwan, and their high labor costs discourage Taiwanese investors from setting up manufacturing operations in these countries. Thus, Taiwan's economic relations with these countries may be conducted mainly by the government in Taipei rather than by the business community. Moreover, most of these countries are not willing to jeopardize their relations with Beijing. Because of the high degree of political instability in these countries, it is sensible for Taipei to be cautious in dealing with them.

A Changing International Environment

The rapidly changing international environment has had and will continue to have a strong impact on China-Taiwan relations in general and Taipei's flexible diplomacy in particular. The collapse of communism in the former Soviet Union and Eastern Europe has fundamentally changed the contemporary international system, which also has strongly affected the dynamics of Beijing-Taipei relations. While the Red Army is no longer a direct threat to the Western alliance, the collapse of the Soviet empire has caused new political tensions within and between various republics. The possibility of direct military confrontation between the two sides has declined dramatically. Rather, they have been able to make significant progress in the areas of both nuclear and conventional arms control and disarmament.

Conversely, the political situation in Russia and most other republics remains highly unstable, largely because of the existing economic crisis, the rapid process of political change, and increased tensions among nationalities. If political developments in these countries continue along the current path, U.S.-Russian relations will continue to improve, and East-West tensions will decline further.

Even if the political situation in these republics becomes chaotic or turns in a conservative and militant direction and their relations with the West grow tense again, becoming a direct security challenge to the West once more is unlikely in the near future. In particular, the changed political and military balance between East and West might not be affected immediately.

The triangular political relationship between Washington, Beijing, and Moscow has been transformed. In Asia, having pulled out its troops from Afghanistan and Mongolia, Moscow has been destroying its SS-20 missiles in accordance with the Intermediate-range Nuclear Forces Agreement and has improved ties with Beijing. It has also cut its economic and military aid to Vietnam, India, and North Korea. These developments have substantially reduced Washington's need to cooperate with Beijing in constraining the Soviet presence in the Asian-Pacific region. They have also significantly improved China's security environment: without Moscow's support, India and Vietnam can no longer challenge Beijing strategically. Rather, both countries have taken initiatives to improve relations with the latter.

Washington, Beijing, and Taipei. Since June 1989, Sino-American relations have undergone several serious political crises. By sending high-ranking officials secretly to Beijing in July and November 1989 and at the same time imposing economic sanctions against China, the Bush administration attempted to maintain its relationship with Beijing while placating the U.S. Congress and public opinion. The White House carefully tried to avoid making strong public criticism of the political repression in Beijing and the reversal of the economic reforms and open-door policy; despite this, the conservatives in Beijing continued to accuse Washington of trying to "overthrow China's socialist system by a 'peaceful transformation.' "[33]

Although Sino-American trade increased to $17.8 billion in 1989 from $13.5 billion in 1988 and Washington lifted some sanctions against technology transfers and loans to China, the American business community remained temporarily reluctant to increase its investment commitments in China, largely because of China's high political risk, weakened economic base, and low import ability. Moreover, while Taiwan's trade surplus with the United States declined and its trade surplus with China increased, the amount of the U.S. trade deficit with China increased dramatically. In 1990, it reached $8.5 billion. The deficit in 1992 reached $18 billion. In October 1990, the U.S. Congress appointed a special team to investigate the trade imbalance between the two countries. In January 1992, having forced Beijing to make compromises, the Office of the U.S. Trade Representative signed an agreement with its Chinese counterparts for the protection of intellectual property. In the next few years, the trade imbalance will continue to be a serious political conflict between Beijing and Washington.[34]

While continuing the debate over what has happened in China and what might happen next, America's China hands are unlikely to reach a consensus on forming U.S. policy toward China. Congress increased its pressure on the Bush administration to take a tougher stance against Beijing. In June 1991 and March 1992, both House and Senate voted to extend conditionally China's most favored nation status. Nevertheless, the Bush administration decided to veto the bill. Meanwhile, by exercising the leverage of MFN debates, Washington has forced Beijing to make compromises in arms control, bilateral trade, human rights, and regional conflicts such as in Indochina.[35] If the United States removes China's MFN status, Taiwan's economic ties with China will be damaged, because a few thousand Taiwanese companies now operating on the Chinese coast are the key exporters to the U.S. market and much of Taiwan's U.S. $5 billion trade with China is Taiwanese-made parts, components, and equipment shipped to China for its processing lines for the U.S. market.

The political tensions between Beijing and Washington since June 1989 have gradually changed the foundation of political cooperation between the two countries on various subregional political and security issues in the Asia-Pacific region. To maintain the region's stability, however, Washington may still have to work with Beijing, especially in the Korean peninsula, Central Asia, South Asia, and Indochina, where the two countries share certain common interests and Beijing continues to play an active and important role.

Since June 1989, political tensions between Washington and Beijing have risen. Beijing has criticized Washington's intervention in China's internal affairs and Taipei's flexible diplomacy, but the Taiwan issue has not become a key source of conflict between Beijing and Washington. Beijing realizes that the main reasons behind Taipei's active pursuit of flexible diplomacy are Beijing's internal crisis, China's strained relationship with most OECD nations, and the rapid progress of democratization and pluralization in Taiwan, which has increased the importance of internal politics in reshaping Taipei's policy toward Beijing as well as its foreign policy in general.

In addition, Washington has been cautious in dealing with Taipei's flexible diplomacy. With the exception of Washington's comments on Taipei's application for GATT, no top U.S. government official has made much of a public policy statement on Taipei's flexible diplomacy. At the policy level, Sino-American political tensions have not been fully translated into support for Taipei. Moreover, Washington's policy toward Taiwan and China will have to be coordinated with its Asian allies and other OECD nations. To date, most of these nations prefer relatively stable relations between Washington and Beijing and between Beijing and Taipei. Therefore, in the near future, Washington is unlikely to encourage Taipei actively to move toward independence. Given Washington's political influence (especially on issues concerning China and Taiwan) among the OECD nations and the lack of interest of other Asian nations, Taipei's flexible diplomacy therefore may not gain strong official support.

These developments will have important repercussions for Beijing-Taipei relations. First, the collapse of the Soviet Union has sharply reduced Beijing's leverage in dealing with Washington. The focus of Sino-American cooperation will not center on containing Soviet expansionism in the region but will be limited to coping with certain subregional security or political issues, especially in Indochina and the Korean peninsula. Washington may readjust its policies toward Beijing and Taipei according to the new balance of power at both global and regional levels.

Second, because of China's political instability, Washington has difficulty in forming a consistent China policy. Beijing's ongoing political repression will continue to invite criticism from the U.S. public and Capitol Hill, thereby undermining both the Bush and the Clinton administration's efforts to improve relations with Beijing. In addition, the Democrats played up the issue of China policy during the presidential election campaign of 1992 and the Republicans will do so subsequently. At the same time, Taiwan's successful experience in political and economic development has rapidly improved its image in the U.S. public, generating new support for the island.

Third, to maintain stability in the region and to avoid giving an excuse for Beijing's conservatives to promote extremist nationalism, the White House is unlikely to give strong public support to Taipei's flexible diplomacy. Nor will it actively encourage the latter to move toward independence. Nevertheless, the U.S. Congress, because of its anger at Beijing's repression of the prodemocracy movement and disappointment at Beijing's human rights record, may increase its political support for Taipei. More important, Washington may take advantage of China's domestic and international vulnerability to separate gradually its policy toward Taiwan from its China policy. Such a possibility will further complicate the debate over U.S. China policy between the White House and Capitol Hill. It may also result in Washington's greater support for Taiwan's increased participation in the international community. Thus, new tensions between Washington and Beijing over the Taiwan issue may soon arise.

Elsewhere. In other parts of the world, attitudes toward the China-Taiwan crisis over flexible diplomacy are mixed. Most OECD nations have been critical of Beijing's suppression of the prodemocracy movement in China, but they have gradually lifted sanctions against Beijing. Both the World Bank and the Asia Development Bank have resumed their lending to Beijing. In most OECD nations, restrictions imposed after June 1989 on technology transfers to Beijing have been relatively ambiguous. Following Prime Minister Toshiki Kaifu's trip to China in August 1991, most OECD nations have lifted their ban on high-level exchange with Beijing. By and large, OECD nations are taking a wait-and-see approach toward China.

This approach, however, has had a certain impact on their policies toward Taipei. Taiwan's economic strength and its competitiveness in international markets have already encouraged many OECD nations to expand their economic ties with Taipei. OECD nations have become more interested in inviting Taiwan to participate in many international economic and business organizations, and a number of them have opened trade offices and consulates in Taipei. They have become more interested in expanding commercial ties with and selling weapons and military technology to Taipei.

These developments, however, have certain limitations. At least in the near future, none of the OECD nations will reestablish diplomatic ties with Taipei at the expense of breaking relations with Beijing. Most of them, especially Germany and England, will continue to take Beijing's reactions into account when they develop bilateral relations with Taipei and consider their policy toward Taipei's application to governmental international organizations such as GATT. Their policy toward Beijing-Taipei relations has just begun to change. The final outcome of this policy change will depend on their assessments of China's future development and their comprehensive strategic calculation.

In Asia, no country except Japan made a significant response to China's political crisis in 1989. No Asian country has openly criticized Beijing's bloody suppression of the prodemocracy movement in June 1989. Rather, North Korea, Vietnam, India, and Pakistan expressed their support, or understanding, of the crackdown and accused foreign or Western countries of intervention in China's internal affairs. Most Asian countries prefer that Beijing-Taipei relations remain peaceful and stable, especially when China enters its political succession.

Taken together, the dynamics of the international environment with which Beijing and Taipei have to deal have changed significantly. Both Beijing's and Taipei's foreign policies and policies toward each other have undergone a transformation. In the near future, these changes are likely to continue. Unless Beijing's domestic politics and its relations with the OECD nations experience another fundamental crisis, most OECD and Asian countries are unlikely to change dramatically their current policy toward the two sides of the Taiwan Strait. Thus, the international dimension of the Beijing-Taipei relationship may remain stable.

Two Chinese Societies

By any measure, the Chinese and the Taiwanese have had two disparate political, economic, and social systems for more than forty years. Their cultural structures also have many major differences. Yet, they are two parts of one divided nation. The gap between their political, social, and economic systems started to narrow between 1978 and 1988, when China's reform and open-door policies were first in effect, but it has now widened again because of Beijing's political and economic crisis and Taiwan's rapid political development since December 1989. In the international community, Beijing and Taipei have acted differently as the result of their distinct positions in the contemporary international system. As a regional power with some global strategic significance, Beijing has played an important and active role in the Asian Pacific region and in the third world. During the past ten years, Taiwan has established itself as a newly industrialized economy; backed by its economic and financial strength, it has become an increasingly active participant in the international market and the international community as a whole.

At present, Beijing and Taipei are still at a turning point. So are relations between them, and between the two of them and other parts of the world. The nature of China's succession politics will bring about great uncertainties in its internal development as well as in its foreign policy in general and its policy toward Taiwan in particular. The relationship with Taiwan has not been the top priority of Beijing's policy makers, because the government has been preoccupied with its internal difficulties and its tense relations with OECD nations. Nevertheless, this situation may change in the next few years if Taiwan's move toward independence accelerates and the political struggle within the Chinese leadership heightens during the succession process.

More important, after the succession, China is unlikely to produce another strong leader like Deng Xiaoping or Mao Zedong, and Chinese citizens, who have learned a great deal from their experience over the past fourteen years and from recent developments in the former Soviet Union and Eastern Europe, are likely to put strong pressure on the government and play a more active role in shaping the country's political structure, economic institutions, and foreign relations. Local authorities, especially those on the Chinese coast, will become more independent in pursuing their own reform and open-door policies, including their relations with Taiwan. In addition, to restore political and economic stability in China, the new leadership will have to improve its ties with the OECD nations, Hong Kong, and Taiwan. Consequently, room for compromises with Taipei will enlarge. These trends may open a wide range of opportunities for Beijing to restructure its relations with Taipei.

Over the next few years, Taiwan will continue to become more democratic, and the influence of native Taiwanese will continue to increase. Under pressure from the opposition and society at large, the KMT will implement more reforms and adapt its own organization to operate effectively in the changed political and social environment. It will gradually relax its control over the broadcasting industry, recruit more talented people who can attract popular votes, and strengthen its ties with the business elites, particularly the younger generation. While a younger generation of local politicians will soon dominate both the National Assembly and the Legislative Yuan, institutionally the KMT is likely to introduce direct elections for president gradually. The KMT will have to learn to share power with the opposition, at least at the local level.

The opposition in Taiwan will continue its struggle for the further redistribution of power and for increased democratization. While continuing to use mass demonstrations to pressure the KMT, it will make more of an effort to compete with the latter in Parliament and demand further change in the political process and institutions. In the foreseeable future, the opposition is likely to devote more energy to public policy issues, while gaining more experience governing the counties under its control. Demand for Taiwan's independence will grow correspondingly. Pressure from the TIM will push the KMT to expand its relations with Beijing.

Meanwhile, the influence of Taiwan's labor, student, women's, and environmental protection movements will continue to rise. If the KMT and various opposition groups fail to make compromises or the KMT internal power struggle spins out of control, Taiwan's political stability will be threatened. In the near future, the TIM may become the main force in the opposition politics; debate over the issue of independence, however, is unlikely to escalate to the point of violence.

In the economic sphere, Taiwan will continue to upgrade its industrial structure, to reform its economic institutions, and to diversify its overseas markets. Under strong internal pressure, Taipei will continue its flexible diplomacy, expanding its relations with other parts of the world and competing against Beijing in the international community. Provoking an internal political crisis, military confrontation with Beijing, and possible regional instability by moving rapidly toward independence are not, however, in Taipei's interests. Taipei may continue its limited support for China's prodemocracy movement while further relaxing restrictions on the expansion of economic relations with coastal regions of China. Nevertheless, such a policy will not be implemented at the expense of Taiwan's fundamental security.

During the past few years, the political and economic development of China and Taiwan has been a major determinant of relations between them. The importance of the international community, especially Washington, in influencing Beijing-Taipei relations has gradually declined. Yet in the international community, Washington and Tokyo will play a more important role in shaping other nations' attitudes toward Taipei. For the next few years, at least, neither peaceful reunification nor Taiwanese independence would be practical or realistic. A hasty jump in either direction could raise tremendous political tensions inside Taiwan and between Taipei and Beijing, possibly provoking a military confrontation that would jeopardize the stability of the entire region.

Beijing-Taipei relations are no longer a zero-sum game but rather a competition in which compromise is possible. To pursue their own interests, Beijing and Taipei will continue to compete for international support; they must, however, develop a comprehensive strategy for dealing with each other. In this regard, both parties should be more flexible, placing more emphasis on the development of their mutual interests and bilateral relations than on any specific format of Taipei's international participation. Rather, under the format of one China, Taipei should be encouraged to increase its international participation. Reducing direct political tensions and increasing contacts, especially at the semigovernmental and even full diplomatic levels, will be most conducive to maintaining a balanced relationship between them. These approaches can prevent a sudden crisis and expand the area of mutual interest between them, enabling both Beijing and

Taipei to survive the current period of uncertainty and will be supported by the international community. They will create an environment in which time and rational policies can work toward a resolution of the complex relationship between the two Chinese societies.

PART EIGHT
Conclusion

18
The Chinese and Their Future

Thomas W. Robinson and Zhiling Lin

The chapters in this volume explore economic, political, and social developments in China, Hong Kong, and Taiwan during the late 1980s and early 1990s. They also note international trends, in Asia and beyond, that affect each of the three Chinese entities and their interrelations. This chapter pulls together various strands and constructs a composite view of Greater China and its three components, inspecting current domestic and international developments and trends and setting forth several alternative futures.

Trends in China, Hong Kong, and Taiwan in the Early 1990s

Let us begin by examining domestic and international developments as they relate to China.

China. Several years after the 1989 Tiananmen incident in China, the situation on the Chinese mainland began to clarify considerably. Most important, the country seemed to recover economically from the 1989 shock and the subsequent two years of doldrums and struggle over the choice of a path to development. The first indication was the signal in mid-1990 that retrenchment from the Zhao Ziyang market-oriented reforms and reversion to central planning were over. The reforms of the 1980s would be kept, and further, rapid growth could resume. Gradually thereafter, through a combination of price, enterprise management, financial, agricultural, housing, and foreign investment reforms, the economy swung back—first to a balance between market and plan, then increasingly toward marketization. The results were a resumption, and then an acceleration, of high rates of growth; a resumption and then an explosion of foreign investment; and the emergence, at least in the southern coastal areas of China, of a reasonably highly developed area.

These trends were accentuated by the January 1992 trip of Deng Xiaoping to Shenzhen, the region adjacent to Hong Kong and the most successful of the special economic zones. There he announced that China would henceforth fully resume marketization; would export the southern, export-led growth strategy to the other two "coasts" of China—borders with various other countries and the Yangtze River Valley; would strive for even higher, deliberately double-digit economic growth; would open the country further to the outside world; and would accelerate all reforms. These initiatives were ratified at the party's Fourteenth Congress in November 1992, when the country was engaged in a frenzy of new ventures and consumer-oriented production. Reforms were broadened further to include such initiatives as stock markets and even their tentative extension to the laggard, state-run industrial sector. The inevitable signs of overheating the economy then appeared: double-digit inflation in some places, wage increases unconnected to productivity, overly rapid credit creation at the local and regional levels, rampant corruption, factories standing idle as primary product resources were detained by transportation bottlenecks, and a failure of the fiscal system because market control mechanisms were not yet sufficiently powerful.

The immediate prospect, therefore, was for a dampening of growth from the top down, and thus for another cycle of stop-start economic development. For the longer term, however, the Chinese economic situation appeared bright, so long as several secular trends could be held in check. Marketization was remaking the economy and converting it into a gigantic example of Asian-based export-led growth. Furthermore, after centuries of isolation, China was joining the world economically. It would participate as a full member of the interdependent group of industrial nations. Because of a combination of high growth rates over a long time and significant upward reevaluation of the country's initial gross national product, China was becoming so large that it could eventually rival the influence of the advanced industrial powers in Asia and around the globe.

Nonetheless, it was equally true that dangerous new factors were emerging that could bring down the whole economic process if not addressed successfully. The great disparity of growth between the southern coastal area and the regions to the north, the inland provinces, and the minority areas next to the former Soviet Union had a disintegrative impact on regional relations. Many began to speak of the possible breakup of the country into several political entities along economic lines, somewhat akin to the developments in Eastern Europe and the Commonwealth of Independent States. Although such a breakup was unlikely, the forces militating in its favor would have to be coped with politically and economically.

446

Another potential danger was the cumulative effects of environmental neglect and mismanagement. These were to be seen most prominently in agriculture and industry. Overfertilization and overuse of the land combined with continual deforestation to make even continuation of present yield levels problematic. Huge increases of industrial coal-burning and lack of attention to industrial waste disposal caused excessive urban pollution and China's emergence as a major contributor to global warming. These developments could only negatively affect economic performance and, if not addressed rapidly and successfully, could bring on disaster.

Finally, China was faced with the problem of population. The national population continued to increase by 15 million each year. Continued immense growth in absolute numbers and the change in the population composition could severely attenuate or even reverse the gains from high economic growth rates. Furthermore, reform in breaking the "iron rice bowl" freed millions to move about the country in search of employment. China could not employ in the urban sector all the increasing numbers of young adults, and could only with increasing cost take on the burden of caring for the rapidly rising number of elderly.

In sum, China's economic prospects seemed reasonably good in the early 1990s, despite the market transition problems and the longer-term problems. The same could not be said of its political prospects. Since Tiananmen, the party had refused to accept responsibility for its repression, had not moved to institute political reforms in the only direction it could—democracy—and had only marginally broadened its basis of rule, and then only within the party. The party modernized its political ideology slightly, and then only in relation to the needs of economic marketization. It continued to govern the country from the top down, on the principles of Leninism-Maoism, intolerant of any political opposition. The result was a dangerous disjunction between the growing wealth of many citizens and the emergence of new interest groups and quasi-classes on the one hand and the stiffness, increasing irrelevance, intolerance, and outmoded administrative practices of the party on the other. Wherever economic development in poor countries proceeded beyond a certain point— such as $1,000 per capita annual income, 40 percent urbanization, and other such measures—further economic progress became closely intertwined with emerging demands for political liberalization. Parts of China were at or approaching that level, and middle-class attitudes were already evident in many places. Moreover, not only was a desire to get rich supplanting Communist party ideology in most people's thoughts and actions but also the party seemed to be losing practical

447

control over many localities and even some cities, as power was being dispersed away from the Beijing center and relocated in a thousand different places around the country.

It also happened that more and more the party was forced to become a political holding corporation, an umbrella under which a cacophony of voices, new and old institutions, emerging classes and orientations, and regional loyalties all competed for power. Trying to cover all activities within its umbrella of control, the Beijing leadership was increasingly forced to extend outward the party's activities. As a result, its capabilities in any given area were stretched increasingly thin. And after the collapse of communism in Eastern Europe and the Soviet Union (to say nothing of Tiananmen), it could not appeal to the presumed verities of Marxism-Leninism-Maoism. Indeed, Marxism was nearly dead in China, mortally wounded by party-dictated changes in basic beliefs: "Marxism does not have the answer to all questions," "market socialism," "seek truth from facts." The best substitute Deng and his followers could come up with was a watery combination of traditional Chinese philosophical beliefs and crass nationalism. That could hold the fort for a while, but not forever. Ultimately, the umbrella would be stretched too thin at some point and the party would break down or would transform itself into autonomous geographical-, institutional-, class-, and age-differentiated factions that would behave increasingly like political parties. And once the umbrella was removed, China would make the definitive transition to another form of government—perhaps democratic, but more probably authoritarian, at least for a time. Probably the whole of the 1990s would have to occur first. But by the beginning of the first decade of the twenty-first century, "evolutionary democratization" could be on China's horizon.

Meanwhile, the party tried to have it both ways. At the Fourteenth Party Congress, held in November 1992, all remaining party elders (including Yang Shangkun and Chen Yun) were officially retired, even from the so-called Central Advisory Commission, which was disbanded. The new Politburo was a carefully balanced amalgam of party, governmental, military, regional, economic, and generational representatives, with a pronounced tilt toward the reformist end of the spectrum. Li Peng, who many believe delivered the formal order for the Tiananmen massacre (although the order originated with Deng Xiaoping and went through Yang Shangkun), was retained as premier, at least for the time being. Nevertheless, his nemesis in terms of emphasis on marketization and faster growth, former Shanghai mayor Zhu Rongji, was promoted to the Standing Committee of the Politburo, and thus became his equal. Both Yang Shangkun and

Yang Baibing were shorn of their power; the latter did keep his Politburo seat but was balanced by Liu Huaqing. Such provincial figures as Li Ruihuan and Tan Shaowen (Tianjin), Xie Fei (Guangdong), Jiang Chunyun (Shandong), and Wu Bangguo (Shanghai) provided geographic diversity, while institutional representation came through Qiao Shi (security), Zhou Jiahua (economic planning), Qian Qichen (foreign relations), Li Lanqing (foreign trade), and Tian Jiyun (finance). Youth was, surprisingly, represented by the elevation to the Standing Committee of Hu Jintao, a former Youth League official and associate of Hu Yaobang. But while the elders were no longer on the official charts, their influence was still considerable under certain circumstances. It was clear that no complete personnel, generational, or policy change could be accomplished until at least Deng was physically removed from the scene. Although reformists seem to have carried the day at the Fourteenth Party Congress, the party still could not bring to its top level representatives of the new ideas and forces in society, since these would challenge the essence of party rule.

Thus, the gap between party and people, evident long before Tiananmen and open for all to see as a result of that event, opened even wider. In the long run, the party could either arrange its own demise gradually through acceptance of the political and social ramifications of the economic reforms, or it could attempt to resist that fate and court the disaster that befell the ruling parties of Eastern Europe and the Soviet Union. For the short term, the party would continue to convince itself that it could modernize the country economically and would continue to govern China through a form of political rule suitable for earlier stages of modernization, when anti-Westernism and anticapitalism were legitimate bases of belief. But the coming era required a reversal of the syllogism: now it was anticommunism, antisocialist economics, and prodemocracy and promarketization that commanded people's loyalties and attention. The party could try to convert itself into the apostle of at least some of these ideas, but in the end it could not go the whole distance without sounding its own death knell. Some years would have to pass before the contradiction could no longer be avoided, and it was surely possible, even probable, that the party in the meanwhile could shed at least part of its Leninist skin. It could theoretically become merely an authoritarian group of power-holders without any particular ideological base except nationalism, and it could govern by force for a further period. That could occupy the 1990s, but not forever.

Hong Kong. By 1991, the countdown to the 1997 transfer of sovereignty over Hong Kong from Britain to China was well under way. The Joint Declaration had been agreed upon in 1984, the Basic Law had been promulgated by Beijing in 1990, and by the end of 1991 the Sino-British Joint Liaison group had held more than twenty meetings on many topics. Four questions would determine how the transition would go and what kind of future Hong Kong would have after 1997: Hong Kong's economic status and success, internationally and in its ties with China; political life in the colony, especially the rise of democracy and its ensuing political parties and elections to the Legislative Council and the Executive Council; the extent to which China appeared willing to abide by the agreements with Britain, or conversely, to which it would interfere in the administration of Hong Kong before the transfer, and whether, and to what degree, China would be willing to carry out the agreements thereafter; and the role of Hong Kong in the emergence of Greater China. These questions were intertwined, but each is analyzed independently below.

The colony had an economic scare because of Tiananmen, the resulting pullback from marketization in China, and the isolating policies of the United States and other countries. But by 1991, this scare had passed as the mainland gradually resumed course, sanctions were slowly lifted, and the door to foreign investment remained open. Of equal importance was the necessity for Hong Kong enterprises to seek mainland markets for their products, to find continuously profitable outlets for their capital, and to lower production costs by locating factories abroad, in lower wage areas. This could only mean moving a significant portion of the colony's new production to China, especially to the Shenzhen special economic zone and to Guangdong province. So successful was this venture that by 1992 more than U.S. $20 billion of Hong Kong money had been invested in Guangdong province alone, and more than five of every six employees of Hong Kong manufacturing concerns lived in that province. Returns on such investments were so great that per capita income in Hong Kong in 1992 grew to more than U.S. $14,000.

The future was not necessarily so rosy. First, the American decision concerning most-favored-nation (MFN) status of China could have a detrimental impact on Hong Kong. If the status were denied or heavily conditioned on human rights criteria, Hong Kong could suffer a significant economic slowdown or even crisis. The Hong Kong government and business community, aware of this danger, were constantly lobbying in Washington for extension, and prospects were reasonably good that an American-Chinese compromise would take place that would safeguard the colony's economic position. This was confirmed, if only for one year, by the Clinton administration's extension of MFN in June 1993.

Second, although Hong Kong in the early 1990s was expanding its economic influence in southern China with gusto and enormous success, it was not clear that the resultant infinity curves would continue. Factor prices in adjacent Chinese provinces could only rise, China's economic boom could only move northward and inland, even farther from Hong Kong, and competition from such ports as Shanghai and from the Yangtze River Valley could only rise. Hong Kong could share in this growth and could redirect itself to strike a balance between the domestic Chinese market and the world economy. Its advantage as a port would always exist. But in the long run, after 1997, it could lose the absolute advantage it held throughout the previous half century as a world financial and service center and as the principal window on, and a springboard to, China.

A major, but as yet unclear, determinant of Hong Kong's future was the changing character of its political life. In the early 1990s, perhaps because of the global drive toward democracy and the popular reaction in Hong Kong to Tiananmen, the British government decided to accelerate democratization in the colony. The governor, Christopher Patten, proposed to accelerate the number of seats directly electable to the Legislative Council ahead of the timetable previously agreed on with China, to separate completely Executive Council and Legislative Council memberships, to lower the voting age to eighteen, to change to a single-vote, single-seat system for geographical constituencies, to replace corporate voting with individual voting in Executive Council functional constituencies, and to expand the franchise and add new functional constituencies for the Executive Council.

This proposal was fully rejected by Beijing as contrary to the Basic Law, and it brought on a political crisis between Britain and China. Both sides deliberately painted themselves into a corner: resolution would be difficult without severe backing down and a loss of face for both. China could not allow Hong Kong's move toward democracy to get so far ahead of that on the mainland—that is, it could not allow any more than marginal reform, since there was as yet none in China—lest democratic pressures from below were to rise. Undoubtedly the crisis would be resolved, because if it were not, China and Hong Kong would both suffer undue economic and, in the case of Hong Kong, financial and social reversals, which would be contrary to Chinese as well as British basic interests.

Nonetheless, it was not clear that China wished to see a successful transition in accord with the Joint Declaration and the Basic Law.

It used the occasion of the British decision in 1989 to construct a new airport to demand a veto on detailed aspects of the project. Even though China signed a joint agreement in 1991 after much blustering and threats, it still refused in 1992 to honor contracts after 1997 unless further financial conditions were met. China appeared to go beyond the Basic Law in 1992 when it appointed its own consultative body in Hong Kong to "advise" it on political developments there, thus short-circuiting the work of the Executive and Legislative Councils. It also unnecessarily took a hand in deciding where the People's Liberation Army would be located in downtown Hong Kong after 1997, it interfered in determining the powers and occupants of the Hong Kong Court of Final Appeals, and it declared members of the United Democrats of Hong Kong—particularly Martin Lee, their leader—*personae non gratae* after their landslide victory, eleven of eighteen contested seats, in the September 1991 elections. The Chinese purpose was to demonstrate that, on issues small and large, Hong Kong could always expect Chinese input and participation and could often expect dissent or even veto, irrespective of the Basic Law.

A final question was Hong Kong's role in the emerging Greater China. In one sense, that role could only be temporary, since reversion to Chinese rule would occur in 1997. But absorption of Hong Kong would take considerable time beyond that date. Even were China to violate the Basic Law in a wholesale manner, Hong Kong would continue to be an important element of the whole into the next century.

Five aspects of Hong Kong's continuing role were apparent in the early 1990s. First, Hong Kong would continue to serve as a link between Taiwan and the mainland regarding trade, investment, personal contacts, and transportation. Hong Kong could find this role declining once direct communications opened between the other two, but the colony's natural and continuing advantages would still allow it to play an important role in the construction of Greater China. Indeed, its very existence was important to the concept and to its success in serving as an intermediate stage, a buffer of whatever indefinite duration, between the extremes of full reintegration under direct mainland rule and Taiwanese independence.

That led to the second aspect: Hong Kong as a talisman of the veracity of China's one-country, two-systems policy toward Taiwan. If the Hong Kong test case were successful, prospects for a closer relationship between island and mainland would improve. China would have to tread carefully with regard to its interference in Hong Kong, and that would provide some opening for Britain's drive to accelerate democracy in the colony before reversion. Hong Kong, in its turn, would supply some impetus for at least a minor break-through in political change on the mainland itself, for China could not afford to get too far out of step with Hong Kong and Taiwan. The third aspect was then obvious: Hong Kong as the unwitting channel between Taiwan and the mainland, concerning political change. If, as seemed likely, Taiwan would further democratize during the 1990s, its example could encourage acceleration of the same process in Hong Kong, and thus more likely in China as well.

The fourth aspect stemmed from the implications for Taiwan-mainland relations of Hong Kong's continued role as generator of economic growth in China. With Hong Kong and Taiwan growing rapidly, with Hong Kong continuing as the most important center of investment, services, and finance for China, and with the colony setting an example for many Chinese regions of the results of export-led growth, the mainland would continue to depend on Hong Kong for its own economic success. Even were the colony's relative economic importance to China to decline, its absolute size would still be quite large and the time it would take for full absorption into the Chinese economy would remain relatively long. Presuming that Taiwan's own economic growth rate remained high, the mainland would have to ensure similar rates of growth to remain competitive. One of the best ways to do so would be to protect Hong Kong's economic health—and hence its sociopolitical solvency.

A final aspect was that Hong Kong would remain a channel for investment funds for China from overseas Chinese everywhere. Taiwan and Singapore, being "overseas Chinese" entities in the extended definition of the term, to some extent could also serve this function, but Hong Kong historically was the major place where Chinese could meet comfortably, efficiently, and on relatively neutral ground. Hong Kong's role might decline as Shanghai's slowly recovered, but the transition could still be lengthy and gradual, with only marginal changes during the 1990s.

Taiwan. If the future for Chinese on the mainland and in Hong Kong was still problematic, the same was not true for those on Taiwan. The Taiwan economy continued in the early 1990s to develop favorably in most respects. Growth rates, slowed because of the global recession in 1990 and 1991 to close to 5 percent, recovered in 1992 to a level above 6 percent and were projected to move to 7 percent for the next several years. Per capita national income surpassed $10,000, and two-way trade rose to approximately $160 billion in 1992, bringing in another $7 billion. Currency reserves were officially above $88 billion, the largest in the world after Japan's, and were probably above $100 billion if funds kept abroad and unofficial money were included. Furthermore, Taiwan investment in the mainland ballooned to more than $16 billion by the end of 1992, mostly as a result of joint ventures with Hong Kong firms, and it became the most significant factor in the rapid economic growth of the Chinese southern coastal provinces. Taiwan would also become a major factor in other economies, thanks in large part to the $303 billion Six-Year National Development Plan for alleviating infrastructural and environmental inadequacies and requiring importation of much equipment and services from abroad.

The political scene was equally encouraging. Once the decision was made in the mid-1980s to undertake the transition from authoritarianism to democracy, political life progressively broadened and opened. The consequence by the early 1990s was a series of elections that, step by step, broadened the franchise and reformed the political system. The first step was the holding of national, provincial, and local elections in late 1989. The Kuomintang allowed itself for the first time since before 1949 to stand in open contest with political opponents. That was a successful test run, as the results were judged to be fair and also favorable to the Kuomintang, which won 70 percent of the total. The second step was the complete replacement of the National Assembly, elected in 1948. The new election took place at the end of 1991, and the Kuomintang again took close to 70 percent of the total, with the opposition Democratic Progressive party garnering most of the rest.

Perhaps the most important step, however, was the Legislative Yuan election of December 1992. There the Kuomintang took only 53 percent of the total, while the Democratic Progressive party increased its strength to 31 percent. These three elections, taken as a whole, signified the victory of democracy on the island. Of perhaps equal importance, they also gave the Kuomintang a degree of legitimacy it had lacked: it had previously ruled by force, but now it could claim to represent the popular will, and this in an entity, 80 percent of the population (or their progeny) of which had been on Taiwan when the Kuomintang first appeared on the scene in 1945.

In addition, martial law having been lifted in 1987, in mid-1991 the party formally terminated the "Communist suppression" period and abolished the accompanying "temporary provisions" under which many constitutional rights were revoked and the military rule of four decades was justified. Not only did that mean that the opposition won the right to organize and compete for power openly; it also meant that citizens could advocate Taiwanese independence, so long as they did so in a nonviolent manner, without fear of incarceration. The consequence was the release of most political prisoners and the return to Taiwan of many who had fought against the Kuomintang from abroad, including the famous P'eng Ming-min, who thereupon returned openly in November 1992. Further, several constitutional amendments were passed strengthening the National Assembly, regularizing the electoral process and terms of holding office, and granting such modern social rights as health insurance and nondiscrimination against women and minorities. By the third year of the decade, therefore, Taiwan had become a pluralistic representative democracy in both form and content.

That did not mean that all political problems were past, of course. The Kuomintang had much additional work to do to modernize itself internally and to broaden its appeal to the Taiwanese majority. The Democratic Progressive party, like the Kuomintang itself, was heavily factionalized and often threatened by extremism. It had yet to learn how to act in a fully responsible manner, it did not yet know how to conduct itself in parliamentary settings, and it was constantly tempted to torpedo the entire democratization process by going to extremes on the question of independence. And the population as a whole was not used to its new freedom. As a result, social unrest, crime, and licentious behavior increased greatly. These could be termed problems of success, but as in all such instances, unexpected political bankruptcy could occur even in the midst of such heady upswings as that of the late 1980s–early 1990s democratic transition.

A final element of success for Taiwan was the initiation and development of contacts with the mainland. Initially this process was carried out by means of citizen visits in 1987. By the end of 1992, more than 3 million Taiwanese had visited the mainland, and perhaps 30,000 mainlanders had visited Taiwan. Journalists and scholars began to be exchanged in 1991, and as of 1992, athletes could participate in each other's sports events, even raising each other's flags and playing respective national anthems. But more important was the establishment of nominally nongovernmental institutions on both sides to conduct direct talks and, someday presumably, negotiations. Taiwan called its body the Straits Exchange Foundation; the mainland termed its institution the Association for Relations across the Taiwan Strait. Both were formed in 1991. Their first meetings in late 1992 were failures, but the ground was broken, and subsequent meetings in 1993 were more successful, especially the historic Koo-Wang talks in Singapore in April.

The one exception to the improved position of Taiwan, within Greater China and internationally, was the island's security. This deteriorated after 1991, because of the mainland's program of military modernization—especially its acquisition of high-tech equipment in increasing numbers—its partial recovery from its nadir in international prestige after Tiananmen, and the accelerated aging of important components of Taiwan's military force. By mid-1992, the situation had reached a critical stage in terms of the most important component: air defense. Taipei's Indigenous Defense Fighter, an improved version of the American F-20, would not come into the inventory in requisite numbers until late in the decade, and a gap opened between mainland offensive capabilities and Taiwanese defenses. This was partially filled by the American sale—unannounced—of Patriot surface-to-air missiles and the sale, announced during the American presidential campaign with much publicity, of 150 F-16s. But the mainland's drive to acquire large numbers of high performance equipment of all kinds could not in the end be countered by Taiwan's efforts alone. Accordingly its security position would only decline or would increasingly be placed in the hands of the United States, its security guarantor. But since the early 1980s the United States had attempted to excuse itself from that function. Although the military balance in the Taiwan Strait was restored for the time by the American sales, Taipei's longer-run security future was increasingly guarded.

International Trends and Emerging Relations between Beijing, Hong Kong, and Taipei

Chapters 15, 16, and 17 examined how post–cold war international trends and relations among the three components of Greater China affected the emergence of the whole. It remains to update that analysis to the end of 1992 and to project trends for the rest of the decade and for the future.

The first years of the 1990s clarified the shape of the future of international relations and how they would influence Asia and Greater China. The 1991 Gulf War, the final demise of communism in the Soviet Union and the subsequent disintegration of that country, and the breakdown of domestic societies on several continents are one factor in that future. They signified the final breakdown of the cold war bipolar system centered on American-Soviet power and ideological rivalry throughout the globe. The disappearance of superpower rivalry meant that a major conflict could be fought and regional aggression stopped under the collective security rules of the United Nations for the first time since 1950. Given continued UN Security Council cooperation among the Permanent Five members, a new global security stability came to replace the cold war balance of nuclear terror. The amazingly rapid and easy demise of communism in the Soviet Union and Eastern Europe meant that Marxism-Leninism as an ideology and a mode of political organization was finished globally. It remained only to witness its replacement in the few remaining Communist-ruled nations—China, Cuba, North Korea, and Vietnam—either by breakdown or by evolution. But there was no longer any doubt as to the future of such rule, or to the eventual victory of democracy and of the market economy as a means to organize the polities and economies of all nations.

The breakdown of domestic order in several nations, Yugoslavia and Somalia being the most obvious, signified the carrying to the extreme the principle of national self-determination, hardly a new factor in international relations. Fortunately, the international community, such as was its organization, increasingly felt a responsibility to deal with such problems. Presuming continued cooperation among the Permanent Five, particularly under American leadership, it was likely that enhanced international, institutional means would be created to address further problems.

A second factor shaping the future was the tentative emergence of a post–cold war international system, as indicated by these three developments. There was still no security overlay, but the assumed solution was collective security as the only way to prevent return to a global or even regional balance of power. The further emergence of global issues, particularly environmental concerns and human rights, was another indication of the new international arrangements. The June 1992 conference on the environment in Rio de Janeiro elevated that issue's importance for many nations, and an ever-increasing number inscribed human rights on their foreign policy agendas. It would take some years, perhaps the rest of the 1990s, to construct a fully operational international system to replace that of the previous half century, but its outlines were visible in the early years of the decade.

The third factor was acceleration of the five trends noted in chapter 16: multipolarity; the democratization-marketization-interdependence triple revolution; domestic policy orientation emphasized above foreign policy; the high-technology emphasis in economic development and as a measurement of national power; and the emergence of global issues. What was a prediction in 1991 became a fact two years later.

A final factor was the political change in the United States attendant upon the election in 1992 of a Democratic administration under President William Clinton. It seemed apparent early in his first year in office that, first, domestic economic and social reconstruction would displace foreign policy as America's principal concern, although a neoisolationist foreign policy would not necessarily follow.

Second, the reduction of American defense capabilities would be quicker and more severe and would affect military commitments more directly than was promised during the election campaign. And third, economic concerns would take priority above national security matters, while European, Middle Eastern, and Russian issues would take precedence above Asian-directed policies, with the exception of economic relations with Japan. Together, these shifts indicated that the United States would play a much less active role in global affairs during the 1990s, taking advantage of the apparent hiatus provided by the end of the cold war to put its own house in order, and returning to full participation and international leadership only toward the end of the decade. At least that seemed to be the White House's game plan. It was doubtful, of course, whether the outer world would cooperate and provide such a benign backdrop. The first international crisis—and there would be many—would require American attention and participation, thus at least partially short-circuiting the hopes of the American president.

These trends had specific reflection in Asia and were of relevance to emerging relations among the three elements of Greater China. The near coincidence of the downfall of communism and the American-led victory in the Gulf War temporarily masked the relative decline in regional American influence. For about two years, America was at the pinnacle: it was the only remaining superpower, and all other nations appreciated American actions in the Middle East and in the cold war and were respectful of—in some cases awed by—American military power. The Soviet Union—or rather, its successor states loosely united in the Commonwealth of Independent States—was temporarily out of the Asian picture, as those components sought to keep their economic and political heads above water. For a while, it therefore appeared that Russia could be ignored.

Bit by bit, however, Russia sought to demonstrate that it not only was a continuing presence in Asia, but had an important role to play there. It signed significant economic, military, and political agreements with China and India, it took a harder-than-expected line toward Japan regarding the Northern Islands issue, and it adopted an approach-avoidance, partner-opponent line toward the United States in Asia. China was, for a time, doubly shocked by the fate of communism everywhere else and by the American military victory. At first Beijing calculated it had better take the low road, lest it be next on the American "hit list." But it recovered and, thanks to a new feeling of confidence born of its economic success and the series of minicrises with the United States on a wide range of issues, it embarked on a much bolder path of regional involvement and even power projection. The net outcome by 1993 was the progressive emergence of relative equality in Asia among the four regional great powers, thus laying the groundwork, if the powers so desired, for constructing a new regional security system and a higher mode of regional international relations.

But high technology, economic development, marketization, and interdependence were the driving variables in post–cold war Asia. These factors formed the core of Japanese relations with the United States and with the smaller states of Asia. Along with democratization, they propelled South Korea, Taiwan, Thailand, Indonesia, India, and most of the other Asian medium powers toward rapid all-around modernization. They also dominated the foreign policy of China and the interrelations among the three components of Greater China. Everyone therefore concentrated on achieving high rates of domestic economic development, and all three tried to create or maintain international conditions favorable to that purpose. China and Taiwan, for instance, were willing to cooperate with each other, or at least not impede each other, in fulfilling the requirements for entering the General Agreement on Tariffs and Trade. Similarly, China was able to rationalize accepting American demands for better treatment of American business in China, made in the so-called 301 and market-opening negotiations. Agreements on a number of economic fronts were thus signed in 1992.

For all the above reasons, none of the major powers or, with the exception of North Korea, the other nations in Asia had any motivation to use force in the conduct of their foreign policies. Consequently, peace reigned in Asia and was likely to continue for the rest of the 1990s. Exceptions were Korea, where the security situation remained volatile; the Spratly Islands, which China could for the first time take in spite of regional opposition; Kashmir, where India and Pakistan could go to war at any time; and Burma, which could implode like Yugoslavia and present a temptation to China or India to intervene. Except for North Korea, however, the likelihood of conflict was reasonably small. Perhaps the case of Taiwan ought to be added to the list of potential trouble spots, as any precipitous movement toward independence—following the coming to power of the Democratic Progressive party, for example—could bring swift mainland military attack. Yet even here the probability of conflict was likely to remain low.

It remains to indicate what likely future relations might emerge among the three sides of the Greater China triangle and how, therefore, the evolution of the whole might proceed. In the middle-to-long term, factors that were constant in the short term would increasingly become variables. This would greatly complicate any composite picture. We can, however, extrapolate trends as they appeared in the early 1990s into a short-term future, and then consider scenarios of the more distant future. "Short term" is defined as the two years beyond the end of 1992, "middle term" as the period ending in 1997, and "long term" as the period thereafter, as distant as the first years of the twenty-first century.

The most important relationship was that between mainland China and Taiwan. As in the past its development depended on the concatenation of domestic developments in the two Chinese entities and the influence of the international milieu. Domestically, the mainland's economy and society evolved rapidly toward pluralism, with impending political change of the same character. In Taiwan, the democratic transition was quite advanced, the economy had produced a modern consumer society, and a new popular culture had emerged out of compatible elements of traditional Chinese culture and modernist attitudes. On the mainland, while the party continued to impose its own cultural norms and to oppose traditional Chinese culture, both modernist and traditional culture experienced revival, amalgamation, and competition with Communist party culture, putting it on the defensive. The consequence, along with the more than half century of separation between China and Taiwan, was that Taiwan began increasingly to think of itself not as an autonomous minority within Greater China but as a separate place.

Other factors, however, pointed in a different direction. The two governments played a cooperative game: by each claiming to be the only government of all China, they discouraged a two-Chinas solution and helped to keep the whole together in most Chinese minds. Neither, at least not yet, countenanced formal independence or formal autonomy for Taiwan. Nor was the use of force by the mainland likely, especially in the context of a reasonable approximation to a balance of military power in the Taiwan Strait and of continued American security guarantorship of the island. Finally, the level of ideological hostility was greatly reduced, trade and cultural exchange were greatly increased, and official contacts were begun.

But that did not indicate that reunification was around the corner, just as the first set of trends did not necessarily indicate that independence was likely. There was no hint on either side of any movement toward acceptance of the other's political system. Taiwanese visits to the mainland showed more clearly the differences between the two places and that Taiwanese citizens felt as much at home in the emerging union of developed, modern countries, East and West, as they did in their original Chinese culture. Taiwan's enhanced international status, together with the mainland's greater foreign policy flexibility, gave Taipei more room to maneuver, internationally and across the strait. Taiwan could resist mainland approaches and play for time until, presumably, communism on the mainland evolved fully away from its traditional forms of organization and ideology.

Neither did that mean final separation. Both peoples still held a one-nation mentality. In Taiwan, even the Democratic Progressive party realized that merely an approach to the gate of independence carried the risk of mainland military response. As Taiwan's security guarantor, the United States was also leaning heavily against formal independence, although it would look with favor on negotiated autonomy. Indeed, China began to see wisdom in going along with Taiwan's policy of seeking a broader role in international institutions: tacitly supporting such a policy acted as a lightning rod against complete independence, and it could also involve the United States in possible new agreements regarding Taiwan's international status.

When these domestic factors concerning mainland-Taiwan relations were set side by side with the international factors noted earlier in this chapter and previously, the weighted average of both pointed roughly in the same direction: neither reunification nor independence. The status quo evident in the early 1990s ought, therefore, to continue through most of the decade. A Taiwan governed by the Democratic Progressive party or a Taipei too successful in regaining international status could, of course, force China to conclude that, step by step, the island was slipping away and that a stop would have to be put to that movement. It is also possible that the United States could tire of its role as a security guarantor and let slip its guard long enough to allow the mainland to think it could conduct an attack without great fear of American retaliation.

But it was more likely that Taiwan would not seek independence; that its diplomatic offensive would reach natural limits; that the mainland would gradually turn in a more liberal, reformist, internationally benign direction and work out a live-and-let-live arrangement with Taiwan; that the United States would strongly encourage the two to negotiate their differences; and that international trends favoring peace, participation, and problem-solving would strongly favor mainland-Taiwan rapprochement. Thus, while the long term could bring about any outcome—even the extremes of forced reunification or negotiated independence—short-to-middle term prospects in the early 1990s seemed likely to continue relatively unchanged. It therefore appeared that the two Chinese parties had a few years still to settle their differences, if they wished to avail themselves of the opportunity.

The future of Hong Kong–China relations was obviously simpler, given the certainty of absorption in 1997. The major determinants were the changing economic-political-social situation in China and the international economy—not international security, since regional or global conflict was relatively unlikely. But the political situation in Hong Kong itself, as well as the reflection in the colony of the mainland situation and Beijing's policies toward Hong Kong, were emerging as variables in their own right, if still less commanding than the others.

Evaluation of Chinese domestic and foreign policy trends led directly to conclusions for Hong Kong–China relations. With the Chinese economy likely to continue to grow and modernize rapidly, to reform through marketization increasingly, and to internationalize and become interdependent successfully, the role of Hong Kong should grow proportionally. Its function as entrepôt and window remaining critical, it would also become China's main service and financial sector, its principal channel for foreign investment, and the chief organizer of production for the vast Chinese internal market. The emerging competition of the Yangtze Valley cities, the various special economic zones, the great industrial centers of north and northeast China, and the interior border provinces would have an impact on Hong Kong, but more in the way of a challenge. Hong Kong would have to redirect its efforts and restructure its economy, but these charges would not signal the beginning of the end of the city-state and its decline into just another—although still important—Chinese city after 1997. Indeed, the spread of the Hong Kong approach to the country as a whole, together with the vastness and hugeness of the future Chinese economy, appeared to guarantee that Hong Kong could both survive and prosper, at least economically, after 1997.

Politically, our previous conclusion was that China was likely to hold itself together but would progressively move away from totalitarianism, through authoritarianism, and finally toward democratic pluralism. Depending on the pace of that transition and the capability of the Beijing regime or regimes to cope with the inevitable rough spots along the way, it should be progressively easier for the Hong Kong–British government to deal with China. Moreover, a Chinese government with a broader and somewhat more liberal base than that of the oldest generation of the Chinese Communist party should be less inclined to take a hard line toward a fully marketized, thoroughly internationalized, culturally globalized, and increasingly democratizing Hong Kong. Conversely, the self-confidence that would accrue from the country's economic success, together with the propensity to substitute nationalism for Marxism-Leninism-Maoism as the ruling ideology, could embolden any Beijing regime to adopt a more forward, interventionist line toward Hong Kong. How Beijing would move between these influences on its Hong Kong policy is difficult to say; "other things being equal," they could roughly cancel each other out.

The one obvious factor that was not equal was the notion that, for economic development, China required both political stability at home and an economically strong, well-governed Hong Kong. That meant moving slowly but inexorably toward democratization at home and not being overbearing or too interventionist toward the colony. Moreover, if one factored in the rapid cultural transformation of China in the modernist direction, with Hong Kong exerting a degree of attraction and influence disproportionate to its size, this conclusion gained strength. Only if one were to postulate a Cultural Revolution–like, antispiritual pollution–like, conservative reaction in the mid-1990s would it be possible to argue to the contrary, and the probability of this reaction was increasingly small.

Moreover, international forces all appeared to favor a reasonable chance that Hong Kong and China could move to the 1997 reversion, and perhaps some years beyond, without major difficulty. While other Asian nations would surely grow in economic strength, possibly diluting Hong Kong's comparative advantage, none appeared to be in line to replace Hong Kong as the locus of trade, service, finance, window, and investment with China. Moreover, the mid-1990s appeared to be a time of economic recovery in the developed market economies, always good news for Hong Kong. Interdependence was marching ahead even more rapidly, engulfing more and more developing economies, including China's. Hong Kong could only benefit from that. Finally, regarding the critical case of American-Chinese economic relations as they concerned Hong Kong, it was likely that most favored nation treatment would continue to be extended to China—that is, that some way would be found in the United States to modify the formal aspects of human rights–laden conditionality, and in China not to lose face over accepting some degree of conditionality. The central problem was not the implications for Hong Kong of American trade treatment of China, but rather of American reaction to China's treatment of the emergence of democracy in Hong Kong.

How China would adjust to the democratic movement in Hong Kong seemed to be the only major cause for concern in the pre-1997 period; after reversion, the fate of Hong Kong democracy would depend strictly on how far China had evolved in the same direction. Since it was unlikely that the mainland would have moved far in comparison with Hong Kong, and since China's policy would undoubtedly be to bring the Hong Kong political situation strictly in line with that of China, prospects for post-1997 Hong Kong democracy were poor.

From the viewpoint of the early 1990s, things could move toward compromise between Britain and China, or the situation could worsen so rapidly as to threaten the entire future of the colony and of all the post-1984 British-Chinese agreements basic to reversion. If both sides were rational, compromise would take place, and some elements of democracy, beyond what was envisioned in the Joint Declaration and the Basic Law, would be preserved. The reasons to think this might transpire were that China could contain within Hong Kong most of the additional measures being asked, and that the economic and social consequences to both sides of the chaos that could erupt in Hong Kong if the democratic movement were stifled might spread to adjacent areas of China. They could then considerably dampen China's economic growth. Since such growth was all the Chinese Communist party had as a raison d'être for staying in power in the eyes of the Chinese people, the party had no choice but to do all it could to ensure continued rapid economic growth. It would therefore have to treat Hong Kong with care, even as concerned democracy. There were limits as to how far China would bend, however, and the questions in the end were, How far would the British government go in pressing China, and how much did the Hong Kong people desire democracy? The latter was indeed real, but opinion in Hong Kong was that popular support of democracy was solid only so long as the Hang Seng stock market index continued to rise. Thus there was a limit to British as well as Chinese tolerance.

The final side of the triangle was that between Hong Kong and Taiwan. Historically, that relationship had been both informal and relatively weak. With no possible political relations between the two, even as in the China-Taiwan case of rival but mutually nonrecognizing governments, all ties had to concentrate on the economic and communications sectors. It was only in 1991 that Britain finally established a commercial-visa office in Taipei, while pro-Taiwan political opinion was strictly controlled, although hardly minimal, in Hong Kong. A major reason for strong economic and communications ties, of course, was the lack of such direct links between China and Taiwan. People and money going between the mainland and Taiwan had to come through Hong Kong, at least formally. There was, however, a large volume of direct China-Taiwan trade, wherein ships with transit documents that read "Hong Kong" headed for the Fujian coast once in international waters. After 1997, even commercial and communications relations would contain a direct, China-controlled component. Finally, since the prospect for opening straight-line links between China and Taiwan were increasingly high, the value of Hong Kong's linkage to Taiwan, while still important, would decline.

All this meant that the Taipei–Hong Kong leg would continue to be the least important of the three components of Greater China. In some respects it was likely to become the missing link, in which case "Greater China" would shrink to a bilateral China-Taiwan entity, or perhaps a two-and-a-half–sided triangle symbolizing the residual nature of the Hong Kong–Taiwan component after 1997. Conversely, some trends pointed to continuation, and even strengthening, of Taipei–Hong Kong relations. It was unlikely that Hong Kong's combination of natural and acquired advantages would decline, absolutely if not relatively, before and even for a period after 1997. Indeed, as the economies of all three Chinese entities continued to grow rapidly, and as Taiwan progressively regained its place in international economic institutions, the importance of Taiwan and Hong Kong to each other was likely to continue. Furthermore, the recovery of Shanghai—Hong Kong's long-time rival—was not certain and was likely to be prolonged; Hong Kong would continue to take steps to ensure its own competitiveness with Shanghai.

And for Taiwan, even in an era of direct trade and communications with China, the Fujian coastal ports were not likely to provide a complete substitute for Hong Kong. To this must be added the political component. With a democratic Taiwan and a democratizing Hong Kong, the two would find a new natural affinity. Hong Kong could, indeed, become a kind of proving ground for mainland-approved democratic experiments of the sort already accepted in Taiwan. Thus, what first would take place in Taiwan might be reproduced with local adaptation in Hong Kong, and then transmitted with care to China. China might therefore develop an interest in preserving some level of Taipei–Hong Kong linkages for political as well as economic-communications purposes.

These counterarguments were not supremely convincing. The Taiwan–Hong Kong side of the triangle would probably still be the weakest of the three. But it would not necessarily disappear or atrophy after 1997.

Putting the Pieces Together—The Future of Greater China

Because so many determinants could vary so greatly in the 1990s and beyond, it was best to adopt an alternative-futures approach and construct several scenarios of varying likelihood. These would serve both as illustrations of the probable end-points of a large number of outcomes and as an indication of some of the possible paths to the future that Greater China might take. Among the many possibilities, we chose three: at one extreme, the sundering of the whole of Greater China under the influence of a breakdown of order on the mainland; at the other extreme, the establishment of a single whole, the consequence of mainland-Taiwan reconciliation; and third, an intermediate future of a rough balance among all three entities, featuring a rapidly developing mainland economy with a much slower movement toward Chinese-style democracy, successful transition to an autonomous Hong Kong, and a live-and-let-live arrangement between Beijing and Taipei.

Worst-case scenarios should always be considered. They illustrate what a combination of the most unpalatable trends might bring, and reality is not always kind to the trends and forces that at any time seem to indicate the likely future. Many things could go wrong, especially in China. Marketization could fail through inability to cope with the many new forces being unleashed, or through overflow by newly emerging party conservatives. Economic growth could therefore be not only stopped but reversed, as it was in the former Soviet Union. The physical environment of China could collapse, as it were, from overutilization and mismanagement of resources, a possibility that could not be excluded and some thought was probable. Furthermore, the polity might prove not to be strong enough to cope with emerging pluralistic pressures, with the consequence of reversion to repressive, party-military totalitarianism. Or the party might prove not to be strong enough to manage the transition, even to an authoritarian stage along the road to democracy, and the country could break down into separatist regions or anarchy. And Chinese society, so hopefully emerging from the dark days of the Maoist–Cultural Revolutionary past, might not be able successfully to ingest all the disparate cultural attractions entering from abroad, or to integrate modernist and traditional cultures in the face of social anarchy. The corruption of society through the frenzy to seek one's own fortune, already evident in the early 1990s and before, could overcome all efforts to contain or channel it.

In Taiwan, the economy could falter because of its own success, as the island's interdependence with the global economy made it too susceptible to the economic ups and downs of the whole, and as other nations sought to contain Taiwan's growth through restrictive trade and other measures. Taiwanese society, like that of the Chinese mainland, could collapse under the combined pressure of international cultural influences and the liberation of domestic groups demanding socioeconomic reforms in their favor. If the Democratic Progressive party were to come to power, for instance, it might not be able to govern the country successfully, because of its own inexperience and divisions within its own ranks. As for Hong Kong, the obvious dangers were an inability to cope with too much economic success—bankruptcy through expansion, as it were—and the effects of too-rapid democratization. The former would demand massive structural changes too quickly of the colony, while the latter would witness breakdown of the procedurally based political consensus, rigidification of the British administration out of fear to proceed either toward further democratization or back toward more direct rule, and an inability of the Hong Kong police to handle the rising tide of crime and other socially unacceptable behavior.

The result of these negative trends would be not only a decisive halt in the trend toward Greater China, but a crisis in all three societies. Once having emerged, it would take considerable time, perhaps decades, to put things right again. The risk of this scenario, of small probability as viewed early in the 1990s, was great enough to frighten all three Chinese societies into taking steps to make sure it—or even some attenuated version—would not come about. That nightmare, interestingly, might be one factor favoring the continued cooperation of all three, so as to move more surely along the path toward Greater China.

The other extreme would be the converse of the above. The entire process—economic, political, and social—described previously in the negative could, in fact, go well in all three Chinese entities. Decision makers in all three capitals could see the wisdom of mutual cooperation. Economic success, the product of that cooperation, could be so great that Greater China would become Asia's largest economy, and with continuing upward potential. The three societies could converge, each the product of a similar set of forces. Taiwan and Hong Kong could be minor variants on the same theme, and China could willingly receive their influences.

Democracy could be the common goal of all three, with Taiwan leading the way, Hong Kong acting as an experimental laboratory for the mainland, and China carefully but surely moving in the same direction. Accordingly, Taiwan-China and Hong Kong–China tensions would subside. The three would begin to act cooperatively in foreign policy, and negotiations for Taiwanese autonomy within a Beijing-centered Greater China would proceed on the assumption that the one-country, two-systems model, successful in the Hong Kong case, could be extended also to the island. Greater China would thereby become a major force in Asian and in global political, security, and economic relations—but a reasonably benign one, given the meliorating role of Hong Kong, Taiwan's full democratization, and China's willingness to learn from both.

Given historical precedents, however, neither of the above extreme scenarios was likely, although neither could be ruled out. More probable was something between them, the product of trends and forces apparent at the beginning of the 1990s and of elements only beginning to emerge on the horizon. In this scenario, many of the elements noted above for each of the Chinese entities would coalesce in a positive manner, but not so rapidly or kindly as to beget a single Greater China. Thus, economic growth in China would depend not only on domestic capital formation and the emergence of a consumer, "demand-pull" economy but also on Hong Kong and Taiwanese investment. Hong Kong's economic growth would increasingly be a function of the ability of the colony's firms to produce for the internal Chinese market. And Taiwan's economic growth would continue to reorient toward movement of capital to the mainland for setting up or strengthening existing Chinese firms as export platforms. Synergy would result. Increasingly, Chinese in all three entities would express themselves through the same cultural democratization, with cultural influence flowing not only from Taiwan and Hong Kong into the mainland but outwardly as well. To an important extent, that would further undermine the Chinese Communist party's ideological hold over the Chinese people, but it would also help build a common approach to the outside world based on modern Chinese nationalism, traditional Chinese culture, and new cultural values shared with other countries.

In the political sphere, there would be important disjunctions between generations on the mainland, as economic modernization made party rule obsolescent and as democracy seeped into China—not just from the traditional Western democracies, but also from the manner in which that form of government was being practiced or approached in Taiwan and Hong Kong. Such disjunctions could produce periodic crises, as for instance during succession, when economic inadequacies spawned political protests, or when the Chinese party refused to move—or was incapable of moving—swiftly enough to satisfy popular demands for broader representation and political pluralism. But the resulting rough spots would not lead to political breakdown; rather, the party at each juncture would retain enough authority and exercise enough repressive force to enable a viable compromise to be found and to produce a periodic redistribution of power—first in the direction of authoritarianism, later of democracy. Taiwan and Hong Kong would lead in this sphere also, but not without their own rough spots. In the Taiwanese case, the movement would surely be toward the union of Greater Chinese and local nationalism, felt by the vast majority of inhabitants of the island. Its political expression would be in the Democratic Progressive party—although the Kuomintang would just as surely seek to revamp itself into a "party of the whole people." The edge of independence would thus be approached, and the prospect for conflict with the mainland would rise concomitantly. But both populace and government would draw back because of fear of war and because of increasingly shared nationalism with their Chinese brothers and sisters on the mainland.

In Hong Kong, pressure for democracy, welling up from below (that is, from Wanchai and Kowloon) and invited from above (from Government House and Whitehall) would be counteracted partially as a result of Beijing's reluctance to see political change take place too fast, and partially as a result of the business community's warning that the economy must continue to take precedence over political preferences. The movement would be in the same direction as in China and Taiwan, but the result would remain within the bounds of the several British-Chinese agreements on the political transition. The upshot, in all three political entities, would be a disjointed, incremental, sometimes very slow-moving and even temporarily stopped, drift toward a watery amalgam of the least common denominator of the political ideologies of China, Hong Kong, and Taiwan. The initial appearance of, talk of, and tentative experiments with common political institutions would, of course, be further off—perhaps well beyond Hong Kong's reversion and also fully into the post–Deng Xiaoping era on the mainland. But once that idea was voiced, the three Chinese entities would imperceptibly begin to slide into an era no longer of one country, two (or three) systems, but rather of not worrying about the number of countries or systems involved or where the eventual center of political gravity would be. Such would be an intermediate version of Greater China.

It remained to factor in a composite reading of the influence, in all three scenarios, of the international component. That was exceedingly difficult, both because of the myriad of relevant international variables and because events and developments within the three components of Greater China were reciprocally linked with trends and forces in the larger sphere. The spectrum of probable international developments of relevance to China, Hong Kong, and Taiwan was not infinite, however; for analytic purposes, it could be reduced to developments in two spheres of activity, economic and security.

469

Economically, three broad alternatives existed: first, a moribund, even declining global economy at one extreme; second, an economy expanding at approximately 4 percent in most geographic areas, with relatively shallow variations in growth rates; and third, an economy characterized by slower growth—approximately 2–3 percent, with some areas, and probably Asia, doing much better than others, such as Africa and Latin America, and with a succession of moderate recessions and recoveries. Although each of these alternatives could be associated with each of the three Greater China scenarios, it was likely that the declining economic alternative would be associated with, and therefore accentuate, the Greater China "disaster" scenario, that the expansionist alternative be linked with the Greater China "harmony" scenario, and that the intermediate alternative be associated with the Greater China "halfway" scenario. Given these assumptions, the conclusions developed in each case not only would not change but, in fact, would be underlined.

The same would be true of three national security alternatives. The worst possibility would be a major conflict involving one or more of the great powers, and probably the United States. That could be in Korea, Cambodia, Kashmir, or Burma in Asia; Iran, Israel, or Iraq in the Middle East; Zaire, South Africa, or Angola in Africa; and the Balkans or former Soviet republics in Europe. A major conflict would draw great-power attention and resources away from the many problems associated with the Greater China disaster scenario, and thus would allow it to proceed even further downward. The best possibility, of course, would be a world at peace, with the various great powers (in this case, including China) cooperating in the construction of a new, higher-order set of regional and global collective security regimes. Such a felicitous future would strongly support the Greater China harmony scenario, since significant global attention and resources could be devoted to the construction of the new Chinese entity, or at least not subtracted from it. A final security future would see minor regional conflicts but no large-scale or protracted wars requiring huge investments by the great powers, and that would also see some progress toward, but not full agreement on, a new security regime.

No unalterable force links the three international economic alternatives and the three national security alternatives with the three Greater China scenarios. Contingency, surprise, and even the order in which expected trends occurred would have to be taken into account. Nonetheless, for analytic purposes it seemed permissible to make that linkage. One reason was that domestic developments in the three components of Greater China and the relations among them did reciprocally influence trends in the international sphere. Prospects for the Asian and global economies and the likelihood of conflict were correlated with the prosperity in and prospects for conflict among the three Chinese entities. The converse also appeared to be true, because each of the three Chinese entities was an important actor in the economic sphere. Mainland China was already an essential element in national security calculations in Asia and was increasingly coming to be so in other regions. Perhaps in the 1960s the components of what three decades later was termed Greater China were so relatively unimportant in Asian regional and global affairs as to deny linkage. But that was no longer the case in the 1990s. And the future would undoubtedly see even firmer demonstrations of that linkage. So far as the roles of contingency, surprise, and order of events were concerned, only detailed forecasts could evaluate their influence, and then only marginally.

Tentative conclusions could be drawn as to the future of the Chinese in the mainland, Hong Kong, and Taiwan portions of Greater China. First, economic, political, and international factors limited the likelihood that a Greater China entity, evident in outline in the early 1990s, would evolve into something more solid later in the decade. Possibly such a trend could be stopped in its tracks or could accelerate somewhat, but there appeared to be no likelihood that the entity would disappear entirely, or that full and complete union of the three would take place during the decade.

Second, the movement toward Greater China was likely to continue, but relatively slowly and by fits and starts. Trends and forces in the three components of Greater China could not be finely put together. Economics would lead politics at times, and in one or another component; at other times the converse would be true. International forces would surely affect the three in some different manner. But the momentum of the drive toward Greater China was, by the early 1990s, sufficiently great to be difficult to slow down, much less stop. The hugeness of the mainland would, however, set an upper limit as to how fast and how far the trend toward full integration could proceed.

That led into a third conclusion: because of the magnitude of the mainland, because Hong Kong would surely be reintegrated on schedule, and because the mainland Chinese economy was likely to continue growing, Beijing would increasingly be in the driver's seat in determining the shape and pace of the formation of Greater China. Taiwan's choice would increasingly be to get whatever "deal" it could out of closer association with the mainland—not necessarily full reintegration, but perhaps negotiated autonomy. Or it could leave

Greater China entirely and try for a much more formal degree of international acceptance, participation, and security guarantorship—not necessarily full and formal independence. Fourth, a Greater China, even in the "intermediate" scenario developed above, would become Asia's most powerful nation and, perhaps by the turn of the century, a true global superpower. Regional and global international relations would therefore be vitally affected: no major regional or global decisions could be taken unless Greater China agreed and took part.

Finally, a Greater China would not have to be governed fully and directly by its most important component, the mainland. The way would be open for creative solutions to the problem of how, politically, to put the three parts together in a peaceful and viable manner. The success of that venture would depend first on the prior success of the democratic transition on Taiwan, second on whether Hong Kong would be permitted to follow suit, and finally on the pace and peaceful nature of eventual democratization on the mainland.

Notes

CHAPTER 2: PLAYING TO THE PROVINCES, *Susan L. Shirk*

1. *Current Digest of the Soviet Press*, vol. 39, no. 8 (1987), p. 8.

2. Deng Xiaoping's choice was also constrained by his own conservatism and the conservatism of the other members of his generation of Communist party leaders. Deng's cohort of leaders are first-generation founders of the Communist revolution in China, whereas Gorbachev belongs to the fourth generation of Communist leaders in the Soviet Union (Jerry F. Hough, *Soviet Leadership in Transition* [Washington, D.C.: Brookings Institution, 1980]). Lee argues that the political nature of the People's Republic of China was shaped by the particular nature of this founder generation that remained in power for over forty years (Hong Yung Lee, *From Revolutionary Cadres to Party Technocrats in Socialist China* [Berkeley: University of California Press, 1991]).

3. The Chinese categories were coarser so the numbers are not strictly comparable. Christine P. W. Wong, "Material Allocation and Decentralization: Impact of the Local Sector on Industrial Reform," in Elizabeth J. Perry and Christine Wong, eds., *The Political Economy of Reform in Post-Mao China* (Cambridge: Harvard University Press, 1985), pp. 253–78.

4. My view of the Chinese system as a hierarchy contradicts Granick's that local governments were principals with their own property rights (David Granick, *Chinese State Enterprises, A Regional Property Rights Analysis* [Chicago: University of Chicago Press, 1990]). In my view, central party officials hold all formal authority and delegate some of it to lower levels of government for three reasons: to improve incentive compatibility, to divest themselves of sole responsibility, and to win the political support of lower-level officials. Granick's observation that legacies of past investments in enterprises give different levels of government a normative claim to a share of enterprise products and profits is correct and important. His evidence for continuity in the relationships of levels of government and enterprises to demonstrate the validity of the property rights hypothesis, however, is not completely persuasive. Moreover, the strongest evidence for hierarchy is one he ignores, namely, the power of the central party authorities to appoint and dismiss regional officials. Bahry's research on the Soviet Union shows that even in the more highly centralized Soviet system, republican officials were expected to assert local interests and were promoted for doing so (Donna Bahry, *Outside Moscow: Power, Politics and Budgetary Policy in the Soviet Republics* [New York: Columbia University Press, 1987]).

5. Robert V. Daniels, "Soviet Politics since Khrushchev," in John W. Strong, ed., *The Soviet Union under Brezhnev and Kosygin* (New York: Van Nostrand-Reinhold, 1971).

6. Tian Yinong, Xiang Huaicheng, and Zhu Fulin, *Lun zhongguo caizheng tizhi gaige yu hongguan tiaokong* (On China's fiscal system reform and macro regulatory control) (Beijing: China Finance and Economics Publishers, 1988).

7. Caizheng bu caishui tizhi zhu. *Caishui gaige shinian* (A decade of financial and tax reform) (Beijing: China Finance and Economics Publishers, 1989).

8. The strategy of achieving market reform by devolving authority and resources to local officials (and thereby allowing them to build up local political machines) made the Chinese and Yugoslav reform drives surprisingly similar. Of course, the reform experiences in China and Yugoslavia were different in other respects. For example, in Yugoslavia the national legislature became the main policy-making arena, while in China, policy making remained within the party and government bureaucracy.

9. Christine Wong, "Central-Local Relations in an Era of Fiscal Decline: The Paradox of Fiscal Decentralization in Post-Mao China" (unpublished paper, 1990), and Barry Naughton, "Macroeconomic Obstacles to Reform in China: The Role of Fiscal and Monetary Policy" (unpublished paper, 1990), have shown that because the central government shifted many of its spending responsibilities to local governments and collected substantial revenues through state corporations and loans from local governments, the net effect of fiscal decentralization was less favorable to local governments than many Chinese and foreign experts believe.

10. *A Decade of Financial and Tax Reform*; Katherine Huang Hsiao, *The Government Budget and Fiscal Policy in Mainland China* (Taipei: Chung-Hua Institution for Economic Research, 1987); Guojia caizheng gailun bianxie zu. *Guojia caizheng gailun* (Introduction to national finance) (Beijing: Finance and Economics Publishers, 1984).

11. In *Chinese State Enterprises*, Granick argues that local governments had greater control over the material products of local factories than over financial profits.

12. When I talk about "local" or "locality," I refer to provinces, autonomous regions, and provincial-level cities.

13. As Donnithorne points out, the Chinese national government was able to draw on the taxable capacity of light industry only by taxing local governments, which was politically much harder than taxing firms. See Audrey Donnithorne, *Centre-Provincial Economic Relations in China* (Canberra: Australian National University, Contemporary China Papers, no. 16, 1981).

14. Ch'ien Tuan-sheng, *The Government and Politics of China* (Cambridge: Harvard University Press, 1961); Arthur Waldron, "Warlordism versus Federalism: The Revival of a Debate," *China Quarterly*, no. 121 (March 1990), pp. 116–28; Madeleine Zelin, *The Magistrate's Tale: Rationalizing Fiscal Reform in Eighteenth Century China* (Berkeley: University of California Press, 1984).

15. Research by Bahry, *Outside Moscow*, shows that in the federal Soviet system, while the republics' share of the budget increased after Stalin, central control over planning and budgeting remained tight.

16. Ch'ien Tuan-sheng, *Government and Politics of China*.

17. John P. Burns, "China's Nomenklatura System," *Problems of Communism*, vol. 36 (September–October 1987), pp. 36–51.

18. Franz Schurmann, "Politics and Economics in Russia and China," in Donald W. Treadgold, ed., *Soviet and Chinese Communism* (Seattle: University of Washington Press, 1967), pp. 297–326. Chinese provincial authority was also closely tied to the military especially during the 1970s after the Cultural Revolution. Many provincial party secretaries served simultaneously as People's Liberation Army political commissars.

19. *A Decade of Financial and Tax Reform.*

20. Nicholas R. Lardy, *Economic Growth and Distribution in China* (Cambridge: Cambridge University Press, 1979); Michel Oksenberg and James Tong, "The Fiscal Reform in China and Its Effects on Interprovincial Variations in Social Services, 1979–1983" (unpublished paper, 1984).

21. *Guangming ribao*, August 23, 1982, Joint Publication Research Service (JPRS), 81938, Economics 271, October 8, 1982; Michel Oksenberg and James Tong, "The Evolution of Central-Provincial Fiscal Relations in China, 1950–1983: The Formal System" (unpublished paper, 1987).

22. Jonathan Unger, "The Struggle to Dictate China's Administration: The Conflict of Branches vs. Areas vs. Reform," *Australian Journal of Chinese Affairs*, no. 18 (July 1987), pp. 15–45.

23. Even in the Soviet Union, with a more centralized institutional setup, leaders with ambitious reform agendas have sought to play provincial leaders against the conservative central bureaucracy. Khrushchev tried to play to the provinces to weaken his rivals and disarm the powerful central ministries. The support of provincial allies in the Central Committee saved Khrushchev when the Presidium (Politburo) tried to get rid of him in 1957 (Bahry, *Outside Moscow*). Gorbachev also built a coalition of support for reform by building a base among provincial party officials; see Timothy J. Colton, *The Dilemma of Reform in the Soviet Union* (New York: Council on Foreign Relations, 1986).

24. Parris Chang, "Research Notes on the Changing Loci of Decision in the CCP," *China Quarterly*, no. 44 (October–December 1970), pp. 169–94; Roderick MacFarquhar, *The Origins of the Cultural Revolution, Volume I, Contradictions among the People, 1956–57* (New York: Columbia University Press, 1974); Kenneth G. Lieberthal and Bruce J. Dickson, *A Research Guide to Central Party and Government Meetings in China, 1949–1989* (Armonk, N.Y.: M. E. Sharpe, 1989); David S. G. Goodman, "Provincial Party First Secretaries in National Politics: A Categoric or a Political Group?" in David S. G. Goodman, ed., *Groups and Politics in the People's Republic of China* (Cardiff: University College Cardiff Press, 1984), pp. 68–82. Goodman challenges Chang's assertion that the provincial leaders promised to support Mao's policies in exchange for greater provincial autonomy by presenting evidence that the provincial leaders were not in complete agreement. While some of them advocated greater financial autonomy, others demanded more central aid to provinces for projects like water conservancy. To argue that provincial officials have political influence in the policy process and that Mao Zedong tried to win their support does not require that they always agree on policy; in

fact, given the very different situations faced by their regions, it would be surprising if they had unanimous policy preferences. Moreover, provincial leaders probably find no inconsistency in their calls for greater financial autonomy and more state aid for particular projects like water conservancy; they wish to have both.

25. For a detailed description of the Great Leap Forward fiscal system see Oksenberg and Tong, "The Evolution of Central-Provincial Fiscal Relations."

26. Cyert and March would call extrabudgetary funds a form of "organizational slack." See Richard M. Cyert and James G. March, *A Behavioral Theory of the Firm* (Englewood Cliffs, N.J.: Prentice Hall, 1963).

27. Sun Yun, "How to Improve Control of Extra-Budgetary Funds," *Caimao jingji*, no. 7, July 15, 1982.

28. Oksenberg and Tong, "The Evolution of Central-Provincial Fiscal Relations."

29. Barry Naughton, "The Third Front: Defense Industrialization in the Chinese Interior," *China Quarterly*, no. 115 (September 1988), pp. 351–86.

30. Oksenberg and Tong, "The Evolution of Central-Provincial Fiscal Relations."

31. Unger, "The Struggle to Dictate China's Administration"; James Tong, "Fiscal Reform, Elite Turnover, and Central-Provincial Relations in Post-Mao China," *Australian Journal of Chinese Affairs*, no. 22 (July 1989), pp. 1–28.

32. Chinese planning was also much more decentralized than Soviet planning. The volume of interprovincial trade in China was depressed because provincial planners sought independent balances. This argument is presented in Thomas P. Lyons, *Economic Integration and Planning in Maoist China* (New York: Columbia University Press, 1987).

33. Author's interview.

34. During most periods the same method of differentiating revenues by the subordination relations of enterprises has been used in the Soviet Union. See Bahry, *Outside Moscow*.

35. The extrabudgetary funds were equal to three times the 1965 amount; see Sun Yun, "How to Improve Control of Extra-Budgetary Funds."

36. *Introduction to National Finance*.

37. Donnithorne, *Centre-Provincial Economic Relations*.

38. Goodman, "Provincial Party First Secretaries."

39. Granick, *Chinese State Enterprises*.

40. *Introduction to National Finance*.

41. Oksenberg and Tong, "The Evolution of Central-Provincial Fiscal Relations."

42. Ibid.

43. Author's interview.

44. According to interviews, the State Planning Commission proposed decentralizing capital construction at the same time (1979) and for the same reason, that is, to divest itself of responsibility.

45. *Renmin ribao*, June 30, 1979, quoted in Akira Fujimoto, "The Reform of China's Financial Administration System," Japan External Trade Research

Organization, *China Newsletter* (March 1980), pp. 2–9; p. 3.

46. Author's interview.

47. Author's interview.

48. Zhao was not appointed premier until 1980, subsequent to the key 1979 meetings deliberating fiscal arrangements, but he may have played a leadership role at the meetings nonetheless.

49. Some provincial advocates pressed for an approach to reform called "local planned economy" that would shift all economic authority from center to provinces. They held up American federalism as the model to emulate. Fang Weizhong, "Some Tentative Ideas on Carrying Out the Reform of the Economic Management Structure," *Renmin ribao*, September 21, 1979, p. 3.

50. Tian Yinong et al., *On China's Financial System Reform*; and Oksenberg and Tong, "The Evolution of Central-Provincial Fiscal Relations."

51. "State Council Notice on Carrying Out the Financial Management System of Apportioning Revenues and Expenditures While Contracting Responsibility according to Levels," *Jingji tizhi gaige wenjian huibian* (Collections of documents on the [state] economic system reform) (Beijing: Finance and Economic Publishers, 1984), p. 841.

52. One interviewee said the number was 500.

53. Author's interview.

54. Tian Yinong et al., *On China's Financial System Reform*, p. 76; and Barry Naughton, "The Decline of Central Control over Investment in Post-Mao China," in David M. Lampton, ed., *Policy Implementation in Post-Mao China* (Berkeley: University of California Press, 1987).

55. Naughton, "The Decline of Central Control."

56. Author's interviews; Guo Daimo and Yang Zhaoming, "Different Viewpoints in a Discussion on the Reform of the Economic Management Structure," *Renmin ribao*, September 21, 1979, p. 3; Fang, "Some Tentative Ideas."

57. Author's interviews.

58. Tian Yinong et al., *On China's Financial System Reform*, says that despite the original intention in 1979 to reform other aspects of the economic structure before tackling financial reform, the clamor from all quarters for more financial power was so deafening that financial reform was undertaken first.

59. This summary description draws heavily on Oksenberg and Tong, "The Evolution of Central-Provincial Fiscal Relations."

60. The ministries must have been reluctant to give up their control over local enterprise expenditures. In a 1979 document on fiscal decentralization, the State Council emphasized that while the central ministries would no longer have authority to hand down local expenditure targets, they still were to "guide the direction, approve the work program, carry out supervision and urging, sum up experiences, and help local enterprises in their sector" (State Council Notice on Carrying Out the Financial Management System of 'Linking Revenues and Expenditures, Sharing Total Revenues, Contracting the Percentages, and Fixed for Three Years'" (1979), *Jingji tizhi gaige wenjian*

huibian (Collection of documents on the [state] economic system reform) (Beijing: China Finance and Economic Publishers, 1984), pp. 803–4.

61. The system was described in "State Council Notice on Carrying Out the Financial Management System of Apportioning Revenues and Expenditures While Contracting Responsibility according to Levels."

62. In 1980, Shanghai 88.8 percent, Beijing 63.5 percent, and Tianjin 68.8 percent; see Oksenberg and Tong, "The Evolution of Central-Provincial Fiscal Relations."

63. *Liaoning jingji tongji nianjian* (Liaoning yearbook of economic statistics), *1987* (Beijing: China Statistics Publishing House, 1987).

64. In July 1979 the State Council had made a preliminary decision to implement a version of fiscal decentralization called "linking revenues and expenditures, sharing total revenues, contracting for percentages, fixed for three years," which was essentially the Jiangsu "sharing total revenues" system; the "apportioning revenues and expenditures while contracting responsibility according to levels" or "sharing fixed revenues" system was introduced on an experimental basis only in Sichuan because it was said to require reforms in other aspects of the economy ("State Council Notice on Carrying Out the Financial Management System of 'Linking Revenues and Expenditures, Sharing Total Revenues, Contracting the Percentages, and Fixed for Three Years'"). After the October meeting of provincial party secretaries and the December National Planning Conference, the State Council announced a change to the "sharing fixed revenues" system.

65. Ibid.

66. Author's interviews.

67. In an earlier document the State Council had stressed that in the fiscal contract negotiations, stability of central revenues and national financial balance had to take priority. Ibid.

68. Tian Yinong et al., "On China's Financial System Reform"; and Oksenberg and Tong, "The Evolution of Central-Provincial Fiscal Relations."

69. Only in part because of a change excluding enterprise depreciation funds from the local revenue base. See "Evolution," Oksenberg and Tong.

70. "The failure to achieve a complete set of reforms has affected the implementation of fiscal reforms"; see *A Decade of Financial and Tax Reform*, p. 232.

71. Author's interviews.

72. The center extended a loan to Liaoning in the meantime. Author's interviews.

73. "Caizheng bu caishui tizhi gaige zhu" (Deepen the reform of the budget management system to promote economic development), *Jingji guanli* (Electronic management), no. 10, 1988, pp. 35–37, 39.

74. Tian Yinong et al., "On China's Financial System Reform," p. 84.

75. *Deepen the Reform of the Budget Management System.*

76. The continued existence of the big pot is illustrated by the widespread "chicken game" between local and central governments over grain procurement funds during 1989–1990. Local governments spent their grain procure-

ment funds for other purposes and then asked the center to bail them out to prevent peasant unrest.

77. That is not to say that fiscal reform did not aggravate regional tensions. For one thing, many provinces were jealous of Guangdong's special financial privileges (author's interviews).

78. Author's interviews; Shanghai's share was increased from 12.1 percent in 1984 to 24 percent in 1985. Tianjin's share was raised from 46 percent in 1984 to 58 percent in 1985. See Tong, "Fiscal Reform."

79. One of them, the Chinese National Petrochemical Corporation, was granted the bureaucratic status of a ministry; all the others were made subordinate to ministries.

80. Author's interviews.

81. Author's interviews.

82. Christine P. W. Wong, "Central-Local Relations in an Era of Fiscal Decline."

83. Author's interviews.

84. Oksenberg and Tong, "The Evolution of Central-Provincial Fiscal Relations"; and Hsiao, *The Government Budget and Fiscal Policy*.

85. Oksenberg and Tong, "The Evolution of Central-Provincial Fiscal Relations."

86. Wang Bingqian, "Report on the Implementation of the State Budget for 1986 and on the Draft State Budget for 1987," *Xinhua* (New China News Agency), April 13, 1987; Foreign Broadcast Information Service *(FBIS), China*, April 15, 1987, pp. K11–21.

87. In one exception to the universal application of these extractions, the center hit up Guangdong and Fujian for loans in 1981 (1.6 billion yuan from Guangdong, 154 million yuan from Fujian) and again in 1982 (the loans were written off in 1983 and never repaid); see Tong, "Fiscal Reform." Officials in Guangdong and Fujian probably calculated that it was worth their while to pay off the center to keep their special privileges (which included capital construction and foreign investment approval authority, planning authority, a separate labor market, and foreign exchange retention as well as fiscal autonomy). From their point of view, the loans were protection money to the organization boss to preserve their profitable franchise.

88. "State Council Notice on Improving the Financial Management System of 'Apportioning Revenues and Expenditures While Contracting Responsibility According to Levels'," (1982), *Jingji tizhi gaige wenjian huibian 1977–83* (Collection of documents on the state economic system reform) (Beijing: China Finance and Economics Publishers, 1984), p. 841.

89. Ibid.; *A Decade of Financial and Tax Reform*; Oksenberg and Tong, "The Evolution of Central-Provincial Fiscal Relations"; and Wong, "Central-Local Relations."

90. Tian Yinong et al., "On China's Financial System Reform," p. 83.

91. *Guangming ribao*, August 23, 1982, *JPRS*, 81938, Economics 271, October 8, 1982.

92. "State Council Notice on Improving the Financial Management Sys-

tem of 'Apportioning Revenues and Expenditures While Contracting Responsibility according to Levels'"; Oksenberg and Tong, "The Evolution of Central-Provincial Fiscal Relations."

93. Wong, "Tax Reform."

94. *Introduction to National Finance*; and *A Decade of Financial and Tax Reform*.

95. The theory of political rent seeking, that is, politicians who intervene in markets to generate political resources for themselves, has been elegantly developed by Robert H. Bates in *Essays on the Political Economy of Rural Africa* (Berkeley: University of California Press, 1983); and *Markets and States in Tropical Africa* (Berkeley: University of California Press, 1983).

96. One group of Chinese reform economists argued that the emergence of problems like local administrative interference and market blockades could not be blamed entirely on the decentralized fiscal system. They were the result of introducing fiscal decentralization into a system characterized by "unified local Party and government leadership and the role played by local Party and government authorities in functioning as the acting owners of enterprise assets under the system of public ownership." See Hua Sheng, Zhang Xuejun, and Luo Xiaoping, "Ten Years of Chinese Reform: Review, Reflection, and Prospects," *Jingji yanjiu* (Economic research), no. 9, September 20, 1988, pp. 13–37.

97. Author's interview.

98. See Susan L. Shirk, *The Political Logic of Economic Reform in China*, chap. 7, for a detailed analysis of the *li gai shui* case (University of California Press, forthcoming).

99. Wong, "Tax Reform."

100. Ibid. Although formally all provinces were on a system of "sharing specific revenues," "because conditions were not ripe," the "sharing total revenues" system was "temporarily implemented." See *A Decade of Financial and Tax Reform*.

101. Author's interview.

102. *Deepen the Reform of the Budget Management System*.

103. During the period from 1979 to 1987, the center accumulated deficits totaling more than 64 billion yuan, while local governments ran surpluses totaling more than 7 billion yuan; see *A Decade of Financial and Tax Reform*.

104. Tian Yinong et al., *On China's Financial System Reform*; "Minister of Finance Addresses Financial Meeting," *Xinhua*, July 24, 1988.

105. Author's interview.

106. Author's interview.

107. *Deepen the Reform of the Budget Management System*.

108. Burns, "China's Nomenklatura System."

109. Author's interview.

110. Xue Muqiao, "China's Current Economic Situation, Analysis and Prospects," *Renmin ribao*, June 3, 1983; *FBIS, China*, June 13, 1983, pp. K34–41.

111. Tian Jia, Zhu Limin, and Cao Siyun, "Further Perfect Reform of Separately Listing Cities in the State Plan," *Shijie jingji daobao*, October 26, 1987, p. 10.

112. For an argument on behalf of giving full provincial-level legal status to central cities see Tian Jia et al., ibid.

113. "State Council Decision to Improve the Method of Local Financial Contracts," *Caizheng* (Finance), no. 10, 1988, p. 1.

114. By 1984, one account listed fifty-two experimental cities in China. *Renmin ribao*, October 20, 1984.

115. Author's interview.

116. Ibid.

117. Ibid.

118. Ibid.

119. *Xinhua*, June 2, 1987; *FBIS, China*, June 5, 1987, p. K13. Most extra-budgetary funds were in the hands of enterprise managers, but a sizable share was controlled by local government officials.

120. Author's interview.

121. "State Council National Forum on Industry and Communications Closed September 1st," *Xinhua*, September 3, 1981; *FBIS, China*, September 8, 1981, pp. 12–13.

122. Jing Ping, "Everyone Must Support Key Construction," *Hongqi* (Red flag), no. 8, April 16, 1983, pp. 16–18.

123. As one article acknowledged, "If we properly curtail the construction of ordinary processing industry projects in our locality or department and concentrate our financial and material resources on supporting the state in the construction of key projects and the development of energy sources and transport in our country, we eventually will benefit, although our immediate earnings will be smaller" (Hua Xing, "The Components Will Be Stimulated When the Whole Is Handled Well," *Xinhua*, April 17, 1983; *FBIS, China*, April 21, 1983, pp. K10–11).

124. Wong, "Central-Local." Han Gouchun, "A Brief Introduction to the System of 'Apportioning Revenues and Expenses between the Central and Local Authorities, While Holding the Latter Responsible for Their Own Profit and Loss in Financial Management,' " *Caizheng*, no. 7, July 5, 1982; *JPRS*, no. 82018, October 19, 1982, pp. 16–19.

125. Rui Jun, "Economists on How to Deal with Inflation in China," *Liaowang Overseas Edition*, October 24, 1988; *FBIS, China*, October 31, 1988, pp. 44–45.

126. Wong, "Tax Reform."

127. Liu Lixin and Tian Chunsheng, "Conscientiously Control the Scale of Investments in Fixed Assets," *Renmin ribao*, February 21, 1983; *FBIS, China*, February 24, 1983, pp. K15–18.

128. In April 1982, the State Council issued a regulation prohibiting regional blockades in purchasing and marketing industrial products (*Xinhua*, April 20, 1982; *FBIS, China*, April 21, 1982, pp. K10–11; also Qi Xiangwu and Hou Yunchun, "Why Is It Necessary to Oppose Regional Economic Block-ades?" *Hongqi*, no. 9, May 1, 1982). Continuing press complaints about protectionist practices indicate that the problem persisted after 1982 (Ying Guang, "On the Socialist Unified Market," *Renmin ribao*, February 28, 1983;

"Do Not Put Up New Blockades in the Course of Reform," *Xinhua*, July 18, 1984; *FBIS, China*, July 23, 1984, pp. K9–10).

129. The pervasiveness of local protectionism is indicated by the fact that when Beijing Mayor Chen Xitong declared that Beijing would stop practicing local protectionism, it was front-page news. According to the press report, local governments' strategies for protecting local products included stipulation that a portion of the earnings derived from the price disparity of color televisions purchased from outside be turned over to local coffers; orders to commercial enterprises specifying the amount of local products that must be sold each month; earmarking loans for the purchase of local goods; and lists of products forbidden to be "imported" from other regions (Chen Yun and Zhang Guimin, "Minister Calls for an End to Local Protectionism," *Xinhua*, April 10, 1990; *FBIS, China*, April 20, 1990, p. 43).

130. Susan L. Shirk, "China: The Bargaining Game," in Hadi Soesastro and Mari Pariguestee, eds., *Technological Challenge in the Asia-Pacific Economy* (Sydney: Allen and Unwin, 1990).

131. The financial link between local governments and their subordinate enterprises was more direct under the "sharing specific revenues" version of the reform than it was under "sharing total revenues." But even under the latter scheme local revenues were tied to the performance of local enterprises.

132. Author's interview.

133. Wong, "Central-Local."

134. An exception was Jiangsu Province. According to their reputation, Jiangsu officials traditionally respected experts and left them alone to make economic decisions. And because its local market was so small, Jiangsu officials encouraged enterprises to go out and compete on the national market instead of protecting the local market (author's interview).

135. For example, the press criticized local officials for giving or reducing taxes for particular enterprises on the one hand and for imposing extra taxes (such as the so-called local energy and transportation construction tax) on all enterprises on the other hand ("Immediately Stop Additional Levies of Local Energy and Transportation Constructional Funds," *Renmin ribao*, November 24, 1984).

136. The best example of this kind of local populism was the record of Li Ruihuan as party secretary of Tianjin. Because the Chinese system lacks elections, we would predict that officials would use rents more for industrial empire building, which translates into bureaucratic power and prestige, than for popular public works, which translates into votes. The fact that a few officials like Li Ruihuan have experimented with the populist strategy suggests that they are gambling on a change in the political system occurring in the future.

137. On local political machines in other Communist countries, see Jerry F. Hough, *The Soviet Prefects* (Cambridge, Mass.: Harvard University Press, 1969); and Jean Woodal, *The Socialist Corporation and Technocratic Power: The Polish United Workers' Party, Industrial Organization and Workforce Control, 1958–80* (Cambridge: Cambridge University Press, 1982). We as yet have little

empirical information about how these local industry-based political machines work in China. For example, is the party secretary the power broker in Chinese provinces and cities as he was in the Soviet Union, or is the broker role played by government leaders instead? Did the shift in power over expenditures from ministries to localities create new conflicts of interest on the local level?

138. "Reducing the Scale of Capital Construction Is an Important Supporting Measure for Reform," *Renmin ribao*, September 2, 1988; *FBIS, China,* September 9, 1988, pp. 64–65.

139. "What Is Unnecessary Should Be Given Up So That What Is Necessary Can Be Achieved," *Renmin ribao*, December 4, 1988; *FBIS, China,* December 15, 1988, pp. 34–37.

140. James C. F. Wang, *Contemporary Chinese Politics, An Introduction* (Englewood Cliffs, New Jersey: Prentice Hall, 1989).

141. Author's interview.

142. Chao Hao-sheng, "Yao Yilin on the Economic Situation in China," *Ta Kung Pao* (Hong Kong), December 23, 1989; *FBIS, China,* December 26, 1989, pp. 24–26.

143. The original financial agreements between center and provinces introduced in 1980 had been described as contracts sharing responsibility as well as resources, but in 1988, the contract notion was reaffirmed.

144. The original 1980 system had intended to eliminate the "eating from the big pot" phenomenon, but in fact center and provinces continued to eat off one another's plates.

145. "Li Peng Chairs State Council Executive Meeting," *Xinhua*, July 12, 1988; *FBIS, China,* July 13, 1988, p. 19; "State Council Decision to Improve the Method of Local Financial Contracts."

146. Appealing to powerful political actors who felt they had been put at a competitive disadvantage by Zhao Ziyang's version of economic reform was a consistent theme in Li Peng's succession strategy. He took up the cause of large state factories as well as high-revenue provinces; see Shirk, *The Political Logic of Economic Reform.*

147. "Li Peng Chairs State Council Executive Meeting."

148. The State Council meeting announcing the contracts for these thirteen high-revenue areas also announced that from then on the terms of all provincial contracts would be made public; see "State Council Decision to Improve the Method of Local Financial Contracts." This measure was probably designed to satisfy the high-revenue provinces that still turned over to the center a high proportion of their revenues. These provinces wanted everyone to recognize their contributions to the public good and wanted to show up the free ride of other provinces.

149. Lin Ruo, "A Successful Attempt to Reform the Financial System," *Renmin ribao*, March 21, 1988; *FBIS, China,* April 6, 1988, pp. 55–57.

150. "State Council Decision to Improve the Method of Local Financial Contracts."

151. Zhang Zhenbin, "My Opinion on Several Questions Regarding Finan-

cial Reform," *Renmin ribao*, March 18, 1988; *FBIS, China*, April 5, 1988, p. 25.

152. Willy Wo-lap Lam, "Further on CCP Central Work Conference," *South China Morning Post* (Hong Kong), November 3, 1989; *FBIS, China*, November 3, 1989, p. 13; David L. Shambaugh, "The Fourth and Fifth Plenary Sessions of the 13th CCP Central Committee," *China Quarterly*, no. 120, December 1989, pp. 852–62.

153. Wang Bingqian, "Report on the Implementation of the State Budget for 1989 and on the Draft Budget for 1990," *Xinhua*, April 7, 1990; *FBIS, China*, April 12, 1990, pp. 16–24.

154. "The Proposals of the CCP Central Committee Said to Have Been Revised Twice," *Ming Pao* (Hong Kong), January 29, 1991, *FBIS, China*; January 30, 1991, pp. 16–17.

155. Cheung Po-ling, "Regions Reported to Get Concessions in Next Plan," *Hong Kong Standard*, November 24, 1990; *FBIS, China*, November 26, 1990, pp. 28–29.

156. Ho Po-shih, "Inside Story of the Seventh Plenum," *Tangtai* (Hong Kong), January 5, 1991; *FBIS, China*, January 8, 1991, pp. 28–30.

157. Lu Feng, "Vigorously Promote the Work of the Cadre Reshuffles," *Renmin ribao*, January 19, 1991; *FBIS, China*, January 25, 1991, pp. 33–34.

CHAPTER 3: PARTY AND ARMY, *Feng Shengbao*

1. Chinese Communist leaders considered that Taiwan, Hong Kong, South Korea, and Singapore had not yet become democracies. The more stability, the faster economic development seems in developing countries.

2. Chong-Pin Lin, "The Extreme Roles of the People's Liberation Army in Modernization: Limits of Professionalization," p. 1. in *Security Studies* (Summer 1992). When Lin argued against the idea that the PLA has withdrawn from politics he correctly cited many Western works. He did not, however, cite works about the PLA withdrawing from economic or cultural activities. Nor did he evaluate the PLA's reform.

3. Ellis Joffe said, "The man-over-weapons doctrine provides a key theoretical underpinning for party supremacy over the army." *Party and Army: Professionalism and Political Control in the Chinese Officer Corps, 1949–1964* (Cambridge: Harvard University Press, 1971), p. 57.

4. Chen Weiming and Zhang Jingming, *Choice of the Epoch* (Beijing: Military Science Press, 1988), pp. 7, 21.

5. Mao Zedong, "Problem of War and Strategy," in *Selected Military Writing of Mao Tse-Tung* (Peking: Foreign Language Press, 1966), p. 275.

6. Deng Xiaoping, "Build Powerful, Modern and Regularized Revolutionary Armed Forces," September 19, 1981, in *Selected Works of Deng Xiaoping (1975–1982)* (Beijing: Foreign Language Press, 1984), p. 373.

7. Joffe, *Party and Army*, p. 57.

8. Lin, "Extreme Roles of the PLA in Modernization," p. 1.

9. Ibid., p. 8.

10. Wang Dong et al., *Strategies in Retrospect* (Beijing: PLA Press, 1987), p. 129.

11. Deng Xiaoping, "The Present Situation and the Tasks before Us," January 16, 1980, in *Selected Works of Deng Xiaoping*, pp. 248–49.

12. This refers to the statement that "we will resolutely uphold whatever policy decisions Chairman Mao made, and unswervingly follow whatever instructions Chairman Mao gave." See *Selected Works of Deng Xiaoping*, p. 400 n. 13.

13. Deng Xiaoping, "The Army Needs to Be Consolidated," January 25, 1975, in *Selected Works of Deng Xiaoping*, p. 11.

14. Chen Weiming and Zhang Jingming, *Choice of the Times* (Beijing: Military Science Press, 1988), p. 21.

15. Deng Xiaoping, "The Army Needs to Be Consolidated," p. 11.

16. Deng Xiaoping, "Peace and Development Are the Two Outstanding Issues in the World Today," March 4, 1985, in *Fundamental Issues in Present-day China* (Beijing: Foreign Language Press, 1987), p. 98.

17. Chen Weiming and Zhang Jingming, *Choice of the Times*, p. 29.

18. Huang Xian, "A Shaking, Reforming and Unquiet Year," *China Daily*, December 31, 1987, p. 6.

19. *World Affairs*, vol. 3, (Beijing). 1988, the 1,000th issue, pp. 2–34.

20. Feng Shengbao, "The Epoch of Peace and Development," Beijing, February 25, 1988. Unpublished.

21. Zhang Zhaozhong, "View the World Looking on Ocean with Critical Eyes" (*lengyan xianyan kanshijie*), *Contemporary Military Affairs*, July 1990, p. 60.

22. Deng Xiaoping, "Safeguard World Peace and Ensure Domestic Development," May 29, 1984; "The Principles of Peaceful Coexistence Have a Potentially Wide Application," October 31, 1984; "Peace and Development Are the Two Outstanding Issues in the World Today," March 4, 1985; "Concrete Actions for the Maintenance of World Peace," June 4, 1985; all in *Fundamental Issues in Present-day China*, pp. 46, 86, 97, 116.

23. Yang Changchun, *Research on Deng Xiaoping's Thoughts concerning Establishment of the Army during the New Period* (Beijing: PLA Press, 1989), p. 29.

24. Chen and Zhang, *Choice of the Times*, p. 30.

25. Ibid., p. 22.

26. Deng Xiaoping, "Build Powerful, Modern and Regularized Revolutionary Armed Forces," September 19, 1981, in *Selected Works of Deng Xiaoping*, p. 372.

27. Deng Xiaoping, "The Army Should Subordinate Itself to the General Interest, Which Is to Develop the Country," November 1, 1984, in *Fundamental Issues in Present-day China*, p. 91.

28. Yang, *Research on Deng Xiaoping's Thoughts*, p. 277.

29. Ibid.

30. Chong-Pin Lin, *Military Modernization of Communist China and Its Influence to Taiwan*, *China Times* (Taipei), December 25–27, 1989. He warns the West, especially Taiwan, that the PLA already has relatively advanced weapons. China, however, has not yet equipped all of its troops with every new

development that other countries have. China is not able to do so and does not consider that necessary.

31. Yang, *Research on Deng Xiaoping's Thoughts*, p. 115.

32. Ibid., p. 143.

33. Ibid.

34. Deng Xiaoping, "Streamline the Army and Raise its Combat Effectiveness," March 12, 1980, in *Selected Works of Deng Xiaoping*, p. 274.

35. Ibid.

36. Deng Xiaoping, "The Army Should Attach Strategic Importance to Education and Training," August 23, 1977, in *Selected Works of Deng Xiaoping*, p. 76.

37. Yang, *Research on Deng Xiaoping's Thoughts*, p. 311.

38. Ibid., p. 321.

39. Ibid.

40. Ibid., p. 323.

41. Cai Shanwu, "Chinese Air Force on the Way to Modernization—Interview with General Wan Hai, commander of the air force of the PLA," *Contemporary Defense Affairs* (Beijing), August 1990, pp. 1–6.

42. Ding Henggao, "Review and Prospects of China's Science Technology and Industry for National Defense," *Contemporary Defense Affairs* (Beijing), June 1990, pp. 89–97.

43. Deng Xiaoping, "On Opposing Wrong Ideological Tendencies," March 27, 1981, in *Selected Works of Deng Xiaoping*, pp. 357–58.

44. During the Cultural Revolution the PLA was sent to support those of the masses who were considered the Left; to help the development of industry and agriculture; to institute military control over some localities, departments, and units; and to give military training to students.

45. Deng, "On Opposing Wrong Ideological Tendencies," pp. 357–58.

46. Mao Zedong, "The Struggle in the Chingkang Mountains," November 25, 1928, in *Selected Military Writings of Mao Tse-Tung* (Peking: Foreign Language Press, 1966), p. 31.

47. It is said that Zhang Guotao "secretly ordered Chen Changhao: 'If Central Red Army Headquarters refuses go down south you should solve it with military force!' Then Ye Jianying found this secret telegraph slip [telegram] and immediately reported to Mao Zedong. Meanwhile Xu Xianqian resisted this conspiracy." Xu Xianqian, however, in his book *Historical Review* did not mention it but told readers that the Central Red Army left quietly. It is said that Marshal Xu never admitted the fact of this "slip." When Ye Jianyin was alive, however, there were rows between the men concerned. Hu Hua, *Chinese New Democratic Revolutionary History* (Beijing: Chinese Youth Press, 1981), pp. 186–87; Xu Xianqian, *Historical Review* (Beijing: PLA Press, 1984), p. 452.

48. The official story was that "under Zhang Guotao's fraudulent order the 20,000-man vanguard units of the Red Fourth Field Army were organized as *xilu jun* (route army), crossed the river fighting toward the west and suffered a disastrous defeat." Marshal Xu Xianqian offered many details that

showed that Mao Zedong and the leadership of the Red Army made up their minds to get through that way to reach the USSR. Mao should be held responsible for their defeat, in Xu's view. Hu, *Chinese New Democratic Revolutionary History*, pp. 186–87; Xu, *Historical Review*, pp. 501–63.

49. Mao Zedong, "Problem of War and Strategy," pp. 271–72.

50. Ibid., p. 272.

51. He Baihai, quoted in "A Day in Beijing under Martial Law," *Contemporary (Dang Dai)* (Hong Kong), September 8, 1990.

52. Yang, *Research on Deng Xiaoping's Thoughts*, pp. 11–12.

53. Deng Xiaoping, "Speech at a Plenary Meeting of the Military Commission of the CC of the CPC," December 28, 1977, in *Selected Works of Deng Xiaoping*, p. 95.

54. *Tan suo* (United States), no. 77 (May 1990), p. 70.

55. Guo Jian, "The CCP's Trilogy Stressing the Control of Army," *Contemporary (Dang Dai)* (Hong Kong), July 21, 1990, p. 15.

56. Zhao Wei, "Perspective in the Political Future of Zhao Ziyang," *China Times Weekly*, December 8–14, 1990, p. 39.

57. Mao, "Struggle in the Chingkang Mountains," p. 31.

CHAPTER 4: MARXISM, CONFUCIANISM, CULTURAL NATIONALISM, *Zhang Shuqiang*

1. Most of the so-called orthodox arguments against present-day capitalism were advanced by Lenin in his *Imperialism: The Highest Stage of Capitalism* (New York: International Publishers, 1939), and *State and Revolution* (New York: International Publishers, 1935).

2. Yu Guangyuan, "It Is Necessary to Reassess Present-Day Capitalism," *Guangming Ribao*, January 23, 1989.

3. See "Bourgeois and Proletarians," in Karl Marx and Frederick Engels, *Manifesto of the Communist Party* (Beijing: Foreign Language Press, 1965), for a concise explanation of their "economic determinism."

4. Yu, "Necessary to Reassess."

5. Liu Weihua, "The Trend in the Socialization of Capital and Surplus Value," *Guangming Ribao*, January 23, 1989.

6. Lu Cong Ming, "Modern Capitalism Reassessed," *Guangming Ribao*, November 21, 1988. Its English translation appeared in *Beijing Review*, January 8–15, 1989. Lu's article presents views more radical than those in Xu Jiantun's article "Re-understanding Capitalism." Its English translation was published in *Beijing Review*, November 18–22, 1988. The concept of "social capitalism," first proposed by the Japanese economist Tsuru Shigeto, aroused great interest among Chinese economists in the mid-1980s. The Chinese Communist party Central Committee's party school sponsored a symposium on the topic in 1988. Tsuru Shigeto's theory is explained in his book *Has Capitalism Changed?* (Tokyo: Iwanami Shoten, 1961).

7. Wu Jian, "Modern Capitalism Is State Monopoly Capitalism," *Guangming Ribao*, January 23, 1989.

8. Hong Yunshan, "On the Transformation of the Capitalist System of Ownership," *Guangming Ribao*, February 13, 1989.

9. Wu, "Modern Capitalism."

10. Hong, "Transformation of the Capitalist System."

11. Li Zheng, "The Phenomenon of Convergence under Two Systems Viewed from the Perspective of Productive Forces," *Guangming Ribao*, September 12, 1988. Wu Bingxi wrote a response, "Some Opinions for Consideration on the Issue of the Convergence of the Two Social Systems," which was published in *Guangming Ribao*, February 13, 1989. In his commentary, Wu states that the philosophy of one system (socialism) eating up the other (capitalism) is "outmoded."

12. Lu, "Modern Capitalism Reassessed."

13. Hong Zhaolong, "Learn from the Scientific Attitude of Marx and Engels toward the *Manifesto*," *Guangming Ribao*, February 29, 1988. Revision of Marxism was a conspicuous and recurrent topic in the media and in academia until June 1989. One outspoken report on the topic appeared in *Wenhui Bao*, June 7, 1988, under the title "How to Comprehend the Need for a Major Development of Marxism?" The author, Li Ling, reported that "Marxist philosophy is facing a crisis. . . . Marxism, as a value system and belief system, has lost the supreme status it used to enjoy." That crisis "essentially is a political crisis." Those sentiments were expressed at a Shanghai conference of graduate students in philosophy held at Fudan University. Another example is Xiong Yinwu's article "Adhere to the Criteria of Productive Forces, and Develop Marxism," published in *Zhengming*, no. 5, 1988. Xiong stated that it is not just some specific principles of Marxism that require revision; its fundamental principles need to be developed. In other words, Marxism has been a fundamentally flawed worldview or ideology.

14. Zbigniew Brzezinski, "The Crisis of Communism: Conflicts in Political Participation," *Chinese Intellectual*, no. 20, 1990. The English original is not available to this author. The quote was translated back into English from the Chinese version by Liang Fujie. Brzezinski's book, *Debacle* (New York: Macmillan, 1989), offers a more comprehensive and in-depth analysis of the weakening of the Communist ideology. The book has been translated into Chinese by the Chinese Academy of Military Sciences and made available through "controlled internal circulation" with the following note: "This book is extremely reactionary and highly deceptive. But it helps large numbers of our cadres to clearly recognize the reactionary nature of the Western monopoly capitalist class headed by the United States and to increase their political immunity so that the struggle against the 'peaceful evolution' can be carried out effectively, and their confidence strengthened in the overall historical trend toward the victory of socialism over capitalism." According to a report in the November 1990 issue of the Hong Kong magazine *Open*, this book sells for seventy yuan on the black market in Beijing—ten times its retail price.

15. Kong Lingdong, "Some Theoretical Problems Concerning Political Democracy in the Primary Stage of Socialism," *Guangming Ribao*, February 15, 1988.

16. Ibid.

17. Brzezinski, "Crisis of Communism."

18. Lin Xie, "Wipe Off the Dust That Has Settled on History: Chinese Research on Bukharin in Recent Years," *Wenhui Bao*, January 17, 1989. The four characteristics of the "new leviathan" were proposed by Su Zhaozhi. Nikolai I. Bukharin's economic principles—particularly his idea of retaining a certain measure of private economy under socialism and the argument that a poor and backward country like Russia would have to creep toward socialism "at a snail's pace"—have also served to justify the official redesign of socialism in China. A snail's pace is interpreted as "at least 100 years," according to Zhao Ziyang's report to the Thirteenth National Congress of the Communist party of China in October 1987. No explanation is given how the estimate was made.

19. Kong, "Some Theoretical Problems."

20. Zhao Ziyang, "Advance along the Road of Socialism with Chinese Characteristics," report delivered at the Thirteenth National Congress of the Communist Party of China on October 25, 1987, *Beijing Review*, November 9–15, 1987, pp. 26–27. The report includes a section on "the primary stage of socialism and the basic line of the party." The primary stage was previously translated as "the preliminary stage," as in "Preliminary Stage of Socialism," by Dai Yannian, in the June 15, 1987, issue of *Beijing Review*, no. 24, pp. 4–5.

21. "The Central Committee's Decision on Reform of the Economic Structure," *Beijing Review*, October 29–November 4, 1984.

22. Zhao, "Advance along the Road," p. 36.

23. Gong Yuezhi, "New Starting Point for the Emancipation of the Mind," *Wenhui Bao*, June 2, 1988.

24. Yan Jiaqi, "China's Current Democracy Movement," paper presented in the forum series "Protest in the Chinese Tradition" at the Center for Chinese Studies, University of Hawaii at Manoa, March 3, 1990. During the talk, Yan emphasized that of all the individual rights, the most important is the right to own property. Without that right, other rights are pointless. His advocacy of private ownership was later cited as evidence of his "counterrevolutionary crime" in Li Jianshen's article "The Turmoil 'Elite' Yan Jiaqi," which appeared in the official *Renmin Ribao* (overseas edition), August 3, 1989. Also see Wen Qun, "Yan Jiaqi on Mr. D[emocracy], Mr. S[cience], and Mr. L[aw] and Today's China," *Zhongguo Qingnian*, no. 3, 1989.

25. Translated from the Chinese text in *Press Freedom Herald*, September 30, 1990.

26. Jiang Yiwei, "On Socialist Commodity Economy and Capitalist Commodity Economy," *Jingji Ribao*, January 26, 1990.

27. Terrel Carver and Li Jun, "Marxism and Reformism," in David Goodman and Gerald Segal, eds., *China at Forty: Midlife Crisis?* (Oxford: Clarendon, 1989), p. 15.

28. Wei Jingsheng, "Democracy or New Dictatorship?" *Tuansuo* (special issue), March 25, 1979. As a reply to a speech given by Deng Xiaoping on March 16, Wei emphasized that "the public must be alert to the possibility of

Deng Xiaoping degenerating into a dictator." (The translation here is mine.) Another English version is included in Gregor Benton, ed., *Wild Lilies: Poisonous Weeds—Dissident Voices from People's China* (London: Pluto Press, 1982). Wei was arrested four days after the publication of the reply, and sentenced to fifteen years of imprisonment on October 16. Many of his ideas were propagated first on the 1978 Democracy Wall in Beijing, then through the 1986–1987 student demonstrations and the 1989 democracy movement. His first major essay that caused a sensation, "The Fifth Modernization: Democracy," has been translated into English by Simon Leys in *The Burning Forest* (New York: Holt, Rinehart and Winston, *New Republic* 1983), pp. 224–40.

29. For the definitive definition of "socialism with Chinese characteristics," see Zhou, "Advance along the Road."

30. Luo Yijun, "Review and Prospect of the Evolution of the Third-Stage Confucianism," *Wenhui Bao*, August 2, 1988.

31. Tang Yijie, "The Creation of a New Chinese Culture," *Dushu*, no. 7, 1988.

32. Chen Xuelu, "Retrospection and the Retrospection of Retrospection," *Wenhui Bao*, May 24, 1988.

33. All quotations from Confucius in this chapter, unless otherwise indicated, are cited from the *Analects*. Quotations from Mencius are all from the book *Mencius*. The translations are mine. In the text, the first number in the parentheses indicates the chapter in the respective book, the second the section.

34. Daniel W. Y. Kwok, *Protest in the Chinese Tradition*, Occasional paper no. 2, Center for Chinese Studies, University of Hawaii at Manoa, 1989, p. 3.

35. See Zhou, "Advance along the Road," p. 28.

36. Ibid., p. 42.

37. Wei, "Mr. D[emocracy], Mr. S[cience], and Mr. L[aw]."

38. Shu Zhaozhi and Wang Yizhou, "1989 Reminds Us," *Zhongguo Qingnian*, no. 1, 1989.

39. Chinese ethicists do not think there is a systematic Marxist moral philosophy. Marxism does not provide an adequate look into moral life, and in that sense is amoral. Such views are summarized in a discussion by five ethicists: "The Predicament of Ethics and Its Way Out," *Guangming Ribao*, January 30, 1989.

40. Xing Lusheng, "Chinese Traditional Culture and the Yan'an Spirit," *People's Daily* (overseas edition), November 30, 1990. The Communist-led Red Army reached Yan'an in 1935 after being forced out of its base area in Jiangxi by the Nationalist forces. The party managed to consolidate its political and military position at Yan'an for a comeback. Therefore those years at Yan'an have always been a source of pride for party veterans. The dark side of those days was revealed in Wang Shiwei's writings. He underwent seventeen days of political repudiation during a "rectification campaign" and was shot in 1947, when the party's Central Committee decided to move away from Yan'an. Wang, a believer in communism, was probably the first writer to be

shot by the party for no reason other than his literary writings. His books are still banned in China.

41. Confucius, *Analects*, chap. 15, sec. 8. This is misquoted in the *People's Daily*. The correct version reads: "No determined scholar or virtuous person will seek to live at the expense of his virtue"—not "at the expense of other people," as this article presents it.

42. Confucius, *Confucius's Teachings on Family*, vol. 7, sec. 32. In the same volume he warned the ruler by comparing him to a boat. The populace can carry the boat or submerge it; the power of a monarch is not absolute.

43. Cited from Lin Yutang's introduction to the *Book of History: Documents of Chinese History*, in Lin Yutang, ed., *The Wisdom of China and India* (New York: Random House, 1942), pp. 696–97.

44. For "protest against tradition" and "protest within tradition," see Kwok, *Protest in the Chinese Tradition*.

45. Cited from Mao Huaixin, "The Role of Confucius and Confucianism in the History of Chinese Culture," *Cultural Studies*, vol. 2, 1987. The two quotes are from Chen Duxiu, "Theory of Compromise and Old Morality," *Xinqingnian*, vol. 7, no. 2 (1921). Mao does not agree with Chen's criticism of Confucianism. He says Chen "either misunderstood the age of Confucianism or failed to see clearly the target of his criticism." Feudal rulers distorted Confucianism to promote subservience, which is not the teaching of Confucius or Mencius. Confucianism is the positive mainstream of Chinese culture.

46. See Confucius, *Analects*, chap. 15, sec. 8, pp. 696–97.

47. See Kwok, *Protest in the Chinese Tradition*. Although Mao does not particularly associate himself with "new Confucianism," his views run counter to the orthodox Marxist critique of Confucianism, representing what may be considered an effrontery against the "moral superiority" of communism. The quote is from Jacques Gernet's *History of the Chinese Culture* (London: Cambridge, 1982), p. 432. The book is not available to me. The quote was translated from Chinese.

48. Liu Zaiping, "Summary of a Seminar on 'New Authoritarianism,' " *Guangming Ribao*, March 24, 1989. The theory came upon the international scene in the late 1970s and became a topic for public debate in China in 1988. Liu's report was based on presentations at the First National Symposium on Modernization Theories in Beijing in November 1988. For a more detailed explanation, see also Shao Gongin and Zhu Wei, "New Authoritarianism: A Painful Dilemma," *Wenhui Bao*, January 17, 1989.

49. Cited from Ding Xueliang, "The East Asia Model and 'New Authoritarianism,' " *Mingzhu Zhongguo*, no. 1, 1990; Tao Gang, "On the Zigzag Theory of National Salvation," *Open*, no. 11, 1990; and Hu Ping, "The China Dream of New Authoritarianism," *China Spring*, no. 6, 1990.

50. For Wei Jingsheng, see Wei, "New Dictatorship?" For Hu Ping, see Hu, "China Dream."

51. Shao and Zhu, "New Authoritarianism."

52. Ibid.

53. Ibid.

54. Ibid. Also see Ding, "East Asia Model," pp. 34–35.

55. "Deng on Issues of World Interest," *Beijing Review*, September 22, 1986, p. 6. Deng made the statement during a CBS interview with Mike Wallace.

56. Huang Wansheng, "Questions and Answers on the Criticism of New Authoritarianism," *Wenhui Bao*, February 22, 1989. See also Bao Zunxin, "Confucian Ethics and the 'Four Little Dragons' of Asia," *Wenhui Bao*, May 12, 1988.

57. Bao, "Four Little Dragons." Bao and Huang are among the strongest critics of new authoritarianism. They not only are critical of its potential role in China but also question the validity of the allegedly causal relationship between Confucianism and economic development in countries like Japan and Singapore. Bao thinks the claim is "pure fiction." He cited Max Weber's *Protestant Ethics and the Spirit of Capitalism* and *The Religion of China: Confucianism and Taoism*; he said that "Confucian ethics was the cultural factor suppressing the development of capitalism in China." Bao is now in prison in China.

58. Mao Huaixin, "Traditional Chinese Culture and the Cultural Exchange between the East and the West," lecture presented at the Center for Chinese Studies, University of Hawaii at Manoa, October 25, 1990.

59. Mencius, *Mencius*, chap. 1, sec. 5. Although the idea can be found in Confucian thinking, it was Mencius who advanced the concept. The concept should not be confused with the Western idea of democracy, because it was proposed, as the reader can see in this particular section, to mobilize the population for wars to restore the "imperial dignity." Also see *Mencius*, chap. 1, sec. 6.

60. C. P. Fitzgerald, *China: A Short Cultural History* (Boulder, Colo.: Westview Press, 1985), p. 75.

61. Quote from Ji Xianlin. See Tao Kai and Lin Chunling's interview, "Build Socialist Modernization in an Optimal Process," *Guangming Ribao*, February 20, 1990. One of the interviewees—Ding Shouhe—said, however, that Japanese capitalists have an abacus in one hand and a copy of *Analects* in the other. "It is the abacus that plays the crucial role."

62. See Chen, "Retrospection."

63. See Bao, "Four Little Dragons."

64. See Jin, "Build Socialist Modernization." Also see the beginning of Bao, "Four Little Dragons."

65. For instance, see Wei, "The Fifth Modernization," p. 234. Wei wanted a European or American type democracy where "they were able to dismiss their Nixon, de Gaulle, or Tanaka, and if they so wish, they can as well call them back. No force would interfere with the free exercise of their democratic prerogative."

66. Many young intellectuals hold this view. For example, see Liu Xiaobuo's interview in the November 1988 issue of *Jiefang Yuebao* (Liberation monthly). The television documentary "River Elegy" also reflects such a view, referring to the current status of the Chinese civilization as the "last

struggles of the ancient nation." See Wang Luxiang, "River Elegy: Script of the Television Series 'River Elegy,' Part III," *Wenhui Bao*, June 28, 1988. Yan Jiaqi, in his "China Is No Longer a Dragon," *People's Daily*, May 23, 1988, emphasized that China must overcome its ethnocentrism. "A China that does not seek progress . . . deserves to groan in pain under attack. . . . We are not descendants of the dragon!"

67. See Bao, "Four Little Dragons."

68. Most of the controversies center around the second part of the six-part series. It was written by Wang Luxiang, then a graduate student of philosophy at Beijing University. See "River Elegy."

69. Cited from Cui Wenhua, ed., *The Great Discussion on "River Elegy" Abroad* (Harbin: Heilongjiang Educational Press, 1988), p. 77.

70. Frederic Wakeman, Jr., "All the Rage in China," *The New York Review of Books*, March 2, 1989, p. 21.

71. Shi Ren, " 'River Elegy' and the Patriotic Spirit," *Wenhui Bao*, December 15, 1988.

72. Zhao Shiyu, "On the Theory of History in 'River Elegy,' " *Guangming Ribao*, August 10, 1988.

73. Alice De Jong, "The Demise of the Dragon: Backgrounds to the Chinese Film 'River Elegy,' " *China Information*, vol. IV, no. 3, Winter 1989–1990, pp. 32–33.

74. Cited from Ye Yang, " 'River Elegy': The Paradox of Tradition," paper presented at the conference "Politics and Ideology in Contemporary Chinese Literature," Duke University, Durham, North Carolina, October 26–28, 1990. Su Xiaokang, Yuan Zhiming, Wang Luxiang, and Zhang Gang managed to leave China after the Tiananmen Square massacre.

75. Li Reihuan, "Some Issues on How to Promote Fine National Culture," *Guangming Ribao*, May 16, 1990.

76. Jiang Zemin, "Patriotism and the Mission of the Intelligentsia of Our Country," *Guangming Ribao*, May 4, 1990.

77. See Li, "Fine National Culture."

78. Guo Zhong, "On 'River Elegy' and the Westernization Faction on the Mainland," *People's Daily*, August 22, 1989. It was first published in the July 1989 issue of the Taiwan magazine *Yuanwang*.

79. Moralizing politics was one of the mistakes committed by Mao Zedong in his last few years. According to Li Zehou, Mao tended to turn political concepts into concepts found in feudal moral philosophy. See Li Rei, "On the Thinking and Practice of Mao Zedong in His Last Few Years," *Guangming Ribao*, February 2, 1989. The article is an introduction to the book *Mao Zedong in His Last Few Years*. The book contains a collection of articles, several of which discuss the connection between China's cultural tradition and Mao Zedong Thought.

80. See, for example, Xu Qixian, "Promote the Spirit of National Self-Respect, Self-Confidence, and Self-Consolidation," *Guangming Ribao*, May 11, 1990. In response to such warnings Luo Yibuo wrote, "We shall never allow the Chinese Communist regime to turn the current conflict between

'democracy and autocracy' into a spurious conflict between 'foreign countries and China.' " See Luo Yibuo, "Crisis and Change in China," *The Chinese Intellectual*, Autumn 1990, p. 75.
81. "China's Economic Plan," *Honolulu Advertiser*, December 31, 1990.

CHAPTER 5: CHINA'S POPULATION, *Judith Banister*

1. State Statistical Bureau of China, *Statistical Yearbook 1990* (Beijing: Zhongguo tongli chubanshe, 1990), pp. 89–90.
2. Census of 1990, Communiqué no. 1, "The 1990 Census," *Beijing Review*, vol. 33, no. 46, November 12–18, 1990 (Hereafter, *Census of 1990*), p. 17. The census communiqués are compiled in Sun Jingxin, "Some Ideas on the Utilization of Data from China's 1990 Population Census" (Paper presented at the Thirteenth Population Census Conference, Honolulu, December 1990).
3. "Minister Says Population to Exceed Target," *Foreign Broadcast Information Service Daily Report-China (FBIS-CHI), 90-004-S*, January 5, 1990, p. 5.
4. Yu Changhong, "AIDS Problem Termed 'Relatively Serious,' " *FBIS-CHI 90-210*, October 30, 1990, pp. 26–27; Cui Lili, "AIDS Challenge for China," *Beijing Review*, vol. 33, no. 48, November 26–December 2, 1990, p. 32.
5. China People's University, Institute of Population Research, "1981 Abridged Life Tables for China as a Whole and Each Province," *Renkou yanjiu* (Population research), no. 1, January 29, 1987, pp. 60–61; Hao Hongsheng, Eduardo Arriaga, and Judith Banister, "China: Provincial Patterns of Mortality" (Paper presented at the seminar "Mortality and Morbidity in South and East Asia," Beijing, August–September 1988), tables 2–7.
6. Judith Banister, "China: Mortality and Health under the Economic Reforms," and Ansley J. Coale, "Recent Mortality Trends in China" (Papers presented at the seminar "Recent Levels and Trends in Mortality in China," Center for Population Studies, Harvard University, Cambridge, Mass., March 1990).
7. In general, old people are likelier to die than young people in any particular time period, so with the same mortality conditions by age a young population has a lower crude death rate than an old population. Crude death rate means deaths in a year divided by the total midyear population.
8. Crude birth rate minus crude death rate equals rate of natural population increase. Net international migration added to the natural population increase rate determines the population growth rate.
9. For details see Judith Banister, *China's Changing Population* (Stanford, Calif.: Stanford University Press, 1987), pp. 152–65.
10. Wang Feng, Nancy E. Riley, and Lin Fu De, "China's Continuing Demographic Transition in the 1980s" (Presented at the Annual Meeting of the Population Association of America, Toronto, Canada, May 3–5, 1990), table 1.
11. To calculate China's total fertility rates for 1987 and 1988, we used 1988 fertility survey data on absolute numbers of births to each single age group

of women fifteen to forty-nine in 1987 and the first half of 1988. Births for all of 1988 were extrapolated from the first six months using the monthly pattern of births reported for 1986 and 1987. See State Family Planning Commission, *Quanguo shengyu jieyu chouyang diaocha quanguo shuju juan, heji* (Data from China's national sample survey on fertility and family planning, summary volume), Beijing, Zhongguo renkou chubanshe, 1990, pp. 90, 92, 193, 195. These births were applied to China's female single-year age structure in 1987 and 1988 reconstructed at the U.S. Bureau of the Census, resulting in unadjusted total fertility rates of 2.52 for 1987 and 2.24 for 1988. Another source estimated a 1987 TFR of 2.59 based on the fertility survey data; see Li Bohua, "Changes in Fertility Rates in China's 28 Provinces, Autonomous Regions and Municipalities Directly under the Central Authorities (1973–1987)," *Renkou yu jingji* (Population and economics), no. 3, June 25, 1990, p. 4. The total fertility rate is the average number of children who would be born alive per woman to a group of women during their lifetimes if they lived through all their childbearing years and conformed as a group to all the age-specific fertility rates of a given year.

12. *Statistical Yearbook 1990*, p. 90.

13. *Census of 1990*, Communiqué no. 1, p. 19.

14. See John S. Aird, *Slaughter of the Innocents: Coercive Birth Control in China* (Washington, D.C.: AEI Press, 1990), on recent official attempts to prevent births outside the government's birth plans.

15. *Census of 1990*, Communiqué no. 1, pp. 18–19, and Communiqué no. 4, "State Statistical Census Communiqué No. 4," *FBIS-CHI-90-229*, November 28, 1990, pp. 23–24. Chinese sources report declines in primary and secondary school enrollment in the 1980s through 1987 and a continuing problem with school dropouts. Yet in the late 1980s, there were greatly increased enrollments in adult education and worker education, as well as vocational, technical, and specialized high schools and universities. The net result seems to have been an increase in educational attainment and literacy, especially among today's adults. Deborah Davis, "Chinese Social Welfare: Policies and Outcomes," *China Quarterly*, no. 119, September 1989, pp. 577–97; and "China Sees Education for More," *China Daily*, December 15, 1990, p. 3.

16. As of 1984, 94 percent of the rural population ages sixty and above received no social security assistance and were completely dependent on themselves and their sons for support. Judith Banister, "The Aging of China's Population," *Problems of Communism*, vol. 37, no. 6, November–December 1988, p. 70.

17. Xin Renzhou and Zhang Yuxian, "Causes of Rural Population Growth and Countermeasures," *Zhongguo nongcun jingji* (China's rural economy), no. 7, July 20, 1990, pp. 8–12.

18. China, State Council Population Census Office and State Statistical Bureau Department of Population Statistics, *Zhongguo 1982-nian renkou pucha ziliao (dianzi jisuanji huizong)* (Data from China's 1982 population census, results of computer tabulation), Beijing, Zhongguo tongji chubanshe, 1985. Hereafter, *Census of 1982*, pp. 478–79.

19. *Census of 1990*, Communiqué no. 1, p. 19.

20. For details, see Susan Greenhalgh, *State-Society Links: Political Dimensions of Population Policies and Programs with Special Reference to China*, Working paper no. 18 (New York: Population Council, 1990).

21. National and provincial data on urban and rural populations were reported in *Census of 1990*, Communiqué no. 2. See *Zhongguo renkou bao* (China Population), November 9, 1990, p. 1. Summarized in "Statistics Bureau Issues Second Census Communiqué," *FBIS-CHI-90-215*, November 6, 1990, pp. 19–20.

22. The 1990 census count of the military population is given in *Census of 1990*, Communiqué no. 2.

23. The 1987 1 percent sample census reported that 5.28 percent of the city populations of China were members of minority groups; see State Statistical Bureau Department of Population Statistics, *Zhongguo 1987 nian 1% renkou chouyang diaocha ziliao, quanguo fence* (Tabulations from China's 1987 1% sample survey, national volume), Beijing, Zhongguo tongji chubanshe, 1988. Hereafter, *Sample Census of 1987*, p. 33. The 1982 census reported that 1.5 percent of the military population consisted of minority individuals; see *Census of 1982*, p. 505. We have applied these figures to 1990 census urban and military totals to estimate the Han and minority portions.

24. Details on which provinces have which birth limitation policies are found in Liu Leiqi, "Jihua shengyu zongshu" (A summary of family planning), *Zhongguo baike nianjian, 1989* (Encyclopedic yearbook of China, 1989) (Beijing: Zhongguo dabaikequanshu chubanshe, 1989), pp. 325–26.

25. Using data on the proportion of Han and minority in rural areas by province from the 1987 1 percent sample census. See *Sample Census of 1987*, p. 33.

26. In February 1990, the director of China's State Family Planning Commission Peng Peiyun was quoted as follows: "But no one, under any condition, is allowed to have a third child. This policy applies to ethnic minorities as well." Zhu Baoxia, "Minister Stresses Family Planning in Rural Areas," *China Daily*, February 13, 1990, p. 1. Yet in October 1990, I visited a Hui minority area where a three-child policy was in effect. I assume that Peng's policy statement is not yet fully implemented.

27. For example, Manchu minority couples in rural Heilongjiang province are allowed two births, regardless of the sex of the first child. "Xinhua Features Manchu Minority Lifestyle," *FBIS-CHI-90-078*, April 23, 1990, p. 44. Minorities are also permitted two children in Hunan province. *Zhongguo jihua shengyu nianjian 1987* (Family planning yearbook of China 1987), Beijing, Renmin weisheng chubanshe, 1988, p. 362. But China's largest minority group, the Zhuang minority in Guangxi province, is subject to the same one-and-a-half-child policy as the rural Han population. In contrast, the Mongols in Inner Mongolian rural areas are allowed three children. "Inner Mongolia Reports Population Statistics," *Joint Publications Research Service*, JPRS-CAR-90-090, December 7, 1990, p. 52. These exceptions have been incorporated into our calculations.

28. In this calculation, we assume that legal exceptions to the one-child limit would allow a TFR of 1.1 births per woman in the one-child-policy areas and that in the one-and-a-half-child policy areas, the TFR from approved births would be 1.6 births per woman to allow for exceptions such as for a handicapped firstborn son and other "special difficulties."

29. See, for example, Banister, *China's Changing Population*, pp. 206–7; Du Xin and Yu Changhong, "The Great Tide of Childbearing in Rural China," *Liaowang Overseas Edition*, no. 43, October 23, 1989, p. 19, in *FBIS-CHI-89-238*, December 13, 1989, pp. 23–25; Pei Gang, "Thoughts on the Present Disarray in Matters of Population Reproduction and Suggested Improvements," *Renkou yu jingji*, no. 5, October 25, 1989, pp. 6–10, in *JPRS-CAR-90-010*, February 7, 1990, pp. 62–67; "Five Million Seek to Change Nationality Identity," *FBIS-CHI-90-145*, July 27, 1990, pp. 21–22; Sten Johansson, Zhao Xuan, and Ola Nygren, "On Intriguing Sex Ratios among Live Births in China in the 1980s," *Journal of Official Statistics*, vol. 7, no. 1, 1991, pp. 25–43.

30. For details see Banister, *China's Changing Population*, pp. 183–221, 355–68; and Aird, *Slaughter of the Innocents*, pp. 28–58.

31. China's 1982 nationwide fertility survey calculated that rural minority women had a total fertility rate of 4.36 births per woman in 1980 and 5.05 in 1981. Li Hechang, Song Tigyou, and Li Cheng, "Current Fertility Status of Women of the Han and Minority Nationalities in Rural Areas," *Analysis on China's National One-per-Thousand-Population Fertility Sampling Survey* (Beijing: China Population Information Centre, 1984), pp. 100–5.

32. Zhang Tianlu, "Woguo shaoshu minzu renkou guokuai zengzhang jiqi wenti" (The rapid growth of the population of China's ethnic minorities and its problems), *Zhongyang minzu xueyuan xuebao* (Journal of the central institute for nationalities), no. 3, May 15, 1990, p. 18.

33. "Prevalence of Contraceptive Use and Fertility," *KIPH (Korea Institute for Population and Health) Bulletin*, no. 16, June 1989, p. 1; *Statistical Yearbook of the Republic of China 1988* (Taipei: Republic of China Executive Yuan, Director-ate-General of Budget, Accounting and Statistics, 1988), p. 35.

34. Blanche Tyrene White, "Population Policy and Rural Reform in China, 1977–1984: Policy Implementation and Interdependency at the Local Level" (Ph.D. diss. Ohio State University, 1985); and Greenhalgh, *State-Society Links*.

35. Tian Xueyuan, "On Changes in the Age Composition of the Population and Policy Options for Population Planning," *Social Sciences in China* (Autumn 1984), pp. 191–206.

36. Data for earlier years compiled and discussed in Banister, *China's Changing Population*, pp. 326–35.

37. This policy shift and its results were traced in Judith Banister, *Urban-Rural Population Projections for China*, Center for International Research, Staff Paper no. 15 (Washington, D.C.: U.S. Bureau of the Census, 1986); and in Judith Banister and Jeffrey R. Taylor, "China: Surplus Labor and Migration," *Asia-Pacific Population Journal* (Bangkok), vol. 4, no. 4, December 1989, pp. 3–20.

38. "Floating Population Nears 80 Million," JPRS-CAR-90-020, March 14, 1990, p. 58.

39. Jeffrey R. Taylor and Judith Banister, *China: The Problem of Employing Surplus Rural Labor*, Center for International Research, Staff Paper no. 49 (Washington, D.C.: U.S. Bureau of the Census, 1989).

40. For details and analysis, see Judith Banister, "China's Population Changes and the Economy," in U.S. Congress, Joint Economic Committee, ed., *China's Dilemmas in the 1990s* (Washington, D.C.: U.S. Government Printing Office, 1991), pp. 234–35.

CHAPTER 6: TRADITIONALIST, MODERNIST, AND PARTY CULTURE, Zhiling Lin

1. Copies of this 1988 film are available at the Library of Congress and at the Foreign Service Institute, Washington, D.C. The author viewed it in China.

2. The classic Chinese debate is recorded in Ten Ssu-yu and John K. Fairbank, *China's Response to the West: A Documentary Survey, 1839–1923* (New York: Atheneum, 1963). See also Mary C. Wright, *The Last Stand of Chinese Conservatism: The T'ung-Chih Restoration, 1862–1874* (New York: Atheneum, 1966).

3. James O'Connell, "The Concept of Modernization," *South Atlantic Quarterly*, Autumn, 1965.

4. See John Woronoff, *Asia's "Miracle" Economies* (Armonk, N.Y.: M.E. Sharpe, 1986) and his extensive bibliography for an entree into this literature, and Hajime Nakamura, *Ways of Thinking of Eastern Peoples: India, China, Tibet, Japan*, Philip P. Weiner ed. (Honolulu: University of Hawaii Press, 1964) for insights into the breadth and limits of the Sinic tradition.

5. 與 人 為 善 and 四 海 之 內 皆 兄 弟 These are popular proverbs, reflected frequently in Chinese literature and art. The originals come from Confucius and Mozi: 我 不 欲 人 之 加 諸 于 我 也 ， 吾 亦 欲 無 加 諸 人("If I don't like other people to impose on me, I don't want to impose anything on others") from the 《 論 語 · 公 冶 長 》 載 子 貢 語 (Confucian analects, Gong Yian Chang, a quotation from Zi Gong); 利 人 乎 即 為 ， 不 利 人 乎 即 止.("Do what benefits others; avoid doing what harms them"), from the 《 墨 子 · 非 樂 上 》(Mozi, Fei Le Shang); and 四 海 之 內 ， 皆 兄 弟 也("People over the world are brothers") from the 《 論 語 · 顏 淵 》 載 子 夏 語 (Confucian analects, Yan Yuan, a quotation from Zi Xia).

6. 自 由 ， 平 等 ， 博 愛 。

7. The best English-language study of the *danwei* is Gail Henderson and Myron Cohen, *The Chinese Hospital: A Socialist Work Unit* (New Haven: Yale University Press, 1984). The author also draws on her own Chinese experience in this description.

8. Martin King Whyte and William L. Parish, *Urban Life in Contemporary China* (Chicago: University of Chicago Press, 1984).

9. "肥 猪 先 宰 " ． " 樹 大 招 風 " ， " 出 頭 椽 子 先 爛."

10. Edgar Schein et al., *Coercive Persuasion* (New York: W.W. Norton, 1961),

and Robert J. Lifton, *Thought Reform and the Psychology of Totalism: A Study of "Brainwashing" in China* (New York: W.W. Norton, 1963).

11. 做 一 天 和 尚 ， 撞 一 天 鐘 .

12. " 榮 宗 耀 祖 " ， " 吃 得 苦 中 苦 ， 方 為 人 上 人 " ， " 衣 錦 還 鄉, These ideals run deep in Chinese popular culture and were always themes of traditional literature, especially drama.

13. Boyd Compton, *Mao's China: Party Reform Documents, 1942–1944* (Seattle: University of Washington Press, 1952).

14. Merle Goldman, *Literary Dissent in Communist China* (Cambridge: Harvard University, 1967), and Mu Fu-sheng, *The Wilting of the Hundred Flowers: The Chinese Intellectual under Mao* (New York: Praeger, 1962).

15. Merle Goldman, *China's Intellectuals: Advice and Dissent* (Cambridge: Harvard University Press, 1981).

16. Franz Schurmann, *Ideology and Organization in Communist China* (Berkeley: University of California Press, 1966), and Hong Yong Lee, *The Politics of the Cultural Revolution* (Berkeley: University of California Press, 1978).

17. Stuart Schram, *The Political Thought of Mao Tse-tung* (New York: Praeger, 1963) and *Chairman Mao Talks to the People* (New York: Pantheon, 1974); John Bryan Starr, *Continuing the Revolution: The Political Thought of Mao* (Princeton: Princeton University Press, 1979).

18. S. Feuchtwang et al., eds., *Transforming China's Economy in the 1980s*, two volumes (Boulder, Colo.: Westview Press, 1988), and Joint Economic Committee, U.S. Congress, *China's Dilemmas in the 1990s: The Problems of Reforms, Modernization, and Interdependence* (Washington, D.C.: Superintendent of Documents, 1991).

19. Merle Goldman, Timothy Cheek, and Carol Lee Hamrin, eds., *China's Intellectuals and the State: In Search of a New Relationship* (Cambridge: Harvard University Press, 1987), and Perry Link, Richard Madsen, and Paul G. Pikowicz, eds., *Unofficial China: Popular Culture and Thought in the People's Republic of China* (Boulder, Colo.: Westview Press, 1989).

20. 傷 痕, written by a Fudan University student, 盧 新 華 (Lu Xinhua), first published in *Wenhui Bao* in Shanghai in 1977.

21. 《 人 啊 ， 人 ！ 》 ， 戴 厚 英, (Dai Houying), Shanghai: Shanghai People's Publishing House, 1981.

22. A convenient edition, with both Chinese and English versions, is 苦 戀 , Taipei: Institute of Current China Studies, 1981.

23. The developments can well be followed in the newsletters of the National Committee on U.S.-China Relations and of the Scholarly Committee for Communications with the People's Republic of China, as well as in the organ of the U.S.-China Business Council, *The China Business Review*.

24. Roger Garside, *Coming Alive: China after Mao* (New York: McGraw-Hill, 1981); Fox Butterfield, *China: Alive in a Bitter Sea* (New York: Times Books, 1982); and Harry Harding, *China's Second Revolution* (Washington, D.C.: Brookings Institution, 1987).

25. 《 丑 陋 的 中 國 人 》 ， 柏 楊, (Buo Yang), Fujian People's Publishing House, 1987.

26. 國以民為本，社稷亦為民而立 ("A nation is based on its people; society is also established for the benefit of its people") from 宋 · 朱熹《四書集註·孟子·盡心下》註語(The Song Dynasty, Zhu Xi, *Full Notes on the Four Books, Notes to Mencius, Jin Xin Xi*); 聖人無常心，以百姓心為心 ("A good ruler should not depend on his own whim; rather, he should look to the will of the people as his guide"), from 《老子》，四章(*Laozi*, chapter 4); "憂民之憂者，民亦憂其憂"，"樂民之樂者，民亦樂其樂" ("If the ruler takes into account the concern of the people, the people in turn will have concern for him"; "The ruler who looks to the happiness of his people will find his people concerned about his own happiness") from Mencius, 梁惠王下 ("Presentation to Liang Hui Wang"); 凡治國之道，必先富民 ("The best way to rule a country must be to enrich the people first"), from 《管子·治國》(Guan Zi, "To rule a country"); and 天之生此民也，使先知覺後知，使先覺覺後覺也 ("The way that heaven created its people was to let those who learned first educate those who learned later, and to let those who have a feel for things educate those who still lack that quality"), from 《孟子·萬章上》(Mencius, "Wan Zhang Shang").

27. Mao Zedong: "On Contradiction," *Selected Works of Mao Tse-tung*, vol. I, p. 314; "The Chinese Revolution and the Chinese Communist Party," *Selected Works*, vol. II, p. 308; "Cast Away Illusions, Prepare for Struggle," *Selected Works*, vol. IV, p. 428; and "On Practice," *Selected Works*, vol. I, p. 206 (Beijing: Foreign Languages Press, 1967). Mao's theory of class struggle was heavily and frequently published in all kinds of official publications, such as newspapers, journals, and textbooks. It became, as the party required, the guideline of all work.

28. "為政以德，譬如北辰，居其所而眾星共之"（《論語·為政》載孔子語）；"不以仁政，不能平治天下"（《孟子·離婁上》）；"興天下之利，除天下之害"（《墨子·兼愛下》）；"天之所覆，地之所載，莫不盡其美，致其用"（《荀子·王制》）

29. This idea is part of the very air that every Chinese citizen must breathe. It appears in all forms of art and literature and throughout official propaganda and party documents. An example is Liu Shaoqi's famous *On the Training of Members of the Communist Party*.

30. Ruth Hayhoe, ed., *Contemporary Chinese Education* (Armonk, N.Y.: M.E. Sharpe, 1984).

31. Amid the rapidly growing literature on the Tiananmen Square incident, see in particular George Hicks, ed., *The Broken Mirror* (Chicago: St. James Press, 1990), and *Huo Yu Xueh Zhi Zhen Xiang* (*The Truth of Fire and Blood*) (Taipei: Institute for the Study of Chinese Communist Problems, 1989).

32. These observations are based on the author's experience in Shanghai surrounding the Tiananmen events; interviews with many Chinese colleagues from Beijing, elsewhere in China, and abroad; a reading of the official Chinese press; Chinese-language journals in China, Hong Kong, and the United States; and the Foreign Broadcasting Information Service, *Daily Report:*

China (Washington, D.C.: National Technical Information Service), for the period 1988–1990.

33. For peasant attitudes, see the authoritative work by William L. Parish and Martin K. Whyte, *Village and Family Life in Contemporary China* (Chicago: University of Chicago Press, 1978).

34. *Wen Hui Bao*, "Dilemmas Created upon Being Confined," November 1990, and *Bowen* (General digest), August, 1989, pp. 18–19.

CHAPTER 7: CHINESE AGRICULTURE, *Jean C. Oi*

1. This chapter was written while I was a national fellow at the Hoover Institution during the 1990–1991 academic year. I thank the Hoover Institution for its support and Scott Rozelle for his comments on the revised draft. All views expressed in this chapter remain my own.

2. For a detailed account of the problems, see Oi, "Peasant Grain Marketing and State Procurements: China's Grain Contracting system," *China Quarterly*, no. 106 (June 1986): 272–90.

3. Other studies that point in this direction include Frederick Crook, "Defusing Peasant Discontent," *China Business Review* (July–August 1990): 12–15; Frederick Crook, "Current Problems and Future Development of China's Agricultural Sector," *The Chinese Association of Agricultural Students and Scholars: First Conference Proceedings* (Cornell University, Ithaca, New York, June 24–25, 1989): 9–19; and Jorgen Delman, "Current Peasant Discontent in China: Backgrounds and Political Implications," *China Information*, vol. 4, no. 2 (Autumn 1989): 42–64, which provides a detailed examination of some of the more technical aspects of the input problems.

4. See Frederick Crook, *China: Agriculture and Trade Report*, Economic Research Service, (November 1989): RS 89-5.

5. Tai Ming Cheung, "China's Grain Yields Fall Short of Targets: Harvest of Woes," *Far Eastern Economic Review* (30 August 1990): 54–56.

6. For details of this see Oi, *State and Peasant in Contemporary China: The Political Economy of Village Government* (Berkeley: University of California Press, 1989), chap. 8.

7. The problem of the "difficulty of selling grain" was not limited to 1983–1984. In areas with abundant harvests or areas that no longer have funds to continue procurements, peasants still are finding it difficult to sell their grain. See, for example, "Why Peasants Households Have Stored So Much Grain," *Nongmin ribao* (30 May 1990): 2, translated in *JPRS-CAR-90-055* (26 July 1990): 79.

8. For further details and documentation see Oi, *State and Peasant*, chapter 8.

9. During this period production costs increased 20.7 percent, but income increased only 8 percent. See Sun Zhunghua, Rural Survey Office, Rural Development Research Center, State Council, "1984–1988 Nian Liangshi Shengchande Weiguan Tanshi," *Zhongguo nongcum jingji* ("A microprobe into

1984–1988 grain production," in Chinese agricultural economy), no. 3 (20 March 1990): 16–24.

10. The study found that income was reduced by 10 percent. See Oi, *State and Peasant*: 175.

11. In 1990 the state further cut the quota from 75 million to 50 million tons. This spells only problems for the peasants. Market prices are already low because of the recent good harvests. See *Far Eastern Economic Review* (30 August 1990): 54–56.

12. Rural Capital Task Force, Cooperative Economy Administration and Management Home Office, Ministry of Agriculture, "Yindao nongcun zijin zengjia nongye touru," *Nongye jingji wenti* ("Guide rural capital; increase agricultural investment," in Problems in agricultural economy), no. 4 (23 April 1990): 20–25.

13. In areas where the promise of production inputs act as an effective incentive—where the government has consistently provided the promised inputs—peasants and local officials still turn to grain production as an economically rational use of labor. Grain production remains a prime source of employment. See Scott Rozelle, "Principals and Agents in China's Rural Economy: A Decision Making Framework of Township Officials, Village Leaders and Farm Households," unpublished ms., Stanford University, 1990.

14. See Oi, "Peasant Households between Plan and Market: Cadre Control over Agricultural Inputs," *Modern China*, vol. 12, no. 2 (June 1986): 272–90.

15. See "1984–1988 Nian Liangshi Shengchande Weiguan Tanshi." The price of plastic mulch has risen from 2,400 yuan to 6,000 yuan to as much as 10,000 yuan per ton. See Wu Huien, Wu Qingsong, and Liu Aijun, Jincheng Municipal Rural Economic Committee, Shanxi, "Study of the Law of Motion of Productivity for the Purpose of Spurring Reform and Development of Agriculture—Theoretical Ideas and Policy Conceptions for the Development of Agricultural Productivity," *Kexue yu kexue jishu guanli* (Science and scientific mnagement), no. 2 (1990): 3–5, and no. 3 (1990): 27–30, translated in *JPRS-CAR-90-048* (5 July 1990): 72–80.

16. According to the Ministry of Agriculture, 60 percent of the 1990 increased grain production was due to the increase in sown acreage. *Far Eastern Economic Review* (30 August 1990): 54–56.

17. This occurred in Shandong in 1988. Author's Interviews, China, 1990.

18. Delman in "Current Peasant" cites a *Nongmin ribao* (Peasant's daily) article that states that in May 1989 national procurement agencies had only half of the funds needed for procuring the spring harvest.

19. In my earlier work, I underestimated this potential and, consequently, was more optimistic about the attractiveness of the sales contracts than may have been warranted. See Oi, "Peasant Grain Marketing."

20. Grain traders from various grain-short areas such as Guangdong, in addition to local enterprises, need to buy large supplies.

21. "1984–1988 nian liangshi Shengchande."

22. Ibid.

23. This category includes businesses and industries that belonged to

township or village governments as well, and individual and jointly owned companies. The following statistics include all four categories. The collectively owned enterprises, however, are the largest of these and produce the most revenues. The following discussion will focus on the collectively owned—township and village owned—enterprises, unless otherwise noted.

24. *Zhongguo tongji nianjian* (1988): 214.

25. Crook, "Current Problems," 12.

26. *Zhongguo Nongye nianjian* (Chinese agricultural yearbook) (ZGNYNJ) (1989): 19.

27. Ibid.

28. Research Office of the State Council, "Town and Township Enterprises as a Motive Force in the Development of the National Economy," *Jingji yanjiu* (Economic research), no. 5 (20 May 90): 39–46, translated in *JPRS-CAR-90-066* (29 August 1990): 34–42.

29. "1984–1988 nian liangshi Shengchande."

30. Some peasants have more opportunity than others to pursue these nonagricultural jobs; the growth of rural enterprises varies in different parts of the country. In spite of the differences in rates of development, however, the number of areas with sizable output are increasing. By 1988 46.6 percent of all counties had rural enterprises whose output value exceeded one hundred million yuan, ten times or more that amount. *ZGNYNJ* (1989): 20.

31. Author's interviews, China, 1988.

32. Often the male workers will return to farming during harvest season.

33. In areas where mechanization and scientific farming techniques are used, farming is producing incomes that rival those earned in industry. In areas such as Jiangsu that have been cited as "advanced," for example, and use modern farming techniques, a couple "contracted 5 hectares of newly reclaimed land and produced 34 tons of grain in 1989 earning 17,000 yuan." See Xinhua English, 0600 GMT (11 June 1990) in *JPRS-CAR-90-046* (26 June 1990): 83–84.

34. "1984–1988 Nian Liangshi Shengchande Weiquan Tanshi."

35. "Yindao nongcun zijin zengjia nongye touru."

36. Ibid.

37. *ZGNYNJ* 1989.

38. "Yindao nongcun zijin zengjia nongye touru."

39. The central state instituted a series of fiscal reforms beginning in the mid-1980s to persuade localities to develop their economies and generate revenue. The central state wanted to create a situation where each level of government would "eat from separate kitchens," as the system is colloquially described. Each level of government down to the township has been made responsible for its revenues and expenditures, after meeting a tax quota to the next higher level of government. Revenues, income, and returns have become, as a result, as important to local governments as to individuals.

40. See Jean C. Oi, "Fiscal Reform and the Economic Foundations of Local State Corporatism in China," *World Politics*, vol. 45 (October 1992), no. 1, pp. 99–126.

41. This is not the total explanation of IOUs, but it helps explain why some localities ran out of funds when special funds were provided.

42. Author's interviews in China, 1990.

43. This view, unfortunately, is not shared by the more conservative leaders, such as Chen Yun, who probably would argue that central planning and control must always play a leading role.

44. This is, of course, one of the most fundamental reforms and would radically alter the system. It involves major economic costs and would require a restructuring of many aspects of the system.

45. For a provincial perspective see Wu Yunbo, Zhou Wenbao, Zhang Chengyuan, Liu Hang, and Xing Wei, Heilongjiang Provincial Government Rural Development Research Centre, "Study of Remedies to Reduce Grain Business Losses in Heilongjiang Province," *Zhongguo nongcun jingji*, no. 5 (20 May 1990): 20–27, translated in *JPRS-CAR-90-064* (17 August 1990): 46–53.

46. This has occurred in Liaoning. See Wang Tieyun and Zhang Shumiao, "Investigation of Cutbacks in State Price Sales of Grain and Edible Oil in Liaoning Province," *Jiage lilun yu shijan* (Theory and practice of price), translated in *JPRS-CAR-90-046*, no. 2 (20 February 90): 24–30.

47. Economists point out that the existence of a dual track does not necessarily cause problems. The two, in theory, can function together. The author thanks Scott Rozelle for this insight. The problem is that the rationing system becomes a source of corruption.

48. I prefer the term "hierarchy of prices" because, in practice, three prices exist, not two. Between the ration price and the free market price is a negotiated price that is often lower than the free market price, but higher than the ration price. See Oi, "Peasant Households."

49. See Oi, "Peasant Households."

50. This may explain why peasants who live in villages that use unified management often seem to have fewer problems under the reforms. In these villages the village leaders, who often have good contacts and know many back doors, procure the needed inputs for the village, thus saving peasants from having to deal with both the market and the supply cooperatives.

51. In addition to the scarce chemical fertilizer and diesel fuel, pesticide has likewise become scarce at state prices.

52. "Yindao nongcun zijin zengjia nongye touru."

53. See "A Survey of Monopoly Management of Agricultural Materials in Hunan," *Hunan Ribao* (Hunan daily), translated in *JPRS-CAR-90-044* (11 June 1990): 60–61.

54. See Delman, "Current Peasant."

55. For an economic examination of such changes see Richard Boisvert and Scott Rozelle, "Grain Policy in China's Provinces: Simulating the Response of Yields to Pricing, Procurement and Loan Policies," unpublished manuscript. 1991. Stanford University.

56. See *JPRS-CAR-90-048* (5 July 1990): 73–80.

57. See Xinhua English, 0600 GMT (11 June 1990) in *JPRS-CAR-90-046* (26 June 1990): 83–84.

58. For an elaboration of this theme see Oi, "Fate of the Collective After The Commune," in Deborah Davis and Ezra Vogel, eds., *Chinese Society on the Eve of Tiananmen: The Impact of Reform* (Cambridge: Harvard University, Council of East Asian Studies, Harvard Contemporary China Series, no. 7, 1990): 15–36.

59. There already are large areas that have unified management (*tongyi guanli*) of key aspects of the agricultural cycle. The numerous news stories about the move toward recollectivization, especially those reports from Hong Kong, are somewhat misleading. They suggest that areas will return to pre-1979 collectivized farming. But what is happening with the *daguimo jingying* (large-size management) is quite different. This large-scale specialized household is using mechanized farming techniques, not communes. This type of enterprise, moreover, has been in existence since the early 1980s. See Oi, "The Commercialization of Rural Government," *Problems of Communism*, (September–October 1986): 1–15.

60. Author's interviews in China, 1990.

61. Sun Yonggang and Ma Lirong, "A New Taste of Village Reform—A Report on the 'Double Guarantee System' of Food Production in Chaodong, Heilongjiang Province," *Jinrong Shibao* (Monetary times) (16 May 1990): 2 and Cheng Weigao, "Survey of Thoughts on the Two-way Contract System in Agriculture," *Renmin ribao* (People's daily) (13 July 1990): 5.

62. Starting around 1989 it tacked on an additional quota called a "negotiated price" quota. It pays peasants a higher price for this grain, but is still lower than the market price. In 1989 in Shandong Province, for example, a negotiated sales price (*yijia*) was added to the regular quota. This was officially termed a "*yijia juancheng pingjia renwu*" (official price quota converted from negotiated-price quota) because the state then sold this grain at the low-ration price. Author's Interviews with China, 1990. Based on a state council decision of November 1988 to abolish this quota, it seems there was also a national quota. ZGNYNJ (1989): 10. My interviews and reports from individual provinces, such as Zhejiang, suggest that they still exist in spite of the state council decision. Perhaps these are now provincial quotas. See Huang Quanwu, "Zehjiang Province Sets Up Negotiated-Price Grain Reserves to Enable It to Share in Basic-Level Difficulties and Makeup Crop-Failure Shortages with Bumper-Harvest Surpluses" *Jingji Ribao* (30 April 1990): 2, translated in *JPRS-CAR-90-045* (19 June 1990): 73–74.

63. Author's interviews in summer 1990. In Zhejiang similar complaints were made that too many funds had been tied up buying such large amounts of negotiated grain. See "Zhejiang Province Sets Up Negotiated-Price Grain Reserves."

64. For elaboration see Oi, "The Shifting Balance of Power in Central-Local Relations: Local Government Response to Fiscal Austerity in Rural China" (Paper presented at the Annual Meeting of the American Political Science Association, Washington, D.C., August 29–September 1, 1991.)

65. See, for example, Zhang Rui and Shen Nongdiao, "Peasant Burdens Have Increased Steadily," *Yunnan ribao* (17 May 1990): 2, translated in *JPRS-CAR-90-056* (27 July 1990): 75–76.

66. See Robert Delfs, "Conservatives behind Chen Yun in Reform Struggle: Thought Control," *Far Eastern Economic Review* (8 November 1990): 19–20.

CHAPTER 8: RETREAT TO CENTRAL PLANNING, *Ellen Salem*

1. John Kohut, "Athletic Prowess Prompts Waves of National Pride," *South China Morning Post*, October 7, 1990.

2. "Conference Outlines Tasks for Next Year," *China Daily*, December 3, 1990.

3. John Kohut, "Harsh Policy for Economy Must Go On," *South China Morning Post*, December 3, 1990.

4. Tan Hongkai, "Local Barriers Hit National Economy," *China Daily*, November 6, 1990; Li Hong, "Materials Ministry to Take On Market Role," *China Daily*, December 4, 1990.

5. Robert Delfs, "Doddering Helmsman: Confusion Spreads as Press Debates Deng's Policy Speech," *Far Eastern Economic Review*, June 29, 1989, pp. 10–11.

6. Ellen Salem, "Things Fall Apart, the Centre Cannot Hold," *Far Eastern Economic Review*, October 21, 1988, pp. 38–41.

7. "How to Remedy the Regional Imbalance," *China Daily*, December 4, 1990.

8. Luise de Rosario, "Peking Decrees Economic Retrenchment the Goal: Three Years Hard Labor," *Far Eastern Economic Review*, November 30, 1989.

9. Willy Wo-Lap Lam, "Old Guard Takes a Firmer Grip," *South China Morning Post*, April 24, 1991.

10. Chris Yeung, "Study Urged to Remove Doubts about Socialism," *South China Morning Post*, November 24, 1990.

11. "Yangtze Delta Zone Hailed for Future," *China Daily*, November 9, 1990.

12. Liu Xing-Li, "Where Did the Government Capital to Help Major Enterprises Go?" *Renmin ribao* (People's daily) (Beijing), November 2, 1989.

13. "The Chinese Economy in 1989 and 1990: Trying to Revive Growth While Maintaining Social Stability," U.S. Central Intelligence Agency Assessment, June 28, 1990, pp. 6–7.

14. "Rural Jobless a Big Problem," *China Daily*, November 10, 1990; Tan Hongkai, "Non-State Sector Is Future Labor Pool," *China Daily*, November 28, 1990; Ru Ruo, "Time to Focus on the Rural Economy," *China Daily*, November 5, 1990; Deng Chuanping, "Labor Ministry Sees Peak in Number of People Entering Labor Market in China," *Beijing Jungji Cankao* (Beijing economic references), September 14, 1990.

15. Zhang Yu'an, "Finance Chief Says Revenue Hike Needed," *China Daily*, December 5, 1990; "Economic Revamp Is Needed Now," *China Daily*, November 20, 1990; "Subsidies a Heavy Burden on Government," *China Daily*, June 25, 1990.

16. Julia Leung, "China Is Paying a Hefty Price for Stability," *Asian Wall Street Journal*, November 1, 1990.

17. Wang Xiangwei, "Clampdown Urged on Tax Dodge Enterprises," *People's Daily*, September 6, 1990.

18. Nicholas D. Kristoff, "At the Businesses Owned by Beijing, the Ink is Red," *New York Times*, November 18, 1990.

19. "State Warns of Financial Situation," *People's Daily*, July 9, 1990.

20. Yuan Zhou, "Township Enterprises Get Boost in Bank Loans," *People's Daily*, November 9, 1990.

21. Chuanping, "Labor Ministry Sees Peak in Number of People Entering Labor Market in China."

22. "Rural Employment Needs Attention," *People's Daily*, December 5, 1990.

23. Tai Ming Cheung, "Looking for Work: China Fears Mounting Unemployment Tolls," *Far Eastern Economic Review*, July 19, 1990.

24. Li Hong, "China to Hold Urban Jobless Rate at 3.5%," *People's Daily*, December 11, 1990.

25. Zhang Bian, "Rural Firms Lead Industry out of Slump," *People's Daily*, September 26, 1990.

26. Ellen Salem, "Closing the Back Door: Peking's Anti-Corruption Drive Will Hit Only Small Companies," *Far Eastern Economic Review*, November 17, 1988, pp. 40–1.

27. Liu Dizhong, "Peninsula Region Links Inlanders to Prosperity," *People's Daily*, December 7, 1990.

28. Lo Dic, "Province Out to Gain from Pudong Plan," *South China Morning Post*, June 20, 1990.

29. Daniel Kwan, "Planners Hit by Row on Reform," *South China Morning Post*, December 6, 1990.

30. "China: Macroeconomic Stability and Industrial Growth under Decentralized Socialism," *World Bank Report 1990*, July 1990.

31. Qu Ying-pu, "Foreign Trade Up 9.9% in November," *People's Daily*, December 12, 1990.

32. Willy Wo-Lap Lam, "Hardliners Dominate in Drafting Plan," *South China Morning Post*, August 28, 1990.

33. "Yuan Mu Says the Economy Is Top Priority," *People's Daily*, December 4, 1990.

34. "Yuan: Success Relies on Reform and Socialism," *People's Daily*, November 19, 1990.

35. *Far Eastern Economic Review*, February 18, 1993, p. 53.

36. *South China Morning Post*, February 9, 1993, p. 10.

CHAPTER 9: SCIENCE AND TECHNOLOGY, *Richard P. Suttmeier*

1. Although this chapter is mainly concerned with the mainland and Taiwan, we should not forget the importance of Hong Kong for the development of Greater China Science and Technology. Like Taiwan, Hong Kong has been making a concerted effort to enhance its own indigenous technical capabilities. This is seen, for instance, in the increased importance of the

Hong Kong Productivity Center and the establishment of the Hong Kong University of Science and Technology. In addition, Hong Kong is likely to play an increasingly important role in technology transfer to and from the mainland, and Hong Kong firms are likely to be increasingly important, high technology, joint venture partners with research institutes, established enterprises, and start-up firms on the mainland.

2. The classic formulation of the tensions between nationalism and cosmopolitanism in modern Chinese history is found in Joseph R. Levenson, *Confucian China and Its Modern Fate* (Berkeley, Calif.: University of California Press, 1958).

3. See, for instance, Manuel Castells and Laura D'Andrea Tyson, "High Technology Choices Ahead: Restructuring Interdependence," *Growth, Exports, & Jobs in a Changing World Economy* (New Brunswick, N.J.: Transaction Books, 1988), pp. 55–96; Bruce Guile and Harvey Brooks, eds., *Technology and Global Industry* (Washington, D.C.: National Academy Press, 1987); Arnold Miller, "Critical Factors in the Development of an Electronics Industry" (Technology Strategy Group. Unpublished paper, 1988); Janet H. Muroyama and H. Guyford Stever, eds., *Globalization of Technology* (Washington, D.C.: National Academy Press, 1988).

4. These points are developed at greater length in Richard P. Suttmeier, "The Changing Context for East Asian Science and Technology" (Unpublished report submitted to the National Science Foundation, August 1990).

5. For a recent assessment of Hsinchu, see "Science Park for Tomorrow," *Asia Technology*, vol. 2, no. 12 (December 1990), pp. 40–42.

6. Denis Fred Simon, "Technology Policy on the Pacific Rim," *Forum for Applied Research and Public Policy*, vol. 5, no. 3 (Fall 1990), p. 70.

7. Ibid.

8. Nan-hien Ma and Nin-sun Wuang, "R&D Management—National Policy on Science and Technology" (Paper presented at the First Science and Technology Task Force Symposium of the Pacific Economic Cooperation Conference, Seoul, Korea, November 4–7, 1990).

9. Zhu Lilan, remarks presented to the first Science and Task Force Symposium of the Pacific Economic Cooperation Conference, Seoul, Korea, November 4, 1990.

10. David J. Teece, "Capturing Value from Technological Innovation: Integration, Strategic Partnering, and Licensing Decisions," in Guile and Brooks, eds., *Technology and Global Industry*, pp. 70ff.

11. William C. Kirby, "Technocratic Organization and Technological Development in China: The Nationalist Experience and Legacy, 1928–1935," in Denis Fred Simon and Merle Goldman, eds., *Science and Technology in Post-Mao China* (Cambridge, Mass.: Harvard University Press, 1989), pp. 23–44.

12. Tai Ming Cheung, "Reaching for the Sky," *Far Eastern Economic Review* (May 4, 1989), p. 73; Lincoln Kaye, "Taiwan's Space-age Dream," *Far Eastern Economic Review* (March 8, 1990), p. 62.

13. The "supply push" approach explains technological innovation as stemming from the new ideas generated by scientific research. In contrast, a

"demand pull" approach explains this innovation as stemming from the identification of technical needs and opportunities, which, in turn, shape the agenda for research. The absence of an effective market mechanism in centrally planned economies and ideologically based commitments to centralizing the organization of research have biased the innovation strategies of such economies against the demand pull approach.

14. Richard P. Suttmeier, "China's High Technology: Programs, Problems and Prospects," in U.S. Congress, Joint Economic Committee, *China's Economic Dilemmas in the 1990s: The Problems of Reform, Modernization and Interdependence*, April 1991, pp. 546–64.

15. Ibid.

16. Li Xu'e, "Some Problems in the Development of China's High Technology Industry," *Zhongguo Keji Luntan* (Forum on Science and Technology in China), no. 6 (November 18, 1990) in U.S. Department of Commerce, Joint Publications Research Service (JPRS), CST-90-008, March 15, 1990. The State Science and Technology Commission Vice Minister Zhu Lilan, whose responsibilities include the 863 Program, recently sounded the theme of high-tech internationalization. He stated that the program would try to expand international cooperation. Zhu also called attention to the role of 863 in encouraging China's overseas students to return to China as a result of its contributions to improving the research atmosphere. *China Daily* (June 13, 1990), in Foreign Broadcast Information Service (FBIS-CHI-90-116. June 15, 1990), p. 29.

17. "Taiwan, Mainland Enhance Science Exchanges." Beijing. *Xinhua.* April 21, 1992. In FBIS-CHI-92-077, April 21, 1992. p. 66. This report is based on an interview with Xu Kunming of the Research Section for Science Exchange across the Strait, under the State Science and Technology Commission.

CHAPTER 10: EFFECTS OF DEMOCRATIZATION, *Yung Wei*

1. Cal Clark, "The Taiwan Exception: Implications for Contending Political Economy Paradigms," *International Studies Quarterly* (September 1987), pp. 327–56; and Alice A. Amsden, "Taiwan's Economic History: A Case of Estatisme and a Challenge to Dependency Theory," *Modern China* (July 1979), pp. 341–79.

2. For a broad discussion of bureaucratic authoritarianism, see Guillermo O'Donnell, *Bureaucratic Authoritarianism* (Berkeley, Calif.: University of California Press, 1988). See also Edwin A. Winckler, "Institutionalization and Participation on Taiwan: From Hard to Soft Authoritarianism?" *China Quarterly*, no. 99 (September 1984), pp. 481–99; and a critique of Winckler's thesis by Ramon H. Myers in "Political Theory and Recent Political Developments in the Republic of China," *Asian Survey*, vol. 27 (September 1987), pp. 1003–22.

3. For discussion of the problems of inequality in economic development, see A.B. Atkinson, *The Economics of Inequality*, 2nd ed. (New York: Oxford

University Press, 1983); and Simon Kuznets, "Economic Growth and Income Inequality," *American Economic Review* (March 1955).

4. For political development on Taiwan and the integration of the mainland and Taiwanese elite, see Yung Wei, "Political Development in the Republic of China on Taiwan," in Hungdah Chiu, ed., *China and the Question of Taiwan: Documents and Analysis* (New York: Praeger Publishers, 1973), p. 74; also see Hung-mao Tien, *The Great Transition: Political and Social Change in the Republic of China* (Stanford, Calif.: Hoover Institution Press, 1989); Richard L. Walker, "Taiwan's Movement into Political Modernity," in Paul S. Sih, ed., *Taiwan in Modern Times* (Jamaica, New York: St. John's University Press, 1973), pp. 359–96.

5. For a discussion on Sun Yat-sen's three stage nation-building theory, see Yung Wei, "Sun Yat-sen and China's Nation-building Efforts," in Paul S. Sih, ed., *Sun Yat-sen and China* (Jamaica, New York: St. John's University Press, 1974); and James A. Gregor, *Ideology and Development: Sun Yat-sen and the Economic History of Taiwan* (Berkeley, Calif.: Institute of East Asian Studies, 1981).

6. With regard to the emphasis of the ROC government on both growth and distribution, see Yung Wei, "Modernization on Taiwan: An Allocative Analysis," *Asian Survey* (March 1976), pp. 249–69.

7. Compared with other countries, the decline in the Gini index for Taiwan is significant. See the following table:

GINI INDEX OF LAND CONCENTRATION IN SELECTED COUNTRIES, 1948–1964

Country	Year	Gini Index (C)	Year	Gini Index (E)	Decline in Gini Index, in percentage $\frac{(C) - (E)}{(C)} \times 100$
Columbia	1960	0.864	1969	0.818	5.32
India	1953–54	0.628	1960–61	0.589	6.14
Mexico	1930	0.959	1960	0.694	27.64
Philippines	1948	0.578	1960	0.534	7.26
Taiwan	1952	0.618	1960	0.457	26.08
U.A.R.	1952	0.810	1964	0.674	16.74

SOURCE: Hung-chao Tai, *Land Reform and Politics* (Berkeley, Calif.: University of California Press, 1974), p. 310.

8. For the discussion of the socio-political effects of land reform, see Martin M.C. Yang, *Socio-Economic Results of Land Reform in Taiwan* (Honolulu: East-West Center Press, 1970).

9. *Report on the Survey of Personal Income Distribution in the Taiwan Area, Republic of China 1985* (Taipei: Directorate-General of Budget, Accounting and Statistics, Executive Yuan, Republic of China, 1986), p. 38.

10. Yung Wei, "Political Development in the Republic of China: Reflections

and Projections," in Yung-Hwan Jo, ed., *Taiwan's Future* (Hong Kong: Union Research Institute and Center for Asian Studies, Arizona State University, 1974), pp. 11–38.

11. Huei-en Peng, *The Political Economy of Taiwan's Development* (Taipei: Feng-yun Publisher, 1990), p. 170.

12. For a review of political reform under President Chiang Ching-kuo, see Yung Wei, "Toward an Institutionalized Development of Democratic Politics: An Outlook on the Political Development in the Republic of China" (Taipei: Research, Development, and Evaluation Commission, RDEC, hereafter; 1987); also see Yang-sun Chou and Andrew J. Nathan, "Democratizing Transition in Taiwan," *Asian Survey*, vol. 28 (March 1987), pp. 277–99.

13. As an example of the effect of these study tours on political reform, see Yung Wei, "A Reflection on the Insight Gained from Party Politics in Great Britain," *The Excellence Magazine* (January 1990), pp. 155–57.

14. In an analysis of the challenges faced by Lee Teng-hui in his ascendancy to the leadership of the government and the party, see Huang Hui-chen, "The Radical Change in the Highest Political Leadership Structure," series reports on the challenges of the 1990s, *China Times* (December 28, 1990), p. 11.

15. Ibid.; also see Jurgen Domes, "The Thirteenth Party Congress of the Kuomintang: Toward Political Competition?" *China Quarterly*, vol. 118 (June 1989), pp. 345–59.

16. Chen Yu-chun, "Democratic Party Operation in a Pluralistic Society," conference on the challenges facing the KMT in the 1990s, held in Taipei, ROC, June 9, 1990; also see Kê Yung-Kuan, "Study on the Democratization of the KMT," in the same conference.

17. Kao Long, "Reform in the KMT, Constitutional Change, and the Development of Party Politics," conference on the challenges facing the KMT in the 1990s, held in Taipei, ROC, June 9, 1990.

18. See Chen Yu-Chun, conference of June 9, 1990, p. 13.

19. "Where Will the 'National Unification Board' Find Itself?" editorial, *China Times* (September 13, 1990), p. 3.

20. *United Daily News* (July 5, 1990), pp. 3–4; and *Central Daily News* (July 4, 1990), pp. 5–6.

21. *United Daily News* (November 18, 1990), p. 2.

22. "An Objective Analysis on the Factors Contributing to the Formation of the National Unification Board," *Min-tsung Daily* (September 14, 1990), p. 2; and Lin Chia-cheng, "A Political Observation on the Formation of the National Unification Board," *Chih-Yiu Shih Pao* (Liberty Times) (October 4, 1990), p. 2.

23. *China Times* (December 20, 1990), p. 1.

24. "CCP Announces the Newest Policies toward Taiwan, Hong Kong, and Macau," *China Times* (December 31, 1990), p. 1.

25. "The Implication of CCP's Announcement That There Is No Timetable for Unification," *China Times* (December 31, 1991), p. 2.

26. For examples, see Ke Yung-Kuan and Kao Long, conference of June 9, 1990.

27. Ibid.

28. Yung Wei, "Socio-political Development in the Republic of China: Analysis and Projection," paper delivered at the American Management Conference on US–Taiwan Economic Relations, Plaza Hotel, New York City, June 15, 1987; and same author's report on "Political Attitudes and Voting Intention of the People in the Taiwan Region" (Taipei: RDEC, 1980), p. 26.

29. "The Tremendous Change in Party Politics in the Process of Democratic Transformation," *China Times* (December 31, 1990), p. 11.

30. Chu Kao-cheng, "Party Politics Is to Fully Express the Will of the People," *China Times* (December 31, 1990); *Chung-Hua Min-Tsu-She-Hui Tang Chi-Fen Tang-Kang* (The basic platform of the Chinese social democratic party), 1990.

31. For a discussion of the political attitude of the middle-class voters, see Yung Wei, "The Emergence of a Middle Class in Taiwan and Its Implications," *China Times*, May 23–25, 1985.

32. See Yung Wei, "The Trend of Political Development (in the ROC) as Seen in the Findings and Six Consecutive Opinion Surveys," a report delivered at the Joint Monthly Meeting, Central Committee of the KMT (May 5, 1986).

33. Data released by Gallup Poll in November 1990.

34. Ibid.

35. See, for example, Yung Wei, "The Unification and Division of a Multi-System Nation: A Comparative Analysis of Basic Concepts, Issues, and Approaches," in Hungdah Chiu and Robert Dowsen, eds., *Multi-System Nations and International Law* (Baltimore: University of Maryland Press, 1981).

36. See Yung Wei, "Dual Recognition and Pragmatic Diplomacy," *Central Daily News* (August 7, 1989), p. 2.

37. For ROC's external relations, particularly those with the United States, see Ramon Myers, ed., *The United States and the Republic of China under the Taiwan Relations Act* (Stanford, Calif.: Hoover Institution Press, 1989).

38. According to an island-wide opinion survey, only 6.4 percent of the voters believed that declaring independence is in the interest of the people in Taiwan. See "The Response of People in Taiwan toward Mainland China Policy: Results of an Opinion Survey" (Taipei: RDEC, June 1989).

CHAPTER 12: RECONCILING CONFUCIANISM AND PLURALISM,
Hei-yuan Chiu

1. Kuo-shu Yang and Hei-yuan Chiu, eds., *Taiwanese Society in Transition* (Taipei: Institute of Ethnology, Academia Sinica, 1988).

2. Directorate General of Budget, Accounting, and Statistics, *Social Indicators in the Taiwan Area of the Republic of China* (1989).

3. Li Shiang Yau, *An Exploratory Study on the Changes of Buddhism in Taiwan since 1950* (unpublished manuscript, 1988).

4. Hei-yuan Chiu and Li-shiang Yau, "On Religious Changes in Taiwanese

Society," in Hei-yuan Chiu and Ying-hua Chang, eds., *Social and Cultural Change in Taiwan* (1986).

5. Rahn Strickler and Chung-chien Hsia, *The Church in Taiwan: Present Situations and Projections* (Taipei: Gospel Movement for the Year 2000, 1990).

6. Hsin-chiang Kao, ed., *Buddhist Priestess Cheng Yen's Meditations* (Taipei: Chiu-Ko, 1989).

CHAPTER 13: "UNGOVERNABILITY" IN THE TWILIGHT OF COLONIAL RULE, Siu-kai Lau

1. See, for example, Ian Scott, *Political Change and the Crisis of Legitimacy in Hong Kong* (Hong Kong: Oxford University Press, 1989).

2. For a discussion of colonial ideologies, see, for example, Phillip Darby, *Three Faces of Imperialism: British and American Approaches to Asia and Africa 1870–1970* (New Haven: Yale University Press, 1987).

3. In the 1988 survey I conducted, 41.6 percent of a total of 396 respondents agreed that Hong Kong should not be taken over by China but should declare independence; 46.7 percent were opposed to the suggestion. The survey was part of the Social Indicators Research Project jointly undertaken by the Centre for Hong Kong Studies (now the Hong Kong Institute of Asia-Pacific Studies) of the Chinese University of Hong Kong, the Social Science Research Centre of the University of Hong Kong, and the Department of Applied Social Studies of the Hong Kong Polytechnic.

4. See Tony Smith, "Patterns in the Transfer of Power: A Comparative Study of French and British Decolonization," in Prosser Gifford and William Roger Louis, eds., *The Transfer of Power in Africa: Decolonization, 1940–1960* (New Haven: Yale University Press, 1982), pp. 90–91.

5. See, for example, Brian Lapping, *End of Empire* (London: Granada Publishing, 1985); and William Roger Louis and Ronald Robinson, "The United States and the Liquidation of British Empire in Tropical Africa, 1941–1951," in *The Transfer of Power in Africa*, pp. 31–54.

6. See Ambrose Yeo-chi King, "Administrative Absorption of Politics in Hong Kong: Emphasis on the Grassroots Level," *Asian Survey*, vol. 15, no. 5 (May 1972), pp. 422–39; and Lau Siu-kai, *Decolonization without Independence and the Poverty of Political Leaders in Hong Kong* (Hong Kong: Hong Kong Institute of Asia-Pacific Studies, Chinese University of Hong Kong, 1990), pp. 5–6.

7. See Lau Siu-kai, *Society and Politics in Hong Kong* (Hong Kong: Chinese University Press, 1982), pp. 102–17; Lau Siu-kai and Kuan hsin-chi, *The Ethos of the Hong Kong Chinese* (Hong Kong: Chinese University Press, 1988), pp. 73–92.

8. In fact, the criterion of performance looms very large in the political legitimacy of governments in the modern age. In the words of Arthur J. Vidich,

In the contemporary world, both in Third World nations and in the industrialized countries, legitimacy processes include production and economic performance as a critical dimension on which legitimacy claims are made. The economic performance of a regime may constitute a major prop for its legitimacy in the eyes of groups and classes which have accepted life style enhancement as a life goal.

See his "Legitimacy of Regimes in World Perspective," in Arthur J. Vidich and Ronald M. Glassman, eds., *Conflict and Control: Challenge to Legitimacy of Modern Governments* (Beverly Hills: Sage Publications, 1979), p. 299.

9. See Lau and Kuan, *The Ethos of the Hong Kong Chinese*, p. 84.

10. Lau, *Society and Politics in Hong Kong*; and Norman Miner, *The Government and Politics of Hong Kong*, 4th ed. (Hong Kong: Oxford University Press, 1986).

11. See Lucien W. Pye, *The Spirit of Chinese Politics* (Cambridge, Mass.: MIT Press, 1968); and Richard H. Solomon, *Mao's Revolution and the Chinese Political Culture* (Berkeley, Calif.: University of California Press, 1971).

12. See Lau Siu-kai and Ho Kam-fai, "Social Accommodation of Politics: The Case of Young Hong Kong Workers," *Journal of Commonwealth and Comparative Politics*, vol. 20 (July 1982), pp. 177–88; Lau and Kuan, *The Ethos of the Hong Kong Chinese*, pp. 63–64; Tsang Wing-kwong, "Class Structure and Social Mobility in Hong Kong: The Weberian Approach" (Ph.D. diss., Chinese University of Hong Kong, 1990).

13. Lau and Kuan, *The Ethos of the Hong Kong Chinese*, pp. 119–43. See also Lau Siu-kai, "Social Change, Bureaucratic Rule, and Emergent Political Issues in Hong Kong," *World Politics* (March 1984), pp. 259–84.

14. See, for example, Hsin-chi Kuan, *Hong Kong after the Basic Law* (Victoria, Hong Kong: Institute for Research on Public Policy, 1990).

15. See Lau, "Social Change"; and Scott, *Political Change*.

16. Notwithstanding the government's perennial claim to represent public interests, Hong Kong Chinese have a strong tendency to attribute self-seeking motives to the government. In a 1985 survey of mine, 61 percent of respondents agreed or very much agreed with the following statement: "Most of the time the Hong Kong government avows that it is the protector of public interests. In reality, it always promotes its own interests." See Lau and Kuan, *The Ethos of the Hong Kong Chinese*, p. 83. It can even be said that there are deep-seated though barely perceptible anti-British feelings among the Hong Kong Chinese.

17. Lau Siu-kai, "The Unfinished Political Reforms of the Hong Kong Government," in John W. Langford and K. Lorne Brownsey, eds., *The Changing Shape of Government in the Asia-Pacific Region* (Victoria, Hong Kong: Institute for Research on Public Policy, 1988), pp. 43–82; and Lau, *Decolonization without Independence*.

18. See Lau Siu-kai, "Institutions without Leaders: The Hong Kong Chinese View of Political Leadership," *Pacific Affairs*, vol. 63, no. 2 (Summer 1990), pp. 191–209; and Lau Siu-kai and Kuan Hsin-chi, "Public Attitude toward Laissez Faire in Hong Kong," *Asian Survey*, vol. 3, no. 8 (August 1990), pp. 766–81.

19. Terry T. Lui and Terry L. Cooper, "Hong Kong Facing China: Civil

Servants' Confidence in the Future," *Administration & Society*, vol. 22, no. 2 (August 1990), p. 159; Terry L. Cooper and Terry T. Lui, "Democracy and the Administrative State: The Case of Hong Kong," *Public Administration Review*, vol. 50, no. 3 (May/June 1990), p. 338; and Ian Scott, "Sino-British Agreement and Political Power in Hong Kong," *Asian Pacific Community*, no. 31 (Winter 1986), pp. 6–12.

20. Lau Siu-kai and Kuan Hsin-chi, *Chinese Bureaucrats in a Modern Colony: The Case of Hong Kong* (Hong Kong: Centre for Hong Kong Studies, Chinese University of Hong Kong, 1986); Kathleen Cheek-Milby, "The Changing Political Role of the Hong Kong Civil Servant," *Pacific Affairs*, vol. 62, no. 2 (Summer 1989), pp. 220–34; and Kathleen Cheek-Milby "The Civil Servant as Politician: The Role of the Official Member of the Legislative Council," in Kathleen Cheek-Milby and Miron Mushkat, eds., *Hong Kong: The Challenge of Transformation* (Hong Kong: Centre of Asian Studies, University of Hong Kong), pp. 256–91.

21. Cooper and Lui, "Democracy and the Administrative State," p. 336.

22. Ken Davis, *Hong Kong to 1994: A Question of Confidence* (London: Economist Intelligence Unit, 1990), pp. 12–22.

23. *South China Morning Post*, March 5, 1992.

24. See *Tasks for the 1990s: Implementing Hong Kong's Strategy for Building Prosperity* (Hong Kong: Hong Kong Economic Survey Ltd., June 1990).

25. Lau, "Social Change"; Lau Siu-kai and Kuan Hsin-chi, "The Changing Political Culture of the Hong Kong Chinese," in Joseph Y.S. Cheng, ed., *Hong Kong in Transition* (Hong Kong: Oxford University Press, 1986), pp. 26–51.

26. Lau, "Institutions without Leaders," p. 198.

27. Ibid., pp. 195–98. See also Lau Siu-kai, "Perception of Authority by Chinese Adolescents: The Case of Hong Kong," *Youth and Society*, vol. 15, no. 3 (March 1984), pp. 259–84; and Leung Sai-wing, *Perception of Political Authority by the Hong Kong Chinese* (Hong Kong: Centre for Hong Kong Studies, Chinese University of Hong Kong, 1986).

28. See, for example, Benjamin K. P. Leung, "Poverty and Inequality," in Benjamin K. P. Leung, ed., *Social Issues in Hong Kong* (Hong Kong: Oxford University Press, 1990), p. 71; Laurence L. C. Chau, "Economic Growth and Reduction of Poverty in Hong Kong," *Philippine Economic Journal*, vol. 18, no. 4 (1979), pp. 570–615; and Steven C. Chow and Gustav F. Papanek, "Laissez Faire, Growth and Equity—Hong Kong," *Economic Journal*, vol. 91 (June 1981), pp. 466–85.

29. Wong's survey is part of the social indicator project mentioned in note 3. See Thomas W. P. Wong, "Inequality, Stratification and Mobility," in Lau Siu-kai et al., eds., *Indicators of Social Development: Hong Kong 1988* (Hong Kong: Hong Kong Institute of Asia-Pacific Studies, Chinese University of Hong Kong, 1991), pp. 145–71.

30. In my own 1988 survey, I found that 74.1 percent of respondents thought that the government should tax the rich more to reduce economic inequality. See Lau and Kuan, "Public Attitude," p. 770.

31. See Joe England, *Industrial Relations and Law in Hong Kong*, 2d ed. (Hong Kong: Oxford University Press, 1989).

32. See, for example, Michel J. Crozier et al., *The Crisis of Democracy* (New York: New York University Press, 1975); Laurence Whitehead, "On 'Governability' in Mexico," *Bulletin of Latin American Research*, vol. 1, pt. 1 (October 1981), pp. 27–47; Claus Offe, " 'Ungovernability': The Renaissance of Conservative Theories of Crisis," in *Contradictions of the Welfare State* (Cambridge, Mass.: MIT Press, 1984); Michael C. Hudson, *Arab Politics: The Search for Legitimacy* (New Haven: Yale University Press, 1977); and Lucian W. Pye, "The Legitimacy Crisis," in Leonard Binder et al., *Crises and Sequences in Political Development* (Princeton: Princeton University Press, 1971), pp. 135–58.

33. Lau and Kuan, *The Ethos of the Hong Kong Chinese*, p. 84.

34. *Ming Pao Daily News*, May 22, 1990, p. 3.

35. See City and New Territories Administration, "Report of an Opinion Poll in November 1990" (Hong Kong: CNTA, November 1990, mimeo.), p. 6.

36. *South China Morning Post*, October 7, 1990.

37. Lau and Kuan, *The Changing Political Culture*," pp. 37–41; and Lau and Kuan, *The Ethos of the Hong Kong Chinese*, p. 102.

38. Anthony B. L. Cheung and K. S. Louie, *Social Conflicts in Hong Kong, 1975–1986: Trends and Implications* (Hong Kong: Hong Kong Institute of Asia-Pacific Studies, Chinese University of Hong Kong, 1991).

39. *South China Morning Post*, April 14, 1990.

40. The decision of Britain in 1989 to grant 50,000 elite families of Hong Kong British nationality might moderately widen the support base of the colonial government. But this is not enough to arrest the decline of colonial authority. Besides, as many of these families might eventually want to remain in Hong Kong, their interests might not coincide with those of the colonial government. In any case, their loyalty to Britain is quite fragile.

41. Despite the fiscal crunch, the government still seeks to enhance its legitimacy through performance. The decision to embark upon the huge Port and Airport Development Scheme is a case in point. The general policy orientation of the government in the near future, however, is the reduction of its role in the provision of social welfare and public services. In fact, the government is articulating a crude form of neoconservatism that emphasizes the free market and the family in meeting personal and social needs. See the governor's 1990 speech in *South China Morning Post*, October 11, 1990.

42. In Annex II of the Joint Declaration, Article 5 reads:

> The two Governments have agreed that in the second half of the period between the establishment of the Joint Liaison Group and 1 July 1997 there will be need for closer cooperation, which will therefore be intensified during that period. Matters for consideration during this second period shall include: (a) procedures to be adopted for the smooth transition in 1997; (b) action to assist the Hong Kong Special Administrative Region to maintain and develop economic and cultural relations and conclude agreements on these matters with states, regions and relevant international organisations.

See *A Draft Agreement between the Government of the United Kingdom of Britain and Northern Ireland and the Government of the People's Republic of China on the*

Future of Hong Kong (Hong Kong: Government Printer, September 26, 1984), p. 5.

43. Both the elites and the people of Hong Kong would like to see a more cooperative relationship between Britain and China, according to some opinion polls. See *South China Morning Post*, July 21, 1990, and November 5, 1990, and *Ming Pao Daily News*, August 1, 1990.

CHAPTER 14: THE 1977 BARRIER AND BEYOND, *Yun-wing Sung*

1. Paul C. K. Kwong, "Emigration and Manpower Shortage," in Richard Y. C. Wong and Joseph Y. S. Cheng, eds., *The Other Hong Kong Report* (Hong Kong: Chinese University Press, 1990), pp. 297–338.

2. Ibid., p. 301.

3. *South China Morning Post*, December 14, 1990.

4. *Hong Kong Industrialist* (December, 1990), p. 26.

5. *Economist*, May 11, 1985.

6. Yun-Wing Sung, "The China-Hong Kong Connection," in James A. Dorn and Wang Xi, eds., *Economic Reforms in China: Problems and Prospects* (Chicago: University of Chicago Press, 1990), pp. 255–66.

7. Kozo Yamamura, "General Trading Companies in Japan: Their Origins and Growth," in Hugh Patrick, ed., *Japanese Industrialization and Its Social Consequences* (Berkeley, Calif.: University of California Press, 1976), pp. 184–85.

8. Charles Stuart, "Search and Spatial Organization of Trading," in M. Lippmand and T. McCall, eds., *Studies in Economics of Search* (North Holland, Amsterdam, 1979), p. 17.

9. John Hicks, *A Theory of Economic History* (London: Oxford University Press, 1969), pp. 47–49.

10. Robert Lucas, "The Mechanics of Economic Development," Marshall Lecture, Cambridge University, 1985.

11. Yamamura, "General Trading Companies in Japan," pp. 184–85.

12. Sung, "The China-Hong Kong Connection," pp. 260–65.

13. *Hong Kong Economic Times*, December 4, 1990.

14. *Wen Hui Pao*, June 30, 1989.

15. *Hang Seng Economic Monthly*, October 1990.

16. *Hong Kong Economic Times*, December 13, 1990.

17. *South China Morning Post*, December 14, 1990.

18. *Hong Kong Economic Monthly*, November 1989.

CHAPTER 15: EVOLUTION OF DIVIDED CHINA, *Byron S. J. Weng*

1. It is a conspicuously curious fact that no specific abstract terminology has yet been developed by scholars or politicians to describe the component units of a divided nation, even though the politics of divided nations has been the subject of special attention for the past four decades. In the book

NOTES TO PAGES 345–348

that made the first attempt to arrive at a kind of general theory on the subject of divided nations (Gregory Henderson, Richard Ned Lebow, and John G. Stoessinger, *Divided Nations in a Divided World* [N.Y.: David McKay, 1974], Henderson, Lebow, and Stoessinger defined divided nations as "countries with marked ethnic homogeneity, a common historical tradition and experience of successful political unity, that have been subsequently divided into two separate political units" (p. 434).

2. See Hungdah Chiu and Robert Downen, eds., *Multi-System Nations and International Law: The International Status of Germany, Korea and China*, Proceedings of a Regional Conference of American Society of International Law (Baltimore: University of Maryland Law School, Occasional Papers/Reprints Series in Contemporary Asian Studies, no. 8, 1981), p. 45.

3. There are a number of "partitioned countries," such as Ireland, India-Pakistan-Bangladesh, Cyprus, Palestine-Israel, and Rwanda-Burundi. They should be distinguished from "divided nations." These countries are partitioned primarily for internal reasons, such as ethnic, religious, or linguistic differences. While the people of a divided nation generally aspire to reunite someday, the peoples of a partitioned country seem to prefer going their separate ways. See Henderson, Lebow, and Stoessinger, *Divided Nations*, p. 434.

4. See John H. Herz, "Germany," in ibid., pp. 3 ff.

5. See Byung-Hwa Lyou, *Peace and Unification in Korea and International Law* (Baltimore: University of Maryland School of Law: Occasional Papers/Reprints Series in Contemporary Asian Studies, no. 2, 1986).

6. "One country, two systems," for instance, would render Taiwan a local unit. "One country, two regions," or "one country, two governments," however, would make the two regions equal.

7. James N. Rosenau, "Pretheories and Theories of Foreign Policy," in R. Barry Farrell, ed., *Approaches to Comparative and International Politics* (Evanston: Northwestern University Press, 1966), p. 65.

8. Weng Song-jan (Byron S.J. Weng), "A Preliminary Study on the Relationships between the Two Sides of the Taiwan Straits in the Coming Decade," *Jiushi Niandai*, no. 193 (February 1986), pp. 24–31.

Henderson and Lebow suggested a paradigm of division that includes a clearly stated hypothesis and a four-stage process. The hypothesis was derived from case studies showing that relations between divided nations change as a function of the degree of stability and legitimacy of each divided state, relations between each divided state and its respective superpower; and relations between the superpowers themselves. The four stages in the division process are: (1) intense mutual hostility, (2) diminishing hostility, (3) rapprochement, and (4) unification. All divided nations begin life in stage one but do not necessarily pass through the other stages, since a solution may be reached by one of the three ways at any point. Henderson and Lebow noted that the shifts from stage one to stage two and from stage three to stage four represent two quantum leaps in the relations between the divided nations. What Henderson and Lebow referred to as quantum leaps were in fact ambiguities that require refinement. Henderson, Lebow, and Stoessinger, *Divided Nations*, pp. 433–42.

9. The description of the new paradigm in this section borrows heavily from both my earlier article (Weng, "A Preliminary Study") and the Henderson-Lebow-Stoessinger paradigm. Henderson, Lebow, and Stoessinger suggest that divided nations troubled by the problems of identity and successor status may solve such problems and normalize their relations in one of three ways: unification by military conquest, the collapse of one side for internal reasons, and mutual acceptance of the status quo. See note 8 above.

10. See Weng, "A Preliminary Study."

11. "Well water shall not violate river water; river water shall not violate well water." This is an old Chinese saying meaning, "Neighbors should stay within their own bounds and be at peace with each other." Jiang Zemin used the first half of this saying at a meeting in 1989 to express his view on mainland-Hong Kong relations. Sensitive Hong Kong people are wary that he did not refer to the last half. Beijing's reference to Hong Kong as "a base to topple the government" or "a forward base" in connection with democratic groups and their activities also frightens some people.

12. Henderson, Lebow, and Stoessinger, *Divided Nations*, p. 439.

13. In Rosenau's words,

> Stated formally, an issue-area is conceived to consist of (1) a cluster of values, the allocation or potential allocation of which (2) leads the affected or potentially affected actors to differ so greatly over (a) the way in which the values should be allocated or (b) the horizontal levels at which the allocations should be authorized that (3) they engage in distinctive behavior designed to mobilize support for the attainment of their particular values.

Hence, "boundaries of political systems ought to be drawn vertically in terms of issue-areas as well as horizontally in terms of geographic areas." Rosenau, *Pretheories and Theories*, pp. 71, 81, and note 90 on p. 74.

14. In 1955, prior to the Bandung Conference, a plane carrying members of the PRC delegation exploded in midair. Sabotage was suspected, whereupon Zhou Enlai laid down certain demands on the Hong Kong British authorities: for example, safety of Chinese officials must be looked after and the territory must not be used as a base by enemies of the PRC.

15. This is controversial, for it may be that the visitation policy since 1987 has afforded Taiwan a greater, more subtle kind of penetration into the mainland.

16. Private drafts of such a law began appearing in Taipei in 1988. The Ministry of Justice floated a semiofficial draft of a law, entitled Provisional Regulations Regarding Relations between the Two Shores of the Straits, in February 1989. In Beijing, the Taiwan Law Research Center of the China University of Political Science and Law circulated a draft of its own in 1989. In Hong Kong, the Chinese Law Programme, Chinese University of Hong Kong, of which the author is the secretary, organized an international conference in May 1990 to discuss the drafts. The papers, all in Chinese, have

since been published. See Weng Songran (Byron S.J. Weng), ed., *Liangan Falu Shiyong zhi Lilun yu Shiwu* (The application of laws between the two shores: theory and practice) (Taipei: Weili Falu, 1992). See also Zeng Xianyi et al., *Haixia Liangan Guanxi Zhanxing Tiaoli* (Provisional regulations on relations between the two shores of the straits) (Taipei: Weili Falu, 1989). A law, retitled Regulations between the Peoples of the Taiwan Region and the Mainland Region, was passed by the Legislative Yuan of the ROC on July 31, 1992.

17. The draft text of the NUC guidelines appeared on the front page of Taiwan's major newspapers on December 21, 1990.

18. These technical difficulties are analyzed succinctly in the editorial of *Ming Pao Daily* (Hong Kong, December 29, 1990).

19. *Wen Wei Po* (Hong Kong, December 31, 1990), p. 2.

20. *China Times* (Taipei, December 21, 1990), p. 1.

CHAPTER 16: POST–COLD WAR SECURITY, *Thomas W. Robinson*

1. An increasingly large literature has emerged on the structure and trends of the post–cold war era. Among others are the following: Zbigniew Brzezinski, *Out of Control: Global Turmoil on the Eve of the 21st Century* (New York: Scribner's, 1993); Samuel P. Huntington, *The Third Wave: Democratization in the Late Twentieth Century* (Norman: University of Oklahoma Press, 1991); Frances Fukuyama, *The End of History and the Last Man* (New York: Free Press, 1992); Graham E. Fuller, *The Democracy Trap: Perils of the Post–Cold War World* (New York: Dutton, 1991); Ali A. Mazrui, *Cultural Forces in World Politics* (Portsmouth, N.H.: Heinemann, 1990); Paul M. Kennedy, ed., *Grand Strategy in War and Peace* (Yale: Yale University Press, 1991); Michael Howard, "Old Conflicts and New Disorders," in *Asia's International Role in the Post–Cold War Era* (New York: Brassey's, Adelphi Paper 275–276, for the International Institute for Strategic Studies, 1993), pp. 2–13; Robert A. Scalapino, "Emerging Patterns of Political and Military Conflicts: Diagnosis and Prognosis," and Kazuo Takashashi, "Emerging Patterns of Social and Cultural Conflicts: Diagnosis and Prognosis," in Rohana Mahmood and Rustan A. Sani, eds., *Confidence Building and Conflict Reduction in the Pacific* (Kuala Lumpur: Institute for Strategic and International Studies, 1992), pp. 34–54 and 71–78, respectively; Robert A. Scalapino, "Pacific-Asia in Transition," in Robert A. Scalapino and Gennady I. Chufrin, eds., *Asia in the 1990s: American and Soviet Perspectives* (Berkeley, Calif.: Institute of East Asian Studies, University of California, 1991), pp. 2–15; Samuel P. Huntington, "The Clash of Civilizations?" *Foreign Affairs* (Summer 1993), pp. 22–49; Joseph S. Nye, "What New World Order?" *Foreign Affairs* (Spring 1992), pp. 83–96; Larry Diamond, "Promoting Democracy," *Foreign Policy* (Summer 1992), pp. 25–46; James Schlesinger, "New Instabilities, New Priorities," *Foreign Policy* (Winter 1991–92), pp. 3–24; Ted Galen Carpenter, "The New World Disorder," *Foreign Policy* (Fall 1991), pp. 24–39; Joseph S. Nye, "Soft Power," *Foreign Policy* (Fall 1990), pp. 153–71; Christopher Layne, "The Unipolar Illusion: Why New Great Powers Will Rise," and Samuel P. Huntington, "Why International

Primacy Matters," *Foreign Policy* (Spring 1993), pp. 5–51 and 68–83, respectively; Adams Roberts, "The United Nations and International Security," *Survival* (Spring 1993), pp. 3–30; and James Mayall, "Nationalism and International Security after the Cold War," *Survival* (Spring 1992), pp. 19–35. For an expression of the author's views on this topic, see his "Domestic and International Trends in Asian Security: Implications for American Defense Policy," *Korean Journal of Defense Analysis* (Summer 1992), pp. 129–46.

2. Joseph A. Camilleri, "The Emerging Security Agenda in the Asia-Pacific Region" (Ottawa: North Pacific Cooperative Security Dialogue, working paper 12, May 1992); Brian L. Job, *The Insecurity Dilemma: National Security of Third World States* (Boulder, Colo.: Lynne Reiner, 1992); Il Yung Chung, ed., *The Asia-Pacific Community in the Year 2000* (Seoul: Sejong Institute, 1991); Leszek Buszynski, "Southeast Asia in the Post–Cold War Era: Regionalism and Security," *Asian Survey* (September 1992), pp. 830–47; Steven Blank, "Soviet Perspectives on Asian Security," *Asian Survey* (July 1991), pp. 646–61; and Tsuneo Akaha, "Japan's Comprehensive Security Policy: A New East Asian Environment," *Asian Survey* (April 1991), pp. 324–40. The annual roundtable conferences on Asian security sponsored by the Malaysian Institute for Security and International Studies (ISIS), beginning in 1987, have concentrated on airing Asian proposals. See, for instance, Mahmood and Sani, eds., *Confidence Building and Conflict Reduction in the Pacific*, and Jawhar Hassan and Rohana Mahmood, eds., *Towards a New Pacific Order* (Kuala Lumpur: ISIS, 1991). While South Korean opinion understandably concentrates on the Korean peninsula, the three English-language journals available to the author have many relevant articles. See the *Journal of East Asian Studies*, *Korea and World Affairs*, and the *Korean Journal of Defense Analysis* for the post-1989 period. Other Asian opinion is recorded in notes 3 and 19.

3. Chinese views are found, among others, in: *Guoji Wenti Yanjiu* (International studies), *Guoji Zhangwang* (World outlook), *Foreign Affairs Journal*, *Guoji Zhanlue Yanjiu* (International strategic studies), *Xiandai Guoji Guanxi* (Contemporary international relations), and *Hoping* (Peace), all organs of various research institutes in Beijing and Shanghai. See in particular Shen Qurong, "Some Questions concerning the Establishment of a New International Order"; Chen Qida, "Newly Emerging Economic Order in Northeast Asia"; Ma Zhongshi, "Partners in Asia-Pacific Economic Cooperation"; Liu Jiangyong, "On the Current Changes in the Asia-Pacific Political Scene"; and Shen Qurong, "Security Environment in Northeast Asia: Its Characteristics and Sensitivities," in *Contemporary International Relations* (Beijing: China Institute of Contemporary International Relations), July 1991, December 1991, February 1992, March 1992, and December 1992, respectively, and Wan Guang, "Challenges Facing the World Today and the Establishment of the New International Order," Beijing Symposium on a New International Order, September 1991. For a survey of this literature, see Samuel S. Kim, "China in and out of the Changing World Order" (Princeton: Center of International Studies, 1991). Vietnamese literature is not easily accessed. The author's impressions of a knowledgeable and active Vietnamese community were

gained during a 1992 visit to the Institute of International Relations in Hanoi, where it was evident that scholars and diplomats at this official research and training institute were well acquainted with post–cold war ideas and the literature. For access to the Vietnamese literature, see Douglas Pike, *Indochina Chronology* (Berkeley: Institute of East Asian Studies, University of California, a quarterly), each issue of which contains an extensive bibliography.

4. Official American post–cold war pronouncements can be found in: U.S. Department of Defense, "A Strategic Framework for the Asian Pacific Rim: Report to Congress," April 1990, February 1991, and February 1992; Adm. Charles R. Larson, "United States Pacific Command Posture Statement 1993"; Winston Lord, "A New Pacific Community: Ten Goals for American Policy," Confirmation Hearing Statement, March 31, 1993; Richard H. Solomon, "Pursuing US Objectives in Asia and the Pacific," *Department of State Dispatch*, April 6, 1992; the White House, *National Security Strategy of the United States*, January 1993; Richard L. Armitage, "The U.S. Security Role in Southeast Asia: Not a Millstone, but a Cornerstone," and Adm. Ronald J. Hayes, "Regional Security Trends," in Dora Alves, ed., *Cooperative Security in the Pacific Basin* (Washington, D.C.: National Defense University [NDU] Press, 1990), pp. 3–16 and 101–10, respectively; Adm. Huntington Hardisty, "Pacific Challenges," in Dora Alves, ed., *Evolving Pacific Basin Strategies* (Washington, D.C.: NDU Press, 1990), pp. 3–12; Hardisty, "A Long-Term Game Plan," in Dora Alves, ed., *Change, Interdependence, and Security in the Pacific Basin* (Washington, D.C.: NDU Press, 1991), pp. 3–14; Adm. Charles R. Larson, "New Perspectives on Asia and the Pacific," in Dora Alves, ed., *New Perspectives for US-Asian Pacific Security Strategy* (Washington, D.C.: NDU Press, 1992), pp. 2–12; Adm. Charles R. Larson, "Playing Catch among the Crystal: Planning Tomorrow's Pacific Security Today," in Ralph A. Cossa, ed., *The New Pacific Security Environment* (Washington, D.C.: NDU Press, 1993), pp. 253–61; and James A. Kelly, "Asia-Pacific Strategic Issues: An American Perspective," in Scalapino and Chufrin, eds., *Asia in the 1990s: American and Soviet Perspectives*, pp. 16–29.

Unofficial American proposals and analyses are many. They include: James A. Winnefeld et al., *A New Strategy and Fewer Forces: The Pacific Dimension* (Santa Monica, Calif.: Rand Corporation, 1992), R-4089/2-USDP; John Y. Schrader and James A. Winnefeld, *Understanding the Evolving U.S. Role in Pacific Rim Security* (Santa Monica, Calif.: Rand Corporation, 1992), R-4065-PACOM; Paul H. Kreisberg, "US Political-Military Policy in the Asia-Pacific," in Alves, ed., *Change, Interdependence, and Security in the Pacific Basin*, pp. 15–32; Kreisberg, "American Security in the Asia-Pacific," in Alves, ed., *New Perspectives for US-Asian Pacific Security Strategy*, pp. 29–48; Walt W. Rostow, "The Pacific Basin and National Security," in Alves, ed., *Cooperative Security in the Pacific Basin*, pp. 17–30; Doug Bandow, "Sounding the Retreat," in Cossa, ed., *The New Pacific Security Environment*, pp. 249–52; William Zimmerman, ed., *Beyond the Soviet Threat: Rethinking American Security Policy in a New Era* (Ann Arbor: University of Michigan Press, 1993); S. J. Deitchman, *Beyond the Thaw: A New National Strategy* (Boulder, Colo.: Westview Press,

1991); Daniel J. Kaufman et al., *U.S. National Strategy for the 1990s* (Baltimore: Johns Hopkins University Press, 1991); Charles E. Morrison, "The United States in Post–Cold War Asia," in Mahmood and Sani, eds., *Confidence Building and Conflict Reduction in the Pacific*, pp. 107–18; Edward A. Olsen, "A New American Strategy in Asia?" *Asian Survey* (December 1991), pp. 1139–55; Sheldon W. Simon, "U.S. Interests in Southeast Asia: The Future Military Presence," *Asian Survey* (July 1991), pp. 662–75; Alan Tonelson, "Superpower without a Sword," *Foreign Affairs* (Summer 1993), pp. 166–81; Richard Rosecrance, "A New Concert of Powers," *Foreign Affairs* (Spring 1992), pp. 64–82; William J. Crowe, Jr., and Alan D. Romberg, "Rethinking Security in the Pacific," *Foreign Affairs* (Spring 1991), pp. 123–40; Morton Halperin, "Guaranteeing Democracy," *Foreign Policy* (Summer 1993), pp. 105–23; Flora Lewis, "The G7 1/2 Directorate," *Foreign Policy* (Winter 1991/92), pp. 25–41; Stanley Hoffmann, "The Case for U.S. Leadership," *Foreign Policy* (Winter 1990/91), pp. 20–38; Robert J. Art, "A Defensible Defense: America's Grand Strategy after the Cold War," *International Security* (Spring 1991), pp. 87–109; Robert J. Art, "A US Military Strategy for the 1990s: Reassurance without Dominance," *Survival* (Winter 1992/93), pp. 3–23; and Samuel P. Huntington, "America's Changing Strategic Interests," *Survival* (January-February 1991), pp. 3–17.

5. Brian L. Job and Frank Langdon, "The Evolving Security Order of the Asia-Pacific: A Canadian Perspective" (North Pacific Cooperative Security Dialogue, working paper 15, September 1992); Mary L. Goldie and Douglas A. Ross, eds., *Pacific Security 2010: Canadian Perspectives on Pacific Security Into the 21st Century* (Toronto: Aurora Paper 10, 1992); Paul M. Evans, "Non-Government and 'Track-Two' Diplomacy and its Potentials," and Peggy Mason, "Asia-Pacific Security Forums: Canadian Views," in Mahmood and Sani, eds., *Confidence Building and Conflict Reduction in the Pacific*, pp. 137–42 and 153–66, respectively; Paul M. Evans, "Emerging Patterns in Asia-Pacific Security: The Search for a Regional Framework," in Hassan and Mahmood, eds., *Towards a New Pacific Order*, pp. 51–68; and David B. Dewitt and Paul M. Evans, "The North Pacific Cooperative Security Dialogue: Setting the Research Agenda" (Victoria, British Columbia, 1991).

6. Peter Hayes, *Pacific Powderkeg: America's Nuclear Dilemmas in Korea* (Lexington, Mass.: D.C. Heath, 1990); James F. Leonard and Gary Milhollin, "North Korea: Do They or Don't They Have the Bomb" (Washington, D.C.: Lawyers Alliance for World Security and Washington Council on Non-Proliferation, 1992); Steven K. Sudderth, "Political and Economic Impacts on the North Korean Threat," in Alves, ed., *Change, Interdependence, and Security in the Pacific Basin*, pp. 201–16; James Cotton, "North Korea's Nuclear Ambitions," in *Asia's International Role in the Post–Cold War Era*, pp. 94–106; Lau Teik Soon, "The Korean Conflict," in Hassan and Mahmood, eds., *Towards a New Pacific Order*, pp. 119–22; Andrew Mack, "The Nuclear Crisis on the Korean Peninsula," *Asian Survey* (April 1993), pp. 334–59; Tong Whan Park, "Issues of Arms Control between the Two Koreas," *Asian Survey* (April 1992), pp. 250–365; Nicholas Eberstadt and Judith Banister, "Military Buildup in the DPRK: Some New Indications from North Korean Data," *Asian Survey*

(November 1991), pp. 1095–1115; Leonard S. Spector, "Repentant Nuclear Proliferants," *Foreign Policy* (Fall 1992), pp. 21–37; Andrew Mack, "North Korea and the Bomb," *Foreign Policy* (Summer 1991), pp. 87–104; Young Sun Song, "North Korea's Nuclear Issue," *Journal of Northeast Asian Studies* (Fall 1991), pp. 61–77; John Simpson, "Nuclear Capabilities, Military Security, and the Korean Peninsula," Ashok Kapur, "Nuclear Arms Control on the Korean Peninsula in a Changing World," and William Epstein, "Nuclear Security for the Korean Peninsula," in the *Korean Journal of Defense Analysis* (Winter 1992), pp. 11–32, 33–54, and 55–70, respectively; Koji Kakizawa, "Japan's Position on Suspected Nuclear Weapons Development by North Korea," and Larry Niksch, "Dealing with North Korea on the Nuclear Weapons Threshold," in the *Korean Journal of Defense Analysis* (Summer 1992), pp. 57–66 and 67–84, respectively; Han Yong-Sup, "Ensuring North Korea's Compliance with Future South-North Nuclear Inspection Agreements," and Curtis A. Gayle, "Nuclear Non-Proliferation and Lessons from the Korean Example," in *Korea and World Affairs* (Spring 1993), pp. 21–44 and 45–56, respectively; Michael J. Mazarr, "North Korea's Nuclear Program: The World Responds, 1989–1992," *Korean and World Affairs* (Summer 1992), pp. 294–318; "Preliminary Report: Carnegie Endowment Delegation Visit to Pyongyang, April 28–May 4, 1992" (Washington, D.C.: Carnegie Endowment for International Peace, May 1992); and James S. Tomashoff, *Conference on Regional Implications of Korean Proliferation* (McLean, Va.: Science Applications International Corporation, 1992).

7. A. James Gregor, "The Spratlys and the Security Environment in the South China Sea," in Cossa, ed., *The New Pacific Security Environment*, pp. 215–32; Mark J. Valenca, "The South China Sea: Potential Conflict and Cooperation," in Mahmood and Sani, eds., *Confidence Building and Conflict Reduction in the Pacific*, pp. 55–70 (this authoritative source contains many useful references); Soendaroe Rachmad, "South China Sea: Necessity for Peaceful Cooperation," in Hassan and Mahmood, eds., *Towards a New Pacific Order*, pp. 129–34; and John W. Garver, "China's Push through the South China Sea: The Interaction of Bureaucratic and National Interests," *China Quarterly* (December 1992), pp. 999–1028.

8. Recent general works on Chinese foreign policy include: Samuel S. Kim, ed., *China and the World*, 3d ed. (Boulder, Colo.: Westview Press, 1993); Thomas W. Robinson and David Shambaugh, eds., *Chinese Foreign Policy: Ideas and Interpretations* (New York: Oxford University Press, 1993); John W. Garver, *Foreign Relations of the People's Republic of China* (Englewood-Cliffs, N.J.: Prentice-Hall, 1993); and Allen S. Whiting, ed., *China's Foreign Relations*, the *Annals*, January 1992. See also Chen Qimao, "New Approaches in China's Foreign Policy: The Post–Cold War Era," *Asian Survey* (March 1993), pp. 237–51; Huo Hwei-ling, "Patterns of Behavior in China's Foreign Policy: The Gulf Crisis and Beyond," *Asian Survey* (March 1992), pp. 263–76; Barber B. Conable, Jr., and David M. Lampton, "China: The Coming Power," *Foreign Affairs* (Winter 1992/93), pp. 133–49; Michel Oksenberg, "The China Problem," *Foreign Affairs* (Summer 1991), pp. 1–16; Samuel S. Kim, "China as a Regional Power," *Current History* (September 1992), pp. 247–52; John W. Garver,

"Chinese Foreign Policy: The Diplomacy of Damage Control," *Current History* (September 1991), pp. 241–46; John Wilson Lewis and Hua Di, "China's Ballistic Missile Programs: Technologies, Strategies, Goals," *International Security* (Fall 1992), pp. 5–40; David Shambaugh, "Peking's Foreign Policy Conundrum since Tiananmen: Peaceful Coexistence vs. Peaceful Evolution," *Issues and Studies* (November 1992), pp. 65–85; Arthur S. Ding, "Peking's Foreign Policy in the Changing World," *Issues and Studies* (August 1991), pp. 17–30; Samuel S. Kim, "Peking's Foreign Policy in the Shadow of Tiananmen: The Challenge of Legitimacy," *Issues and Studies* (January 1991), pp. 39–69; Roxane D. V. Sismanidis, "China's International Security Policy," *Problems of Communism* (July-August 1991), pp. 49–62; David Shambaugh, "China's Security Policy in the Post–Cold War Era," *Survival* (Summer 1992), pp. 88–106; Robert S. Ross, "Chinese Pacific Security Policies in the 1990s," in Alves, ed., *Evolving Pacific Basin Strategies*, pp. 39–60; and Parris H. Chang, "China and the Great Powers to the Year 2000," in Alves, ed., *Change, Interdependence, and Security in the Pacific Basin*, pp. 33–50.

Most of the details of post–cold war Chinese policy are found in Beijing's bilateral relations with the United States, Russia, and Japan. In the American case, see, in a large literature, Ding Xinghao, Zhiling Lin, and Thomas W. Robinson, eds., *New Ideas and Concepts in Sino-American Relations*, Report of a conference held in Washington, D.C., sponsored by the American Enterprise Institute, 1992; Barber Conable, Jr., et al., *The United States and China: Relations at a Crossroad* (Washington, D.C., and New York: Atlantic Council and the National Committee on U.S.-China Relations, 1993); William T. Tow, ed., *Building Sino-American Relations: An Analysis for the 1990s* (New York: Paragon House, 1992); Harry Harding, *A Fragile Relationship: The United States and China since 1972* (Washington, D.C.: Brookings Institution, 1992); David Shambaugh, *Beautiful Imperialist: China Perceives America, 1972–1990* (Princeton: Princeton University Press, 1991); *The Future of U.S.-China Relations* (Washington, D.C.: Center for Strategic and International Studies, 1992); Ding Xinghao, "Managing Sino-American Relations in a Changing World," *Asian Survey* (December 1991), pp. 1155–69; Nancy Bernkopf Tucker, "China and America, 1941–1991," *Foreign Affairs* (Winter 1991/92), pp. 75–92; Steven I. Levine, "China and America: The Resilient Relationship," *Current History* (September 1992), pp. 241–46; Robert G. Sutter, "Tiananmen's Lingering Fallout on Sino-American Relations," *Current History* (September 1991), pp. 270–74; Roger W. Sullivan, "Discarding the China Card," *Foreign Policy* (September 1992), pp. 3–23; Robert G. Sutter, "The Crisis in U.S.-China Policy, 1991: The Role of Congress," *Journal of Northeast Asian Studies* (Winter 1991/92), pp. 3–24; and Yangmin Wang, "The Politics of U.S.-China Economic Relations: MFN, Constructive Engagement, and the Trade Issue Proper," *Asian Survey* (May 1993), pp. 441–62.

Sino-Soviet (Russian) relations and Sino-Japanese relations are covered in notes 10 and 11, respectively.

9. David G. Haglund, ed., *Can America Remain Committed? U.S. Security Horizons in the 1990s* (Boulder, Colo.: Westview Press, 1992); Frank Gibney,

The Pacific Century: America and Asia in a Changing World (New York: Walker, 1992); Robert G. Sutter, East Asia and the Pacific: Challenges for U.S. Policy (Boulder, Colo.: Westview Press, 1992); Robert W. Tucker and David C. Hendrickson, The Imperial Temptation (New York: Council on Foreign Relations Press, 1992); John Lewis Gaddis, The United States and the End of the Cold War: Implications, Reconsiderations, Provocations (New York: Oxford University Press, 1992); Nayan Chanda, "The US Southeast Asian Security Policy for the 1990s," in Alves, ed., Change, Interdependence, and Security in the Pacific Basin, pp. 261–80; Jonathan Pollock, "The United States in East Asia: Holding the Ring," in Asia's International Role in the Post–Cold War Era, pp. 69–82; and Charles L. Glaser, "Nuclear Planning without an Adversary: U.S. Planning for the Post-Soviet Era," International Security (Spring 1992), pp. 34–78.

American-Japanese relations are covered in: William S. Dietrich, In the Shadow of the Rising Sun: The Potential Roots of American Economic Decline (University Park: Pennsylvania State University Press, 1991); Mike Muchizuki et al., Japan and the United States: Troubled Partners in a Changing World (Washington, D.C.: Brassey's, 1991); Hisahiko Okazaki, "The US-Japan Alliance in Historical Perspective," and Robert A. Scalapino, "The Evolving Japanese Security Policy and the United States," in Alves, ed., Evolving Pacific Basin Strategies, pp. 79–86 and 93–106, respectively; Michael Nacht, "From Competitive Allies to Potential Adversaries: The US-Japan Security Relationship," and John E. Endicott, "Can the US-Japanese Security Partnership Continue into the 21st Century?" in Alves, ed., Change, Interdependence, and Security in the Pacific Basin, pp. 87–102 and 103–16, respectively; Hisahiko Okazaki, "US-Japanese Alliance in the Changing World," and John E. Endicott, "US-Japanese Security Cooperation in the New International Order," in Alves, ed., New Perspectives for US-Asian Pacific Security Strategy, pp. 111–30 and 131–48, respectively; Oh Kwan-Chi, "Economic Aspects of US and Japanese Policies in East Asia: A Korean View," in Alves, ed., Cooperative Security in the Pacific Basin, pp. 85–100; Howard H. Baker, Jr., and Ellen L. Frost, "Rescuing the U.S.-Japan Alliance," Foreign Affairs (Spring 1992), pp. 97–113; Michael Nacht, "The United States and Japan: Building a New Relationship," Current History (April 1991), pp. 149–51ff; Yoichi Funabashi, "Japan and America: Global Partners," Foreign Policy (Spring 1992), pp. 24–39; I. M. Destler and Michael Nacht, "Beyond Mutual Recrimination: Building a Solid U.S.-Japan Relationship in the 1990s," International Security (Winter 1990/91), pp. 92–120; and Joseph S. Nye, "Coping with Japan," Foreign Policy (Winter 1992/93), pp. 96–115.

Some sources on American-Russian relations are: Banning Garrett and Bonnie Glaser, "US-Soviet Military Competition in Northeast Asia: The Case for Confidence-Building Measures," and William E. Berry, "Gorbachev's Security Initiatives in the Pacific Basin: Implications for the United States into the 1990s," in Alves, ed., Evolving Pacific Basin Strategies, pp. 123–40 and 159–84, respectively; Dimitri K. Simes, "America and the Post-Soviet Republics," Foreign Affairs (Spring 1992), pp. 73–89; Alexander Dallin, "America's Search for a Policy toward the Former Soviet Union," Current History (October 1992), pp. 321–26; Paul Goble, "Forget the Soviet Union," *Foreign Policy* (Spring 1992), pp. 51–65; and Marshall Brement, "U.S.-U.S.S.R.: Possibilities in Partnership," *Foreign Policy* (Fall 1991), pp. 107–24.

10. Tim Jackson, *The Next Battleground: Japan, America, and the European Market* (New York: Houghton Mifflin, 1993); Daniel Burstein, *Turning the Tables: A Machiavellian Strategy for Dealing with Japan* (New York: Simon and Schuster, 1993); Nathaniel B. Thayer, "Strategic Problems from the Japanese Perspective," in Alves, ed., *Evolving Pacific Basin Strategies*, pp. 87–92; James E. Auer, "Japan's Changing Defense Policy," in Cossa, ed., *The New Pacific Security Environment*, pp. 81–96; Gerald L. Curtis, "Assessing Japanese Foreign Policy in the 1990s," in Scalapino and Chufrin, eds., *Asia in the 1990s: American and Soviet Perspectives*, pp. 150–69; Takashi Inoguchi, "Japan in Search of a Normal Role," in *Asia's International Role in the Post–Cold War Era*, pp. 58–68; Itaru Umezu, "The Future of Japan in the Asia-Pacific," in Mahmood and Sani, eds., *Confidence Building and Conflict Reduction in the Pacific*, pp. 79–86; *Asian Survey*, special issue: *Japan's Redefining Its International Role* (June 1993); Peter J. Katzenstein and Nobuo Okawara, "Japan's National Security: Structures, Norms, and Policies," and Thomas U. Berger, "From Sword to Chrysanthemum: Japan's Culture of Anti-Militarism," *International Security* (Spring 1993), pp. 84–118 and 119–50, respectively.

Japanese-Chinese relations are covered in: Allen S. Whiting, *China Eyes Japan* (Berkeley: University of California Press, 1990); Jonathan D. Pollock, "China and Japan in the New Pacific Era," in Alves, ed., *New Perspectives for US-Asian Pacific Security Strategy*, pp. 87–110; Uldis Kruze, "Sino-Japanese Relations," *Current History* (April 1991), pp. 160–63ff; and *China Quarterly*, special issue: *China and Japan: History, Trends, and Prospects* (December 1990).

11. *The National Interest*, special issue: "The Strange Death of Soviet Communism" (Spring 1993); Ed A. Hewitt with Clifford G. Gaddy, *Open for Business: Russia's Return to the Global Economy* (Washington, D.C.: Brookings Institution, 1992); Gilbert Rozman, ed., *Dismantling Communism: Common Causes and Regional Variations* (Baltimore: Johns Hopkins University Press, 1992); James H. Billington, *Russia Transformed: Breakthrough to Hope* (New York: Free Press, 1992); Robert G. Kaiser, *Why Gorbachev Happened* (New York: Simon and Schuster, 1992); William Hauner, *What Is Asia to Us? Russia's Asian Heartland Yesterday and Today* (Cambridge, Mass.: Unwin and Hyman, 1990); Donald S. Zagoria, "Soviet Policy in East Asia: The Quest for Constructive Engagement," in Alves, ed., *Change, Interdependence, and Security in the Pacific Basin*, pp. 143–68; Vladimir I. Ivanov, "The USSR Breakup: New Strategic Realities in the Pacific Basin," in Cossa, ed., *The New Pacific Security Environment*, pp. 53–81; Gennady I. Chufrin, "Soviet Defense Strategy in the Asia Pacific Region in the 1990s," Evgeny Ivanov, "Peace, Security, and Cooperation in Asia and the Pacific: A View From Moscow," Coit D. Blacker, "Changing Times—The Making of Soviet Policy in Asia," Alexis D. Bogaturov, "The Situation in Northeast Asia: A Search for Common Understanding," and Konstantin O. Sarkisov, "Forging a New System of International Relations in Asia and the Pacific," all in Scalapino and Chufrin, eds., *Asia in*

the 1990s: American and Soviet Perspectives, pp. 30–37, 38–48, 60–69, 70–80, and 81–93, respectively; Sergei Karaganov, "Russia and Other Independent Republics in Asia," in *Asia's International Role in the Post–Cold War Era*, pp. 21–30; Gennady Chufrin, "The Future Role of the CIS in the Asia-Pacific Region," in Mahmood and Sani, eds., *Confidence Building and Conflict Reduction in the Pacific*, pp. 99–108; V. P. Fedotov, "The Positive and Negative Factors Influencing Peace in the Pacific in the Short- and Medium-Terms," and Alexandre Nikolaevitch Panov, "Processes and Structures in Asia and the Pacific and Soviet Policies," in Hassan and Mahmood, eds., *Towards a New Pacific Order*, pp. 21–32 and 163–76, respectively; Robert L. Canfield, "Restructure in Greater Central Asia: Changing Political Configurations," *Asian Survey* (October 1992), pp. 875–87; Shafiqual Islam, "Moscow's Rough Road to Capitalism," *Foreign Affairs* (Spring 1993), pp. 57–66; Jude Wanniski, "The Future of Russian Capitalism," *Foreign Affairs* (Spring 1992), pp. 17–25; Steven White, "Russia's Experiment with Democracy," *Current History* (October 1992), pp. 310–13; Mark Kramer, "Soviet Foreign Policy after the Cold War," *Current History* (October 1992), pp. 317–22; Paul Goble, "Russia and Its Neighbors," *Foreign Policy* (Spring 1993), pp. 79–88; Vladimir P. Lukin, "Our Security Predicament," *Foreign Policy* (Fall 1992), pp. 57–75; James Rupert, "Dateline Tashkent: Post-Soviet Central Asia," *Foreign Policy* (Summer 1992), pp. 175–92; Boris Z. Rumor, "Central Asia's Gathering Storm," *Orbis* (Winter 1993), pp. 89–106; Martha Brill Olcott, "Central Asia's Post-Empire Politics," *Orbis* (Spring 1992), pp. 253–68; *Problems of Communism*, special issue: "Moscow, August 1991: The Coup de Grace—A Symposium" (November-December 1991); and Steven E. Miller, "Western Diplomacy and the Soviet Nuclear Legacy," *Survival* (Autumn 1992), pp. 3–27.

Post–cold war Russian-Chinese relations are covered in: Lowell Dittmer, *Sino-Soviet Normalization and Its International Implications, 1945–1990* (Seattle: University of Washington Press, 1992); Tai Ming Cheung, "Ties of Convenience: Sino-Soviet/Russian Military Relations in the 1990s," manuscript, June 1992; Vladimir I. Kulikov, "Soviet-Chinese Relations in the Beginning of the 1990s: Inertia and Alternatives," in Scalapino and Chufrin, eds., *Asia in the 1990s: American and Soviet Perspectives*, pp. 127–34; J. Richard Walsh, "China and the New Geopolitics of Central Asia," Hung P. Nguyen, "Russia and China: The Genesis of an Eastern Rapallo," and Bin Yu, "Sino-Russian Military Relations: Implications for Asian Security," in *Asian Survey* (March 1993), pp. 272–81, 285–301, and 302–16, respectively; Gerald Segal, "China and the Disintegration of the Soviet Union," *Asian Survey* (September 1992), pp. 848–68; John W. Garver, "The Indian Factor in Recent Sino-Soviet Relations," *China Quarterly* (March 1991), pp. 55–85; Pi Ying-hsien, "Chiang Tse-min's Visit to Moscow and Peking-Moscow Relations," *Issues and Studies* (December 1991), pp. 100–111; William B. DeMills, "Dynamically Modelling Peking-Moscow Rapprochement," *Issues and Studies* (February 1991), pp. 12–35; and Huan Guocang, "The New [Chinese] Relationship with the Former Soviet Union," *Current History* (September 1992), pp. 247–52.

12. Andrew Mack, "Naval Arms Control and Confidence-building for

Northeast Asian Waters" (North Pacific Cooperative Security Dialogue, working paper 13, August 1992); Alex Gliksman, "Arms Production Spread: Implications for Pacific Rim Security," in Alves, ed., *Evolving Pacific Basin Strategies*, pp. 61–78; Hwang Dong Joon, "Regional Arms Production Cooperation and Pacific Security," in Alves, ed., *Change, Interdependence, and Security in the Pacific Basin*, pp. 117–42; M. Susan Pederson and Michael J. Cusak, "The Implications of Proliferation in China, Korea, and the Subcontinent," in Cossa, ed., *The New Pacific Security Environment*, pp. 155–82; Ryukichi Imai, "Nuclear Proliferation in the Post–Cold War World," Gong Ro-myung, "The Consequences of Arms Proliferation in Asia: I," and Gerald Segal, "The Consequences of Arms Proliferation in Asia: II," in *Asia's International Role in the Post–Cold War Era*, pp. 31–41, 42–49, and 50–61, respectively; Andrew Mack, "The Case for Nuclear Weapons-free Zones in the Pacific: The Rorotonga Treaty and a Northeast Asian Nuclear-Free Zone," in Mahmood and Sani, eds., *Confidence Building and Conflict Reduction in the Pacific*, pp. 191–212; Andrew Mack, "Arms Control and Arms Limitation in the Pacific: Problems and Prospects," and Desmond Ball, "Towards Arms Control and Reduction in the Pacific," in Hassan and Mahmood, eds., *Towards a New Pacific Order*, pp. 69–86 and 111–14, respectively; and Michael T. Klare, "The Next Great Arms Race," *Foreign Affairs* (Spring 1993), pp. 136–52.

13. Jo Dee Catlin Jacob, ed., *Beyond the Hoppo Ryodo: Japanese-Soviet-American Relations in the 1990s* (Washington, D.C.: AEI Press, 1991); Hiroshi Kimura, "Gorbachev's Japan Policy: The Northern Territories Issue," *Asian Survey* (September 1991), pp. 798–815; Richard deVillfranca, "Japan and the Northern Territories Dispute: Past, Present, Future," *Asian Survey* (June 1993), pp. 610–24; Rajan Menon and Daniel Abele, "Security Dimensions of Soviet Territorial Disputes with China and Japan," *Journal of Northeast Asian Studies* (Spring 1989), pp. 3–19; and Peggy L. Falkenheim, "The Soviet Union, Japan, and East Asia: The Security Dimension," and Mari Kuraishi Horne, "The Northern Territories: Source or Symptom?" *Journal of Northeast Asian Studies* (Winter 1989), pp. 43–59 and 60–79, respectively. Russian-Japanese relations are often reduced to this issue, in which case see: Gilbert Rozman, *Japan's Response to the Gorbachev Era, 1985–1991: A Rising Superpower Views a Declining One* (Princeton: Princeton University Press, 1992); and Konstantin O. Sarkisov, "Soviet-Japanese Relations: Paradigm of a Territorial Problem," in Scalapino and Chufrin, eds., *Asia in the 1990s: American and Soviet Perspectives*, pp. 170–78.

14. Frank Gibney, *Korea's Quiet Revolution: From Garrison State to Democracy* (New York: Walket, 1992); Lee Young Ho, "The Korean Peninsula in a Changing Environment: Prospects for Peace and Unification," in Alves, ed., *New Perspectives for US-Asian Pacific Security Strategy*, pp. 161–72; William Pendley, "Korea and Asian Security," in Cossa, ed., *The New Pacific Security Environment*, pp. 97–102; Ahn Byung-joon, "Managing Reunification in the Korean Peninsula," in *Asia's International Role in the Post–Cold War Era*, pp. 83–93; O Chang Rim, "Consideration of the Immediate Issues with Regard to Korea's Reunification," and Han Song-joo, "Korea and the Emerging

International Relations in East Asia," in Hassan and Mahmood, eds., *Towards a New Pacific Order*, pp. 101–4 and 105–10, respectively; Kang Suk Rhee, "Korea's Reunification: The Applicability of the German Experience," *Asian Survey* (April 1993), pp. 360–75; Jia Hao and Zhuang Qubing, "China's Policy toward the Korean Peninsula," *Asian Survey* (December 1992), pp. 1137–56; Peggy Falkenheim Mayer, "Gorbachev and Post-Gorbachev Policy toward the Korean Peninsula," *Asian Survey* (September 1992), pp. 757–72; Kyung Ae Park and Sung-Chull Lee, "Changes and Prospects in Inter-Korean Relations," *Asian Survey* (May 1992), pp. 429–47; Eugene and Natasha Bazhanov, "Soviet Views on North Korea," *Asian Survey* (December 1991), pp. 1139–55; Nicholas Eberstadt, "Can the Two Koreas Be One?" *Foreign Affairs* (Winter 1992/93), pp. 150–65; Hong Yung Lee, "Future Dynamics in Sino-Korean Relations," *Journal of Northeast Asian Studies* (Fall 1990), pp. 34–49; Keun Lee and Chung H. Lee, "Trade between Bohai of China and Korea: An International Perspective," *Journal of Northeast Asian Studies* (Winter 1990), pp. 15–35; Young-shik Bae, "Soviet–South Korea Economic Cooperation Following Rapprochement," *Journal of Northeast Asian Studies* (Spring 1991), pp. 19–34; Tun-jen Cheng and Lawrence B. Krause, "Democracy and Development: With Special Attention to Korea," *Journal of Northeast Asian Studies* (Summer 1991), pp. 3–25; and Young Whan Kihl, "North Korea's Foreign Relations: Diplomacy of Promotive Adaptation," *Journal of Northeast Asian Studies* (Fall 1991), pp. 30–45. Aside from the above, the most complete sources on Korean developments are the three English-language South Korean journals: *Korea and World Affairs*, *Journal of East Asian Affairs*, and *Korea and World Affairs*, as well as the Korean-language *Sino-Soviet Affairs*. Each issue contains several relevant articles, and the total since 1990 is massive.

15. Raymond H. Myers, ed., *Two Societies in Opposition: The Republic of China and the People's Republic of China after Forty Years* (Stanford, Calif.: Hoover Institution Press, 1991); Simon Long, *Taiwan: China's Last Frontier* (New York: St. Martin's, 1991); Chi Su, "The International Relations of the Republic of China during the 1990s," Edward I-hsin Chen, "The Post–Cold War US Policy toward the Two Sides of Taiwan Straits in a Neo-Realist Perspective," and Hungdah Chiu, "Koo-Wang Talks and the Prospect of Building Constructive and Stable Relations across the Taiwan Straits," papers for the Twenty-second Sino-U.S. Conference on Contemporary China, Washington, D.C., June 1993; Cheng-tian Kuo, "The PRC and Taiwan: Fujian's Faltering United Front," *Asian Survey* (August 1992), pp. 683–95; Jia Qingguo, "Changing Relations across the Taiwan Straits: Beijing's Perceptions," *Asian Survey* (March 1992), pp. 277–89; Tiemo Kracht, "German Unification Policies since 1949: Implications for China," *Issues and Studies* (December 1991), pp. 29–59; Emerson M.S. Niou, "An Analysis of the Republic of China's Security Issues," *Issues and Studies* (January 1992), pp. 82–95; Wu An-chia, "The ROC's Mainland Policy in the 1990s," *Issues and Studies* (August 1991), pp. 71–80; Dennis Van Vranken Hickey, "U.S. Policy and Taiwan's Reintegration into the Global Community," *Journal of Northeast Asian Studies* (Spring 1992), pp. 18–33; Dennis Van Vranken Hickey, "Will Inter-China Trade Change Taiwan or the

Mainland?" *Orbis* (Fall 1991), pp. 517–32; Tsai Wen-hui, *In Making China Modernized: Comparative Modernization between Mainland China and Taiwan* (Baltimore: University of Maryland School of Law, 1993); and Thomas W. Robinson and Zhiling Lin, "Domestic and International Determinants of Chinese Reunification," *Journal of East Asian Affairs* (Summer/Fall 1992), pp. 424–546.

16. Edith T. Morante, *Burmese Looking Glass: A Human Rights Activist on the Forbidden Frontier* (New York: Grove, 1993); Thomas R. Lausner and David E. Morey, *Towards Democracy in Burma* (Washington, D.C.: Institute for Asian Democracy, 1992); Bruce Matthews, "Buddhism under a Military Regime: The Iron Heel in Burma," *Asian Survey* (April 1993), pp. 408–23; and Josef Silverstein, "Burma in an International Perspective," *Asian Survey* (October 1992), pp. 951–63.

17. Ashutosh Varsshney, "India, Pakistan, and Kashmir: Antimonies of Nationalism," *Asian Survey* (November 1991), pp. 997–1019; Devin T. Hagerty, "India's Regional Security Doctrine," *Asian Survey* (April 1991), pp. 351–63; Pratap Bhano Mehta, "India's Disordered Democracy," *Pacific Affairs* (Winter 1991/92), pp. 536–53; Sumit Ganguly, "Ethno-Religious Conflict in South Asia," and Thomas P. Thornton, "The United States and South Asia," *Survival* (Summer 1993), pp. 88–109 and 110–28, respectively; Paul Brass, "The Punjab Crisis and the Unity of India," in Paul Brass, ed., *Ethnicity and Nationalism: Theory and Comparison* (New Delhi: Sage Publications, 1991), p. 210; Ifitkhaar H. Malik, "Ethnicity and Contemporary South Asian Politics: The Kashmir Conflict as a Case Study," *Round Table* (April 1992), pp. 203–14; Gurharpol Singh, "The Punjab Problem in the 1990s: A Post-1984 Assessment," *Journal of Commonwealth and Comparative Politics* (July 1991), pp. 175–91; and Sumit Ganguly, "Avoiding War in Kashmir," *Foreign Affairs* (Winter 1990/91), pp. 57–73.

18. Robert L. Hardgrave, "South Asian Internal Politics and Policies," Vladimir N. Mosalenko, "Interstate Relations in South Asia," and Leo E. Rose, "South Asia Foreign Policies in the Context of Sino-Soviet-U.S. 'Normalization,' " in Scalapino and Chufrin, eds., *Asia in the 1990s: American and Soviet Perspectives*, pp. 194–210, 211–22, and 223–35, respectively; Francine Frankel, "India's Post–Cold War Perspective," in Cossa, ed., *The New Pacific Security Environment*, pp. 145–54; Raju Thomas, "The Security and Economy of a Reforming India," and Stephen Cohen, "The Regional Impact of a Reforming India," in *Asia's International Role in the Post–Cold War Era*, pp. 62–82 and 83–93, respectively; Thomas P. Thornton, "India Adrift: The Search for Moorings in a New World Order," *Asian Survey* (December 1992), pp. 1063–77; Seyyed Vali Reza Nasr, "Democracy and the Crisis of Governability in Pakistan," and Krishna K. Tummala, "India's Federalism under Stress," *Asian Survey* (June 1992), pp. 521–37 and 538–53, respectively; Ramesh Thakur, "India and the Soviet Union: Conjunctions and Disjunctions of Interests," *Asian Survey* (September 1991), pp. 826–46; Devin T. Hagerty, "India's Regional Security Doctrine," *Asian Survey* (April 1991), pp. 351–63; Rasul B. Rais, "Pakistan in the Regional and Global Structures," *Asian Survey* (April 1991), pp. 378–92; John W. Garver, "The Indian Factor in Recent Sino-

Soviet Relations," *China Quarterly* (March 1991), pp. 55–85; Charles H. Percy, "South Asia's Take-off," *Foreign Affairs* (Winter 1992/93), pp. 166–74; George Perkovich, "A Nuclear Third War in South Asia," *Foreign Policy* (Summer 1993), pp. 85–104; Mohammed Ayoob, "Dateline India: The Deepening Crisis," *Foreign Policy* (Winter 1991/92), pp. 166–84; Brahma Chellaney, "South Asia's Passage to Nuclear Power," *International Security* (Summer 1991), pp. 43–72; Pratap Bhano Mehta, "India's Disordered Democracy," *Pacific Affairs* (Winter 1991/92), pp. 536–52; Sandy Gordon, "Resources and Instability in South Asia," *Survival* (Summer 1993), pp. 66–87; Rodney W. Jones, "Old Quarrels and New Realities: Security in Southern Asia after the Cold War," *Washington Quarterly* (Winter 1992), pp. 105–28; Arthur G. Rubinoff, "The Multilateral Imperative in India's Foreign Policy," *Round Table* (June 1991); S. D. Muni, "India and the Post–Cold War World: Opportunities and Challenges," *Asian Survey* (September 1991), pp. 862–74; Ishtiaq Hossain, "Regional Order in South Asia: *Sine Qua Non* for Indian Foreign Policy," *Asian Thought and Society* (May–September 1992), pp. 203–14; and Seymour Hersh, "On the Nuclear Edge," *New Yorker*, March 29, 1993, pp. 56–73.

19. James W. Morley, ed., *Driven by Growth: Political Change in the Asia-Pacific Region* (New York: M. E. Sharpe, 1992); Paul Kennedy, *Preparing for the Twenty-first Century* (New York: Random House, 1993); John M. Lee et al., *To Unite Our Strength: Enhancing the United Nations Peace and Security System* (Lanham, Md.: University Press of America, 1992); Richard P. Cronin, *Japan, the U.S., and Prospects for the Asia-Pacific Century: Three Scenarios* (New York: St. Martin's, 1992); James Chace, *The Consequence of the Peace* (New York: Oxford University Press, 1992); John W. Lewis and Mikhail L. Titarenko, eds., *Peace, Security, and Cooperation in the Asia-Pacific Region* (Stanford, Calif.: Stanford University Center for International Security and Arms Control, 1989); Andrew Mack, "Reassurance versus Deterrence Strategies for the Asia-Pacific Region," Canberra: Australian National University, 1991; Ralph A. Cossa, "The New Pacific Environment: Defining the Challenges," Richard Halloran, "An Age of Uncertainty: Asia Approaches the 21st Century," and Zakaria Haji Ahmad, "The Next Generation: Asian Leadership," in Cossa, ed., *The New Pacific Security Environment*, pp. 3–18, 19–36, and 233–48, respectively; Walt W. Rostow, "Let's Organize the Pacific Basin Now," and Charles E. Morrison, "The Future of Democracy in the Asia-Pacific Region: The Security Implications," in Alves, ed., *Evolving Pacific Basin Strategies*, pp. 13–24 and 107–22, respectively; Edward A. Olsen, "The End of the Cold War and Northeast Asian Security," and Sheldon Simon, "Tension Reduction and Northeast Asian Security," in Alves, ed., *Change, Interdependence, and Security in the Pacific Basin*, pp. 169–200 and 235–60, respectively; Robert A. Scalapino, "Toward Democratization and Stability in Asia," and Donald C. Hellmann, "Future Strategic Options in the Pacific: A Nichibei Condominium?" in Alves, ed., *New Perspectives for US-Asian Pacific Security Strategy*, pp. 13–28 and 149–60; Lawrence E. Grinter and Young W. Kihl, "Security Cooperation in Northeast Asia: Patterns and Prospects," and Robert A. Scalapino, "Regionalism in the Pacific: Prospects and Problems," in Alves, ed., *Cooperative Security in*

the Pacific Basin, pp. 47–68 and 255–74, respectively; Donald S. Zagoria, "Major Power Relations in East Asia," in Scalapino and Chufrin, eds., *Asia in the 1990s: American and Soviet Perspectives*, pp. 49–59; Chung-min Lee, "What Security Regime in North-East Asia?" in *Asia's International Role in the Post–Cold War Era*, pp. 5–20; Jusuf Wanandi, "Asia-Pacific Security Forums: Rationale and Options," Paul Dibb, "The CSBM Agenda in the Asia-Pacific Region: Some Aspects of Defence Confidence Building," Robert W. Grey, "The Practical Aspects of Establishing a Maritime Surveillance Regime," and Kevin P. Clements, "The United Nations Peacemaking and Peacekeeping Role: Problems and Prospects," in Mahood and Sani, eds., *Confidence Building and Conflict Reduction in the Pacific*, pp. 143–52, 167–76, 177–90, and 213–24, respectively; Robert A. Scalapino, "The Prospects for Peace in the Pacific-Asian Region: A Balance Sheet," in Hassan and Mahmood, eds., *Towards a New Pacific Order*, pp. 5–20; Steven John Stedman, "The New Interventionists," and James Schlesinger, "Quest for a Post–Cold War Foreign Policy," *Foreign Affairs*, "America and the World 1993," pp. 1–16 and 17–28, respectively; Bruce Russett and James S. Sutterlin, "The U.N. in a New World Order," and John Lewis Gaddis, "Toward the Post–Cold War World," *Foreign Affairs* (Spring 1991), pp. 69–83 and 102–22, respectively; Edward C. Luck, "Making Peace," and Doug Bandow, "Avoiding War," *Foreign Policy* (Winter 1992/93), pp. 137–55 and 156–74, respectively; Gregory Flynn and David J. Scheffer, "Limited Collective Security," *Foreign Policy* (Fall 1990), pp. 77–101; Lisa L. Martin, "Interests, Power, and Multilateralism," *International Organization* (Autumn 1992), pp. 765–92; Oran J. Young, "Political Leadership and Regime Formation: On the Development of Institutions in International Society," *International Organization* (Summer 1991), pp. 281–308; Donald Crone, "The Politics of Emerging Pacific Cooperation," *Pacific Affairs* (Spring 1992), pp. 50–72; *Problems of Communism*, special issue, "Towards a Post-Communist World" (January–April 1992); and Peter Polomka, "Towards a 'Pacific House,' " *Survival* (March–April 1991), pp. 173–82.

20. The field of security and economics is finally emerging after a long gestation period. See David B. H. Denoon, ed., *Constraints on Strategy: The Economics of Western Security* (New York: Pergamon-Brassey's, 1986); Denoon, *Real Reciprocity: Balancing U.S. Economic and Security Policies in the Pacific Basin* (New York: Council on Foreign Relations Press, 1993); Andrew L. Ross, ed., *The Political Economy of Defense: Issues and Perspectives* (New York: Greenwood Press, 1991); Craufurd D. Goodwin, ed., *Economics and National Security: A History of Their Interaction* (Durham, N.C.: Duke University Press, 1991); Ethan Barnaby Kapstein, *The Political Economy of National Security* (Columbia: University of South Carolina Press, 1992); Helen Milner and David Baldwin, *The Political Economy of National Security: An Annotated Bibliography* (Boulder, Colo.: Westview Press, 1990); Nicole Ball, *Security and Economy in the Third World* (Princeton: Princeton University Press, 1988); Lee D. Olvey, James R. Golden, and Robert C. Kelly, *The Economics of National Security* (Wayne, N.J.: Avery Publishing Group, 1984); Robert Gilpin, *The Political Economy of International Relations* (Princeton: Princeton University Press, 1987); Joan Edelman Spero,

The Politics of International Economic Relations, 4th ed. (New York: St. Martin's, 1990); Michael Mastandono, Economic Containment: COCOM and the Politics of East-West Trade (Ithaca, N.Y.: Cornell University Press, 1992); and Daedalus, "Searching for Security in a Global Economy" (Fall 1991).

21. Henry Bienen, ed., Power, Economics, and Security: The United States and Japan in Focus (Boulder, Colo.: Westview Press, 1992); Clyde V. Prestowitz, ed., Powernomics: Economics and Strategy after the Cold War (Lanham, Md.: Madison Books, 1991); Stuart Harris, "The Economic Aspects of Pacific Security," and Peter Ackerman, "A Reply," in Asia's International Role in the Post–Cold War Era, pp. 14–30 and 31–35, respectively.

22. Wayne Sandholtz et al., The Highest Stakes: The Economic Foundations of the Next Security System (New York: Oxford University Press, 1992); Jagdish Bhagwati, Political Economy and International Economics (Cambridge, Mass.: MIT Press, 1991); Finding Common Ground: U.S. Export Controls in a Changed Global Environment (Washington, D.C.: National Academy Press, 1991); Jagdish Bhagwati and Hugh T. Patrick, eds., Aggressive Unilateralism: America's 301 Trade Policy and the World Trading System (Ann Arbor: University of Michigan Press, 1990); Mary Brown Bullock and Robert S. Litwak, The United States and the Pacific Basin: Changing Economic and Security Relationships (Washington, D.C.: Woodrow Wilson Center Press, 1991); Cal Clark and Steve Chan, eds., The Evolving Pacific Basin in the Global Political Economy (Boulder, Colo.: Lynne Reiner, 1992); William H. Overholt, "Pacific Asia after the Oil Crisis and US Recession: Lessons in Resilience," in Alves, ed., New Perspectives for US-Asian Pacific Security Strategy, pp. 71–87; Edward J. Lincoln, "Developments in the Japanese Economy and Their Implications for the Asian Region," in Scalapino and Chufrin, eds., Asia in the 1990s: American and Soviet Perspectives, pp. 170–94; and Bill Emmott, "The Economic Sources of Japan's Foreign Policy," Survival (Spring 1992), pp. 50–70.

23. The field of economic development is large. Only a few recent sources are provided here, as they pertain to military modernization in Asia. Stephan Haggard, Pathways from the Periphery: The Politics of Growth in the New Industrialized Countries (Ithaca, N.Y.: Cornell University Press, 1990); Ezra Vogel, The Four Little Dragons: The Spread of Industrialization in East Asia (Cambridge, Mass.: Harvard University Press, 1991); Ivan L. Head, On a Hinge of History: The Mutual Vulnerability of South and North (Toronto: Toronto University Press, 1991); Chris Dixon, Southeast Asia in the World Economy (New York: Cambridge University Press, 1991); China Quarterly, special issue, "The Chinese Economy in the 1990s" (September 1991); Chu-yuan Cheng, "The ROC's Role in the World Economy," Issues and Studies (November 1992), pp. 30–48; Chu-yuan Cheng, "Mainland China's Modernization and Economic Reform: Process, Consequences, and Prospects," Issues and Studies (November 1991), pp. 78–102; Dali L. Yang, "China Adjusts to the World Economy: The Political Economy of China's Coastal Development Strategy," Pacific Affairs (Spring 1991), pp. 42–64; Charles E. Ziegler, "Soviet Strategies for Development: East Asia and the Pacific Basin," Public Affairs (Winter 1990/91), pp. 451–68; Robert Wade, "East Asia's Economic Success: Conflicting Perspectives, Partial In-

sight, Shaky Evidence," *World Politics* (January 1992), pp. 270–320; and Wendy Frieman and Thomas W. Robinson, "Costs and Benefits of [Chinese] Interdependence: A Net Assessment," in Joint Economic Committee, 102nd Congress, *China's Economic Dilemmas in the 1990s: The Problems of Reforms, Modernization, and Interdependence* (Washington, D.C.: Government Printing Office, 1991), pp. 718–74.

24. Colin S. Gray, *Weapons Don't Make War: Policy, Strategy, and Military Technology* (Lawrence, Kans.: University of Kansas Press, 1993); Eugene B. Skolnikoff, *The Elusive Transformation: Science, Technology, and the Evolution of International Politics* (Princeton: Princeton University Press, 1993); Eric H. Arnett, ed., *Science and International Security: Responding to a Changing World* (Washington, D.C.: American Association for the Advancement of Science, 1990); and Richard P. Suttmeier, "The Technological Emergence of the Pacific Rim: Threat or Opportunity to the U.S.?" ms., February 1992.

CHAPTER 17: CHANGING CHINA-TAIWAN RELATIONS, *Guocang Huan*

1. *World Journal* (New York), August 20, 1991.
2. *The Nineties* (Hong Kong), no. 7, 1991, pp. 24–27.
3. *World Journal*, February 24, 1991.
4. *China Times Weekly*, July 20–26, 1991, pp. 8–9, 12.
5. *People's Daily* (overseas edition, Beijing), July 25, 1991; *The Nineties*, no. 7, 1991, pp. 24–27; and *World Journal*, June 7, 1991.
6. *World Journal*, June 9, 1991.
7. *Asian Wall Street Journal*, August 29, 1991.
8. *World Journal*, August 29, 1991.
9. *World Journal*, February 27, 1991.
10. See, for instance, *The Nineties*, no. 7, 1991, pp. 22–23.
11. *World Journal*, August 23, 1991, and *China Times Weekly*, pp. 48–49, 58–62.
12. *World Journal*, January 23, 1992.
13. *China Times Weekly*, June 8–14, 1991, pp. 30–31.
14. *World Journal*, February 26, 1991, and *China Times Weekly*, February 10–16, 1991, pp. 18–41.
15. *World Journal*, September 4, 1991.
16. *China Times Weekly*, August 3–9, 1991, pp. 52–54.
17. *China Times Weekly*, July 27–August 2, 1991, pp. 14–20, and August 10–16, 1991, pp. 42–43.
18. *The Nineties*, no. 8, 1991, pp. 30–32.
19. *New York Times*, September 5, 1991.
20. *World Journal*, October 25, 1990.
21. *China Times Weekly*, March 17–23, 1990, pp. 8–44.
22. *China Times Weekly*, September 1–7, 1990, pp. 68–75, and April 28–May 4, 1990, pp. 20–26.
23. *The Nineties*, no. 3, 1991, pp. 74–75, and no. 7, 1991, pp. 43–45.
24. *China Times Weekly*, August 31–September 6, 1991, pp. 45–49.

25. Ibid., pp. 42–44.

26. *World Journal*, June 3, 1991.

27. *World Journal*, September 5, 1991.

28. *World Journal*, June 26, 1991.

29. *World Journal*, January 6, 1991.

30. *The Nineties*, no. 3, 1991, pp. 71–73.

31. *World Journal*, June 24, 1991.

32. *World Journal*, June 19, 20, and 26, 1991.

33. Donald Zagoria, "Taiwan and Asian-Pacific Region" (Paper presented to a conference on the Republic of China and new international order, August 20–23, 1991, Taipei). Sponsored by the *China Times* in Taiwan.

34. *Chengming* (Hong Kong), no. 2, 1990, pp. 6–8.

35. *Chengming*, no. 9, 1991, pp. 6–10.

Index

Glenn C. Loury
Department of Economics
Boston University

Sam Peltzman
Sears Roebuck Professor of Economics
   and Financial Services
University of Chicago
   Graduate School of Business

Nelson W. Polsby
Professor of Political Science
University of California at Berkeley

Murray L. Weidenbaum
Mallinckrodt Distinguished
   University Professor
Washington University

Research Staff

Leon Aron
Resident Scholar

Claude E. Barfield
Resident Scholar; Director, Science
   and Technology Policy Studies

Walter Berns
Adjunct Scholar

Douglas J. Besharov
Resident Scholar

Jagdish Bhagwati
Visiting Scholar

Robert H. Bork
John M. Olin Scholar in Legal Studies

Michael Boskin
Visiting Scholar

Karlyn Bowman
Resident Fellow; Editor,
   The American Enterprise

Dick B. Cheney
Senior Fellow

Lynne V. Cheney
W.H. Brady, Jr., Distinguished Fellow

Dinesh D'Souza
John M. Olin Research Fellow

Nicholas N. Eberstadt
Visiting Scholar

Mark Falcoff
Resident Scholar

Gerald R. Ford
Distinguished Fellow

Murray F. Foss
Visiting Scholar

Suzanne Garment
Resident Scholar

Patrick Glynn
Resident Scholar

Robert A. Goldwin
Resident Scholar

Gottfried Haberler
Resident Scholar

Robert W. Hahn
Resident Scholar

Robert B. Helms
Resident Scholar

Jeane J. Kirkpatrick
Senior Fellow; Director, Foreign and
   Defense Policy Studies

Marvin H. Kosters
Resident Scholar; Director,
   Economic Policy Studies

Irving Kristol
John M. Olin Distinguished Fellow

Michael A. Ledeen
Resident Scholar

James Lilley
Resident Fellow; Director, Asian
   Studies Program

Chong-Pin Lin
Resident Scholar; Associate Director,
   Asian Studies Program

John H. Makin
Resident Scholar; Director, Fiscal
   Policy Studies

Allan H. Meltzer
Visiting Scholar

Joshua Muravchik
Resident Scholar

Charles Murray
Bradley Fellow

Michael Novak
George F. Jewett Scholar in Religion,
   Philosophy, and Public Policy;
   Director, Social and
   Political Studies

Norman J. Ornstein
Resident Scholar

Richard N. Perle
Resident Fellow

William Schneider
Resident Fellow

William Shew
Visiting Scholar

J. Gregory Sidak
Resident Scholar

Herbert Stein
Senior Fellow

Irwin M. Stelzer
Resident Scholar; Director, Regulatory
   Policy Studies

Edward Styles
Director of Publications

W. Allen Wallis
Resident Scholar

Ben J. Wattenberg
Senior Fellow

Carolyn L. Weaver
Resident Scholar; Director, Social
   Security and Pension Studies

A NOTE ON THE BOOK

*This book was edited by Dana Lane, Ann Petty, and Cheryl Weissman
of the staff of the AEI Press. The index was prepared by Patricia Ruggiero,
and the figures were drawn by Hördur Karlsson.
The text was set in Palatino, a typeface designed by the twentieth-century
Swiss designer Hermann Zapf. Coghill Composition Company,
of Richmond, Virginia, set the type, and Data Reproductions Corporation,
of Rochester Hills, Michigan, printed and bound the book,
using permanent acid-free paper.*

The AEI PRESS is the publisher for the American Enterprise Institute for
Public Policy Research, 1150 17th Street, N.W., Washington, D.C. 20036;
Christopher C. DeMuth, publisher; *Edward Styles*, director; *Dana Lane*, assistant
director; *Ann Petty*, editor; *Cheryl Weissman*, editor; *Mary Cristina Delaney*,
editorial assistant (rights and permissions).

D